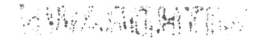

The French Revolution
in Miniature

The French Revolution in Miniature

Section Droits-de-l'Homme,
1789-1795

Morris Slavin

PRINCETON UNIVERSITY PRESS

PRINCETON, NEW JERSEY

Copyright © 1984 by Princeton University Press
Published by Princeton University Press, 41 William Street,
Princeton, New Jersey 08540
In the United Kingdom:
Princeton University Press, Guildford, Surrey

Library of Congress Cataloging in Publication Data will be
found on the last printed page of this book

ISBN 0-691-05415-0

Publication of this book has been aided by a grant from the
Whitney Darrow Fund of Princeton University Press

This book has been composed in Linotron Garamond

Clothbound editions of Princeton University Press books
are printed on acid-free paper and binding materials are
chosen for strength and durability. Paperbacks, while satisfactory
for personal collections, are not usually suitable for library rebinding.
Printed in the United States of America by Princeton University Press
Princeton, New Jersey

for
Sophie and Jeanne

Contents

List of Figures

Figure 1 is reproduced by courtesy of Félix Gatier.
Figures 2-5, 8, and 9 are from *La Révolution française* by
Armand Dayot (Paris: Ernest Flammarion, n.d.).

List of Maps

List of Tables

Preface

This study seeks to present the French Revolution *d'en bas*, through the experiences of one section of Paris, Droits-de-l'Homme. Although the works of Jaurès, Lefebvre, Soboul, and others have great merit, none traces the history of a particular neighborhood through the events of the Revolution. This may seem surprising in light of the immense bibliography on the French Revolution in general, and on its course in the city of Paris, in particular. The reason cannot be due to lack of sources. My own study has convinced me that there is a vast amount of material to be examined by scholars. It is even conceivable that a forty-eight-volume history of the sections of Paris might be launched some day.

Such an enterprise, obviously, would be a vast microhistory. Perhaps this is one reason why no such work has appeared. If the history of one section is an isolated story, if it has no application to the Revolution as a whole, then its appeal must remain limited. Yet, unless it can be demonstrated that each individual section reacted to the Revolution in a unique way—a patent absurdity—such a study must give an insight into the Revolution itself. This is not to say that variations in geography or in social composition were not reflected in diverse politics, in clashing ideologies, or in class antagonisms. The sections in the center of the capital differed from those of the West end, yet even these differences were muted during certain periods because all of Paris responded to shortages, to threats of counterrevolution, and to foreign intervention in the same way. There were no sections whose politics were consistently bourgeois or purely *sans-culotte*.

I have avoided reciting the well-known events of the Revolution except to summarize them briefly for purposes of continuity and in order to jog the memory of the reader. In doing so, I have attempted to hold the interest of the specialist without driving away the general reader interested in the French Revolution. The narrative, thus, is concerned with developments in section Droits-de-l'Homme. Some of these are unique to the section; others are reactions to the mood in the capital. Throughout, I have laid emphasis on the origin, growth, and decline of the revolutionary institutions that appeared in the section. The political and administrative organs in the districts and sections after 1789 reflected the Revolution on a local level. They are worth examining at close hand, for only thus, it seems to me, can the impact of the Revolution on a neighborhood be seen. In addition to this, I have sought to reveal the popular mentality of the sectionnaires, although this is limited for the most part to the militants and activists for whom records exist. A number of these are interesting personalities in themselves, made more so by their political role. A few, like Jean Varlet and Antoine Descombes, approach the modern, professional revolutionary.

This study, then, focuses on the history of section Droits-de-l'Homme from 1789 to 1795, years that witnessed profound social and political changes. It begins with the birth of the sixty districts and their evolution into the forty-eight sections, which yielded, in turn, to the twelve arrondissements. I have referred to developments in sections Arcis, Homme-Armé, and Réunion, neighbors of Droits-de-l'Homme, in order to compare or contrast a popular reaction, the function of an institution, or the evolution of a political program. These three, together with Droits-de-l'Homme, composed the seventh arrondissement of the capital. In tracing the social and political fluctuations in section Droits-de-l'Homme I have attempted to discuss its contribution to the larger struggle, to examine its organs of power and of administration, and to present its leaders and its militants. The jolt of the dramatic days of the Revolution, its *journées*, is examined in some depth in an effort to see this movement from below.

What justification can there be, however, for selecting section Droits-de-l'Homme from among the forty-eight neighborhoods of the capital? The answer is more historical than logical. After I had published an article on the activities and ideas of a young militant by name of Jean Varlet, a resident of the section, Professor Marc Bouloiseau, of the University of Paris, suggested that I attempt a study of the environment in which the young Varlet functioned. My interest in the latter was stimulated by a study I had made of a group of revolutionaries dubbed *enragés* by their less sympathetic contemporaries. The result is this exploration of section Droits-de-l'Homme, first known as Roi-de-Sicile, which had grown out of district Petit-Saint-Antoine and a portion of district Blancs-Manteaux.

Since "no man is an island entire of itself," I owe much to colleagues and friends who have encouraged me with their suggestions and criticisms. The late Richard Brace read the manuscript in its early stages, as did Professor Edward T. Gargan. I have benefited much from their advice. My former mentor, John Hall Stewart, was generous with a number of invaluable suggestions. Professor Guido Dobbert, a historian turned sociologist, and my colleague at Youngstown State University, has spent countless hours with me feeding quantitative information into the computer and helping me unravel its mysteries. I owe him a great debt which it is a pleasure to acknowledge. Mrs. Hildegard Schnuttgen, reference librarian of Youngstown State University, has given me invaluable assistance in tracking down books often unavailable in the more frequented libraries. Edgar L. Feige and George V. Taylor read Chapter I and raised a number of important questions that forced me to rethink some of my early conclusions. Walter Markov read the entire manuscript and encouraged me to seek its publication, and the late Albert Soboul was kind with suggestions and replies to my inquiries in the early stages of my research. Needless to say, none is responsible for whatever errors in judgment I may have made.

I want to thank also the many archivists and librarians of various establishments in Paris. Mme Devaux of the Archives Nationales, Mme Felkay, formerly with the Archives de Paris, MM. Dérens and James of the Bibliothèque historique de la Ville de Paris, and MM. Gighnac and Coutarel of the Archives Préfecture de Police—all deserve my warm thanks for making my task more pleasant and gratifying. A former student of Professor Marc Bouloiseau's, John Weber, was kind enough to turn over a number of bibliographic references that saved me some weeks of work when I first began my research. My colleague and mathematician, Professor Steve Kuzarich, has helped me unravel a statistical tangle. I owe much, also to my colleague and friend, Professor Renée Linkhorn, whose profound knowledge of the French language has kept me from stumbling over a number of obscure eighteenth-century expressions. My friend and colleague, Professor Agnes M. Smith, has read several chapters of the manuscript and has been generous with her suggestions. My graduate student, Francis Butvin, has spent numerous hours transferring raw data onto computer cards. The Media Center has reproduced a number of documents to illustrate the text, and Miss Janet Sebulsky and Mrs. Susan Fogaras spent many hours in typing the manuscript.

Portions of this book appeared in my article, "Section Roi-de-Sicile and the Fall of the Monarchy" in *Bourgeois, Sans-Culottes, and Other Frenchmen*, edited by Morris Slavin and Agnes M. Smith (Waterloo, Ontario: Wilfred Laurier University Press, 1981), and is used by permission of the publisher.

I should like to thank also my university for granting me two quarters of leave and the Youngstown Education Foundation for helping me financially in my sojourn in Paris. The Youngstown State University Graduate Council has been generous with funds throughout the period of research and writing.

Finally, I want to thank my wife, Sophie S. Slavin, for encouraging me in the task of research and for creating an atmosphere conducive to study and writing.

Abbreviations

A. de P.	Archives de Paris (formerly Archives de la Seine)
A.N.	Archives nationales
A.P.P.	Archives préfecture de police
B.H.V.P.	Bibliothèque historique de la Ville de Paris
B.N.	Bibliothèque nationale
B.V.C.	Bibliothèque Victor Cousin
Br. M.	British Museum

ABBREVIATIONS OF PUBLISHED WORKS FREQUENTLY CITED

A.P.	*Archives parlementaires* . . .
B. & R.	Buchez and Roux, *Histoire parlementaire* . . .
Annales historiques	*Annales historiques de la Révolution française*

A Word of Explanation

A work cited for the first time is always quoted in full, after which the author's last name with the volume number and page is given. Where several works of an author are listed a key word of the title is always indicated. For example: references to Lacroix's *Actes de la Commune de Paris pendant la Révolution* are given simply as Lacroix, with the volume and page number following. Aulard's *La Société des Jacobins* . . . is cited as Aulard, *Jacobins*.

The journals referred to for the first time are preceded by their call number in the Bibliothèque nationale, after which the *côte* is dropped. In a number of cases journals in the Bibliothèque historique de la Ville de Paris are cited without their call numbers. This procedure is also followed for the collection of revolutionary newspapers and journals in the Widener Library of Harvard University. Youngstown State University also possesses a number of standard works and journals such as the *Moniteur*, Marat's *l'Ami du peuple*, Hébert's *Le Père Duchesne*, Babeuf's *Journal de la liberté de la presse* and his *Tribun du peuple*, the *Journal de Paris*, etc. In addition to the above there are a number of publications on microfilm in my possession. To have listed call numbers of all these would have led to needless confusion.

In citing references to the F⁷ collection of the Archives nationales, the number of the carton with its dossier is given when the individual is presented for the first time. After the first citation the number of the dossier is dropped. The latter are not too accurate, as everyone who has worked in these files knows.

If the spelling of streets is not always consistent it is because there are several acceptable variations in the eighteenth century. For example: Bourg-Tibourg was often spelled Bourtibourg; Moussy appears at times as Moussi, and Tisseranderie was spelled often as Tixeranderie. The streets of the section with their various spellings are listed in the key to Map 1. In using the French word *rue* for the English *street* I have done so consciously—for effect, style, and sound. Rue du Temple is simply more authentic than Street of the Temple or street du Temple.

With few exceptions, French terms and quotations from the French have been translated into English. On occasion the original was left after I had translated it for the first time. For example: *procès-verbal* may mean minutes of a meeting, a record of the proceedings, or a report of various agencies and officials. In such cases I have used the French term. In the case of the *comité de bienfaisance* it seemed better to give its American equivalent, which is a relief or welfare committee. The latter conforms to the French as well as the former, since welfare in the United States is often relief, not the general welfare of the preamble of the Constitution of the United States.

The French Revolution
in Miniature

Figure 1. The Marais

INTRODUCTION:
The Setting

By an unbelievable incompetence, the Constituent Assembly had created in Paris forty-
eight hotbeds of perpetual agitation, and had
donated . . . in advance to the insurrection its
organic law, its privileges, and its immuni-
ties. There was formed within each section a
nucleus of leaders who continually demanded
meetings and who there had adopted the most
incendiary and the most unconstitutional of
motions.
Louis Mortimer-Ternaux,
Histoire de la Terreur, 1792-1794, I, 27.

It is the sections, in effect, which have prepared, created the great revolutionary movements; exercised this surveillance which prevented or held off failures; found, collected
money, when one no longer knew where to
get it; enrolled, paid the volunteers who flew
to the front.
Ernest Mellié, *Les Sections
de Paris pendant le Révolution française*, p. 4.

The Marais district, which embraces section Droits-de-l'Homme, is a
vast triangle on the right bank of the Seine, bounded by the river and
stretching north to the Place de la République, which acts as its apex.
The great boulevards lead to this point, following the old ramparts of
the city, with the streets Beaubourg and Temple swinging to the
northeast. Historically, the Marais was a marsh (hence its name), which
was gradually drained and transformed into meadows, farmlands, and,
finally, into the suburbs of Paris.[1] Some of the more famous mansions

[1] See the map of the Marais area (Fig. 1) and of the section (Map 1), which make
clear the general outline. See also: Jacques Wilhelm, *La Vie quotidienne au Marais au
XVIIIᵉ siècle* (Paris, 1966), pp. 7-8; Yvan Christ et al., *Promenades dans le Marais*

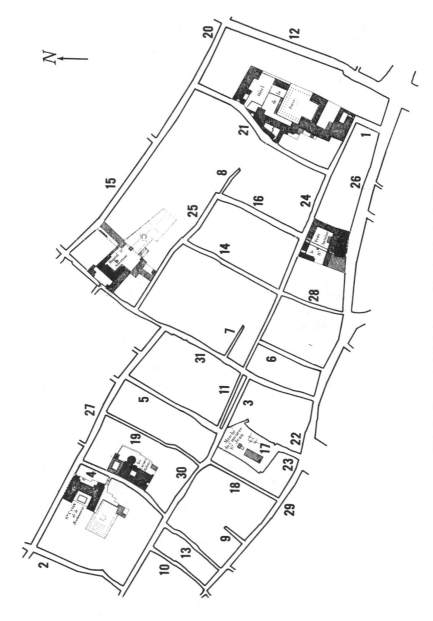

N

Map 1. Streets and Cul-de-sacs of Section Droits-de-l'Homme

Streets and Cul-de-sacs of Section Droits-de-l'Homme
as They Appear on Verniquet's Map of 1790

(Alternative spelling in parenthesis)

1. Ballets (Balets)
2. Bar-du-Bec (Barre-du-Bec) (now Temple)
3. Bercy
4. Billettes (now des Archives)
5. Bourg-Tibourg (Bourtibourg)
6. Cloche-Perce (Cloche-Perche)
7. Col-de-Sac d'Argenson (now Impasse de l'Hôtel-d'Argenson)
8. Col-de-Sac Coquerelle (Col-de-Sac Coquerie) (now Rosiers)
9. Col-de-Sac St. Feron (now Rivoli)
10. Coq (now Verrerie) (Coq-St. Jean is Rivoli)
11. Croix-Blanche (now Roi-de-Sicile)
12. Culture-Sainte-Catherine (now Sévigné)
13. Deux-Portes (now des Archives)
14. Ecouffés
15. Francs-Bourgeois
16. Juifs
17. Marché-du-Cimetière-Saint-Jean
18. Mauvais-Garçons
19. Moussy (Moussi)
20. Neuve-Sainte-Catherine (now Francs-Bourgeois)
21. Pavée (Pavée-au-Marais)
22. Place Baudoyer
23. Renaud-le-Febvre (Renard-le-Fèvre until-1854) (also Renaud-Lefevre)
24. Roi-de-Sicile (Droits-de-l'Homme)
25. Rosiers
26. Saint-Antoine
27. Sainte-Croix-de-la-Bretonnerie
28. Tiron
29. Tisseranderie (Tixeranderie) (now Rivoli)
30. Verrerie
31. Vieille-du-Temple (Vieille-rue-du-Temple)

Total of 31 streets and alleys

Note: rue Potterie (Poterie) appears on Verniquet's map but is outside the section proper. Coquilles can be treated as a separate street (as it appears on the map) although it was not part of the section and fused with Temple.

of Paris, such as the *hôtels* de Soubise, d'Ormesson, de Beauvais, and de Carnavalet graced its streets. The many churches, convents, hospitals, and poorhouses of the quarter gave it a history and a tradition that were rooted in the earliest beginnings of the city. Such structures as the Bastille, the Temple, the Hôtel de Ville were destined to act as stages for the most dramatic events throughout the Revolution. A number of ecclesiastical institutions erected on sites that went back to the very foundations of the city's history were to hold inhabitants of districts and, later of sections, whose purpose and outlook had nothing in common with their former occupants. One such example is the ancient "basilica" dating from the fourth century, on whose location was built the magnificent church of Saint-Gervais with its mixture of the Gothic and Renaissance styles. It was to house electors and revolutionaries after 1789, many of whom were to come from the neighboring district of Petit-Saint-Antoine, out of which the future section Droits-de-l'Homme was to be formed.

Although it is true that many mansions of the Marais quarter had been abandoned by their former owners on the eve of the Revolution, it would be an exaggeration to accept uncritically some contemporary accounts of the "sad" nature of this region, as it was described in the reign of Louis XIII. At one time, the Marais had been the neighborhood most frequented by pleasure-seeking Parisians. A number of its streets and mansions housed prostitutes and their madames. Its cemetery of Saint-Jean (in the heart of section Droits-de-l'Homme) witnessed public executions of criminals, or those deemed to be such by the harsh standards of the past. Its Théâtre du Marais presented Corneille's *Cid* for the first time in 1636, and Beaumarchais was to construct his own playhouse within its confines in 1790.[2]

That division of the Marais which formed the future section Roi-de-Sicile (called Droits-de-l'Homme after the overthrow of the king), was composed of thirty-one streets and alleys,[3] almost all originating

(Paris, [1964]), pp. 19-20, an attractive and an informative book; Jacques Hillairet, *La Rue Saint-Antoine* (Paris, 1970); and the same author's *Dictionnaire historique des rues de Paris*, 2 vols., 5th ed. (Paris, n.d.), II, 420-421.

[2] Girault de Saint-Fargeau, *Les Quarante-huit quartiers de Paris* (Paris, 1846), p. 105; Hillairet, *Dictionnaire*, II, 641.

[3] This count is based on a map of Edmonde Verniquet, an architect of section Jardin-des-Plantes (Sans-Culottes), B.H.V.P., *Atlas du plan gén'l de la ville de Paris* (1791), map no. 37. See Map 1 and its key for a fuller explanation.

in the earliest period of the Middle Ages. The majority of these could trace their beginnings to the thirteenth century, and a number went back even to the twelfth and eleventh centuries. Although mansions and ordinary dwellings changed, decayed, were demolished, or rebuilt in the course of time, few inhabitants or visitors of the section would have been unaware of this long history. The very name of the section, Roi-de-Sicile, came from its street, which dated back to the thirteenth century, and took its title from a *hôtel* owned by Charles of Anjou, king of Naples and Sicily. The street ran on an east-west axis between a short passage called Ballets (absorbed by the present rue Malher) to its east, and by rue Vieille-du-Temple to the west. Just south of rue Roi-de-Sicile and running parallel to it was the better-known rue Saint-Antoine. In 1266 Charles built his mansion, which later became *l'hôtel* Saint-Paul and in 1698 took the name of La Force after a duke of the same name. It was destined to become the scene of the September massacres, during which many aristocrats, including Mme de Lamballe, attendant to Marie Antoinette, were to lose their lives. The structure became a prison for males in 1780 known as La Grande Force, and confined debtors and those detained by police for the less serious crimes. Five years later, an adjacent building known as the *hôtel* de Brienne was given the name of La Petite Force to house women prisoners. For a time a common sewer was the only means of communication between the two buildings. By 1792 the sexes were mixed and all distinction between the structures ceased.[4]

During the seventeenth century, rue Saint-Antoine was the principal artery of the Marais quarter, dotted with beautiful mansions like the *hôtels* de Mayenne, de Sully, and de Beauvais. Picturesque processions of royalty, enthusiastically acclaimed by crowds, contrasted sharply with those that took the same route (from La Bastille to les Halles or the Place de Grève), composed of pitiful victims who had been condemned to be burned, beheaded, broken on the wheel, hanged, or quartered. It was along this street that de Launay was lynched after

[4] Hillairet, *Dictionnaire*, II, 357-358; de Saint-Fargeau, *Quartiers de Paris*, p. 103. See also Félix and Louis Lazare, *Dictonnaire administratif et historique des rues de Paris et ses monuments* (Paris, 1844), p. 595. This source is valuable because the streets of the quarter Marché-Saint-Jean of the seventh arrondissement still retained much of their eighteenth-century character before the demolitions of Baron Haussmann altered or destroyed them.

surrendering the Bastille, while his officers and men were massacred on their way to the Hôtel de Ville. From 13 June to 28 July 1794 prisoners from the Conciergerie were transported along the same route to be guillotined on Place du Trône-Renversé (Place de la Nation, today), undoubtedly jeered by many who had warmly applauded them in the past. The street itself was divided among the four sections that were to form the future seventh arrondissement (l'Indivisibilité, de l'Arsenal, de la Fidelité, and des Droits-de-l'Homme), and on 4 July 1793 the word Saint was removed by the Convention to become simply Antoine.[5]

On the north side of the street was a famous religious house, le Petit-Saint-Antoine, which gave its name to the district out of which the section was to be created. It was begun in 1095 as a charitable institution, founded by a gentleman from Dauphiné to give refuge to the sick who had eaten grain infected with fungus. The illness (ergotism: "mal des ardents") gave rise to a curse as in the oath: "May the fire of Saint-Antoine burn you." This *hospice* became the monastery of Petit-Saint-Antoine in 1619 and shortly thereafter was joined to the Order of Malta. It was closed down in 1790, but not before it had seen the meeting of electors from its district draft a list of grievances and elect officers and deputies to the National Assembly. The structure was sold by the government in 1798 and was demolished six years later.[6]

The street had also witnessed tournaments within palisades constructed for this purpose, during one of which Henry II was accidentally killed in 1559. Promenades were conveniently located for the courtiers of the neighboring royal residence at Place Royale (des Vosges), and St. Vincent de Paul was almoner at the convent des Filles de la Visitation Sainte-Marie from 1632-1666. The same convent held Mazarin's niece, Hortense Mancini, a prisoner. It, too, was suppressed in 1790 and its chapel became the seat of a popular club where, among others, Théroigne de Mericourt spoke in favor of women's

---

[5] Hillairet, *Saint-Antoine*, pp. 7-8, 15, 17, 55, 57-58.

[6] *Ibid.*, pp. 242-244. For the early history of the street, see Hillairet's *Dictionnaire*, II, 376, wherein the author points out how it was created from earlier and older streets and alleys. The streets l'Aigle and Pont-Perrin became Saint-Antoine in the fifteenth century. Today it is 603 meters long (1,978 feet); Lazare, *Dictionnaire*, pp. 22-23.

rights. (A Phrygian cap may still be seen sculptured above one of its doors.) The main portal is ornamented by two Corinthian columns, and on its pedestal are two sculptures representing Charity and Religion; the façade to the right was reserved during the Revolution for the posting of placards carrying the latest decrees and laws adopted by public authorities—a nice mixture of symbols from the old regime and the new.[7]

Among the oldest structures on the street is the *hôtel* de Mayenne, whose historical roots go back to 1378 when Charles VI purchased a mansion for his brother, Louis d'Orléans, which became *hôtel* de Boissy in 1562, de Mayenne (or Maine) in 1617, and after several transfers was purchased in 1759 by d'Ormesson, a master of requests. Ironically enough, his son, who had inherited it in 1775, became a petty commander in the National Guard under Lafayette. He wisely refused to become mayor of Paris in 1792, was arrested during the Terror, and freed after the 9th of Thermidor.[8]

Equally noteworthy was the *hôtel* de Sully, built in 1624-1630 for a banker and speculator, who sold it to the duke of Sully in 1634. After enlarging it, the latter gave it to his son-in-law, Maréchal de Rohan. In 1725 Voltaire was tricked into accepting a dinner invitation to this *hôtel*, but was beaten by lackeys of the proprietor instead, and after presuming to challenge Rohan to a duel was imprisoned in the Bastille for his pains. Sometime later it passed to a relative of Turgot, and became *hôtel* de Boisgelin, then was sold in 1800 to various commercial establishments. The bas-reliefs in the court represent the Elements and the Seasons, and a beautiful stairway leads upward under a paneled ceiling decorated with floral ornaments and lovely medallions.[9] After the expulsion of the Jesuits in 1762, a building originally given to them in the sixteenth century was turned over to the priory de Sainte-Catherine-du-Val-des-Escoliers, on the other side of the street and well within the future section of Droits-de-l'Homme. The future library, Bibliothèque historique de la Ville de

---

[7] Hillairet, *Saint-Antoine*, II, 376-377. The site of the convent bears the number 17. For additional architectural features of the convent, see Christ, *Promenades*, p. 102.

[8] Hillairet, *Dictionnaire*, II, 377-378; *Saint-Antoine*, pp. 138-139; Christ, *Promenades*, pp. 103-107.

[9] Hillairet, *Dictionnaire*, II, 378-379; Christ, *Promenades*, p. 114.

Paris, was housed in its halls in 1773, and held some 1,200,000 volumes on the eve of the Revolution.[10]

The busy street offered crowds five cafés where individuals could refresh themselves, play chess or dominoes, learn the news of the day, or simply enjoy the atmosphere around them. Fountains were also available for the weary or thirsty, the most famous being la Fontaine des Tournelles. A market, marché-Sainte-Catherine, was located there, and omnibuses "for the comfort and freedom of the bourgeois" ran along the street. A number of schools, both private and free, could also be found on the street.[11]

If a visitor proceeded west along Saint-Antoine he would have come to a square called Place Baudoyer, which originated in an enclosure of the eleventh century. A number of streets led to it, among which were Pourtour-Saint-Gervais (now François-Miron), Tisseranderie, named after the weavers who inhabited it, and a short street called Renaud-Lefèvre (which disappeared along with Tisseranderie when Rivoli was built in 1854). All these streets proceeded to a small square, which at its southern end was in the twelfth century the site of a cemetery of the church Saint-Jean-en-Grève; in 1313 it was closed in favor of a larger one on rue de la Verrerie to its north. In the eighteenth century the square served as a market called marché du Vieux-Cimitière-Saint-Jean, or, simply, marché Saint-Jean. A tall cross resting on a solid pedestal was placed among its stalls. Attempts were made at different times to forbid the wandering of pigs through the market, but the monks of Petit-Saint-Antoine insisted on the right to feed their pigs, and continued to defy the authorities successfully.[12]

Place Baudoyer was also connected by rue de la Tisseranderie, which curved in an arc toward the north, and joined rue de la Coutellerie. The latter ran close to the Place de Grève, the square before the Hôtel de Ville. Construction of Tisseranderie had begun in the eleventh century and it was opened for traffic for the following century. It

[10] The priory itself was founded at the beginning of the thirteenth century in Champagne by four professors of the University of Paris, and the first stone of the church Sainte-Catherine was laid by St. Louis in 1229. Christ, *Promenades*, p. 118; Hillairet, *Dictionnaire*, II, 380.

[11] Hillairet, *Saint-Antoine*, pp. 60-69.

[12] Hillairet, *Dictionnaire*, I, 158. The name Baudoyer comes from Baudacharius, a defender of Paris about A.D. 700. The first gate on rue Saint-Antoine was called Baudoyer. Lazare, *Dictionnaire*, p. 56.

served a number of important structures in the section, such as *l'hô-pital* Saint-Gervais, *l'hôtel* de Coucy, and several properties that had belonged to the Knights Templars (now on rue de Lobau). Tisseran-derie ran from east to west and received a number of small streets and cul-de-sacs.[13] Pascal and Scarron, the latter having married the future Mme de Maintenon, were among the more famous men who lived on the street. The *hospice* de Petit-Saint-Antoine stood nearby, and at what is now no. 230 de Rivoli was the site of the Terrasse des Feuil-lants, where Jean Varlet, the *enragé* and political activist of the sec-tion, harangued crowds. The *salle du manège royal* witnessed the trial of Louis XVI and from its podium was proclaimed the first French Republic.[14]

From Place Baudoyer one could have skirted the cemetery of Saint-Jean, and proceeding north, would have come to rue de la Verrerie, which for a long time was one of the most important streets of the Right Bank. Together with rues Roi-de-Sicile and Saint-Antoine, it constituted the great east-west axis of the capital, taking its name from a glass works built on the street in 1185. Much later, a broth-erhood of glass painters and enamelers was installed on it. The street was enlarged by Louis XIV for his trips from the Louvre to the Cha-teau de Vincennes, and was favored as the route taken by foreign ambassadors to his court.

The cemetery called Neuf-Saint-Jean, or cemetery Verd, had been opened in 1393 to replace an older one. This burial place was shaped in the form of an axe whose cutting edge was turned to the east, and the handle corresponded to a lane that connected it to rue de la Ver-rerie, upon which it opened. Rows of houses surrounded it on three sides. In the eighteenth century, inhabitants of these buildings insti-tuted proceedings against a factory that was removing the soil from the cemetery following the inhumation of cadavers. It was finally closed down in 1772 because of the unhygienic practice of reusing graves while the corpses were still not completely decayed. Sold in 1793, its site was absorbed by the market of Saint-Jean, which became one of the larger marts for fruit and vegetables.

---

[13] These will be discussed below. Tixeranderie is now part of the great boulevard Rivoli, whose history is developed by David H. Pinkney in *Napoleon III and the Rebuilding of Paris* (Princeton, 1958). See also Lazare, *Dictionnaire*, p. 636.

[14] Hillairet, *Dictionnaire*, II, 351.

XVI in January 1793. Residents of the section would have been aware, naturally, of this structure and the drama connected with it.[19]

On the extreme west end of the section was Bar-du-Bec (Temple, today), which extended from la Verrerie to Sainte-Croix-de-la-Breton-nerie, then continued as Sainte-Avoye. Beyond the boundaries of the section it led to that Temple which held the royal family prisoner after Louis' dethronement. The origins of this street go back to 1300, when a rue Gentien connected Tisseranderie and la Verrerie. In the fifteenth century it was called des Coquilles, and then Bar-du-Bec, named after a church in the Eure.[20] Bougainville, the famous navi-gator, was born on the street in 1729, and Mme de Sévigné lived on Sainte-Avoye between 1651 and 1669. A *hôtel* de Gentien built in the thirteenth century gave way in the fifteenth century to the *hôtel* des Coquilles, with its decorations of shells over its doors and windows.

To the east of rue Bar-du-Bec and running parallel to it, just be-yond the monastery of Sainte-Croix-de-la-Bretonnerie and the convent des Carmes-Billettes, was the street of Billettes (des Archives, today). The monastery was continually occupied from the thirteenth century to the Revolution by members of an order that originated in 1211. Its main entrance was from a cul-de-sac des Billettes which adjoined it and opened on the gardens of the monastery. (In 1299 the street was called des Jardins.) Within its cavern was interred the first pres-ident of Parlement, Jean de Popincourt, who died in 1430. On the eve of the Revolution it was inhabited by five old monks "crushed by old age and infirmities," and was about to have been closed when the revolutionaries carried out this task in 1790 and sold the structure in 1793.[21] The Carmes-Billettes occupied almost the whole of a small

---

[19] Hillairet, *Dictionnaire*, II, 515-518. In 1391 the street witnessed an assassination of a constable by the chamberlain of the duke of Orléans, brother of Charles VI, in an intrigue of the heart. The chamberlain, Pierre de Craon, obtained a pardon from the king of England, but had his house demolished. The site then was converted into the cemetery Saint-Jean, then into the market Saint-Jean. Lazare, *Dictionnaire*, p. 110. The *hôtel* Carnavalet was on the corner of Francs-Bourgeois and Culture-Sainte-Catherine, just outside the boundaries of the section. No. 52 is the site of a *hôtel* owned by the wife of the last *prévôt des marchands* of Paris. She was killed in 1789 at the age of sixty-five. For the architecture of the *hôtel* Lepeletier de Saint-Fargeau, see Christ, *Promenades*, pp. 233-234.

[20] Hillairet, *Dictionnaire*, II, 543. The abbé du Bec had his *bar* (*barre*) or seat of justice on this street. Lazare, *Dictionnaire*, p. 47.

[21] Christ, *Promenades*, p. 175; Hillairet, *Dictionnaire*, II, 493.

block. The original order can be traced back to Philip the Fair, who installed the brothers (frères hospitaliers de la Charité Notre-Dame) in 1295. They were eventually replaced by another order of Carmelites who maintained the church until it, too, was closed down and sold during the Revolution.[22]

East of Billettes was a street called Moussy, which ran parallel to the former from la Verrerie to Sainte-Croix-de-la-Bretonnerie. Begun at the end of the thirteenth century, it was known as Franc-Mourier and held a number of old houses that still stand today. Until the end of the last century, one of these had belonged to the bishops of Beauvais, among whom was Pierre Cauchon. The future marquise de Pompadour inhabited it in 1727.[23] Parallel to Moussy and just east of it was Bourg-Tibourg, located also between la Verrerie and Sainte-Croix. It was already completed as a street in 1180, and still has a number of old buildings standing on it.[24]

To its east was rue Vieille-du-Temple (sometimes called Vieille-rue-du-Temple) already in existence in 1270. It ran between Place Baudoyer and Francs-Bourgeois, and took its name from the Templars, whose first structure was located nearby (on present Lobau). Many old houses still remain, and a number are standing on sites that go back to the early history of Paris. Among these were a *hôtel* that belonged to Marie de Fourcy, wife of a marshal of France. Another was owned by the bishop of Troyes since 1450 and inhabited by a marquis de Crillon during the Revolution. One of the better-known structures was the *hôtel* des Ambassadeurs de Hollande, which goes back to 1655. Beaumarchais wrote his *Marriage of Figaro* there in 1776. The main gate is adorned on the exterior with two sitting figures representing Fame, and bas-reliefs under the arch display heads

[22] Christ, *Promenades*, pp. 173-174; Hillairet, *Dictionnaire*, I, 103. The name of the street may come from a type of toll (a block of wood was suspended from the door of the customhouse; technically, a *billette* was, among other things, a customhouse receipt). The Lazares think, however, that the name came from the hospitalers of Notre-Dame, who wore *billettes* or labels for recognition. Lazare, *Dictionnaire*, p. 75.

[23] Hillairet, *Dictionnaire*, II, 169. A municipal magistrate, Jean de Moussy, who was *échevin* (magistrate) in 1530, seems to have given his name to the street by the beginning of the sixteenth century. Lazare, *Dictionnaire*, p. 473.

[24] Hillairet, *Dictionnaire*, I, 233. The name of the street comes from a small market town, Thiboud or Thibourg. Lazare, *Dictionnaire*, p. 92.

of the Medusa. The interior is decorated with a large bas-relief of Romulus and Remus being found by the shepherd Faustus and bears the date 1660. The shutters (*vantaux*) carry medallions expressing representations of Force and Truth, Peace and War, and Ceres and Flora. The "court of honor" has four sundials with Latin mottoes in gold letters. A gateway under the arch, decorated with pilasters and busts, leads to another large court. The interior is decorated by the best painters of their day. Descendants of Le Tellier owned it during the Revolution, but had converted it into a dance hall. After that it underwent various changes and owners.[25]

The magnificent *hôtel* de Rohan, although just beyond the limits of the section (being north of rue Francs-Bourgeois) had various names until the architect, Pierre-Alexis Delamair, built the present structure between 1705 and 1708. Delamair constructed the *hôtel* de Soubise at the same time. The *hôtel* Rohan (officially called Strasbourg) presents a sober and austere façade "suitable for lodging a bishop." The main gate of the stables is dominated by a relief sculptured in 1738 that is considered to be the most beautiful French figure of the eighteenth century. It is the work of Robert Le Lorrain, who created the tomb of Richelieu and the church of the Sorbonne, and represents the horses of Apollo, full of movement and life. A passage to the left leads to an alley along the common gardens of the *hôtels* Strasbourg and Soubise. The powder found in the Bastille after its fall was stored in *hôtel* Rohan, and shortly thereafter Tallien installed a revolutionary club within its walls—undoubtedly after the powder was removed. The *hôtel* de Soubise, as is well known, became the seat of the Archives nationales, whereas the *hôtel* Strasbourg is now the home of the National Press.[26]

A visitor curious to see La Force could have walked along rue Saint-Antoine and seen its entry, an extremely low door, even before he turned north on a very short street called des Ballets. This street disappeared when the prison was demolished in 1848, and the present rue Malher took its place.[27] Another approach to the prison was along

[25] Hillairet, *Dictionnaire*, II, 636-637; Lazare, *Dictionnaire*, p. 631. See also Christ, *Promenades*, pp. 203-204, for the architecture of this structure.

[26] Hillairet, *Dictionnaire*, II, 638. Christ, *Promenades*, pp. 188-194.

[27] Hillairet, *Dictionnaire*, II, 94. The street was only 34 meters (111.5 feet) long. Lazare, *Dictionnaire*, p. 44.

rue Pavée, by turning north from Roi-de-Sicile, or south from rue
Neuve Sainte-Catherine. That part which ran from Roi-de-Sicile to
Francs-Bourgeois had existed since 1235, and when it was paved in
1450 it received the name that it still carries. Voltaire's niece, Mme
Denis (Louise Mignot) lived on the street in 1744. The *hôtel* d'An-
goulême, which was built in 1580 for a mistress by Henry II, better
known by its present name, Lamoignon, stands on the corner of Pavée
and Francs-Bourgeois. It is one of the oldest structures in Paris, and
is renowned for its façade over the gate of the courtyard and the
roofing over the principal buildings. The main entry is on rue Pavée.
Over the principal door is a circular pediment dating to 1718, with
two figures of children, one of whom holds a mirror and the other a
serpent symbolizing Truth and Prudence, traditionally the most important qualities of a good magistrate. At the upper end of the courtyard is the main building of three floors and a side wing. The Corinthian pilasters on the lower two floors are the oldest in Paris. In
1759 Antoine Moriau, *procureur du roi*, deposited his library of 14,000
volumes and 2,000 manuscripts, which was opened to the public in
1763. It is this collection that later served to enrich the Bibliothèque
historique de la Ville de Paris, which acquired the building in 1968
as an annex of the Carnavalet museum. During the Revolution the
hôtel served as a seat of commercial and industrial activity.[28]

West of Pavée and running parallel to it between rue Roi-de-Sicile
and Rosiers was rue des Juifs (now Ferdinand-Duval). Both Rosiers
and des Juifs were part of the ancient Jewish ghetto. In 1715 there
were only seventeen Jews in Paris, if the list compiled by the police
of that date is accurate. On the eve of the Revolution their number
had grown to some 500 individuals, reflecting a microcosm of European Jewry. Most were poor shopkeepers, peddlers, or workmen.[29]
From the thirteenth to the fifteenth century, des Juifs was an extension at a right angle of Rosiers which ran above it, and only in 1500
did it take its present name. Today, as is well known, a number of
Jewish shops with their owners may still be found on Rosiers, although none of them is a descendant of that original colony which
first resided on the street in the thirteenth century. The well-known

[28] Hillairet, *Dictionnaire*, II, 246-247; Lazare, *Dictionnaire*, p. 531.
[29] Arthur Hertzberg, *The French Enlightenment and the Jews* (New York, 1968), pp.
133, 135.

Conventionnel, Boissy d'Anglas, lived on des Juifs in 1804. A number of old structures still stand, one of the more interesting being at no. 20, which was called *hôtel* des Juifs in 1728, and which was inhabited by members of the *cour des aides*.[30]

La rue Rosiers originated from a roadway of the enclosure built by Philip Augustus, and was referred to by this name as early as 1230, after a neighboring garden of roses. An old cul-de-sac, called Coquerie since 1540, extended from it eastward. The street has many old houses still standing today.[31] Just above it was the *hôtel* Saint-Gervais, or Saint-Anastase, founded in 1171 by the son of a mason, and rebuilt and reconstructed later. In the fourteenth century it became the seat of Augustinians or Hospitalers of Saint-Anastase. During the eighteenth century it belonged to the family d'Ecquevilly, who sold it in 1792 before its final confiscation by the revolutionary government shortly thereafter. A chapel constructed alongside was demolished in 1758 and was replaced by various shops.[32]

Between Rosiers and Roi-de-Sicile, west of des Juifs, was a street called Ecouffes, opened in the thirteenth century. It had several titles, but settled for its present name after a sign representing a kite (*milan*, then termed *escoufle*, a bird of the hawk family). During the seventeenth century, Desmarets de Saint-Sorlin, the first chancellor of the Académie Française, lived on the street, which accommodated some ancient structures that still stand.[33] Directly south of Ecouffes was rue Tiron, which ran into Saint-Antoine and was already built up by 1250. Its name was derived from an occasional lodging house (*pied-à-terre*) which in 1270 belonged to an abbey of Tiron. This street was one of nine in Paris that had been reserved by St. Louis to house prostitutes (*femmes prostituées tenant bordel en la Ville de Paris*).[34]

West of Tiron was Cloche-Perce, built in 1250 and called then Renault-le-Fèvre. It took its present name in 1636, after a bell colored blue (or *perse*). In 1739 Voltaire lived at *l'hôtel meublé* de Brie, and his sister resided on the street, as well. The central portion of the street was absorbed by the boulevard de Rivoli in 1854.[35]

[30] Hillairet, *Dictionnaire*, I, 518; Lazare, *Dictionnaire*, p. 352.

[31] Hillairet, *Dictionnaire*, II, 366; Lazare, *Dictionnaire*, pp. 162, 598.

[32] Christ, *Promenades*, pp. 243-245; Hillairet, *Dictionnaire*, II, 50.

[33] Hillairet, *Dictionnaire*, I, 465; Lazare, *Dictionnaire*, p. 192.

[34] Hillairet, *Dictionnaire*, II, 560; Lazare, *Dictionnaire*, p. 636.

[35] Hillairet, *Dictionnaire*, I, 361-362; Lazare, *Dictionnaire*, p. 144.

West of the cemetery Saint-Jean was a street called Mauvais-Garçons, which at one time had connected Tisseranderie and la Verrerie.
In the early Middle Ages it had been inhabited by *des filles publiques*,
and took its name in 1539 after French and Italian adventurers who
had desolated Paris in 1525 at the time of Francis I's captivity. In the
fifteenth century butcher apprentices (*garçons bouchers*) lived on it and
disturbed the neighborhood with their brawls and rioting.[36] The street
must have lost its former reputation by the eighteenth century, as
there appears nothing on the eve of the Revolution to distinguish it
from others in the section.

Between Tisseranderie and la Verrerie was a street, Deux-Portes,
originally called Entre-Deux-Portes in 1281. It ran parallel to Mauvais-Garçons and ended just west of Billettes on la Verrerie. Like a
number of neighboring streets it, too, was absorbed by the present
des Archives.[37] The last street on the west, which connected la Verrerie and Tisseranderie was du Coq. In 1273 it was called André-
Malet, but in the fifteenth century took its name of Coq from a sign
showing a rooster. Like so many others of this neighborhood, it disappeared when Rivoli was built in the nineteenth century.[38]

During the time that the neighborhood was still district Petit-
Saint-Antoine, before it had become section du Roi-de-Sicile, it included a street called Poterie which ran between la Coutellerie and la
Verrerie, west of Coquilles. North of la Verrerie it became la rue
Renard, which is the name it carries today. When the Revolution
broke out, German Jews had a synagogue on rue Brisemiche, nearby.
A second synagogue was opened on rue Renard in 1789, but was
closed during the Terror, after its gold and silver objects were transferred to the Mint. The street was also the site of a court dealing with
merchants and those with whom they had business relations. It was
sold as national property in 1793.[39]

---

[36] Hillairet, *Dictionnaire*, II, 114; Lazare, *Dictionnaire*, p. 244.

[37] Hillairet, *Dictionnaire*, I, 102. In the early 1300s the street opened on Tisseranderie under an arcade of a house; Lazare, *Dictionnaire*, p. 566. I have discussed its
main features under Billettes, above. The present street, des Archives, absorbed Deux-
Portes; les Billettes; la rue de l'Homme-Armé (the name of a neighboring section),
which extended between Sainte-Croix-de-la-Bretonnerie and les Blancs-Manteaux, built
between 1137 and 1180; and la rue du Chaume, which ran between Blancs-Manteaux
and Rambuteau.

[38] Hillairet, *Dictionnaire*, I, 103; Lazare, *Dictionnaire*, p. 161.

[39] The amount of gold and silver confiscated from the synagogue totaled a mere 27

In addition to the principal and secondary streets of the section that
we have discussed, there were a number of passages, lanes, and alleys.
Croix-Blanche, dating from the fifteenth century and named after a
sign on the street, ran between Bourg-Tibourg and Temple, and was
almost a short extension of rue Roi-de-Sicile.[40] Just south of it was
Bercy-Saint-Jean (or Bercy-au-Marais) which began at rue Vieille-du-
Temple and ended at rue Bourg-Tibourg, south of Croix-Blanche.[41]
A Col-de-Sac d'Argenson (called today impasse de l'Hôtel d'Argenson)
ran east from rue Vieille-du-Temple, above Roi-de-Sicile. This blind
alley had a *hôtel* that belonged to several important persons connected
with Parlement until bought by the count of Argenson, who enlarged
it and whose heirs sold it, ultimately, to the marquis de Villette. The
marquis' descendants had possession of it until 1792, when they, too,
sold the property. A number of old houses still stand on this short
street.[42] The total number of streets and alleys that appear on the map
of Verniquet outlining the limits of section Droits-de-l'Homme are,
thus, thirty-one.[43]

---

livres, 17 sols, 6 deniers. In 1789 the court of merchants had judged some 80,000
cases. Hillairet, *Dictionnaire*, I, 242-243; II, 330-331. Poterie was in the seventh
arrondissement, but in the *quartier* Arcis. Lazare, *Dictionnaire*, p. 572.

[40] Hillairet, *Dictionnaire*, II, 357; Lazare, *Dictionnaire*, p. 167.

[41] Verniquet's map of 1791 gives the name as rue Bercy, but Hillairet makes clear
that this was Bercy-Saint-Jean, which fused with rue Roi-de-Sicile in 1868. The Lazares
call it Bercy-au-Marais, which was 70 meters (c. 230 feet) long. *Dictionnaire*, p. 65.

[42] Hillairet, *Dictionnaire*, I, 647-648. That its dimensions must have been modest
may be seen from the present size of its successor. The impasse measures 37 by 3
meters (121.36 by 9.84 feet). Lazare, *Dictionnaire*, p. 31. This cul-de-sac had never
been laid out.

[43] This excludes Poterie. See Key to Map 1 for the list.

I

The Socioeconomic Base

Writing in the *Tableau de Paris*, its publisher saw the Marais as a world of boredom and intolerance. He was convinced that

> there reigns . . . the total accumulation of all the old prejudices. . . . There one may see the old grumblers, gloomy enemies of all new ideas. . . . They call the philosophes people to be burned at the stake (*gens à bruler*). . One sees there antique furniture, which seems to concentrate the prejudices and ridiculous customs.
>
> Even the pretty women that a fatal star has consigned to this sad quarter, dare not receive anyone but the old military men or the old gentlemen of the robe.[1]

Today scholars question the literary exaggerations of Mercier. Although the Marais was losing many of its wealthier residents to the new *quartiers*, enough wealth, and the influence that accompanies it, remained to maintain traces of its past glory. A population of almost 120,000 subdivided into a dozen classes with their myriad professional and occupational groups could hardly have ceased their normal activities. If some of these enterprises were not as vigorous and dynamic as in the past, they still reflected life, work, and growth.[2]

Of the social classes in the Marais, the nobility of both robe and sword was by far the wealthiest and the most powerful. Constituting but 5 percent of the population, it held more than 70 percent of all

[1] Louis-Sebastien Mercier, *Tableau de Paris* (Amsterdam, 1782), I, 272-273.

[2] Two studies analyzing the position and wealth of the Marais nobility and bourgeoisie are D. Roche, "La Noblesse du Marais," in *Recherches sur la noblesse parisienne au milieu du XVIIIe siècle* (Paris, 1962), pp. 541-578; and M. Vovelle and D. Roche, "Bourgeois, rentiers, propriétaires, éléments pour la définition d'une catégorie sociale,' " in *Actes du quatre-vingt-quatrième congrès national des sociétés savantes* (Paris, 1960), pp. 419-452.

personal property in the district. Together with the value of real estate, its total holdings rose to 75 percent.[3] It was this wealth, in addition to the prestige of ancient blood, that gave the nobility its preponderant social weight. All classes were linked to it economically, and, consequently, were dependent upon it. As Roche puts it:

> Members of the Parlement and of the councils, the military, the gentlemen of the robe—all give a certain countenance to the quarter. Everyone draws activity from it: domestics, wholesale merchants, and artisans, but also men of law, linked to the nobles by their business. The Revolution will be necessary to drain off the inhabitants of the Marais, and to modify, not the setting, but the social reality of the eighteenth century.[4]

The flight of the nobility at the outbreak of the Revolution was bound, therefore, to disorganize profoundly the economic life of the Marais.

In contrast to the castelike rigidity of the Marais nobility was the mobility of the bourgeoisie. Relatively open, this comparatively young class was rapidly losing traces of its rural origins. The city, with its complex relations among the classes, helped draw closer the commercial middle class, a portion of the liberal profession, and the bourgeoisie proper.[5] Marriage, of course, was an important means of rising socially.[6] Moreover, although the wealth of the bourgeoisie was far below that of the nobility, it was considerably higher than that of the artisans. The bourgeoisie possessed real estate, of course, but 70 per-

[3] Roche, "Noblesse," pp. 543, 570. The nobility numbered 3,850 persons and made up 5.01 percent of the inhabitants. For its investments in land, fiefs, and seigneuries, town property, offices, and regiments, see Roche's discussion, pp. 555, 557, 560, and 566-569.

[4] *Ibid.*, pp. 568-569.

[5] "The bourgeoisie of the Marais is a category socially open, relatively young, reflecting partially the attractive role exercised by the city." Vovelle and Roche, "Bourgeois," p. 424. The authors define the word and explain the social category of *bourgeois* in the following way: in medieval terms it was an inhabitant of a town. The nineteenth century saw the bourgeois as one whose revenue proceeded essentially from industry and finance capital. The eighteenth century viewed him as a commoner, but one who was idle by living off interest or investments (*rentes*). *Ibid.*, pp. 419-420.

[6] By the middle of the eighteenth century, fewer than a third of those who married daughters of the bourgeoisie were Parisians, in contrast to more than two-thirds of their fathers-in-law. *Ibid.*, p. 422; 28 percent as against 67 percent.

cent of its wealth was in bonds or dividends.[7] This, more than any other single factor, made it a class apart.[8]

The poor and near-poor played a minor role in eighteenth-century political life. They were far too busy scrabbling for a living. Where there was little or no industry or commerce, as in most of the neighborhoods of section Roi-de-Sicile, their plight was doubly hard. What little business existed was concentrated in portions of the streets of Ecouffes and of Juifs, near the La Force prison. The peddlers of the streets of Fourcy and of Nonnains d'Hyères, the stonemasons living in furnished rooms of rue de la Mortellerie, and the day laborers of section Maison-Commune, Arsenal, Place-Royale, and Roi-de-Sicile were uninterested in politics. The Revolution would awaken some of them, but without property, education, or leisure they would sink back to the lower depths again.

If the Marais numbered 120,000 people, what was the total population of the capital and of its individual sections on the eve of the Revolution? A number of demographic studies that have appeared in the last decade have sought to answer this question.[9] Lack of documents for various sections makes it difficult to be certain of the answers. Moreover, eighteenth-century statistics, as is well known, are often inaccurate, incomplete, and unreliable. This is especially true of its population figures. Early statisticians multiplied the number of births by a coefficient often adopted arbitrarily, then verified the figure by taking a sample in order to arrive at an approximate number of inhabitants. Thus, Paris was thought to have 650,000 people in 1789, which, in theory, included the floating portion of the popula-

[7] *Ibid.*, pp. 426-428. Thirty-seven percent of bourgeois adults left fortunes of more than 20,000 livres upon their deaths. Half in the Marais district left behind over 50,000 livres, and four transmitted fortunes of over 100,000 livres, thus approaching the wealth of the nobility. *Ibid.*, p. 430.

[8] In Chartres (employed by the authors as a model representing the provincial bourgeoisie in contrast to that of Paris), the bourgeois was much less likely to be a *rentier* and much more probably a *propriétaire*, that is, one who lived off the revenue derived from land. *Ibid.*, p. 437.

[9] Martine Sévigrand, "La Section de Popincourt pendant la Révolution française"; Anne Goeury, "La Section Grange-Batelière pendant la Révolution"; and F. Rousseau-Vigneron, "La Section de la Place des Fédérés pendant la Révolution," in *Contributions à l'histoire économique et sociale de la Révolution française* (Paris, 1970).

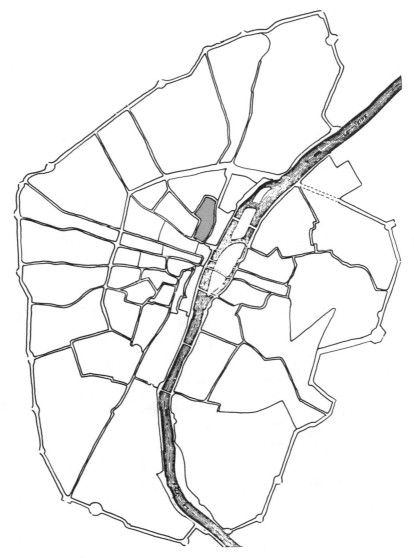

Map 2. Plan of Sections of Paris
Section Droits-de-l'Homme is shaded.

tion—the poor wage-workers, vagabonds, women workers, immigrants, and child laborers.[10] Contemporary sources varied in their estimates, but none dipped much below 650,000 or rose significantly higher than 700,000.[11]

If it is difficult to obtain an exact figure of Parisians during the Revolution, it is no less so for section Droits-de-l'Homme. From 1793 to 1807, population statistics fluctuate around the figure of 11,000. Only the returns of 11 pluviôse, Year III (30 January 1795) give a substantially larger figure of 12,321.[12] If the latter returns are accu-

[10] Marcel Reinhard, *Nouvelle histoire de Paris. La Révolution 1789-1799* (Paris, 1971), pp. 118-119. The author quotes contemporaries who repeated that "Paris ne 'peuplait' pas" ("Paris does not 'repeople' itself").

[11] *Réimpression de l'ancien moniteur depuis la réunion des Etats-generaux, jusqu'au Consulat (mai 1789-novembre 1799)* (Paris, 1858-1863), VIII, no. 145, p. 481, 25 May 1791, "Population de France de l'année 1790," thought that there were between 641,751 and 660,165 people in Paris in 1790. These figures were arrived at by multiplying the coefficient of 33 by the 20,005 births or the 19,447 deaths reported for the capital.

Arthur Young thought that Paris numbered 725,333 in 1791. Marcel Reinhard, *Etude de la population pendant la Révolution et l'empire* (Gap, 1961), pp. 26-27. This was approximately the same time that the "Tableau de la population, 27 Mai 1791" gave Paris 647,472 inhabitants. The *Almanach royale, Année commune M.DCC.XCI*, edited by Laurent d'Houry (Paris, 1791), p. 529 gave Paris 680,000 for 1790 and repeated the same figure for the following three years.

If the number of workers who lodged in hotels and in furnished rooms, as reported by the Châtelet (the police court), was indeed one-fifth or one-sixth of the labor force, the total number of inhabitants could have risen to 700,000. The General Council of Paris published a report of its commission in 1791, which began with the premise that the capital contained 700,000 inhabitants. Thus, there seems to have been a consensus among contemporaries that the capital held between 650,000 and 700,000 people.

George Rudé, "La Population ouvrière parisienne de 1789 à 1791," in *Annales historiques de la Révolution française*, no. 187 (January-March 1967), pp. 15-33, *passim*. A. de P., I AZ 145, *Rapport des commissaires chargés de l'examen des mémoires concernant les approvisionnemens en grain . . . par M. Regnault. Lu au Conseil-général de la Commune* ([Paris], 20 November 1791), 24 pp. See also A.N., F[7] 3688[4], "Etat général de la population de Paris, nombre des citoyens," accompanied by a letter dated 11 pluviôse, Year III (30 January 1795), which reported the population of Paris to be 636,772. Jeffrey Kaplow in *The Names of Kings; the Parisian Laboring Poor in the Eighteenth Century* (New York, 1972), pp. 18-19, is convinced "that Paris contained at least 700,000 people and perhaps 50,000 more on the eve of the Revolution, floating population included."

[12] A.N., F[7] 3688[4], "Etat général de la population de Paris, nombre des citoyens."

rate, the section must have suffered a considerable exodus, as district Petit-Saint-Antoine reported a total of 19,425 individuals in the census of 1790.[13] The "scientific" nature of these surveys may be gauged from the method of gathering data on 28 prairial, Year V (16 June 1796), which gave section Droits-de-l'Homme a total of 11,710 "inhabitants." Among the latter were 34 horses and 50 "dead defenders"![14] Other returns are no less questionable.[15]

Whether the population of section Droits-de-l'Homme numbered more than 12,000 or less, a more significant question is the approximate density of this population. There is hardly need to stress that a high density in a district or section is often an indication of the latter's relative affluence or poverty, and all the social tensions that crowded conditions bring in their train. It was this problem that the Russian scholar, N. Karéiev, sought to resolve. Using various plans of the capital drafted during the eighteenth century, and especially that of Verniquet and the *Almanach de l'an III* (reproduced by Mellié), he finally decided to measure the area himself.[16] Then, finding the same

Section Droits-de-l'Homme is no. 26, with the following figures: under the heading "se nourrissent chez eux," 10,807; "par les traiteurs," 1,514; "quantité des bouches par section," 12,321.

[13] A.N., D IVbis 13, 252^b. The original document gives an erroneous total of 19,432; the total number of active citizens is also wrong: 2,247, which should be 2,229. Another document A.N., D IVbis 52, "Recensement général des habitans de la Ville de Paris," 1790, gives quite different figures for the district: 17,814; active citizens numbered 2,207.

[14] A.N., F^20 123, Département de la Seine, Commune de Paris, "Denombrement de la population de la Commune de Paris, et des chevaux qui existent dans ce canton." The total figure was broken down into the following: 3,133 men; 3,962 women; 1,684 boys; 2,597 girls; or 11,376 inhabitants. Men would have formed 27.54 percent of the total. Rue Saint-Antoine held the most residents—402 men and 497 women, whereas la Croix-Blanche had the least, with 9 men and 16 women.

[15] A.N., F^20 381, 11(?) fructidor, Year III (28 August 1794); the same in A.N., F^20* 19. The exact number given was 11,015. A.N., F^7* 2498, p. 207, 5 ventôse, Year III (23 February 1795) gave an even figure of 11,000. A.N., F^11 1181, 6 nivôse, Year IV (27 December 1796), when section Droits-de-l'Homme was given 11,844. Reinhard's figure in *La Révolution*, Annexe, IV, 434, based on A.N., F^20 123-124, is 11,488, but is an error. A.N. F^20 255. The seventh arrondissement contained a total of 2,055 houses and a population of 45,009. The residents in section Droits-de-l'Homme, thus, composed almost 24 percent of the arrondissement.

[16] Karéiev, *La Densité de la population des differentes sections de Paris pendant la Révolution*, translated by J. Patouillet (Paris, 1912), pp. 6-7.

confusion in the population statistics of the city, he resolved, fin: that the survey of the Year V (1797) by the *bureaux de bienfaisanc 48 sections*, which counted the number of "mouths to feed," was most accurate. The latter gave a total figure of 551,347 for the capital, not including those serving in the army or the "non-domiciled."[17]

The *Plan de Paris* (Map 2) and the table of population and area (Table 1) demonstrate that section Arcis, neighbor of Droits-de-l'Homme, had the highest density, with 580 people per 1,000 sq. *toises*, or 479 per acre. The smallest, Champs-Elysées, had a mere 9 per acre, a ratio of 53 to 1. Section Droits-de-l'Homme numbered 289 per acre, which compared with its neighbors in the seventh arrondissement as follows: Beaubourg (Réunion) had 260, Enfants-Rouges (Marais, Homme-Armé) numbered 109, and Hôtel-de-Ville (Maison-Commune, Fidelité) counted 251 per acre. The median for the sections on a scale from 580 to 11 was 212.35 per acre (or 175.5 per 1,000 sq. *toises* as in Table 1). Section Droits-de-l'Homme, thus, had about 77 individuals per acre above the median. These figures can be compared with London of 1801, which within its walls included 380 acres with a population of 63,832, thus having 168 persons per acre, a little below the median figure for the sections of Paris a decade earlier. The total area of section Droits-de-l'Homme was 1.08 sq. mi. or 692.2 acres.[18]

Forty years before the Revolution, the city housed its population in 23,565 dwellings, making an average of 29.70 inhabitants per structure.[19] According to the census of 1790 for district Petit-Saint-Antoine, 19,425 residents occupied 659 houses; thus the district would have had 29.47 persons per house, almost the same figure as for the rest of Paris. The census of 1807, as seen above (10,779 individuals occupying 509 houses), would have made the concentration of 21 individuals per house, a marked reduction from the survey of 1790. This corresponds to the trend during the last decades of the eighteenth century for Paris, which was to lose population to the newer districts and faubourgs, a tendency aggravated still further by the Revolution.

[17] The above figure, according to Karéiev, corresponds to that of the Year XI (1800), and is the first to merit belief. *Ibid.*, pp. 8 and 9.

[18] Reinhard, *Révolution*, p. 414, citing *Recherches statistiques sur la Ville de Paris*, V, Tableau no. 65, to which the number of sections has been added. Marché-Saint-Pierre was formerly no. 31, section Droits-de-l'Homme.

[19] Kaplow, *Names of Kings*, p. 20.

TABLE 1.

Population and Area of the Sections of Paris, 1790-1800

No. of Sections	Population			Area (square meters)			Inhabitants per 1,000 sq. Toises
	1792	An III	An IX	According to Girault de St.-Fargeau	According to F. et L. Lazare	Square Toises*	
1	12,600	12,600	10,702	666,800	620,124	131,375	74
2	8,000	8,000	6,844	2,629,800	2,743,427	573,500	11
3	12,850	12,850	10,736	1,890,000	1,830,786	449,375	23
4	14,000	20,400	16,098	280,000	265,000	64,500	251
5	20,400	14,000	11,321	630,000	482,786	149,625	75
6	12,987	12,987	9,928	330,000	307,562	68,500	147
7	11,570	11,570	9,997	930,000	958,095	243,350	39
8	11,800	13,615	10,310	284,000	250,560	37,125	259
9	6,612	9,950	9,764	130,000	73,416	22,125	444
10	7,011	12,472	8,842	120,000	122,028	30,000	294
11	9,869	13,000	9,264	130,000	99,664	28,125	330
12	13.000	9,869	8,807	780,000	153,343	33,325	266
13	12,472	7,011	7,941	—	174,558	35,000	224
14	9,950	12,550	10,446	150,000	122,994	20,000	360
15	13,645	13,511	12,710	190,000	118,376	35,000	360
16	11,000	11,722	10,891	150,000	122,771	27,875	388
17	14,722	11,000	8,861	80,000	79,296	15,500	555
18	12,550	13,747	11,844	140,000	153,266	27,250	438
19	12.000	12,550	8,711	90,000	88,337	15,200	580
20	13,800	11,800	9,073	780,000	772,979	175,750	51
21	12,000	6,582	8,695	800,000	841,862	200,000	43
22	13,315	13,800	10,473	1,448,600	1,303,500	322,375	32

23	25,000	12,030	10,052	1,021,600	896,782	210,500	48
24	13,747	11,230	8,192	1,890,000	1,913,980	449,500	17
25	15,000	14,500	10,649	1,040,000	1,002,045	234,750	45
26	12,550	21,000	15,478	2,760,000	2,767,706	626,875	27
27	11,000	25,000	22,603	—	279,317	62,125	364
28	13,840	12,000	9,679	650,000	596,788	139,375	62
29	11,015	15,000	12,623	200,000	186,516	40,500	315
30	8,974	11,000	8,089	250,000	266,089	61,873	132
31	10,500	11,015	8,865	210,000	181,758	37,500	239
32	11,230	8,974	8,221	150,000	167,975	27,000	304
33	14,450	13,840	11,886	420,000	442,301	93,625	123
34	21,000	10,500	7,929	330,000	574,706	96,875	82
35	5,257	—	4,703	110,000	168,130	23,000	204
36	11,780	11,780	10,550	150,000	217,668	34,375	310
37	3,581	—	5,051	—	127,147	17,850	297
38	11,000	11,000	12,829	2,980,000	3,260,714	728,625	17
39	10,878	10,878	13,790	680,000	726,758	160,000	86
40	21,516	21,516	18,206	380,000	364,174	86,875	204
41	16,600	16,600	16,553	280,000	286,903	60,000	274
42	17,600	17,600	18,348	1,260,000	1,169,522	268,875	67
43	17,000	17,000	17,565	1,510,000	1,637,153	332,875	52
44	14,490	14,490	12,054	211,000	183,008	36,750	325
45	22,645	22,645	22,368	340,000	309,830	72,625	320
46	19,907	16,000	12,613	1,030,000	1,387,410	391,000	32
47	16,000	19,907	11,992	780,000	991,828	197,750	60
48	12,741	12,741	14,580	—	2,234,199	406,000	35

* One square *toise* = 36 square feet.

SOURCE: N. Karéiev, *La densité de la population des différentes sections de Paris pendant la révolution*, translated by J. Patouillet (Paris, 1912).

District Petit-Saint-Antoine had received a projected plan for the reorganization of Paris as early as 20 August 1789, drafted by commissioners of the Commune on 12 August.[20] That the census of 1790, which listed twenty-one streets for the district, was inaccurate has already been mentioned. Added to the erroneous totals of population is the inexplicable omission of a main street like Roi-de-Sicile—despite the registrar's assurance to his superiors in an introductory note that his figures were based on the work of census commissioners "after the most rigorous examination, and the most exact investigation," neither of which was true.[21] Furthermore, the map of Verniquet indicates clearly that the district contained another dozen short streets and alleys not mentioned in this report. Finally, the scheme that was to form the basis of the new political division depended on the number of active citizens residing in each district, making it even more difficult to understand how whole streets could be omitted from this survey.

As we bear these caveats in mind, what did the census of 1790 reveal about district Petit-Saint-Antoine? Table 2 has been rearranged on the basis of the total number of inhabitants per street, in descending order. The table demonstrates that Marché-Saint-Jean had the highest number of dwellers per house, about 67 individuals, followed by Verrerie with 59 and Tisseranderie with 58. The lowest concentration was on rue Culture-Sainte-Catherine with 5, succeeded by Poterie with 6. The median for the number of individuals per dwelling is 12, shared by Pavée and Coquilles. A word of caution is necessary in dealing with percentages of active citizens for the last four streets of the table. It seems hardly conceivable that Coq, with 90 individuals living in 11 different houses would have 40 active citizens, a ratio of one active citizen for every 2.25 persons. Where were the children and servants, it might be asked. Deux-Portes and Culture-Sainte-Catherine show an equally high proportion—about one per three.

If the percentages of active citizens are accepted, then it could be

[20] B.N., Lb[40] 1489, *Extrait des déliberations prise dans l'assemblée des comités du district du Petit-Saint-Antoine*, p. 1.

[21] The street Roi-de-Sicile was simply inserted between des Billettes and Pavée without a single figure either for the number of houses or the number of inhabitants on the street. Moreover, Cloche-Perce and Tiron are combined for no apparent reason. A.N., D IVbis 13, 252[b].

argued that these streets were the most affluent of the neighborhood. On the other hand, the tax assessments of real estate and personal property (discussed below) do not bear out such a conclusion. The poorest street, from the point of view of number of active citizens, was Marché-Saint-Jean with fewer than 5, followed by Billettes with about 8. Verrerie, despite its relative concentration of people per structure, numbered fewer than 12 active citizens, while Tisseranderie had 8, and Saint-Antoine fewer than 5. The majority of streets, as is evident, had houses with one, two, or three active citizens living in them.

This wide dispersion of active citizens on most of the streets makes clear that although a number of the latter were undoubtedly more desirable than others, rich and poor resided on the same streets and occupied, probably, the same houses, with the traditional separations of bourgeoisie and professional classes living on the lower floors while the poor took the upper, with the poorest in the garrets. Rues du Coq and des Deux-Portes, with their high percentage of active citizens, were on the extreme west side of the district, whereas rue Culture-Sainte-Catherine, with its next higher ratio of active citizens, was on the east side. The relatively small number of active citizens on Marché-Saint-Jean might have been due to its having been a cemetery, or, more likely, to the noise and refuse that the market would have brought in its train. The proportion of active citizens to the total number of inhabitants in the district and in the section remained constant. In 1790 Paris had a total of 78,090 active citizens. In 1789 the 2,229 active citizens of district Petit-Saint-Antoine formed 2.2 percent of all actives in the city; in the fall of 1790 section Roi-de-Sicile held 1,699 active citizens, which was the same percentage of all active citizens of Paris.[22]

Whether one were an active citizen and could afford to live on the lower floors, or were a passive citizen and had to inhabit the upper stories, the more crowded neighborhoods could not have been very pleasant. For one thing, the streets on which these houses stood were so narrow, and the structures themselves so tall, rising to seven and eight stories, that the sun seldom shone into the rooms. The poor who sought shelter in their hovels suffered especially from lack of

[22] Etienne Charavay, ed., *Assemblée électorale de Paris, 18 novembre 1790-15 juin 1791* (Paris, 1890), I, Préface, p. IX.

TABLE 2
Number of Individuals and Active Citizens, District Petit-Saint-Antoine, 1790

Streets	No. of Individuals	No. of Houses	No. of Indiv. Per House	Active Citizens	Active Citizens per Dwelling	Percentage of Active Citizens per Street
Tisseranderie	3,879	67	57.89	321	4.79	8.27
Verrerie	3,747	64	58.54	434	6.78	11.58
Marché-Saint-Jean	2,673	40	66.82	123	3.07	4.60
Saint-Antoine	2,175	87	25.00	402	4.62	18.48
Billettes	1,974	64	30.84	154	2.40	7.80
Vieille-du-Temple	1,791	58	30.87	197	3.39	10.99
Rosiers	807	54	14.94	124	2.29	15.36

Juifs	504	35	14.40	110	3.14	21.82
Mauvais-Garçons	317	29	10.93	35	1.20	11.04
Francs-Bourgeois	301	27	11.14	42	1.55	13.95
Cloche-Perce &						
Tiron	232	22	10.54	51	2.31	21.98
Ecouffes	219	23	9.52	52	2.26	23.74
Pavée	210	17	12.35	35	2.05	16.66
Bercy	162	12	13.50	25	2.08	15.43
Coquilles	107	9	11.88	18	2.00	16.82
Poterie	94	16	5.87	19	1.18	20.21
Culture-Sainte-						
Catherine	92	17	5.41	30	1.76	32.60
Coq	90	11	8.18	40	3.63	44.44
Deux-Portes	51	7	7.28	17	2.42	33.33
Total	19,425	659	29.47	2,229	3.38	11.47

SOURCE: A.N., D IVbis 13, 252[b], Division de Paris d'après le plan de M[r] Dezauche.

sunlight. Physicians were observant enough to realize that the dampness and darkness of these streets made for ill health among their inhabitants. A concerned reformer suggested, for example, that the proportion between "the height of houses, relative to the length of streets, be rigorously observed. On several very narrow streets, the houses are of a stupendous height, and these streets are like infected wells where one breathes the most unwholesome air."[23]

Moreover, the residents of these edifices, which were often badly constructed, paid high rents. In 1790, 3 percent of the Parisians expended from 1,600 to 10,000 livres annually on rent. The majority (58 percent) spent 40 to 200 livres a year.[24] The percentage of a workingman's budget spent on rent is difficult to determine, but it must have averaged less than 10 percent.[25] The badly furnished rooms of the *maisons garnies* received the poor and the disinherited, who often moved every three months in order to avoid paying rent. (Unlike the custom in the United States, rent was paid quarterly in France.) This lack of stability often punished the principal tenants and proprietors who were left to settle the rent of their runaway lodgers.[26] The crisis was not eased until 1791, when many artisans left Paris because of unemployment in the luxury trades caused by emigration of the nobility and clergy. Later, the *levée en masse* contributed to easing the

[23] Charles L. Chassin, *Les Elections et les cahiers de Paris en 1789* (Paris, 1888-1889), III, 369-370, "Additions aux differentes projets de cahier."

[24] Reinhard, *Révolution*, p. 42, "L'Echelle de loyers en 1790," citing a document found among papers of a deputy. The great mass of poor who paid less than 40 livres for their hovels do not appear in the record cited. These would have included the overwhelming majority of the workingmen whose budget Rudé analyzed.

[25] Rudé gives the following approximation of the percentage of several workingmen's budgets spent on rent: a builder's laborer in 1789 and 1790 expended 3 sous of his 30 sous budget for rent, or 10%; his "effective" income being but 18 sous, the percentage for rent would have been 16.66%. A journeyman carpenter spent 6% or 10% of his "effective" income. For a journeyman carpenter in 1793, rent would have been 7.5% or 10.5% "effective." A journeyman locksmith in 1793 spent 5.45% or 7.69% "effective" for rent (my percentages). George Rudé, *The Crowd in the French Revolution*, Appendix VII (Oxford, 1959), Table 2, pp. 251-252.

[26] B.N., 8º L⁷K 42192, Jean de La Monneraye, *La Crise du logement à Paris pendant la Révolution* (Paris, 1928), p. 6. As late as 1847 it is estimated that 610,000 persons were ill-housed in the capital. Adeline Daumard, *La Bourgeoisie parisienne de 1815 à 1848* (Paris, 1963), pp. 12, 23. The author found that 52.5 percent who paid less than 150 francs a year were poor.

housing problem by removing many young men from the city. Shortly thereafter, the harsh law against foreigners forced many of them to flee the capital, thus making more dwellings available. Not until 1795 was this trend reversed again, and the housing crisis reappeared.

How did the inhabitants of these houses earn a living? It is well known that the labor force in the urban centers of eighteenth-century France was composed, largely, of artisans and craftsmen. The vast majority who toiled in the capital inhabited this world of the artisan—often indistinguishable from the small retailer who manufactured his own goods and then sold his products in a shop to which his living quarters were attached. The militia list of 13-14 July 1789, which carries a total of 1,214 names of volunteers for the Parisian Guard who resided in district Petit-Saint-Antoine, reflects this world of the craftsman and presents a kind of infrastructure, a *physionomie sociale*, of section Roi-de-Sicile.[27] Of these 1,214 names 316 failed to give their occupation, or the secretary did not record it. Thus, a total of 898 residents of district Petit-Saint-Antione may be classified by occupation as in Table 3.[28]

It is obvious that categories of occupations can be shifted and interchanged. The 22 wine merchants, for example, could just as easily be classified as retail merchants as in the food and drink division. More important is to realize that it is impossible to know the exact nature of the occupations. The 29 *menuisiers* are divided into 11 master cabinetmakers or joiners, 6 *compagnons*, and 12 designated simply as *menuisiers*. Whether some or all of them should be listed under the

---

[27] This list is on microfilm in my possession taken from B.H.V.P., MS 742, fols. 262-282. It has been reproduced by Georges Lecocq in *La Prise de la Bastille et ses anniversaires d'après des documents inédits* (Paris, 1881). Its importance consists in the fact that it makes it possible to use the services of a computer in analyzing the occupations of district Petit-Saint-Antoine. The total of 1,214 names was arrived at by counting every name, or, as in several instances, someone's garçon or domestic, initials, brothers, fathers, or sons of the signatories. Unless otherwise listed, MS 742 refers to the above folios.

[28] Five individuals who lived outside the district proper signed the *procès-verbal* of July 13-14. Two of these lived in alleyways or passages that must have been unrecorded in official sources (a coachman on Neuve-Saint-Gilles and a merchant on Col-de-Sac-Grespine), two who failed to give their occupation lived just south of rue Saint-Antoine, on rue de Jouy, and an innkeeper had his establishment on Geoffroy Lasnier. They might have found it convenient to walk across the street (rue Saint-Antoine) and sign, or had a relative or friend record their names with the secretary.

TABLE 3

Occupations of 898 Signatories of *Procès-verbal* of District Petit-Saint-Antoine, 13-14 July 1789

Occupations	Number	Percentage of Total (round figures)
Bourgeois and propertied	116	9.5
Merchants (wholesale and retail)	33	2.7
Legal profession	80	6.5
Physicians, teachers, architects	27	2.2
Civil servants	15	1.2
Clerks, *auditeurs*, controllers	38	3.1
Building trades	100	8.2
Servants and concierges	35	2.8
Transport workers, garçons, workers	44	3.6
Food and drink	77	6.3
Clothing and shoes	102	8.4
Metal and wood	64	5.2
Personal care	15	1.2
Furnishing	83	6.8
Miscellaneous professions	39	3.2
Miscellaneous trades	30	2.4
Total identified	898	73.9
Unidentified	316	26.0
Grand total	1,214	100.0

SOURCE: B.H.V.P., MS 742, fols. 262-282.

building trades (as joiners) rather than under furnishings is probably a matter of personal choice. There are some 10 members of the nobility on the list, but since they lived off their property or *rentes*, it seems more logical to group them under "bourgeois and proprietors." In other words, sociologically the noblesse cannot be linked to bourgeois gentlemen, but in terms of their economic links and source of income (unless they held certain offices in the state, of course), they can be classified under the same category. Were the 3 *écrivains* writers or journalists, in our sense, or did they simply practice their profession by writing letters, messages, drafting documents (like notaries), for illiterates in their neighborhoods? It is impossible to say. Bearing these caveats in mind and exploiting other sources available, it is thus possible to form a fair idea of the social structure of the population in the future section Droits-de-l'Homme.[29]

The 116 bourgeois or propertied gentlemen in the district form the highest percentage (10 percent) of all socioeconomic categories. Together with the 10 *négociants* and other wholesalers, this large number of individuals may illustrate that even if the Marais neighborhood was depressed, as observed by various contemporaries, district Petit-Saint-Antoine had its share of wealthy subjects. More important is the political influence that would be exerted by this group after 14 July, an influence that would favor conservative or moderate conduct. Joined by members of the legal profession (7 percent) they would tend to be constitutional monarchists, then republicans of the Feuillant or Girondist persuasion—some undoubtedly supporting the Montagnards before, finally, completing their political evolution in the Thermidorian camp. In short, these two groups would tend to form a solid base for opponents of the more radical elements in the section, that is, the local Jacobins and Cordeliers.

The link between manufacturing and commerce was so close in eighteenth-century Paris that it is impossible to separate the many artisans from the petty bourgeoisie. If the following categories are added together—the building trades, clothing and shoe industries, food and drink business, metal trades, furnishing, wood and transport workers, personal care, and the 30 in miscellaneous trades—it would give a total of 482 individuals, or 40 percent in commerce and the crafts. To these could be added various *commis*, teachers, musicians, architects, physicians, and so on—a solid base tending to favor the more radical politics of the Convention and Commune. There is hardly need to emphasize that individuals and even whole groups might differ radically from their confrères in the same occupation for a hundred and one reasons. Nevertheless, if economic and sociological groups and classes have any meaning in history, the politics of the propertied and of the propertyless differ in large part because of these disparities.

The thirty-three garçons and workers were obviously too few (3

[29] See the interesting and perceptive article by R. B. Rose, "How To Make a Revolution: The Paris Districts in 1789," in *Bulletin of the John Rylands University Library of Manchester*, 59 (Spring 1977), pp. 426-457. Professor Rose's figures differ somewhat from mine.

percent), and too poor, to play an independent role. Moreover, the traditional hierarchy of the guild still prevailed, although artisans in twenty-two crafts were affiliated to journeymen societies (*sociétés compagnoniques*), among which were metal, construction, textile, leather, and paper-manufacturing workers.[30] Masters continued their customary exploitation of journeymen and apprentices, however, until the abolition of guilds in March 1791.[31] Of course, there were far more than thirty-three working people in the section, as will be demonstrated below when the number of employees and employers is analyzed. The thirty-five servants, concierges, and doorkeepers (3 percent) were too dependent on their masters economically and psychologically to do more than scrape for a living once emigration from the capital began on a mass scale.

If to the legal profession are added members of various liberal professions—civil servants, commissioners, physicians, teachers, architects, sculptors, musicians, clerics, engineers, writers, the one librarian, and the students, a total of 72 individuals (6 percent), the 152 persons (80 of the legal profession plus the 72 above) would form a bloc of 13 percent). Their influence would be far greater than their numbers, however, because of their position in society. It is interesting to note the wide variety of crafts practiced by one or two individuals in the district.

As for the signatories of the list (a number of whose biographies are sketched below in connection with the organization of the district), there were Jean-François Dufour, an *avocat au parlement* and future president of the district assembly; Champion de Villeneuve, one of the secretaries and a future minister of Louis XVI; Bellart, an *avocat* who was to become a celebrity under the Restoration; the historian Aneilhon; Proudhomme, the famous publisher of the journal *Révolutions de Paris*; Miller de Precarré, substitute to the *procureur général*; Colon de Thévenot, the inventor of stenography; and William Playfair, agent of the Ohio (Scioto) Land Company.[32]

---

[30] Jean Jacques, *Vie et mort des corporations; grèves et luttes sociales sous l'ancien régime* (Paris, 1948), p. 92.

[31] "From the beginning of the seventeenth century particularly, masters busied themselves less to teach the craft to an apprentice than to get service from him." Alfred Franklin, *La Vie privée d'autrefois; arts et métiers; modes, moeurs, usages des parisiens du XIIe au XVIIe siècle* (Paris, 1889), p. 51.

[32] Lecocq, pp. 24-25. William Playfair (1759-1823), listed as an "English engi-

A mere eleven were illiterate, recorded by the secretary as unable to sign their names, among whom were two bourgeois, a master shoe-maker, a master tiler, two merchants, and the rest *compagnons* and workers. The overwhelming mass of signers were obviously the solid core of the district: literate, propertied, or possessed of a profession or occupation, with fixed residences in the neighborhood. The 1,214 individuals were united not only in protecting their property against the *gens sans aveu* but against the arbitrary power of the king and his officials, as well.

In addition to the 898 individuals whose occupations may be gleaned from the militia list, there were workingmen who were paid in *assignats* by their employers. The exchange of these *assignats* of large denomination for smaller notes is another source of classification of the labor force in the section.[33] The first thing that strikes an observer is the relatively large number engaged in the building and furniture

---

neer" was born near Dundee, Scotland, and moved to Paris where he took out a patent for a rolling mill in 1789. He succeeded Joel Barlow as agent of the Ohio Land Company and participated in the attack on the Bastille. Playfair left France in 1793 and violently attacked the Revolution in a number of brochures. Upon his return after Waterloo, he launched a journal, but was forced to leave France again after a widow whose husband had been killed in a duel brought charges against him. *Dictionary of National Biography* (London, 1909), XV, 1,300-1,301.

[33] A.N., F^{30} 145, "Administration des finances. Eschanges d'assignats contre numéraire pour faciliter la paye des ouvriers." Figures are based on the total entries under individual employers divided among the three years. It is possible, of course, that some of the master workmen who ran an enterprise in 1790 continued to manage it in 1791 even though no *assignat* notes were exchanged for small denominations in the latter year. The figures listed by Frédéric Braesch in his "Essai de statistique de la population ouvrière de Paris vers 1791," *La Révolution Française*, 63 (1912), 306, do not correspond to my findings, and a number of occupations listed by him for the section do not appear in this collection at all. In only a few instances are the figures not clear. A Fournier, under date of 16 March 1791, appears to be a mason who employed an average of 5.2 workers, and is so listed by me. A Filliot, an *entrepreneur de terrasse*, employed 25 workers at an unspecified date. I have placed this entry in the year 1790, which made for an average of 20 workers for him. The jeweler Boiteau employed 6 men on 6 December 1791, followed by an entry for the same date of what appears to be 8; on 14 May he employed 8, followed by an entry for the same date of what appears to be 6. A mason Petit employed a number of workers on 3 February 1790, and, possibly, 33 workers for 17 March 1791. These figures are not clear, however, and I have omitted this entry from the total number.

Evidently, what Braesch did was to use the final (top) figure for the year 1791, rather than the average employed based on all figures reported for the year.

trades. Masons, carpenters, cabinetmakers, and locksmiths formed a large proportion of the total work force. The addition of painters, plasterers, roofers, plumbers, upholsterers, and glaziers, made these trades a clear majority of the crafts listed. Out of the labor force of 1,031 that supposedly prevailed in the section in 1791, masons alone numbered 598, painters 94, and carpenters-cabinetmakers 44.[34] Assuming that there were 67 employers and 1,031 workers in the section, the average number of workers per employer would have been 15.3, slightly below the overall average for the capital, which was 16.6. The actual figure of workers in the section is closer to 1,143, however, if categories of workers omitted from Frédéric Braesch's list are added.[35] This, in turn, would have made an average of 17 workers per employer (on the basis of 67 employers), a figure slightly higher (by 0.4) than the average for the capital.

The great majority must have lived in the section in which they worked, although there is evidence that this was not always the case.[36] Masons made up the largest number of wage-workers employed, reaching 723 at their height and dropping to 223 at their lowest point. One master mason engaged 114 men at the peak of the season in 1791, and another hired 95 during the same year, in contrast to the mere 12 occupied in the summer of the previous year.[37] Several employers

[34] The above figures are based on Braesch, "Essai." I have corrected the number of workers in the section to 1,031 (based on Braesch's own figures, p. 306, in contrast to his 1,028 as given in his table on p. 315).

[35] *Ibid.*, pp. 315, 316. Ile St. Louis had 305 workers with 28 employers, whereas section Ponceau had 5,288 laborers and 242 employers. There was large industry only in faubourgs St. Denis (with an average number of workers of 31.8), des Halles (27.9), Jardin des Plantes (25.7), and Fontaine de Grenelles (25.5). Section Roi-de-Sicile was substantially below these sections.

Only one baker is listed, employing 6 men. Yet, at the time of bread rationing 12 bakers were employed by the civil committee to supply bread in the section. A. de P., 4 AZ 53, 20 October 1793. Not a single butcher is given, yet in 1795 there were 35 butchers and an unspecified number of workers employed by them. A.N., D III, 256³, d. 10, pc. 59, 19 prairial, Year III (7 June 1795). A more glaring omission is that the list in question carried but one shoemaker employing 6 men. A survey in the fall of 1794 reveals that there were 67 cobblers, without specifying, however, the number of workers employed by each. A. de P., 4 AZ 356, 9 vendémiaire, Year III (30 September 1794). Those three categories would add an additional 112 workmen and/or employers.

[36] Rudé, "La Population ouvrière," p. 30.

[37] A.N., F³⁰ 145, Guanguet residing on Mauvais Garçons. In October 1790 he

TABLE 4

Number of Wage-Workers and Employers

Occupation	No. of wage-workers	No. of employers
Manufacturer of rope	16	1
Locksmith	103	6
Saddler	8	2
Smelter	4	1
Glazier	6	2
Upholsterer	15	2
Shoemaker	6	1
Dressmaker	3	1
Hatmaker	10	1
Tailor	8	1
House painter	87	9
Roofer	23	2
Painter-gilder	72	6
Carpenter	89	8
Building contractor	61	3
Mason	723	18
Plumber	9	1
Tiler	15	2
Mirror maker	12	1
Blacksmith	21	3
Maker of inlaid ware	8	1
Earthwork contractor	25	1
Plasterer	79	1
Baker	6	1
Coppersmith	4	1
Goldsmith	16	1
Total	1,429	77

SOURCE: A.N., F[30] 145. The totals are based on the highest number reported for each year, 1790-1792. Three additional employers were listed: Vauban, a mason, Quatremère, a merchant grocer-apothecary, residing on rue Verrerie (Marché-Saint-Jean), and Grodard, but none reported any workers under him. I have not included them in the 77 employers of labor.

hired as few as 2 workers, however,[38] with the highest number of laborers engaged in construction by one employer being 32.[39] The number of carpenters occupied, like the number of masons, fluctuated with the season—from the high of 24 to the low of 8.[40] One plasterer employed as many as 79 workmen, whereas a painter-gilder hired 30 men,[41] and a locksmith engaged 60 workers.[42] The highest number of house painters employed in the section was 20;[43] some master workers expanded their labor force considerably, with one baker hiring 6 men,[44] a painter-sculptor employing 8, and a jeweler engaging 16 men at the height of the employment curve.[45]

---

employed 24 workers; a year later, his labor force had risen to 114. This is a good illustration of the great fluctuation of employment in the section. The detailed figures are as follows: for 1790, 27 January, 30 workers; 14 October, 24; 10 April, 50; for 1791, 19 May, 91 workers; 18 August, 104; 13 October, 114; 19 January 1792, 76 workers. A labor force of 114 was most unusual. "According to the census of 1896, 98 percent of all establishments employed fewer than 50 workers." Michelle Perrot, *Les Ouvriers en grève, France 1871-1890* (Paris, 1974), I, 55. Feuillet, residing at 13 rue des Rosiers, was a signatory of the *procès-verbal* of 13-14 July. MS 742. The figures are for 13 October 1791 and 23 June 1790, respectively. A.N., F[30] 145.

[38] A.N., F[30] 145. Veste, a master carpenter residing at no. 10 Cloche-Perce, employed 2 workers on 16 March 1791; Jean Garnier, also a master carpenter, residing at no. 22 rue de la Poterie, and signatory of the list of 13-14 July, employed 2 men on 15 December 1790. Mosset, a glazier residing on Mauvais-Garçons, employed 2 workers on 30 July 1790. Michel, a tiler, of no. 21 Roi-de-Sicile, employed 2 workers on 7 April 1791. René Hébert, a painter-gilder, of no. 50 Saint-Antoine, and signatory of the *procès-verbal* of 13-14 July, employed 2 workers on 19 November 1790. In April he had hired 15 men. Capillon, also a painter-gilder, residing at Sainte-Croix-de-la-Bretonnerie, employed 2 men on 20 August 1791.

[39] *Ibid.*, Girardin, an *entrepreneur de bâtiments*, residing at no. 37 rue Avoye and no. 46 de la Verrerie, employed 32 men on 16 March 1790. A year later he listed only 6.

[40] *Ibid.*, Jacques Joseph Quitton, master carpenter, residing at no. 82 rue Vieille-du-Temple, and signatory of the militia list of 13-14 July, employed 24 men on 2 March 1790; on 7 September 1791 he listed only 8.

[41] *Ibid.*, Dubois, a master plasterer, formerly of the municipality of Belleville, then residing at no. 35 rue Saint-Antoine. Dupré, a painter-gilder, residing at no. 13 rue de la Verrerie, and signatory of the list of 13-14 July, hired 30 men on 4 August 1790. The following year (1 August 1791) he employed 20 men.

[42] *Ibid.*, Grenier, residing on rue de Bercy, employed 60 men on 12 March 1790. In November he was to employ a mere 4.

[43] *Ibid.*, Lasue, master painter, residing on rue Saint-Antoine, employed 20 men on 3 March 1790.

[44] *Ibid.*, Calli, residing on rue des Ecouffes, employed 6 men on 16 March 1790.

[45] *Ibid.*, Daverne, a painter, sculptor, etc., residing at no. 113 rue Vieille-du-

The total number employed for each occupation listed (using the highest number of wage-workers reported between 1790-1792), is shown in Table 4.

Of the 77 employers, 17 were alone in their occupation, although this obviously did not preclude the existence of self-employed craftsmen in the same occupation, or others who had no need to exchange *assignat* notes either because of cash on hand or because of the temporary position of their hired workers. If the number of workers employed gives any indication of the profits earned, then the differences among them must have been more than quantitative. An employer of 114 masons was on a different economic scale from a glazier who directed the labor of 2 men. The sharp variation in numbers employed by the same master craftsman is also striking. All work seemed seasonal, and fluctuated greatly from quarter to quarter and from month to month. What happened, it may be asked, to workers laid off by their employers? How many had skills to leave one occupation in temporary decline and shift to another in temporary ascent? The difference between 1,429 and 624 (the lowest number of workers employed) meant that in an off season, 805 laboring men had to find work, obtain relief, beg, or turn to petty crime.

According to Braesch's figure, the number employed in 1791 by the section's 16 employers was 666 workers, each employer hiring above the average of 15.3 for the section. The figures vary from the 16 engaged in the manufacture of rope to the 95 working for a mason. Thus 51 employers hired the remaining 365 workmen.[46] This means that approximately 24 percent (23.8 percent) of the employers hired 64 percent of the labor force, while 76 percent employed 36 percent. A master workman with 95 laborers under him might still call himself a *sans-culotte* in the Year II, but his status was obviously different from his neighbor who employed only two men and who also considered himself a *sans-culotte*. Yet both would enjoy a higher position,

Temple. Boiteau, a jeweler, residing on rue de la Verrerie, employed 16 goldsmiths throughout the months listed for 1790.

[46] Braesch, "Essai," p. 306. Thirteen of these were master masons. It is questionable if the statistical method employed by Braesch is accurate in determining the number of workers in section Roi-de-Sicile. A detailed examination based upon all the figures listed give the following averages: for the year 1790, an average of 911.19 were employed by 74 employers; in 1791, there were 574.80 employed by 42 entrepreneurs; in 1792, an average of 258.50 were employed by 10 employers.

economically and socially, than that shared by their respective work-men.

How was this labor force recruited? Various trades did their hiring at designated squares or streets. Fullers, for example, had two places in the section: one near the Place Baudoyer, where they hired men by the year, the other at the church of Saint-Gervais, where they em-ployed by the day. Carpenters gathered on the street of Ecouffes, while masons and unskilled laborers were hired on the Place de Grève.[47] As for the number of hours they worked, it is difficult to be precise, since the work schedule was usually set by the sun. This meant they worked as long as sixteen hours a day during the summer and about eight hours in wintertime.[48] Sometimes the working day was indi-cated by the ringing of church bells; night work by candlelight was forbidden because it would make for an imperfect product, it was believed. Wages remained low, as unemployment and poverty were chronic. The best-paid workers were carpenters, masons, and other construction workers, who averaged 30-40 sous a day, about double the earnings of other trades.[49]

In addition to the labor force, the amount and worth of the sec-tion's real and personal property are important factors that present further evidence of its economic and social base. Tables 5 and 6 seek to analyze this base as well as the economic trends for the years 1791-1793—the data for 1794-1795 unfortunately being unavailable. De-spite this latter omission it is possible to arrive at certain conclusions.

The value of real estate property (*propriété foncière*) for the year 1792 and an incomplete list for 1793 give an indication of the relative wealth by street. Table 5 compares assessments of landed property by street in the years 1792 and 1793.

Table 5 demonstrates that the ownership of real estate was widely distributed throughout the section. There appear to be no distinct, identifiable rich or poor neighborhoods. But the table reflects tend-encies of a more subtle kind. Of the nineteen streets listed, only two show no change in assessment, while eleven are increased and six decreased. Yet, although the assessments of these six streets fall, their means rise from 87.7 percent (Ste. Catherine) to 3.5 percent (Bercy).

[47] Franklin, pp. 59-61.

[48] *Ibid.*, p. 119.

[49] Jacques, p. 79. The average wage for most workers was 18 to 22 sous per day.

This means that fewer taxpayers paid more in 1793 than they did in the previous year. The two streets that suffered no change in assessment (Bar-du-Bec and Paveé) still reflect a substantial increase in their means—35 percent and 42 percent, respectively. In four cases both assessments and means grew (from 36.3 percent for Rosiers to 21.1 percent for Juifs). In seven streets the means are decreased, but in each case the number of properties assessed is increased. The percentage of increase mounts from a meaningless .0013 percent (for Saint-Jean) to 18 percent for Roi-de-Sicile. In the latter case, the total tax from the street climbs by 16.7 percent. A more dramatic illustration of this trend is that of Francs-Bourgeois, where the total tax increases from 26,500 to 52,700, a rise of 99.2 percent.

Furthermore, of the nineteen streets examined, fourteen had their maximum assessment raised from 228 percent (Ste. Catherine) to 12 percent (for Bercy and Ecouffes). Among the five whose maximums were lowered the decrease ranges from 53.6 percent (for Roi-de-Sicile) to 7.1 percent (for Billettes). A similar trend may be noted for the minimum assessments. In thirteen cases it is lowered (by 27 times for Ecouffes and 15 times for Rosiers) to 5.2 percent (for Coq). In five instances the minimum is decreased from 86.8 percent (for Saint-Jean) to 6 percent (for Bar-du-Bec), whereas Pavée reflects no change.

What conclusions can be drawn from the above? It seems that the civil commissioners were attempting to maximize the receipts from the tax *foncière* despite the drop in the total number of assessments. It is obvious that in a number of cases fewer taxpayers had to make up the difference. With hardly an exception, whenever the number of assessments is increased, the mean decrease is quite modest, that is, the total take is not redistributed among the larger number of taxpayers, thereby decreasing the rate per individual. On the contrary, appraisals are increased despite the additional number of taxpayers. In fourteen cases, where the maximum was raised, the range of the increase was much larger than in the five cases where it was lowered. Moreover, it is possible that where the minimum rises spectacularly, this could be due to the fact that a number of taxpayers on the lower end of the scale are dropped from the rolls. In general, the manner in which the tax *foncière* was applied could have been a manifestation of the tendency "to soak the rich" in the section.

The number of national estates (*biens nationaux* or *domaines nation-*

TABLE 5
Tax *Foncière*, 1792, 1793

Streets	1792					1793				
	N	Range	Median	Mean	Total	N	Range	Median	Mean	Total
Bar-du-Bec	7	3600-1600	2000	2128	14,900	7	5500-1500	2500	2871	20,100
Bercy	17	2500-350	800	841	14,300	7	2800-300	600	871	14,813
Billettes	13	4500-400	1200	1511	19,640	18	4180-490	1200	1422	25,420
Bourg-Tibourg	22	7000-300	1550	2271	49,960	26	10000-650	1300	2425	63,040
Bretonnerie	20	5000-200	1600	1530	30,610	26	6000-600	1550	1949	50,680
Cimetière St. Jean	30	5180-680	1200	1466	43,980	31	3700-700	1250	1464	45,400
Cloche-Perce	12	2900-350	1020	1237	14,840	11	4800-500	1550	1982	21,800
Coq	4	2040-1140	1280	1435	5,740	5	2500-1200	1700	1760	8,800
Coquerelle	5	900-300	420	524	2,620	6	650-420	510	523	3,140
Ste. Catherine	10	3650-340	1800	1509	15,090	9	12000-500	1600	2833	25,500
Deux-Portes	10	4000-600	1500	2165	21,650	6	6000-700	1675	2703	16,250

Ecouffes	22	2500-22	1100	24,502	21	2800-600	1550	1518	24,440
Francs-Bourgeois	8	6600-1000	2600	26,500	19	8500-600	1400	2778	52,790
Juifs	20	3400-300	1120	26,760	24	4000-490	1150	1621	38,900
Pavée	11	6000-600	1500	24,600	11	10600-600	1500	3172	24,060
Roi-de-Sicile	22	6900-400	1280	89,820	42	3200-600	1200	1388	47,160
Rosiers	30	3200-20	880	35,360	35	4000-300	1000	1244	43,560
St. Antoine	40	6840-600	1800	96,840	52	8800-430	1625	2174	113,050
Tisseranderie	21	5800-120	1300	30,400	15	2880-750	1500	1604	24,060
Temple				84,620					none
Verrerie				79,440					none

NOTE: All figures are rounded.

SOURCE: A. de P., D. 4L¹ 39, and D. 4L¹ 40, *Régie de l'enregistrement et du domaine national. Sommier des rôles de contribution foncière.* (Register #50). For 1792, Col-de-Sac d'Argenson, rues Ballets and Tiron are omitted because each lists two properties only, as is Col-de-Sac-Saint-Feron which gives three properties. Place Baudoyer and Neuve-Sainte-Catherine are not listed. Argenson, Ballets, and Tiron each had only two properties listed, for 1793. The important streets of la Verrerie and Vielle-du-Temple (for 1793) are missing.

aux) in the section totaled 170 throughout the entire revolutionary period.[50] Saint-Antoine had the most, with thirteen individual properties, followed by Roi-de-Sicile with eleven. Bercy, Francs-Bourgeois, and Tisseranderie each had one.[51] Most experienced a common history in being leased, sold, and leased again. In 1792 there were only two such properties listed in the section (if the tax rolls can be accepted as being accurate), which increased to ten the following year. These varied in value from 3,500 livres to a mere 420 in 1793.[52] A dozen public properties, mostly charitable institutions (*hôtels Dieu*), also appear on the tax rolls. Cloche-Perce listed four such institutions worth from 3,000 to 500 livres, and several other streets counted a number of poorhouses and hospitals appraised at from 3,300 livres to 1,050.[53] A number of these holdings were sold at fairly high prices, while others were rented for substantial returns (although this is more true of the period before 1792 and after 1795 than during the time of falling property values). One *hôtel Dieu* on rue Saint-Antoine, for example, assessed at 34,146 francs, was rented at 1,897 francs per quarter (632.33 francs per month) on 1 October 1791, while another piece of property that had belonged to an émigré and had been valued at 72,000 francs brought only 45,000 livres when sold as late as 11 ventôse, an V (1 March 1797). A mansion on rue Francs-Bourgeois, appraised at 216,000 francs, was seized by the authorities under the charge that its owner had emigrated, only to be restored to his heirs who proved the contrary. Rue Bourg-Tibourg presented an example of a piece of property that had originated as a factory, valued at 144,000 francs; and La Force prison was appraised at 450,000, bringing a rent

[50] H. Monin and L. Lazard, *Sommier des biens nationaux de la Ville de Paris* (Paris, 1920), II, 372-399, wherein each street is listed with the history of each property traced.

[51] *Ibid.*, II, 372-375, 391-393, 375-379, 396—in the respective order.

[52] For the year 1792, one property on Saint-Antoine was assessed at 1,820 livres, and the other, on rue Cloche-Perce, was valued at 1,000 livres. The following year the *domaines nationaux* were assessed as follows: Bretonnerie, 3,500; Saint-Antoine, 2,300; Rosiers, 1,800; Roi-de-Sicile, 900; Coquerelle, 650, 570, two at 450, and one at 420. A. de P., 4L¹ 39 and 4L¹ 40, *Régie de l'enregistrement*.

[53] A hospital on rue Saint-Antoine was assessed at 3,300 livres; one on Bretonnerie was valued at 1,600. Cloche-Perce carried the following evaluations: 3,000, 1,500, 1,300, and 500. Saint-Jean listed two at 1,700 and 1,050, respectively, followed by Juifs with 2,400, Renaud-Lefebvre at 3,150, Roi-de-Sicile at 1,200, and Tiron with 1,240 livres. *Ibid.*

of 25,000 francs. In the early years of the Revolution a number of properties brought substantially more money when sold than their original appraisal seemed to warrant. One such example was a house on Saint-Antoine and rue Tiron valued at 40,500 francs but sold for 72,100 livres in 1791.[54] It seems clear, therefore, that before the great decline in property values in 1792 the section had its share of valuable property, and the buying and selling of real estate, buildings, and other assets must have propelled a number of Rougons on their way to fame and fortune.[55]

That the Revolution gave an impetus to the spirit of equality may be seen in a spirited objection made by a resident of section Droits-de-l'Homme to the practice of selling large blocks of property to a few individuals. One sale of five houses on rue Sainte-Croix-de-la-Bretonnerie, placed at auction "en bloc," roused a protest from citizen Vial (probably member of the *comité de bienfaisance*), who wrote: "One could have sold them in five individual lots, or at least not to have undertaken the auction of all so long as they could be disposed by individual auction." This brought consent by the official in charge who ordered: "Sell them separately. You will carry out the wish and spirit of the decree which is to create many small proprietors, because they are more attached to the Constitution than the larger ones and the entrepreneurs who buy them in order to resell them at higher prices."[56]

In addition to these individual properties, there were twenty-five *jardins de luxe* (pleasure parks) in the section, five on rue de la Verrerie, four on Francs-Bourgeois, three on Vieille-du-Temple, two each on rue des Juifs and rue Pavée, and one on each of the following streets: Culture-Sainte-Catherine, Moussy, Temple, Rosiers, Sainte-Croix-de-la-Bretonnerie, Deux-Portes, Bar-du-Bec, and Droits-de-l'Homme.[57]

---

[54] Monin and Lazard, II, no. 3120, p. 372; no. 3129, p. 374; no. 3143, p. 379; no. 3144, p. 379; no. 3187, p. 389; no. 3122, p. 372. In 1792, La Force prison was assessed at only 6,900 livres A. de P., 4L¹ 39, *Régie de l'enregistrement*.

[55] See Further, A.N., Q² 207, p. 135, ff. for section Droits-de-l'Homme, "Documents de la régie des domaines nat'aux," volume 10.

[56] A.N., C 141, no. 135, fol. 34, signed by Vial, *citoyen actif*, Paris, 9 December 1791, cited by Monin and Lazard, II, 399. The reply was written in the margin of the *Journal de la vente des biens nationaux*, A.N., C 141, no. 135, 17. I have omitted two slight errors of repetition in translating the above.

[57] A. de P., 3 AZ 287, pcs. 39, 47-51, n.d., "Liste des jardins de luxe de la

TABLE 6

Tax Mobilière, 1791-1793

Streets	(N)[a]	1791				1792				1793			
		Highest	Lowest	Median	Total	Highest	Lowest	Median	Total	Highest	Lowest	Median	Total
Bercy	(15)	2800	400	800	15,425	2100	300	600	11,867	420	60	120	2,310
Bourg-Tibourg	(23)	6600	600	1680	57,880	4950	450	1260	40,424	990	90[b]	254	7,845
Bretonnerie	(22)	6000	600	1230	41,426	4500	450	922	32,469	900	90	180[c]	6,790
Cimetière-St. Jean	(60)	3000	50	700	51,451	2250	37	525	37,397	450	7	105	7,708
Cloche-Perce	(12)	3250	350	1750	18,740	3250	262	1020	15,054	483	52	180	2,807
Croix-Blanche	(13)	9000	400	1480	30,080	6750	300	1111	21,961	1350	60	223	4,392
Ecouffes	(20)	2800	600	1475	30,590	2100	450	1106	22,942	435	90	237	4,788
Juifs	(24)	4025	440	1150	36,479	3018	330	862	27,391	605	66	172	5,467
Pavée	(11)	10068	600	1500	34,886	7551	450	1125	23,764	1510	90	225	5,247
Roi-de-Sicile	(31)	4000	500	1250	49,298	3000	375	907	37,689	600	75	187	7,560
Rosiers	(34)	4000	300	1000	44,952	3000	225	750	33,324	600	45	150	6,875
Temple	(45)	5450	600	2000	100,304	4387	450	1500	76,523	877	90	300	15,648
Tisseranderie	(26)	2600	500	1325	35,660	1950	375	993	26,043	390	75	198	5,422
Verrerie	(47)	8000	600	1600	93,147	6000	450	1200	70,689	1200	90	240	13,931

[a] Of the 14 streets, all but 4 (Pavée, Croix-Blanche, Cloche-Perce, and Bercy) have a minimum of 20 properties listed. Twelve streets had fewer than 10. These are: Ballets (2), Mauvais-Garçons (7), Faron (3), Renaud-Lefebvre (5), Deux-Portes (6), Billettes (9), Tiron (3), Coq (4), Coquerel (7), Moussy (5), Francs-Bourgeois (8), and Bar-du-Bec (7). Their ranges and medians are too sparse for a meaningful analysis. Culture Ste. Catherine, Neuve Ste. Catherine, and Place Baudoyer do not appear.

[b] The entry for 1793 reads 40 instead of 90 (item 32), but must be an error since the decrease for this item is out of proportion with all other entries. Were this entry correct, the rate of decline between 1791 and 1793 would be 93 percent.

[c] There ae 23 entries for 1793 because Eglise St. Croix was added as a *domaine national*, assessed at 160 livres.

SOURCE: A. de P., D. 4L¹ 37 and D. 4L¹ 38, *Régie nationale de l'enregistrement et des domaines. Sommier des rôles de la contribution mobiliaire.* Register #52. Individual entries are in the latter record; the former is a copy by a secretary from the original individual entries.

Most belonged to private individuals, although no. 10 rue Pavée listed several tenants. The *jardin* on rue Temple belonged to a *religieuse* of Saint-Gervais.[58]

Although the value of real estate is an important source that indicates the distribution of wealth in the section, a more complete record exists of personal property, *propriété mobilière*, for the years 1791-1793. Table 6 compares the assessments made of this property for the years 1791, 1792, and 1793.

Table 6 illustrates that the decrease in percentage (with only two significant differences)[59] among the highest, lowest, and median figures is constant. These differences are 25 percent for the period 1791-1792; 80 percent for 1792-1793; and 85 percent for 1791-1793. How is it possible to account for the increases of the tax *foncière* in contrast to the across-the-board lowering of the tax *mobilière*? One possible explanation lies in the larger number of contributors to the latter as against the number of taxpayers to the former, that is, 503 individuals, compared with the 314 individuals (in 1792) who paid the tax *foncière*. An 80 percent cut would satisfy both the wealthier and the poorer taxpayers. Moreover, real estate is more visible than personal effects (*états*). On the other hand, mansions (*hôtels*) that are taxed may satisfy the humbler citizen during a time of hostility to wealthy property holders. At the same time, an 80 percent decrease on his property tax appeals to the wealthier citizen. Furthermore, land does not depreciate, unlike houses, shops, and personal effects. In times of extreme food shortages, even an acre or two enables its owner to grow some vegetables and to keep chickens and pigs to supplement his meager diet. Finally, the continued drop in value of the *assignat* was bound to be reflected in the rising price of real estate.

Does Table 6, therefore, illustrate a real decline in property values,

---

section des Droits-de-l'Homme." A twenty-sixth is listed on no. 3 Cloche-Perce, but no one was identified as its proprietor.

[58] *Ibid.* In two cases it is not clear whether a *jardin* is involved, or some other property. On rue de la Verrerie, for example, a large shop (*magazin chez quatre maire*) is given, and on Sainte-Croix-de-la-Bretonnerie no description of the property is listed.

[59] The two differences may be due to an error of the clerk. Temple shows a decrease of 19 percent for the highest figures between 1791 and 1792. Bretonnerie reflects a 19 percent drop in the median for the same years. Item #13 for the latter, however, yields a 72 percent decrease (1792-1793) and a 79 percent drop (1791-1793). Item #17 (1793) is illegible.

or is this decrease the result of a political-administrative decision by the civil commissioners of the section? It is difficult to be precise in replying to this question. The uniformity of the decreases in percentage for the years 1791-1793 points to a political or an administrative judgment. Yet, unless the assessments were based on nothing but the whims of civil commissioners—a conjecture without foundation—they must have reflected the declining property values in the section. The fall of the *assignat*, coupled with shortages of necessities, raised prices (as is discussed below). The war, internal revolts, the levy *en masse*, the attack on private property, the general uncertainty—all contributed to this crisis. If the latter factors helped empty the capital, however, because men of draft age were swept up into the armed forces while others returned to their original homes in the provinces because they could no longer make a living in Paris, what would have happened to property values when so many houses, shops, and commercial buildings stood empty? Whether civil commissioners grasped this economic trend in theory or not, the practical ruling made by them, as shown by the decreasing assessments, reflected this sad reality. Thus, there is little doubt that section Droits-de-l'Homme was suffering an economic depression—a partial explanation, surely, for the radicalization of that sector of its population which saw in political measures a means of ameliorating its economic condition.

II

The Districts and
the Fall of the Bastille

The attack on the Bastille, which unleashed the Revolution, was but the culmination of a long struggle, as is well known, between the middle classes and their allies against ·the privileged orders of clergy and nobility. Every effort at reform of the most glaring injustices and irrationalities of the Old Regime was rejected out of hand by aristocrats and their dependents—a policy so rigid and unyielding that it finally brought on a financial and political crisis, which, in turn, aggravated class antagonisms during the period of the so-called pre-revolution preceding the outburts of 14 July.[1] The financial emer-

[1] See, for example, Jean Egret, *La Pré-Révolution française (1787-1789)* (Paris, 1962). Most general studies of the French Revolution begin with a description of the period between 1787-1789 as preliminary to the Revolution proper.

For different points of view as to the class nature of the Revolution, see Elizabeth L. Eisenstein, "Who Intervened in 1788? A Commentary on the Coming of the French Revolution," *American Historical Review*, 71 (October 1965), 77-103, and Eisenstein, Jeffrey Kaplow, and Gilbert Shapiro, "Class in the French Revolution: A Discussion," *ibid.*, 72 (January 1967), 497-522. Daniel L. Wick, "The Court Nobility and the French Revolution: The Example of the Society of Thirty," *Eighteenth Century Studies*, 13 (Spring 1980), 263-284 argues that "The Court nobility in the Society of Thirty may have been loyal or at least sympathetic to Louis XVI, but they were not loyal or sympathetic to the *ancien régime*" (p. 282). None of this disproves the bourgeois nature of the Revolution, however. To do so, the author would have to demonstrate that the Thirty did, indeed, make the Revolution, or contribute in a major way to it. See also, George V. Taylor, "Noncapitalist Wealth and the Origins of the French Revolution," *American Historical Review*, 72 (January 1967), 469-496.

The "Revisionist" view criticizing the Marxist tenet and citing de Tocqueville and Cochin is presented by François Furet, *Penser la Révolution française* (Paris, 1978). Patrice Higonnet, *Class, Ideology and the Rights of Nobles during the French Revolution* (Oxford, 1981) seeks to reconcile the two points of view and argues that both have useful things to say.

gency, itself the result of decades of war and extravagance,[2] forced Louis to summon the Estates-General, and, thereby, opened a new chapter in the conflict so long in the making. The elections and the *cahiers* of 1789 enabled reformers of all classes to mount their offensive against the regime of privilege, and, of equal importance, for formerly obscure commoners to assume positions of political leadership and responsibility. Paris, divided for administrative and electoral reasons at first into twenty quarters, then into sixty districts, followed by forty-eight sections, and, finally, into twelve arrondissements, witnessed the decisive intervention of the people (the *populace*, as conservatives termed them) in primary and electoral assemblies, which transformed the nature of the Revolution. It was in the neighborhoods of the capital that the Revolution was made. "The districts are the focus where the civic action of Parisians is concentrated; the districts provide for everything," wrote a historian of the Paris Commune.[3]

In addition to the historic split between bourgeois and noble, between the Third Estate and the upper two orders, there developed profound differences within the ranks of the commoners. Some of these were rooted in inequality of class; others were of the traditional variety between rich and poor, still others were based on corporate interests jealous of any encroachment on their historic privileges. Spokesmen of the Third Estate were often in a difficult position, therefore, for on the one hand they had to champion the general goals of their class vis-à-vis the clergy and nobility, and on the other hand they were not anxious to share their growing power with that large mass of artisans, petty shopkeepers, and poor workers whose aspirations and hopes were often in contradiction to their own. Yet those deemed conservative by their more radical brothers repudiated with indignation efforts of the king's ministers to deny them the right to choose their own representatives or to elect their own presiding officers. "It is the very essence of [the principle of] representation that it be the free expression of the will of all citizens,"[4] they wrote. Among

[2] A good, popular account is C.A.B. Behrens, *The Ancien Régime* (London, 1967).

[3] Sigismond Lacroix, *Actes de la Commune de Paris pendant la Révolution*, Série I, *Collection de documents relatifs à l'histoire de Paris pendant la Révolution française* (Paris, 1894-1900), I, Introduction, p. VII.

[4] "Mémoire et consultation sur la question suivante: Quels sont le moyens que doivent employer les habitans de Paris pour obtenir de nommer eux-mêmes leurs Représentans aux prochains Etats généraux . . . ," 18 December 1788, Chassin, *Elections*, I, 79-80. The protest carried 108 signatures.

the signatories to this complaint are such well-known personalities as Lafayette, the abbé Morellet, Hébert, and de la Harpe. Others demanded a better proportion of representatives from the capital and a broader electorate.[5]

The Royal Letter of Convocation and the *règlement* of 24 January 1789, followed by that of 28 March, outlined the rules under which the elections to the Estates-General would be conducted. Article XXIX of the latter regulation assured Paris special status in sending delegates to the Estates-General.[6] These regulations were further interpreted in the decree of 13 April 1789, which convoked members of the Third Estate who were born or naturalized Frenchmen, twenty-five years of age or older, with a fixed domicile in their *quartier*, paying at least six livres head tax.[7] These limitations on the right to vote and the consequent deprivation of a large mass of Frenchmen having spokesmen in the Estates-General encouraged a spirit of resentment and opposition among the more outspoken. They saw their exclusion from the political process as unjust, and warned that it would only encourage riots as "a prelude to a general insurrection" of the *quatrième ordre*.[8] One gentleman, whose title indicated that he was not of the lower order himself, declared that it was the disfranchised who enriched the other classes of the Third Estate, and that, moreover, their interests differed from those who were able to pay the six livres tax and who wanted to keep them in a state of dependence and servitude.[9] Spokesmen of the Third Estate were aware of this opposition, naturally—an opposition that complicated their own struggle with the privileged.

[5] "Mémoire des habitans de la ville de Paris au Roi," *ibid.*, I, 94-99.

[6] Jérôme Mavidal, Emile Laurent, Marcel Reinhard et al., *Archives Parlementaires de 1787 à 1860*, Série I (Paris: 1879-in progress), I, 547. Article XXIX reads: "Nulle autre ville que celle de Paris n'enverra de députés particuliers aux Etats généraux. . . ." The various regulations are in this volume, pp. 543-544, 544-550, 656-657. For a fine survey and translation of the main documents leading to the convocation of the Estates-General, see John Hall Stewart, *A Documentary Survey of the French Revolution* (New York, [1951]), pp. 25-41.

[7] "Règlement fait par le roi en interprétation et execution de celui du 28 mars dernier, concernant la convocation des trois états de la Ville de Paris," articles 12 and 13. A.P., I, 658, 659.

[8] "Protestation et déclaration," in Chassin, *Elections*, I, 469; "Du 20 avril," p. 476.

[9] "Au Directeur général des finances," 28 April 1789, signed by Le Chevalier de Moret, *ibid.*, I, 477-478.

The royal ordinance of 13 April had invited Parisians to make known their grievances through their electoral districts by depositing their observations and complaints in a special box placed for that purpose at the entrance of the Hôtel de Ville.[10] The primary assemblies, composed of all eligible voters in the district, were to meet in a church reserved for this purpose. In addition to drafting *cahiers*, they were enjoined to choose delegates to an Assembly of Electors who would then reduce the sixty individual *cahiers* into a general one for the whole of Paris.[11] These electors would also send deputies to the Estates-General to represent the Third Estate. The number of electors designated by each district was proportional to the total number of delegates sitting in primary assemblies. Upon completing these two tasks, namely, drafting the *cahier* and sending delegates to the Assembly of Electors, the district assemblies were to be dissolved. Events did not permit such a development, however. To draft a list of grievances and to elect delegates necessitated reports, discussion, committee meetings—all of which, in turn, led to the growth of a political consciousness that was to inaugurate the Revolution. The districts did not dissolve themselves; on the contrary, they helped overthrow the Old Regime.

The two districts that formed the future section of Droits-de-l'Homme, first known as Roi-de-Sicile, were Blancs-Manteaux and Petit-Saint-Antoine. The former had made up the ancient quarter of the Marais, and was destined to lose its identity by being divided between sections Droits-de-l'Homme and a neighboring section called Enfants-Rouges.[12] Bordering the district of Blancs-Manteaux was the

[10] A. de P., 1 AZ 113, *Ordonnance pour avertir les habitans de la ville et des fauxbourgs de Paris, de déposer dans un coffre, à l'Hôtel-de-Ville, leurs mémoires & observations, destinés à la reduction du cahier de ladite ville, pour les Etats-généraux* ([Paris], 15 April 1789), 4 pp.

[11] Duvergier, I, 73-89, 22 December-January 1790, decree relative to the constitution of primary and administrative assemblies.

[12] Its official name was district de l'Eglise des Blancs-Manteaux, and it was formed from the following streets: running in a northerly direction along rue Bar-du-Bec, it continued along rue Saint-Avoie; then east along rue des Blancs-Manteaux to rue Vieille-du-Temple; south to rue de Bercy; then west along de Bercy and rue de la Verrerie to rue Bar-du-Bec. A. de P., 1 AZ 113, *Etats-généraux convocation des habitans du tiers-état de la ville et fauxbourgs de Paris* (15 April 1789), 24 pp.; B.H.V.P., 100.65, districts (en général), a collection of 23 brochures; the above reference is to no. 110 bis, *Supplément de la feuille*, no. 23, p. 1153 (20 April 1789).

former quarter of La Place Royale, which assumed the name of Petit-Saint-Antoine.[13] The electoral assemblies that met, respectively, in the church of Blancs-Manteaux and in that of Saint-Gervais, experienced the same general problems and took many of the same steps as did many of their neighbors among the sixty districts of the capital.[14]

Of the 11,706 who voted for the 407 electors to represent the Third Estate, district des Blancs-Manteaux counted 176 ballots for its 8 electors, whereas district du Petit-Saint-Antoine reported 214 voting for 7 electors.[15] The former was among the nine districts with between 150 to 200 voters, whereas the latter was one of eight with from 200 to 250 voters. Three districts had fewer than 50 voters; four counted more than 400. A total of eleven districts chose 7 electors, with Petit-Saint-Antoine among these. Eight districts, including Blancs-Manteaux, selected 8 electors.[16] The number of electors chosen by the districts was in excess of the official regulations set at 100. Thus, Blancs-Manteaux, for example, had been limited to 2 electors, and Petit-Saint-Antoine was granted but 3.[17]

The primary assembly of district Blancs-Manteaux met on 21 and 22 April in its church of the same name. The order of business,

[13] The official name was district de l'Eglise du Petit-Saint-Antoine, and it was formed as follows: beginning on the north at the corner of rue des Francs-Bourgeois and rue Vieille-du-Temple, it ran east to rue Culture-Sainte-Catherine; south to rue Saint-Antoine; west along Saint-Antoine and rue de la Tisseranderie to rue des Co-quilles; north along the latter street, then east along rue de la Verrerie to rue de la Poterie. A. de P., 1 AZ 113, *Etats-généraux*, p. 20; B.H.V.P., 100.65, no. 110 bis, pp. 1160-1161.

[14] "Extrait du journal de Hardy du mardi 24 avril," in Chassin, *Elections*, II, 301-302. Hardy was a member of the assembly of district des Mathurins, but was aware of what went on in the assemblies of other districts, as well. The royalist journal, *L'Ami du roi*, admitted that the assemblies of the Third Estate were expected to be noisy and disorderly (expected, undoubtedly, by those who shared the journal's views), but were found to be tranquil and orderly. The writer of the report observed that all *cahiers* revolved about the same theme. Some wanted to demolish the Bastille; almost all wanted to remove the *prévôt des marchands*, the magistrates (*échevins*), and the counsellors, and to replace them with freely elected citizens. "Extraits de *L'Ami du roi*," 21 April 1789, written by Montjoie, *ibid.*, II, 303-306.

[15] "Etat-général des electeurs nommés pour le tiers état de Paris," *ibid.*, II, 317-318, 319. The *procès-verbal* of district Petit-Saint-Antoine gave 208 voters, as discussed in Chapter I.

[16] *Ibid.*, II, 322-324.

[17] *Ibid.*, II, 325-332 contains an analysis of the 407 electors by profession.

resolutions adopted, and the heated discussion animating the body all testify to the rapid quickening of political awareness permeating members of the Third Estate in the district. This was expressed from the very beginning in forceful opposition to efforts limiting the scope of their deliberations by royal officials; the electors demanded an equal number of representatives to the combined number of the first two orders, and insisted on the right to choose their own president, in defiance of royal authority.[18] Of special interest is their stress on the right to instruct their deputies and to express their will. Referring to their representatives as *mandataires* (mandatories or proxies), the assembly asserted that its deputies were never given power to act independently of their constituents. On the contrary, they were meant "to execute faithfully the thinking and will of the citizens."[19] This form of direct democracy was to reappear among the demands of popular clubs and assemblies later.

The assembly requested, furthermore, like others elsewhere, the immediate enactment of measures guaranteeing "the natural rights of Man and of the Citizen," the right to think, speak, write, and publish one's beliefs, the right to property, and the recognition of the principle that government was established for the purpose of assuring to each his essential rights. These universal principles were followed by thirteen propositions outlining the basic constitutional beliefs of the electors of 1789: the French monarchy was hereditary, legislation was the product of the general will, judicial power was exercised by magistrates or judges, all taxes were levied without distinction on all citizens alike, and so on. The assembly recognized the need for reform and protested bitterly its lack of power "to express its own views and to fulfill its high duty."[20] The minutes recorded reports from various delegates that almost all districts had elected presidents in opposition to those appointed for them by the authorities. Furthermore, they had protested against the limitation on the number of electors by official regulations, as seen above. In defiance of these regulations the assem-

[18] Almost all primary assemblies rejected the presidents appointed for them by that ancient executive officer of Paris, the *prévôt des marchands*. B.H.V.P., 923.645, Georges Garrigues, *Les Districts parisiens pendant la Révolution française* (Paris, n.d.), p. 10.

[19] B.H.V.P. 100.65 (28), *Cahier d'instructions données par l'Assemblée de Paris, tenue en l'église des Blancs-Manteaux, le mardi 21 avril 1789, & le lendemain mercredi, sans désemparer* ([Paris], 21 April 1789), p. 3.

[20] *Ibid.*, pp. 7-8.

bly chose eight electors, instead of the prescribed three, holding, moreover, that it had the right to select electors from all of Paris rather than limiting its choice to the district alone.[21]

The primary assembly of district Petit-Saint-Antoine met the same day, 21 April, in its own church, completing its deliberations on the following day. Its 214 members, after questioning the right of royal officials to appoint its officers, like its neighboring district Blancs-Manteaux, decided to ignore the formal instructions and chose, instead, a president, a secretary, and eight tellers from its own body. In a final act of defiance it expelled the *prévôt*'s officer from the hall, over his loud protests.[22]

The assembly then proceeded to form ten bureaus consisting of twenty-one members each. These, in turn, were to elect by simple plurality two of their colleagues; the twenty members so elected were charged with drafting the *cahier* to be presented to the primary assembly, which would then adopt the document with whatever modifications or amendments it chose. Once again, in defiance of the ordinance, it was decided to appoint seven electors, rather than the three allotted by law, the argument being that since the total number of electors was set at 300 (not 100 as at first), one-sixteenth of that number should give the district a minimum of five electors.[23]

The elections having been concluded, the critical problems of the Old Regime still confronted deputies and electors alike. In a short time, the latter realized that to solve these problems the ancient in-

[21] *Ibid.*, pp. 29-35; A.P., VI, 686-688.

[22] B.H.V.P., 100.65 (106), *Procès-verbal du tiers état . . . du Petit-Saint-Antoine* ([Paris], 21 April 1789), pp. 21-24. The tellers were an architect, an attorney, a caterer, two *avocats*, a wholesale merchant, a grocer, and a shopkeeper.

[23] *Ibid.*, pp. 24-25, 30. Not all district assemblies endorsed this view, however. Electors of district Sainte-Elisabeth pointed out that although they had a total of 316 active citizens, they had elected only four delegates and an equal number of substitutes. B.N., Le[23] 127, *Remonstrance de messieurs les Electeurs du district de Sainte-Elisabeth, à Messieurs les Electeurs des autres districts* ([Paris], [1789]), 4 pp. Maurice Tourneux in his monumental collection, *Bibliographie de l'histoire de Paris pendant la Révolution française* (Paris: 1890-1913), I, no. 837, mistakenly lists the assembly of district Saint Germain-de-Près under Petit-Saint-Antoine. The same defiance of official regulations and opposition to royal authority appears in this assembly as in those of Blancs-Manteaux and Petit-Saint-Antoine. B.H.V.P., 100.70 (18), *Procès-verbal de l'assemblée partielle de l'ordre du tiers-état de la Ville de Paris, tenues à l'abbaye Saint-Germain-de-Près, le 22 et 23 avril 1789*, 24 pp.

stitutions of the country had to be not modified but totally destroyed. To carry out such a task, however, the great mass of common people had to be mobilized and brought into political life. Here the economic crisis helped stir thousands who otherwise might never have become involved.

It is true, of course, that "the men of 14 July did not fight for goodies!" as Gonchon, spokesman for faubourg Saint-Antoine, declared to the Assembly in January 1792.[24] Yet it cannot be denied that, as George Rudé has concluded, "the most constant motive of popular insurrections during the Revolution . . . was the compelling need of the *menu peuple* for the provision of cheap and plentiful bread and other essentials."[25] Furthermore, as Georges Lefebvre wrote, "the municipal revolution was successful because the political crisis coincided with an equally violent economic crisis. Had bread been cheaper, the brutal intervention of the people, which was indispensable to assure the destruction of the ancient regime, might never have occurred, and the bourgeoisie would have triumphed less easily."[26] Contemporary accounts give instances of the food crisis in the spring and early summer of 1789 that help explain the desperate behavior of crowds in the capital.[27] Competition with England; the growing unemployment, caused partly by this competition and partly by the general uncertainty; speculation and engrossment—all had an adverse effect on the price and the availability of bread. Necker reported on 1 July the purchase of large amounts of grain and flour. Yet he admitted that "the multitude" blamed the high cost of bread on speculation as "the prime cause" of this increase.[28] Bread was the capital question between April and October 1789.[29] One pamphleteer began with, "Ce

[24] Cited by Albert Mathiez, *La Vie chère et le mouvement social sous la Terreur* (Paris, 1927), p. 47. The original quotation is: "Les hommes du 14 juillet ne se battent pas pour des bonbons!"

[25] Rudé, *The Crowd*, p. 200.

[26] Georges Lefebvre, ed., *Documents relatifs à l'histoire des subsistances dans le district de Bergues pendant la Révolution (1788-an V)* (Lille: 1914), I, xxxviii.

[27] The royalist journal, *l'Ami du roi*, 3e cahier, p. 39, gave a graphic report on the shortages of necessities, the long lines before the doors of bakeries, and the "detestable" bread sold when it was available, cited by B. & R., II, 40.

[28] From his report in Chassin, *Elections*, II, 549.

[29] *Ibid.*, II, 571-579. Chassin gives extracts from four brochures as typical of the many on the subject. A number of writers were eloquent with indignation on the situation of the poor.

que personne n'a dit encore je le dirai!" Attacking monopoly and the high price of bread, he demanded that the various assemblies occupy themselves with this problem at once.[30] "What's the good of a wise Constitution to a people emaciated by hunger?" another asked. "Feed the people, open the ateliers, give land for cultivation," he urged.[31] "When I see some people eat up in one meal what would suffice to maintain some ten families for a year, this makes me f_____ mad, and plenty," raged the *Père Duchesne*.[32]

In addition to the economic and financial crisis, political unrest grew as the great question of whether the Estates-General would vote by head or by chamber continued to agitate Paris. The Electoral Assembly of the capital, having refused to dissolve itself, decided to remain in a state of permanence during the approaching meeting of the Estates.[33] The growing unrest began to affect the armed forces, as was to be expected. Soldiers were beginning to side with the people against orders of their officers.[34] Persistent rumors of the approaching military intervention by the king and the growing menace of Swiss mercenaries and other loyal regiments against the National Assembly, coupled with the growing anarchy or fear of such, persuaded a number of leading electors and officials of the capital that a reliable armed force commanded and staffed by the middle class was essential. Nic-

[30] "Cahier du quatrième ordre," *ibid.*, II, 582-586. "What no one has yet dared to utter I will say." Among other charges, he attacked the posting of soldiers at the doors of assemblies directed against "the *populace*."

[31] "Quatre cris d'un patriote à la nation," *ibid.*, II, 586-587. "Of the twenty-five million people who inhabit my country, at least eighteen million die of hunger," he wrote, and warned of "a terrible insurrection . . . not far away of twenty million poor without property."

[32] "La colère du Père Duchene à l'aspect des abus," *ibid.*, II, 587. The original combines a vulgar expression by dividing the word *fâcher* thus: "Quand je vois des hommes manger en un seul repas ce qui suffirait à la subsistance de dix familles dans un an, cela me f . . . âche, et beaucoup."

[33] "Permanence de l'Assemblée du Tiers," on a motion of an *avocat* Oudet, conforming to a resolution of 22 April to remain in permanence and to correspond with the electoral corps and with the deputies of the Estates-General, *ibid.*, III, 245-246.

[34] See the various reports by Hardy, as "L'Agitation de Paris du 25 juin au 2 juillet 1789," *ibid.*, III, 449-453, 465-468. A letter written by a *garde-française* to his colonel accused the latter of treating his men like slaves. "Dans votre system, il faut n'être plus ni français, ni citoyen, ni fils." In another letter he complained that the army was represented only by the nobility. B. & R., II, 35.

olas de Bonneville, a freemason and cofounder with Claude Fauchet of the Cercle social, a club interested in political and social reforms, was the first to move on 25 June, to arm the citizens in a *garde bourgeoise*. Two weeks later, on 7 July, the electors of Paris agreed to constitute themselves as a provisional commune.[35] These two decisions—to create an armed force and to assume the powers of a municipal government—laid the foundation for the victory of the bourgeoisie and its supporters on and after 14 July.

On 12 July the Electoral Assembly sitting at the Hôtel de Ville resolved that "the districts be convoked immediately." The following day, 13 July, the tocsin was heard in almost all parishes from 6 a.m. on. A large crowd invaded the Hôtel demanding arms, a demand that the unfortunate assembly could not meet. Among the hurried resolutions adopted by the electors was one to establish a Permanent Committee (*un comité permanent*) that would meet without interruption, destined to act as the executive committee of the provisional municipal government of Paris.[36] At 2 p.m. the Permanent Committee appointed commissioners to formalize the creation of the Parisian militia and immediately proclaimed its organization.[37]

The general assembly of district Petit-Saint-Antoine met the same day to implement the measures resolved upon by the Assembly of Electors. As its former president, Jérôme-Louis Trudon, had resigned because of age and infirmity, the assembly elected in his stead Jean-François Defour, an *avocat au parlement*. Meanwhile, La Force prison

[35] Séances des électeurs de Paris du 10 et du 11 juillet," in Chassin, *Elections*, III, 474-477. The resolution of the Assembly of Electors on July 7 read: "and the deputies of the provisional representatives of the Commune to place before the Bureau of the National Assembly the act of the Constitution ratified by the districts." The first articles of this constitution were to provide for an annually elected municipality and the establishment of a bourgeois militia. *Ibid.*, p. 477.

[36] Bailly wrote that on the evening of 14 July "the Permanent Committee was active without pause," and described dramatically its role during the siege of the Bastille. B.N., La[33] 8, *Mémoires de Bailly*, 3 vols. (Paris, 1821-1822), I, 369, 375-385 in Saint-Albin Berville and Jean François Barrière, *Collection des mémoires relatifs à la Révolution française* (Paris, 1820-1828).

[37] Chassin, *Elections*, III, 497. "Hôtel de Ville lundi après-midi, 13 juillet 1789 arrêté du comité permanent. . . ." The decree provided for the organization of 16 legions from the 60 districts, each legion to be divided into 4 battalions (3 legions to have 3 battalions each), the battalions to be composed of 4 companies each of 200 men, and so on. Also in B. & R. in 16 articles, II, 94-95.

had been broken into by "vagrants" (*gens sans aveu*) and its inmates, most of whom were being held for debt, freed. It was essential, therefore, to organize a citizen guard against these "ill-intentioned persons" who, allegedly, were menacing persons and property, and equally important to beat back the gathering forces of the counterrevolution.[38] When the Assembly of Electors resumed its sessions about 4 p.m., delegates from the district reported on the measures taken to organize this bourgeois guard, and the meeting formally approved the emergency measures taken "until the Assembly of Electors can, upon deliberation with all districts, agree on a general rule."[39] District des Blancs-Manteaux resolved to rely on the prudence of its electors, whose powers it confirmed and extended, urging them to act "in the name of the country." Furthermore, it called on all citizens of the district to assemble at 5 p.m. under arms and to use them as judged necessary.[40]

By the evening of 13 July, steps had been taken by the district assemblies, the *comité permanent*, the Assembly of Electors, by various bureaus and commissioners, and by the command of the hastily formed bourgeois guard to confront royalty and the attempted counterrevolution. It is difficult to see anything that smacks of "mob" action in these well planned and executed steps. Communication and personal contact had been made long before between the National Assembly and its supporters in the districts of Paris. The action of the following day was merely the logical culmination of plans decided upon the day before—themselves the result of the struggle of some months previous. When the session of the Assembly of Electors had been formally concluded by 8 p.m., large crowds still remained to hear reports of what had taken place in Versailles. Not until midnight did many in the crowd, which included electors, finally disperse.[41]

---

[38] B.H.V.P., MS 742, fols. 262-273. The signatories with their occupations have been analyzed in Chapter I. The organization of the district's sixteen companies is in folio 274.

[39] Chassin, Elections, III, 499-500, 503.

[40] *Ibid.*, III, 501.

[41] *Ibid.*, III, 503-507, *passim*. Hardy's observations on the dramatic events of 13 July are especially instructive. "In the afternoon, the same popular movements, the same agitations, the same rumors continued," he wrote, and noted the good order of his district's militia together with many insurgents armed in every conceivable fashion. *Ibid.*, pp. 507-510. See also the review of events in B. & R. II, 96-101.

The dramatic events leading to the fall of the Bastille have been the subject of numerous studies.[42] There is no need, therefore, to do more than to note that for vividness of detail, none can take the place of contemporary accounts. The *procès-verbal* of the assembly of district Petit-Saint-Antoine gives an exciting view of the siege, as reports were incorporated into the minutes by Bellart, secretary of the assembly. Interestingly enough, they follow in their main outline the accounts given to the Assembly of Electors and the Permanent Committee. The general assembly of the district met early on 14 July, and immediately appointed three of its members to seek arms and ammunition from the *prévôt des marchands*, a hopeless task. Meanwhile, reports began to stream in that a crowd had gathered before the Bastille, that a bridge

Figure 2. The Siege of the Bastille

---

[42] Among the more recent is that of Jacques Godechot, *La Prise de la Bastille 14 juillet 1789* (Paris, 1965).

had been lowered to facilitate entrance into the fortress (presumably while negotiations were going on with de Launay), but that this act had proved to be a trap for the unwary, who now faced great danger. The garrison had begun to fire on "the unfortunate victims of their confidence," and it was this "act of treachery" that had resolved the crowd to storm the prison. The arrival of the *gardes-françaises* who came running to assist their fellow citizens determined the successful outcome of the action. In the words of the secretary, "their valor, joined with that of the people and with the bourgeois militia, carried the fortress." Then, waxing poetic, he described the scene before the town hall: "the cannon, the firearms, the flags, the wounded, the prisoners—all this riotous and imposing gathering creates a spectacle that inspires at one and the same time contradictory feelings—horror and satisfaction, pleasure and fear."[43] Thousands of citizens had come out of their homes to honor and applaud those "who had saved the city from danger." Then followed a personal observation of the secretary in the form of a question: why was it, he asked, that victory had not appeased the desire for vengeance? "The traitors are guilty," he admitted "but the law has condemned them just as public opinion has." The *vainqeurs de la Bastille*, some of whom had shed blood and seen their relatives and friends die in the siege, could hardly have replied in the detached and philosophical manner demanded by the question.

The fall of the Bastille changed radically the balance of forces. Popular intervention had saved and guaranteed the continued existence of the National Assembly, and as the secretary of district Petit-Saint-Antoine observed, "indeed it seemed that the life of the city had changed all of a sudden."[44] Hardy made essentially the same

[43] A. de P., 4 AZ 813. Chassin refers to this *procès-verbal* as registering "the act of de Launay's treason," but gives Champion de Villeneuve, future minister of Louis XVI, as secretary of the proceedings, and cites no. 487 of Fillon's *Inventaire* by Charavay, as proof. *Ibid.*, III, 541-542 n.1. Bellart might have transcribed the minutes from de Villeneuve, or more likely, might have taken down the reports and proceedings simultaneously.

[44] *Ibid.* In a document entitled "Siège de Paris prise de la Bastille," under date of "Le mardy 14e juillet 1789," the same dossier gives the following brief summary of events: At 11 a.m. faubourg Saint-Antoine beat the general alarm. From "midy" to 3 p.m. the Bastille was besieged and taken. Four cannon fired on the fortress. De Launay's head was cut off between 6 and 7 p.m.

In a dossier entitled "Vainqueurs de la Bastille," there is a document signed by

comments in his journal, and thought that the conquest of the fortress in less than three hours was "a miracle,"[45] while the duke of Dorset's flattering remarks on the surprising discipline of the people and the relative peacefulness of the event are too well known to require comment.[46]

As ancient institutions dissolved, the districts stepped into the breach. Beginning with the ratification of Jean-Sylvain Bailly as mayor of Paris and of marquis de Lafayette as commander of the National Guard, they went on to reorganize their administrative structure. Each district elected officers to preside over its primary assembly, and appointed committees to take charge of finances, accounts, the police, the armed forces, the poor, provisions, justice, and so on. To coordinate their work they formed a Central Bureau of Correspondence where their delegates exchanged information and decided on common action. What seemed chaotic on the surface actually contained a high degree of harmony and common purpose.[47] To systematize its work, the Permanent Committee was subdivided into three departments: provisions, police, and National Guard,[48] and on 25 July changed its name to Provisional Committee without in any way changing its functions.[49]

One of the problems troubling the authorities was the provisional and, technically speaking, illegal structure of the city government. Efforts to resolve the problem led to numerous disputes between the municipal government (that is, the Paris Commune) and the individual districts. On 18 July the Assembly of Electors convoked the districts for the purpose of electing deputies who would constitute them-

---

Louis granting pensions to widows, orphans, and wounded of the "conquerors of the Bastille." It also names those worthy of citation for courageous conduct. By 16 August 1791, the original number of 880 "conquerors" had been augmented to 910. A.N., F^{10} III, Seine 27.

[45] Chassin, *Elections*, III, 575-576.

[46] *Ibid.*, III, 542.

[47] Lacroix, *Actes*, I, Introduction, pp. VII-VIII.

[48] A. de P., 1 AZ 137; 4 AZ 697; 4 AZ 680; 4 AZ 813; Lacroix, *Actes*, I, 16-17. "Comité-permanent, établi a l'Hôtel de Ville, provisoirement autorisé, jusqu'à l'établissement d'une municipalité régulière et librement formée par l'election des citoyens des districts." A. de P., 4 AZ 680, 21 July 1789.

[49] Lacroix states that it was not a separate committee, as Buchez and Roux as well as Louis Blanc thought; Lacroix, *Actes*, I, 17-21.

selves as a duly recognized municipal body, a legal commune. While awaiting the formation of this institution, the electors formed a committee of sixty members to carry on the pressing daily work, divided into four bureaus of fifteen members each: correspondence, police, subsistence, and military. To legalize its proceedings, each district was requested to elect one delegate, the sixty delegates so elected to constitute the Provisional Committee.[50] On 19 and 21 July, fifty-five districts formally endorsed the election of Bailly and Lafayette, and were urged by the former to create a permanent organization for Paris. The first meeting of the delegates was scheduled for 25 July, marking the formal opening of the Paris Commune, the municipal government of the capital.

Although concerned with administrative details, the assembly of district Petit-Saint-Antoine remained alert to the larger political developments. Having been informed on 15 July that Louis had agreed to withdraw his troops from around Paris, it evinced its suspicion upon learning on the morrow that his troops had not yet been withdrawn. When it realized that the cannon of the bourgeois militia had been left unguarded, it hastened to warn the military committee of the Hôtel de Ville of this neglect; and to scotch rumors that flour and other provisions could have been poisoned, it suggested that the latter be examined by savants of the Academy of Science.[51] Yet, on the whole, the mood of the district was optimistic. The assembly drafted a flattering address to Lafayette after receiving a letter from him praising the courage of its participants in the events of 14 July.[52] At the same time, it addressed the new mayor, Bailly, as the "pilot" who had brought the ship safely home through raging storms.[53] The assembly of district Blancs-Manteaux limited itself to thanking the electors for having drafted the *cahiers* and for having elected deputies to the Estates-General, adding that this was done by illegally extending their powers, and calling for new elections to establish the Paris Commune.[54]

[50] Lacroix, *Actes*, I, Introduction, p. xii. A. de P., V.D.* 5, 18 July 1789, 6 pp.

[51] A. de P., 4 AZ 813. Chassin, *Elections*, III, 546-547 n. 3.

[52] B.N., Lb⁴⁰ 296, *Adresse à M. de La Fayette*, 21 July 1789; A. de P., 1 AZ 158, *Adresse à M. de La Fayette, Général de la milice parisienne; par l'Assemblée générale du district du Petit-Saint-Antoine*, 21 July 1789.

[53] B.N., Lb⁴⁰ 295, *Adresse à M Bailly*, 21 July 1789; A. de P., 1 AZ 158, 21 July 1789.

[54] B.N. MSS, Nouv. acq. fr. 2681, fol. 303, 21 July 1789; B.H.V.P., 100.65

Two days after the fall of the Bastille, the district assembly of Petit-Saint-Antoine heard with alarm that the demolition of the fortress was endangering the lives of prisoners allegedly still held in its secret dungeons. Disturbed by this rumor, it called the former jailers, Lassinotte father and son, to testify before it; both men swore that there were no secret cells in the Bastille and that the work of razing the structure, therefore, endangered no one. Shortly thereafter it was reported that there had been but seven prisoners at the time of its siege, and that all seven had been released "by the hand of patriotism."[55] In order to avoid such needless, and, at times, dangerous rumors from gaining credence, the president alone was authorized, henceforth, to present reports to the assembly.

Having chosen its delegates to the first assembly of the Commune, the district proceeded to establish a more permanent administration by electing a treasurer, a commission of finances of eight members and a military committee of fourteen, with one delegate assigned to the Commune's military board. Finally, it ratified the appointment of eight secretaries.[56] Several of these posts were to undergo modification in both number and structure, whereas others were to be added as the district's political life developed. Yet, on the whole, it showed a marked flexibility as the volume of its business increased.

This flexibility resulted from the myriad tasks performed by committees created by the districts as they linked their neighborhoods together by correspondence or oral exchange of views. Resolutions or motions were usually transmitted by special delegates; hence, the close sharing of opinions. Moreover, these committees also acted as agents of execution by placing seals on papers and personal effects, seizing grain, confiscating guns and powder, drawing up budgets, and carrying out police functions. Among the latter duties was the organization of patrols, the inauguration of house visits, and the disarmament of suspects. On the eve of their dissolution they had acquired many powers, including the supervision of theaters, lodging houses, and publications, and the arrest of counterrevolutionaries and other

---

(30 bis), *District des Blancs-Manteaux*, 21 July 1789, 2 pp. This was signed by Godard, one of its presidents, whose contribution is discussed below, and by Chappe d'Oreval, one of its secretaries.

[55] A. de P., 4 AZ 813, 16 July 1789.

[56] A. de P., 4 AZ 777, 18 July 1789.

lawbreakers. At times they tended to ignore their own assemblies, and had to be reminded of their subordinate role in the administration of the districts.[57]

The first assembly of the Commune, composed of 122 representatives elected by the districts, met on 25 July to 18 September 1789. The second followed on 19 September, and concluded its business on 19 November. Although it constituted itself as the municipal government of the capital, it was long in becoming a regular body. The City Council and heads of departments were not established until 8 October. Its most powerful official, the *procureur*, and his two substitutes, were elected on 14 and 15 October, and were not installed until 11 November, thus ending the last vestige of the municipal organization of the Old Regime. The department of police took up its functions on 16 November, and the police tribunal assumed its duties the following day. Not until October 1790 was it possible to recognize the municipal government of Paris as a definitive institution.

Its different departments and bureaus were the following: 1. office of the mayor; 2. the Assembly of Representatives composed of 240 members, each district electing 4 delegates (the City Council [Conseil de ville] included another 60 representatives, each district electing a fifth delegate for this purpose, thus making a total of 300 delegates elected); 3. the *procureur* and his two substitutes elected by the Assembly of Representatives; 4. the City Council, presided over by the mayor, and divided into nine departments (in addition to the *tribunal contentieux* [a court to settle disputed claims], there were eight administrative departments; these included subsistence and provisions, police, office of public institutions, public works, hospitals, public property, taxes, and the Parisian Guard [National Guard]; each department was chaired by a lieutenant of the mayor, elected by the City Council); 5. the town bureau (*bureau de ville*), composed of 21 principal officers, who met under the mayor; 6. an elected police

---

[57] Garrigues, pp. 51-54, 60-77, *passim*. The author points out that members of district committees were often *avocats*, counsellors in the Parlement, and lawyers. The majority were nobles who had rallied to the bourgeoisie. Members of committees of districts Blancs-Manteaux and of Petit-Saint-Antoine were in the latter category.

Mercier gives an amusing description of gentlemen of the law in the following passage: "A superficial taint of pedantry, always inseparable from the robe, the position between a man of letters and a professor of a university." *Tableau*, II, 41-42.

tribunal, also chaired by the mayor or his substitutes; and 7. the *comité des recherches* (investigating committee), a high government police committee, composed originally of 6 members from the Assembly of Representatives.[58]

With the adoption of a provisional plan on 12 August, each district elected one committee charged with executing the ordinances passed by the Commune or one of its departments. In addition to this duty, it supervised public health and—especially important—exercised police powers. The committees included a president who was chosen from the five representatives of the district to the Hôtel de Ville, and who presided over the district's general assembly; a vice president; the commander of the district's armed force constituted as a battalion; and thirteen to twenty-one members without specific public function, that is, ordinary citizens. Finally, there was a salaried secretary-registrar. All of these officials were elected by the general assembly of the district.[59]

Both districts Blancs-Manteaux and Petit-Saint-Antoine sent *avocats* to represent them in the first assembly, an indication of the relatively conservative stage of the Revolution and the traditional prestige still shared by members of the legal profession. Blancs-Manteaux elected two men, Blondel and Picard. The former was an *avocat au parlement*, had been coopted to the Assembly of Electors on 25 July 1789, and was elected and reelected twice as one of the presidents of the Assembly of Representatives of the Commune. He was a member of numerous delegations and was a signatory to important decrees, which included the installation of a new committee of subsistences and the adoption of regulations on discipline for the National Guard (both in September 1789). Blondel served as commissioner for examining the papers found in the Bastille, was elected as one of the presidents in the second Assembly of the Commune and was a signatory to the municipal plan presented by the Assembly of Representatives to the districts. District Blancs-Manteaux withdrew his mandate in the dispute between the districts and the Commune over the municipal plan

[58] Lacroix, *Actes*, II, Introduction, pp. IX, X-XI. Each of the departments was subdivided into an office (bureau) under an administrative head. The National Guard was placed under a commanding general elected by the districts and assisted by a military committee composed of delegates elected ad hoc by them.

[59] *Ibid.*, II, Introduction, p. XII and n. 1.

to be adopted and retired him from active political life on 11 December 1789.[60]

The second delegate, Picard, had also been an *avocat au parlement* and was elected as one of the presidents of the Assembly of Representatives. He was appointed as a commissioner to visit municipal prisons (8 August 1789) and was signatory to the decree banning the staging of the drama, *Charles IX*, [61] as being contrary to the new order of things.

District Petit-Saint-Antoine sent Jean-François Dufour, an *avocat au parlement*, former elector, member of the Commune's police committee, and later charged with the task of centralizing funds for the poor (in January 1790). He was a signatory to many decrees dealing with municipal affairs, and on 8 October 1789 congratulated the women of La Halle for their march on Versailles. Elected as secretary to the Hôtel de Ville, he became an assessor to the municipal tribunal, and on 10 December 1790 helped launch a subscription for funds to relieve the poor.[62] The second representative was Nicolas Oudart, an *avocat au parlement*, former elector, and member of the municipal investigating committee. Among the many duties he carried out was to act as one of the commissioners to establish a true list of the *vainqueurs de la Bastille* (as pensions and prestige were involved). He also was a member of the Committee on Subsistences, was returned to the second Assembly of the Commune, and as a commissioner elected to address the National Assembly suggested the best means to acquire church property (19 June 1790).[63] One hundred twenty-five members of the first assembly were returned to the second assembly, among whom were future deputies of the legislature and the Convention; others were to hold important positions in the revolutionary government.

Of the five representatives from Blancs-Manteaux, three had served in the first assembly. In addition to Blondel, there was Pierre-Marie-Auguste Broussonet, thirty years old, a member of the Royal Society of Agriculture and its secretary, as well as member of the Academy

---

[60] *Ibid*, Index, pp. 155-156. It is strange that despite the political activity of Blondel and his signature on many documents, his first name remains unknown.

[61] *Ibid*., Index, II, 654.

[62] *Ibid*., Index, p. 320.

[63] *Ibid*., pp. 629-630; for Oudart's role as president of section Droits-de-l'Homme at the time of the arrest of Jean Varlet, see the chapter on The Popular Society.

of Sciences. He was also a member of the *conseil de ville* and Committee on Subsistences (8 September 1789). On 30 January 1790 he was elected secretary of the Assembly of Representatives of the Commune.[64] The third representative was François Gorguereau, forty years of age, an *avocat au parlement*, president of his district and a commissioner for an examination of the papers found in the Bastille.[65] He was to be elected as deputy to the Legislative Assembly while still residing in the section.[66] To these were added Jacques-Louis Maugis, an *avocat au conseils* (that is, practicing before the Royal Councils) and elected secretary of the Assembly of Representatives (4 November 1789),[67] and Charles-Paul de Montmorency, an *abbé*, who was added to the police committee (3 October 1789). He congratulated the women of La Halle for their march on Versailles, was replaced as representative to the Commune, and retired from political activity in December 1789.[68]

On 10 October, Broussonet was replaced by César-Gabriel Filleul, age forty-one, former head clerk of finances, a *conseiller de ville*, and an administrator of subsistences for the department of Paris. He was especially active in matters relating to the sale and administration of national estates.[69] On 7 December 1789, among those who replaced former representatives was Ambroise-Jean-Baptiste-Pierre-Ignace Gattrez, age forty-five, *avocat au parlement* and active on various commissions as representative to the Commune.[70] The second representative was Phelippes de la Marnière, *conseiller au Châtelet*, and, like many others, one who served without pay.[71] The last was Jacques Godard, twenty-eight years old, an *avocat au parlement*, president of his district, and deputy to the Legislative Assembly. He was secretary for a short

[64] *Ibid.*, p. 193.

[65] *Ibid.*, p. 397. Gorguereau replaced Picard upon his resignation. Lacroix, *Actes*, I, 415.

[66] "M. Gorguereau, député de Paris, malade depuis plusieurs jours, est admis à prêter le serment du 10 août." A.P., XLVIII, 117, 14 August 1792.

[67] Lacroix, *Actes*, I, 579.

[68] *Ibid.*, p. 603.

[69] *Ibid.*, pp. 362-363; II, 681.

[70] *Ibid.*, III, 714; Index, pp. 381-382.

[71] *Ibid.*, Index, pp. 477-478; III, 714. Thus, Blancs-Manteaux had replaced Blondel, Gorguereau, Maugis, and Montmorency by Broussonet, Gattrez, de la Marnière, and Jacques Godard, as discussed below.

time to the lawyer and member of the Academy, Gui-Jean-Baptiste Target, who championed the cause of deaf-mutes and spoke in behalf of the Jews both in the Commune and in the National Assembly. Godard was active on numerous commissions as representative to the Commune, suggested means to acquire ecclesiastical property, and was a member of the Cercle social and the Amis de la vérité, the masonic gatherings led by de Bonneville and the *abbé* Fauchet. He was elected deputy to the Legislative Assembly on 20 September 1791, but died shortly thereafter, on 4 November 1791, ending what appears to have been a brilliant career.[72] One of the interesting controversies between him and the mayor of Paris deserves more than a passing notice.

Bailly had refused to take a new oath demanded of him by representatives of the Commune, holding that an honest man need not swear that he was such. On the charge that he had arbitrarily imprisoned a man who had insulted a public functionary in the street, he argued that he possessed this power of arrest by virtue of his position as president of the police tribunal. Godard reasoned that the mayor had assumed an unacceptable independence and an arbitrary tone contrary to fundamental principles of liberty. Do not those who demand that the mayor swear that he will carry out his duties have the right to inquire if he had, indeed, carried them out faithfully? he asked. Moreover, in imprisoning individuals allegedly guilty of breaking the law the mayor had gone further in an illegal direction than had agents of the Old Regime. He had not drafted a *procès-verbal*, for example. More than twenty unfortunates were sitting in La Force prison because of this arbitrary action or because of negligence.[73] The dispute be-

[72] *Ibid.*, Index, pp. 393-396.

[73] B.N., Lb[39] 4211, *Réfutation des principes exposés par M. le Maire de Paris, dans sa lettre à M. le Président de l'Assemblée nat'le par une société de citoyens légalement réunis en vue du bien public, au cirque national, et coalisés à la confédération générale des Amis de la vérité* ([Paris], [1790]), 19 pp. The first half of the brochure contains the mayor's letter; the last carries Godard's reply. As early as November 1789 Prudhomme had attacked the "arbitrary power" of the mayor to arrest and hold an individual for three days without trial. At the same time he denounced Brissot for arguing that the government had the right to arrest a man for calumny. This belief, wrote Prudhomme, held essentially that government could stop a man from expressing dangerous opinions. To put an end to such acts of tyranny he advocated the public examination of those arrested. *Révolutions de Paris*, no. XVIII, 7-14 November 1789, "Etat actuel de la commune et de la municipalité de Paris."

tween Bailly and Godard went no further but reflected the determination of the elected representatives to hold their municipal officers within the limits of the concept embraced by the term, *mandat impératif*, under which representatives acted as mere proxies to carry out the will of the voters.

District Petit-Saint-Antoine reelected three of its five representatives to the Second Assembly of the Commune. These were Dufour, Oudart, and Jacques-Hilaire Mennessier, forty-five years old, *avocat au parlement*, and a commissioner on examining the question of *ateliers de charité* (12 August 1789). He served on numerous other commissions while a representative to the Commune; among them was to examine the papers in the Bastille and to investigate the military regulations. Mennessier was elected secretary of the committee that drafted the plan for the municipality of Paris, and served as secretary of the Assembly of Representatives of the Commune (28 April 1790).[74] The fourth member was Anne-Clement-Félix Champion de Villeneuve, secretary of the district's assembly, as discussed above, an *avocat au conseils*, and a *conseiller de ville*. He served as an administrator of the department for public establishments (*département des établissements publics*), was a member of the *comité de la confédération nationale*, and contributed to many commissions and delegations from the Commune, serving as a member of the commission that dealt with the disposal of ecclesiastic property and of the department of public works (fifth department of the Commune). On 16 November 1790 he was a delegate to the National Assembly to honor the National Guards of Nancy (in the notorious affair which saw the arrest and execution of a number of soldiers who objected to the control of funds by their regimental officers), and was also interested in the cause of deaf-mutes.[75] In 1791 he was appointed to the Court of Cassation, and on 21 July 1792 became minister of the interior under Louis XVI.[76] The last representative was Jean-Baptiste-François Guyet, fifty-six years old, an *avocat au parlement*, and member of several commissions and delegations.[77]

The ages and occupations of these representatives show them to be

---

[74] Lacroix, *Actes*, Index, pp. 582-584.
[75] *Ibid.*, pp. 223-224.
[76] Braesch, *La Commune*, p. 295.
[77] Lacroix, *Actes*, Index, p. 417.

almost all in their middle years and members of the legal profession. Only one was an ecclesiastic, one interested in or involved in agriculture, and one a commissioner of finance. The Revolution was still bourgeois, as distinct from its later, democratic phase. Active citizens tended to elect—as was to be expected—men of property. Little change could be anticipated in the social physiognomy of the Commune until war, shortages, political factionalism, and clashes of personality had done their work.

III

From District to Section

The intervention of the common people had changed the complexion of French politics after 14 July. Their clash with defenders of the old order had made them less tolerant and more impatient with those who felt that the revolt had gone far enough. On 30 July Jacques Godard, as one of the presidents elected by the assembly of district Blancs-Manteaux, reported on a speech of Necker's to the Commune and to the Electoral Assembly in which he had warned them against substituting popular justice for that of the regular courts. He had termed their acts "bloody executions," citing the example of Baron Pierre-Victor de Besenval, who had been charged with treason. The latter was a lieutenant-colonel of the Swiss Guards who had encouraged de Launay to prolong his resistance in the Bastille, or so it was charged. The Electoral Assembly of Paris had decreed a general pardon and threatened that "it regards henceforth as enemies of the Nation only those who would trouble, by whatever excess, public tranquillity." Godard emphasized that this declaration had made a terrible impression, having emanated from an "illegal assembly . . . of a few citizens without commission." The surest way to disarm the people was to calm their agitation by responsible authorities themselves taking the lead against such decrees, he urged.[1] Whatever the merits of Godard's remarks, they reflected the differences between the districts and the electors on the future course of the Revolution. In a few months these differences would manifest themselves even on purely

[1] B.N., Lb⁴⁰ 234, *Extrait des registres des délibérations du district des Blancs-Manteaux relativement à la députation qu'il a faite à l'Assemblée nationale, sur l'arrêté des électeurs, du 30 août* [sic, juillet] 1789. ([Paris], 30 July 1789), 14 pp. The quotations are from pp. 4 and 5. Lacroix gives the date of the amnesty as 27 July: *Actes*, I, 56, 58-59. The deliberations of the Commune on this case are in *Actes*, I, 53-55. Those who opposed a general amnesty argued that it would only encourage further plots. A. de P., V.D.* 450, 30 July 1789.

administrative questions between the neighborhoods of the capital and their representatives in the Paris Commune. If the Electoral Assembly had expressed the political sentiments of the voters before 14 July, it was questionable whether it continued to do so, at least on some matters of concern to the districts, after the fall of the Bastille.

Upon completion of Godard's report, the district assembly repudiated formally the amnesty decreed by the Electoral Assembly, holding this act illegal, and pointing to the Commune as alone possessing the right to act in its name. The delegates then moved to present their resolution to the National Assembly and transmit copies to the Commune and the other fifty-nine districts. Shortly thereafter the Commune added its own voice to that of district Blancs-Manteaux,[2] whose resolution had aroused widespread support and precipitated a heated debate in the National Assembly. The latter adopted the essential arguments of the district on the need to punish traitors, but added that de Besenval was to be held under the safeguard of the law.[3] The pressure of public opinion and threats of violence had obviously affected the action of the National Assembly.

Throughout the month of August the two districts continued to improve their administrative organs, to retire officers and to elect their replacements, to send delegates to the Commune and to receive its instructions, and to open their halls to all citizens of their respective neighborhoods.[4] On 29 July they extended invitations to their fellow-citizens to attend services for the dead whose sacrifices had assured "the triumph of public liberty."[5] On 22 August the assembly of district Petit-Saint-Antoine made plans to conduct its own services scheduled for 2 September.[6] A chapter in the history of the districts

[2] B.N., Lb[40] 234, *Extrait des registres* pp. 7-9; B.N., MSS, Nouv. acq. fr. 2681, fols. 304-310; A. de P., V.D.* 5, pièce 450, 30 July 1789. Most early sources spell Besenval's name with a "z". Lacroix gives the spelling as Besenval, *Actes*, I, 58-59.

[3] A.P., VIII, 308-314, 31 July 1789. The decree is reprinted in A. de P., 1 AZ 139, 31 July 1789, which reads that "if the person of Sir Baron de Bezenval is again detained, he should be delivered to a secure place, and under sufficient guard." See also Brissot's reports of this affair in his *Le Patriote françois*, no. IV, pp. 3-4, 31 July 1789; no. V, pp. 1-3, 1 August 1789; no. VI, pp. 1-2, 3 August 1789; and the "Supplément" to no. V, pp. 1-2, 1 August 1789.

[4] B.H.V.P., MS 800, fols. 309, 310, 475, 479, 535, 547, 553, 555; MS 742, fols. 283, 284, 289, 291.

[5] B.H.V.P., MS 814, fol. 485.

[6] B.V.H.P., MS 800, fol. 485.

had come to an end. They had established a viable local government and had successfully repulsed an attempted counterrevolution.

Not all counterrevolutionaries had been subdued, however, nor had local authorities solved the pressing problem of shortages of foodstuffs, especially of bread, as the *journée* of October 5 and 6 was to demonstrate. The reasons for the women's march on Versailles are complex, though hunger and the provoking behavior of reactionary officers made overbold by too much wine appeared as the immediate cause. As large numbers of women, supported by hundreds of men, arrived from their different quarters to the square of city hall, then broke into the Hôtel de Ville, it was obvious that the Commune had lost control of the situation.[7] Thousands of individuals, with weapons of every description, milled about inside, filled the avenues and streets leading to the Place de Grève, and tried to set fire to official papers of the municipality because, as one of them put it, "they are the work of the representatives of the commune, all bad citizens, and who deserve the lantern, M. Bailly and M. de la Fayette being the first."[8] To what extent this sentiment was shared by the women as they prepared to march is difficult to say, but if widespread, it demonstrates how far in esteem the representatives of the Commune had fallen since the halcyon days of July. Yet, amidst the din and tumult, the constant ringing of the alarm bell, the destruction and pillage, many brave men and women risked their lives to extinguish torches held in the hands of incendiaries and to guard the municipal treasury until help could arrive.[9]

As the seven to eight-thousand women began to march, led by Stanislas-Marie Maillard, a *vanqueur de la Bastille*, their ranks swelled by methods not unlike those of press gangs in their search for sailors,[10]

---

[7] The following sources give dramatic versions of these events: B. & R., III, 70-131; *Moniteur*, II, no. 68, pp. 11-12, 5 to 8 October 1789; no. 69, pp. 17-20, 9 October; no. 70, pp. 25-30, 10 October; no. 71, pp. 33-36, 10 to 11 October; no. 72, pp. 41-47, 12 October; no. 75, pp. 65-66, 68-70, 15 to 20 October; Lacroix, *Actes*, II, 165-195; A.P., IX, 346-348, 349-350, 405-406.

[8] B. & R., III, 72.

[9] Among these men was Jacques-François Pic, clerk for Hotte de Pontcharaux, *procureur au parlement*, of rue des Billettes in district Petit-Saint-Antoine. Lacroix, *Actes*, II, 167 n. 1.

[10] Desmoulins uses this expression in his *Révolutions de France et de Brabant*, III, 365, cited by B. & R., III, 111. Buchez and Roux state that Maillard proposed to save public order by leading the women to Versailles, away from the Hôtel de Ville.

a far more serious confrontation occurred between Lafayette and the grenadiers he ostensibly commanded. One of their spokesmen, demanding that Lafayette proceed with them to Versailles, was reported to have observed that the soldiers had no intention of bayonetting hungry women in search of bread, that shortages were due to poor administration in the Commune, and that "the source of the malady is at Versailles." It was essential to bring the king to Paris, to punish the Flanders regiment for insulting the flag, and, finally, if the king was too feeble, to depose him and create a council of regents instead. The general tried to dissuade them by haranguing them on their duty, but he was drowned out by shouts of "à Versailles!"[11] There is evidence that Lafayette himself was threatened, according to the memoirs of Desmoulins, who reported that a grenadier cried out to him "accompanying this word with a very significant gesture of his gun: *General, to Versailles, or to the lantern.*"[12] Lafayette had to admit to the Commune that he could no longer resist the demands of his troops before it authorized him to depart for Versailles with his 60,000 men.[13] Thus the common soldiers, forcing their officers to place themselves at their head, followed the women some hours behind.[14]

The historic events outside the chateau of Versailles, the clash between the palace guards and the crowd, the introduction of a delegation to see Louis, the appearance of the women with Maillard at the bar of the National Assembly, the near massacre of the royal family and the intervention of Lafayette's troops to save the chateau, and the final triumph of the insurgents as the king agreed to accompany them to Paris—all these are well known and need no further elaboration.[15]

If so, his actions and remarks in the National Assembly were in contradiction to his earlier proposal.

[11] B. & R., III, 75-76; *Moniteur*, II, no. 70, p. 26, 10 October.

[12] Cited by B. & R., III, 110, italics added.

[13] Lacroix, *Actes*, II, 171. "Le général palit, et promenant un regard douloureux sur les nombreux bataillons qui l'investissaient, donne l'ordre de départ. Un cri de joie universelle fait retentir les airs." B. & R., III, 77.

[14] That officers of the National Guard had lost complete control of their men is clear from the sources. See the interesting discussion of Louis Gottschalk and Margaret Maddox, *Lafayette in the French Revolution Through the October Days* (Chicago and London, [1969], chapter XIV, "October 5," pp. 329-349, and chapter XV, "October 6," pp. 352-385.

[15] See the sources cited above. Especially noteworthy is the deposition of Lecointre,

Some months later an investigation was conducted into these events and a number of depositions taken. Among the latter was that of Françoise Rolin, an illiterate flower girl, age twenty, residing on rue de la Poterie (district Petit-Saint-Antoine), in the house of a cloth merchant. She had been asked by several market women to join them on their way to city hall, and told that if they were not satisfied they intended to proceed to Versailles. Starting their march about noon, they arrived at their destination between 4 and 5 p.m., after a heavy rain. Although refused entry at the palace gate, after an exchange of shots she was admitted to see the king with four others, led by Mounier, who was presiding at the moment over the National Assembly. After being pushed violently and kicked by a Swiss guard she was permitted, finally, to see the keeper of the seals, and to come out of the palace with another girl (Lovison Chabry, age seventeen, a worker in a wood-carver's shop). The latter had a document signed by the king (evidently promising relief), which was not believed by the crowd, who accused their own delegation of having been bribed, and threatened to lynch them. Françoise Rolin managed to accompany the delegation to the king's apartment, where Louis signed some papers in their presence, which were taken to the National Assembly. Once in the hall of the Assembly, Rolin and others made known their demand to have the king come to Paris, and when an unknown gentleman tried to bribe them to be quiet they refused. By 10 p.m. Rolin was back in Paris, having arrived by carriage, and turned over the papers to officials in the Hôtel de Ville, who gave her supper, and enabled her to be back home by 5 a.m.[16]

Among other deponents was an elected member of the Commune who had been an *avocat* practicing before the Parlement, age forty-two, by name of Gérard-Henri de Blois. Most women, he reported, were young; wore white, their hair dressed and powdered, and "hav-

---

who commanded the Versailles militia, B. & R., III, 115-117. Among other events he describes was his refusal to allow the queen's carriages to depart from the chateau. Buchez and Roux also cite the journal *Vieux tribun du peuple* of 1790, p. 123, and Desmoulins. Mounier's account from his *Exposé justificatif* is also interesting, *ibid.*, pp. 80-85.

[16] *Procedure criminelle instruite au Châtelet de Paris sur la dénonciation des faits arrivés à Versailles dans la journée du 6 Octobre* 1789, deposition 187, 23 April 1790, translated by Philip Dawson, ed., *The French Revolution* (Englewood Cliffs, N.J., [1967]), pp. 63-64.

ing examined the clothing, figures, and faces of all these women, he noticed very few of them who could be put in the class of vile populace."[17] Among his other observations was that he had heard the grenadier tell Lafayette that "it is necessary to go to Versailles" and a short time later, that the general was in danger.[18]

Thus, once again, as on 14 July, the intervention of the common people—bourgeois and *sans-culotte*, flower girl and militiaman, craftsman and lace worker—had changed the direction of the Revolution toward a more popular tendency.[19] Yet, the persistent problem of bread and other necessities remained to plague both Commune and National Assembly. Even while the women were making their way to Versailles, Parisian authorities busied themselves with finding provisions. Traditional measures having proved fruitless, battalion commanders were authorized to purchase grain in the countryside around the capital by offering 30 livres per *septier* (240 pounds). Meanwhile, the General Council made available 1,000 pounds of rice to each of the three districts that made up faubourg Saint Antoine, and bread for National Guardsmen when they returned from Versailles.[20]

This intervention of the government to make available a normal supply of foodstuffs in times of dearth or famine had a long history behind it. Ancient custom had established a tradition in France that the state had a legal right to intervene between the cultivator and the consumer,[21] especially during times when freedom of commerce cou-

[17] *Ibid.*, Deposition 35, 24 December 1789, p. 57.

[18] *Ibid.*, p. 58. Other depositions of interest are those of Jeanne Martin, a practical nurse, age forty-nine, forced by the women to accompany them, who testified that she saw no men dressed as women, and that the queen was insulted by the "common people." Deposition 82, 5 March 1790, *ibid.*, pp. 59-62. Marie-Catherine-Victoire Sacleux, mistress of a cleaning and dyeing establishment, age thrity-one, testified that she had been unable to obtain bread Saturday, Sunday, and Monday, and so joined the women. Deposition 105, 19 March 1790, *ibid.*, pp. 62-63. Marie-Rose Barré, a lace worker, age twenty, was forced to join the women on Pont Notre-Dame, and was one of four delegates to see the king.

[19] That conservatives were not averse to using popular pressure on the court may be seen throughout the early days of the Revolution. When Mirabeau warned Mounier, for example, that "Paris is marching on us," the latter is said to have replied: "so much the better, we shall soon be a republic." B. & R., III, 78.

[20] Lacroix, *Actes*, II, 169-170.

[21] Georges Afanassiev, *Le Commerce des céréals en France au dix-huitième siècle* (Paris, 1894), pp. 1, 4-5, 6-25, *passim*.

pled with a poor harvest raised prices to new heights.[22] The royal decree of 23 April 1789, and those that followed, sought to ease the dangerous situation by prohibiting the export of grain and by making large purchases for release to markets of the realm.[23] These edicts had done little to ameliorate the situation, however, as testified by violent outburts against merchants who tried to sell grain outside their particular locality. Many large cities of France, including its capital, experienced widespread hunger in the summer of 1789.[24]

Shortages and high prices were encouraged further by the prohibition placed upon the continued existence of corporations and guilds.[25] At the same time, the appearance of *assignats* led to the gradual extinction of metallic currency and to the reduction in the quantity of money.[26] By the end of 1789, the *assignat* had dropped 5 percent, harbinger of financial disasters to come.[27]

To deal with the crisis, the Permanent Committee of the Commune established a Committee on Provisions and asked each district to take an immediate inventory of grain and flour in possession of its bakers. Informed of this resolution by President Dufour at its Assembly of Electors, district Petit-Saint-Antoine hastened to appoint four of its members to execute the order. Meanwhile, the threat of shortages often interrupted the normal business of the assembly. On 18 July, for example, it was startled by an elector from faubourg St. Antoine who demanded an immediate vote on relief for workers if it wished to avoid disorders.[28] The same day the *comité permanent* had resolved to disarm all "vagabonds," a loose term that could be applied to hungry men and women, and to break up all unauthorized gather-

---

[22] "The establishment of the freedom of commerce in 1787 aggravated the effects of the poor harvest and contributed, in part, to provoke the most grievous rise in prices that had ever been seen in the eighteenth century." Lefebvre, *Subsistances*, I, XXXIX.

[23] Pierre Caron, *Le Commerce des Céréals* (Paris, 1912), pp. 29-31.

[24] Pierre Emile Levasseur, *Histoire des classes ouvrières et de l'industrie en France de 1789 à 1870* (Paris, 1903-1904), I, 36. There were riots in Reims, Caen, Orléans, Lyon, Nancy, Marseilles, Laon, Etampes, Angers, etc.

[25] Charles Schmidt, *L'Industrie; instruction, recueil de textes et notes* (Paris, 1910), p. 6.

[26] Seymour E. Harris, *The Assignats* (Cambridge, 1930), pp. 4-5.

[27] Pierre Caron, *Tableau de dépréciation du papier-monnaie* (Paris 1909), p. LII.

[28] B.H.V.P., *Extrait des déliberations de l'assemblée général des électeurs* (18 July 1789), 14 pp.

ings.[29] Asked to establish committees to enforce this order the districts were encouraged to take other measures to assure public security. A week later district St. Leu published an appeal for public order.[30]

To assure the safe arrival of convoys, armed force was used regularly. Commanders of platoons of district Petit-Saint-Antoine were given wide discretionary powers, and were often forced to disperse crowds bent on pillage, crowds of "unfortunates," as one officer termed them.[31] On 29 July the platoon began escorting boats carrying grain and flour on the Seine and, at the same time, soldiers were forced to scatter large crowds made desperate by hunger and ready to plunder.[32] On 25 August the assembled committees of the district informed the Commune of their resolution to come to the assistance of bakers operating in Petit-Saint-Antoine by alerting authorities upon the arrival of flour, and offering armed escorts to assure its safe arrival.[33]

These shortages and armed clashes led to accusations by the district that the Committee on Provisions appointed by the Commune did not represent the true interests of the district, that it was composed of former electors and others who had never performed public service, and that, consequently, it could not know the true needs of the people. Only the duly elected representatives of the districts, they argued, had the legal right to take measures for supplying the capital. When the mayor replied that in such matters it was essential to use the experience of former administrators, the committees of Petit-Saint-Antoine found his reasons unacceptable and charged, moreover, that too many foreigners were influencing the Committee on Provisions, and that the flour on sale was of inferior quality. The committees also criticized the inefficient operation of flour mills in Paris and its en-

[29] A. de P., 4 AZ 697.

[30] B.H.V.P., 100.65 (30), M. Parelle, *Motion, ou cri d'un citoyen françois* ([Paris], 25 July 1789), 3 pp.

[31] B.H.V.P., MS, 768, fols. 6-11, 29 July to 12 August 1789. These contain a number of observations of Bezancour, aide-de-camp to Lafayette, and the reports of Delangle and Blay, commanding grenadiers who were given the task of escorting boats laden with grain and flour destined for Paris. One of the convoys was stationed at a bridge on the Seine, from which point it would pick up boats and escort them into the city.

[32] *Ibid.*, On 31 July and 1 and 6 August the officer in charge reported that he convoyed boats with supplies and was forced to repel pillagers.

[33] Lacroix, *Actes*, I, 336.

virons, and the continued engrossment of cereals; they demanded, furthermore, that steps be taken to force farmers to thresh the grain in their possession, halt profiteering, and take an inventory of the supplies on hand. In an effort to bend the Commune to their will, the committees resolved to publish this resolution and to ask their brother districts for support.[34]

On 29 August the mayor reported that thirty-two flour mills had ceased operations because of lack of grain, as farmers had stopped trading with the capital because they feared seizure of their products on the rivers Aisne and Oise.[35] It was becoming obvious that shortages were not due to simple malevolence, as so often was charged by irritated officials who resorted more and more to armed force.[36] When the captain of the third company reported to the assembly of Petit-Saint-Antoine that 300 pounds of flour had been spilled at the market of la Halle, of which 200 pounds had been spoiled, the assembly noted the gravity of this loss. Although admitting that it was an accident, it resolved that the Commune take steps to assure that such incidents would not occur in the future.[37] Had the times been normal, it is difficult to believe that the spoiling of 200 pounds of flour would have called for such concern.

The turbulence caused by shortages forced the mayor and his fellow magistrates to issue periodic appeals to the people to remain calm and to use the legal machinery for redress of grievances. The pathetic nature of these admonitions may be gathered from the following, not untypical invocation:

> Citizens, in the name of Heaven . . . in the name of your duty, of your own interests, . . . of your own rights, let there be an end to

[34] B.H.V.P., MS 742, fols. 285-288, 27 August 1789; MS 800 fol. 487, 22 August 1789. Bailly defended the Commune's Committee of Provisions as having performed invaluable services, and attributed the attack of district Petit-Saint-Antoine to envy and personal rancor. *Mémoires*, II, 293-294, cited by Lacroix, *Actes*, I, 314.

[35] B.H.V.P., MS 742, fol. 291; MS 800, fol. 487.

[36] B.H.V.P., MS 799, fols. 29, 30, 34, "Assemblée des représentans de la Commune." After a disturbance involving two bakers and an armed patrol, on 12 September, representatives of the Commune could recommend only an increase of guards for markets and bakeries.

[37] B.N., Lb⁴⁰ 1489 and 1489*, 7 October 1789; B.H.V.P., 100.65 (103); Br. M., F. 60** (19).

insurrections, to uprisings, to unlawful assemblies. What! Why do you revolt: Your king, is he not among you? Is he not a Citizen? The National Assembly, does it not occupy itself with your welfare?
. . .

> Are you not free? Is not the Nation now sovereign? . . . If you are wronged, if you complain of abuses, address your grievances, your demands to the Legislative Body, to your representatives, and you shall be satisfied.[38]

Hungry men and women needed more than well-meaning exhortations, however. Nor did the mayor's commitment to the policy of the free circulation of grain win over many demonstrators.[39] On 21 October rioters lynched an innocent master baker by name of François, in the district of Notre-Dame, for allegedly hiding a few loaves of bread. Upon investigation it was revealed that these loaves had been set aside, without his knowledge, by his journeymen for their own consumption.[40] This was but a forerunner of troubles yet to come. Soon the districts began to campaign for direct control of supplies, to send commissioners to inspect markets, and to purchase grain in the countryside. None of these measures seemed to help, however, and martial law had to be proclaimed on 22 October to assure provisions for the capital and to maintain order.[41] To protect its inhabitants from butchers who slaughtered unhealthy animals and who sold low-quality meat, commissioners of district Petit-Saint-Antoine began to inspect their shops.[42] Nothing seemed to help, however, as these problems continued throughout the Revolution.

In addition to questions of administration and of provisions, the districts faced the pressing need of establishing a new military structure. The unreliability of the old professional army and its aristocratic

---

[38] A. de P., 1 AZ 138, *Adresse de l'Assemblée général des représentans de la Commune de Paris* ([Paris], 15 October 1789), 7 pp. The above quotation is from pp. 5-6. This appeal was also carried in B.N., 8° Lc² 260-261, *Journal de la municipalité et des districts de Paris*, no. III, pp. 17-20, 21 October 1789; and no. IV, pp. 25-27, 23 October 1789.

[39] B.H.V.P., MS 799, fol. 285, 20 October 1789.

[40] A. de P., 1 AZ 137, ([Paris], 21 October 1789, 7 pp. The contingent of National Guardsmen was simply pushed aside, and the baker lynched on the spot.

[41] Garrigues, pp. 225-232, *passim*.

[42] B.N., MSS, Nouv. acq. fr. 2680, fols. 36-38, 39-42, 16 March 1790.

officer corps, the suspicion hovering around the guard of the king and his mercenaries, the professional jealousies and petty divisions in the traditional military organization—all called for a drastic reorganization. Above all, the events of 14 July underscored the need for a military force composed of bourgeois troops, of citizen-soldiers, who would be loyal to the new order. On 16 July the Assembly of Electors invited the districts to send delegates to the Hôtel de Ville for the purpose of organizing a Parisian militia to bear the name of National Guard, a proposal endorsed by the districts.[43] Petit-Saint-Antoine formed the third battalion of the fifth division, whereas Blancs-Manteaux organized the seventh battalion of the same division.[44]

Three days before the invitation of the Commune to send delegates to city hall, the assembly of Petit-Saint-Antoine resolved that all inhabitants of the district should form a "bourgeois militia to be in active service at all times."[45] The total number of men under arms was to be divided into sixteen companies, each numbering twenty-three men (later modified), with the commander and noncommissioned officers to be elected by the company. Members of the guard were to arm themselves at their own expense and to carry arms while in service. Pistols, strangely enough, were forbidden as being too dangerous, without explanation as to whether they were unsafe to their bearers or to the civil population. No uniform was adopted for the time being; instead a green cockade was to be worn for purpose of recognition. Membership was limited to the following as stated in the resolution: "No one may be admitted into the bourgeois guard except the inhabitants having a dwelling in the district, their sons, workingmen living in the district and paying a head tax as well as workingmen who live with their masters within the district."[46]

The requirement of a head tax and a fixed abode, coupled with the regulation that individuals must buy their own uniforms, guaranteed the bourgeois nature of this militia, as few workers could afford the 4 *louis* for a uniform.[47] The age limit was set at sixteen, and two

[43] Alexandre Tuetey, *Répertoire général des sources manuscrites de l'histoire de Paris pendant le Révolution française* (Paris, 1890-1914), I, no. 184, 16 July 1789.

[44] Lacroix, *Actes*, I, 193-194.

[45] B.H.V.P., MS 742, fols. 273-274, 13 July 1789.

[46] *Ibid.*

[47] Garrigues, p. 171.

patrols were formed for active duty, with another two in reserve at guard headquarters. These were expressly forbidden to leave their district except when called upon for assistance by other districts. At the first sign of alarm all were to march immediately to the general place of assembly, and for the time being the hall of a church was to serve as headquarters of the militia.[48]

On 18 July President Dufour reported to the district assembly that the Permanent Committee had decided to impose a levy for the support of the newly created militia, equal to half the head tax. Control of the armed force was entrusted to a military committee of fourteen, among whom were two nobles, four men connected with the law, two architects, two engineers, two bourgeois, an auditor of accounts, and one whose occupation was not given. Five of the committee were signatories of the militia list of 13-14 July.[49] The assembly also elected eight members to the Committee of Finance, among whom were three lawyers, one bourgeois, two merchants, an entrepreneur engaged in construction, and one consul.[50] Nicolas Denegeau was elected as representative of the military committee to the *bureau général de l'Hôtel*

---

[48] B.H.V.P., MS 742, fols. 273-274.

[49] A. de P., 4 AZ 777, 18 July 1789. The committee members were as follows (an asterisk denotes signatories of the militia list):

1. *Husquin, de Bleville, avocat, no. 8, Roi-de-Sicile
2. *Dufour, fils, avocat, no. 12, rue des Juifs
3. *Mussey, procureur au parlement, no. 7, rue des Juifs
4. Gerard, avocat
5. Vareau, architecte
6. *Le chevalier de Beaulieu, no. 7, rue Tiron
7. Le chevalier de Thierri
8. *Pierre Petit, architecte, no. 9, rue des Juifs
9. Denfer, ingénieur
10. *Guillaume Viot, ancien directeur de coches d'eau, no. 46 rue Saint-Antoine
11. Deau, Profession not given
12. Datiller, bourgeois
13. Decamp, bourgeois
14. Herbault, auditeur des comptes

[50] *Ibid.* (an asterisk denotes signatory of the militia list):

1. Galland, entrepreneur des bâtiments
2. *Jean Popelin, avocat au parlement, rue de la Tisseranderie
3. Maginnel, consul en exercise
4. *Frederick Balthazard Colmet, procureur au parlement, no. 37, rue des Rosiers
5. Potidard, bourgeois
6. *Antoine Jacquotot, conseiller en l'amirauté, Deux-Portes-Saint-Jean
7. Badouleau, marchand
8. Bassacotte, marchand de vin, ancien garde en sa communauté

de Ville (replaced by Viot on 8 August), whose formation had been requested by Lafayette.[51] This was followed by the election of eight deputies to the *bureau de l'Hôtel de Ville*, six of whom were related to the law, one being a merchant, and one an architect.[52] The assembly then ratified the election of four vice presidents and eight secretaries, and concluded its business for the day.[53]

The creation of a National Guard aroused a heated debate on its social composition and future role.[54] Was it to be a people's militia or a bourgeois guard? Special companies of grenadiers, riflemen, and barrier guards had introduced mercenaries, in addition to paid soldiers, while Lafayette's role in militarizing the guard had aroused suspicion and then hostility against him. "Some citizens," said a spokesman of Petit-Saint-Antoine, "forgetting that all of us make up an army of brothers, are seeking to break this precious equality in the defense of which all of us are devoted." The battalion of the district had even dared refuse entry to its president.[55] This dispute between civilian and military authorities was brought before the Commune, which appointed a commission to investigate the charges and countercharges on 27 October 1789. Two days later it reported that according to the battalion commander the argument arose over the regulation that limited membership on the military committee to officers.

[51] A. de P., 3 AZ 284, B.H.V.P., MS 800, fol. 544. Tourneux, in his *Bibliographie*, II, no. 7234, wrongly lists B.N., Lb40 297, *Extrait des délibérations du district des Petit-Augustins*, 6 August 1789, 3 pp. under district Petit-Saint-Antoine. This is an address by an Agut of the first battalion of the Garde-françoise of rue de Bablylon, praising the decision to recognize merit in the service by granting medals to deserving guardsmen.

[52] A. de P., 4 AZ 777 (an asterisk denotes a signatory of the militia list of 13-14 July):

1. Mocassieur, notaire
2. *Descrez, procureur au Châtelet, Roi-de-Sicile
3. *Champion de Villeneuve, avocat au conseils, no. 64, rue Saint-Antoine
4. Jabeneau Dematroits, procureur au Châtelet
5. *Jacques Hilaire Menessier, avocat au parlement, no. 91 rue de la Tisseranderie
6. *Jean Louis Bleve, architecte expert, rue des Ecouffes
7. Chassanerier, marchand
8. Guyet, avocat au parlement

[53] *Ibid.* The names of these officers are not given in the *procès-verbal*.

[54] B.N., Lb39 7837, Coque (soldat-citoyen du district Saint-Germain-l'Auxerrois), *Très-sérieuses observations sur la mauvaise organisation de la Garde nationale-parisienne . . .* ([Paris], 15 September 1789), pp. IV-58.

[55] Cited by Garrigues, p. 182, no source given.

The president of the district admitted that he had no right to oppose assemblies of the battalion, nor to preside over them, but observed, however, that the battalion should address its complaints to the general assembly rather than take unilateral action—a proposal agreed to by the commander. The commissioners noted, therefore, that both parties to the dispute had been reconciled.[56] This tension between officers and men, and between the battalion and the assembly, was to take on a class significance as the Revolution became more radical.

The general assembly of Blancs-Manteaux, like that of Petit-Saint-Antoine, opposed the growing trend to professionalize the Parisian Guard. Its assembly disapproved unanimously the regulation of 20 October that had authorized the formation of six paid companies as proposed by Lafayette.[57] On the important principle of the right to convoke itself, that is, without permission of civilian authority, its battalion had adopted a resolution in direct opposition to the decision of the district assembly.[58] Although Lafayette's effort to create a separate artillery corps had met a rebuff (an important defeat, as it turned out later), the commander of the National Guard had succeeded in transforming the armed force from a citizen militia into a semi-professional military corps loyal to him and to his staff.[59]

On the important principle of who could enroll in the guard, the assembly of district Petit-Saint-Antoine ruled that only those with fixed dwellings could register. When a delegation of notary clerks protested against this restriction, the president assured them that the assembly had acted strictly in conformity with Article 3 of the official regulations, adding that the district's position on this question was in opposition to that of the Commune and its military committee.[60] Young men employed in commerce, finance, business, and the arts,

---

[56] Lacroix, *Actes*, II, 439, 27 October 1789; II, 459, 29 October 1789.

[57] *Journal de la municipalité*, no. VIII, p. 63, 2 November 1789.

[58] Garrigues, p. 188.

[59] *Ibid.*, pp. 186-187, 192. "The Parisian National Guard became a military aristocracy, losing the democratic character which it possessed at its formation" (p. 172).

[60] B.H.V.P., MS 800, fol. 526, 12 August 1789. Dufour referred to the "patriotic" position of the district on this question. Article 3 of Title I of the military regulations read: "Every citizen, domiciled, married or unmarried, from the age of twenty to age fifty, shall be carried on the general list of citizen soldiers, and subject to march when required." Lacroix, *Actes*, I, 147.

but who lacked a permanent residence, petitioned the military committee of the Commune to form a voluntary corps, but were refused.[61]

Since more volunteers had registered than were needed, the district assembly of Petit-Saint-Antoine ruled that the men who were to compose the four companies would be selected by lot. These, in turn, would elect their officers, the whole totaling 412 officers and men.[62] Geoffroy de Charnois was elected battalion commander on the second ballot, and Lemerle de Beaulieu was chosen captain.[63] President Dufour then delivered a patriotic address urging the newly elected officers of the battalion never to forget that "the soldiers are your equals, that they are citizens." The ceremony was concluded by an oath of allegiance to the nation and king.[64]

The enrollment of 412 men raised the question of where to lodge them, and how to meet this expense. Another practical problem was how to provide some mark of distinction between professional and nonprofessional troops. After some discussion it was decided that unpaid troops would wear epaulettes.[65] Among the 425 men who had enrolled, it was found that eleven were under age twenty. These were made supernumeraries or cadets. Officers, it was ruled, could serve for one year and be reelected once, but not for the third year in the same grade. Finally, citizens of the district were asked to bring their guns to the commander, for which they would be paid.[66]

On 29 August district Blancs-Manteaux asked the Benedictines to lodge its soldiers temporarily,[67] and on 9 September it invited the Commune to attend the ceremony for the blessing of its battalion banner, which was done in the church of Blancs-Manteaux three days

[61] Lacroix, *Actes*, I, 252-253. The districts were asked to pronounce themselves on this question by the representatives of the Commune on 16 August. Evidently Petit-Saint-Antoine favored the petition, according to Dufour.

[62] B.H.V.P., MS 800, fols. 541-542, 10 August 1792.

[63] B.H.V.P., MS 800, fols. 503, 511, 12 August 1789; fol. 527, 14 and 15 August 1789; B.N., Lb[40] 1488, *Extrait des registres des délibérations du district de Petit-Saint-Antoine* ([Paris], 13 August 1789), 8 pp. A total of 224 ballots were cast for the above on 12 and 13 August.

[64] B.H.V.P., MS 800, fol. 499, 15 August 1789.

[65] *Ibid.*, MS 800, fol. 494, 18 August 1789; B.N., MSS, Nouv. acq. fr. 2680, fol. 29, 18 August 1789. Lacroix, *Actes*, I, 471, on the difficulty of finding lodging for professional troops.

[66] B.H.V.P., MS 742, fols. 291, 294-307, 29 August and 3-5 September 1789.

[67] Lacroix, *Actes*, I, 385.

later. The oration delivered by the ex-president of the district, Godard, reflected the new feelings of confidence and defiance: "You have no further conquests to make; but you should conserve those that you have made. . . . Remember that a monarch is not accustomed to seeing his will limited so easily; that he watches for a favorable moment when he can break his yoke; that if he is clever, he lulls the people by words."[68] The speaker reminded his audience, however, that true liberty lay in submission to law, and that to prevent anarchy they should support their representative assembly. In short, like a good bourgeois, he warned against both a royalist counterrevolution and a peoples' democratic revolution on the Left.

Some weeks later the assembly protested that the guard was forming too slowly, that it was essential to have troops "ready to repel that despotism to which all governments tend."[69] A critic accused his co-citizens of laziness and indifference, and admitted that military service would always be insufficiently rewarding for the rich. "No man," he urged, "from age twenty to fifty domiciled [in the district should] exercise any public function in the capital, before first having served in the National Guard."[70] This proposal was adopted by the assembly, which then appointed four commissioners to present its resolution to the Commune, the National Assembly, and the king.

The assembly of district Petit-Saint-Antoine drafted a number of grievances and distributed them among the districts. It complained that the manner in which the king's officials received the National Guard was in sharp contrast to the way the former Paris Guard had been received,[71] a criticism that reflected the conflict between the districts and royal judicial authorities in the Châtelet. The spokesmen of Petit-Saint-Antoine confessed that "the members of the committee are amazed at the difficulty which they encounter with commissioners

[68] B.N., Lb⁴⁰ 235, *Discours prononcé dans l'église des Blancs-Manteaux le samedi 12 septembre 1789. A l'occasion de la bénédiction des drapeaux du district des Blancs-Manteaux. Par M. Godard, avocat au Parlement, ex-président du district* (Paris, 1789), 23 pp. The quotation is from pp. 4 and 10.

[69] B.H.V.P., 100.65 (31), *Motion faite à l'Assemblée générale du district des Blancs-Manteaux, par M. B. Garde nationale du district* ([Paris], 17 October 1789), p. 1.

[70] *Ibid.*, p. 3. His exact words were, "before having the honor of being a National Guardsman."

[71] B.H.V.P., 100.65 (104), *Du District du Petit-Saint-Antoine aux représentans de la Commune* ([Paris], 20 October 1789), 3 pp.

of the Châtelet when the National Guard brings law breakers to them," and demanded an end to the humiliation suffered by offenders who were paraded before one official after another.[72]

Petit-Saint-Antoine was aware also that the king's judicial officials were opposed to trials of nobles upon being denounced by the Commune's special police court, the *comité des recherches*. Marat had been menaced by the Châtelet for his role in denouncing Baron de Besenval, and was saved from further persecution only when district Cordeliers took him under its protection. It did the same for Danton when he was threatened by the authorities sometime later. Petit-Saint-Antoine strongly endorsed the action of the Cordeliers of 20 March 1790 with its own resolution,[73] thus demonstrating its distrust of royal authority.

On 27 April 1790 Petit-Saint-Antoine sent four commissioners to the National Assembly to examine the procedure of the court of Châtelet relating to the circumstances of 5-6 October 1789.[74] The opposition of the districts was such that the Châtelet did not dare investigate these events, and their continual antagonism led, finally, to its suppression in October 1790.[75] The district also expressed its alarm at the inactivity of police as winter approached, when troubles would undoubtedly mount, aggravated as they would be by shortages and lack of fuel; it urged, therefore, that the police duties of the districts and their legal rights, in general, should be clarified.[76] That these fears were real was soon demonstrated when a sentinel on duty was murdered. In an address to Lafayette, the district assembly of Petit-Saint-Antoine assured all that it would not be frightened by its enemies, and offered Lafayette an additional guard. The marquis prudently accepted the offer.[77]

[72] *Journal de la municipalité*, No. VI, pp. 44-45, 28 October 1789.

[73] Garrigues, p. 207. A. de P., 1 AZ 136, pc. 293, 18 Mai 1790, deals with the attempt to arrest Danton (spelled "Danthon").

[74] Garrigues, pp. 214-215.

[75] *Ibid.*, p. 196.

[76] B.H.V.P., 100.65 (104), *Du District du Petit-Saint-Antoine*. A few weeks later the Commune, under the signatures of mayor Bailly, Condorcet as president, and five secretaries of the General Council, denied responsibility for the dismissal of the guard by the king. B.N., Lb[40] 36, *Assemblée des représentans de la Commune de Paris* ([Paris], 14 November 1789), 3 pp.

[77] B.N., Nouv. acq. fr. 2680, fols. 32-33, 28 December 1789.

By the end of the year, districts Blancs-Manteaux and Petit-Saint-Antoine had established more than the rudiments of a working administration. Their committees and officials executed the decrees of their assemblies as well as those of the municipal government. Considering the immense work of building an organization almost from scratch, they had accomplished their task surprisingly well. The political experience gained between April and December matured them and encouraged them to maintain an independence and a jealous guardianship over that direct democracy which this experience represented. More complex and less successful was their effort to deal with food shortages, a problem that could not be resolved within the narrow limits of a neighborhood. Yet their pressure and suggestions, their initiative and resolutions, impelled the Commune to deal with this question and to adopt emergency measures that were to become national in scope. The districts were to contribute much to the ultimate solution of this nagging problem. Finally, they had created a responsive military weapon, an armed militia ready to defend the conquests of 14 July. The fate of the nation and its Constituent Assembly rested in no small measure on the political attitudes of this bourgeois guard. The districts thus held the key to the future course of the Revolution. Blancs-Manteaux and Petit-Saint-Antoine had contributed their share to this course.

Successful as the districts appeared in resolving many of the pressing problems that had risen after 14 July, their very success had brought them into conflict with the municipal authorities. The clash between districts and Commune broke out in earnest during the fall of 1789 and continued into the spring of the following year. Delegates to the second Assembly of Representatives of the Commune, installed on 19 September, had been given only a provisional and limited mandate by the districts, who insisted that their primary function was to draft a plan for the municipality of Paris. Once drafted, it was to be approved or rejected by the districts themselves. In other words, these delegates were to be mere proxies of their constituents, not truly representatives. Their argument was based on the concept of direct democracy rather than on representative government, and had strong historic roots. Under the Old Regime a deputy was expected to defend the interests of his own class, not to represent all France. Since each estate theoretically knew its own interests, it could direct the mission of its delegate. This obligation imposed by the electors upon their delegates to vote in a predetermined manner upon questions considered in advance was what was meant by the term *mandat impératif*.[78] The resolution of district Blancs-Manteaux of 21 April 1789 which spoke of mandatories was in this tradition.

Not all district assemblies shared this view, however, as may be seen when a dispute broke out between advocates of *censure* (that is, the right by the districts to exercise critical control over their delegates to the Commune) and those who looked upon them as their representatives.[79] Both Blancs-Manteaux and Petit-Saint-Antoine had given their nominees powers in conformity with the decree of the representatives of the Commune, that is, limited mandates, although in the course of developments the former, at least, reflected uncertainty in its stand.[80] By the end of November it had repudiated the strong resolution of district Cordeliers which sought to limit the powers of its commissioners to the Commune.[81]

This resolution, adopted by the Cordeliers on 11 and 12 November 1789, was destined to be a frontal challenge to the very concept of representative government. It resolved unanimously that its representatives to the Commune take an oath pledging to oppose in advance any measure deemed prejudicial to the common rights of their

---

[78] See Camille Koch, *Les Origines françaises de la prohibition du mandat impératif* (Nancy, 1905). M. Genty, "Mandataires ou représentants: un problème de la démocratie municipale. Paris, 1789-1790," in *Annales historiques*, no. 207 (January-March 1972), pp. 1-27.

Louis XVI had specifically asked that the Estates-General meet without instructions, as a representative assembly. *Moniteur*, I, no. 10, p. 93, 20-24 June 1789. For the arguments of Sieyès against the *mandat impératif* and those of Talleyrand and Barère, see A.P. VIII, 200-203, 207. Jean Jacques Rousseau, *Du Contrat social*, in C. E. Vaughan, ed., *The Political Writings of Jean Jacques Rousseau* (Cambridge, 1915), II, 96, wherein appears Rousseau's famous statement that the general will cannot be represented.

[79] Lacroix, *Actes*, II, 642, 468 n. 1. Bailly wrote that an "unceasing war" between him and representatives of the Commune had begun as early as 30 August 1789. *Mémoires*, II, p. 317. Prudhomme in his *Les Révolutions de Paris*, no. XVII, pp. 6-7, 31 October-7 November 1789, argued for direct democracy and endorsed the view of district Saint-Germain-des-Prés that "the rights of the Commune reside only in the districts."

[80] Lacroix, *Actes*, II, Introduction, pp. V, VIII-IX, XIII-XIV, 2-3.

[81] *Ibid.*, III, 34-35. There is no indication how Petit-Saint-Antoine voted.

constituents, and to agree that they were revocable at the will of their district assembly, despite regulations to the contrary adopted by the Assembly of Representatives of the Commune. Cordeliers invited the other districts to join it, thus forcing the Commune to take up its challenge.[82]

Needless to say, the Assembly of the Commune repudiated this resolution. It held:

> Considering that the deputies of a district, from the moment they become Representatives of the Commune, no longer belong to the individual district, but to the Commune as a whole; that according to the principle adopted under art. VII of title III of the *Project of a municipal plan*, provisionally accepted by the majority of the districts, they cannot be revocable at the will of those who had commissioned them, and that it is to the Commune alone that they must submit their resignations. . . .
>
> Considering finally that if each district, after having elected its deputies, desires to bind them by the *mandats impératifs* and by new oaths, the result will be that each district, individually administered and possessed of contrary will, would expose the city of Paris to all the disorders of anarchy; . . .
>
> Unanimously declares null and of no effect the resolution and formula of the oath prescribed by district Cordeliers, the 11th and 12th of the present month, together with the oath sworn consequently by MM. Périlhe and Croharé. . . .[83]

The right to recall their delegates to the Commune was won temporarily by the districts when the National Assembly ruled in favor of the Cordeliers.[84] This was followed by the dispute over the principle of *permanence*, that is, the right of the districts to convoke themselves without waiting to be summoned by higher authority. As early

[82] *Ibid.*, II, 638-639. The resolution was signed by Danton as president of the district assembly.

[83] *Ibid.*, II, 640. Article VII of Title III held: "No representative belonging to the Commune as a whole may be recalled by the assemblies of the districts." *Ibid.*, p. 639 n. 2. Périlhe and Croharé were replacements by the district to the Commune, which refused to accept the resignation of the original three delegates.

[84] *Ibid.*, III, 33, 35. The National Assembly adopted unanimously the report of Treilhard to let things rest as they had been on the tenth of the month. *Journal de la Municipalité*, no. XVIII, pp. 140-42, 25 November 1789.

as 13 July, Petit-Saint-Antoine had resolved to convene its assembly in order to maintain public order, menaced by "ill-intentioned persons," as discussed above. All citizens were invited to meet in the church of Petit-Saint-Antoine in order to occupy themselves with public business. Among its more important decisions was the express determination to remain in permanent session and to dissolve itself only by its own act.[85] District Blancs-Manteaux also decided somewhat later to meet, resolving to hold a general assembly every Thursday in addition to its regular meeting. The assembly invited its brother districts to inform its committee of the time and date of their meetings "so that it might correspond with them upon general affairs, and form a joint assemblage, so necessary for [common] views and operations."[86]

The decree on municipalities passed by the National Assembly on 14 December viewed sectional assemblies as possessing solely the function of conducting elections; once done they were to dissolve themselves.[87] Had the districts submitted to this ruling, however, they would have surrendered their direct participation in the government, and become ordinary citizens gathered in their assemblies. The direction of government thus would have been left in the hands of a few representatives. The assemblies did not necessarily want to exercise executive functions, especially in matters of administration, but insisted on the right to intervene in these matters if circumstances demanded. "At bottom, the question debated under the guise of *permanence* was that of direct communal government, opposed to communal government by delegation."[88] This, of course, is the essence of the dispute on the *mandat impértif*, as well.

[85] B.H.V.P., MS 742, fols. 233-234, "Procès-verbal de l'Assemblée gén'le," 13 July 1789. Several hundred signatures endorsed this resolve.

[86] B.N., MSS, Nouv. acq. fr. 2681, fol. 314, 9 October 1789; Etienne Charavay, *Catalogue des autographes et des documents historiques . . .* (Paris, 1900), no. 51, p. 13.

[87] Duvergier, I, 63-67; A.P., X, 564-571. Article 24 stated: "After the elections, the active citizens of the community may not remain assembled, or reassemble in communal body, without an express convocation ordered by the general council of the commune hereinafter mentioned. Said council may not refuse it if it be requested by one-sixth of the active citizens in communities of fewer than 4,000 inhabitants, or by 150 active citizens in all other communities." I have used the translation of Stewart, *Documentary Survey*, p. 122.

[88] Lacroix, *Actes*, IV, 405.

In February-March 1790 the districts took the initiative in drafting a plan for the municipal government of Paris that was presented by the mayor at the bar of the National Assembly on 23 March.[89] Bailly expatiated on the theme of permanence and requested an end to the provisional status of his administration, whose powers were both uncertain and ineffective. The commissioners of fifty-three districts who had gathered in the Evêché (the archbishop's palace) a week previously gave their adherence to a municipal plan which embodied their doctrine of popular sovereignty. "A General Council . . . is not suitable for the Commune of Paris," they wrote. "Its districts, its population, demand that the functions of the General Council be exercised directly by the Commune in its sections."[90] Forty districts pronounced themselves in favor of this scheme,[91] which was presented to the National

[89] A. de P., 1 AZ 138, *Discours de M. le Maire de Paris a l'Assemblée Nationale* ([Paris], 22 March 1790), 7 pp.; A. P., XII, 333-334, 23 March 1790; Lacroix, *Actes*, IV, 407. The address of de Beauvais de Préau, president of district Prémontrés, was entitled *Adresse de la Commune de Paris dans les soixante sections à l'Assemblée nationale; Journal de la municipalité*, no. 69, pp. 562-563, 25 March 1790.

[90] A. de P., 1 AZ 138, *Règlement général pour la municipalité de Paris* ([Paris], [10 April 1790]), 70 pp. Lacroix gives the title of this plan as *Esprit de règlement général pour la Commune de Paris*, in *Actes*, IV, Introduction, p. VIII.

[91] Brissot's *Patriote françois*, no. XXV, pp. 2-3, 25 August 1789, denied that there was disorder or war among the districts, and praised the moderation of the people. As early as 23 July 1789, Mirabeau criticized the anarchy among districts, citing disturbances in the city and blaming them for lack of authority in the municipality. A. P., VIII, 264.

B.N., MSS, Nouv. acq. fr., 2680, fol 34, 16 January 1790. One pamphleteer suggested that the sixty representatives to the council be equally divided among nobles, lawyers or bourgeois, and manufacturers. B.H.V.P., 100.65 (1), M. de Joly, *Plan de municipalité proposé aux membres composant le comité chargé par l'assemblée des représentans de la Commune de travailler au plan d'organisation du corps muncipal de la Ville de Paris* (Paris, n.d.), 26 pp. *Révolutions de Paris*, no. XVII, p. 3, 31 October-7 November 1789 wrote that "the organization of municipalities is above all the real crisis of the Revolution."

See the resolutions of districts Capucines, 11 September; Pré-montrés, 31 October; and Cordeliers, 25 February 1790. A. de P., V.D.*5, pcs. 456, 483, 464. See also the following in A. de P., 1 AZ 138: M. Bouvouloir, *Principes généraux et observations sur la formation de la municipalité de Paris* (1790), 36 pp., in which the author presents a conservative but able critique; M. Maugis, *Esprit du règlement général pour la Commune de Paris* (1790), 7 pp.; M. Peuchet, *Réflexions sur la permanence des assemblées générales des districts de Paris* (9 March 1790), 7 pp.; Duport (a deputy from Paris), *Réflexions sur l'intérêt de la Ville de Paris dans la division du royaume en départemens*, 16 pp.

Assembly on 10 April as the project of the Commune, and signed as such by Bailly. Among adherents to this plan was district Petit-Saint-Antoine.[92]

The rejection by the districts of the Commune's design for reorganizing the municipality led the representatives of the latter, ultimately, to resign. Petit-Saint-Antoine, like the majority of the districts, refused to accept the dismissal of its delegates,[93] although two did: Blancs-Manteaux and Saint-Honoré.[94] The battalion of the former, however, in marked contrast to the district assembly, expressed its regrets to the Commune on the resignation of its representatives. The president of the Council, Godard, himself a member of Blancs-Manteaux, replied graciously and thanked the delegation for their "heroic role" in the past.[95]

The districts had won, but their victory proved to be inconclusive, as the National Assembly reiterated its principle adopted 14 December 1789, namely, that "after the elctions, the active citizens may not remain assembled in communal body, without a convocation ordered by the municipal body."[96] The sections, formed from districts by the same law, continued to demand the right of permanence, however, and to make use of an article of the law that did not forbid them to deliberate in assembly. The right of convocation, clumsy though it was in that it required at least fifty active citizens of the section to demand a meeting, was used adroitly by their leaders. They would win the struggle for permanence, but only after shortages and the war had transformed the political situation.

This quarrel between the districts and Commune revealed another important, if secondary consideration—the special position of Paris. The Assembly of Representatives of the Commune wanted the capital to become the center of a great department, that is, to enjoy the same dimensions as other departments. The Constitutional Committee of the National Assembly, on the other hand, was willing to "honor"

[92] A. de P., 1 AZ 158, *Extrait du registre des délibérations du district du Petit-Saint-Antoine* ([Paris], 9 April 1790).

[93] B.N., MSS, Nouv. acq. fr. 2680, fols. 43, 64, 13 April 1790.

[94] B.N., MSS, Nouv. acq. fr. 2644, fols. 316-317; B.H.V.P., 100.65 (29), *Délibération du district des Blancs-Manteaux* ([Paris], 27 May 1790), 4 pp.; Lacroix, *Actes*, IV, p. xv.

[95] Lacroix, *Actes*, V, 132-133, 26 April 1790.

[96] Duvergier, I, 180, Title I, article 19, decree of 21 May-20 June, 1790.

Paris by raising the city itself, surrounded by a green belt of suburbs, into a separate department, thus restricting its size in contrast to the other eighty-two departments. Between these two proposals the districts hesitated. A slight majority, thirty-four out of sixty, ratified the proposal of the representatives of the Commune, among these being Blancs-Manteaux and Petit-Saint-Antoine,[97] while twenty-six districts accepted the proposal of the Constitutional Committee for Paris to remain a small department.

Basing themselves on the will of the majority of the districts, Representatives of the Commune addressed the National Assembly on 28 December in favor of Paris being established as a large department, that is, larger in size than the National Assembly was willing to allow. The Constitutional Committee, profited by the division between districts and Commune, however, rendered homage to the city for its patriotism, but persisted in its own plan. On 13 and 19 January, the National Assembly endorsed the plan of its Constitutional Committee.[98] Thus Paris remained what it had been in its territorial dimensions, but was to be both municipality and department.

On 1 June 1790 the mayor was asked, once again, to convoke the districts in order to elect commissioners for another assembly in the Evêché. The purpose of this meeting was to consider various proposals on the division of the capital into sections.[99] As early as 21 July 1789, Brissot de Warville had outlined a municipal plan for Paris upon which he elaborated on 12 August. Essentially he argued for a balance between "anarchy" and "despotism." The general rule ought to be, he wrote, that "a few should point the way, the many should make the choice." All power was derived from the people and could be delegated only by the people. This called for a large body of representatives, staggered elections, and the principle of an electoral college.[100] Brissot's project became the basis of discussion among the

[97] A.N., D IV*bis* 13, 251, 19 December 1789; A. de P., 1 AZ 138, "Tableau du voeu des différens districts, relativement à l'étendue du département dans lequel la capitale doit être placée," p. 8.

[98] Lacroix, *Actes*, III, pp. VI-VII.

[99] B.N., Lb⁴⁰ 1226, 4 June 1790, "Lettre circulaire aux présidents des sections sur la projet de la division des sections de la capitale."

[100] B.N. Lb⁴⁰ 15, J.-P. Brissot de Warville, *Motifs des commissaires, pour adopter le plan de municipalité, qu'ils ont presenté à l'assemblée gén'le des représentans de la Commune* (Paris, 20 August 1789), 29 pp., 52 pp. The first portion is his plan of 21 July; the

delegates of the first Assembly of the Commune, and laid the foundation for the plan of Condorcet in its Second Assembly.[101]

The decree of the National Assembly of 21 May-20 June 1790 established the definitive organization of the municipality of Paris.[102] In scrapping the sixty districts and substituting for them the forty-eight sections, the Assembly took every precaution to allow the Parisians themselves to reveal their preferences. Delegates of the districts were joined by four representatives of the *conseil de ville* (elected on 26 May), who met jointly in the Evêché from 6 to 14 June 1790. Two basic plans were under consideration: the one proposed by Jean-Claude Dezauches, an ordnance-surveyor and vice president of district de Saint-Etienne-du-Mont; the other by Edmonde Verniquet, an architect of the Jardin-des-Plantes. Forty-six districts adhered to the plan of Dezauches, eight to that of Verniquet, and six rejected both.[103] At the time of Gossin's report of 22 June to the National Assembly, fifty-two of the districts rallied to its support. It was destined to remain as the basis for the administration of Paris for the next seventy years.[104]

The reduction of sixty districts to forty-eight sections entailed the disappearance of some divisions, obviously. After a year's existence, however, few, if any, districts were willing to surrender their identity. The plan of Verniquet had as its major objective the convenience of elections and the efficiency of its civil and military service. Of the total active citizens, who numbered 97,631 by the end of 1789, 31,792

---

second is that of 12 August. Other copies are: A. de P., 1 AZ 137, *Motifs des commissaires, pour adopter le plan de municipalité* (Paris, August 1/89), 52 pp. Brissot's remarks are on pp. 3-27. B.H.V.P., 100.65, *Projet d'une déclaration de droits de la Commune* ([Paris], n.d.), 79 pp.

[101] Lacroix, *Actes*, III, Introduction, p. III; A number of district assemblies referred to Brissot's project as "plan provisoire" or "plan Brissot," to meet at least once a week in general assembly. It was adopted by twelve districts. Garrigues, p. 20.

[102] Duvergier, I, 179-190. Title I, Art. 3 read: "The city of Paris shall be divided into forty-eight parts termed sections, each to be equal, insofar as possible, in proportion to the number of active citizens."

[103] Lacroix, *Actes*, V, 561-562. The plan of Dezauches was adopted by the assembly of commissioners of the districts on 14 June, by the Constitutional Committee on 21 June, and by the National Assembly on 22 June 1790. Lacroix, Index, "Dezauches."

[104] Lacroix points out, *ibid.*, V, 562, that the forty-eight sections were called *divisions* under the Directory, then *quartiers* after 1812, retaining the same limits, and disappeared only in 1860 as required by the transformation of an enlarged Paris.

lived south of the Seine, while 65,839 lived north of the river. Verniquet thus divided the southern part of the capital into fifteen sections and the northern portion into thirty-three sections. Districts Blancs-Manteaux and Petit-Saint-Antoine were in the north, of course.[105]

In defending his proposal, Verniquet argued that he had divided the sections into equal divisions insofar as possible, bearing in mind the number of active citizens in each section, as well as the total number of citizens actually enrolled. Nor had he ignored the number of passive citizens (whom he equated with indigents). In addition to noting the concentration of active citizens, he had carried out a careful survey of such physical features of future sections as gates, covered and open markets, and access to them by quays, boulevards, and principal streets, and had attempted to form the sections into regular polygons.[106]

District Blancs-Manteaux supported the plan of Verniquet rather than that of Dezauches because according to the former it would have preserved its existence, whereas by the latter plan it would have been divided between districts Petit-Saint-Antoine (section Roi-de-Sicile) and Capucins (Enfants-Rouges). Despite its arguments, ultimately it failed to save itself from extinction.[107] District Petit-Saint-Antoine, on the other hand, not only succeeded in preserving itself but added a portion of district Blancs-Manteaux within its boundaries.[108]

On 27 April 1790 Démeunier reported for the Constitutional Committee of the National Assembly on a "plan of municipality appro-

---

[105] A.N., D IV^b 13, 252^c. Faubourg Saint-Honoré numbered 32,647 active citizens, while faubourg Saint-Antoine had 33,192.

[106] A.N., D IVbis 13, 252^a; A.N., D IVbis 13, 252^c.

[107] A.N., D IVbis 13, 252^c. See Verniquet's plan for Blancs-Manteaux, which was to have been the thirtieth section. A.N., D IVbis 13, 252^a. There is a detailed sketch of district Blancs-Manteaux in D IVbis 13, 252^c.

[108] A.N., D IVbis 13, 252^h. The arguments above appear to have been developed by Dezauches, probably with the advice of members of the assembly and its committees. This dossier is entitled "Division de Paris d'après le plan de Mr Dezauches." In A.N., D IV^b 13, 252^a is the plan of Verniquet (misspelled Duviquet) entitled "Division de Paris d'après le plan de Mr Verniquet, architecte." His plan called for the twenty-seventh section being Minimes, and does not mention Petit-Saint-Antoine. An interesting but shopworn map of the sections is A.N., N II Seine 235, entitled "Plan de la Ville de Paris période révolutionnaire 1790-1794." Section Droits-de-l'Homme is no. 31.

priate for the city of Paris,"[109] that became the basis of the decree adopted by it between 21 May and 20 June. On 22 June Gossin reported on the organization of Paris into forty-eight sections. Essentially, it followed the general outline of Dezauches and Verniquet. The 97,631 active citizens were divided into three regions: the south with 31,792, the northeast with 32,647, and the north with 33,692. The south was given fourteen sections, the northeast eighteen, and the north sixteen.

The reporter acknowledged that the committee discussed the problem arising from the dissolution of districts Enfants-Rouges, Blancs-Manteaux, Saint-Severin, and Petits-Augustins, and reviewed the argument of Blancs-Manteaux for its continuation as a separate entity, suppressing, instead, district Saint-Jean-en-Grève. The spokesmen for Blancs-Manteaux pointed out that the position of Mont-de-Piété and its police force and troops gave it an advantage of defense against popular agitation. Gossin reported, however, that Saint-Jean had a population of 16,000 and was the arena for all kinds of extremist manifestations. It needed, therefore, continuous watching, and should not be divided among stronger neighboring sections. Blancs-Manteaux, on the other hand, offered no such inconvenience.[110]

Gossin admitted, furthermore, that good arguments could be found for naming the sections after great men of the past or for some historical incident in the history of Paris. The committee rejected this idea, however, deciding to take the names of well-known squares, fountains, or monuments, or in the absence of such, to name the section after its principal streets. That this was not carried out, or eventually proved unsatisfactory, may be seen in a report to the General Council of 17 nivôse, Year II (6 January 1794). "The names of most streets of Paris," the report stated, "are either barbarous, ridiculous, or patronymic. In general they are insignificant, and all together present no reasonable pattern" (aucun motif). Many places were named after individuals of the Old Regime, others after politicians, still others after saints. Moreover, some of the streets carried the same name as a commune which resulted in postal confusion. In order to put an end to all this, the reporter recommended simple names of one word, if possible.[111]

[109] A.P., XV, 305-314, "Annexe"; p. 650, 22 May 1790.
[110] Ibid., XVI, 417.
[111] A.N., AD XVI, 70, Rapport au conseil général de la Commune de Paris sur quelques

Whatever the names of the forty-eight divisions, a new organization for the capital had been created. Nor were violent wrenchings of loyalties or political transformations visible in this alteration of district Petit-Saint-Antoine and parts of Blancs-Manteaux into section Roi-de-Sicile. The changes that did appear were brought about not by geographic mutations but by events outside the limits of topography. Nor would the new structure per se limit the practice of the *mandat impératif* or of *permanence*. On the contrary, should the government fail to solve the persistent problem of shortages and of high prices, launch a foreign adventure and meet defeats, or stumble in dealing with the counterrevolution, the sections would take the initiative once again as their predecessors, the districts, had done on 14 July.

---

mesures à prendre en changéant les noms des rues, 17 nivôse, an II, 4 pp. At the time of the report Paris had about 900 streets, 30 quais, 12 bridges, 28 alleyways, courts, or former cloisters, 26 squares, 20 markets, 9 enclosures (*enclos-ou l'on passe*), and more than 100 blind alleys. *Ibid.*, p. 3.

The boundaries of section Roi-de-Sicile (looking north) were as follows: beginning with rue du Coq, to the right, from rue Tisseranderie to la Verrerie; la Verrerie, to the right, from du Coq to rue Bar-de-Bec; from the latter, to the right, to Sainte-Croix-de-la-Bretonnerie; from the latter to rue Vieille du-Temple; from the latter, to the right, from Sainte-Croix-de-la-Bretonnerie to rue des Francs-Bourgeois; from Francs-Bourgeois and Neuve-Sainte-Catherine, to the right, up to rue Culture-Sainte-Catherine; from the latter, to the right, from Neuve-Sainte-Catherine to rue Saint-Antoine; Saint-Antoine, to the right, from Culture-Sainte-Catherine, up to rue de la Tisseranderie; Tisseranderie, to the right, up to rue du Coq. A.P., XVI, 433, 22 June 1790. This is from the report of Gossin on the organization of Paris into forty-eight sections; Duvergier, I, 179-190. See the map of the section.

─────── IV ───────

From Varennes to
the Fall of the Monarchy

Louis' flight to Varennes, like the fall of the Bastille, opened a new chapter in the history of the Revolution. Although a number of democrats and popular societies had mistrusted him from the very beginning, it was rare to find the kind of criticism of his policies and of his office that became common after 20 June 1791. On 21 June, the

Figure 3. The Demonstration of 20 June 1792

Cordeliers petitioned the Assembly to recognize the new situation, that France was *"free and without a king."*[1] When this appeal was refused, the Cordeliers and their supporters of the Amis de la vérité decided on a demonstration at the Champs de Mars. The resulting "massacre" drew a line of blood between the democratic and bourgeois parties, and defeated, for the time being, the popular movement in favor of a republic.[2]

Military defeats and growing food shortages radicalized the Parisians, however, and placed conservatives on the defensive. The third anniversary of the Tennis Court Oath, 20 June 1792, proved to be a dress rehearsal for the fall of the monarchy, as activists of faubourgs Saint-Antoine and Saint-Marcel demanded to march in armed procession, ultimately joined by thousands of supporters from the militant sections of the capital. The municipal and departmental authorities, sharply split on the political tasks before them,[3] too weak to resist the demonstrators, and fearful of unleashing a civil war, decided to legalize the coming manifestation by placing the regular officers of the National Guard and representatives of the Commune at its head.[4]

[1] Albert Mathiez, *Le Club des Cordeliers pendant la crise de Varennes et le massacre de Champs de Mars* (Paris, 1910), p. 31.

[2] *Ibid.*, pp. 54-105, *passim* for the sessions of the Cordeliers of 24, 26, 28, 30 June and 9-12 July, together with numerous letters and petitions from affiliated societies in the provinces. The dramatic events leading up to the massacre are described, pp. 117-121, 123-128, 128-150, *passim*. The proclamation of martial law against "the factious" and "the seditious" is in A. de P., 1 AZ 145, *Extrait du registre des délibérations du corps municipal* (Paris, 1791), "Procès-verbal," 15 pp.

A. de P., 1 AZ 145, *Municipalité de Paris. Par le maire et les officiers municipaux* (Paris, 3 August 1791), 3 pp., contains the harsh law against sedition. A publication of 4 pp. under the same title as above for 5 August 1791 proclaimed the withdrawal of the red flag and its substitution by the white flag on the Hôtel de Ville.

[3] A week before the demonstration, the conservative directory of the Paris department had assured Roland, minister of the interior, that it had succeeded in isolating "the Jacobin intriguers." A.N., F^ic III, Seine 27, d. 4, 12 June 1792. At first, the directory insisted that the municipal authorities suppress the armed demonstration by force, if necessary. See the letters between Mayor Pétion, who suggested mixing prudence with a legal approach, and the directory. B.H.V.P., MS 806, fols. 281-282, 284, 296. See also his eloquent and convincing defense of the "multitude" in an address to the Jacobin Society, which it published and distributed. B.N., Lb^40 2273, *Société des amis de la constitution séant aux Jacobins*, "Règles Générale[s] de ma conduite" (Paris, 12 July 1792), 7 pp.

[4] A.N., BB^30 17, "Pièces relatives à l'événement du 20 juin 1792." There are

Although reports indicate that the crowd was in a carefree mood, a number of spokesmen, among whom was Jean Varlet, a young militant of section Roi-de-Sicile, declared harshly that "the people, the true sovereign, is here to judge ['the traitors']."[5]

The consequent invasion of the Tuileries by the huge throng led to an investigation of those responsible. Among the officers and men interrogated were those of section Roi-de-Sicile as they appeared before the justice of the peace from their own section, Louis-Gille-Camille Fayel, whose membership on this court was to cost him his life more than a year later.[6] Among the witnesses heard was Pierre Mussey, second in command of the fourth battalion of Petit-Saint-Antoine, who gave one of the more articulate and detailed accounts describing the march of his detachment, the huge crowds, the position taken by the troops, and the role of two of the municipal officers. Arriving in the queen's apartment, he found but a handful of soldiers and abandoned rifles. His detachment held back several surges of the armed crowd during which his captain, Etienne Lasne, was wounded by a demonstrator. After forcing its way into the Salle de Jeu, the mass entered the bedroom and rifled the beds, looking for the queen. When the crowd had finally left, his troops searched the premises carefully with the help of officers of the Tuileries to make sure that none of the "madmen" was hiding in the apartment.[7] Others added to the account. All were critical of the municipal authorities and blamed them for not using force.

It was evident that both officers and soldiers of the section felt indignant and humiliated by the events of the day. Louis-François Bidault fils, for example, stated that his uniform had been run through

---

forty-one items in this dossier. A dramatic narrative is Laura B. Pfeiffer's *The Uprising of June 20, 1792* (New York, 1970, reprinted from the edition of 1913, Lincoln, Neb.).

A.N., BB[30] 17, *Compte rendu par le maire, et procès-verbaux dressés par les officiers municipaux, sur les événemens du 20 juin 1792* (Paris, 1792), 15 pp.

[5] *Moniteur*, XII, no. 174, p. 717, 22 June 1792. A.N., BB[30] 17, reported in the *procès-verbaux* of the municipal officers Mouchet, Guird, and Thomas. See also A. de P., 1 AZ 145, *Compte rendu par le maire, et procès-verbaux dressés par les officiers municipaux sur les événemens du juin 1792*, 82 pp., and Roederer's long account to the department in B.H.V.P., MS 806, fols. 306-323.

[6] A.N., F[7] 4704, d. 1, 14 and 15 frimaire, Year II (4 and 5 December 1793).

[7] A.N., BB[30] 17, 25 June 1792.

by a weapon and that he had been forced to sheathe his bayonet while "indecent" remarks about "M. and Mme Veto" were shouted. Jean-Baptiste-Marie-Louise la Reguse, a volunteer of the battalion of Isle-de-Saint-Louis, blamed Santerre, the popular leader and "Bastille conqueror," and reported that Legendre (not identified but probably the well-known Jacobin) had called Louis "perfidious" to his face. Jean-Baptiste Turot, grenadier of battalion Petit-Saint-Antoine of the section, testified how his company of thirty men had repulsed the crowd attempting to storm into the Tuileries, and had only ceased their defense at the orders of municipal officials. Many, he reported, were drunk and armed with pistols, while one had a scythe.[8] These witnesses, however, did not represent the great majority of guardsmen who had marched with their fellow demonstrators.

Having taken depositions of the witnesses, Fayel was in a difficult position, as he could hardly have ordered the arrest of the mayor even if he had the legal right to do so. On the other hand, he could not simply exonerate him, and so he tried to compromise by declaring that it appeared to him that both mayor and municipal officials had acted under duress. The law of 24 August 1790 (Title 2, Article 13), concerning the organization of the judicial department, forbade judges, by reason of their functions, to summon administrators before them.[9] He was opposed to calling the mayor and municipal authorities before the court, therefore, prior to submitting them to an interrogation by the directory of the department. This correct legal position, whatever his sympathies, was not enough to save him from future charges of sitting on a counterrevolutionary court. The position of moderates was, indeed, a difficult one.

On 11 July the country was proclaimed in danger.[10] Two weeks later (25 July) the sections were made "permanent,"[11] and the gren-

---

[8] *Ibid.* Other witnesses were Jacques Cuvillier, corporal of grenadiers of Petit-Saint-Antoine, rue de la Verrerie; François Martin Chauvreau, rue Cloche-Perce; Vincent Balieu, rue de Deux-Portes-Saint-Jean; Jean Quentin Guffroy, Cemetière-Saint-Jean. All were fusiliers of the battalion of Petit-Saint-Antoine (26 June 1792).

[9] Duvergier, I, 312. The twelve titles are listed by Duvergier, pp. 310-333.

[10] A.P., XLVI, 110-111, 4 July 1792. Jean Debry (of Aisne) reported the proposed decree (in nineteen articles). The definitive text appeared the following day, 5 July, pp. 133-134.

[11] A.P., XLVII, 143, on a motion of Thuriot. A.N., AD XVI, 70, 28 July 1792; B.H.V.P., 104.095, 28 July 1792, a printed sheet headed "Loi relative à la permanence des Assemblées de Section [sic] dans Paris."

adiers, elite troops of the National Guard, were suppressed on 30 July. This egalitarian tendency was strengthened further by the admission into the armed forces and the sectional assemblies of workers and petty bourgeois with their pikes. To coordinate this movement, a Central Bureau of Correspondence was established by the municipality, stimulating the energies of the sections by its circulars and reports.[12] Shortly thereafter the revolutionaries received help from an unexpected source. The duke of Brunswick's manifesto, threatening the total destruction of Paris, helped set the stage for the overthrow of the king.

During the last week of July, section Roi-de-Sicile had adopted a resolution that it would act according to circumstances,[13] a noncommital position that reflected the indecisive struggle between republicans and monarchists within its ranks. On 31 July section Mauconseil adopted its famous motion for the dethronement of the king,[14] to which section Roi-de-Sicile declared its adherence on 2 August. The following day (3 August), it participated in the delegation of the sections, with Mayor Pétion at their head, bearing a petition to the Legislative Assembly against royalty. The appeal demanded the dethronement of Louis, in line with the resolution of Mauconseil, and was signed by the section's president and future police commissioner, Pierre Auzolles.[15] This trend was completely reversed the next day, 4 August,[16] and on the following day (5 August), the section called on the municipal authorities to maintain order.[17] The directory of the

[12] Braesch, *Commune*, pp. 104-134, *passim*; Ernest Mellié, *Les Sections de Paris pendant la Révolution française* . . . (Paris, 1898), p. 116.

[13] B.N., Lb⁴⁰ 3442, Fritz Braesch, *Procès-verbaux de l'Assemblée générale de la section des Postes, 4 décembre 1790 - 5 septembre 1792* (Paris, 1911), p. 148, read by section Postes on 29 July. Braesch was not acquainted, however, with the contents of this resolution. There is no mention of it in Louis Mortimer-Ternaux, *Histoire de la Terreur, 1792-1794, d'après des documents authentiques et inédits*, 2nd ed., II (Paris, 1870), which deals with the events leading up to the overthrow of the monarchy.

[14] The resolution stated that Louis had lost the confidence of the nation. The section no longer recognized him as king of the French. Cited by Mortimer-Ternaux, II, 174-175. The full version of the resolution is in B. & R., XVI, 247-248.

[15] A.P., XLVII, 425-427, 3 August 1792.

[16] Mortimer-Ternaux, II, 430. Mortimer-Ternaux lists 14 sections as adhering to the resolution, 16 rejecting it, 10 taking no action on it, and 8 leaving no record of their vote. *Ibid.*, II, 443-444. The Assembly rejected the resolution and invited all to abide by the law. A.N., AD XVI, 70, 4 August 1792.

[17] Tuetey, *Répertoire*, IV, no. 2074, 9 August 1792.

department gratefully acknowledged this conservative position and congratulated the section for its resistance to the "deviations of a factious section."[18]

The course of this struggle is made even clearer in the adoption and partial repudiation of Jean Varlet's motion to dethrone the king, introduced by him on 5 August. The petition embodying this resolution was presented to the Legislative Assembly, signed, appropriately enough, on the Champs de Mars, by the *fédérés*, who, it will be recalled, had arrived from various departments of France to celebrate the anniversary of the fall of the Bastille. Their central committee (*comité central des fédérés*) sat in the hall of the Jacobins and met with commissioners of the republican sections (who assembled in the Hôtel de Ville as an "illegal Commune"). The Jacobin Club, on the eve of the insurrection, had transformed itself into an armed battalion, like that of the *fédérés* from Marseille and Brest, the former of whom having arrived in Paris on 29-30 July with their famous marching song.[19] The petition, therefore, was an instrument by which the republicans hoped to rally support for their position. It began: "The country is in danger; these terrible words mean that we are betrayed."[20] The orator then launched into a sharp attack on royalty and on the role of Louis. "Gentlemen," the speaker challenged, "among you sit some favorites of the court." This brought on a violent outburst from the deputies of the Right, but the petitioner continued to attack the "monstrous" power of the king to corrupt and to veto legislation. When he denounced the one-sided "contract" between the people and the king, deputies of the Left and their supporters in the galleries burst into applause. Varlet ended his discourse by proposing to veil the Declaration of the Rights of Man as symbolic of the political state of France, to dethrone Louis, to convoke the primary assemblies, and to introduce universal manhood suffrage.[21] His petition, unanimously adopted

[18] *Ibid.*, IV, no. 2076, 9 August 1792. The letter was written by Roederer, the *procureur-général-syndic* of the department to sections Roi-de-Sicile and Jardin-des-Plantes. The contents of their resolutions were communicated to the assembly, where they were heard "with interest."

[19] Braesch, *La Commune*, pp. 144-145, 185-186. According to Braesch, 39 out of 48 sections were "democratic" on the eve of the insurrection, p. 162.

[20] *Moniteur*, XIII, no. 220, p. 340, 7 August 1792.

[21] *Ibid.*, p. 341. The above embraced his proposals in the first four articles. The remaining articles (twelve in all), demanded the removal of nobles from general staffs,

by the general assembly of the section, was to be communicated to the other sections by twenty-four commissioners taken from its assembly.[22]

That Varlet himself was not clear as to the outcome of the struggle in his section may be gathered from his statement that "the section . . . [was] yielding to judgment which it [the petition] has undergone and desir[ed] to let public opinion decide on this work."[23] On 7 August the conservatives won a partial victory when they forced Pierre Auzolles to resign as president of the section and replaced him with their own man, Louis Fayel, the justice of the peace. This struggle was not resolved, as will be seen, until the very morning of the insurrection. The following day Roi-de-Sicile repudiated the resolution of section Quinze-Vingts of 4 August, which threatened to launch an insurrection if the king were not deposed. The conservative majority argued that the proposal was unconstitutional because, according to the municipal code, sections could not concern themselves with anything but communal matters, and the use of public force was reserved to the mayor and municipal officers.[24] In less than a week the section had made a complete turnabout from its resolution of 2 August. That

---

a decree of accusation against Lafayette, raising an additional 400,000 men for the armies of France, the recall of "the patriotic ministers" (that is, the Girondin ministers), the renewal of all directories in the departments, the demission of all ambassadors, severe laws against speculation and engrossment, and the dismissal of all commanding officers appointed by the king. After some dispute, the petitioners were accorded the honors of the session.

[22] B.N., Lb[39] 10728, *Voeux formés par les français libres* (Paris, 1792), 8 pp.; Br. M., F 65* (2), same title, place, and date of publication. Varlet's version of his program varies slightly from that contained in the *Moniteur*. He makes sixteen demands instead of twelve. No. 7, for example, asks for 250,000 troops instead of 400,000, but it is essentially the same in all other respects. Braesch gives the full title of the brochure and the three editions that he found of this work. *La Commune*, p. 165 n. 2.

[23] Cited by Braesch, *La Commune*, p. 166, italicizing the last clause.

[24] A.N., C 161, 350, pc. 26, 8 August 1792, "Extrait des registres des délibérations de l'assemblée générale de la section des Droits-de-l'Homme." This was adopted unanimously and was to be communicated to the National Assembly to demonstrate that the section abided by the Constitution. It was signed by Fayel, president, and Ruquet, secretary. Tuetey, *Répertoire*, IV, no. 1991, 8 August 1792. This was done under the pretext that it had no reason to deliberate on the resolution (*qu'il n'y a pas lieu à délibérer*) and inviting section Quinze-Vingts "to confine itself within the precise provisions of the Constitution," not necessarily a harsh condemnation of its action. Mortimer-Ternaux called this action "an energetic protest," in II, 431.

the conservatives held the initiative at this time may be gathered from the attack made by a citizen of section Mauconseil on Varlet's petition, which, he charged, had originated in a popular society. Many of the signatures were fraudulent, he accused, and cited two names to prove it.[25]

If the democrats had their spokesman in Varlet, the conservatives had their champions, as well. One, who simply signed himself "A citizen of section du Roi-de-Sicile," argued that although the section contained more than 2,000 active citizens, only 100 to 130 had bothered to vote on the question of the abdication of the king. Among the latter were passive citizens and even nonresidents, he charged. Accusing the opposition of intimidating the monarchists and then forcing through their own petitions, he revealed that they employed the extraordinary commission formed by the thirty-three radical sections since 23 July, thus bypassing the legal Commune, where they were outnumbered.[26]

Throughout the evening of 9 August the struggle within the assembly of the section continued. Fayel, as president, frustrated the demands of the insurrectionists by adjourning the session and carrying off the register of proceedings to his home. The republicans then installed their own president, Paulet, a constitutional priest. Only at 3 a.m. did the assembly, which must have been a mere rump, send three commissioners to the Hôtel de Ville. One of them, Paul-Henri Pollet (not to be confused with Paulet), resigned his commission at 8 a.m. on 10 August.[27] The victory of the radicals was inconclusive, therefore, until the very moment of the insurrection.

[25] *Moniteur*, XIII, no. 222, p. 357, 9 August 1792. Charles Brunot is the citizen mentioned. Tuetey, *Répertoire*, IV, no. 1987, 6 August 1792 gives the name as Bruneaut.

[26] B.H.V.P., MS 104.095, *Observation sur la demande qui a été faite de la décheance du Roi* ([Paris], 6 August [1792]), 4 pp. On the basis of the section's action regarding the resolutions of Mauconseil and of Quinze-Vingts, Braesch wrote: "I think, therefore, that one can consider this section as being also on the list of the moderately conservative sections." *La Commune*, p. 166. One can argue, however, that the participation of the section in presenting the petition of 3 August and in adopting Varlet's resolution of 6 August makes it difficult to characterize its political conduct on the eve of 10 August with any degree of accuracy.

[27] Mortimer-Ternaux, II, 431. The author says that Pollet feared the responsibility but offers no proof for this remark. This resignation did not prevent Pollet from playing a role as member of the civil committee or from being elected to the Commune.

Figure 4. The Insurrection of 10 August 1792

The insurrection of 9-10 August was initiated by a Central Committee of the *fédérés*, numbering forty-three members, among whom
was a committee of five called the Secret Directory of the Insurrection.
It was this body that ostensibly met in three successive sessions to
plan the overthrow of the king. On the eve of 10 August it coopted
nine others and then launched the attack.[28] Before the final assault,
the movement in the sections rose and fell as armed sectionnaires were
called out, only to return, and as factional struggles swayed majorities
in the assemblies.[29] Commissioners of the sections, the newly re-
formed National Guard, the Jacobin Club now acting as an armed
battalion, the *fédérés*—all moved together as if by instinct. This is not
to deny that the many moderate sections remained neutral and awaited
results, but the active forces settled the issue. As the sound of the
tocsin brought an orderly mobilization of the armed battalions, marching
as citizens of the section rather than as units of the National Guard,

[28] B.H.V.P., 8⁰ 959751, *Articles, notes, et extraits d'articles de J. L. Carra, tirés des
annales patriotiques . . . 1793 l'an II de la République*, Article XXXVI, pp. 54-56, 30
November 1793. B. & R., XVI, 269-272.

[29] Braesch, *La Commune*, pp. 145, 162-173. See also A. de P., 1 AZ 146, *Tableau
général des commissaires des 48 sections*, below.

Antoine-Jean Gailliot, marquis de Mandat,[30] the royalist commander of the guard, was replaced by the popular militant Antoine-Joseph Santerre, just before the attack on the Tuileries. The Swiss could not hold out against the overwhelming odds against them,[31] and by noon the chateau was in the hands of the revolutionaries.

Who had made this revolution? Braesch, who wrote the definitive study of the event, concluded that it was largely the work of passive citizens. It was they who had invaded the assemblies to replace majorities, broke down church doors to sound the tocsin, and seized arms from royalists to use against the king. June 20 had largely been their work, after which they had retired into the shadows, only to emerge again by the end of July and early August, but not as mere spectators now. They had won, in practice, universal suffrage, which the Legislative Assembly decreed only on the morrow; had overthrown the Paris Commune, which they had no hand in electing; and had replaced the officers of the National Guard. Thus, in one night, they had transformed Paris and all France. All that followed merely sanctioned their work—replacement of the general staffs, establishment of a new municipal government, adoption of universal suffrage, abdication, not only of the king, but of royalty itself.[32]

The men from section Roi-de-Sicile who sat as commissioners on the illegal Commune were representative of this change.[33] Most were

[30] Mandat was charged with having moved troops without permission of the mayor. He had posted troops at the Tuileries, he insisted, by express orders of Pétion, which protest did not save him from being lynched shortly later. Maurice Tourneux, *Procès-verbaux de la Commune de Paris* (Paris, 1894), pp. 1-2.

[31] A. de P., 4 AZ 961, 10 August 1792, "Commissaires de la majorité des sections réunis avec pleins pouvoirs pour sauver la chose publique": "The general assembly decrees that the Swiss prisoners be conducted immediately to the Abbaye." Signed by Huguenin and Coulombeau. The original document containing the transfer of power from the legal Commune to the commissioners of the sections is in A.N., C. 156, 304, p. 27, "L'Assemblée des commissaires de la majorité des sections réunis avec plein pouvoir de sauver la chose publique . . . ," 10 August 1792. This document is signed by Huguenin, president, and Martin, secretary.

[32] *La Commune*, pp. 217-219, 220.

[33] A. de P., 1 AZ 146, *Tableau général des commissaires des 48 sections qui ont composés le Conseil-général de la Commune de dix août mil sept cent quatre-vingt-douze, l'an premier de la République française* (Paris, 10 August 1792), 21 pp. This is the list referred to by B. & R., XVI, 410, which formed the basis for Braesch's study, "Liste, par ordre alphabétique, des individus ayant fait parti du conseil général de la commune, du 9

family men with fixed residences in the section, holding local government posts, enjoying modest incomes as members of the liberal professions or as artisans with small shops of their own. Paul-Henri Pollet, for example, was thirty-two years old, a school teacher, residing on rue Roi-de-Sicile,[34] and future member of the section's civil committee. He was replaced almost immediately, on 10 August, possibly because he was lukewarm to the attack on the Tuileries. His substitute was Jean Chevalier, appointed by the General Council together with three other men to serve at Temple prison where Louis and his family had been confined.[35] In November Chevalier was given police powers with his colleagues to maintain order in the prison.[36]

Etienne-Pierre Leclerc was fifty-seven years old, residing on rue des Juifs, the father of three children, two of whom had participated in the attack on the Tuileries. Before 14 July 1789 he was employed as clerk-registrar in the Hôtel de Ville and as assistant to the head of the Bureau of Provisions. As the Revolution unfolded he joined the Cordelier and Jacobin clubs, the Société fraternelle des deux sexes, and the Club central et électoral—all the more politically conscious societies of the capital. It was as a member of the latter organization that he prepared for the insurrection. Moving from one modest post to another, he occupied a seat on the revolutionary tribunal of the third arrondissement, became director of the jury for six months, then sat on the criminal court. He always claimed to have been on good terms with patriots and was an intimate of Marat.[37]

---

août, à minuit, au 17 août soir," *La Commune*, pp. 245-264. Mortimer-Ternaux's work differs in some essential respects with the above. The list of 288 names contains more names than the total membership on the General Council because of the confusion immediately following the events of 10 August. *Ibid.*, p. 265.

[34] The *Tableau général* gives no information on Pollet. See references to him in the chapter on the civil committee, below.

[35] Tuetey, *Répertoire*, VIII, no. 720, 10 September 1792. See also *ibid.*, VI, no. 418, 30 August 1792.

[36] *Ibid.*, VIII, no. 781, 18-21 November 1792. Braesch's reference to Tuetey, VI, no. 569 is in error, as it deals with a justice of the peace, Le Chevalier, mentioned by the committee of section Roule, presumably its surveillance committee. The list of 13 July has a Jean-François Chevalier, a master tailor, residing on rue Saint-Antoine, opposite rue des Jouy, B.H.V.P., MS 742, fols. 262-282.

[37] A.N., F⁷ 4774⁹, d. 1, "Réponse aux questions proposée à par le Comité de sureté générale pour Etienne-Pierre Leclerc ci devant administrateur de la police de la Commune de 10 aoust et depuis juge du tribunal du 3e arrondt de Paris détenu à

Leclerc was accused of having stolen a watch from a victim of the September massacres (discussed below), but successfully refuted this "slander" and was confirmed as a judge shortly thereafter. On 13-14 messidor, Year II (1-2 July 1794), he was arrested by the Committee of Public Safety and sent to La Force prison, where he remained for more than three weeks until the 9th of Thermidor. Although released by the Committee of General Security, he was refused the restoration of full citizenship rights, and, consequently, was not returned to his former position in the Office of National Estates. Leclerc stressed his devotion to the Revolution, which had begun with the wrongful seizure of his property by a bishop in an unexplained action. In a summary of his revolutionary conduct, he revealed that as one of the commissioners appointed to watch over the imprisoned king he had insisted that Louis be moved into less comfortable, but more secure, quarters. Protesting that he had never signed any petition that threatened to compromise liberty, he insisted that he had always behaved properly. Rearrested by the Thermidorians of the section on 6 prairial, Year III (25 May 1795), he was accused of being somehow responsible for a letter sent by the police which, allegedly, had encouraged the massacres. A more specific charge was that he had manifested "indecent joy" at seeing victims of "tyranny" go to their execution. He was then sixty years old.[38] Although there are no documents that mention his ultimate fate, it can be assumed that he was freed with other victims of the Thermidorian reaction, shortly before the attempted royalist coup of Vendémiaire.

Jean-Baptiste-Pierre Lenfant resided on rue Saint-Antoine. He was elected to the Commune on 10 August and was appointed assistant police administrator at the end of the month. Unfortunately, there is no information on his early political life. As an *administrateur de l'habillement* he was arrested, probably, on a charge of peculation, on 12 nivôse, Year II (1 January 1794), by order of the Committee of Gen-

la force"; Tuetey, *Répertoire*, V, Introduction, pp. x-xiii. See also the scattered references to him in Braesch's *La Commune*.

[38] A.N., F⁷ 4774⁹. The general assembly voted his arrest for allegedly demanding the extermination of all prisoners, including those in the Temple (that is, Louis XVI and his family) before departing for the front. His motion was supported by the assembly of the section and taken to the Commune, it was charged, thus contributing to the massacres of September. B.V.C., MS 120, fol. 163, 6 prairial, Year III (26 May 1795).

eral Security. Found innocent, he was released on 21 ventôse (11 March).[39] Like Leclerc, he was rearrested on 6 prairial, Year III (25 May 1795), by the Thermidorian assembly of the section for having signed "an infamous letter" as a member of a police administration that, allegedly, had defended the September massacres. Lenfant wrote an eloquent denial of this charge, protesting that he had never denounced any "unfortunates," although being aware that many reputations had been made in the section by "vociferous declamations against them."[40] During the unfortunate events of September he had never left the Hôtel de Ville, nor had he ever been a judge in any prison while these horrors were taking place.[41]

The civil committee confessed that it knew no witness who could testify that Lenfant had indeed signed the notorious letter, and admitted that no such signatures existed. After the surveillance committee of the seventh arrondissement recommended that Lenfant be freed, the Committee of General Security ordered his provisional release under the surveillance of the section's authorities. Lenfant appealed for full freedom and had his petition endorsed by two Representatives of the People, Roy and Reynaud. There is no indication of the final outcome of his appeal, although it can be assumed that the Committee of General Security would hardly have ignored a petition signed by deputies of the Convention at a time when it was releasing prisoners with far fewer endorsements.[42]

Claude Coulombeau was forty years old, a lawyer by profession, residing on rue des Francs-Bourgeois. He was elected a commissioner on 10 August, and shortly thereafter became secretary-registrar of the Commune, in which position he served for more than a year. Arrested

---

[39] A.P.P., A A/136, fol. 49. Auzolles lifted the seals from his papers.

[40] A.N., F⁷ 4774¹⁷, d. 1, 8 prairial, Year III (28 May 1795). The *procès-verbal* was signed by Grandjean, president of the assembly, and Boudard, secretary. It was revealed that although the letter in question had not been found at Robespierre's home, none of its signatories denied its existence when it had been disclosed to the Convention. This type of reasoning foreshadowed the totalitarian frameups of our own day. On the obverse side of this document was a notation that Leclerc recognized the existence of the letter in question, and had only denied signing it, not its existence. Lenfant's denial bears no date, although Tuetey, *Répertoire*, V, Introduction, p. XIII, places it as sometime in thermidor.

[41] B.V.C., MS 120, fols. 163-165, 7 prairial, Year III (27 May 1795).

[42] A.N., F⁷ 4774¹⁷.

as a Dantonist in floréal, Year II (April-May 1794), he was released after the death of Robespierre. Coulombeau was a prodigious worker, as a glance at the thousands of documents transcribed by him reveals. When the General Council complained about certain irregularities, he wrote that his work was "immense, beyond human power. . . . I am usually at work fourteen hours in the Hôtel de Ville; very often I spend there eighteen to twenty hours."[43]

Mareux, pére, resided on rue Saint Antoine. Nothing is known of him except that he was appointed to the assembly by commissioners during the night of 9-10 August.[44] The last name carried on the list of the *Tableau général* is that of Rumel. He was already sitting in the Hôtel de Ville during the night of 9-10 August (possibly as an observer), when he was elected by the section on 10 August. Nothing more is known about him,[45] nor about a commissioner by the name of Berle, who was also elected the same day.[46]

According to the General Council, of the commissioners listed, all but Pollet and Rumel had fulfilled their duties by remaining at their posts.[47] After 17 August additional commissioners were elected to the Commune, some serving without a clear mandate and others remaining only briefly. In addition to Chevalier, mentioned above, an F. Giraud served as president of the General Council after 6 Septem-

[43] Mortimer-Ternaux, II, 451 and n. 3. The quotation is from Braesch, *La Commune*, p. 277. Braesch calls him an "honnête homme."

[44] His name appears in the *Tableau général*. Braesch added the *père* and considered the possibility that his name might have been Mareuil, *La Commune*, p. 258. There is a Mareux on the list of those who signed up for the bourgeois militia, 13 July, who resided at no. 46, rue Saint-Antoine, but his occupation is not given. B.H.V.P., MS 742, fols. 262-282.

[45] Mortimer-Ternaux, II, 451. Braesch gives the name of Romel as an alternative to Rumel, *La Commune*, p. 262.

[46] His name is not mentioned in the *Tableau général* nor by Mortimer-Ternaux. B.N., MSS, Nouv. acq. fr. 2691, fols. 143-144, mentions him, however. Braesch cites this source in *La Commune*, p. 246. Mortimer-Ternaux lists only Lenfant, Coulombeau, and Rumel as commissioners, but quotes Buchez and Roux as including Pollet, Leclerc, and Mareux. Braesch accepts the list of Buchez and Roux as constituting the "illegal Commune" rather than that of Mortimer-Ternaux. According to Buchez and Roux, twenty-eight sections sent a total of eighty-nine representatives to the Hôtel de Ville. Huguenin of section Quinze-Vingts presided over the assembly, to which section Roi-de-Sicile sent a representative. Braesch, *La Commune*, pp. 222-224.

[47] This is indicated by an asterisk placed before each name in the *Tableau général*.

ber. He might have been François Giraud, who became a member of
the Commune on 2 December. An order for the arrest of an apprentice
baker was signed by him on 6 September.[48]

The last commissoner was Philippe Hardy, thirty years old, a master shoemaker by trade and captain in the armed forces residing on
rue des Juifs. He had volunteered for the bourgeois militia on the eve
of 14 July, and must have been elected to officer rank shortly thereafter. Arrested on 21 September 1793 for ostensibly giving asylum to
a member of the former nobility and for helping a Princess Talmont
make her escape from Paris, he was freed within a few weeks. At the
time of his arrest he was employed as a registrar in the police court.
On 2 October the revolutionary committee reported that after an examination of his papers it found nothing suspicious. Hardy petitioned
for his release from La Force prison, citing deputy Réal who could
testify to his poverty—proof of his virtue, evidently. On 14 brumaire,
Year II (4 November 1793), the assistant public prosecutor wrote a
letter in his favor, countersigned by the judge of the court of the 17th
and 1st arrondissements.[49] It can be assumed that he was freed shortly
thereafter.

These commissioners from Roi-de-Sicile sat with others from the
"ultrademocratic" sections (to use the characterization of Frédéric
Braesch), representing those sections that marched against the Tuileries.
Collectively they constituted the core of the revolutionary movement
against the monarchy. The contrast in types of occupation and social
position of these men with former spokesmen of districts and sections
is striking. The latter represented the active citizens in the primary and
electoral assemblies, in the Commune, or on the many committees
during the period of the constitutional monarchy. Many of these were
members of the upper bourgeoisie or professional and governing classes;
if not actually belonging to these groups, they were closely allied to
them. The new men of the Commune were small employers, not *sans-
culottes* (or *hommes du peuple*), although about one-third were journey-

[48] Tuetey, *Répertoire*, VII, no. 1234, 16 September 1792. Braesch is careful to
explain that his "Liste des membres de la Commune révolutionnaire nommés après
le 17 août 1792" is quite tentative and uncertain. *La Commune*, pp. 641-643.

[49] A.P.P., A B/327, p. 420, 22 September 1793; A.N., F⁷ 4739, d. 1. It is
difficult to say if this Hardy was the same who was elected to the civil committee. I
am assuming that he was. See additional information on his role in the chapter on
the civil committee.

men and master workers. In addition to these was the relatively high number of manufacturers and merchants, but few from large industry or commerce. The real leaders were a compact group of petty masters or patrons whose politics was represented by the men of letters and of the law.[50]

From the fragmentary data available on the commissioners of section Roi-de-Sicile, it is evident that not one was independently wealthy, or had practiced law before Parlement, or—with the sole exception of Coulombeau—was a member of the legal profession, or was engaged in commerce or manufacturing. Although, probably, these men were known to their neighbors, it should be noted that with the possible exception of Chevalier and Mareux, not one had signed the *procès-verbal* of district Petit-Saint-Antoine when its militia was being formed on the eve of 14 July. It is conceivable, of course, that they had long resided in the neighborhood,[51] but politically speaking, they were new men who had been brought forth by the passive citizens who had made the insurrection of 10 August.

As for Braesch's division of the sections between the "moderately conservative" and the "moderately democratic"—this is a more subtle contrast. Of the twenty-three sections "moderately democratic," only eight failed to send representatives to the illegal Commune. Most conservative sections remained silent and awaited the outcome.[52] On the basis of this analysis, it seems difficult to argue that a section which had not sent commissioners to the Hôtel de Ville at the decisive moment of 9-10 August was "moderately democratic" while one which did (like Roi-de-Sicile), was "moderately conservative." Is it not pos-

[50] Braesch, *La Commune*, pp. 265, 266-268, 269, 271, 272. Of the 206 members whose occupation is known, 18 were lawyers and 8 were *avocats*. There were 12 men of letters, 27 were in the liberal professions, and 4 were bourgeois. Twenty-five were in the construction industry and 16 were in the clothing industry. *Ibid.*, pp. 265-266.

[51] See the interesting discussion of Richard Andrews, "Refléxions sur la conjuration des égaux," in *Annales: économies, sociétés, civilisations*, 29 (1974), 73-106. The author argues that no sectional insurrection ever succeeded, or, indeed, could have succeeded, without the agreement and/or leadership of important men in the neighborhoods. These were usually descendants of people who had immigrated to Paris in the 1730s and 1740s and who had begun modestly enough, before gradually establishing themselves in a profitable business or craft. The offspring of these immigrants composed the real elites of the sections.

[52] Braesch, *La Commune*, pp. 224-225.

sible to hold that what determined the political complexion of a section was not so much its position on the resolutions of sections Mauconseil and Quinze-Vingts, but rather its ultimate action during the night of 9-10 August?

In an apology written shortly after the insurrection, section Roi-de-Sicile replied to accusations made against it by section Quinze-Vingts for its equivocal conduct in the past. Appealing to its critics as old friends who had shed blood in common against "tyranny," it admitted that there had been two sections formerly—that of "the patriots" and that of "counterrevolutionaries." Now, however, there was but one section of patriots, whose deliberations were open to the public. The authors hastened to repudiate all past resolutions contrary to the principles of liberty as the work of the former "cabal" in the section.[53]

The intention of the announcement was to dispel the charge of uncivic behavior made against the section and to reassure its friends in the neighboring sections that the conservative party had, indeed, been defeated. Indirectly, it must have acted as a warning to the former members of the "cabal" that the democrats were firmly in control, as manifested by the unanimous support of the active sectionnaires who adopted the address. Moderation, at least as defined in pre-10 August terms, was now out of favor; conservatism, needless to say, was even more so.

The revolutionary waves, however, were to display troughs as well as crests, since one could never be certain, after all, of a decisive victory. The more perceptive surely must have known that in times of flux nothing was permanent. When Pétion resigned as mayor after being elected to the Convention, section Droits-de-l'Homme (as Roi-de-Sicile was called after 21 August 1792), together with Quatre-Nations, Faubourg-Montmartre, Luxembourg, and Arsenal all asked him to remain in his former position. Had the moderates in these sections raised their heads again? They seem to have found their voice,

---

[53] B.N., Lb[40] 3246, *Adresse des citoyens de la section du Roi-de-Sicile à leurs frères de la section des Quinze-Vingts et de toutes les sections de Paris* (Paris, n.d.), 1 p. It was signed by Pollet, president, Huguet, secretary, and 300 citizens of the section. This must have been published between 10 August and 21 August 1792, when the section changed its name.

for Pétion was not the leader of the more militant revolutionaries.[54] After the September massacres there was a predictable reaction in some sections, and a number of them sent their commissioners to the General Council on the evening of September 9 to discuss the matter. Among these were delegates of section Droits-de-l'Homme.[55] The vacillation of the section was to continue, despite "unanimous" resolutions to the contrary. Democrats and conservatives were ultimately dependent on the general course of the Revolution, as its history was to prove.

Among the first steps taken by the victorious revolutionaries was to remove those officers of the armed force who had proved unreliable in the events of 10 August. The general assembly of the battalion of Petit-Saint-Antoine elected commissioners to recover the weapons and cartridges in the hands of Jean-Baptiste Herbault and Pierre Mussey, ex-commanders of the battalion.[56] The following day (11 August), the section convoked its citizens to hear Herbault attempt to justify his actions,[57] an attempt that failed. Two days later (13 August), the provisional commander, Norman, elected after the demission of Herbault, invited the battalion to hear the reading of an address to the Legislative Assembly. Moreover, he requested the section to convoke its general assembly in order to elect a military committee of twelve members, designed to act as a disciplinary body over its armed forces.[58] The creation of such a committee was further evidence of the mistrust that remained in placing too much authority into the hands of commanding officers, and was a manifestation of the democratic trend in the politics of the day.

On 22 September the general assembly censured its former commanding officers,[59] although the exact role of the battalion during the morning of 10 August remains unclear. A coachman declared that he had heard the cannoneers cry "vive le roi!" as they attended the review

---

[54] Braesch, *La Commune*, p. 539: "The moderates wanted to use this name [Pétion's], still popular, to bring about a change in feeling in their favor."

[55] *Feuille de Paris*, 10 September 1792, cited by Braesch, *La Commune*, p. 638. The other sections were Tuileries and Invalides.

[56] Tuetey, *Répertoire*, IV, no. 2176, 10 August 1792.

[57] *Ibid.*, IV, no. 2177, 11 August 1792. B.N., MSS, Nouv. acq. fr. 2691, fol. 146, 11 August 1792, signed by Pointard, Collet, and Hague.

[58] Tuetey, *Répertoire*, IV, no. 2268.

[59] B.V.C., MS 120, fol. 132.

of Swiss troops by the king.[60] This was corroborated by a volunteer serving in the battalion, who added that his comrades and he had difficulty in leaving the chateau.[61] This report was contradicted, however, by another witness who claimed that the cries were "vive la nation!"[62] What probably happened was that while the officers of the armed force remained loyal to the monarchy, the men were hostile and manifested their opposition as best they could. Lieutenant Amable-Antoine. Picard declared to the committee of surveillance that Roederer, the *procureur-général-syndic* of the department, warned the troops at 7 a.m. against riotous assemblies, but that a municipal official told them to repel force with force. The fight with the Swiss troops broke out an hour later.[63]

Another question that had to be settled was what to do with Louis, still formally not removed from the throne. Varlet, as one of the leaders of the republican party, advocated prompt measures to dethrone the king, without waiting for the explicit convocation of the primary assemblies. In addition, he suggested that the dauphin be removed from the care of those whose influence might corrupt him. Blood ties, he pointed out, were more important to him at present than the future of a great empire. Only a different type of education could change his present loyalties, something which could be accomplished by a tutor who would teach him that the duty of kings was to defend the weak. Varlet added in his petition to the Legislative Assembly a demand that it enact laws against profiteering and speculation in currency. "Universal peace to all people; harsh war against all tyrants," he concluded.[64]

While petitions and resolutions were being presented to the municipality and the National Legislature, the assembly of the section appointed a commission to repossess its register from the former president, Fayel.[65] On 21 August the section requested to change its name

[60] Tuetey, *Répertoire*, V. no. 398, August 1792.

[61] *Ibid.*, IV, no. 2307, 11 August 1792. Lebeque reported to section Arcis that when the review passed before the king, cries of "vive le roi" were heard.

[62] *Ibid.*, IV, no. 2309, 11 August 1792. Report of Phulpin of rue de la Verrerie. He claimed that they had to threaten an officer to get out of the Tuileries.

[63] *Ibid.*, IV, no. 2328, 15 August 1792.

[64] A.N., C 161, 351, 12 August 1792; Tuetey, *Répertoire*, V, no. 17. About 120 citizens endorsed this petition by their signatures.

[65] B.N., MSS, Nouv. acq. fr., 2691, fol. 137.

from Roi-de-Sicile to Droits-de-l'Homme, the name it was to retain until 1796. This was accorded by the General Council.[66] The Rights of Man, obviously, held meaning that the obscure king of Sicily no longer possessed. On 2 September, Varlet was elected with two other members by the general assembly to make judicial investigations (*pour faire des perquisitions*) and to receive testimony and declarations by anyone who wished to lodge complaints or give reports of recent events. These would be directed, of course, against moderates and other opponents of the revolutionists in the section.[67]

Throughout the month of September the section adopted measures to regulate its internal life. Its citizens did everything from patrolling the barriers to finding lodging for the *fédérés*, from demanding uniforms for volunteers to making haversacks by its women. On 2 September the section was authorized by the General Council to seize horses from persons who had not been licensed by the municipality after 10 August. Its new military officers, confirmed in their election by the general assembly on 22 September, reviewed troops departing for the front. The following day, the section's civil committee distributed new civic cards, destined to play an important role in the life of private citizens. On 27 September it unanimously hailed the proclamation of the French Republic, and on the 30th drafted an address to the newly elected Convention.[68]

The address reflected suspicion of the preceding two legislative bodies, and, at the same time, patriotic support for the newly constituted Convention. Pointing to past "betrayals" of the people by former legislators who cloaked their evil machinations under the mask of patriotism, the petitioners boldly announced that all this was changed when "the whole people" rose up guided by the slogan "the annihi-

---

[66] Tourneux, *Procès-verbaux*, p. 49: "this request was received by lively applause."

[67] B.H.V.P., MS 748, fol. 119.

[68] B.V.C., MS 120, fols. 132 and 133. The first entry is for 10 September 1792. On the requisition of horses, see A. de P., 4 AZ 966, 2 September 1792.

That there must have been confusion and overlapping in the sometimes frantic efforts to establish a functioning administration after the insurrection may be taken for granted. A letter from the *procureur-général-syndic* to section Droits-de-l'Homme and to others, for example, rejected their complaints that they were not receiving copies of laws and decrees adopted by the Commune. The failure, he wrote, was due to their own negligence, as the municipality was distributing sufficient numbers of copies. B.N., MSS, Nouv. acq. fr. 2691, fol. 221, 13 September 1792.

lation of kings: live free or die." Although the events of 10 August
were bloody, they had their effect. The question now was whether the
Convention was worthy of its sublime mission. Within the Convention itself were speculators and the factious whose very existence
threatened the whole of France. The decree of the Convention, however, which had abolished the monarchy, had saved France. Millions
of men stood ready to support the Republic, ready to spill their blood
for the safety of the country. The Convention could rely on them as
they swore "to live free or to die."[69] Thus ended this declaration,
which began critically and concluded on a note of warm support for
the new legislature. Yet it must have occurred to more than one
deputy sitting in the chamber to wonder—who enjoyed the real power,
the National Convention or the sections and their Commune?

This question had already been posed in concrete fashion during
the first days of September, when the terrible massacres broke out.
That they were a manifestation of popular hysteria, of fear, and of a
desire for vengeance can hardly be doubted. Victims of the attack on
the Tuileries filled the hospitals, and funeral processions throughout
the month of August of those who succumbed, inflamed passions still
further. The battalions of Petit-Saint-Antoine and of Blancs-Manteaux
each lost one man, but the military ceremony accorded them must
have added to the somberness of the general mood.[70] Hatred of the
Swiss, accused of firing nicked bullets and a mixture of glass buttons,
was universal,[71] while the official report on the state of the wounded
in the hospitals and a description of their wounds contributed to the
desire for revenge.[72]

[69] A.N., C 233, 190, 30 September 1792. A slightly different version is in B.N.,
Lb[40] 1796, and in Lb[40] 1796 A, *Adresse presentée à la Convention nationale le 30 septembre
1792, l'an ler de la République française, par les citoyens Gattrez, Oudart, Pointard, Gasnier*
(Paris, 1792), 4 pp. This is reproduced in A.P., LII, 243.

[70] Tuetey, *Répertoire*, IV, no. 2629, 15 August 1792. François Nativel died of his
wounds on 10 August. Jean Lallemand, a porter of section Marais, died on 6 September. *Ibid.*, IV, no. 2668, 7 October 1792. As late as 4 November, Momoro, president of section Théâtre-Français, invited the sections to attend the ceremony honoring
the dead of 10 August. B.N., MSS, Nouv. acq. fr. 2647, fol. 2.

[71] Braesch, *La Commune*, p. 474. The interrogation of a frightened Swiss guardsman, Jean Julien Cavietzel, by the revolutionary committee of section Bondy makes
clear this hatred and fear. A.P.P., A A/75, fol. 21, 30 August 1792.

[72] A. de P., 4 AZ 962, 11 August 1792, "Etat de blessés apportés à l'hôtel Dieu
dans la journée du 10 aoust et celle du 11. Jusqu'à unze [sic] heures du matin."

Sections held masses for the dead, and the Commune staged a general funeral on 26 August. Slogans for vengeance were in evidence everywhere. The discovery of compromising letters from émigrés and the appearance of crude publications describing alleged acts of treason aggravated the feeling of insecurity made sharper by the perennial shortages. News of the investment of Verdun frightened the patriots further. Against this background appeared an alarming proclamation issued by the Commune at 2 p.m. on Sunday, 2 September, warning that the enemy was at the gates and calling upon all to repel the invader.[73]

In the evening of 2 September large groups of men invaded the prisons and began their summary judgments and executions. The day being Sunday, thousands of Parisians were outdoors. It was hardly possible for them to have remained ignorant of what was transpiring behind the walls. Yet not one person interfered. Not one magistrate, not a single guardsman, not one member of the *fédérés* budged. Efforts of commanders of the Guard and commissioners sent by the Legislative Assembly to halt these killings proved vain. It is difficult to believe, therefore, that these executions did not enjoy overwhelming support among the inhabitants of Paris.[74]

La Force prison has the dubious distinction of experiencing the most prolonged of the massacres, from the night of 2-3 September to the 7th. Of the 700 prisoners within its walls 161 perished, including Mme Lamballe.[75] As to who were the executioners from section Droits-de-l'Homme (it can be assumed that it furnished its share), it is impossible to say. Of the thirty or thirty-one sections whose assemblies met on 2 September, eighteen did not occupy themselves with the massacres at all, or if they did, failed to mention it in their *procès-verbaux*. No trace of these proceedings in the assembly of Droits-de-l'Homme exists, if it did meet.[76] By 6 September the dominant tendency was to halt the massacres, but at the same time to justify them.[77]

[73] B. & R., XVII, 406-409, *passim*; Braesch, *La Commune*, p. 478.

[74] See Robespierre's convincing explanation of the atmosphere prevailing at the time of the massacres, and his refutation of the charge that the municipality should have proclaimed martial law. B. & R., XX, 210-211.

[75] Pierre Caron, *Les Massacres de septembre* (Paris, 1935), pp. 91-92. Caron's work is the definitive study on this subject. Tuetey, *Répertoire*, VI, no. 1896.

[76] B.V.C., MS 120, fol. 132 begins with the proceedings of 10 September.

[77] Caron, *Massacres*, pp. 334-335. On 15 February 1793 the general assembly of

Whoever was responsible for them, they reflected the growing intolerance of dissent, and, especially, of royalism. Politically, the shift in section Droit-de-l'Homme was to the left. Former patriots now developed differences as the war and shortages continued to aggravate conditions of life. These revealed themselves in mass riots in the month of February and in an attempt by Jean Varlet in March to push the Revolution still further to the left.

section Droits-de-l'Homme supported the resolution of section Butte-des-Moulins against attempts to prosecute the participants of "2 and 3 September." B.V.C., MS 120, fol. 135. Braesch says categorically that "it was section Poissonière that took the initiative in the massacres." *La Commune*, p. 484. Caron is convinced that those general assemblies which voted in support of dispatching prisoners did so not before they were launched (which would have been the motivation for them), but during or even after they were finished. "It is not possible under these circumstances to speak of 'cause,' " he wrote. *Les Massacres*, p. 339.

V

From the Fall of the Monarchy
to the Fall of Robespierre

In whose hands lay the ultimate source of power now that the king had been overthrown? If it can be argued that until the fall of Louis there existed an uneasy balance between the Legislative Assembly and the court, the events of 10 August destroyed this equilibrium. It is true that political power had been seized by the bourgeoisie on 14 July 1789, and that the traditional structure on which Louis' authority rested had been destroyed by the events that had culminated in the fall of the Bastille. Nevertheless, the attempt to create a limited monarchy carried with it the implication of ruling jointly with a monarch. The intervention of the sections and the Commune created a different situation, however, since they wanted no king at all. The Commune possessed the means now to mobilize the only organized armed force in the capital, the Parisian National Guard, and, in an emergency, could call out the sections as well. This is not to deny that the Legislative Assembly, about to be replaced by the Convention, still retained much authority and respect. Nonetheless, its status and influence had been diminished in the eyes of thousands of revolutionaries. Although the nature of sovereignty is indivisible in revolutionary situations, it is possible to speak of dual power (*dvoevlastie*, to use Trotsky's well-known term in describing the uneasy balance between the Provisional Government and the Petrograd Soviet), that is, a sharing of power between the national assemblies and the Paris Commune.

Despite this potential strength, which rested on the *menu peuple* of the city, the social and economic condition of the latter had not improved, as the Revolution had neither elevated their status nor raised their living standards. Hungry and miserable, they were becoming

disillusioned and disheartened.[1] Hébert paraphrased their disappointment in a bitter diatribe: "We no longer believe anyone. . . . They
steal from us, plunder us as in the past; we no longer have either
money or provisions. There is no bread, f . . . at any price . . . we
are without work. . . . For four years now have we suffered. What
have we gained from the Revolution?"[2]

This mood of apathy and depression could be traced to the drastic
decline of living standards. The cost of the war, the further fall of the
assignat, the steep rise in the price of bread—all struck at the mass of
urban consumers.[3] "Our first concern is bread," wrote Hébert,[4] and
Saint Just admitted: "What has destroyed the grain trade . . . is the
excessive use of paper money. . . . The farmer who does not want to

---

[1] Chaumette admitted that the great mass of poor "remain in the same condition
and have gained nothing from the Revolution but the right to complain of their
misery." Cited by Jean Jaurès, *Histoire socialiste (1789-1900)* (Paris, 1901-1909), *La
Convention*, IV, 1,054. Babeuf agreed in a letter to Chaumette that "the catchwords
of the revolution . . . have not changed for the better its mode of existence . . .
resulting . . . in an apathy, a discouragement, a general indifference." Claude Ma-
zauric, ed., *Babeuf textes choisis* (Paris, [1965]), p. 155, 7 May 1793. Marat admitted that "a clever rascal" could undermine faith in the Revolution by contrasting the
price of food prior to its outbreak with its cost in the spring of 1793. Quoting an
imaginary complainant, he wrote: "What have we gained from the revolution. . . .
It was better under despotism with all its abuses." B.N., Lc² 227, *Publiciste de la
République française*, IV, no. 224.

[2] B.N., Lc² 508, *Le Père Duchesne*, IV, no. 233, p. 5, 5 May 1793.

[3] See the table of prices for wheat in B.N., 8°S 21478 (1), Octave Festy, *L'Agriculture pendant la Révolution française* (Paris, 1947), p. 88 n. 3. C. E. Labrousse,
Esquisse du mouvement des prix et des revenus en France au XVIIIe siècle (Paris, 1932), pp.
105, 304. Labrousse points out that the increase in prices for the period 1734-1817
was unique in comparison to the three preceding centuries. From 1789 this increase
attained exceptional force. Between the base period of 1726-1741 and "the great
intercyclical period" 1771-1789, the average increase was 60 percent. The price of
wheat rose 56 percent. *Ibid.*, p. 240 and n. 3. The author argues that as against
relatively immobile wages, the continuous price climb was an absolute trend.

[4] *Le Père Duchesne*, IV, no. 341, p. 3, n.d. More than half of the popular budget
went for bread. See Rudé's *The Crowd*, Appendix VII, p. 251: a laborer in Reveillon's
factory spent 80 percent of his earnings on bread; a builder's laborer expended 67
percent; a journeyman locksmith and carpenter gave 40 percent. The policy of army
suppliers to double prices on the promise of immediate delivery aggravated both
shortages and price rises. Fernand Gerbaux and Charles Schmidt, eds., *Procès-verbaux
des comités d'agriculture et de commerce* . . . III (Paris, 1908), 63-64, 14 February 1793
(49th session).

put paper in his drawers is loth to sell his grain."[5] Popular pamphlets directed against profiteering began to appear in greater profusion, and irritated their readers further. One, entitled *Donnez-nous du pain, ou égorgez-nous!* (Give Us Bread, or Cut Our Throats!), made quite an impact. Written anonymously by a man of some education, it was one of the more moving appeals of the day:

> So it has come to this, frightful monsters reeking of crime! . . . Excellent patriots who possess no other treasure but their arms and virtue, are condemned to perish of hunger and poverty in the midst of abundance! A woman was forced to kill her unfortunate son and to hang herself. And you have the nerve to hear this with the most criminal indifference![6]

Another, written in the patois of the streets, reflected profoundly this popular discontent. Addressing their "mandatories" in a threatening manner, it demanded action to curb runaway prices and drastic measures against profiteers. If the Convention could not provide bread, they would seize it from the hands of speculators, they threatened.[7]

On Sunday, 24 February 1793, the price of soap in the capital had suddenly risen from 14 sous per lb. to 22 sous. Laundresses, made desperate by this attack on their living standards, seized whatever soap they could find, and began to distribute it at prices that had prevailed prior to 1789. The following day, 25 February, mass pillaging broke out,[8] a spontaneous and popular movement, as the police reported.[9]

[5] A.P., LIII, 663, 664, 29 November 1792.

[6] B.N., Lb[41] 201, *Donnez-nous du pain, ou égorgez-nous!* (Paris, Faubourg Saint-Marceau), 7 pp. "Famine is deaf," he wrote, "but aren't there arms?" Tuetey in his *Répertoire*, IX, Introduction, p. I, singles this out as one of the two pamphlets reflecting the growing discontent in the winter of 1793. The second brochure is discussed below.

[7] B.N., Lb[41] 2886, *Le Dernier cri des sans-culottes qui demandent du pain, à la Convention nationale* (Paris, n.d.), 8 pp., signed by Durandé. The author points out that the condition of the *sans-culottes* was no better with the execution of the king. Why should the currency of a republic be worth less than that of a king, he asked, and ended on a call to action: "Come then, fellow, bread like rain; and with arms in hand the whole universe will tremble." The literature on how to deal with the food crisis is much too vast to list. Everyone wrote on it, including many who developed the concept of "granaries of abundance" where grain could be stored against times of famine or shortages.

[8] A.P., LIX, 150-151, 24 February 1793. C.A. Dauban, *La Démagogie en 1793 à*

When news of this riot reached the general assembly of section Droits-de-l'Homme, many rose immediately and hurried to rue de la Verrerie, where a grocer's shop was being pillaged.[10] A spokesman of the section admitted in the General Council, however, that the sound of the tocsin proved ineffective, as his fellow citizens failed to respond; no one reported with arms to his place of assembly.[11] Realizing the seriousness of the crisis, the assembly demanded that the General Council petition the Convention to lower the price of necessities.[12]

The section also issued a stern warning against "intriguers" who sought to destroy Paris and the Republic. Although the assembly recognized the desperate plight of the poor, it was convinced that the authorities had taken salutary measures to assure abundance. True patriots, it reminded its readers, must unmask plotters who exploited

---

Paris, ou histoire, jour par jour, de l'année 1793 (Paris, 1868), pp. 76-77; B.N., Lc² 763, *Le Bulletin des Amis de la vérité* (Paris, 1793), I, no. 57, 25 February 1793. The bureau of police reported that soap worth 14 sous was sold at 32 sous, which was a cause of the riot. Tuetey, *Répertoire*, IX, no. 432. *Révolutions de Paris*, no. 190, pp. 389-392, 23 February-2 March 1793. Prudhomme wrote that the smallest shops were treated like the largest; only a few Jacobin grocers were untouched. *Ibid.*, p. 392 n. 1. Yet some were heard to remark, as they refused to participate, that they would rather break their children's arms than allow them to touch such goods. Some laundresses stated that they would rather beg than pillage. *Ibid.*, p. 393.

B.N., Lc² 563, *Mercure universel*, XXIV, 420, 27 February 1793, reproduced only the condemnation by the General Council of "the unfortunate circumstances" of the events of February 25.

[9] Thirty-two of the forty-eight sections are mentioned in the records of the Prefecture of Police. Merchants lost from one-half to two-thirds of the value of goods seized. George Rudé, "Les Emeutes des 25, 26 février 1793 à Paris," in *Annales historiques*, 25 (1953), pp. 33-57, *passim*. Paolo Viola in *Annales historiques*, no. 214 (October-December 1973), pp. 503-518, argues that the riots of 25 February and the abortive insurrection of 9-10 March 1793 had little in common. The first was spontaneous, closely linked with demands for the *maximum*; the second had the endorsement of the Jacobins against the journals of the Girondists. In any case, the *enragés* did not lead the movement of 25 February despite what Marat, Jaurès, and Mathiez wrote. A.P.P., A A/75, fol. 68, 25 February 1793. The *procès-verbal* of a merchant-butcher by name of Brisset is in fol. 70, 26 February 1793.

A.P.P., A A/248, fols. 69-70, 25 February 1793. Of the fifty arrested whose occupations were listed, it seems clear that they were workers, artisans, petty merchants, and shopkeepers, not just the poor. Rudé, "Les Emeutes," p. 49.

[10] B.V.C., MS 120, fol. 135, 25 February 1793.

[11] *Moniteur*, XV, no. 59, p. 565, 28 February 1793.

[12] *Ibid.*, p. 566.

shortages, and should support the law that would ultimately destroy speculators and engrossers. When Antoine-Ignace-François Descombes, an important militant, warned of plots by enemies he was warmly applauded.[13] The section, like its sisters and the Convention itself, could not, or would not, examine the real causes of shortages and hunger. It was easier to blame them on "intriguers."[14]

Needless to say, victims of the riot received no compensation. A grocer-apothecary, Nicolas-Denis Quatremère, of section Droits-de-l'Homme, residing on rue la Verrerie, testified at the police bureau that a crowd of about 2,000 persons had invaded his shop for five hours. They seized his merchandise, which included soap and sugar, the total cost of the goods being worth 4,156 livres 10 sous. He had recovered but 781 livres from the pillagers, suffering a loss, therefore, of 3,375 livres 10 sous; in addition, much that remained was now spoiled and worthless.[15] This forfeiture must have made it extremely difficult to remain in business, and doubly so under the threat of future outbursts.[16]

Despite the condemnation of this popular effort to control prices, the section continued to advocate government intervention in the economic process. As early as 27 September 1792, Droits-de-l'Homme had endorsed a petition of section Mirabeau against speculation in currency,[17] adopting a resolution to this effect and appointing two

[13] B.N., MSS, Nouv. acq. fr. 2716, fol. 65, *Adresse de la section des Droits—au peuple de Paris* ([Paris], 27 February 1793). The last paragraph is from the minutes of the assembly under date of 27 February. This address was signed by Angar, president, Bernard, vice president, and Vaubertrand, secretary. A biographical sketch of Descombes is in the chapter on the revolutionary committee.

[14] It is revealing that when a deputy proposed that all authorities of the capital be held accountable for attacks on property and persons, the Convention passed on to the order of business. A.N., AD XVI, 70, 5 March 1793, "Décret de la Convention nationale relatif à la responsabilité des autorités constitué[s] de la Ville de Paris, pour les atteintes portées aux propriétés & à la sûreté des personnes."

[15] A.P.P., A A/136, no. 19, 26 February 1793. Quatremère is listed in the collection, A.N., F[30] 145 for 1 August 1791, wherein he complains of a "considerable debit," but reports no workers under him. The soap, he reported, had cost him 2,208 livres and the sugar was worth 675 livres.

[16] The Convention ruled that those who had suffered losses in the riots of 25 February should petition the courts prescribed by the law of 25 February. A.N., AD XVI, 70, 21 June 1793.

[17] B.V.C., MS 120, fol. 133.

commissioners to act in its name.[18] Government intervention was not always possible, however, especially when hungry men and women became impatient of bureaucratic record keeping. When the police commissioner of section Droits-de-l'Homme arrived to take stock of deliveries made to Gouffe, a baker in the section, he found such a crowd before the doors of her bakery that he simply could not get inside to make his count. Auzolles's estimate of the number of four-pound loaves contained in the wagon before her shop differed from hers by 25½ loaves. This difference, if true, would have given her a possibility to speculate, but as the police commissioner could not make the count, little was done to halt this infraction of the law.[19]

The *sans-culottes* were disappointed in the results of the riot of 25 February, as prices failed to decline. Added to the economic woes were the military defeats of Miranda and of Charles-François Du-mouriez in Belgium. Shortly thereafter the counterrevolution raised its head in Brittany and the Vendée. Rumors began to circulate that another purge was essential if the country were to be saved, and volunteers from the departments who had come to the capital began to attack the Girondins as traitors. On 9 March they declared themselves to be in a state of insurrection against the "factionalists" of the Convention and the journals of Gorsas and Brissot.[20]

The call to insurrection on 10 March proved abortive; the tocsin did not ring and no one moved. A commissioner from section Finis-tère revealed in the General Council that four men had demanded its sounding in order to mobilize support for the arrest of certain deputies.[21] One of the four agitators was Varlet, who had accused the Commune of being "infected with aristocracy."[22] He had been recognized by a member of section Marat as leading a delegation of section Unité accompanied by four fusiliers on the night of 10 or 11

[18] A. de P., 3 AZ 287, 28 February 1793.

[19] A.P.P., A A/136, fol. 26, 20 March 1793.

[20] A.N., F⁷ 4445. Mortimer-Ternaux, *Histoire*, VI, 184-185. The purpose of the insurrection was to impose the will of its supporters on the "factions" in the Convention and to break the presses of Brissot and Gorsas.

[21] *Journal de Paris*, III, no. 71, p. 283, 12 March 1793. Jacques Roux (of all people), demanded the arrest of these "four disorganizers." B. & R., XXV, 62, Commune, 10 March 1793.

[22] Adolphe Schmidt, *Tableau de la Révolution française* (Leipzig, 1867), I, 149, 10 March 1793.

March.[23] Santerre verified that he had heard talk of insurrection (undoubtedly some remarks of Varlet), but hastened to add that since its purpose was to overthrow "tyrants," while at present the people themselves ruled, there was nothing to fear and that the Commune should put an end to this agitation. Hébert added that the agitators were in secret correspondence with Prussia, and Chaumette joined the chorus by accusing the popular societies of scheming with Prussia and Britain.[24] Varlet's intemperate accusation must have rankled the leaders of the Commune.

A group of forty men did break the presses of Gorsas, and another sacked Condorcet's *Chronique de Paris*. Aside from this, the military patrols reported the usual infractions but nothing of an alarming nature.[25] Varlet, meanwhile, had drafted an address that he presented to the Cordeliers Club. Although adopted by it and by section Quatre-Nations—an indication of dissatisfaction with conditions among an important sector of public opinion—when the latter section read its resolution to the General Council, it was repudiated decisively. The Council condemned Varlet as an "intriguer" and ordered its secretary to transmit all such resolutions to the Convention.[26] A number of agitators demonstrated in the Convention and then dispersed to the various quarters of the city to spread the message, but received no support.[27]

Having failed in this effort, Varlet demanded that the Jacobins help free his fellow agitator, Fournier l'Américain. Boldly declaring that "moderation was out of season," that it was undermining the Repub-

[23] A.N., F⁷ 4608, d. 2 (dossier Bonneville). The revolutionary committee of section Marat (Théâtre-Français) interrogated François Bonneville, who reported that he had recognized "citizen Varlet."

[24] *Journal de Paris*, III, no. 71, p. 287, 12 and 13 March 1793; Tuetey, *Répertoire*, IX, no. 462, 11 and 13 March 1793.

[25] A.N., AF IV, 1470, 11 March 1793, "Garde nationale parisienne. Commandant-général Citᵉⁿ Santerre." A citizen was arrested for crying "long live the king"; another for insulting a patrol; a fire in a bakery was extinguished, and so on. Most reported "nothing else." The patrol of the fourth legion wrote "nothing new."

[26] B.H.V.P., MS 808, fol. 485, 15 March 1793. Reproduced in *Moniteur*, XV, no. 77, p. 718, 18 March 1793; and Mortimer-Ternaux, *Histoire*, VI, 491-492, 493-494.

[27] See the study of this attempted insurrection by A. M. Boursier, "L'émeute parisienne du 10 mars 1793," in *Annales historiques*, no. 208, April-June 1972, pp. 204-230.

lic, he called on the people to save themselves by an insurrection, now incumbent upon them as the most sacred of duties. When he sought to repeat his speech delivered to the Cordeliers, however, many Jacobins began to shout, "We're not at the Cordeliers; order of business." The tumult became so great that the presiding officer was forced to suspend the proceedings, and, in order to calm his supporters, allowed Varlet to read his address. The latter's attack on Dumouriez excited another outburst, however, and he was forced to leave the tribune. Shortly thereafter he was expelled from the society. Billaud-Varennes replied to Varlet that although he was no partisan of Dumouriez, the latter could not afford a defeat for his own sake.[28] The young revolutionary was to prove to be the better prophet.

Although the Convention had arrested Fournier l'Américain (12 March), it could prove nothing against him. Upon his release, the latter published a violent attack on Marat, charging him with responsibility for his arrest.[29] The following day the Convention sought to bring charges against the insurrectionary committee, but could not prove its existence.[30] Gohier reported to the Convention on 19 March that some members of the Jacobin Club had met in a cafe, but that these meetings could hardly be considered subversive, although he did mention some "dangerous agitators"—Varlet, Fournier, Lazowski, and others.[31] No one was touched, however.

Varlet openly regretted that the insurrection had failed, as he boldly declared to a large crowd on the Terrasse-des-Feuillants, repeating what he had proclaimed in the Jacobin Club: that an insurrection was still essential and legitimate, and that it had merely been postponed; that he hoped that the apathy of the Jacobins would be replaced by the energy of the women of 5 and 6 October; that he trusted the Convention would proscribe the sale of metallic currency, decree the death penalty for speculators and engrossers, execute Roland and Brissot, and erect the guillotine on the court of the Manège.[32] Without

---

[28] F. A. Aulard, ed., *La Société des Jacobins, recueil de documents pour l'histoire du Club des Jacobins de Paris* (Paris, 1889-1897), V, 85-86, 12 March 1793.

[29] A.N., F⁷ 6504, d. 2.

[30] The minister of justice reported to the Convention on the existence of a committee of insurrection and on the events of 9 and 10 March. Tuetey, *Répertoire*, VIII, no. 2210, 13 March 1793.

[31] *Ibid.*, IX, Introduction, p. XXIV.

[32] Aulard, *Jacobins*, V, 85-86; Tuetey, *Répertoire*, IX, no. 472, 16 and 17 March 1793.

realizing it himself, perhaps, Varlet was taking the road to the successful overthrow of the Gironde less than three months away. Although repudiated by most active revolutionaries for the moment, his willingness to risk all in March contributed, undoubtedly, to his being elected president of the insurrectionary committee on the eve of 31 May.

News of French defeats in Belgium made Paris more tense than ever. Dumouriez had written his letter of defiance to the Convention on 12 March; on the 18th he suffered his disastrous rout at Neerwinden. The municipal authorities reacted by tightening restrictions on passports, and on March 28 they began to round up suspects. The following day they placed guards at the barriers and proceeded to institute house searches.[33] The Gironde, by its close alliance with Dumouriez, now stood condemned in the eyes of many patriots. Some were bound to ask if the war itself, launched with *panache* and bravado, had not been a criminal adventure. The charge, just or not, placed Brissot and his colleagues in a difficult position.

These developments were subtly changing the loyalties of section Droits-de-l'Homme. Moderates were no longer in full control of the general assembly as a process of radicalization began that was to triumph in the last days of May. The contest for control of the revolutionary committee on 19-20 May culminated in the triumph of the radicals, but before this decisive engagement came to a head the moderates lost support of the sectional assembly. That this development occurred may be seen in the initiative taken by that body, which launched the movement to convoke a revolutionary committee of the sections destined, ultimately, to overthrow the Gironde. On 27 March 1793 its general assembly adopted a resolution declaring "that after deliberating on the dangers facing France" it had unanimously "risen to save the country and liberty." To this end it urged its sister sections to send commissioners to a central point, where they would occupy themselves with the means to save the country from a "liberty-killing faction."[34] News of the treachery of Dumouriez had aroused a storm

[33] *Ibid.* Tuetey, *Répertoire*, IX, Introduction, pp. XXIII-XXIV and no. 478, 18 and 19 March 1793.

[34] Charavay, *Catalogue*, p. 28, no. 106, item #2, letter under the signature of Dubois, president, and Varlet, secretary, 28 March 1793, informing section Gravilliers that a meeting would be held in the Evêché, on Saturday, 30 March at 10 a.m.; B.N., MSS, Nouv. acq. fr. 2647, fol. 120 (Paris, 4 April 1793), 4 pp. Two hundred copies of this brochure were sent out over the signatures of Descombes, secretary.

of indignation in section Droits-de-l'Homme, which led to the adoption of the resolution.[35]

The following day twenty-seven sections responded by sending commissioners to the Evêché. On 1 April they assumed the name of "Central Committee of Public Safety and of Correspondence with the Departments."[36] Its roots may be traced to an assembly of ninety-six commissioners of several sections charged with discussing the problem of provisions.[37] Section Cité suggested the creation of a federation of all sections to defend the republic, and communicated this resolution after 2 November 1792 to section Poissonière and then to others. By January 1793 a sort of central committee had been formed in Paris supported by the Jacobins, fédérés, and popular societies. The seed planted by section Droits-de-l'Homme, therefore, found fertile ground.[38]

When a delegation of commissioners appeared before the General Council on 1 April, asking that the Commune pay the expenses of its office, upon the recommendation of Chaumette it was so ordered.[39] It appeared, therefore, that Evêché's revolutionary committee was organized on 1 April, receiving at the same time official recognition by the municipal authorities as a representative committee of the majority of sections sitting in the Evêché. The very same day, however, a storm of opposition was aroused in the conservative sections by this action. The hall of the Evêché was also the seat of the electoral corps of the department of Paris, where its assembly was in permanent session. On 2 April it vigorously protested the organization of the Evêché committee and specifically denounced Varlet and others of section Droits-de-l'Homme.[40]

B.N., Lb[40] 1792, is the same as the preceding with a defense of the section's actions of 2 April, and a renewal of its invitation to the sections to send commissioners to the Evêché, 7 April; A. de P., V.D. *9, no. 1025, 27 March, Year II, "Extrait. . . ."

[35] B.V.C., MS 120, fol. 135, 27 March 1793.

[36] Aulard, Jacobins, V, 118, 1 April 1793; Tuetey, Répertoire, Introduction, p. XXVII.

[37] Moniteur, XIV, no. 302, p. 309, 28 October 1792.

[38] Henri Calvet, "Les Origines du comité de l'Evêché," Annales historiques, 7 (1930), 12-23, passim.

[39] Moniteur, XVI, no. 95, p. 37, 5 April 1793.

[40] Charavay, Assemblée electorale, III, 465-466, 2 April 1793; Moniteur, XVI, no. 96, p. 467, 6 April 1793; Tuetey, Répertoire, IX, Introduction, p. XXVII; Jaurès, La Convention, IV, 1,257.

A number of sections, together with the Jacobin Club, joined this denunciation and repudiated the Evêché committee. Section Mail, which had sent observers to the Evêché, upon hearing that the commissioners had adopted the name of "Central Assembly of Public Safety Corresponding with Departments under the Security of the People," revoked the powers of its commissioners.[41] The following day, the Convention responded to section Mail by resolving that it had merited well of the country, and threatened war on this "new tyranny" that menaced the Convention.[42] Sections Butte-des-Moulins and Beaurepaire also repudiated the Evêché committee and were accorded the honors of the session by a grateful Convention.[43] On 2 April, sections Arsenal, Marais, Gravilliers, and Arcis, neighbors of section Droits-de-l'Homme, withdrew the powers of their commissioners. The General Council, which just twenty-four hours before had endorsed the assembly of commissioners by funding its office, now reversed itself and withdrew the funds appropriated.[44] The Jacobins, meanwhile, were addressed by delegates of sections Mail and of Gravilliers on why they had repudiated the Evêché committee. They, too, were applauded and invited to the honors of the session. The society then passed a motion that any member who failed to withdraw from the Evêché committee would be expelled from the organization.[45]

This counterattack by the more conservative sections brought an about-face in section Droits-de-l'Homme itself. A delegation to the Convention appeared, with its spokesman demanding the dissolution

[41] A.N., AD XVI, 70 *Extrait de procès-verbal de l'Assemblée générale permanente de la section du Mail*, 1 April 1793, 2 pp. The title adopted by the committee appears in other documents as Central Committee, rather than Central Assembly. In either case, it implied a challenge to the regularly constituted authorities and was so regarded by them.

[42] *Ibid.*, 2 April 1793; B.H.V.P., 104.095, *Décret de la Convention nationale du 2 avril 1793, l'an second de la République françoise* (Troyes, 2 April 1793), 4 pp. It also called upon the mayor to report on what he knew of the assembly of commissioners. Barère warned that the nation was endangered by both Brunswick and "the system of slander . . . of Marat," and denounced the Comité central of the Evêché. *Moniteur*, XVI, no. 94, pp. 35-36, 3 April 1793.

[43] A.P., LXI, 131, 3 April 1793. Butte-de-Moulins asked the Convention to dissolve the Evêché committee, while Beaurepaire prohibited its commissioners from further attendance at the Evêché.

[44] *Moniteur*, XVI, no. 96, p. 45, 6 April 1793.

[45] Aulard, *Jacobins*, V, 123.

of the Evêché committee. Needless to say, the thankful Convention offered them, too, the honors of the session.[46] Thus the factional divisions and vacillations that had characterized the sections on the eve of 10 August were being repeated over the question of the revolutionary committee sitting in the Evêché.

Varlet and his friends replied to this "vilification and misinterpretation" by republishing the resolution adopted by the section on 27 March. Although acknowledging that the Evêché committee had made an error in adopting the title of Committee of Public Safety, which thus gave the appearance of being a constituted authority, this was done only through thoughtlessness and in an excess of enthusiasm, they pleaded. Because of this one mistake was it proper "to abandon a measure so useful to public safety?" they asked. "No, citizens, you must sense the need to unite at this time of crisis when the most explicit perfidy leads us to the ruin of the Republic."[47] Never had liberty run greater dangers, it continued. Now was the time for all patriots to form a united front in order to expose the traitors. Once again, it urged that commissioners meet on the following Sunday, 7 April, to deliberate on means to save the Republic.[48] This vigorous counterattack won over the General Council, which resolved to give the section honorable mention in its *procès-verbal*, and so informed the other forty-seven sections.[49] It was evident that the struggle to create the Evêché committee was still not resolved.

Meanwhile, the General Council had created a correspondence committee with the 44,000 municipalities the same day, 2 April, as a counterweight to the Girondin federation of departments.[50] The following day it established "an uninterrupted correspondence between

[46] A.P., LXI, 131, 3 April 1793.

[47] B.N., MSS, Nouv. acq. fr. 2647, fols. 120-121, *Extrait de registre des délibérations de l'Assemblée-générale de la section des Droits de l'Homme* (Paris, 4 April 1793), 4 pp. The quotation is on p. 3. This is signed by the vice president, Rattier, in the absence of Angar, president of the assembly, and by Descombes, secretary.

[48] *Ibid.* When the section learned of Arsenal's recall of its commissioner it acknowledged that it was a mistake for the Evêché committee to have assumed the title of Committee of Public Safety. B.V.C., MS 120, fol. 136, 2 April 1793.

[49] B.N., MSS, Nouv. acq. fr. 2691, fol. 245, 2 April 1793; MSS, Nouv. acq. fr. 2647, fol. 120, 2 April 1792. This was signed by Pache and Coulombeau.

[50] A.N., F[10] III, Seine 13, April 1793. The resolution was signed by Destournelles, vice president, and Coulombeau, secretary. A.N., C 355, 1865, 2 April 1793.

the forty-eight sections and itself," and called on the sections to send commissioners to meet with it.[51] On 5 April it invited section Droits-de-l'Homme, among others, to elect delegates to meet jointly with the General Council at 5 p.m. every day.[52] Shortly thereafter, it reported that ninety-six commissioners had met.[53]

On 4 April, section Droits-de-l'Homme was informed by the Commune that Dumouriez had been outlawed by the Convention, and four days later section Bon-Conseil petitioned the assembly to remove the Girondin leaders.[54] Section Halle-au-Blé issued its famous challenge to the Convention on 10 April, accusing its members of being profiteers, and warning the Montagnards that if they were incapable of saving the Republic the section would do it alone.[55] The General Council now joined the movement and asked the expulsion of twenty-two deputies of the Convention by name, communicating this demand to the municipalities of France. On 18 April it published and circulated this resolution throughout the capital, which the Convention rejected as "slanderous."[56] Meanwhile the mayor, together with his municipal officers and administrators of the department, met at the Jacobins the same day and drafted a petition for a *maximum*. The Convention failed to act on this request, however, and, instead, referred it to its Committee of Agriculture. That evening the General Council proclaimed itself to be in a state of revolt so long as provisions were not assured.[57]

Section Droits-de-l'Homme adopted a strong resolution in support of its cocitizens of the capital on 27 April, and read it to the Convention the following day. "Why do you allow continual attacks on Parisians within your midst?" it asked. "Paris . . . is the foyer of the whole Revolution," the goal of the foreign coalition. Parisians captured by the enemy were treated worse than other Frenchmen, as everyone knew. Of course there was more heat, more defiance, more

[51] B.N., MSS, Nouv. acq. fr. 2691, fol. 248, 3 April 1793. This was signed by Pache, mayor, and Coulombeau, secretary.

[52] *Ibid.*, fol. 252, 5 April 1793.

[53] *Ibid.*, fol. 254.

[54] *Ibid.*, fol. 250, 8 April 1793.

[55] B. & R., XXV, 320-322.

[56] The Commune published 12,000 copies of its resolve. For the debate on the role of the Commune in this episode, see A.P., LXIII, 32-35, 20 April 1793.

[57] *Moniteur*, XVI, no. 111, p. 177, 21 April 1793.

agitation, more disquiet in Paris than elsewhere. Precisely because of this one should be able to harness this energy to serve the cause of revolution. "The great art of the legislator is to make it serve the public cause," for no power on earth could extinguish this movement, the spokesman concluded.[58] This subtle attack on the Gironde under the guise of defending the capital, with the implication that those who assaulted Parisians were in league with the enemies of France, proved effective. The Convention accorded the battalion the honors of the session and voted to insert the petition in its *Bulletin*.

Equally effective was the action of radicals who began to invade the general assemblies of their neighboring sections under the guise of fraternizing with their colleagues. By combining the forces of several sections, they could impose their will, temporarily, on a vacillating section where a resolution adopted the previous evening would be repudiated the following night, only to be reaffirmed shortly there-after. Often it was the support or rejection of the revolutionary assembly in the Evêché that became the point at issue, while at other times it was the acceptance or condemnation of a particular resolution that divided an assembly. Sometimes a motion was passed late at night, after the majority had already dispersed, or the president of the assembly had officially adjourned the meeting.[59]

The struggle to radicalize the assemblies lasted through the month of May and even after the overthrow of the Gironde. In faubourg Saint-Antoine, as might be expected, the three sections of Montreuil, Popincourt, and Quinze-Vingts were in the hands of revolutionaries. Five sections—Gravilliers, Marchés, Contrat-Social, Lombards, and Bon-Conseil had united to purge themselves of moderates, now dubbed

[58] A.N., AD XIV, 70, 27 April 1793, 4 pp.; Br. M., F.R. 57 (18), *Adresse de la section armée des Droits-de-l'Homme à la Convention nationale* (Paris, 27 April 1793), 4 pp. This was signed by Pollet, president, and Picard, fils, secretary; A.P., LXIII, 544-545, 28 April 1793. The address was given in connection with the presentation of a new banner to the section's battalion. On the same day it was presented at the Hôtel de Ville and was received by the mayor. B.V.C., MS 120, fol. 137, 28 April 1793.

[59] See, for example, the proceedings as recorded by the revolutionary committee of section Contrat-Social in A.N., C 355, 1862, 46 *pièces* from 9 March to 20 May 1793, and especially the valuable collection in A.N., C 355, 1864, which contains a detailed record of developments in section Mail for the period between 18 April and 24 May 1793.

"aristocrats." Section Unité adhered to this pact. Soon they were joined by sections Droits-de-l'Homme, Arsenal, Arcis, Réunion, Marais, Temple, Faubourg-Montmartre, and Bondy. La Cité was also a citadel of radicalism. On the Left Bank, the patriots dominated the sections Marseilles and Sans-Culottes. Thus the latter were preponderant in twenty sections, as against conservatives or moderates who also dominated twenty sections, mostly in the west. The equilibrium was unstable, however, and did not begin to shift decisively until 2 June.[60]

On 19 May section Droits-de-l'Homme was invaded by numerous delegations from sections Contrat-Social, Bon-Conseil, Unité, Lombards, Gravilliers, and Marchés. Amidst the highest enthusiasm and fraternal exchanges it received the pledge of Guiraud, president of section Contrat-Social, to assist the *sans-culottes* of the section against the so-called "aristocrats." Moderates were now denounced as "monsters" far more to be feared than tyrants because "they mislead public opinion and chill patriotism in order to deliver a mortal blow to liberty." The assembly then adopted unanimously the principle that when several sections met together their joint sessions were to be considered as one and the same and their deliberations as common to all. One immediate result was the replacement of members of the section's revolutionary committee, now thought to be too moderate.[61]

The dismissal of former members of the revolutionary committee was not a unanimous process, and a number of these were retained on the new committee. When a participant suggested that present members be allowed to speak in self-defense before being dismissed, he was loudly applauded. The only charge against the vice president was

[60] Albert Soboul, *Les Sans-culottes parisiens en l'an II. Mouvement populaire et gouvernement révolutionnaire 2 juin–9 thermidor an II* (Paris, 1958), pp. 25-27. This authoritative work is indispensable for the study of the sections of Paris.

[61] B.V.C., MS 120, fols. 138-141, 19 May 1793. A member of section Droits-de-l'Homme spoke movingly on how moderates and counterrevolutionaries were taking advantage of the gap left by the departure of patriotic *sans-culottes* of the section for the Vendée. Hence he welcomed the aid proffered the section against "aristocrats." Fol. 140. See also A. de P., 1 AZ 159², *Procès-verbal*, 20 May 1793, 4 pp.; B.H.V.P., 104.095, *Section des Droits-de-l'Homme. Procès-verbal de la séance du 20 mai, 2e* (n.d.), 4 pp. For developments in the section prior to 19 May, see references in A.N., AD I, 70; A. de P., 1 AZ 159²; B.H.V.P., 100.65*; and B.V.C., MS 120. The date of 20 May is often cited, rather than 19 May, for the reorganization described above and below.

a supposed "violent interruption" made by him during the reading of an unspecified patriotic address. When the question was put to the vote, the assembly decided to retain Pollet as president and Descombes as secretary (for the remainder of the session), but replaced the vice president by a militant and future commissioner on profiteering, Carron.[62]

All members of the revolutionary committee were elected by an assembly that included militants of the six sections sitting jointly with Droits-de-l'Homme. The atmosphere must have bordered on hysteria, as the following incident demonstrates. A member arose to make a stirring appeal against "the counterrevolutionary banners waving in our midst." The assembly then burned "the uncivic banners . . . [in] an outburst of patriotism and horror of despotism permeating all hearts."[63] When Descombes pointed out that his appointment deprived a good patriot from serving, as he was already a member by virtue of his being secretary of the body, the assembly elected Ravel in addition.[64] In an effort to guarantee the permanence of its decision, the assembly resolved to regard anyone who dared challenge the action taken by the meeting as a "disturber and enemy of public affairs." After singing "the hymn to liberty, Allons enfans de la patrie," the assembly rose and gave witness to "the most touching feelings of fraternity."[65] A week later "the regenerated section" was called upon,

[62] The revolutionary committee was now composed of the following: Eude, captain of cannoneers; Pétaud, vice president; Carron, also a vice president; and Rattier, Dupaumier, Duclos, Descombes, Dubois, Deschamps (père), Guéneau, Gervais, Joiris; adding shortly thereafter, Thiébart (fils), Bernard, and Mazin.

In A.N., F[7]* 2497, p. 24, 20 May 1793, "Extrait des registres des délibérations de l'Assemblée générale de la section des Droits-de-l'Homme dans sa séance de ce jour," there is a slightly different version of the proceedings. Pollet presided as former members installed the newly elected members after the oath. Deschamps was elected president, and Guéneau secretary. It was agreed to organize "a definite committee" on 22 May. This was signed by Deschamps and Guéneau.

[63] B.H.V.P., 104.095, Procès-verbal de la séance du 20 mai, passim. The former vice president was refused the floor.

[64] Descombes wrote in his own justification, later, that it was he who had organized the fraternization with others "to confound the aristocrats in his section." B.N., Ln[27] 5894, Descombe(s), électeur, membre du Conseil général de la Commune de Paris, et secrétaire-greffier de la section des Droits-de-l'Homme ([Paris]; [1794]), 16 pp. The reference is to pp. 8-9.

[65] B.H.V.P., Procès-verbal. This was signed by Ravel, secretary, Pétaud, vice president, and Descombes, secretary-editor. Five hundred copies of this procès-verbal were printed.

in its turn, to come to the assistance of its neighboring section, Arsenal, against the latter's own "aristocrats." The section went in a body with the president at its head to help their fellow militants.[66]

Thus, unlike the time of troubles and vacillations experienced by Droits-de-l'Homme on the eve of 10 August, the section was now firmly in control of those who supported the Mountain against the Gironde. Still, three or four of the men elected had deep roots in the Revolution, being signatories of the militia list of 13-14 July.[67] Although the political break with the past was evident, eight (or half) of the men elected on 19-20 May were members of the first committee,[68] thus indicating a certain continuity of personnel if not of politics. Like other Jacobins of the capital, they had become disillusioned with Girondist policies. Shortages, high prices, and the war had done their work, for moderates now became as suspect as former royalists. This trend was dramatically underscored by the insurrection against the Gironde as a new chapter in the history of the Revolution and in that of section Droits-de-l'Homme was about to begin.

This political change was itself a partial reflection of the sharpening economic crisis. It is enough to mention that an *assignat* note of 100 livres, which in May had been at 52, fell in June to 36.[69] In comparison to 1790, prices rose steeply on all necessities: beef was up 136 percent, salted pork 33 percent, wheat 27 percent, potatoes 700 percent; table wine sold at 16 sous a pint. A rough estimate is that necessities, including rent, had risen about 100 percent. Wages, too, had gone up, but for most workers, not in the same proportion as prices.[70]

[66] B.V.C., MS 120, fol. 143, 26 May 1793. Section Arsenal staged its purge on 24 May, precipitated by delegates from section Fraternité over the Commission of Twelve. After thirty to forty members left the hall in protest, the parties were divided into seventy-five radicals and sixty "others." Presumably, had those who walked out remained, the moderates would still have controlled the section. A.N., C 355, 1859-1860, 24 May 1793.

[67] These were Louis-Pierre Thiébart, fils (discussed below in the chapter on the Civil Committee); Mazin, an upholsterer; and Clement-René Bernard, a painter. Three Dubois appear on the list: Jean, a bourgeois, Louis, a carpenter, and Joseph, a mason. One of the latter two could have been the Dubois elected. B.H.V.P., MS 742.

[68] These are discussed in Chapter IX on the revolutionary committee. Their names are: Duclos, Eude, Gervais, Dupaumier, Guéneau, Descombes, Pétaud, and Mazin.

[69] Caron, *Tableau*, Introduction, p. LII. By August it was down to 22, rose to 48 in December, and then resumed its downward course again in 1794.

[70] See the figures compiled in A.N., F[11] 218 and the discussion of Rudé, *The Crowd*, Appendix, VII, Table 3, p. 252 n. 2.

Police spies reported open talk of insurrection, discontent with authorities, and general dissatisfaction with the state of society and government. An observer for the Commune wrote one week before the revolt: "We should not fool ourselves, for the uprising is *inevitable* and *very close*, if we do not adopt measures of relief for the people."[71] Another admitted "that all citizens were discontented with deputies of the Convention," and were calling for another 10 August.[72] A third observer spoke of "a dissatisfied people, which hates the Convention."[73]

Deputies of the Convention were aware of this unrest, of course, and of the assembly of commissioners in the Evêché formed by the sections in response to this dissatisfaction. To frustrate their plans, the Convention, on a motion of Barère, established the Commission des Douze to examine all resolutions and acts of the Paris Commune and its sections, in an obvious attempt to chill their ardor for an insurrection.[74] Among the questions posed by the commission to the authorities of the capital were demands for information on the "preachings of a Varlet."[75] The orator of section Droits-de-l'Homme had established by now a more than local reputation.

Although the mayor sought to reassure the Convention and its commission that all measures of precaution had been taken,[76] the latter was less than satisfied with Jean-Nicolas Pache's assurances. It was especially critical of Hébert's *Père Duchesne*, which it accused of calling daily for massacres and assassinations. Citing the publisher's justification for using intemperate language in calling for the extermination of "traitors" without which his journal "would lack punch," the commissioners observed ironically: "What language for a magistrate of the people to use."[77] Vigée, reporting for the commission, proposed that

[71] A.N., C 256, 488-489, pc. 18, 23, 24 May 1793, emphasis in original.

[72] A.N., C 355, 1868, pc. 21, 22 May 1793, reported by Legrand.

[73] A.N., F^{1c} III, Seine, 27, pc. 27, 30 May 1793, a perceptive report by Dutard for the department of Paris.

[74] A.N., C 355, 1866, 21 May 1793. The dossier of 8 pièces is entitled "Commission extraordinaire des Douze du 21 Mai au 28 du d. an 1793"; B. & R., XXVIII, 131-132; the latter lists members of the commission, p. 161.

[75] A.N., C 355, 1866, 22 May 1793.

[76] *Ibid.*, and A.N., C 256, 488-489, pc. 15, 25 May 1793.

[77] A.N., C 355, 1867, *Rapport très précis de la Commission des Douze* (n.d.), 5 pp. The commission quoted Hébert (underscoring his remarks): "Il avoue que ses expressions figurées, dans un stile qui, sans exagérations, n'auroit aucune sel."

in addition to certain security measures to be taken, all sectional assemblies adjourn by 10 p.m. and their minutes and registers be turned over to the commission. Despite the protests of Danton, the proposals were adopted by the Convention.[78]

Wasting no time, the commission issued warrants of arrest against Hébert, Varlet, and other critics,[79] with the Ministry of Justice dispatching two gendarmes into section Droits-de-l'Homme to seize Varlet. In defiance, his section immediately appointed three commissioners from its assembly to accompany him on his way to prison, and took him under its own safeguard.[80] Nor did this challenge to the commission stop there, for the arrest of Hébert and Varlet aroused a storm of protest from the Commune and the other sections. Delegates sent by the General Council demanded the immediate release of their magistrate. It was then that Isnard, presiding over the Convention, made his intemperate reply that if threats against the Convention continued, "soon they will search on the banks of the Seine [to see] if Paris had ever existed." While the party on the Right applauded, his remarks were greeted with loud indignation by the Left.[81]

Sixteen sections, among which was Droits-de-l'Homme, adopted a petition for the release of Hébert and Varlet, their spokesmen accusing the commission of behaving tyrannically in hopes of establishing a new despotism. "Do you think," asked a delegate, "that we have broken the scepter of tyranny to bow our heads under the yoke of a new despotism?"[82] Soon thirty-three sections sent delegates to the Evêché determined to "save the Republic," an action resulting from an invitation of section Temple to send two delegates each to the

[78] *Moniteur*, XVI, no. 145, pp. 459-460, 25 May 1793, and no. 146, pp. 467-468, 26 May 1793; B. & R., XXVII, 185-197, *passim*.

[79] A.N., C 355, 1866, 25 May 1793.

[80] B.V.C., MS 120, fol. 143, 24 May 1793. Hébert was interned in the Abbaye prison. B. & R., XXVII, 204. He was arrested for his article in the *Père Duchesne*, no. CCXXXIX, wherein he denounced the Girondins as counterrevolutionaries in the pay of Pitt. *Ibid.*, pp. 208-212. "It is within the Convention, yes, f . . . it, it is among the representatives of the people that the foyer of the counterrevolution exists now." Calling upon the *sans-culottes* to rise, he warned that "the poison" of moderation was more dangerous than the arms of the Austrians. *Père Duchesne*, no. 239, pp. 1-8, n.d.

[81] B. & R., XXVII, 225, 25 May 1793; *Moniteur*, XVI, no. 147, p. 480, 27 May 1793.

[82] A.N., C 256, 488-489, pc. 7, 26 May 1793; B. & R., XXVII, 233.

Commune for this purpose. Why, asked section Temple, in its petition to the Convention, had it arrested Hébert and Varlet, "whose patriotism is generally recognized." It demanded that they be released under the guarantee of the sections. Section Droits-de-l'Homme had unanimously approved the address of the Commune and had elected two commissioners to carry this approval to the General Council.[83] A number had endorsed the threat of section Faubourg-Montmartre, which on 25 May warned that it would go en masse to bring back by force the records of its proceedings, as they were the depository of "the sovereign people." On the morrow it resolved to stage a demonstration demanding the dissolution of "the despotic and counterrevolutionary Commission of Twelve."[84]

While the sections and Commune were mobilizing against the Commission of Twelve, Robespierre delivered a forceful address against "the Brissotins," after which the Jacobins declared themselves to be in a state of insurrection against "the corrupt deputies."[85] The Convention itself became an arena of combat between partisans of the Gironde and their enemies of the Mountain, spurred on by the constant demonstrations and petitions of the radical sections.[86] On 28 May Cité called on the sections to send representatives to the Evêché to deliberate on how to save the Republic, a call to which thirty-three sections responded by sending two commissioners each. Among them were Varlet and Eugene-Honoré Gervais of Droits-de-l'Homme, the former having been released with Hébert on 27 May. The section having declared itself in permanent session on 29 May, now endowed its commissioners with unlimited powers.[87] Varlet was about to give

[83] A.N., C 256, 488-489, pcs. 20, 31. The commissioners elected were Picard and Rattier, their commission signed by Collet, president, and Pointard, secretary. Section Temple's resolution is in the same dossier, pc. 20, 25 May 1793.

[84] *Ibid.*, pcs. 40, 8.

[85] Aulard, *Jacobins*, V, 208, 26 May 1793. A fuller version is in B. & R., XXVII, 243-244, 26 May 1793.

[86] A.P., LXV, 355-356, 477-481; B. & R., XXVII, 249, 251-270. See especially the petition of Unité, A.N., C 256, 489, pc. 13, 28 May 1793, endorsed by section Droits-de-l'Homme, *ibid.*, pc. 26; the eloquent attack on Isnard by section Arcis, *ibid.*, pc. 8, 29 May 1793; and that of Beaurepaire, which threatened to "stamp on the brow of each one of you [deputies] the mark of our reprobation" if they betrayed the aspirations of the people. *Ibid.*, pc. 9, 29 May 1793.

[87] B.V.C., MS 120, fol. 143, 28 and 29 May 1793.

the signal for the insurrection of 31 May which, among other results, was to put an end to the Commission of Twelve.[88]

The sixty-six delegates who met in the Evêché on 29 May spoke for thirty-three sections that had determined to resort to extraordinary measures, that is, to take illegal action, to bring an end to the political crisis. During the night and morning of 30-31 May, this revolutionary assembly declared Paris to be in insurrection against "the aristocratic and liberty-oppressive faction" (the Girondins), and announced its own state of permanence.[89] Its first act was to elect a committee of nine members (*comité des neuf*), to direct the insurrection, which later assumed the name of Comité central révolutionnaire,[90] and to organize itself into ten different departments.[91] Many of its members were not yet thirty years old; Varlet, who gave the signal for the insurrection, was but twenty-nine.[92] Although it usurped the powers

[88] The Commission was temporarily cashiered on 27 May, reestablished the following day, and permanently suppressed on 31 May. See the debate on this question in B. & R., XXVII, 276-283, 287, 292; *Moniteur*, XVI, no. 149, pp. 491-496, 29 May 1793; no. 150, pp. 500-504, 30 May 1793; no. 151, p. 509, 31 May 1793; no. 152, pp. 521-524, 1 June 1793.

[89] *Inventaire des autographes et des documents historiques composant la collection de M. Benjamin Fillon*, séries I and II (Paris, 1877), p. 64, no. 546 ("Paris déclaré en insurrection"), items 1 and 2. The latter contains a communication addressed to section Droits-de-l'Homme.

[90] A.N., BB³ 80, d. 16, pc. 49, "Liste des membres composant le Comité central et révolutionnaire du département de Paris." Marquet of section Bonne-Nouvelle heads the list, with Varlet's name being third. This carton is the most significant collection on the insurrection of 31 May-2 June. Unless otherwise noted, the references are to the *44e carton*, which contains documents of the Department of Police, the General Council of the Commune, the department of Paris, and the General Assembly of the Commissioners of the forty-eight Sections (the Evêché assembly). In addition, as will be seen below, reports of the sections are in a dossier entitled "Etat produit par les sections qui dans les journées des 31 mai, 1er et 2 juin ont marché sous les drapeaux de la liberté."

[91] A.N., BB³ 80, d. 16, pc. 51. Its ten bureaus were: correspondence with the Committee of Public Safety and Committee of General Security, interior police, public works, émigrés, legislation, armed force, finance, ministerial correspondence, *procès-verbaux*, and correspondence with the interior. Exercising these powers made it virtually the real government of France. For a few days, perhaps, it became just that.

[92] At first the committee was known as the Committee of Nine. On 31 May it coopted an important militant of section Cité, Claude-Emmanuel Dobsen, which made it the Committee of Ten, and was so referred to in numerous documents. The

of the legally constituted authorities, the committee clearly recognized its own subordination to the sections that had created it.

The Revolutionary Central Committee launched the insurrection on
31 May by suspending the powers of the mayor, the municipal officers, and the General Council of the Commune, the act of suspension
being signed by Jean Varlet.[93] This order, together with that of sounding
the alarm in the sections, made Varlet, for a brief moment, the chief
figure of the insurrectionary committee, no mean achievement for a
man still in his twenties.[94]

Although Varlet's contribution to the insurrection was important
and even dramatic, the role of his section was more modest, its general assembly being more a recipient than initiator of revolutionary
acts. As the section received directives and messages from the Evêché
committee, the General Council, and the directory of the department,
it took the usual steps common to most sections during these three
days of revolution. On the morning of 31 May it was informed of the
department's decision to send commissioners to the Jacobins, thereby
enlarging the revolutionary committee of the Evêché.[95] It is doubtful
if anyone sitting in the assembly realized the implication of this move
in reference to the future role of its own commissioner, Jean Varlet,
as it had more practical questions to consider—one being the need to
obtain guns and shells. Its revolutionary committee, having received

---

same day (31 May), the authorities of the department of Paris with their communes
added eleven members, and the General Council of Paris appointed four members,
thus enlarging the original committee to twenty-five members. See the remarks by
Paul Sainte-Claire Deville, *La Commune de l'an II. Vie et mort d'une assemblée révolutionnaire* (Paris, [1946]), p. 87.

[93] A.N., BB³ 80, d. 16, pc. 21, 31 May 1793. Varlet signed it as provisional
president, with Fournerot as secretary. The document carries the appointment of four
commissioners to carry out this suspension. See also pc. 36, 30 May, signed by the
Comité des Neuf.

[94] Mathiez exaggerated when he wrote that "The Revolution of May 31-June 2 was
made by . . . three men: Varlet, Jacques Roux, and Leclerc d'Oze." "Les Enragés
contre la Constitution de 1793," *Annales révolutionnaires*, 13 (1921), 303; *La Vie chère*,
p. 206.

[95] The section elected a total of four commissioners—Varlet and Gervais (on 29
May) and Descombes and Dupaumier. There is no mention of the election of the
latter two in the minutes of MS 120, but Descombes records the four delegates in
his *Descombes, électeur, membre du Conseil général*, p. 5.

the order to arrest suspects, advised a thorough search of lodging houses and furnished rooms in its own section and throughout the city, and communicated this suggestion to other committees.[96]

The insurrection of 31 May unleashed a flurry of activity in the committee. As directives from the Commune dealing with public safety began to arrive, the revolutionary committee launched a number of sweeps throughout the section to pick up suspects. The latter included a gendarme without identification, an individual who had declared that Marat should be assassinated, and another who had dared to proclaim that all revolutionary committees should be abolished—a charge denied by him, especially with reference to the committee of section Droits-de-l'Homme.[97]

The following day, 1 June, many suspects who lacked cards of identity were brought before the committee, but after an interrogation they were returned to their respective sections. The committee took steps to carry out the decree of the Revolutionary Central Committee and the Commune to disarm all suspects and to arm patriots with the weapons confiscated. The forced loan on the wealthy, the purpose of which was to help dependents of soldiers and volunteers, was also implemented. Among measures of security taken by the section was the enrollment of patriotic citizens to help the section's armed force carry out the arrests decreed by the central authorities. The commander of the armed force reported that he had dispatched cannoneers with their pieces to the Place du Carousel, as ordered by the commanding general of the Parisian National Guard, François Hanriot.[98]

That there was some opposition to the insurrection in the section may be gathered from the interrogations conducted by the committee. A citizen by name of André Déon was brought before it by an armed patrol of section Marais. He had gone to the church Saint François,

[96] B.V.C., MS 120, fol. 143, 31 May 1793; A.N., BB³ 80, d. 16, pc. 209, n.d., carrying the name of Houdaille, member of the revolutionary committee of the section. The document was addressed to the Revolutionary Central Committee entitled "A la commission de Salut public, séante à la maison commune" and signed by Deschamps, president, and Guéneau, secretary.

[97] A.N., F⁷* 2497, p. 27, 31 May 1793. The *procès-verbal* was signed by the suspect, Gaillard.

[98] *Ibid.*, p. 28, 1 June 1793.

it was charged, demanding to see the written orders of those who were sounding the alarm, but having no civic card on his person, he was immediately sent to Minimes prison. Another case involved a charge of abuse, made by Lieutenant Bernard of the section's first company against a domestic by name of Baumon, as the former was rounding up those who had failed to report upon sound of the general alarm. Among the latter was a citizen Doré residing on rue Mauvais-Garçons whose domestic, Baumon, had allegedly abused verbally the lieutenant in line of duty. Surprisingly, it was Baumon, not Doré, who was brought in under armed guard, interrogated, and sent to Minimes prison.[99]

On the last day of the insurrection, 2 June, the committee continued to interrogate those brought before it who lacked cards of security, returning them, as before, to their own sections. Upon receiving a warning by commissioners of section Popincourt of possible damage to national buildings by certain inhabitants of section Droits-de-l'Homme who allegedly planned to tear out the wood in these structures for fuel, the committee notified its armed force to take the necessary precautionary measures. It also received orders from the Revolutionary Central Committee to suppress all unpatriotic journals and to distribute the proceeds from this act of confiscation among the section's poor. The committee stopped issuing passports upon receiving a decree from the Commune to this effect, and drew up a list of indigent patriots who had served under arms during the three days of the insurrection, as it continued to enforce military regulations that required service in the armed force of the section's companies. Its last decree for the day was to order the illumination of all houses in the section.[100]

The second in command of the section's armed force, Garnier, reported a dramatic chase after a suspect who somehow managed to jump into a carriage and get away—this, despite the fact that Garnier was on horseback.[101] Meanwhile, the section's commissioners were meeting with others and promoting the insurrection. By the evening

[99] *Ibid.*, pp. 28-29.

[100] *Ibid.*, p. 29, 2 June 1793. When the corporal of the 1st company reported that a citizen by name of Adancourt had refused to carry his gun, that is, to patrol, he was brought in under armed guard.

[101] A.N., F7* 2514, pp. 15-16, 3 June 1793. Garnier describes how he broke up a brawl between four gendarmes and the suspect. Whether possession of a knife truly made him a suspect is not made clear by Garnier's testimony.

of 2 June, the assembly of the section was gratified to hear from the Commune how wisely and prudently the revolution was developing.[102] Like other sections, it experienced moments of frustration and doubt, but also determination and bold action.[103]

The Revolutionary Central Committee appointed Varlet and two others to draft a declaration on the status of the arrested deputies at its evening session of 4 June. Wasting no time, on the following day Varlet enjoyed the rare pleasure of reading to the Commune the committee's draft, consisting of a number of preliminary articles against the leading Girondins.[104] Meanwhile, the men arrested were lightly guarded and were even allowed to visit their wives,[105] which enabled many to escape and organize an uprising of numerous departments, the so-called Federalist revolt, that endangered for a time the very existence of the Republic. When a number of disaffected militants, including the *enragés*, ideologically linked to Varlet, spoke out against the government of the Terror, one of their charges was the lackadaisical and irresponsible effort in guarding these deputies.[106] For the time being, however, the directives of the Central Committee were for moderation; its president, Marquet, reminded the police that although suspects were to be arrested according to law, they were to be treated in a manner "worthy of free men," and admonished them to conduct themselves properly.[107] The Revolutionary Central Commit-

[102] B.V.C., MS 120, fol. 144, 31 May, 1 and 2 June 1793.

[103] A.N., BB³ 80, d. 16. "Sections et comités des sections de Paris" contains a collection of decrees and resolutions of the sections as they prepared for the *journée* of 31 May. Most are brief notations of election of commissioners to the Evêché assembly. A detailed recital of events and resolutions of the General Council for 30-31 May is in B. & R., XXVIII, 305-322, *passim*.

[104] B.N., BB³ 80, d. 3, pcs. 89 and 164, 4 and 5 June 1793. On 5 June the name of the Revolutionary Central Committee changed to Revolutionary Central Committee of the Commune of Paris. Tuetey, *Répertoire*, IX, Introduction, p. C.

[105] BB³ 80, d. 16, pc. 228, n.d. The revolutionary committee of section Unité reported from the *hôtel* du Patriote Holandais, where the deputies were supposedly under guard, that "several had left at night to visit their wives." They were unarmed, however, and were supposed to be guarded by "two good citizens." *Ibid.*, D.5, pc. 89, 4 June 1793.

[106] See, for example, the charge of Leclerc in his journal B.N., Lc² 704, *l'Ami du peuple*, no. XXIV, 15 September 1793. See my article, "Théophile Leclerc: An Anti-Jacobin Terrorist," in *The Historian*, 33 (May 1971), pp. 398-414.

[107] BB³ 80, d. 16, pc. 58, 5 June 1793. Marquet had received complaints from those imprisoned in section Butte-des-Moulins of harsh treatment by the police.

tee agreed, moreover, to draft an address explaining that it had placed the arrested deputies under its own protection.[108]

Needless to say, those Girondin deputies who had escaped had a different view of the *journée* of 31 May-2 June from its defenders. Among them was Bergoeing, a deputy of the department of the Gironde and a former member of the Commission of Twelve. In the testimony compiled against the insurrection he quoted a number of observers, all of whom verified the alleged desire of the revolutionaries to exterminate the Girondin deputies. Writing in the heat of battle, he redefined suspects as "all those who are not friends of anarchy." Among these "anarchists," Varlet received more than his share of attention as Bergoeing cited the young *enragé*'s fifteen articles of 22 May, when he supposedly proposed to kidnap deputies, priests, nobles, and lawyers before staging an insurrection.[109]

In a testimony by a Bernard T. of Bordeaux, Bergoeing quoted from his report on what he allegedly heard on 16 May from the lips of a young man (Varlet) dressed in the uniform of a National Guardsman. He had mounted a chair placed on the Terrasse des Feuillants in the Tuileries and was quoted as follows:

> Before departing for the Vendée, I must tell you what to do to foil the schemes of the f . . . Blacks [reactionaries]. For you see their design by the cards of privilege that they give to aristocrats like themselves. It is high time to finish with them. We must no longer guillotine cooks, coachmen, the poor fellows of *sans-culottes*; but we should chop off the heads of Convention members like the Brissotins, Girondins, etc. You understand me.[110]

A number of women, allegedly, were also told by Varlet: "wait a while; in three of four days we are going to accomplish something."[111]

---

[108] *Ibid.*, d. 16, pc. 160, 5 June 1793. On 29 June the prisons of Paris held a total of 1,335 individuals in confinement; a little over a hundred of these were military prisoners, plus five hostages. A.N., C 261, 564, pc. 16.

[109] B.N., Lb⁴¹ 715, *Bergoeing; député du département de la Gironde, & membre de la Commission des Douze, à ses commettans, et à tous les citoyens de la République* (Caen, 1793), 44 pp. The quotation is on p. 4; reference to Varlet is on pp. 6-7. A major portion of this brochure is reproduced by B. & R., XXXVIII, 108-126, as are other pamphlets, notably those of A. J. Gorsas, pp. 4-29, and J.B.M. Saladin, deputy of the department of the Somme, pp. 30-54.

[110] *Bergoeing*, p. 22.

[111] *Ibid.*, p. 39.

Whatever the truth of Bergoeing's witnesses, there can be no question that Varlet's public propagandizing for the overthrow of the Girondin leaders had helped propel him into a leading role on the eve of 31 May. Yet it is significant that he was not elected to the new Revolutionary Central Committee, called after 8 June, the Committee of Public Safety of the Department of Paris.[112]

The 40 sous voted by the Convention to subsidize the poorer *sans-culottes* for bearing arms were duly paid, the number under arms reflecting the popular nature of this uprising.[113] Hardly was the subsidy voted when a delegation of section Droits-de-l'Homme arrived on 4 June before the General Council, to repudiate this indemnity. Like so many resolutions in the past, this, too, was authored by Varlet, its argument simply put being that it was improper to accept money for service to the *patrie*. Destournelles, the vice president presiding, replied that although their sentiments were "sublime," poor patriots who had made pecuniary sacrifices could accept "with honor" the promised indemnity. To receive help to live was a small price to pay for the blood shed by the poor *sans-culotte*.[114] "What an admirable example you show!" continued the vice president, "one can recognize the true *sans-culotte* there, model of all virtue." The General Council applauded the feelings expressed by the delegation and ordered the publication of its proceedings on this matter and their wide distribution.[115] This generous gesture, and the no less generous response of the Commune, was to change into a feeling of hostility when Varlet continued to manifest his opposition to the revolutionary government.

The uncertain behavior of the Convention with respect to the in-

[112] Tuetey, *Répertoire*, Introduction, p. CIV; Henri Calvet, *Un Instrument de la Terreur à Paris: le Comité de salut public ou de serveillance du département de Paris (8 juin 1793–21 messidor an II)* (Paris, 1941), pp. 10, 78-79. Jean-Henri Hassenfratz, who also played a key role in the insurrection, was not elected, either.

[113] A.N., BB³ 80, d. 16, pcs. 1, 2, 21, 22; dated 3, 6, 7 June, 21 (?) July 1793. See Henri Calvet's study, "Remarques sur la participation des sections au movement du 31 mai–1er-2 juin 1793," *Annales historiques*, 5 (1928), 366-369. Section Droits-de-l'Homme does not appear among the thirty-three sections listed.

[114] B.N., MSS, Nouv. acq. fr., 2647, fol. 179, 4 June 1793. The question involved and the consequences that followed are discussed more fully in the chapter on the Welfare Committee.

[115] *Ibid.*; this was signed by Destournelles, vice president, Dorat-Cubière, secretary-registrar, and Coulombeau, secretary-registrar.

surrection, the ambivalent reports of its committees regarding the role of the Commune, the uneasy feeling that its freedom of deliberation had been compromised, the heated defense of its action by the Revolutionary Central Committee—all pointed to the vacillations of the Convention and its committees immediately after 2 June.[116] Only after the growing threat to Paris by foreign invaders, the widening Federalist revolt, the early victories of Vendéens, and the establishment of communications between the Girondists and London and Piedmont, did the Convention swing to the side of the Mountain and the Commune.[117] This was reflected in its resolution that "The National Convention declares that during the *journées* of 31 May, 1st, 2 and 3 June, the Revolutionary General Council of the Commune and the people of Paris contributed powerfully to save the liberty, unity, and indivisibility of the Republic."[118] The Revolution was now given its formal justification, but the struggle in the sections between the patriots and moderates linked to counterrevolutionaries continued for some time after 2 June.[119]

The conversion of the Committee of Nine into the enlarged committee of twenty-five carried Dobsen into the presidency and removed Varlet from this key position.[120] The implication of this move was not lost on the latter. Writing in the fall of 1794, he analyzed the

[116] See, for example, the report of Barère directed against the Commune, in the Convention on 6 June, and Robespierre's reply. B. & R., XXVIII, 167-168, 169-171; and Billaud-Varenne's proposals in the Jacobins to organize the country for defense, *ibid.*, pp. 160-161. The Jacobins' eloquent defense of the insurrection is *ibid.*, pp. 134-140. On 4 June the Commune reacted indignantly to rumors of its alleged usurpation of power, *ibid.*, p. 157. Calvet points out that many sections were divided in their attitudes to the insurrection. *Instrument*, pp. 30-31. Thirty-four sections had no representatives on the new committee, that is, the Committee of Public Safety of the Department of Paris. *Ibid.*, pp. 79-80.

[117] B. & R., XXVIII, 141-155, *passim*.

[118] *Ibid.*, XXVIII, 202, 13 June 1793.

[119] Calvet, *Instrument*, pp. 82-86, *passim*. Calvet quotes observers who spoke of a "scission cordelière" (a Cordeliers split), which he explains: "a Jacobin minority, preponderant within the Cordeliers, and which followed probably the Enragés, detached itself from the revolutionary mass and preached for more vigorous action." *Ibid.*, p. 85. Varlet was among the latter.

[120] Chaumette in his *Mémoires* does not even mention Varlet, but speaks of Dobsen (spelling his name d'Obsent), as president of the Evêché assembly. "Deuxième Récit," p. 185. See Guérin's interesting analysis of Dobsen's role, I, 120-129, *passim*. The cooption of Dobsen is in A.N., BB³ 80, d. 16, pc. 135, 30 May 1793.

events of 31 May. Among those elected to save the country, he affirmed, were true republicans together with a number of "the most destructive of factions." This "league of Caligula" saw nothing in the overthrow of the Brissotins but the possibility of developing a vast scope for their ambition: "The insurrectionary committee contained the germ of a revolutionary government, conceived secretly at the very beginning. The false insurgents substituted Robespierre for Brissot; for federalism, a revolutionary dictatorship, decreed in the name of public safety. As for me, I was too sincere to be initiated into it; I was set aside."[121]

That there was opposition to the insurrection among the revolutionists there can be no doubt. Testifying at the trial of Chaumette, after the execution of the Hébertists, Marchand revealed that: "as a member of the Revolutionary Central Committee on 31 May, I saw Chaumette bend all his efforts to shackle this glorious revolution, to denounce at every moment all measures that public safety demanded, shout, cry, tear his hair, and make the most violent efforts to convince us that the Central Committee was effecting the counterrevolution. His behavior was such that one could have taken him for a mad man."[122]

Varlet became suspicious of Dobsen's role on the morrow of his own demission, and accused him of having "hindered the operations of the revolutionary committee."[123] He must have been aware, of course, that Dobsen had been dispatched by the newly enlarged Evêché committee to the Committee of Public Safety of the Convention to ask for instructions. This meant that another body had been introduced into a directing role of the insurrection.[124] Louis-Pierre Dufourny ex-

---

[121] B.N., Lb⁴¹ 1330, Jean Varlet, *Gare l'explosion!* ([Paris]), 15 vendémiaire, an III (5 October 1794), 16 pp. The quotation is from pp. 5-6. Another brochure containing the same material is B.N., Lb⁴¹ 4090, *L'Explosion* ([Paris]), du 10 vendémiaire, an III (1 October 1794), 15 pp.

[122] Cited by Mortimer-Ternaux, VII, p. 391 n. 1. The author states that of all the leaders of the Commune, Chaumette alone did not want to act illegally. This means, of course, that he opposed the insurrection.

[123] B. & R., XXVII, 355, 1 June, in the Commune. Varlet moderated his criticism by adding that "nevertheless he does not wish to question the civic conduct of this citizen." *Moniteur*, XVI, no. 155, p. 542, 4 June 1793.

[124] A.N., BB³ 80, d. 16, pc. 16; Fillon, *Autographes*, p. 66, no. 547, item 12, 31 May 1793, where Dobsen's name is spelled Dopson.

ulted in the Year III that he had stopped "the conspirators of 31 May
. . . the men of blood," by taking measures to nullify their actions.[125]
That this was no vain boast may be seen when, almost a year after
the insurrection, Robespierre revealed that "on 31 May, Dufourny
gained admittance into the committee of insurrection; when he saw
that the popular movement would succeed, he retired from the committee and sought means to render it impotent."[126] Official authorities, anxious to hold the insurrecton within acceptable limits (acceptable to the Jacobins and deputies of the Mountain), mistrusted
revolutionaries like Varlet who wanted to push the Revolution further.
Pache must have spoken for many of them when he stated regretfully,
"this is what happens . . . every time you place a Varlet at your head;
it will serve you right."[127]

That Varlet was cognizant of these differences can be seen in his
bold remarks on 1 June regarding the mayor who "has not been instructed during the past twenty-four hours. . . . He thinks that being
clothed with legal authority, he could be harmful to the revolution."[128] This mistrust was based on more than personal pique at
having been removed as president of the Revolutionary Central Committee. One explanation for it lies in a revealing item published by
the *Chronique de Paris* under the heading of "Journée du 31 mai." It
observed, "many misguided people, making no distinction between
the Plain and the Mountain, accuse the whole Convention of responsibility for the tremendous rise in prices, and believe that they can
find an end to their troubles in its dissolution."[129] Varlet was no
partisan of representative government, promoting, rather, the traditional aims of champions of the *mandat impératif*. The active intervention of devoted militants, acting through their commissioners in the
Evêché, must have reinforced his faith in direct democracy, and he
would hardly have regretted the dissolution of the Convention. Indeed, one member of the Committee of Nine, the Spaniard Gusman,

[125] Cited by Calvet, *Instrument*, p. 46.

[126] Aulard, *Jacobins*, VI, 52, 16 germinal, an II (5 April 1794); B. & R., XXVII,
209. Robespierre had Dufourny expelled from the Jacobins.

[127] Cited by Deville, p. 89. ("Voilà ce que c'est . . . chaque fois que vous mettrez
un Varlet à votre tête, il vous en arrivera autant.")

[128] B. & R., XXVII, 355, 1 June 1793; *Moniteur*, XVI, no. 155, p. 542, 4 June
1793.

[129] B.N., Lc² 218, no. 153, p. 3, 2 June 1793.

Figure 5. The Fall of Robespierre, 9 Thermidor, Year II

is said to have told Sebastien Mercier that the chiefs of the Jacobins, Robespierre and Marat, should be removed, together with the Girondins.[130] True or not, men like Varlet would hardly have been satisfied with the mere replacement of the Girondins by the Montagnards, since their aim was to go beyond the acceptable limits of the Jacobins.

When Robespierre and the Montagnards were finally removed from the political scene, Varlet could hardly have rejoiced at this turn of fortune. The kind of revolution his partisans and he had in mind had little in common with that prepared by the Thermidorians. Like others, including Babeuf, the *enragés* might have been fooled for a short time, but it was not long before they learned the true nature of the regime established on the bones of Robespierre, Saint Just, and Couthon.

Historians who have examined the events that led to Robespierre's fall from power cite a variety of factors for this event—from the rain that fell in the early hours of 10 thermidor to the vacillations and hesitations of the "Incorruptible" himself. There is little doubt that the execution of the Hébertists and Dantonists and the domestication

[130] Deville, p. 118.

of the Commune alienated thousands of formerly loyal *sans-culottes*. An additional factor that estranged more working people than any other measure was the publication of a new salary schedule by the Commune on 5 thermidor (23 July). It was a table drafted on 21 messidor (9 July) and made public on the eve of the conflict between the Robespierrists and the future Thermidorians. The decree of 5 thermidor lowered wages considerably. A first-class carpenter's earnings fell from 8 livres to 3 livres 15 sous; a baker's apprentice from 15 livres to 6 livres.[131] Other categories of workers had their earnings reduced correspondingly.

When the events of 9 thermidor unfolded, workers who had been bitterly disappointed with the *maximum* of 9 germinal, Year II (29 March 1794) continued their opposition. The attempt of the mayor, Jean-Baptiste-Edmond Fleuriot-Lescot, to blame the new *maximum* on Barère was much too late to convince the *sans-culottes* that Robespierre was on their side.[132]

Workers in the *ateliers* of section Droits-de-l'Homme had engaged in a demonstration for higher wages (23 brumaire, Year III–12 November 1794), and the following month joined in a mass outpouring of 15,000 workingmen, a manifestation that so disturbed the revolutionary committee that it sent dispatches for help to the Committee of General Security, the police, and the National Guard. Two of its members reported that the Convention and its committees were uneasy over unrest in several shops manufacturing arms, and had asked that a careful surveillance be conducted in the section to see what might be uncovered.[133]

---

[131] A.N., F[12] 1544[30], *Tarif du maximum des salaires, façons, gages, main-d'oeuvres, journées de travail dans l'étendue de la Commune de Paris*, 63 pp.; A.N., Collection Rondoneau, AD XI, 75 (same title as above with the following addition: "présenté par la Commission du commerce et des approvisionnemens de la République au Comité de salut public le Vingt deux Thermidor l'an 2e de la République une et indivisible"), 30 pp.; B.N., Lb[40] 1154 M*.

For the impact of this salary schedule on the *sans-culottes*, see G. Rudé and A. Soboul, "Le Maximum des salaires parisiens et le 9 Thermidor," in *Annales Historiques*, 26 (1954), 1-22.

[132] Rudé and Soboul, pp. 16-17. The authors conclude that Robespierre satisfied the bourgeoisie but lost the *sans-culottes*. *Ibid.*, p. 22.

[133] A.N., F[7]* 2498, p. 75; 22 frimaire (12 December), p. 118; and 17 nivôse, Year III (6 January 1795), p. 148. Houet and Milliet reported to the revolutionary committee of the section.

The fateful events of 9-10 thermidor have been recited and analyzed by both contemporaries and their historians, and require no further elaboration in these pages. A glance at the sources makes obvious the vacillations, divisions, and uncertainties that swept the sections throughout the early hours of the struggle.[134] There is little doubt that a more determined Commune could have succeeded, once again, in imposing its will on the Convention, but even if it had failed, the struggle for power might not have been resolved in favor of the Convention with so little effort. The neat reports of official committees with their justifications and apologies hardly correspond to the confused events as they unfolded in the sections. As might be expected when neither Convention nor Commune had emerged as clear victor in the early hours of the conflict, many sections hesitated to declare themselves, and did the prudent thing by awaiting developments, a policy followed by section Droits-de-l'Homme as well.

The minutes of its revolutionary committee, rewritten after the event, seek to give the impression that with the exception of the cannoneers and a few misguided individuals, local authorities and the section as a whole stood solidly behind the Convention from the very beginning. This was far from true. To begin with, the president of the sectional assembly, Pierre Duclos, joined the Commune by taking the oath of allegiance to the General Council, not to the Convention. The section's representative to the Commune, Jean-Louis Eude, remained loyal to that institution throughout the decisive moments of struggle, and Jean Ponsard, who was elected president of the civil committee on 10 thermidor,[135] also took the oath of loyalty to it, as he confessed later. Furthermore, the officers and men who composed the battery of cannoneers expressly repudiated the decree of the Convention that had outlawed the rebellious Commune. It is true, of course, that both the revolutionary and civil committees, as might be

[134] See the following: B.N., R4899 bis 12, N.E. Karéiev, *Neizdannie Protokolie Parizhskikh Sektsii 9 Thermidora II (Documents Inédits . . .) Mémoires de l'Académie impériale des sciences de St. Petersbourg, VIIe série*. Vol. XII, no. 4 (St. Petersbourg, 1914). A.N., AF II, 47 is a rich collection of minutes of the revolutionary committees and reports of commanding officers of the armed forces of the sections. A.N., F⁷ 4432 contains a fine collection of ten *plaquettes* that include excerpts of the *procès-verbaux* of civil and revolutionary committees of many sections.

[135] A.N., AF II, 47, pl. 367, pc. 43; F⁷ 4774⁷⁹, d. 2, 16 thermidor, Year II (3 August 1794).

expected, proved loyal to the Convention. Yet the commander of the section's battalion lost control over the armed forces and was arrested by the insurgents. Had a few commanding officers in key sections declared boldly for the Commune, the outcome of 9 thermidor might have been quite different. As it was, their support of the Convention and the lack of firm leadership by the General Council in the early stages of the rebellion proved decisive in the victory of the Thermidorians.

Although the Committee of Public Safety had called upon the president of the section to convoke the general assembly, Duclos had turned over the message to the General Council, thus reflecting the confusion and division among the men who led the section. In his absence, the hastily summoned general assembly appointed its vice president, Richebourg, to take the chair, and Auzolles to act as secretary of the emergency session.[136] Failing to receive the order to convoke the sectional assembly, the meeting of the latter body started late; the general alarm was sounded throughout the section only by 3 p.m. By then the civil and revolutionary committees had assembled, the former sending commissioners to seek information from the Convention. Why did the commissioners not approach their sister sections for information? The answer, as the revolutionary committee reminded Barras some days later, was that it was illegal to communicate directly with other sections.[137]

Shortly after hearing the general alarm (about 3:30 p.m.), Etienne Lasne, commander of the section's armed force, attempted to ascertain by whose orders it was being sounded. Upon learning that the call to assemble the company at the Hôtel de Ville had originated with Hanriot, Lasne told his sergeant-major that he was washing his hands of the whole affair. This unequivocal reply convinced the latter to disobey the order of the commander of the National Guard and to stay in place with his men.[138]

The refusal to carry out the orders of Hanriot led to a sharp conflict between the cannoneers of the section commanded by Captain Eude

---

[136] A.N., AF II, 47, pl. 367, pc. 43, "Extrait du registre des délibérations de l'assemblée permanente de la section des Droits-de-l'Homme."

[137] *Ibid.*, pl. 367, pc. 46, 14 thermidor, Year II (1 August 1794), "Au Citoyen Barras."

[138] *Ibid.*, pc. 42, 17 thermidor, Year II (4 August 1794).

and his lieutenant, Picard, and the infantrymen commanded by Lasne. A serious clash was avoided only because neither side wished to shed blood.[139] Fayölle, second in command under Lasne, justified his delaying tactics later, but admitted that he could have ordered the companies of infantry to attack with their bayonets.[140] Whether such an attack would have succeeded is problematical, however, for the revolutionary committee confessed that it bowed temporarily before the will of the cannoneers because they were manning their guns. Moreover, Picard had arrested the battalion commander, Lasne, and had deprived him of his rank (probably on orders of the municipal authorities sent by the Commune).

This action brought a protest from Second Lieutenant Michon, of the 8th company, who was also arrested for his pains. The two officers were taken to the Hôtel de Ville, where Lasne witnessed (as he testified later), the president of his section, Duclos, take the oath to the Commune. Although harangued by the mayor, Fleuriot-Lescot, he stubbornly refused to authorize the removal of the cannon from the section. This defiance led to his being turned over to the Executive Commission, together with Lieutenant Michon.[141]

Although Eude had made several efforts to move the cannon, as ordered by Hanriot, he had failed to do so—even after the arrest of Lasne. This was not due to any reluctance of the cannoneers to follow him, since they were convinced that they were about to save the country once again.[142] After an exchange of insults and threats between the revolutionary committee and the cannoneers, Eude proclaimed that the people no longer recognized the Convention and its committees. About 9 or 10 p.m. he succeeded, finally, in bringing the cannon to the Place de Grève.[143] Only when it became widely

---

[139] A.N., F7* 2497, pp. 134-136. The minutes of the revolutionary committee are rich in detail on the events of the night and early morning, but reflect some jumble in chronology. Karéiev has confused this collection, A.N., F7* 2497, under the heading of section Homme Armé. *Documents inédits*, pp. 54-58.

[140] A.N., AF II, 47, pl. 367, pc. 45, 15 thermidor, Year II, "Cinquième légion quatrième section rapport depuis le 9 trois heures après midy." This report was made out by the second in command, Fayölle.

[141] *Ibid.*, pc. 42, 17 thermidor, Year II, "Force armée parisienne, de la section des Droits-de-l'Homme. 5me légion. 4me section. Etat-major."

[142] A.N., W 79, d. 3, 9-10 thermidor, Year II, Comité civil de la section des Droits-de-l'Homme (Canoniers de la section des Droits-de-l'Homme).

[143] A.N., F7* 2497, pp. 134-138, *passim*. In their reply to Barras, the committee

known in the section that the Commune had been outlawed was it possible for the revolutionary committee to have arrested Eude and Hanriot's aide-de-camp, Florant Bouquet, together with some twenty cannoneers.[144] When, some days later, Barras demanded an hour-by-hour report from the committee on what had transpired in the section, they gave him what surely must be a classic retort: the members of the committee, they wrote, were republicans, not writers![145]

The civil committee, like the revolutionary committee, had remained in continual session throughout the night and had dispatched observers to the Convention to ascertain the state of political support for the warring institutions. Upon the release of the section's officers, whom it received "with joy" during the evening of 9 thermidor, it resumed its regular business on the morrow.[146] The general assembly, on the other hand, played a passive role, following rather than directing events in the section because most of its active citizens were under arms, and the leading elements were engaged in permanent session in the civil or revolutionary committee. It did send a delegation to the Convention "to assure it of its devotion,"[147] but exactly at what stage this took place is difficult to say—probably after the weakness of the Commune had become clear to all. By 2 a.m. the assembly finally concluded its session.[148]

The fall of Robespierre had precipitated Duclos' own downfall. As

---

reported that the cannon were taken by Captain Eude after 10 p.m. A.N., AF II, 47, pl. 367, pc. 46, 14 thermidor, Year II (1 August 1794). Eude might have confronted the revolutionary committee after placing the cannon before the Hôtel de Ville and after the arrest of Lasne.

[144] A.N., F7* 2497, p. 137; A.N., W 79, d. 3. According to the civil committee's minutes, it had learned of the outlawry of the municipality at 1:30 a.m. on 10 thermidor, suspiciously late.

[145] A.N., AF II, 47, pl. 367, pc. 46, 14 thermidor, Year II, "Au Citoyen Barras." This was signed by Deschamps, Temponnet, Donzel, Cordier, Mazin, Bernard, Gervais, and Bertram.

[146] A.N., AF II, 47, pl. 367, pc. 43, 10 thermidor, "Suite de la séance permanente du 10 thermidor, 17 heures du matin." By 5 p.m. Collet presided and Richebourg acted as secretary.

[147] B.V.C., MS 120, fol. 159.

[148] A.N., W 79, d. 3, 9-10 thermidor, "Comité civil de la section des Droits-de-l'Homme." This document was made out much later, conforming to the register of 28 frimaire, Year III (18 December 1794), and carried the signatures of Collet as president and Grandhomme, secretary-registrar.

can be readily understood, he was confused and bewildered by the rapidly changing situation, but as president of the section he was forced to respond to events.[149] It is possible, of course, that he tried to straddle the two forces, Convention and Commune, as long as he could, but his own recital of events as he reacted to them has the ring of authenticity about it. Noting that there was strong support for the two Robespierres in the Commune and among the Jacobins, and having received no directive of any kind from the Great Committees, he renewed his oath of loyalty to the Commune. It was this "unfortunate act" that led to his arrest. Duclos appealed to the Committee of General Security that he had been misled by the "guilty municipal authorities," called attention to his youth, and submitted a certificate that carried the names of twenty-five cannoneers, which bore out his patriotic conduct. His wife added, with justice, that his sole crime had been to preside over the section during the events of 9 thermidor. The Committee of General Security admitted that there was no evidence against him, and released him, finally, on 21 October 1795. Despite this lack of evidence, he had remained in prison for fifteen months.[150]

More serious was the charge against Jean-Louis Eude, captain of the battery of cannoneers, arrested with his lieutenant and men for supporting the "rebellious Commune." Eude argued in his defense that he was duty-bound to obey his superior officers, and that when the arrest of Lasne occurred the Commune had not yet been declared in a state of rebellion. Citing an official of that body who had appealed: "Citizens, I ask that you obey the voice of the Magistrates of the People and allow the cannon to be brought out" (underscored), Eude insisted he could hardly be blamed for obeying a legitimate order. Finally, he emphasized that he had been among the first to march with his battery under the orders of Bourdon de l'Oise to execute the orders of the Convention. A search of his home had revealed nothing suspicious, and there being no warrant for his arrest he was released, presumably with the men of his company about a year after the dramatic events that had brought about his arrest.[151]

[149] A.N., F⁷ 4684, d. 3.

[150] Ibid.; an undated document addressed to Courtois admitted that there was no evidence against him.

[151] A.N., F⁷ 4684, 13 thermidor, Year III (31 July 1795).

In addition to Duclos and Eude, three other officials were also investigated by the Committee of General Security. Jean Ponsard had "mistakenly" taken the oath to "the rebellious Commune," as he confessed.[152] Brought before the revolutionary tribunal, he was acquitted and released. Philippe Hardy, captain of the 2d company, was placed under arrest by the revolutionary committee but was aquitted by the Committee of General Security on 27 frimaire, Year III (13 December 1794), with an admission "that citizen Philippe Hardy . . . was unjustly arrested. . . ."[153] Finally, Jean-François Millet, like Ponsard a member of the civil committee, was charged with being a "zealous partisan of the Commune," and after the *journée* of prairial was stripped of his post and shadowed by the police.[154]

The arrested officers and cannoneers published in October-November 1794 a justification of their conduct during the events of 9 thermidor,[155] in which they argued that so long as the Paris Commune remained a legal body it was their duty to obey their superior officers. Citing four specific orders that had emanated from the General Council—two to bring their cannon to the Hôtel de Ville, and two to arrest their battalion commander, who had refused to carry out these orders of the Commune—the cannoneers maintained that at the critical moment they had submitted to the orders of the convention and had marched against the Hôtel de Ville.[156]

Although their arguments have some merit, it is difficult to deny the long persistence of the cannoneers' support of the Commune. Surely the division between the main body of the section's armed force and its cannoneers was more than a mere difference in interpretation of the military orders received by Lasne as against Eude. Historians have long noted the more radical political behavior of the artillery as com-

[152] A.N., D III, 256³, d. 10, pc. 41; A.N., F¹ᵇ II, Seine 18, where his name is spelled "Fansard."

[153] A.N., F⁷*, 2497, p. 136, 10 thermidor, an II. His name is spelled "Ardy." Also A.N., 256, F⁷ 4739, d. 1 and 2.

[154] A.N., F⁷ 4774⁴⁵, d. 2; A.N., F⁷ 4748, d. 2 (dossier Pierre Jacob); F⁷ 4774⁴⁶, d. 4 (dossier J. F. Millet).

[155] B.N., Lb⁴¹ 1476, *Mémoire justicatif de la conduite de la compagnie des canonniers de la section des Droits-de-l'Homme, à tous les républicains français* (Paris, Brumaire, an III), 11 pp. The slogan on the title page was: "Innocence in chains," and below, "Severity, Justice." The same work in B.N., MSS, Nouv. acq. fr. 2687, fols 5-10.

[156] *Ibid.*, pp. 3-6.

pared with the infantry in the National Guard of Paris.[157] Moreover, in an ultimate test, the far greater firepower of the artillery as against the riflemen could have made the cannon a decisive weapon. What was lacking in the Commune was a determined leader, as was clearly realized by junior officers like Picard. It is difficult to say what the level of political consciousness of individual cannoneers was, but that they were more devoted to the municipality than to the Convention, at least in the early stages of the struggle, is clear. Had Hanriot or his adjutant general, Fontaine, given a forthright order from the very beginning to men like Eude, and brought up the cannon of those sections that responded to his original orders, encircling the Convention, the outcome of 9 thermidor could have been different. Lacking orders after bringing the cannon to the Place de Grève, and allowing the opportunity to impose their will on the Convention to slip by, the Eudes and the Picards had no alternative but to surrender. Later they would have to invent excuses for their "treacherous" behavior.

Fifty-six cannoneers and officers (of whom eighteen were native Parisians) were arrested and imprisoned on 10 thermidor. Nine of these were still in their teens, two being only sixteen years of age, whereas twenty-six were in their twenties, including Captain Eude (age 25) and Duclos, president of the section (age 24). Ten were in their thirties; eight were in their forties, including Lieutenant Picard (age 46); and two were in their fifties.[158] A year after their arrest the section finally intervened on their behalf,[159] after their families petitioned the Committee of General Security to bring them to trial, pleading the direst poverty.[160] Most were released on 30 frimaire, Year III (20 December 1795); on 10 nivôse (30 December) another group of eighteen was freed.[161]

---

[157] Soboul, pp. 1,003-1,005. Cannoneers of sections Invalides, Mutius-Scaevola, Popincourt, Quize-Vingts, Faubourg du Nord, and Droits-de-l'Homme rallied to the Commune. *Ibid.*, p. 1,005. The loyalty of the cannoneers of section Homme Armé to the Convention was in dramatic contrast to its neighbor of Droits-de-l'Homme. A.N., AF II, 47, pl. 366, pc. 1, 15 thermidor, Year II (2 August 1794).

[158] A.P.P., A B/326, 10 thermidor, Year II. Two were arrested on the 12th and one on the 16th. The age of Florant Bouquet, former aide-de-camp of Hanriot, was not given.

[159] B.V.C., MS. 120, fol. 159, 20 thermidor, Year II (7 August 1795).

[160] A.N., W 79, d. 3, n.d.

[161] A.P.P., A B/326; A.N., F7* 2498, p. 132, 30 frimaire, Year III (20 December 1795); B.V.C., MS 120, fol. 160, 10 nivôse, Year III; (30 December 1794); A.N., F7* 2498, p. 143, 12 nivôse, Year III (1 January 1796).

Among the officers arrested was Amable-Antoine Picard, forty-six years of age, a master smelter, residing on rue de Portant Gervais and a signatory of the militia list in July 1789.[162] Lasne had denounced him, as was seen, for having stirred up the cannoneers against him.[163] Letters to the Committee of General Security stressed his familial and patriotic virtues,[164] and after section Fidelité added its appeal for his release, he was freed on 4 messidor, Year III (22 June 1795).[165] The sergeant-major of the battery, Charles Sonnois, was twenty-eight years of age, residing on rue Droits-de-l'Homme at the time of his arrest. Lasne had denounced him specifically, and others called him "one of the most rabid [of enemies]." After the usual testimonials on his behalf he was released on 26 fructidor, Year III (12 September 1795).[166] Freed at the same time as Sonnois were the oldest cannoneers, by name of Jean-François Baudet, who was fifty-five years old, residing on rue de la Tisseranderie, and Jacques-François-Denis Dariencourt, a commissioner in the Bureau de distribution de l'habillements. There was no charge against the latter, and just how he became a victim of the arrests in the section is difficult to discover.[167]

In addition to the arrests of the section's cannoneers, the attack on former martyrs and symbols of the Revolution by the Thermidorians and those to their right reflected the new political climate in Droits-de-l'Homme as well as in the whole of the capital. The removal of the ashes of Marat from the Panthéon and of his bust from theater lobbies and other public buildings on 20 pluviôse, Year III (8 February 1795), revealed the course of the Thermidorians as eloquently

---

[162] At the time that he signed the list, his address was rue Vieille-du-Temple. B.H.V.P., MS 742.

[163] A.N., F⁷ 4684, d. 3, n.d. (dossier Duclos). His first names are given in the "*ecrou*" of La Force, A.P.P., A B/326.

[164] *Ibid.*, 7 and 8 floréal, Year III (26 and 27 April 1795); A.N., F⁷ 4684. Roger and Perrin were appointed by the general assembly to intercede on his behalf, 10 floréal, Year III (29 April 1795).

[165] A.N., F⁷ 4774⁷², d. 4.

[166] A.N., F⁷ 4684, d. 3 (dossier Duclos). His first name, residence, and age as well as date of his release are given in A.P.P., A B/326.

[167] A.N., F⁷* 2498, p. 34, 20 vendémiaire, Year III (11 October 1794) was the date of Dariencourt's arrest. The letter to the section on his behalf is dated 30 germinal, Year III (19 April 1795), at which time a commission to intervene for him was appointed by the assembly. It still took five months before his release, despite the fact that there was nothing against him. A.N., F⁷ 4684 (dossier Duclos).

as did the closing down of the Jacobin Club and the trial of Carrier. A number of violent incidents had occurred at theaters of the rue Feydeau, Favart, and Cité, where partisans and enemies of the revolutionary martyr clashed around his image. In several cafés petitions were openly solicited to demand that the Convention "deapotheasize" the remains of Marat and remove his statue from public halls.[168] Section Lepeletier, destined to initiate the attempted monarchist coup against the Convention in vendémiaire, followed the lead of the Convention, and on the same day removed the images of Marat and of the man whose name it still bore, burning the civic crowns that had adorned them.[169] Soon it became a sport of "the gilded youth" to overturn symbols of the Revolution.[170] The memory of Marat continued to attract his partisans against his defamers, however. The general assembly of section Droits-de-l'Homme witnessed a sharp confrontation between former militants who rallied around his bust, and the *muscadins* who were determined to remove it from the hall.

On the day of the Convention's action, a Thermidorian delivered a heated address against "the men of blood," demanding that the assembly remove immediately the hateful image. A vehement discussion followed, with opponents arguing that the decree in question was officially unknown. Efforts to learn the exact language of the law by reading the *Journal du soir* to the assembly only called forth further disturbance, and Dommanget, who presided, was forced to suspend the session. On the following day tempers flared again and violence broke out in the hall. Carron, the former commissioner on profiteering, struck two zealous partisans who had made the motion to remove the image, thus aggravating the disturbance so that the secretary was unable to read the controversial decree. As a result of this riot, Carron, Roger, Houdaille, Bernard, Renaudin, and Perrin—that is, the former militants of the section—were summoned to appear before the surveillance committee of the 7th arrondissement to answer charges against them.[171]

Jean-Pierre Carron, the partisan of Marat, was a mason by trade,

[168] Aulard, *Paris*, I, 12-19 pluviôse, Year III (31 January-7 February 1795).

[169] *Ibid.*, I, 467.

[170] *Ibid.*, I, 416, 438, 442, 447, 453, 456, 457, 463, 464.

[171] B.V.C., MS 120, fol. 160, 20 pluviôse, Year III (8 February 1795); A.N., F⁷ 4634, d. 3, 20, 21 pluviôse, Year II.

residing on rue des Droits-de-l'Homme. The Thermidorians characterized him as "a man known for his ferocity and one of the zealous
defenders of the tyranny of the triumvirate."[172] When the unknown
young man who had made the proposal to throw out the bust of Marat
had called all Maratists "drinkers of blood," Carron had risen in reply
and had asked the assembly to wait for the decree of the Convention
on this matter. Others supported Carron in their testimony: Roger
added that he had never seen the young man before; Houdaille emphasized that the motion to await the ruling of the Convention had
been adopted unanimously, and Pierre-Etienne Renaudin, a shoemaker residing on rue Bourg-Tibourg, also sustained the testimony
of Carron in its essentials. Finally, Jean-Michel Perrin, a musician
residing on rue des Billettes, gave virtually the same evidence. After
deliberating on the testimony, the committee held that Roger and
Carron had not behaved like good republicans and asked the president
of the section to reprimand them. As for the others, they were asked
to be more gentle and fraternal in their behavior in the future.[173]

This quiet admonition was followed by a decision adopted by the
surveillance committee that was quite out of character with its mild
ruling. It is possible that a directive from higher authorities who took
a graver view of the fracas in the general assembly caused the committee to change its mind. For after summoning Lasne, commander
of the armed force, Dommanget, president of the assembly, and Collet, its secretary, the surveillance committee transmitted its testimony, gathered on 24 pluviôse, to the Committee of General Security, asking how it should proceed in the matter. The following day,
the latter replied: all the accused were to appear before it on the
morrow.[174]

After interrogating Carron and searching his premises, which yielded
nothing but the usual revolutionary journals and the *procès-verbaux*

---

[172] *Ibid.* The register of the Committee of General Security described him as the
principal author of the troubles that broke out in the general assembly in opposition
to the removal of the bust of Marat. A.N., F⁷* 699, Year III. His name is spelled
Caron in the register.

[173] A.N., F⁷ 4634, 26 pluviôse, Year III, "Septième comité de surveillance séant
rue Avoye, no. 160 section de la Réunion," signed by Turtreau, president, and
Maillet, secretary.

[174] A.N., F⁷* 2498, pp. 198-199, 23, 24 pluviôse, Year III (11 and 12 February
1795).

drafted by him as commissioner on profiteering, it sent him to La Force and imprisoned Houdaille on 28 pluviôse (16 February). Undated letters by Carron and his wife asking for his release followed soon thereafter. The former commissioner protested that he had never denounced anyone (if true, how effective could we have been against speculators and engrossers?), and declared that it was he who had prevented the armed force of the section from joining "the rebellious Commune on the 9th of thermidor," another exaggeration. Nevertheless, he was released on 8 May 1795, only to be rearrested on the day of the insurrection of 1 prairial, and sent to the Maison d'Arrêt Egalité, on rue Jacques. Although there is no indication of how long he languished in prison after his arrest, he was probably released about the same time as his colleagues of the section who suffered a similar fate, that is, on the eve of the vendémiaire coup.[175] As for Renaudin and Perrin, they were kept under surveillance by the police because of their role in the affair of the busts of Marat.[176]

The riot in section Droits-de-l'Homme was no isolated incident, as proposals to discard martyrs of the Revolution struck at the very heart of the cult that had moved so many revolutionaries.[177] Those who sought to defend their revolutionary symbols became objects of suspicion and of surveillance by the authorities, among whom was Lelièvre, a second-hand goods dealer, residing on rue de la Verrerie. Although he held no official position (so far as it is possible to determine), he must have been active in the sectional assembly and its popular society. Viar, one of the first to be elected to the section's revolutionary committee, was another. He had removed to section Indivisibilité at the time of his surveillance and was described as a "wicked man" in the police dossier.[178] Former militants such as Dassin, Gervais, Carron, Cornet, and Beudelot were also watched and

---

[175] *Ibid.*

[176] A.N., F7* 699, Year III.

[177] A.P.P., A A/163, fols. 359-361, 15 pluviôse, Year III (3 February 1795) is an interesting example of an effort by a number of young men in section Lombards to replace the bust of Marat with that of the Virgin. The armed force had to be called out to quell the riot that followed.

[178] A.N., F7* 699. This register contains brief comments on the revolutionaries under surveillance with such characterizations as *"perturbateur, fanatique, Septembriseur, enragé,"* and so on.

were ordered by the Committee of General Security to report regularly to the police of their arrondissement.[179]

So long as the Thermidorians could balance themselves between Right and Left, there was no need to incarcerate former militants as a class; it was sufficient to arrest individual "trouble makers" and intimidate the rest. Their stubborn presence, however, given an upswing in the popular movement, could endanger this precarious balance, because as experienced revolutionaries they knew how to channel mass discontent and direct it against the temporary victors of yesterday. Were this to happen, it would not be enough, obviously, to place these militants under surveillance. It would be necessary to remove them from the political scene altogether—their ultimate fate after the uprisings of germinal and prairial.

[179] A.N., F⁷ 4597, plaque 8, pcs. 24, 25, 4e jour complémentaire, Year III, and 2 vendémiaire, Year IV (20 and 23 September 1795), dossier Beudelot. These and others arrested after the insurrection of prairial are discussed in the chapter below dealing with the hunger uprisings of germinal and prairial.

VI

Shortages and the Struggle
for the *Maximum*

Among the many difficulties and concerns faced by the *sans-culottes* as consumers, the most pressing were shortages of bread and flour, and, when available, the high price of necessities. The Convention, like the Commune and the sections, recognized this and sought to deal with the whole complex of what Mathiez termed *la vie chère*. It established a Committee of Agriculture on 1 October 1792 for this purpose, and its first session, held jointly with the Committee of Commerce, considered a law against speculators and engrossers.[1] At its very next meeting it discussed seriously means of establishing a price ceiling on grain,[2] a demand increasingly being voiced by general assemblies, popular clubs, and numerous journalists and pamphleteers. Being wedded to the principle of freedom of trade, however, it could not seriously attack the problem at its source. Moreover, its prejudice against "agitators" who sought to bring their unpopular views before it doomed the committee's proposals to failure. Not that the committee lacked enlightened members who realized that the traditional checks of supply and demand were unworkable in time of revolution and war. When Roland, for example, reported that scarcity of supplies was caused by "agitators" and that regulation of trade would only aggravate the crisis, a member of the committee replied that "the principles of the minister, true in periods of calm, were not applicable

[1] The first session of the committee was held on 15 October 1792. Gerbaux and Schmidt, *Procès-Verbaux*, III, 1. The law would have compelled owners of grain to declare the amount on hand and to send a portion of it to market. Export of grain was to be forbidden. *Ibid.*, pp. 2-4.

[2] *Ibid.*, III, 6, 17 October 1792. One member suggested using the average daily wage as a base for fixing the price of grain, whereas another would have included the cost of rent.

in time of revolution."[3] In any case, despite this opposition, the sections and communes of various departments continued to demand price control of necessities.[4]

In late November 1792 section Droits-de-l'Homme issued an address to the Convention demanding bread. Assuring the "legislators truly republican" that its members preferred "the stormy seas of liberty" to "the calm waters of tyranny," it called for them to strike down the profiteers, and appealed to the minister of interior to provide bread.[5] In December its general assembly adopted a resolution that called for proscribing all speculators. While its patriots fulfilled their duty to the victims of 10 August and to the volunteers at the front, profiteers were undermining the Republic by their "shameful speculation" in paper currency, it complained, and called on the Convention to halt this practice. Giving substance to its resolve, the assembly called on the sections to send commissioners to the Evêché to prepare a joint petition embodying this demand.[6] The agitation of section Droits-de-l'Homme reflected the desperate plight of the *menu peuple* which, in turn, aroused a vast popular movement to regulate, seize, or distribute grain in one department after another. Riots lasted for days. "We are in the presence of a class movement, inorganic often and dispersed, but profound and vigorous," wrote Mathiez.[7] This class movement promoted the gradual break of the Convention from the

[3] *Ibid.*, III, 24, 26-28. This was certainly a more honest appraisal of the situation.

[4] *Ibid.*, III, 71-92, *passim*, for the numerous petitions asking for relief. On 16 March, La Rochelle demanded that grain be declared national property. The petitions are numbered from 529 to 583, p. 91, no. 4. A long list of departmental communes addressing the Convention is on p. 114, no. 1, 22 April 1793.

[5] B.N., Lb⁴⁰ 1797, *Addresse à la Convention nationale* (Paris, 27 November 1792), 4 pp. Two months previous to this, on 22 September 1792, section Panthéon-Français had petitioned the Convention for a law authorizing regulation of the price of grain, meat, and wine, and a ceiling on a predetermined unit of weight. A.N., F¹¹ 218.

[6] B.N., Lb⁴⁰ 1790, *Extrait de registre des délibérations de la section générale & permanente des Droits-de-l'Homme* (Paris, 20 December, Year I [1792]), 3 pp., signed by Descombes as president and Dubois, secretary.

[7] "Les Subsistances," *Annales révolutionnaires*, IV, 172, 304-305. When the Girondists attempted to honor the memory of Simoneau, mayor of Etampes, as a "martyr of the law," killed in a food riot, 3 March 1792, Robespierre condemned this scheme. "Simoneau," he stated, "was no hero; he was a citizen regarded generally in his country as an avid profiteer on public provisions." B. & R., XIV, 268.

traditional policies defending freedom of trade and its eventual adoption of strict regulation through the *maximum*.

Paris still consumed 1,500 sacks of grain (490,500 pounds) daily—grain that at times was not easy to find.[8] Its bakeries supplied themselves from two sources: the provinces, where purchases were made directly by the baker or his agent, and the flour market, the Halle de Farines, whence the municipality's Administration of Provisions bought its supplies.[9] The difficulty of procuring provisions and the rising complaints over the policy of subsidizing bakers led section Droits-de-l'Homme to present its petition to the General Council on 15 June 1793, for a *maximum*.[10] Once again, as during the duel with the Gironde, Varlet was among its inspirers. This time the section's delegates were attacked by Hébert for introducing the resolution when the Convention was considering the adoption of a Constitution. Others pointed to possible alarm that would be caused by raising the threat of shortages, and Pache blamed counterrevolutionaries in the general assemblies for the agitation with their "use of the word Subsistences."[11] When the delegates replied that their petition did not speak of shortages but, rather, on the need to curb high prices, the municipal authorities remained unmoved.[12] They were coming under increasing attacks from the sections, who were to challenge their control of provisions during the coming months of July and August.[13]

The continued pressure of the sections finally forced the Convention to adopt a subterfuge. Rather than vote a general *maximum*, it accepted the proposal of Billaud-Varenne for a stringent law against profiteers as a way to lower prices, embodied in its decree of 26 July making speculation a capital crime.[14] Hastily drafted, ill-defined, tar-

---

[8] Calvet, *Instrument*, p. 202. The rate of daily consumption remained fairly constant from 1790 through 1810, about 1,500 sacks of 327 lbs. each. Soboul points out that both Tuetey (*Répertoire*, IX, no. 1189) and Mathiez (*Vie chère*, p. 320) made an error in quoting the amount consumed in Paris as being 4,500 sacks. *Sans-culottes*, p. 158 n. 21.

[9] Calvet, *Instrument*, pp. 202-203.

[10] B.V.C., MS 120, fol. 144, 9 and 15 June 1793.

[11] B.H.V.P., MS 769, fol. 50, 15 June 1793.

[12] *Affiches de la Commune*, no. 3, 16 June 1793; *Moniteur*, XVI, no. 169, p. 658, 18 June 1793.

[13] See the discussion of this sectional movement in Mathiez's *Vie chère*, pp. 258-290, *passim*; and Soboul's *Sans-culottes*, pp. 117-135, *passim*.

[14] Henri Calvet, *L'accaparement à Paris sous la Terreur. Essai sur l'application de la loi du 26 juillet 1793*. Commission de Recherche . . . (Paris, 1933), p. 13.

dily promulgated, the law proved unenforceable. Juries, often composed of merchants, were reluctant to convict violators. Yet, despite opposition of dealers, traders, and legislators, the sections continued to press for the enforcement of the law, not its abrogation. They demanded that juries be composed of "true *sans-culottes*," because they were the most numerous and the most virtuous. Their commissioners protested that the authorities "struck the small merchant, not the rich man," and held it to be "immoral to judge the monopolizers, the egoists, the most rabid enemies of their fellow citizens, by other monopolizers, by merchants, by moderates, by beings who wear but the mask of patriotism."[15] Despite this warm support, the law, after numerous amendments and revisions, was ultimately suppressed.[16]

On July 31, delegates from thirty-nine sections met in the Evêché to examine the state of provisions in the capital. Among the twenty-four commissioners named to inspect the reserves of food was Temponnet of section Droits-de-l'Homme. This movement of the sections[17] ultimately ended in a vast workers' demonstration of 4 and 5 September,[18] which was able to impose its will on the reluctant Convention,[19] leading to the adoption of a general *maximum* of 29 September

[15] Calvet, *L'accaparement*, nos. 308, 315-318, 320. On the demands and petitions of the sectional delegates, see A.P., LXXVI, 235, 8 October 1793 and LXXVII, 454, 23 October 1793.

[16] "The law of July 26 . . . did not destroy the profiteers." Calvet, *L'accaparement*, pp. 35-36.

[17] B.N., LB⁴⁰ 3334, *Rapport des commissaires des quarante-huit sections sur les subsistances* ([Paris], [August] 1793), 10 pp. B.N., MSS, Nouv. acq. fr. 2715, fol. 32, 6 August 1793. The resolution of Droits-de-l'Homme was received by the civil committee of section Révolutionnaire (formerly Pont-Neuf).

[18] *Le Républicain français*, no. 294, p. 1191, 6 September 1793, contains probably the most complete and dramatic version of this *journée*. *Mercure universel*, XXXI, pp. 103-105, 7 September 1793, quoted the mayor as saying that shortages were common to all large cities and were due to activities of dealers, proprietors, and farmers. This reply is also carried in the *Journal de Paris*, no. 249, pp. 1001-1002, 6 September 1793. B. & R. also cite *Journal de la montagne*, no. XCVI, in XXIX, 26-27.

[19] B. & R., XXIX, 39-40. "This was the high point of the popular movement. The Convention bowed before it—for the last time." Walter Markov, "Robespierristen und Jacqueroutins," *Maximilien Robespierre 1758-1794, Beiträge zu seinem 200. Geburtstag* (Berlin, 1958), p. 194. Edmond Soreau, "Les Ouvriers aux journées des 4 et 5 septembre 1793," *Annales historiques*, 14 (1937), 436-447, wrote that the *journées* were due to political rivalries and shortages "that were in part fictitious" (p. 447). The Commune, he continued, "allowed itself to be led" by the sections. This misses

1793.[20] The base for the price of commodities was to be the average price for the year 1790 plus one-third. Wages were to be the average for the same year plus one-half. Thus, an article that sold for 3 livres in 1790 was to sell now for 4 livres; a worker who earned 30 sous would now earn 45.[21] The adoption of the *maximum* by the Convention, it should be added, had been preceded by submission of a petition endorsed by foty-three sections, among whose signatories was Droits-de-l'Homme.[22]

With all its imperfections, the general *maximum* enabled the working people in the towns to survive. In those centers of the country where the *sans-culottes* had the political strength to enforce price ceilings, the *maximum* saved many from near starvation. Where *sans-culottes* composed a majority of revolutionary committees charged with enforcing the *maximum*, price ceilings on wages were beneficently neglected while being enforced on prices of commodities.[23] Where farmers and merchants staffed the key committees, the consumer received little benefit. Enough has been written to contrast the status of the urban consumer in 1793 with his situation in 1795 to underscore the deterioration of his economic position after the abrogation of the *maximum*.[24] That it could not have solved the basic economic problems seems obvious. The demands made by the war, the fall of the *assignat*,

the mark in ignoring the real economic crisis and the elemental force of the demonstrators, not to say the important role played by the sections. When Soreau states that "Robespierre said nothing," he ignores his effort to halt the Jacobins from joining the demonstrators.

[20] The law was divided into four sections that: required a declaration by cultivators or proprietors on the quantity of grain on hand, prohibited its sale outside of public markets, fixed a *maximum*, and forbade its export. Caron, *Commerce*, pp. 60-68. The reporter of the decree was Laurent Lecointre. A.P., LXXIII, 691-696.

[21] Duvergier, VI, 193-195; A.P., LXXXV, 321-323; B. & R., XXIX, 11-14, 29 September 1793.

[22] A.N., D III, 255-256[1], d. 1, 29 September 1793, "Pétition à la Convention nationale relative à un juré spécial contre les accapareurs." The last section is Droits-de-l'Homme.

[23] "The even more unpopular maximum on wages the [revolutionary] committees neglected almost entirely, perhaps because the majority of the members were workingmen themselves." John Black Sirich, *The Revolutionary Committees in the Departments of France, 1793-1794* (Cambridge, 1943), pp. 156-157.

[24] "The difficulties of the *maximum* period were trivial with those of 1795. . . . I am inclined to attribute the troubles of 1795 not so much to the *maximum* policy as to the premature discontinuance of that policy." Harris, *Assignats*, pp. 155-156.

the disruption of trade, the general uncertainty—all these were be-yond the power of a purely administrative act to resolve. A social system based on individualism and private property could not easily borrow the methods of a system based on collectivism and nationalized property forms. Lefebvre sums it up well:

> In order to have applied the *maximum* to the letter it would have been necessary to have nationalized, if not landed property, at least the commerce in cereals and the manufacture of bread, to have carried off the crop of the cultivator . . . stored it in warehouses and distributed it to the municipalities which, converting the bak-ers into municipal workingmen could have admitted the people under their administration into one large cooperative commune . . . the economy of [private] property would have found itself modi-fied.[25]

The Convention never ceased affirming, however, that it desired to maintain individual property and continued to disavow the "agrarian law," its policy being to multiply the number of property holders by selling them the confiscated estates of the émigrés and parceling out the communal lands. Between such a policy and the actual conditions of applying the *maximum* was a profound contradiction.

In order to enforce the *maximum* and to guarantee supplies, an in-ventory of flour on hand and the daily production of bread had to be reported. The twelve bakeries in section Droits-de-l'Homme that sold bread to holders of ration cards were frequently examined by com-missioners appointed for this purpose at the time of its distribution.[26]

---

[25] Lefebvre, *Subsistances*, I, LXXX.
[26] A. de P., 4 AZ 53. The names of bakers and amount of flour held follow:

	Total	Daily
1. Rogers, 61 rue Vieille-du-Temple	40	4
2. Calix, 11, rue des Droits-de-l'Homme	5	2½
3. Lessie, 1, rue des Juifs	10	1½
4. Courtin, 8, rue St. Antoine (buys daily)	?	3
5. Bernet, 62, Coulture Ste. Catherine (rue)	6	3
6. Beauden, 4, rue St. Antoine	20	?
7. Perreau, 13, rue St. Antoine	20	3
8. Rousseaux, 113, rue de la Verrerie (buys in the Halles market)	?	?
9. Garnier, 124, rue de la Verrerie	6	3

It would have been difficult enough to satisfy the demands of 12,000 people in a dozen shops under normal conditions; in time of shortages and long queues, aggravated as these conditions were by frequent inspections, it was almost impossible to maintain the traditional civilities between buyers and sellers.

How much bread was consumed in the section? It is impossible to give an exact figure because of inaccurate statistics, the frequent changes in the amounts rationed, and the different figures for the total number of people in the section. In addition to this there is the technical problem of arriving at an exact figure on the amount of bread yielded by a given quantity of flour. Sources vary from 24.5 percent to more than 29 percent, as explained below. According to the Agence des subsistances générales, a sack of flour weighing 325 pounds yielded 420 pounds of bread, which is slightly more than 129 percent of the weight of the flour.[27] In the Year III, Auzolles as police commissioner and Dommanget as president of the section's civil committee questioned the baker Calix on his operation of the bakery. According to the latter, 273 pounds of flour produced about 340 pounds of bread.[28] This made for a ratio of 124.5 percent of bread to flour, an obvious difference between his estimate and that of the Agency of Subsistences.

Fortunately, there exists a list of the number of people fed by baker Perreau.[29] According to this record, she supplied bread to 795 "mouths" by providing 291 heads of families daily. Assuming that her daily

10. Bizouard, 4, rue de la Verrerie	30	5
11. Delestans, 32, rue Bourtibourg	?	2½
12. Saigot, 31, rue St. Antoine	20	5
Grand Total	157	32½

If one were to add 52½ sacks for the three bakers who omitted their totals (including Courtin, who bought daily), based on an average of 17.5 sacks per baker, it would give a total of 209.5 sacks of flour.

[27] A.N., F¹¹ 1181, 6 nivôse, Year IV (27 December 1795), "Etat de distribution des farines aux quarante-huit sections de Paris."

[28] A.P.P., A A/136, fol. 222, 25 messidor, Year III (13 July 1795). When put to the test, the 273 lbs. of flour actually produced 337 lbs. of bread, but Auzolles demonstrated that because of an error in the scales, not of Calix's making, he was losing about three pounds per sack.

[29] B.H.V.P., MS 769, fols. 166-176, "Table alphabétique des noms propres des chefs de famille qui se fournissent chez la Cne Perreau Boulangère de la section des Droits-de-l'Homme rue Saint Antoine."

consumption of flour remained constant (which, of course, it did not), the 3 sacks[30] (of 325 pounds per sack) would have amounted to 975 pounds of flour per day. This meant that she produced a total of 1,213.87 pounds of bread (by the 24.5 percent formula) or 1,257.75 pounds (using the 29 percent formula). The latter figure would have given each "mouth" 1.58 lbs. of bread daily. The total amount consumed by each family varied greatly, of course, as the list reveals the numbers fed ranged from 1 to 6 (in one case, 8).

The above figures cannot be accepted literally, however, because the amount rationed changed during the course of the section's existence. At the time of the cited interview with baker Calix, according to his own testimony, the ration per person was a mere 6 ounces.[31] It would be more important, obviously, to know how much bread was consumed by various age groups, occupational classifications, social classes, men as against women, and children and infants. Rudé has shown that workers consumed 4 pounds of bread per day.[32] Unfortunately, it is impossible to tell how many on Perreau's list are workers. When it is realized that there was no substitute for bread, and that labor was arduous and the hours long, an average of one pound or even double this amount hardly sufficed to replenish the energy expended in work. When even the one pound became unavailable, life itself must have become tenuous. Small wonder that bread shortages led men and women to demonstrate, riot, and revolt.

In addition to taking an inventory of the flour on hand, commissioners checked the weight of loaves baked. Auzolles found in one instance that several batches of bread weighed less than the prescribed five pounds, but others were slightly more. To balance this difference, he redistributed the amount with the consent of the baker.[33] More important than occasional infractions of weight was the constant speculation in foodstuffs. Rousseville observed that "the infractions of the law of the *maximum* on commodities and subsistences continue to take shape in the environs of Paris like a branch of commerce."[34] One way

[30] As reported on 20 October 1793 in A. de P., 4 AZ 53, cited above.

[31] A.P.P., A A/136, fol. 222, cited above.

[32] *The Crowd*, Appendix VII, Tables 2 and 3, pp. 251-252.

[33] A.P.P., A A/136, fol. 47, 27 frimaire, Year II (17 December 1793). This involved three batches of bread at baker Courtin's, who blamed the error on the negligence of her *garçons*.

[34] A.N., F¹ᶜ III, Seine 27, 16 prairial, Year II (4 June 1794).

of checking on bakers who speculated was to examine individual loaves
of bread to see if each carried an identifying mark of the baker. Unmarked bread was immediately suspect.[35] The revolutionary committee was also kept busy in an effort to halt violations of the price
ceiling, another source of complaints.[36] Yet it recognized that in some
cases the *maximum* was unfair to retailers. Inspecting the price of sugar,
in one instance, they discovered that merchants would have to sell at
a loss to abide by the law, and so informed the General Council,
which referred their report to the Administration of Subsistences.[37]

The quality of bread sold was also an important cause of concern
for the revolutionary committee and the police commissioner of the
section. The former invited section Arcis to appoint two commissioners to accompany it in examining a flour mill located on Pont Notre-
Dame.[38] Periodic inspections of bakeries were held, and the sifters
and bolters examined to uncover any use of impure ingredients in the
flour.[39] Baker Rousseaux indignantly protested that she "had never
sifted nor bolted the flour, that she had always used that which the
administration had sent her without changing it or adulterating
it. . . ."[40]

Wine was also examined for its purity and wine cellars checked.
Cheaper brands were inspected especially carefully. In one instance
Auzolles and commissioners on profiteering, Carron and Casset, tasted
the wine of a merchant who was selling it at 16 sous per pint, noting

[35] A.P.P., A A/136, fol. 164, 23 pluviôse, Year III (11 February 1795). Elizabeth
Pileus, a widow Verdot, pleaded the necessity to provide for her children, and blamed
the absence of an identifying mark on the negligence of her *garçon.* Her bread was
seized and given to the *comité de bienfaisance* for distribution among the poor.

[36] A.N., F⁷* 2497, p. 74, 21 nivôse, Year II (10 January 1794).

[37] *Journal de la montagne*, no. 76, p. 603, 9 pluviôse, Year II (28 January 1794).

[38] A.N., F⁷* 2497, pp. 59-60, 16 brumaire, Year II (16 November 1793).

[39] A.P.P., A A/136, fols. 98, 147, 148, 11 prairial and 1er jour complémentaire,
Year II (30 May and 17 September 1794). On 28 fructidor, Year II (14 September
1794), the Agence provisoire des subsistances et approvisionnemens of the Commune
wrote the police commissioner that the department was convinced the bakers were
engaging in illegal trade in flour with pastry shops. *Ibid.*, fol. 149.

[40] *Ibid.*, fol. 147 (17 September 1794). In her quaint orthography she wrote: "n'a-
voir jamais ni Bluté ni Tamisé la farine quelle a toujours employé celle que lui a
envoyé l'administration sans y rien changer et sans ladenaturer. . . ." Rousseaux (or
Rousseau) and his wife owned the bakery jointly, as sometimes he is cited, sometimes
his wife.

that it changed color to deep violet, while the better grade, selling for 20 sous, retained its original color. Upon examination of the wine cellar they discovered that the cheaper wine had been made from last year's grapes, which were partly rotten. What must have been doubly embarrassing was that the wine cellar belonged to Ladoubé, a member of the section's civil committee, although managed by another for him.[41] Spoiled wine, or wine suspected to be such, when found outside the section, was duly reported to the General Council.[42]

The denunciations, interrogations, and arrests of those suspected of having violated the law of the *maximum* from the time of its promulgation to its abrogation on 24 December 1794 hardly varied. Often these accusations against individual merchants or pedlars were false or exaggerated, quite possibly the result of individual malevolence or personal pique. Confiscation of goods seized in contravention of the law yielded invariably modest sums, and individuals involved were often small retailers, hawkers, or widows desperately trying to feed a large family. Their customers, however, were often in the same dire circumstances or even worse. Moreover, after standing in line for hours only to find the shelves empty, or having to pay an extra sou beyond the price ceiling, produced short tempers on both sides. Furthermore, the tirades of Hébert, Jacques Roux, and Théophile Leclerc that made ordinary commercial transactions suspect increased popular suspicion of all businesses.

Irate consumers often brought their complaints to the police commissioner, who did what he could to satisfy them. A typical charge involved an alleged effort of a hawker, pedlar, or merchant to charge above the *maximum*. A widow Marigny, seventy-five years old, for example, was accused of demanding twelve sous for potatoes that should have gone for ten. Admitting that she wanted the higher price in an effort to move a larger quantity she denied, nevertheless, that she had refused to sell at the lesser rate. Auzolles confiscated one-half bushel of white potatoes found in her greenhouse and deposited the proceeds of its sale in the treasury of the Commune.[43] Denounced again the

[41] *Ibid.*, fols. 50, 51, 6 pluviôse, Year II (25 January 1794). François Poupart, 103 rue Vieille-du-Temple was arrested for selling improper mixtures of liquor. A.N., F7 4774⁸¹, d. 4, 27 June 1793.

[42] *Journal de la montagne*, no. 11, p. 8, 4 frimaire, Year II (24 November 1793).

[43] A.P.P., A A/136, fol. 62, 11 germinal, Year II (31 March 1794). Two witnesses refuted her denials.

following month for not selling her eggs on the open market, she offered the excuse that the pressure of the crowd would have broken them. Moreover, she had bought the eggs in question above the *maximum* and tried to sell them for more than the law allowed. Once again her produce was confiscated and the sum realized was placed in the treasury.[44] Refusal to sell publicly, even fragile commodities such as eggs, brought confiscation.[45]

Residents of the sections also took their complaints to the police commissioner. On 27 June 1794, a member of the neighboring section, Homme-Armé, accused a woman pedlar of charging beyond the *maximum*. After investigating the complaint, Auzolles released her but transmitted the *procès-verbal* to the national agent for final action.[46] Shortly thereafter the revolutionary committee and Carron, the commissioner on profiteering, prosecuted three women who had bought their quota of butter and eggs and then attempted to resell them at a slight profit, the total sum involved being a mere six eggs and one pound of butter. Upon examining their bread cards, however, Auzolles concluded that they were not speculators and released them.[47] On the other hand, the pleas by a widow Laimon that she had not declared a certain amount of butter because she could not sell vegetables to her customers without it was rejected and the butter confiscated.[48] The following day cheese was seized when it was found that its pedlars were in violation of the law.[49] These not atypical examples illustrate the pathetic nature of the "profiteers" in the section. As for the real profiteers, the large wholesale merchants, engrossers, and speculators—these do not appear in the pages of the police commissioner.

Shortages also made for ill feeling between ordinary citizens and commissioners of the section bent upon enforcing the *maximum*. The former accused officials of taking more than their share or of allowing

[44] *Ibid.*, fols. 87, 88, 26 floréal (15 May).

[45] *Ibid.*, fol. 63, 15 germinal, Year II (4 April 1794), involving femme Desbrosser, whose 21 dozen eggs brought 21 livres.

[46] *Ibid.*, fol. 104, 9 messidor, Year II.

[47] *Ibid.*, fols. 75, 76, 28 germinal, Year II (17 April 1794).

[48] *Ibid.*, fol. 77, 5 floréal, Year II (24 April 1794). The 31½ lbs. of butter brought in 50 livres 8 sous deposited in the treasury.

[49] *Ibid.*, fols. 78, 79, 6 floréal.

others to do so, charges denied by the commissioners.[50] The section's representative to the General Council, Eude, was forced to defend administrators of Droits-de-l'Homme as having executed the law to the letter. Nevertheless, the Council referred these complainants to the administration of police.[51] On occasion, exasperated consumers accused merchants of selling products of poor quality and blamed the civil and welfare committees for it. One especially voluble protestor, a painter by name of Dariencourt, was brought to the guard house amidst much indignation. He hastened to clarify his accusation by explaining that he had not meant to imply anything derogatory against members of the committees. What he meant, he asserted, was that they were in position to choose the better grades of meat, because they happened to be on the spot when the meat arrived. This gave them no greater advantage, he added prudently, than other citizens who also happened to be in the shop at the time of its delivery.[52]

When shortages had become acute, in March 1794, Auzolles noted that large crowds waited for the distribution of a mere one-quarter pound of butter and three eggs per person. Those who used the pretext of purchasing supplies for others and could not prove it were arrested on the spot.[53] Eude reported to the Commune on the amounts distributed, which were seldom beyond modest levels—a total of 650 pounds of butter (one-half pound per individual) and 3,000 eggs (probably about two eggs per person).[54] Occasionally members of the section's armed force received a special distribution of butter and eggs.[55]

Those who purchased meat outside regular channels also had it

---

[50] B.H.V.P., MS 769, fols. 258, 259, 12 germinal, Year II (1 April 1794). The accused commissioners sent a copy of the testimony of a Bousrain after interrogating him, in order to convince the General Council of "the loathsome nature of his accusation."

[51] *Journal de la montagne*, no. 136, p. 1099, 9 germinal, Year II (29 March 1794).

[52] A.P.P., A A/136, fol, 95, 3 prairial, Year II (22 May 1794).

[53] *Ibid.*, fol. 56, 17 ventôse, Year II (17 March 1794).

[54] *Journal de la montagne*, no. 119, p. 944, 22 ventôse (22 March). A week later, 157 lbs. of butter and 3,600 eggs were sold, 6 eggs per person. A.N., F⁷* 2497, p. 93, 30 ventôse (20 March). Between 24 ventôse and 4 germinal (14 and 24 March) a total of 38,239 eggs and 2,777 lbs. of butter was distributed. *Journal de la montagne*, no. 135, p. 1092, 8 germinal, Year II (28 March 1794).

[55] A.N., F⁷* 2497, p. 94, 2 germinal, and p. 109, 24 germinal, Year II (22 March and 13 April 1794), when they received one-half pound of butter and 6 eggs. On the following day they received a dozen eggs.

confiscated and the proceeds deposited in the municipal treasury. A cook, by name of Jacques Legrand, for example, had his sheep seized, which he had just purchased in Vincennes.[56] Hardy, the civil commissioner, reported stopping a wagon containing a sack of meat, but by the time he found the commissioner on profiteering the vehicle had disappeared, leaving behind the meat.[57] Those who attempted to sell meat obtained through private individuals for resale to caterers, an illegal operation, had it confiscated and often faced arrest.[58] Carron seized a man working for a caterer who admitted that he had purchased thirty-seven pounds of mutton in Vincennes for which he had paid sixteen sous per pound. He was freed, however, when two butchers guaranteed his appearance if summoned. When the caterer, Nicolas Coquet, appeared, he attempted to deny that there was any law forbidding him to buy meat, and when it was read to him, proffered the excuse that he had been too preoccupied to have heard of it. Although neither man was held, the meat in their possession was confiscated.[59] These arrests and seizures continued throughout the month of thermidor, in most cases the men being released but the meat in their possession seized and proceeds from its sale deposited in the common treasury.[60]

Hungry men and women naturally would doubt bakers who seemed to have sufficient bread for themselves in spite of shortages outside. This may be an explanation for the charge by a woman worker against the baker Rousseaux that he had a salted ham (*cochon salé*) at home. Upon examination, the latter testified that he had, indeed, slaughtered a pig two and one-half months ago, but had reported it to the commissioners on profiteering. Moreover, he had to feed his wife, six children, and two baker-journeymen. This was verified by the police after an examination of his home.[61]

[56] A.P.P., A A/136, fols. 101, 102, 30 prairial, Year II (18 June 1794). He had paid 36 livres for it.

[57] *Ibid.*, fol. 105, 25 messidor, Year II (13 July 1794). It realized a sum of 81 livres 1 sou for the treasury.

[58] *Ibid.*, fols. 109-112, 28 messidor, Year II (16 July 1794).

[59] *Ibid.*, fols. 115, 116, 3 thermidor, Year II (21 July 1794).

[60] *Ibid.*, fol. 117, 4 thermidor (22 July); fol. 119, 7 and 8 thermidor (25 and 26 July); fol. 124, 9 thermidor (27 July), a normal day so far as enforcing the *maximum* was concerned.

[61] *Ibid.*, fol. 74, 28 germinal, Year II (17 April 1794).

When tempers became strained as shortages continued, violent acts bordering on riots flared up. One such incident is illustrative of what must have been typical in the capital. A woman complained at a *charcutier's* that its proprietor sold nothing but bones, a charge taken up by the crowd ouside his doors. Gervais, of the revolutionary committee, ordered the crowd to disperse and tried to arrest the woman protester, Marie-Catherine-Emilie Blanches, femme Marquet, a laundress age forty-three, mother of four children and resident of section Arcis. Finally, an armed force had to be called out with a corporal in charge. The wrathful laundress kicked him in the shins, but, finally subdued, was brought before Auzolles. She had refused to leave, she admitted, because she felt her protest was just, although she agreed to make amends for her behavior. Auzolles released her.[62]

The same day corporal Doussot reported that he had to disperse a crowd of eighty persons outside the doors of a greengrocer, Eleonor-Colombe Diot, on rue Vieille-du-Temple. So many were willing to testify on her behalf, however, calling the charges against her slanderous, that Auzolles had a difficult time persuading the crowd to disperse. One woman by name of Mouilleron was held for spreading false accusations against Diot, but she, too, had her partisans who were willing to swear to her patriotism (including the health officer and the commissioner of saltpeter), so that she was also released.[63]

At times the crowd would defy orders of the revolutionary committee or its agents and even prevent the police commissioner from arresting a particularly effective spokesman. One such incident involved a pregnant woman who was agitating a sympathetic crowd in the marketplace. When Auzolles made an effort to seize her, the crowd released her from his grasp. Not having an armed force with him, the police commissioner was forced to let her go, as he reported to the revolutionary committee.[64] Shortly thereafter Auzolles arrested five women who were protesting against shortages, one of them being the wife of the official printer of the Convention, Laurens Oudot, of section Panthéon-Français, who had come into the section looking for

[62] *Ibid.*, fol. 89, 28 floréal, Year II (17 May 1794).

[63] *Ibid.*, fols. 90-92, 28 and 29 floréal, Year II (17 and 18 May 1794). The decision in this case was made by Auzolles together with two commissioners of the section, but it is not given.

[64] A.N., F⁷* 2497, p. 112.

cheese. The others were working women who had begun their search for food at 6 a.m., and were accused of forming "a riotous assembly." After the mother of one had promised the police commissioner she would keep her away from any such gatherings in the future, a promise concurred in by the rest, Auzolles decided to release them all.[65]

The many reports entered by the police commissioner in his minute book reveal the desperate search for bread and fuel throughout the Year III. Near panic broke out on one occasion, according to a descriptive report of a commissioner for the distribution of fuel. So large was the crowd that he had to close the doors, after a desperate cry went up: *"Citizens, we're stifling. Save us! Close the door."* In frustration, the crowd began to chase the commissioner, tossing brickbats at him because he had halted the distribution of charcoal. One young man pursued him to the square of Droits-de-l'Homme, shouting *"You will give me charcoal. It has been three days that I've waited at the door without getting any."* When the commissioner asked the guard to arrest the young man as a "subversive," the guardsmen refused under the pretext that their commanding officer was absent. Finally, when a young man was brought in by the patrol it turned out that he was not the one in question.[66]

On 2 prairial, Year III (21 May 1795), in the very midst of a major insurrection, agitation in front of bakeries of the section continued. A house painter by name of Jean-Louis Biair, thirty-three years old, residing in section Bonne-Nouvelle, was arrested for demonstrating before Rogers' bakery on rue Vielle-du-Temple. Holding up crusts of bread covered with mold that he had just purchased in a shop of section Popincourt, he complained bitterly against the Administration of Subsistences. Upon his arrest, he insisted that in showing the morsels of bread he had no subversive intentions but merely wanted the Convention to know of these abuses. Asked what he had done yesterday (that is, when the insurrection started), he replied that he had joined his company at the first sound of the general alarm and had remained with it throughout the day. Then he showed his *carte de securité* and satisfied the police commissioner that all was in order.[67]

---

[65] A.P.P., A A/136, fol. 96.

[66] *Ibid.*, fol. 182, 20 ventôse, Year III (10 March 1794), emphasis as in the original.

[67] *Ibid.*, fol. 205.

The matter was not settled, however, because a witness, François Monvoison, commissioner on the distribution of bread, who had been present at baker Rogers' establishment, accused Biair of loudly blaming the existing government for his plight and the poor quality of bread in the city. The accused admitted that in resisting arrest he might have struck Monvoison inadvertently in making his getaway. Auzolles released the accused in custody of his section, adding that Biair had not meant to create a disturbance; that he had showed more imprudence than evil intent, since no riot resulted from his lonely action.[68]

It is surprising that the authorities made so little effort to have food available in the section following this second insurrection. Three days later the baker Courtin reported that her meager supply of bread was soon exhausted, not everyone having received his share. A woman in the crowd cried out that she would rather be guillotined and cursed the Republic, taunting the crowd for their cowardice in accepting the meager rations distributed. Had it not been for the commissioner on the distribution of bread, Nicolas, who immediately marched her off to the civil committee, a serious riot might have ensued. It turned out that she was a married woman, Elizabeth-Laurence Edrut, forty-nine years old, and a native of Cochin China. Admitting that she had cried out that she preferred death to the small portion of bread allotted her, she emphasized that it was dire *need* that had forced her to desperation. After some discussion, and upon her promise of good behavior, the civil committee released her.[69]

Injustices arising from loss of one's place in queues must have been frequent, as the following incident illustrates. A François Legous, thirty-seven years old, employed at the Théâtre des Variétés, residing on rue de Berry, was brought to the police by an armed force, accompanied by Grandjean of the *comité de bienfaisance* stationed at a butcher shop of the widow Duhamel. There had been much pushing and shoving, and Grandjean had had a difficult time maintaining order. The accused had been twelfth in line at 6:30 a.m. and had been relieved by his son, a lad of ten, some hours later. When Legous returned he found that the boy had been pushed back to the end of the line. In trying to reestablish his original place in the queue he clashed with

---

[68] *Ibid.*, fols. 205-206.
[69] *Ibid.*, fol. 202, 5 prairial, Year III (24 May 1795). Italicized in original.

Grandjean, lost his temper, and accused him of being a rogue. Now that he was calm he was ready to make amends, he confessed. Article XIX of the police code was then read to him, which punished an insult of a public functionary in the course of his duty. He was about to be sent to La Force by Auzolles, who consulted with Dommanget and Doublet of the civil committee, and the *procès-verbal* was to be sent to the *police correctionnelle*, an action that could have resulted in serious consequences. Legous pleaded that as a father and a worker he was needed by his family and he appealed to go free on bail. Upon the testimony of Mathurin-Etienne Lez, employed in the Bureau of Subsistence, that Legous was a man of probity and that he was willing to deposit bail for him, the committee members and police commissioner gave him provisional freedom.[70]

Candles were also in short supply, and a careful inventory of the tallow on hand was taken by Thiébart fils, on 6 vendémiaire, Year III (27 September 1794). His report showed that the six chandlers in the section each had received 2,000 pounds of tallow from the Administration of Subsistence, which should have produced a total of 1,860 pounds of candles. At the time of the report, however, there were only 318 lbs. of candles on hand.[71] When the revolutionary committee asked the civil committee to furnish vouchers for their purchase, the latter admitted that it was impossible to procure them and agreed to appeal to the Committee of General Security for help.[72]

As the Year IV unfolded, there was no change either in the problems or in the method of resolving them by the section. The police commissioner continued to examine the bakers, now increased to thirteen, to make certain that all had enough flour until the end of the month. Inspection of the quality of flour and bread also continued, including the weight of loaves baked.[73] An additional problem that

[70] *Ibid.*, fol. 219, 24 messidor, Year III (12 July 1795).

[71] A. de P., 4 AZ 356. The amount held by five of the chandlers was divided as follows: Olivier, 269 lbs.; Chamay, 220; Geoffroy, 220; Tourneau, 222; and Houry, 220—a total of 1,142 lbs. of candles. Due to various deductions, however, the amount on hand was 318 lbs., as above.

[72] A.N., F7* 2498, p. 374, II fructidor, Year III (29 July 1795).

[73] A.P.P., A A/136, fols. 245, 246, 248, 27, 28 pluviôse and 20 germinal, Year IV (15, 16 February and 9 April, 1796). The carton, A.N., F11 218, contains much material on the problem of subsistence. Many dossiers are for Year IV. In the winter of 1796 the total number of bakeries in Paris was 400, and of butcher shops, 150. B.H.V.P., MS 799, fol. 284, 4 pluviôse, Year IV (23 January 1796), art. 3, pc. 4.

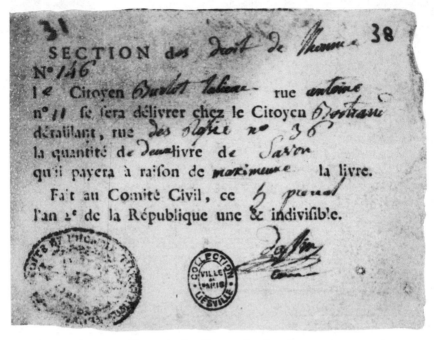

Figure 6. Certificate to Purchase Soap

arose was the refusal of some bakers to accept *assignats*. In one case reported to the police, the baker Ferreau had demanded metallic currency and threatened to withhold the bread ration card of a pensioner whose wife had to pay an excessive amount in coin.[74]

As mentioned above, rents rose between 1789 and 1791 before declining, only to resume the upward climb again in 1795, when the real housing crisis began. Refugees from invaded departments, suspects, and émigrés who returned after 9 thermidor, in addition to working people seeking employment in the arms manufactories—all swelled the search for rooms. Moreover, one could not acquire a bread card without a fixed residence. The Directory estimated that 100,000 new arrivals had sharpened the housing crisis by October 1795. Added

---

[74] *Ibid.*, fol. 252, 19 thermidor, Year IV (6 August 1796). The complaint was launched by Antoine-Louis Querroy, "pensionnaire de la République." On 3 vendémiaire, Year V (24 September 1796), Louise-Julie Thorillon, wife of a copper worker, complained that bakers would not accept her money, a practice that was illegal. *Ibid.*, fol. 253.

to this was the fall of the *assignat*, which struck proprietors especially hard as the real value of their rents declined. Justices of the peace were swamped by suits initiated by the principal tenants (*locataires*) against the eviction notices of their landlords, at a time when it was becoming impossible to obtain any kind of lodging in Paris. Where proprietors could not expel their tenants they neglected maintenance and repairs of their properties, ignoring the necessary hygiene, which struck, above all, at the poor.[75]

Despite this, the economic terror in the section did not appear to be unduly harsh. Few arrests were recorded by the police commissioner for violating the *maximum*, although confiscation of goods seems to have been frequent. Whether it ameliorated the plight of consumers, however, is another matter. It could not, after all, add to the quantity of necessities available in the section's markets; on the other hand, it did redistribute the goods available more equitably. Without price controls and declaration of goods on hand it is difficult to see how many could have survived at all during the harsh years of war and high prices. Here, again, it is the sectionnaires who must be credited or blamed for the imposition and execution of the *maximum*.

[75] La Monneraye, *Crise*, pp. 13-22, *passim*.

TABLE 7

Occupations of 407 Electors, 21 April 1789

Occupations	Paris[a]		District Petit-Saint-Antoine[b]		District Blancs-Manteaux[c]	
	Number	Percentage	Number	Percentage	Number	Percentage
legal profession	170	41.76	72	34.44	83	40.48
avocats			44	21.05	51	25.36
procureurs			14	6.69	22	10.73
notaires			1	0.47	0	0.00
conseillers			3	1.43	4	1.95
agrée			1	0.47	1	0.48
huissiers			8	3.82	5	2.43
engaged in commerce, manufacturing, investments, master workers, merchants	137	33.66	111	53.11	76	37.07
négociants			5	2.39	5	2.43
commerçants			5	2.39	2	0.97
marchands			45	21.53	28	13.65
bourgeois			16	7.65	10	4.87
master workers & artisans			40[d]	19.13	30[e]	13.17
public functionaries	32	7.86	14	6.69	20	9.75
physicians, surgeons, pharmacists	23	5.65	1	0.47	7	3.41
men of letters & professions	15	3.68	6	2.87	6	2.92
artists	13	3.19	2	0.95	1	0.48

academicians	12	2.94	2	0.95	10	4.87
military	5	1.22	0	0.00	2	0.97
not given	0	0.00	1	0.47	0	0.00
Total	407	99.96	209[f]	99.95	205	99.98

[a] "Relevé des 407 électeurs au point de vue des professions," in Chassin, *Élections*, II, 325-332. Chassin breaks down the list of *hommes de loi*, for example, into 95 *avocats*, 42 *notaires*, and 33 attached to various tribunals. He groups merchants, bourgeois, master workers, and artisans into one group, but then divides them according to their specific pursuits.

[b] B.H.V.P., 100.65 (106), *Procès-verbal du tiers-état, composant le premier district du quartier de la Place Royale, convoqué en l'église de petit Saint-Antoine, le mardi 21 avril 1789* (Paris, 1789), 42 pp. The *procès-verbal* gives the number of electors as 208, but is in error. There are 210 names on the list, but one is repeated, a Barnabé Henry, a master bushel-maker, residing on Cimetière-Saint-Jean. He appears no. 41 on the list, and again as no. 121. It is possible, of course, that one of the above was a father while the other was a son, but neither the designation *père* nor *fils* appears in the list.

[c] B.H.V.P., 100.65 (28), *Cahier d'instruction donnés par l'Assemblée de Paris, tenue en l'église des Blancs-Manteaux, le mardi 21 avril 1789, & le lendemain mercredi, sans désemparer* ([Paris], 21 April 1789), 36 pp. "Noms, qualités et domicile[s] des votans," pp. 9-28. The cahier mentions 212 voters in the assembly in justifying its election of 3 electors and 5 substitutes, p. 34.

[d] A total of 34 (or 16.26 percent) are listed as master workers; 6 (or 2.87 percent) are listed simply as artisans without the designation *maître*.

[e] Twenty-seven (13.17 percent) are listed as master workers, 3 (1.46 percent) as artisans.

[f] A number of professions listed could be designated under several different divisions. For example: Jacques-Remi Baure appears as an "ancien garde des archives de Monseigneur Comte d'Artois." He is listed under "Men of letters & professions," although he could appear as an archivist or a librarian. A Jean-Louis Blesve is listed as an "architect expert syndic de la communauté." He appears under the designation "Fonctionnaires publics," rather than under the architects, who are grouped under "Men of letters & professions."

VII

The Primary, General, and Electoral Assemblies

Prior to the fall of the Bastille, the elections held in Paris in the spring of 1789 returned, as might be expected, men from the business and professional classes, almost to the exclusion of other social categories. Table 7 illustrates this trend clearly.

The essentially bourgeois nature of the electors in the capital is reflected in districts Petit-Saint-Antoine and Blancs-Manteaux, as well. In the former, a total of 307 individuals out of 407 (or 75 percent), belonged to the first two categories, that is, either law or business. Out of 209 electors of Petit-Saint-Antoine, 183 (or 87.5 percent) and 159 (or 77.5 percent of the 205 electors) from Blancs-Manteaux were members of these two professions. A mere six artisans in Petit-Saint-Antoine and three in Blancs-Manteaux appear among this group of merchants, bourgeois, lawyers, and master workers. Needless to say, no women participated in the electoral process. If the above groups are added to those of the liberal professions, it is obvious that the electors in the capital and in the two districts belonged to the middle class. This would not preclude, of course, a wide differential of incomes among individual members of different groups, or between various professions.

The four bankers among the electors of Paris could have enjoyed an income not far below that of some of the wealthier nobles of the city. Socially and economically they would have been on a different level from the lower merchants or members of the academic profession. The few nobles, or those public functionaries who had served the *ancien régime*, tended to link their fortunes and their future to the great majority of the solid middle class, as was made evident during the early days of the Revolution.

It should be noted that only one member of the medical profession

(a surgeon) was elected in district Petit-Saint-Antoine, and not a single military man, although both professions had their share of residents in the district. Blancs-Manteaux sent seven of the former and
two of the latter, thus being but slightly behind the capital as a whole
in terms of percentage. Whereas Paris listed fourteen bourgeois among
its electors (3.43 percent), both districts had larger percentages of this
classification (7.65 percent for Petit-Saint-Antoine and 4.87 percent
for Blancs-Manteaux). More important is the substantially higher figure of electors from the ranks of merchants and master workers in
Petit-Saint-Antoine—53 percent as against 33 percent for the capital.
Blancs-Manteaux also enjoyed a larger proportion in this category, but
only by 4 percent. On the other hand, the ratio is in favor of the
capital for the legal profession, by 7 percent and 1 percent, respectively. The number of academicians differed markedly in the two districts: almost 5 percent in Blancs-Manteaux as against not quite 1
percent in Petit-Saint-Antoine. In other categories the differences are
of little significance.

It is interesting to note that the larger number of *avocats* among
the electors aroused sharp objections from several observers of the
scene. One critic felt that their proportion among the deputies should
be limited to one in twenty; the rest ought to be artisans, merchants,
and men in other occupations, he wrote.[1] Another citizen accused the
avocats of sacrificing the interests of the Third Estate in order to pro-
mote that of their own corps.[2] When an *avocat* came to the defense of
his profession, claiming that his colleagues sacrificed their all for the
principle of justice,[3] another critic replied that the reason why so
many of them were elected was not because of their superior knowledge of political economy or their character but because of their "end-
less chatter," and accused them of being devoted to Parlement and to
the general abuses of the regime.[4] In short, from the very beginning

---

[1] *Avis pour l'exclusion des gens de robe* by an unnamed author cited by Chassin, *Elections*, II, 332.

[2] *Ibid.*, II, 332-333. It was their ability to speak that made their arguments so
seductive, he wrote.

[3] "Réponse d'un avocat aux idées d'un citoyen de Paris," Chassin, *Élections*, II,
333-334.

[4] "Ils s'alarment, les citoyens honnêtes, parce qu'ils connaissent vos préjugés, votre
ignorance et votre foi vénal. . . . Y-a-t-il, parmi tout ce fatras de livres de jurispru-
·dence, de publicistes, d'apprétistes, etc. un seul principe qui soit conforme aux règles

of the Revolution there were already those who wanted to broaden both its role and the number of its participants.

As might be expected, a large proportion of the electors in district Petit-Saint-Antoine, a total of seventy-six, signed the militia list of 13-14 July. This makes for almost one-third of the electors, or 32.34 percent, and 6.26 percent of the militia list, an especially high ratio in the former case.

Six months after the destruction of the Bastille a decree establishing primary assemblies provided for the convocation of all eligible and active citizens in their canton for the purpose of choosing electors. These, in turn, were to meet to select representatives to the National Assembly and officials for the department and the district. Upon completing the task assigned to them, the two assemblies were to dissolve, not to reconvoke until the next elections made their reassembly mandatory.[5]

The elections in Paris held in September 1790 returned a total of 781 electors, of whom 45.1 percent were merchants and 30.6 percent members of the legal profession,[6] demonstrating once again the bourgeois composition of the electoral college. The seventeen electors chosen in section Roi-de-Sicile had a slightly different social physiognomy from that of Paris as a whole, in that eleven members were of the legal profession and only two were in business. The rest had one member each as a police commissioner, a former nobleman without a listed occupation, an auditor of accounts, and a counsellor to the admiralty court. Seven held office rank in the National Guard, of whom three were noncommissioned officers. Almost all were younger men or in their early middle age, seven being in their thirties, eight

---

de la saine politique? Citez-m'en un seul, je vous en défie. . . ." "Replique d'un citoyen de Paris à la réponse d'un avocat," Chassin, *Elections*, II, 335.

[5] Duvergier, I, 73-79, sections 1 and 2, 22 December 1789.

[6] Charavay, *Assemblée électorale*, Préface, pp. XII, XIII nn. 1, 3, and 4. Most were wholesale or retail merchants, 353 in all; 239 belonged to the legal profession, divided among 145 *avocats* or lawyers, 29 notaries, 13 magistrates, 12 commissioners at the Châtelet, 14 *procureurs* at the Châtelet, 11 bailiffs-appraisers (*huissiers-priseurs*), and 15 *procureurs au Parlement*. Twenty-seven were doctors or surgeons, 21 ecclesiastics, 19 architects, 14 scholars (*savants*), 13 apothecaries, 18 booksellers or publishers, 4 publishers, 2 actors, 4 teachers, 1 dramatic actor, and 1 fencing master. Of these electors, 54 sat on the General Council of the Commune, 78 were commanders of the National Guard, and 81 were members of the Jacobin Club.

in their forties; one was fifty-seven, and one sixty-five. It is strange that of the fifteen men in their thirties and forties only two (Junot and Gagnier) had volunteered for the Parisian militia in July 1789. The reasons could have varied, of course, from the accidental and personal to social and political factors. In general, it is clear that their social and economic rank corresponded to the mass of electors from the rest of the sections of Paris.[7]

Some nine months later, when elections for primary assemblies began on 16 June 1791, section Roi-de-Sicile with 1,811 active citizens sent eighteen electors, a gain of one over the previous year.[8] The number of voters, as so often happened, fluctuated from a low of 102 to a high of 327, with the last session ending on 19 June.[9] Among the electors returned were such well-known political figures as Chenier, Brissot, David, Santerre, Momoro, Fournier l'Américain, Legendre, and others.[10] Members of the legal profession now numbered 131, a marked reduction from the 239 of the previous year, whereas the number of ecclesiastics rose from 24 to 39. Both the Jacobins and the Feuillants registered successes—this, despite the disturbing repercussions caused by the king's flight to Varennes.[11]

Of the eighteen electors of section Roi-de-Sicile six were judges, one was an assessor to a judge, one an auctioneer, three were merchants, two were "notables," one a solicitor, one an accountant, one a *huissier-commissaire-priseur*, and two were military officers. As in the preceding year, most were in their early middle age: six were in their thirties, seven in their forties, three in their fifties; one was sixty-five, and one seventy-five. Ten of these had served as electors in 1790.[12]

---

[7] A.N., B I, 1; Charavay, *Assemblée électorale*, I, 48-50. These seventeen electors are listed in the appendix to this chapter.

[8] B.H.V.P., MS 806, fol. 228, "Du procès-verbal de la séance de l'assemblée primaire de la section du roi de Sicile," 19 June 1791; Charavay, *Assemblée électorale*, II, Préface, VII.

[9] Charavay, *Assemblée électorale*, II, Préface, V, VII n. 1.

[10] *Ibid.*, II, Préface, XIII, XIV. The total number of electors in the department was 964, with 827 coming from the sections and 137 from the cantons outside Paris. In 1790 there had been 913, so there was a gain of 51 for the year 1791. More than half had never served in the capacity of electors; of the total from Paris (827), only 385 had been elected in 1790.

[11] *Ibid.*, II, Préface, XIV, XV.

[12] *Ibid.*, II, 41-42. The ten electors serving again were Mussey, Morel, Pointard, Gérard, Boursier, Fayel, Oudart, Billaudel, Herbault, and Gorguereau.

In short, there was no significant change in social status, age, or occupation among the electors in the section.[13]

Of the twenty-four deputies elected to the Legislative Assembly, one was a resident of section Roi-de-Sicile, François Gorguereau, a judge and elector, age forty-three and native of Bourges. He had received 243 more votes than had Brissot, becoming the tenth deputy elected, while the latter came in twelfth.[14] The election of these men and their eight substitutes was recognized as a triumph for the patriots of the Left.[15] The last of the twenty-four deputies was elected on 28 September 1791—this, after a sharp division had split members of the Right who left the Evêché assembly to form their own in Sainte-Chapelle. Upon the selection of jurors, judges, and various administrators, including curés, the work of the primary assembly finally came to an end on 12 August 1792.[16] After this date a new chapter opened in the choice of deputies for the Convention.

The electoral assembly of 1792 showed a marked contrast with its predecessors of the two previous years.[17] The new electors chosen by the primary assemblies of Paris had begun selecting their delegates on 27 August, that is, shortly after the overthrow of the king—a change that was bound to be reflected in their social structure. There had been 829 electors in the capital in 1791; now the sections chose 850 out of a total of 990, with the number in section Roi-de-Sicile remaining at 18. As might be expected, few priests and nobles were returned to the electoral assembly in 1792. Of the 990 electors, a mere 195, or less than 20 percent, had sat in previous assemblies. A number of sections did not reelect any of their former electors, whereas fifteen sections, including Roi-de-Sicile (now Droits-de-l'Homme), had reelected only 2 (3, if an elector of 1790 is included).[18]

---

[13] Charavay observes that the number of electors connected with the legal profession had declined from 239 to 131, whereas the clergy had increased from 24 to 39. *Ibid.*, II, Préface, XIV. In section Roi-de-Sicile there were now eight electors connected with the law (six judges, one assessor, and a lawyer), a decline of three. The electors, with their occupation, age, and residence, are listed in the appendix to this chapter.

[14] *Ibid.*, II, Préface, XXVI, XXIX.

[15] *Ibid.*, II, Préface, XV, XXVII-XXIX.

[16] *Ibid.*, II, Préface, XXXI-LVII, *passim*.

[17] The electors with their occupation, age, and residence are listed in the appendix of this chapter.

[18] *Ibid.*, III, Préface, III-IX, *passim*, and pp. 52-54. The 18 electors with their occupation, age, and place of residence are listed in the appendix to this chapter.

Among the new electors were Robespierre, Hébert, Vincent, Dobsen, Lazowski, Jacques Roux, and Jean Varlet, the last enjoying an official position for the only time during his long career in the Revolution. Disputes centered around the question of whether the primary assemblies had the right to reject deputies chosen by their electoral assemblies, that is, whether electors were mere proxies or mandatories of their primary assemblies. A number of conservative sections tried to use this weapon against their radical opponents, thus demonstrating that the concept of the *mandat impératif* could be used against the Left as well as the Right. Twenty-five sections did deliberate and vote on ratifying or rejecting the choices made by their electoral assembly, whereas a number simply ratified the action of their body.[19]

Nicolas Oudart of section Droits-de-l'Homme, an elector and president of the civil tribunal of the 3d arrondissement, was elected president of the criminal court (28 January 1793),[20] and Jean-François Millet, an elector, and Alexandre-Guillaume Le Roy, a lawyer, were elected clerks to the civil tribunal (on 15-22 March 1793).[21] These three were active in the politics of the section, holding a number of local posts, and because of this were to be harassed by the Thermidorians after the fall of Robespierre and, especially, after the insurrection of prairial. It should be noted, also, that Descombes, linked to the Hébertists in the spring of 1794, and Coulombeau, the secretary-registrar of the Paris Commune, were among the electors of the section.

The social composition of these electors was as follows: nine were of the liberal profession (Auzolles, Cheval-de-Saint Hubert, Pollet, Dufour, Le Roy, Descombes, Coulombeau, Oudart, and Richebourg); four were merchants or businessmen (Ladoubé, Sauvegrain, Thérouenne, and Gagnier); two were artisans (Grenier and Hardy); and three were government employees (Millet, Varlet, and Vaubertrand).[22] In the previous body, eleven had been of the liberal profes-

[19] *Ibid.*, III, Préface, x, LVIII, *passim.*

[20] *Ibid.*, III, Préface, LXXXIV.

[21] *Ibid.*, III, Préface, LXXXIX. Bazard, a wine merchant, residing at no. 60 rue Saint-Antoine, was elected to the new administration of the department. *Ibid.*, III, 615.

[22] The liberal profession includes a *receveur des rentes* and a *huissier-priseur* (Hubert and Richebourg).

sion, thus there was a drop of two from the previous group; merchants rose from three to four; none was a professional military man (there had been two previously); and three were government employees. The number of young men now markedly increased. In the previous body there had been none in the twenties; now there were two. Six had been in their thirties; now there were ten. Thus, two-thirds of the electors were not yet forty. Those in their forties had dropped from seven to four; those in their fifties from three to two, and no elector was over fifty. The youth of the body is perhaps a clearer indication of the change in personnel after 10 August 1792 than the occupational divisions—a sign of radicalization in every revolution of modern times.

On 6 October 1790, section Roi-de-Sicile had sent three men to the General Council. These were: Anne-Clément-Félix Champion, introduced in a previous chapter, Félix-Pierre Geoffroy, fils, age twenty-nine, an *avocat au parlement*, residing on rue des Deux-Portes-Saint-Jean-en-Grève; and André Gérard, fils, age thirty-three, and also an *avocat au parlement*, residing on rue Saint-Antoine.[23] In December 1791, the last was reelected to the Council and had been elected assistant judge of the court of the 1st arrondissement.[24]

The general assembly of the section met on 11 October 1790, and verified the presence of 136 (?) active citizens before proceeding to the vote. Billaudel received 130 votes as president and Pointard 91 as secretary. On the following day, 196 active citizens participated in verifying the 17 electors chosen, a process that was finally completed on 14 October.[25]

[23] A. de P., 1 AZ 137, "Liste générale des cent-quarante-quatre citoyens élus par les 48 sections pour composer le Conseil général et le corps municipal de la Ville de Paris," 1790. Champion received 911 votes, Gérard 179, and Geoffroy 110. Robiquet, p. 390.

[24] A. de P., 1 AZ 145, *Liste générale des soixante-quinze citoyens élus par les quarante-huit sections pour composer le Conseil-général, le corps et le bureau municipal de la Ville de Paris* (21 December 1791), p. 4. Tuetey, *Répertoire*, V, no. 3992, 10 December 1791. He had been elected assistant judge in the capacity of being a "distinguished deputy to the Commune." Although Gérard was rejected by 15 sections, he received enough votes from the rest to be admitted into the General Council. A. de P., 1 AZ 145, *Liste générale*.

[25] A.N., B I, 2. The record speaks of 126 citizens being present, but since Billaudel received 130 votes this must be an error, or else he received less than the total reported. On 12 October, 219 active citizens were present but 23 ballots were ruled invalid.

In February 1793, section Droits-de-l'Homme had elected Descombes, Gattrez, and Eude to the General Council.[26] The result of
the balloting was deposited with the Commune, which admitted Descombes and Eude but rejected Gattrez. The Council then decreed that
those sections from which any delegates had been rejected by the
General Council were to proceed to reballot on 5 March.[27] Gattrez
had been attacked by several citizens, including two women, for alleged misconduct in office. The sectional assembly came to his aid,
however, in a unanimous show of support, and allowed him to publish
a reply to his "slanderers," a reply that was transmitted to the Convention. Several of his colleagues urged him not to blow the controversy out of proportion, as his patriotic reputation was perfectly secure. Enough rancor had been generated, however, so that the General
Council rejected his election to the Commune.[28]

On 10 June the Convention convoked the sections to complete
election of delegates to the Commune. By the middle of July, 144
representatives had been elected and the *Commune définitive* opened its
first session on 7 August. The social composition of this Commune
contrasted sharply in some respects with that of the *Commune provisoire*
that had preceded it. Formerly there had been 37 bourgeois, now
reduced to 21; the number of priests had declined from 8 to 2. More
important, perhaps, was the increase of artisans and workers, from 12
to 32, closely associated with 39 merchants and tradesmen. In addition to these were 14 artists and an asssortment of men from the
liberal professions.[29]

More revealing of the change that had occurred politically was the
contrast between the constitution adopted by the Constituent Assembly and that of the Convention. Although destined to remain abor-

[26] B.H.V.P., *Affiches de la Commune*, "Liste générale des 144 citoyens élus par les
48 sections pour composer le Conseil-général, le Corps et le Bureau municipal de la
Ville de Paris," 19 February 1793.

[27] B.H.V.P., *Affiches de la Commune*, 2 March 1794.

[28] B.H.V.P., 100.65, no. 379, "Roi-de-Sicile," 2 February 1793 (Paris), 8 pp.;
B.N., Lb[40] 1791, *Section des Droits-de-l'Homme* (Paris, 2 February 1793), 4 pp. This
is signed by Thiébart, president, and Eude, secretary per interim.

[29] Saint-Clair Deville, pp. 99-101. Out of the 15,191 who voted, 11,881 cast
their ballots for Pache as mayor. Coulombeau, of section Droits-de-l'Homme, was
reelected secretary-registrar. Deville characterizes the men who filled the new posts
as "brutal fanatics . . . without pity." *Ibid.*, p. 116.

tive, the Constitution of 1793 became a weapon in the hands of the Convention against federalism and other forms of domestic opposition, its democratic provisions and unifying role appealing to both moderates and radicals. As another symbol of republican patriotism, it roused further the energies of the *sectionnaires* and, at the same time, traded social aspirations of the *sans-culottes* for dubious, if not empty political forms. Few revolutionaries saw through this sham, however. Jacques Roux alone had the courage or foolhardiness to attack it openly on the floor of the Convention, and suffered a disastrous defeat as a result.[30]

Although the *enragés* like Roux attacked the Constitution of 1793 from the Left because it failed to proscribe speculation and to hold down the cost of living, there were far more numerous opponents on the Right. The latter were opposed to its democratic features and its alleged threat to property. The revolutionary committee of section Droits-de-l'Homme spoke of "the malevolent" who were trying to influence "weak men" to vote "no" on its adoption—without identifying them, however. Among the weapons used by the committee to break this resistance was the condemnation of former so-called "anticivic" petitioners (supporters of a constitutional monarchy and other moderates) by linking them to opponents of the new Constitution.[31]

Like other sections, Droits-de-l'Homme offered its homage to the Constitution adopted by the Convention as its spokesmen read an address that began: "The triumph of Virtue is assured at last. A Popular and Republican Constitution founded upon the eternal principles of Liberty, of Equality, of Indivisibility, has been adopted." Then followed the admonition to the legislators to consolidate this work by establishing a system of public instruction that would teach citizens their duty and the practice of virtue.[32] Its delegation, together with ordinary citizens and an armed contingent, was received by the Convention on 7 July, as a spokesman assured the representatives that the Constitution had been adopted unanimously.[33]

[30] A.N., W 20, 1073, 25 June 1793. See my article entitled, "Jacques Roux: A Victim of Vilification," in *French Historical Studies*, III (Fall 1964), 525-537.

[31] A.N., F7* 2497, p. 35, 25 June 1793.

[32] A.N., C 262, d. 578, pc. 27 n.d. A pledge to avenge the assassination of Marat followed. This was signed by Pétaud, president of the sectional assembly.

[33] A.P., LXVIII, 380, 7 July 1793. The address is reproduced *ibid.*, p. 711, 14 July 1793.

The Constitution was read in the section amidst frequent interruptions of applause. Upon its completion all rose simultaneously with cries of "long live the Republic, long live the Constitution!" Although it was unanimously accepted, all were asked to sign the document with their names and addresses clearly marked, for the sake of correct procedure. To emphasize their adherence (and to overawe the opposition), members of the assembly voted out loud. Even the old and the sick were brought into the hall to add their votes.[34] These measures brought the number voting to 1,738, and the register was left open for latecomers so that there should be "no single complaint." The assembly then addressed its representatives, praising their work as assuring the well-being of 25 million Frenchmen because they had laid "the foundations upon the eternal principles of equality."[35] On 17 September 1795, the list of citizens who had so enthusiastically signed the act of adoption of the Constitution of 1793 was burned by act of the assembly of the section.[36] By then, of course, a different kind of constitution was being considered.

In addition to primary and electoral bodies, sectional assemblies played an important role in the political process, embodying most fully the expression of popular democracy. Gathered in primary assemblies, as seen above, voters expressed their preferences for political tendencies amd administrative personnel; meeting in general assemblies, they deliberated, discussed, and resolved in common. Under the regime based on a property qualification, suffrage had been limited to active citizens; by the spring and summer of 1792 the assemblies witnessed a flood of new participants, as discussed above, formerly passive both legally and in practice. Yet, despite the removal of barriers against the propertyless (formally on 11 August 1792), the number of participants in the active, political life of the section remained small, a phenomenon that remained constant for the whole revolutionary period. The municipal law of 21 May-27 June 1790 provided for the convocation of a sectional assembly upon the demand of fifty active citizens.[37] Until the adoption of the principle of per-

[34] A.N., B 11, 23, liasse 3e, pc. 218, 17 July 1793. The secretary wrote: "A touching spectacle, this first use of sovereignty by the French people; it is the happiest omen."

[35] *Ibid.* The *procès-verbal* was signed by Ravel as president.

[36] B.V.C., MS 120, fols. 168-169.

[37] Title IV, Art. 1.

manence, on 25 July 1792, however, there were few occasions for the implementation of this law.[38] Permanence was, in turn, suppressed on 9 September 1793, when sessions were limited to two a week, then twice a *décade*, and a subsidy of 40 sous was granted to poorer citizens to encourage their attendance.

The municipal law of 1790 spoke at some length on the organization of primary assemblies, but said little on the regulations and practices of general assemblies. It stipulated the election of a president and secretary for the latter, but provided little else. By 1793–Year II, the general assembly was conducted by a president assisted by an executive committee (*bureau*) and a secretary-registrar to draft the *procès-verbal*, tellers to count votes, and censors to maintain order. The executive committee was renewed monthly by a standing vote or by acclamation. Sessions began by reading the *procès-verbal* of the previous meeting followed by decrees of the Convention and ordinances of the Commune. This procedure, together with discussion of the questions of the day, took far longer than had been foreseen when the meetings were legally limited to open at 5 p.m. and close at 10 p.m.[39]

Moreover, sessions were often disorganized and agitated, lacking procedural safeguards and the elements of parliamentary order; there was much shouting and demand for the floor. To end this confusion, section Droits-de-l'Homme separated its women from the men,[40] an indication that those who attended sectional meetings must have had other interests in addition to politics. Moreover, meeting halls were not conducive to good order, as churches and chapels were hardly designed for deliberative assemblies. That participants were aware of this may be seen in the continued demands of the sections for better places in which to meet.[41]

[38] See the discussion in Chapter III and in Mellié, pp. 104-106. The regular *procès-verbal* of section Droits-de-l'Homme begins only with 16 September 1792. B.V.C., MS 120, fol. 132. The assembly declared itself permanent again on 13 January 1793 (there is no definitive indication when, if ever, after July 25 the practice of permanence ceased). It was during this session that it elected Descombes and Deschamps to correspond with the Jacobins. A.N., F[7]* 2497, unpaginated.

[39] Mellié, p. 107; Soboul, pp. 583-584.

[40] B.V.C., MS 120, fol. 135, 19 February 1793.

[41] Soboul, p. 584. There are many references to commotion and disorder in the general assemblies of section Droits-de-l'Homme. Not infrequently the president was forced to suspend proceedings by covering himself, that is, by putting on his hat.

Until the sections were made permanent (25 July 1792), meetings of their general assemblies were relatively few. Section Postes, whose record is quite complete, met 50 times from 4 December 1790 to 25 July 1792, that is, about 20 months. Robespierre's section, Piques, met 76 times from 16 June to 27 September 1792,[42] that is, about 15 weeks. Section Droits-de-l'Homme met 118 times from 10 September 1792 to 5 November 1795,[43] that is, about 38 months, or about 3.1 times per month. Historians have pointed out that the number of voters and participants in the primary and general assemblies was small during the period of the property qualification (from December 1789 to July 1792). Yet when distinction between active and passive citizens disappeared (11 August 1792) and the composition of the membership changed, the number of participants failed to increase. Even after the overthrow of the king, when political feeling was at a high point, the number of voters was still modest,[44] with no more than one-ninth or one-tenth of the active citizens voting in August 1792. Only 14,137 voted for mayor, while one-fourth of the assemblies had a mere 50-60 individuals participating out of some 2,000 or 3,000 eligible voters. In the election for the General Council a handful, about one-twentieth, bothered to cast their vote, and some sections had no more than 15 to 20 voters. Hébert and Chaumette were elected with 56 and 53 votes, respectively.[45] No wonder that section Panthéon-Français complained that despite its 4,000 voters a mere "150, 100, or even less" bothered to vote.[46]

Of the 1,811 active citizens in section Droits-de-l'Homme, plus an additional number of former passive citizens who could have approximated this number, 289 voted for the mayor in 1792.[47] This is 15.95 percent of the active citizens, or 7.97 percent of all eligible citizens, if it can be assumed that the original list of 1,811 had doubled in August 1792. Coulombeau, the secretary-registrar of the General

[42] Mellié, p. 94.

[43] This is based on the entries in B.V.C., MS 120, and assumes that all sessions were duly recorded by Victor Cousin.

[44] Although abstentionism was the dominant political characteristic of the period of the property suffrage, the entry of the *sans-culottes* into the political process did not magnify this trend significantly, wrote Soboul, p. 588.

[45] Mellié, pp. 90-91.

[46] *Moniteur*, XIV, no. 299, p. 281, 25 October 1792.

[47] B.V.C., MS 120, fol. 132.

Council, received a mere 25 ballots out of 155 in section Droits-de-l'Homme.[48] Two weeks after the insurrection against the Gironde, 212 chose the commander of the National Guard, but in the municipal elections of July a mere 56 expressed their preference for representatives to the General Council.[49] A year later, on 14 germinal, Year II (3 April 1794), 283 exercised their right of suffrage for representatives to the Commune.[50]

Section Arsenal became concerned over the great number of absentees, and discussed what means should be adopted to bring them to its assembly. It resolved officially to respect both persons and opinions, in an obvious appeal to politically conscious residents who were boycotting or avoiding the assembly out of fear of expressing themselves. The resolution was discussed in the assembly of section Droits-de-l'Homme, which voted its adherence to it,[51] and, in addition, decided to keep a register of the names of citizens who attended its sessions,[52] hoping thereby to encourage their presence.

A month after the fall of Robespierre, the section cast 224 ballots for the election of new jurors.[53] According to the *procès-verbal* of 5 prairial, Year III, the Thermidorians purged one-sixtieth of the members of the general assembly.[54] If this is an accurate estimate, and the number so purged was 34[55] then the assembly must have numbered 2,040 citizens who were eligible to attend its sessions. In the Year VII the primary assembly of the section was composed of 2,300 residents,[56] a figure not too far removed from that for the Year III. The number who participated in the political life of the section, either by attending the general assembly or by voting at its meetings or those of the primary assembly, thus was quite small.

[48] Braesch, *La Commune*, p. 1,159, cites Mortimer-Ternaux's statement to the effect that only one out of twenty voted for the new Commune after 10 August 1792, as against one out of ten for the preceding one.

[49] B.V.C., fol. 144, 17 June 1793; fol. 144, 18 July 1793.

[50] *Ibid.*, fol. 157.

[51] *Ibid.*, fol. 134, 4 January 1793.

[52] A.N., F⁷* 2497, 4 January 1793, unpaginated.

[53] B.V.C., MS 120, fol. 160, 10 fructidor, Year II (27 August 1794).

[54] *Ibid.*, fol. 162.

[55] A.N., F⁷ 4774⁴⁵, d. 2 (dossier André Michel). This is limited to prairial 5, and does not include another thirty-one arrested later, as is described below in the chapter on the insurrection of prairial.

[56] A.N., F²⁰ 381.

On the eve of the royalist insurrection of vendémiaire, when so much was at stake, only 591 voted in favor of section Lepeletier's resolution condemning the two-thirds decrees of the Convention.[57] The substantially larger vote on the Constitution of the Year III, swelling to 1,721 votes, expressed more fully the political concern of the section,[58] yet in terms of the number of participants it hardly differed from the 1,738 votes cast for the Constitution of 1793.[59] In both cases, it can be assumed that there was pressure by the respective partisans of the Right and the Left to encourage as large a vote as possible. The political nature of the two votes was, of course, diametrically opposed. If it can be assumed that the moderate vote remained constant in both elections, it would seem that the politically conscious Left and the equally conscious Right balanced each other in the section.

The 591 votes cast on 7 September 1795 were the high point of the electoral process in the section. A week later (15 September), it dipped to 520, with no clear majority for the candidates registered,[60] whereas the second vote recorded only 448 ballots. On the 10th vendémiaire (2 October), just three days before the royalist coup, the secretary noted that the number of voters was diminishing daily. On the last day of the month, 31 October 1795 (10 brumaire, Year III), only 98 voted for the justice of the peace. The following day, however, 225 voters cast their ballots for unspecified candidates, and the day after (12 brumaire–2 November), 283 voted for administrators of the department.[61] On 19 messidor, Year IV (7 July 1796) the total number of voters in the seventh arrondissement was given as 9,560. The primary assembly (no. 1), which met in the church of Blancs-Manteaux, recorded 762 voting, while that which met in the church of Petit-Saint-Antoine (no. 10) had 673 voters, in both cases indicat-

[57] B.V.C., MS 120, fol. 166, 21 fructidor, Year III (7 September 1795). (The two-thirds decree is discussed in the chapter on the insurrection of vendémiaire). Mellié points out that the polls were open from 7 a.m. to 10 p.m., for three days, 23-25 fructidor, p. 92. This was an obvious effort by the Right to turn out a large vote against the Convention.

[58] *Ibid.*, fol. 167, 26 fructidor, Year III (12 September 1795).

[59] A.N., B II, 23, liasse 3e, pc. 218, 17 July 1793.

[60] B.V.C., MS 120, fol. 168, 29 fructidor (15 September).

[61] *Ibid.*, fol. 169, 11 and 12 brumaire, Year IV (1 and 2 November 1795).

ing a relatively low participation.[62] Electors listed as having the right to vote in the primary assembly in the 7th arrondissement on 1 germinal, Year V (21 March 1797), numbered 527, with the total "invariably fixed for three years" as being 807 electors.[63]

· The figures cited above illustrate that whether the regime was bourgeois and *censitaire*, revolutionary and democratic, or Thermidorian-Directorial, the mass of qualified voters in the section abstained from the political process. Daily cares and the pursuit of bread were undoubtedly important reasons for this, mixed with some skepticism, if not cynicism, of politics in general. Lack of tradition, illiteracy, and the absence of mass political parties also contributed to this political abstentionism. It is possible also that some "voted with their feet," to use Lenin's well-known expression, because of their disappointment with the Revolution.

Section Droits-de-l'Homme was among the first to refuse the 40 sous subsidy voted to encourage poorer citizens' attendance at sectional meetings by compensating them for time lost from work. From the very beginning the measure was controversial. To begin with, it was never made clear whether it was designed to compensate wage workers for time lost from work—an understandable and just proposal—if the government wished to encourage their attendance at sectional meetings, or was aimed at subsidizing the poorer *sectionnaires*. In either case, it was often applied unfairly and arbitrarily. Section Montagne, for example, excluded domestics from its benefits,[64] while some officials used it to build a base of political support for themselves.[65] The *comité des secours publics* revealed in a letter to the sections that abuses of the *droits d'assistance* were widely prevalent, many receiving the subsidy who were not qualified and others never attending assembly meetings at all.[66] Section Indivisibilité complained to the General Council that some of its members inscribed themselves as being present when the assembly opened at 5 p.m. and then left shortly thereafter; others falsified their attendance while doing

[62] A.N., F[20] 381, Département de la Seine, 19 messidor, Year IV. "Tableau de distribution des assemblées primaires des douze arrondissements du canton de Paris, et désignations des locaux ou elles se tiennent."

[63] B.H.V.P., MS 150, fol. 120, 1 germinal, Year V.

[64] B.V.C., MS 120, cited by Soboul, p. 592.

[65] Soboul, pp. 594-596, *passim*.

[66] Tuetey, *L'Assistance*, IV, #380, 7 messidor, Year II (25 June 1794).

guard duty; and still others had their cards presented by their friends. Of the 99 so inscribed for the subsidy, 49 failed to respond when their names were called.[67] On the other hand, some sections took extreme precautions to guard against these abuses.[68]

As to the number who received the subsidy in individual sections, it is difficult to give accurate figures. Mellié estimated that about one-third of the citizens in their assemblies collected the 40 sous.[69] The neighbors of section Droits-de-l'Homme varied greatly in their practice. Section Arcis, with 855 indigents receiving relief, subsidized 340 of them, or almost 40 percent. Homme-Armé paid the 40 sous to 98 of its 358 poor on relief, this being about 27 percent, while Maison-Commune, with 4,258 on relief, subsidized only 195, or 4.5 percent.[70]

Since no records exist on the number subsidized in section Droits-de-l'Homme, we can only speculate. The divergence between the low percentage of section Maison-Commune and the high of section Arcis does not indicate with any degree of accuracy the number receiving this aid in each section. If one were to apply the guess of Mellié that about one-third of those attending meetings were paid, it still would be difficult to arrive at an exact figure. Assuming that the 212 who voted for the commander of the National Guard on 17 June 1793 and the 283 who balloted for representatives to the General Council on 14 germinal, Year II (3 April 1794) represented a fair picture of the number participating in general assemblies of the section during important periods, the number subsidized would have been about 82, or 6.48 percent of the 1,265 on relief in section Droits-de-l'Homme.[71] This is pure speculation, however, because the number who attended

[67] *Moniteur*, XX, no. 240, p. 498, 30 floréal, Year II (19 May 1794). The Council referred this complaint to the Committee of Public Safety.

[68] Mellié, pp. 147-149, especially in reference to section Gravilliers.

[69] *Sections*, p. 150. He did not think that this number was excessive "in an epoch of poverty." In section Théâtre-Français the subsidy lasted from 15 September 1793 to 30 thermidor, Year II (17 August 1794), with a total of 11,774 livres paid in eleven monthly installments, varying from 824 to 1,198 livres. In section Mont-Blanc the total disbursed was 8,352 livres. The average number subsidized in 66 assemblies of section Théâtre-Français was 89; in Mont-Blanc it was 64.

[70] Soboul, pp. 597-598.

[71] The average of 212 and 283 being 247, one-third of this sum is 82. The latter is 6.48 percent of the 1,265 on relief in the section.

general assemblies was much smaller. It can be assumed, of course, that a subsidy would have encouraged many to attend in order to collect it, whatever merit or futility they saw in sectional politics. On the other hand, it is difficult to believe that a politically conscious section like Droits-de-l'Homme would have had a mere 6.5 percent of its poor subsidized while its next door neighbor, Arcis, paid 40 percent of its indigents on relief. One inhibiting factor in raising this figure in the section could have been the violent agitation of Varlet against the 40 sous.

With the exception of laborers, journeymen, and the poor of section Arcis, few seem to have benefited by this subsidy, and those who did lost both status and dignity, being looked down upon as *des citoyens diminués*, that is, lower-class citizens. In general, the attacks against "the men of 40 sous" reflected an antagonism between property owners and simple workingmen, as Soboul has shown. Although Varlet's opposition was to the principle itself, not to its supposed beneficiaries, it must have contributed to diminishing the number paid in the section. This form of relief was finally suppressed on a motion of Bourdon de l'Oise with the support of Cambon on 4 fructidor, Year II (21 August 1794).[72]

The impact of elections on the political life of a section cannot be circumscribed by the number of voters alone, however. It is possible that those who chose to exercise the suffrage expressed, by and large, the sentiments of many who failed to vote. Even if this was not true, however, the orations, pamphlets, journals, placards, and debates must have raised the general political consciousness of the *sectionnaires*. On the other hand, the effort to encourage poorer citizens to take part in the electoral process and to attend assembly meetings proved a failure. Had their elementary economic needs been satisfied it is possible that they might have been more attracted to this type of activity. As it was, their long hours of labor and search for bread left them little time for politics, even if they were attracted by it.

[72] *Moniteur*, XXI, no. 336, p. 555.

APPENDIX

Electors from Section Roi-de-Sicile

1. BILLAUDEL, LOUIS, *avocat*, former *procureur au parlement* and president of the section, 37 years old, residing at 2 rue Cloche-Perce. He had been a *procureur* in 1785, a volunteer in the 2d company of the battalion of Petit-Saint-Antoine, assessor to the justice of the peace of the section, an attorney-at-law (*avoué*) and an elector in 1791.

2. POINTARD (misspelled as Pointart), CLAUDE-CHARLES, *avocat au parlement*, secretary of the section, 45 years old, 1 rue Pavée. He had been a volunteer in the 2d company of the battalion of Petit-Saint-Antoine, an elector in 1791, and a justice of the peace of the section in 1792.

3. MOREL, CHARLES-GILBERT, formerly of Vindé, *avocat*, 32, 9 rue Bar-du-Bec, parish of Saint-Jean. He was born in Paris 20 January 1759; was counsellor in the Parlement in 1778, member of the Jacobins in 1790, elected judge in 1790, elector in 1791 and 1796, peer of France in 1815, member of the Academy of Sciences in 1824; died in Paris on 20 December 1842. Morel was a former noble (Morel de Vindé), an *avocat* by profession, and had been elected among the first ten judges (29 November 1790). He was elected judge of the tribunal in the 1st arrondissement on 26 January 1791 and signed an order, together with others, remanding prisoners held in the Abbaye to the municipal authorities who had ordered their arrest. (Lacroix, 2e série, I, 441, 457; II, 263 and note 2; III, 126. See the brief sketch of his family by J. François Bluche, *L'Origine des magistrats du Parlement de Paris au XVIIIe siècle* in *Paris et Ile-de-France*, vols. V-VI, 1953-1954 [Paris, 1956], p. 322.)

4. FAYEL, LOUIS-GILLES-CAMILLE, *avocat* and *procureur au parlement* and captain of the 4th company of the battalion of Petit-Saint-Antoine, 42 years old, 107 rue de la Tisseranderie. He had been a *procureur* in 1779, a justice of the peace of the section in 1790, an elector in 1791.

5. MUSSEY, PIERRE, former *procureur au parlement* and captain of

the 1st company of the battalion of Petit-Saint-Antoine, 49 years old, 7 rue des Juifs. He had been a *procureur* from 1777 to 1790, an assessor to the justice of the peace of the section in 1796, an elector in 1791, and a notable in 1814.

6. GORGUEREAU, FRANÇOIS, *avocat au parlement*, 40 years old, 7 rue Bar-du-Bec. He was born in 1750, member of the Jacobins in 1790, elected judge in December 1790, an elector in 1791, deputy of Paris to the Legislative Assembly, elector in 1796.

7. ABRIAL, ANDRÉ-JOSEPH, *avocat au parlement*, 40 years old, 16 rue Sainte-Croix-de-la-Bretonnerie. He was born in Annonay (Ardèche), 19 March 1750, commissioner of the king to the court of the 6th arrondissement of Paris in 1791, minister of justice in 1799, senator, count as of 26 April 1808, peer of France; died in Paris 14 November 1828. As *commissaire du roi* he helped prosecute Santerre on 4 March 1791 for going to Vincennes without Lafayette's permission. (Lacroix, 2e série, II, 258; III, 68 and note 1.)

8. JAQUOTOT, ANTOINE-EDME-NAZAIRE, counsellor in the admiralty court (*conseiller en l'amirauté*), 32 years old, rue des Deux-Portes-Saint-Jean. He was member of the General Council of Paris in 1792, second lieutenant of the 2d company of the battalion of Petit-Saint-Antoine, judge of the peace and notable in 1801.

9. BOURSIER, PIERRE, haberdasher (*mercier*), 65 years old, residing at Cemetière-Saint-Jean. He was an elector in 1791.

10. OUDART, NICOLAS, *avocat*, elector of 1789, 40 years old, 49 rue des Billettes (not Balais as in Charavay). He was an *avocat* in 1776, member of the *comité des recherches* of the Commune in 1789, member of the Jacobins in 1790, elected judge in December 1790, an elector in 1791 and in 1792.

11. VIAR, JEAN-HONORÉ, *avocat au parlement*, 57 years old, 51 rue Saint-Antoine.

12. TESSIER, JEAN-FRANÇOIS-RODOLPHE, formerly du Tillier, citizen, 30 years old, 3 rue des Rosiers. He was police commissioner of the section in 1790.

13. GATTREZ, AMBROISE, JEAN-BAPTISTE-PIERRE-IGNACE, *avocat*, 45 years old, 126 rue de la Verrerie. He was an *avocat* since 1782, member of the General Council of the Commune in 1792, and captain of the 2d company of the battalion of Blancs-Manteaux.

14. GÉRARD, ANDRÉ, *avocat*, 33 years old, 50 rue Saint-Antoine.

He had been an *avocat* since 1781, member of the General Council of the Commune in 1790, corporal of the 5th company of the battalion of Petit-Saint-Antoine, elected substitute judge in June 1791, elector in 1791, judge of the court of the 1st arrondissement in 1792.

15. JUNOT, EDME-ANTOINE, *avocat* and former *procureur au parlement*, corporal of the 4th company of the battalion of Petit-Saint-Antoine, 33 years old, 8 rue Roi-de-Sicile. He had been a *procureur* since 1786. On the list of 13-14 July. (B.H.V.P. 742.)

16. GAGNIER (mispelled Gasnier), JEAN-BAPTISTE, grocer, 30 years old, 50 rue Saint-Antoine. He was sergeant-major of the 2d company of the battalion of Petit-Saint-Antoine. On the list of 13-14 July. (B.H.V.P., MS 742.)

17. HERBAULT, JEAN-BAPTISTE, auditor of accounts (*auditeur des comptes*), captain of the 5th company of the battalion of Petit-Saint-Antoine, 47 years old, 64 rue Saint-Antoine. He had been an auditor since 1764, elector in 1791, justice of the peace and notable in 1801.

JUNE 1791

1. GUYET, JEAN-BAPTISTE-FRANÇOIS, substitute judge of the court of 1st arrondissement, 58 years old, 9 rue Tiron.

*2. MUSSEY, PIERRE, captain of the 1st company of the 3d battalion of the 5th division of the National Guard, 49 years old, 7 rue des Juifs.

*3. MOREL, CHARLES-GILBERT, judge of the court of the 1st arrondissement, 32 years old, 9 rue Bar-du-Bec.

*4. POINTARD, CLAUDE-CHARLES, assessor to the justice of the peace, 46 years old, rue Pavée.

*5. Gérard, ANDRÉ, substitute judge to the court of the 1st arrondissement, 34 years old, 50, rue Saint-Antoine.

*6. BOURSIER, PIERRE, merchant, 75 years old, Marché-Saint-Jean.

*7. FAYEL, LOUIS-GILLES-CAMILLE, justice of the peace of the section, 42 years old, rue des Ecouffes.

8. GEOFFROY DE CHARNAY, FÉLIX-PIERRE, notable of the municipality, 30 years old, rue des Deux-Portes-Saint-Jean. He had been commander of the battalion of Petit-Saint-Antoine in 1790.

9. CHAPPUIS, ANDRÉ, commander of the 3d battalion, 65 years old, 16 rue Saint-Antoine.

10. BOUCHARD, JEAN-CLAUDE, assistant (or deputy-adjunct) no-

table, 54 years old, 9 rue des Juifs. He had been employed in the farming of taxes and was a signatory of the list of 13-14 July. (B.H.V.P., MS 742.)

*11. OUDART, NICOLAS, judge of the court of the 3d arrondissement, 42 years old, 4 rue des Billettes (not Ballets as in Charavay).

12. VERPY, ANTOINE-LOUIS, *huissier-commissaire-priseur*, 31 years old, 108 rue de la Tisseranderie. He had been a *huissier commissaire-priseur* in 1783 and sergeant of the 5th company of the battalion of Petit-Saint-Antoine. Verpy had volunteered for the Parisian militia on 13-14 July. (B.H.V.P., MS 742.)

*13. BILLAUDEL, LOUIS, attorney-at-law (solicitor—*avoué*), 38 years old, no. 2 Cloche-Perce.

14. LADOUBÉ, LOUIS-JEAN, wine merchant, 48 years old, rue Bar-du-Bec, at the corner of rue Sainte-Croix-de-la-Bretonnerie. He had been a volunteer of the 4th company of the battalion of Blancs-Manteaux.

15. SANTERRE, CÉSAR, man of law, 51 years old, 88 rue Vieille-du-Temple.

*16. HERBAULT, JEAN-BAPTISTE-GABRIEL, auditor of accounts (*auditeur des comptes*), captain of the 5th company of the 3d battalion of the 5th division of the National Gurad, 48 years old, 64 rue Saint-Antoine.

*17. GORGUEREAU, FRANÇOIS, judge of the court of the 5th arrondissement, 41 years old, 7 rue Bar-du-Bec.

18. TOULLET, FRANÇOIS-GILBERT, merchant grocer, 35 years old, 112 rue de la Verrerie, second lieutenant of the 2d company of the battalion of Blancs-Manteaux.

SOURCE: Charavay, *Assemblée électorale*, II, 41-42. The asterisk denotes a former elector.

AUGUST 1792

1. AUZOLLES, PIERRE, a former teacher and collector of lotteries, age 36, no. 37 rue Bourtibourg.

*2. LADOUBÉ, LOUIS-JEAN, wine merchant, age 50, rue Bar-du-Bec.

3. CHEVAL-DE-SAINT HUBERT (Bonaventure-Hippolyte-Hubert), *receveur des rentes*, age 40, 57 rue Saint-Antoine.

4. POLLET, PAUL-HENRI, teacher, age 32, 36 rue du Roi-de-Sicile.

**5. OUDART, Nicolas, president of the court of the 3d arrondissement, age 41, no. 42 rue des Billettes.

6. SAUVEGRAIN, JEAN-BAPTISTE-FRANÇOIS, butcher, age 39, Marché-Saint-Jean.

7. DUFOUR, JEAN-BAPTISTE, surgeon, age 50, 22 rue des Rosiers. His name is on the list of 13-14 July. (B.H.V.P., MS 742.)

8. MILLET, JEAN-FRANÇOIS, age 38, 50 rue Saint-Antoine, elected clerk of the civil court, 20 March 1793, and assigned to the court of the 4th arrondissement.

9. THÉROUENNE, ADRIEN-FRANÇOIS, cloth and haberdashery merchant (*marchand-drapier-mercier*), age 33, 29 rue Saint-Antoine.

**10. GAGNIER, JEAN-BAPTISTE, grocer, age 35, 53 Saint-Antoine.

11. LE ROY, ALEXANDRE-GUILLAUME, *avocat*, age 35, 17 Mauvais-Garçons. He was elected clerk to the civil court and assigned to the 2d arrondissement.

12. DESCOMBE(S), ANTOINE-IGNACE-FRANÇOIS, a master of languages, age 28, 20 Sainte-Croix-de-la-Bretonnerie.

13. COULOMBEAU, CLAUDE, *homme de loi*, age 40, 21 Francs-Bourgeois.

14. GRENIER, FRANÇOIS, locksmith, age 34, 22 rue de Bercy.

15. RICHEBOURG, FRANÇOIS-JACQUES, *huissier-priseur*, age 46, 6 Mauvais-Garçons. He became justice of the peace of the section.

16. VARLET, JEAN, employed in the post office, age 27, 6 rue Tiron.

17. HARDY, JEAN, cobbler, age 36, 14 Cloche-Perce. His name appears as Hardi on the list of 13-14 July. (B.H.V.P., MS 742.)

18. VAUBERTRAND, JEAN-CLAUDE, a clerk at Sainte Pelagie prison, age 33, 33 Roi-de-Sicile. He became assessor to the justice of the peace of the section.

SOURCE: Charavay, *Assemblée électorale*, III, 52-54.

*Ladoubé had been an elector in September 1791.

**Gagnier had been an elector in the first assembly of September 1790, and Oudart had been an elector in both previous electoral assemblies.

The original list (or a copy of it) is in A.N., B I, 14 with a slight variation in order of names. The document is marked no. 31.

VIII

The Civil Committee

Although the general, primary, and electoral assemblies were first in importance to sectional politics, the leading administrative organ was the section's civil committee, which acted as the intermediary between the neighborhood and the municipal authorities. These committees were established by the Municipal Law of 21 May-27 June 1790 as organs of surveillance and execution of the ordinances of the Commune. Charged expressly with supporting the work of police commissioners, who had consultative voice within the committees, they also transmitted information and advice to municipal and departmental administrations. Originally composed of sixteen members and later reduced to twelve, they elected their own president and met once a week, with one committeeman remaining on duty for twenty-four hours. Among their many functions was the apportionment of taxes in the section.[1]

As the tasks demanded by the Revolution increased, so did the powers of the civil commissioners. Before long they not only corresponded with the municipality and executed its ordinances but added many other duties to their original obligations. Among these were affixing and removing seals, taking the census of inhabitants, inspecting lodging houses, delivering various types of certificates, converting *assignats* into specie, and giving relief to the poor.[2] On 11 August 1792 these committees were suppressed by the Commune, and a new decree was issued on 15 August that provided for their election by the general assemblies of the sections.[3] This meant that their powers

[1] Duvergier, I, 179-180; A.P., XVI, 425, 22 June, Title IV, Arts. 4-11.

[2] Mellié, p. 164. The author discusses how these powers grew, pp. 158-164, *passim*. For example, one commissioner had to be present at all spectacles; others had to inspect women teachers of the public schools.

[3] *Moniteur*, XIII, no. 233, p. 449, 20 August 1792. General assemblies were authorized to elect commissioners to supervise the execution of the decrees of the General Council that all mount guard personally.

were now drastically reduced as they became emanations, creatures of general assemblies.[4]

Because of this, their role, for some time, was a contradictory one. On the one hand they were representatives or proxies of the sectional assemblies; on the other hand, as administrative bodies they were dependent on the Commune whose decrees they were bound to execute. Partly because of this contradiction they remained removed from politics throughout 1793–Year II. On 31 May-2 June, for example, they remained quiescent and were overshadowed by the revolutionary committees.[5] During the events of 9-10 thermidor, however, they did meet jointly with the revolutionary committees.[6] It was only with the reorganization of Paris by the law of 7 fructidor, Year II (24 August 1794) that they recovered their former importance. Their powers were enhanced further by the Committee of General Security on 3 prairial, Year III (22 May 1795), when it ruled that all petitions presented by individuals disarmed after the insurrection of 1-2 prairial were to carry observations of the civil committee attached to them. A few months later (14 vendémiaire, Year III–5 October 1794) they were charged with delivery of certificates of civic conduct.[7]

In addition to the foregoing, food shortages and the high cost of living forced the committees to rivet their attention on these problems. The distribution of bread and meat demanded their special consideration. Many of these matters were closely linked to food shortages, which struck the poor especially hard—one reason for their joining the relief committees in common deliberations. In this respect there was no clear division between the two bodies.[8]

As late as the winter of 1794, members of these committees received no salaries. The municipality did grant 1,200 livres to each committee for office expenses (18 January 1791), and on 2 April 1793

---

[4] Mellié reproduces the instructive resolution of section Gravilliers aimed at limiting the powers of its civil committee and subordinating it to its assembly, pp. 166-167.

[5] *Ibid.*, p. 168. Mellié found no reference to these events in the *procès-verbaux* he examined.

[6] This is discussed at some length in reference to the two committees of section Droits-de-l'Homme, above.

[7] Mellié, pp. 170-171.

[8] *Ibid.*, p. 171. See the discussion on this question as it applies to section Droits-de-l'Homme in the chapter on the *comité de bienfaisance*, below.

the Commune appropriated 3,000 livres per section to pay off debts incurred since the overthrow of the king. Expense allowances were increased from 1,200 to 1,500 livres (1 January 1793), and another 400 livres were allotted some four months later.[9] It was on the initiative of section Observatoire that twenty-six sections endorsed its demand for salaries from the Convention; included among the petitioners was Droits-de-l'Homme.[10] One factor that must have contributed to the request was the knowledge that members of revolutionary committees had been paid 3 livres a day since 5 September 1793, a subsidy that was increased to 5 livres on November 8. Furthermore, Observatoire argued that capable and devoted family men needed a salary to perform their duties, and bitterly attacked their wealthier colleagues as tending to form a despotism of the propertied unless balanced by poorer citizens.[11] As a result of this pressure and, possibly seeing the justice of the case, the Convention finally authorized the payment of 3 livres per day to members of civil committees on 6 floréal, Year II (25 April 1795).[12] After some complaints as to what constituted actual performance of duty and how to verify the presence of committee members, the law was completed by acts of 23 fructidor, Year II (9 September 1794), and 28 vendémiaire, Year III (19 October 1794).[13]

Before the enactment of these laws, section Droits-de-l'Homme again adhered unanimously to the effort made by section Révolutionnaire in this case to broaden the subsidy voted on 25 April.[14] With the re-

[9] *Ibid.*, pp. 174-175. The Commune also allowed an additional 300 livres to those police commissioners whose services had not been interrupted since 1 August 1792, that is, those who had proved their loyalty to the Revolution.

[10] A.N., C 280, 769, pcs. 45-63. 22 brumaire, Year II (12 November 1793), and pc. 55, 26 October (5 brumaire, Year II).

[11] A.N., C 280, 769, pc. 39, 5 brumaire, Year II (26 October 1793). Mellié cites section Observatoire's petition of 29 pluviôse, Year II (8 February 1794) to the Convention for compensation without referring to its much earlier proposal.

[12] Duvergier, VII, 154, 6 floréal, Year II (25 April 1793). *Moniteur*, XX, no. 218, p. 315, 8 floréal, Year II (27 April 1794).

[13] Duvergier, VII, 273, 302. *Moniteur*, XXI, no. 355, pp. 714-715, 25 fructidor, Year II (11 September 1794); XXII, no. 32, p. 288, 2 brumaire, Year III (23 October 1794). Art. 3 provided for the reduction of the number of commissioners to twelve, one-fourth of whom were to be renewed quarterly.

[14] A. de P., V.D. *9, no. 1026, 24 fructidor, Year II (10 September 1794). This was signed by Grandhomme, secretary-registrar.

duction of membership of civil committees to twelve and their renewal quarterly by the Convention's Committee of Legislation, it was
also decreed that a published list of members proposed by the latter
be provided to each deputy of the Convention. This was a precautionary measure taken by the Thermidorians to eliminate any former militant who might have slipped by the surveillance of his section. The
civil committees were finally abolished on 17 vendémiaire, Year IV
(11 October 1795).[15]

The administrative or technical nature of their jobs enabled these
bodies to escape the purges from 10 August 1792 to the Year III.
Most members belonged to the upper ranks of the *sans-culottes*, and
the revenue gained from a shop or profits earned from trade enabled
them to stay on without a subsidy in the early days of the committees'
existence. Many were able to continue practicing their profession or
to supervise their business and yet find time to carry out their duties
on the committee, while the more fortunate lived off their investments.[16]

Of 343 civil commissioners in the Year II, 91 or 26.53 percent
lived off their property or investments; 252 or 73.47 percent continued to practice their trade or profession. All occupations were represented, with the first, numerically, being merchants engaged in the
food business, followed by those in the wine trade, tailors, hairdres-
sers, and so on. Retired shopkeepers, as might be expected, were more
numerous than former artisans, being 36 or 10.5 percent as against
13 or 3.79 percent of the latter. Among the liberal professions, architects led all others, followed by sculptors, painters, *avocats*, public
health officials, surgeons, and civil servants (*employées*). These, added
to commissioners who at one time belonged to the liberal professions,
formed 20 percent of the total. The mass of commissioners were
craftsmen or shopkeepers, 201 of the 343, or 58.6 percent. If former
artisans or tradesmen were added, this group would have totaled 250
or 72.89 percent, almost three-fourths of the civil commissioners.[17]

How do the members of the civil committee of Droits-de-l'Homme
compare with those of Paris as a whole? By the end of 1792 the

[15] Mellié, p. 177.
[16] Soboul, p. 602.
[17] *Ibid.*, pp. 442-443. Soboul breaks down some of the occupational categories still
further.

section had submitted a list of twenty-six names to the General Council, from which sixteen members were to be elected, as provided by the municipal decree of 21 May 1790. The committee was chaired by Etienne Décourchant, with Pavas Le Roy as its secretary-registrar and Pierre Auzolles as police commissioner of the section.[18] Of these, twenty-one are identified by occupation and may be classified as follows: The largest number, ten, were members of the liberal professions, of whom three were teachers (Pollet, Descombes, and Auzolles); four were bailiff-appraisers (Richebourg, Martin, Thiébart père, and Saulnier); two were collectors of *rentes* (Hubert and Michon); and one was a *procureur au parlement* (Boussière). The next group was engaged in business or lived off their property or investments. Thiébart fils, was of the latter group, Gagnier was in the grocery business, and Ladoubé in wine; Giboy had been in some business (unspecified) but had gone bankrupt; and Sauvegrain was a butcher. The three artisans were Hardy, a cobbler (probably a master cobbler); Roger, a cabinet-maker; and Ponsard with no listed occupation but described as "of little education." The last group was made up of three civil servants: Décourchant, a former *procureur-général à la chambre des comptes*; Vaubertrand, a clerk; and Le Roy, in the police administration.[19] The social composition of this committee is, therefore, overwhelmingly on the side of the upper ranks of the petty bourgeoisie and the more "respectable professions." Whether they can be characterized as *sans-culottes* is largely a matter of definition, and other factors in addition to their social position would have to be considered. The small number of artisans is revealing of the socially conservative nature of this civil committee.

[18] A. de P., 4 AZ 1233, 19 December 1792. The names and signatures (in order of their appearance) are as follows: Décourchant (president), Pollet, Hubert, Hardy, Sauvegrain, Roger, Vaubertrand, Rossignol, Richebourg, Ponsard, Martin, Millet, Groux, Alexandre (no signature), Thiébart (no indication if père or fils), Descombes, Dassin, Saulnier, le Bourcier (probably Boussière), Garnier (Gagnier), Ladoubée (Ladoubé), Michon, Ravel, Giboy (père), Auzolles (commissioner of police), and Le Roy (secretary-registrar). This document was signed by Décourchant and Le Roy.

[19] This analysis is based on a number of sources, the two primary documents being A.N. F^{1b} II, Seine 18, 14 vendémiaire, Year III (5 October 1794), and A.N., D III, 256^3, d. 10, pc. 41, 15 ventôse, Year III (5 March 1795). Other sources and individual dossiers are listed below in discussing members of the committee. Characterizing Ponsard as an artisan or laborer of some sort is an assumption on my part, based on the fact that he was uneducated.

By the Year II this occupational structure did not change; if anything, the tendency to appoint men of the liberal professions was
strengthened. Of the nine men whose occupations can be verified,
seven were of the liberal professions, one was in business, and only
one was an artisan.[20] After the 9th of thermidor, in frimaire, Year III
(November-December 1794), the civil composition of 160 commissioners whose occupations are known (out of a total of 198), changed
markedly in a bourgeois direction. Property holders living off bonds,
rent, or interest now numbered 46.2 percent, in contrast to the 26.2
percent of the Year II, a significant change, whereas merchants and
artisans made up 50 percent, a decrease from the 58 percent of the
previous year. The number who belonged to the liberal professions
rose from the 12 percent before thermidor to 20.6 percent at the end
of 1794, and for purpose of social analysis should be included with
the propertied classes. Other categories remained in the same proportion to the total number as they had been in the Year II.[21] As for
their powers, they tended to grow, especially after the suppression of
the revolutionary committees. In addition to their customary administrative duties, they began to exercise surveillance over the general
assemblies, and as official bodies having the endorsement of the Convention's Legislative Committee were made independent of the sectional assemblies. Furthermore, in contrast to revolutionary committees, retired members numbered 26.2 percent as against only 4.6
percent of the former. Finally, administrative rather than political
duties tended to attract the more steady and qualified men to them.
Yet both civil and revolutionary committees were made up of moderates, not reactionaries, and often stood between former terrorists, or

[20] Members of the liberal profession were: Dufour, a public health officer; Saulnier,
a bailiff; four in the legal profession—Faugé, a notary, Porcher and Guyet, lawyers,
and Folles, unspecified. Lambin was a head tenant of a lodging house, Doublet was
a glazier. These men are discussed below and their dossiers given.

[21] B.N., Lc[38] 1090-1095, *Noms des citoyens présentés par le Comité de législation pour
compléter le comité civil de la section des Droits de l'Homme* ([Paris], n.d.), Imprimé par
ordre de la Convention nationale, frimaire, Year III; A.N., D III, 255-256[1], d. 3,
p. 182, same title. The analysis of the social composition of the civil committees is
in Kåre D. Tønnesson, *La Défaite des sans-culottes; mouvement populaire et réaction bourgeoise en l'an III* (Paris, 1959), p. 49 n. 44. In addition to the above two sources, the
author utilized the document in Br. M., F* 61-11, 20, 21, 27. See my references to
the first two sources below.

those accused of being such, and the general assemblies bent on vengeance.[22]

In March 1795, eighteen members of the civil committee of section Droits-de-l'Homme appeared on the new list, of whom seven had been retained from the earlier list of 1792; one individual was appointed sometime later.[23] Of the new appointees whose occupation is known, two were artisans and four were members of the liberal professions.[24] The thirteen commissioners whose pursuits are given were divided among four artisans, seven of the liberal professions, one *rentier*, and the last a master tenant. These figures are too meager to demonstrate any significant shift in terms of class structure from the list of December 1792, however. The number of artisans had increased by one, from three to four; members of the liberal professions still made up almost half of the total (in December 1792 they numbered ten out of twenty-one as against the seven out of the eighteen now). Those living off their investments dropped slightly (in December they were six of twenty-one as against one on the present list); and one could be regarded as being in business (the master tenant). Who were these individuals on the committee and what was their history?

Etienne Décourchant was sixty-five years old when he became president of the civil committee, married and the father of one son, residing on rue des Ecouffes. He had been a *procureur-général* at the Chambre des comptes before the Revolution, and, since then, lived with the help provided by his old mother in faubourg Saint-Germain. This fall in status and dependence on his mother for a living is a pointed commentary on what happened to men like Décourchant during the Revolution. Could he have welcomed the change? In any case, the

---

[22] Tønnesson, pp. 48, 49, and n. 43. See the many examples in the police dossiers of individual members after the prairial insurrection, below.

[23] Although the committee was composed of twelve members, a number of refusals to serve or resignations necessitated replacements, which accounts for the larger figure. The seven from the list of December 1792 were: Pollet, Ponsard (for a man characterized as of "little education" he must have possessed endearing qualities to remain in his post), Thiébart fils, Hardy, Rossignol, Boussière, and Michon. Lambin was appointed in 1793 or the Year II.

[24] The artisans were: Jambon, a wig maker, and Dupré, a house painter. The members of the liberal professions were: Le Lorgne, a collector of *rentes*; Dommanget, a *procureur*; and Jolly, a bailiff. Lambin was head tenant of a furnished house, as noted above.

revolutionary committee of the section described his character as "gentle." Despite his age he became active politically, attended meetings of the general assembly, and offered his services freely. Perhaps it was his "gentle" character and moderate opinions that enabled him to mix easily with the patriots as well as with their enemies. In addition to his serving on the civil committee, he became president of the section's welfare committee, after a tie vote with his colleague, Joseph Giboy, on 25 August 1793. For a brief time he was also employed in the Bureau of Emigrés, whose supervisor testified that his conduct had always been correct and that he had been a model to his confreres, who respected him highly.[25] Despite his agreeable character, he was arrested by order of the General Council on 4 November 1793 under the Law of Suspects of 17 September and condemned to prison on 9 December "until the peace."[26]

What was the charge against him? He was accused of having enjoyed close relations with Fayel, the former justice of the peace, who had been condemned for counterrevolutionary activities. It seems that he had written one letter to him in an official capacity when he had been chairman of the civil committee. In addition to this, he had the misfortune of having lived in the same house with the condemned justice. Décourchant protested that his relations with Fayel had been superficial and purely formal, a protest that failed to convince the authorities.

Perhaps one explanation for his imprisonment lay in the arrest and execution of his son by the revolutionary tribunal. He had been accused of having made the statement that, if ordered, he would fire on the people. Décourchant's son protested that this was a "slander" and pointed to his action on 10 August 1792, testifying that when he had heard Roederer, the *procureur-général-syndic* of the Paris department order the cannoneers to repel force with force, he had made the cannon inoperative by removing the wad of cotton; besides, neither of the two cannons was loaded. Furthermore, he had received a unanimous

[25] A.N., F⁷ 4665, d. 3. See the testimonials of Targé, assistant secretary, 6 fructidor, Year II (23 August 1794), and a letter of Claude Joseph Ricard, the same date. This dossier is filed under Courchant and is also spelled Courchamp. See d. 2.

[26] *Ibid.*, "Tableau" of the revolutionary committee, 4 prairial, Year II (23 May 1794); and a letter from his wife asking for his release, n.d. She revealed that he was 67 years of age and had been in prison for ten months.

testimonial of his conduct from the general assembly of his section.[27] Neither his objections, nor the witnesses in his behalf saved him from the guillotine in the end.

Was this affair a manifestation of the class struggle in the section? It is not possible to rule out some class hostility to Décourchant because of his former position, his superior education, and the alleged enmity of his son to the insurgents of 10 August. Yet much of his trouble could have been caused by frightened men anxious to prove their patriotism at a time when "gentleness" was no revolutionary virtue. Even the most superficial contact with a condemned counter-revolutionary and being the father of another such person were sufficient grounds to convict him. An example of this may be seen in the following incident. When a member of the civil committee reported to the general assembly that Décourchant had been arrested, it sent six commissioners to city hall to obtain information. The delegates returned with the message that he was being held as a suspect, and that according to law it was left to higher authorities to proceed with the interrogation. Not one voice was raised in protest; on the contrary, the assembly proceeded to the business of the day.[28]

Yet it is surprising that he was not liberated after the fall of Robespierre, as so many victims of the revolutionary tribunal were. Décourchant remained in prison until the middle of vendémiaire, Year II (about the first week of October 1794), that is, eleven months. The seals were lifted form his papers but he was never permitted to resume his duties with the civil committee.[29]

Décourchant's colleague, Joseph Giboy, was already in his sixties

[27] *Ibid.* The "Tableau" of the revolutionary committee (F^7 4665 for 4 prairial, Year II–23 May 1794) states that he had been condemned by the revolutionary tribunal. Jean Décourchant was a sergeant-major instructor of artillery, 25½ years of age when arrested and interrogated on 4 January 1793 on the charge that he was an accomplice in the conspiracy of the court on August 10. Décourchant protested that not only was he innocent but that he was worthy of being esteemed by the *sans-culottes*, "whom he had served honorably in the *journée* of 10 August," adding that he had not left his post for a moment. He was executed on 12 January 1793. Henri A. Wallon, *Histoire du tribunal révolutionnaire de Paris avec le journal de ses actes* (Paris, 1880-1882), II, 345-346.

[28] A.N., F^{1b} II, Seine 18, 15 brumaire, Year II (5 November 1793).

[29] *Ibid.*, "Mise en liberté du cit^{en} Décourchant père. Levée de ses scellés" (no date); A.N., F^{1b} II, Seine 18, 14 vendémiaire, Year III (5 October 1794).

when he was appointed to the civil and welfare committees. Accused by Charpentier, a former resident of the section, of having links with past terrorists, and charged by another personal enemy of having accompanied Payan, the national agent, to the Commune on 9 thermidor, Giboy was arrested in April 1795. Writing from prison, he replied that Charpentier had been a *huissier* for a justice of the peace widely known for his royalist views, and that when he had applied for a certificate of civic conduct, Giboy, as president of the section, had done his best to deny it to him, thus making him into a personal enemy ever since. As for the charge relating to Payan, Giboy pointed out that he had accompanied the agent at 2 p.m., whereas the Commune was not outlawed until 5 p.m. Moreover, he was not acquainted with "the agents of tyranny," the whole business being a concoction of his personal enemies, not one accusation possessing any merit.[30]

In the fall of 1794, Giboy had been accused by a Charger who styled himself as an expert scribe (*expert écrivain*) that he had been condemned as "a fraudulent creditor," was fined, and had been indicted in a criminal case for using a false title. Despite this he had been elected at the end of 1792 to the civil committee and had served as commissioner of relief for a year. Although excluded from the committee by lot, he was trying now to reenter it. Bankrupts, wrote Charger, lost their right to hold office, yet men like Giboy continued to serve on various committees. "Can relief be entrusted to a man who had always cheated his fellow-citizens?" he asked.[31]

As a result of Charpentier's accusations, the general assembly removed Giboy from the *comité de bienfaisance* and deprived him of the right to bear arms. The civil committee ruled on 22 fructidor, Year III (8 September 1795) that the conflict between him and his accusers was purely of a judicial nature, adding that this should not prejudice his political rights. Testimonials given in his favor persuaded the committee to recommend his rearmament and full restoration of his civic rights. Eight days later (30 fructidor–16 September), the Committee of General Security ordered his immediate release and restored him to full citizenship.[32]

[30] A.N., F⁷ 4725, d. 1.

[31] A.N., D III, 256³, d. 10, pc. 6, 4 brumaire, Year III (25 October 1794).

[32] A.N., F⁷ 4725. Giboy was 63 years old when he was arrested at his home, on rue Saint-Antoine. A.N., F¹ᵇ II, Seine 18.

Unlike the two men above, Philippe (Jean) Hardy came from humbler ranks. A master cobbler by trade, he was elected captain of the
section's armed force, and probably was the commissioner who served
as representative to the "illegal Commune" during the morning of 10
August. Like others in the section, he was imprisoned after 9 thermidor and then released on 27 frimaire, Year III (13 December 1794).[33]
The civil committee considered him to be unqualified to serve on it,[34]
a possible manifestation of class prejudice.

Like Hardy, Antoine-Simpsonien Roger was an artisan, a cabinet-
maker by occupation, residing on rue Vieille-du-Temple, and had
served as an elector in April 1789 from district des Blancs-Manteaux.
Arrested on 4 prairial, Year III (23 May 1795), on the charge of
seeking to undermine the loyalty of a military detachment, he was
accused also of being a "partisan and an agent of tyranny" before the
9th of thermidor. Roger denied making any subversive proposal to
the troops, and pointed out that as banner carrier of the detachment
he had not quitted his post for a moment, as could be verified by his
commanding officer. As for the accusation that he had been a partisan
of terror, Roger argued that having to fulfill the role of soldier, civil
commissioner, and assessor to the justice of the peace left him little
time "to court the tyranny." Nor had he ever served on any jury
except that of 17 August 1792 to judge the conspirators of 10 August.[35]

On the charge that he had compromised his colleagues of the civil
committee, he asked: "My colleagues are men of education. Was it
by my eloquence? Me . . . a simple carpenter? . . . Was it by intim-

---

[33] A.N., F^{1b} II, Seine 18; A.N., F^7 4739, d. 1. Charavay in *Assemblée électorale*, III,
54 gives his first name as Jean. He resided at no. 14 rue des Cloches-Perce. Jean
Hardi, a master cobbler, was a signatory of the list of 13-14 July. The only difference
between the names is that he spelled it with an "i" at the end instead of a "y," and
his first name is given as Jean rather than Philippe on the list. When serving as
commissioner to the Commune he resided on rue des Juifs. B.H.V.P., MS 742.

[34] A.N., D III, 256^3, d. 10, pc. 41, 15 ventôse, Year III (5 March 1795), "Liste
des citoyens proposés pour remplacer les membres du comité civil de la section des
Droits de l'he qui ont été proposé au comité de législation de la Convention Nale."
Although the document itself contains no date, the insert by the Committee of
Legislation (pc. 42) is given as above.

[35] A.N., F^7 4774^{97}, d. 1. These responses to the charges against him were written
in Plessis prison on 30 prairial, Year III (18 June 1795).

idation? In one word, why didn't they complain then? Why does this 'inculpation' appear only now?" Furthermore, he denied that he had deliberately deprived butchers in the section of a living by limiting the number who serviced the welfare committee, and cited the minutes of the joint sessions of the civil and welfare committees to prove it. On the charge that he had menaced the president of the section because of his unwillingness to hold an illegal assembly on the eve of the attempted insurrection of 12 germinal (1 April), Roger pointed out that on the contrary, it was he who had urged his fellow citizens to take their grievances to the legal authority, namely, the civil committee, and had helped close the doors of the chamber to prevent an illegal assembly. As for being intimate with another accused, Perrin, he had accepted some refreshments in his company, but this did not make him a drunkard. Moreover, drunkenness was a vice, not a counterrevolutionary crime. Finally, on the charge that he had insulted members of the welfare committee, can you imagine, he asked, an assembly being influenced by a drunkard?

Signatures attesting to his devotion and probity were offered on his behalf the following month. The civil committee submitted its own investigation to the Committee of General Security on 24 messidor, Year III (12 July 1795). Denying his link to "the tyrants" of prethermidor, it saw him, rather, as being tied to those who had always considered themselves alone as the true patriots in the section. He had always been a partisan of the Revolution and had fulfilled his duties. During the insurrection of 1 prairial, he had expressed his disapproval of the demonstrators at the bakeries and had even proposed measures to protect the distribution of bread. As for his role on the tribunal of 17 August 1792, the committee knew nothing of this.[36] Roger, at times, was warmed by the wine he drank, and, as a result, expressed himself rather strongly in meetings, but, the committee hastened to add, that this was partly due to his lack of education. If he troubled some sessions it was only because of too much wine, rather than because he wanted to act in a negative manner on public matters. Seeking to explain the action of the general assembly in linking Roger to the Robespierrists of the past, the committee wrote that "the agents of tyranny preceding 9 thermidor" were singularly attached to men who indulged themselves in drink and who

[36] *Ibid.*

sought, by this means, to corrupt others. The "terrorists," thus, could have used him, which was why the assembly regarded men of this stamp partisans of tyranny. The Committee of General Security found these explanations convincing and ordered his provisional freedom under surveillance of the section. After a request by Roger for full liberty so that he might return to his trade, the Committee agreed and ordered his rearmament.[37]

There is less information on other members of the committee, although their character and ability were assessed by the civil committee when it presented candidates for its own replacement to the Legislative Committee of the Convention. Adrien-Désiré Thiébart père, an elector of district Blancs-Manteaux in April 1789, was forty-six years old in 1793, residing on rue Mauvais-Garçons.[38] Employed as a bailiff appraiser (*huissier-priseur*), he was described by the civil committee as "intelligent and honest."[39] His son, Louis-Pierre Thiébart fils, was a signatory to the list of 13-14 July, living in the home of his father.[40] At the time when he was appointed a national agent (3 vendémiaire, Year III–24 September 1794) he had moved to rue Vieille-du-Temple. Thiébart fils lived off his investments and was described as "blunt in manner" (*brusque main grand*) and a good worker. Of the two Thiébarts, the younger was the more active politically.[41]

Paul-Henri Pollet, the school teacher who sat briefly as the section's commissioner on the revolutionary General Council of 10 August, was elected to the Commune on 17 August 1792. Among the first to be appointed to the civil committee, he continued to serve on it until its last days in 1795. His colleagues described him as "intelligent and

[37] *Ibid.* He was released provisionally on 1 thermidor, Year III (19 July 1795) and was given definitive freedom on 14 thermidor (1 August). In A.N., F7* 699 for the Year III Roger is identified as both cabinetmaker and a justice of the peace. He was a participant in the affair connected with the removal of the bust of Marat on 20 pluviôse, Year III (8 February 1795), discussed above.

[38] B.H.V.P., 100.65 (28), *Cahier d'instruction*, lists Thiébart as an *avocat* and a *huissier priseur* residing on rue de Singes, but fails to give his first name. A.N., F7 4775[28], d. 2. This is a certificate of residence of 3 pluviôse, Year II (22 January 1794) giving his age and residence. The second document, dated 10 nivôse, Year II (30 December 1793), testifies that he was not on the list of émigrés arrested.

[39] A.N., D III, 256[3], d. 10, pc. 41. His first name is given *ibid.*, pc. 60.

[40] His name was spelled Thiébard on the list, living at 23 rue Mauvais-Garçons. B.H.V.P., MS 742.

[41] A.N., D III, 256[3], d. 10, pc. 41.

honest."[42] Another signatory of the 13-14 July list for the militia was Gabriel-Christophe-Agnet Rossignol, established on rue des Juifs, and living off his investments. He, too, was described as being "exact and honest."[43] François-Jacques Richebourg, forty-six years old, resided on rue des Mauvais-Garçons, and was employed as a bailiff-appraiser. Upon the death of Claude-Charles Pointard on 15 September 1795, he became justice of the peace. His colleagues praised him as "a man correct with everyone [*propre à tout*, literally, correct with everything], and a great worker."[44]

Jean Ponsard was established on rue Vieille-du-Temple and was described as "of little education." As was seen above, he was arrested after presenting himself to the revolutionary committee, to whom he admitted that he had "mistakenly" taken the oath of allegiance to the Commune on the 9th of thermidor.[45] Jean-François Millet was thirty-eight years old, residing on rue Saint-Antoine. He was one of the electors of the section in the fall of 1792 and was appointed as clerk of the civil court of the 4th arrondissement. Arrested by the Thermidorians of the general assembly after the failure of the insurrection of prairial, he was charged with having "presided over all revolutions up to the 9th of thermidor," an exaggeration the assembly must have been aware of.[46]

Dassin was a painter who lived on rue des Mauvais-Garçons, had served on the revolutionary committee, and was active in the popular society of the section. After the insurrection of prairial, according to the *procès-verbal*, "at the mere mention of his name the assembly rose spontaneously, wanting no discussion, reflecting its profound indignation" because of his alleged role in denouncing so many "honest

[42] A.N., D III, 256³, d. 10, pc. 41; A. de P., 4 AZ 356, 19 December 1792; and 4 AZ 356, 5e jour sans-culottide, Year III (21 September 1795). His name is spelled occasionally as Paulet. His residence is given as no. 36 rue des Droits-de-l'Homme except in A.N., D III, 254, d. 4, pc. 5, a placard, where his address appears as no. 12 rue Roi-de-Sicile.

[43] B.H.V.P., MS 742. A.N., D III, 256³, d. 10, pc. 41.

[44] A.N., F¹ᵇ II, Seine 18; A.N., D III, 256³, d. 10, pc. 41; Charavay, *Assemblée electorale*, I, 48; II, 41.

[45] A.N., F⁷ 4774⁷⁹, d. 2, 16 thermidor, Year II (3 August 1794). Occasionally, his name is spelled Poinsard. See his role on the 9th of thermidor.

[46] A.N., F⁷ 4774⁴⁵ (dossier André Michel), 5 prairial, Year III (24 May 1795). Charavay, *Assemblée électorale*, III, 53.

citizens" who had perished on the guillotine. This hostility was undoubtedly due to his membership on the section's revolutionary committee, rather than on the civil committee. He was charged with being allied with the Jacobins and the insurrectionary Commune on 9 thermidor and of having boasted that he had the power to guillotine anyone he wished. The Thermidorian police described him as a former "agitator" until the 9th of thermidor, since which he had become "less turbulent."[47]

In contrast to the pro-Jacobin Dassin was Bonaventure-Hippolyte Hubert (Cheval-de-Saint Hubert), who was installed on rue Saint-Antoine; he was forty years old and a collector of *rentes* by profession. On 3 April 1794 he resigned as representative to the Commune, protesting that he had never been a noble, nor had ever supported the nobility. The general assembly highly praised his past contributions as president, member of the civil committee, participant in the popular society, and as a juror. Expressing its regret that he was leaving Paris, it resolved that he had the esteem of the section as it granted him a certificate of civic conduct.[48]

Another artisan was Jean-Baptiste-François Sauvegrain, thirty-nine years of age and a master butcher by occupation, residing in his shop in the market Saint-Jean. He had donated 31 livres to the Legislative Assembly as a patriotic gift (14 June 1792), and later complained that he had been accused of bad faith in signing a seditious petition. Sauvegrain served as an elector for the Convention from his section (27 August 1792),[49] and the following month wrote to "the wise Roland" suggesting that the Convention prohibit the sale of meat three days a week in order to solve the food crisis. Roland replied politely that although the proposal had merit it would not work, as buyers would simply stock up on the eve of prohibited days.[50]

---

[47] B.V.C., MS 120, fol. 162, 5 prairial (24 May 1795), A.N., F⁷ 4774⁴⁵; A.N., F¹ᵇ II, Seine 18; A.N., F⁷* 699; A.N., F⁷ 4748, d. 2, 5 pluviôse, Year III (24 January 1795). A.N., F³⁰ 145 gives his profession and address as no. 20 Mauvais-Garçons.

[48] B.V.C., MS 120, fol. 158; Charavay, *Assemblée électorale*, III, 52.

[49] A.N., B I, 14, "Extrait des registres de délibération de la section des Droits-de-l'Homme convoquée primaire le 27 août, l'an 4eme de la liberté de 1ere de l'égalité." This was signed by Bazard, president, 28 August 1792. Charavay, *Assemblée électorale*, III, 53.

[50] A.N., F¹¹ 218, 26 September 1792.

Jean-Claude Vaubertrand was a clerk in Sainte-Pelagie prison, age thirty-three, residing on rue Roi-de-Sicile. He had been an elector of district Petit-Saint-Antoine in April 1789, was an assessor to the justice of the peace in the section, and filled the post of secretary of the assembly during the riots of 25 February 1793.[51] In 1792, he, too, served as an elector. Another elector of 1792 was Jean-Baptiste Gagnier, thirty-five years old, a grocer living on rue Saint-Antoine.[52] Charles-Denis Saulnier was an elector of district Petit-Saint-Antoine in April 1789, and was probably a signer of the militia list of 13-14 July. He resided on rue des Mauvais-Garçons and was employed as a bailiff in the police court of appeals of the Paris department. Although reelected to the civil committee in the Year III, he was forced to resign because he could no longer carry out his duties as both commissioner of the committee and as bailiff of the court, he wrote.[53]

Saulnier wrote a critique of the practice of holding a plurality of offices, pointing out in his letter to the Committee of General Security that a number of persons had concentrated several functions under one head, which, although it did not appear incompatible with the law, still could be prejudicial to public affairs. In Paris, he contended, zealous republicans had been entrusted with a variety of functions—judges, assessors, members of civil and welfare committees. Military functions were also concentrated in a few hands. The Convention should decree, he suggested, that those who held several positions that required their presence at the same time should resign from one or several of them and their places be filled by others.[54] There is no indication that the Committee took notice of his suggestion, however.

Among the last group was Charles Boussière, a *procureur au parlement*, established on rue des Juifs, and described as "educated and

---

[51] Charavay, *Assemblée électorale*, III, 54; B.N., MSS, Nouv. acq. fr. 2716, fol. 65.

[52] Charavay, *Assemblée électorale*, III, 53.

[53] A.N., D III, 256³, d. 10, pcs. 32, 33; 1, 3 messidor, Year III (19, 21 June 1795); *ibid.*, D III, 254, d. 4, pc. 5, a placard that gives his address as no. 17 rue des Mauvais-Garçons; A.N., F¹ᵇ II, Seine 18. There is a Charles-Denis Saunier, a *huissier à cheval*, who lived at no. 17 Mauvais-Garçons, on the list of 13-14 July. He could have been the Saulnier in question. B.H.V.P., MS 742.

[54] A.N., F⁷ 4775¹⁴, d. 1. "I may be mistaken," he apologized, "but my concern is that of a true republican." Saulnier signed himself simply as a citizen of section Droits-de-l'Homme.

honest."[55] He had served as an elector in April 1789 from district Petit-Saint-Antoine, was on the section's welfare committee, and was appointed to the Bureau of Emigré Estates. In contrast to him was Louis-Jean Ladoubé, a wine merchant, who lived on rue Bar-de-Bec and termed ironically as "good in his business of wine and without much understanding of affairs of the committee."[56] Another member of the liberal profession was Pierre Michon, fifty-five years old, a collector of *rentes*, residing on rue des Droits-de-l'Homme. He served on the Central Commission of Welfare sitting in the Palace of Justice, but resigned from the civil committee because of ill health.[57] Finally, four names appear on the list in the fall of 1793 for whom there is no information. It is probable that although their names were submitted they did not serve on the committee.[58]

After the fall of Robespierre, the membership and social composition hardly changed, reflecting the technical and nonpolitical nature of the civil committee. Among the new members was a glazier, a public health officer, a notary, an assistant to the justice of the peace, and a former attorney.[59] Jean-Nicolas Lambin had resigned as a mem-

---

[55] A.N., F[1b] II, Seine 18; A.N., D III, 256³, d. 10, pc. 41. There was a Le Boursier who was a member of the civil committee residing at no. 1 rue Pavée; there is no indication that he was a different person from Boussière despite the difference in spelling. He was listed as an *assesseur* on a placard in A.N., D III, 254, d. 4, pc. 5. Another source lists Le Boursier, the *assesseur*, as an architect by profession. A.N., D III, 254, d. 4, pc. 10, 3 frimaire, Year III (23 November 1794).

[56] A.N., D III, 256³, d. 10, pc. 41; A.N., F[1b] II, Seine 18. The reference in A. de P., 4 AZ 1233 spells his name as Ladoubée.

[57] A.N. F[1b] II, Seine 18; A.N., D III, 256³, d. 10, pc. 68, 1 floréal, Year III (9 April 1795). Michon explained in a letter to Aumont, of the Civil and Police Administration, that he was confined to his room. His illness was verified by Cosson, surgeon and public health officer, and countersigned by Lelorgne and Lepin for the committee. A.N., D III, 255-256¹, d. 3, pcs. 48, 49, 50.

[58] These are Alexandre, Martin, Groux, and Ravel. Descombes is discussed at some length in the next chapter on the revolutionary committee. On 21 nivôse, Year II (10 January 1794), the popular society of the section was asked by the general assembly to present a list of eight candidates as replacements for the civil committee. The society named a number of candidates, some of whom became members of the committee. B.H.V.P., MS 748, fol. 121. See further reference to this in the chapter on the popular society.

[59] A.N., F[1b] II, Seine 18, 4e jour sans-culottide, Year II (20 September 1794). Jean-Pierre Doublet, a glazier residing on rue Bourg-Tibourg, was also a member of the welfare committee. Dufour, the public health officer and surgeon, surrendered

ber in order to apply for the newly created post of secretary. The committee endorsed his petition and shortly thereafter he assumed his new duties.[60] In late December and early January (1794-1795), a number of replacements were made. Among them were two *avocats*, a *receveur des rentes*, and a former *substitut* at the Châtelet.[61] In each case the civil

his post because he was too busy ministering to his patients. Fillon, *Autographes*, p. 66, no. 547, item #7. Faugé was a notary who served as secretary of the general assembly during its important session of 31 May 1793. He resigned from the committee in September 1794. B.H.V.P., MS 748, fol. 58, 6 brumaire, Year III (27 October 1794). Folles was an assistant to the justice of the peace, residing at no. 32 rue des Droits-de-l'Homme. The committee made no observation on his character, possibly because it had had no time to become acquainted with him. A.N., F^1b II, Seine 18. Jacques-Guillaume-Gabriel Chappe, an attorney, had been proposed for the committee on 3 nivôse, Year III (23 December 1794) by the Committee of Legislation. A.N., D III, 256³, d. 10, pc. 34. He served as president in floréal, Year III (May 1795).

    [60] *Ibid.*, pcs. 19 and 20, 16 messidor, Year III (4 June 1795).

    [61] A.N., D III, 255-256¹, d. 3, pc. 2, frimaire, Year III (November-December 1794), and A.N., D III, 256³, d. 10. Porcher was an *avocat* residing on rue Vieille-du-Temple, and had been an elector from Blancs-Manteaux. He was characterized by the committee as "educated and fit for any duty." At the time of his departure from the committee (about 5 March 1795), Porcher was a judge. The civil committee replaced him on 12 pluviôse, Year III (31 January 1795), *ibid.*, pc. 30. B.H.V.P., 100.65 (28), *Cahier d'instruction*.

    Louis-Joachim Lelorgne (or Le Lorgne) was a national agent, a *receveur des rentes* by profession, residing on rue Bourg-Tibourg, and dubbed "very limited." He had been an elector in April 1789 from district Blancs-Manteaux. Boulanger was a former *substitut* at the Châtelet, residing on rue des Billettes. His name appears on the list published by the Committee of Legislation in A.N., D III, 255-256¹, d. 3, pc. 182, "Noms des citoyens presentés par la comité de législation, pour completer le comité civil de la section des Droits-de-l'Homme." Although this document is undated, under section Cha(s)lier the date "Frimaire l'an III," p. 8, appears. The same is true of the list in B.N., Lc³⁸ 1090-1095. There is one difference between the two documents in reference to section Droits-de-l'Homme. In the former, the name of Pollet is stricken out in ink and "Guyet homme de loi rue Tiron No.6" is written in. The latter document allows the name of Pollet to appear as printed.

    Guyet was an *avocat* and judge residing on rue Tiron. He served in the latter capacity during the winter of 1794. The committee wrote that he was "educated and fit for any duty." (He could have been Jean-Baptiste-François Guyet, former *avocat au parlement* and an elector of Petit-Saint-Antoine in April 1789.) A.N., D III, 256³, d. 10, pc. 41. To Porcher, Lelorgne, Boulanger, and Guyet the Committee of Legislation added eight others: Ladoubé, Thiébart père, Hardy, Richebourg, Rossignol, Thiébart fils, Boussière, and Doublet. A.N., D III, 255-256¹, d. 3, pcs. 2 and 182; B.N., Lc³⁸ 1090-1095. Thiébart fils resigned because of ill health on 27 nivôse, Year

committee was asked to find replacements among men known "for their morality, their civic conduct, and their talents."[62]

By the end of January the General Council presented six names to the Committee of Legislation.[63] Their ages and occupations reflect a general conservative trend evident in the section after thermidor. It is apparent that until the dissolution of the Convention the personnel of the committee remained quite stable, as it continued to characterize candidates and members not in political terms but by psychological traits. Such expressions as "a good citizen," "an honest man," or "educated and honest" abound.[64] Did the committee use these cap-

III (16 January 1795), his resignation being accepted a week later. A.N. D III, 255-256[1], d. 10, pcs. 56, 57, 58. These include testimonials of Truchon, the public health officer, and are countersigned by members of the committee, Rossignol and Guyet. B.H.V.P., MS 748, fol. 60, 5 pluviôse, Year III (24 January 1795).

[62] 5 pluviôse, Year III (24 January 1795). Porcher, Guyet, and Thiébart (fils?) resigned on 12 pluviôse, Year III (31 January 1795). A.N., D III, 256[3], d. 10, pc. 30.

[63] Ibid., pc. 31, 7 pluviôse, Year III (26 January 1795).

[64] Ibid., pc. 41. The ages of a number of the commissioners appear ibid., pc. 68, 1 floréal, Year III (9 April 1795). The conversion of Lambin from commissioner to a paid secretary made for sixteen members, twelve of whom now served at a time. The following left the committee: Thiébart fils, Ladoubé, Porcher; Gamain, the patissier, described as "a good commissioner, but not being able to write except his name"; Guyet, Richebourg, and Doublet. Ibid., pc. 41.

By March 1795 the committee consisted of the following: Pollet; Chappe, characterized as "a good citizen"; Jambon, a wigmaker, age 45, residing on rue des Billettes, described as an "honest man and of little education"; Ponsard; Regnault fils, residing on rue Pavée, characterized as "intelligent and honest"; Gaillard, described as "an honest man"; Claude Dupré, 50 years old, a house painter, and an elector from Petit-Saint-Antoine in April 1789, residing on rue de la Verrerie. The committee paid him the compliment of observing that he had acquitted himself "perfectly of all functions confined to him by the section." Henry-Noël Lepin, age 58, a former phamacist, was described as "a good citizen"; Henry Dervin, age 33, a former bailiff-appraiser, was called "an honest man"; Jean-Jacques Blacque, age 63 was "educated and honest"; Pierre-Jean-Baptiste Latourneur (La Tourneur), age 49, a chandler, was "an honest man." The others, mentioned above, were Thiébart père, Hardy, Rossignol, Boussière, and Lelorgne. Jean-Nicolas Lambin, as pointed out above, became secretary of the committee. He, too, was described as "an honest man."

When a quarter of the committee was renewed the following month, the members proposed were Jambon; Dupré; Jacques Dommanget, age 36, a former procureur at the Châtelet; Antoine Jolly, age 60, a former bailiff-appraiser and elector in April 1789 from district Blanes-Manteaux; Michon; and Rémy Bigot, age 50, a former

tions to avoid taking a political position? It is conceivable that this, indeed, was so. More likely, however, it was an expression of the way the committee regarded its members—efficient or non-efficient, educated or ignorant, devoted or indifferent—another indication of its relatively technical nature. It should be noted that the employment of the term *hommes probes* by the committee differs sharply from the pejorative denomination *honnêtes gens*, resented so bitterly by the *sans-culottes*. This would not have prevented them, of course, from being the "honorable gentlemen" despised by the militant revolutionaries.[65]

Among the many functions performed by the civil committee, the granting or refusal of certificates of civic conduct was one of the more important.[66] Their possession assured the bearer that his patriotism and devotion to the Revolution were formally acknowledged and that he was entitled, therefore, to all rights and privileges appertaining to such recognition. Lack of such testimonial deprived him of the right to practice his profession or occupation, and excluded him from all public posts. Furthermore, denial of this evidence made the individual subject to all the harassment imposed on priests and ex-nobles, which during periods of tension and fear could be a heavy burden indeed.[67]

employé. All six were nominated by the general assembly of the section and show a continuing conservative trend. *Ibid.*, pc. 68, 1 floréal, Year III (20 April 1795).

On the eve of the dissolution of the Convention the committee consisted of the following: Michon, Blondel, Jolly, Chappe, Gaillard, Bigot, Dervin, François-Nicolas Chalour, Doublet, Lelorgne, Lepin, Dommanget, Lambin (secretary), and Pierre-Louis Piault.

[65] A.N., C 271, pl. 666, pc. 27, 8 September 1793, "Adresse de la société des sans-culottes de Beaucaire amis de la Constitution à la Convention nationale," in which the members boast of being "poor and virtuous" and of knowing their friends who had delivered them from the nobility, clergy, and feudality, "those whom the aristocrats call anarchists, factious, Maratists; we also know our enemies, those who are called *honnêtes gens*, the friends of law and order." After 2 June 1793 they began to use the term *honnêtes gens* ironically to describe moderates. Soboul, p. 414.

[66] B.H.V.P., MS 748, fols. 139-192 (beginning with 11 January 1794), contain lists of citizens examined by the civil committee of the section. Although the power to issue these certificates was a prerogative of the revolutionary committee until 14 vendémiaire, Year III (5 October 1794) (Article 1), I am treating this development, for purposes of continuity, under the civil committee.

[67] A.N., F⁷ 7461, d. 4, Louis-Marie Lambin protested the refusal of the revolutionary committee of section Droits-de-l'Homme to grant him a certificate of civic conduct because he had not taken up arms on an unspecified date. He explained that he had been collecting rent due on that day, but had reported to his quarter and was with his patrol until 11 a.m., when he was dismissed with the others.

Before granting such a certificate the committee would pose questions to the applicant such as the following:

For what purpose do you request a certificate of civic conduct?
Show your receipt of patriotic contributions.
Show your receipt of personal taxes.
Show your certificate of service in the National Guard.
What have you done for the Revolution?[68]

Upon satisfying the members that the applicant was indeed a good and trustworthy patriot, a certificate of his *civisme* was duly delivered.[69] Another document was then drafted which bore a description of the citizen to whom the testimonial had been granted. Residents of the section at times submitted to a scrutiny by their general assembly before receiving the coveted voucher; on occasion the Jacobin Club, the Cordeliers, and the popular societies of a section were called upon to examine the civic conduct of employees in various administrations.[70] Occasionally a civic card was included in a police dossier as evidence of a prisoner's probity and patriotism.[71]

Replacement of a lost civic card required the appearance of two witnesses before the revolutionary committee (later before the civil committee), who affirmed upon oath that the bearer would not abuse the privilege of such card if reissued. The petitioner and his witnesses then signed a formal statement to this effect in the presence of the committee.[72] Citizens making application for their civic cards were required to announce their request in advance so that their names might appear on a list to be presented before the general assembly of the section. After the revolutionary committee examined the list, and

[68] A.N., F⁷* 2498, p. 56, 6 vendémiaire, Year II (27 September 1793). Although this is extracted from the section's revolutionary committee, the questions asked by the civil committee were similar in nature.

[69] B.H.V.P., MS 748, fol. 59. On 27 vendémiaire, Year III (18 October 1794), the civil committee requested a printed form for these certificates. A.N., D III, 256³, d. 10, pcs. 23, 24, 25.

[70] *Ibid.*, fol. 138, 20 messidor, Year II (8 July 1794).

[71] A.N., F⁷ 4774³⁷, d. 1, 27 January 1793. Jean-Baptiste Martin was employed at the National Lottery. His certificate was signed by Vaubertrand, secretary, and Le Roy, clerk.

[72] A.N., F⁷* 2498, p. 49, 30 vendémiaire, Year III (21 October 1794); B.H.V.P., MS 748, fol. 66, 2 pluviôse, Year III (21 January 1795).

Figure 7. Certificate of Residence

if no objection was raised, they were accorded the permit.[73] The civil committee also gave certificates that persons were not on the list of émigrés issued by the department.[74]

In addition to certificates of civic conduct, inhabitants of the section were furnished with evidence of residence, or, if they had lived at their present address for less than six months, a certificate of presence. Witnesses and signatures were needed and the document was registered with the police.[75] The following month this decree was supplemented by another providing for delivery of these warrants by committees of the section who were to appoint two commissioners to take charge of this regulation. Lodging houses were required to keep a register of their guests, including those staying overnight.[76] The affidavit itself carried the heading "Commune of Paris"; below was "Certificate of Residence," and beside it the words "Delivered Free." Then followed a declaration of the president and commissioners of the section referring to decrees of the National Assembly of 24 June, 13 December 1791, and 31 March 1792, and conforming to the decree of the General Council of the Commune of 26 June 1791 and of the municipal body of 9 April 1792. This was followed by the names and addresses of two witnesses together with the name, age, address, and description of the person applying, and the duration of residence at his present address. The document was signed by the applicant, the witnesses, the president, commissioner, and secretary-registrar of the section, and countersigned by a municipal officer and a secretary-registrar of the municipality.[77]

[73] See the list for 20 and 29 prairial, and 5, 10, 14, and 15 messidor, Year II (17, 18, 23, 28 June, and 2 and 3 July 1794) in A. de P., 3 AZ 287, fols. 43-50; and for 27 brumaire and 8 frimaire, Year III (17 October and 28 November 1794).

[74] A.N., F⁷ 4665, d. 2, Henry Edme Decomble, former tapestry weaver, 3 prairial, Year II (22 May 1794), residing at 117 rue Vieille-du-Temple.

[75] A. de P., 1 AZ 145, *Arrêté concernant la délivrance des certificats de résidence et de présence dans la Ville de Paris*, 9 April 1792, 4 pp., 6 articles. Article 2 provided for certificates of presence.

[76] *Ibid.*, 10 May 1792, 7 pp., in nine articles. Article II dealt with delivery of the certificates; Article IV provided for the maintenance of registers in which entries had to be made consecutively. The need to keep records for overnight guests was underscored in this article.

[77] See, for example, the certificate of Anne-Catherine-Henriette Bernard, widow Duport, of section Droits-de-l'Homme in A.N., F⁷ 4595, d. 1, 26 nivôse, Year II (15 January 1794); also a blank form in B.H.V.P., MS 748, fol. 46.

Citizens were also furnished with vouchers authorizing them to vote in assemblies of the section and as proof of their having taken the prescribed oath provided by the law of 10 August.[78] During the period of the *censitaire* (the property requirement for exercising the suffrage), those active citizens who had enrolled in the National Guard had their own writ.[79] Passports, which during moments of tension or panic were difficult to procure, were issued to applicants if they aroused no suspicion. The document carried the heading of the department, commune, and the section, the latter written in. Then came the statement that it was being delivered in execution of the law of 28 March 1792 (old style) followed by the date of the new, revolutionary calendar. Below this appeared the name of the bearer, his occupation, and address, followed by his physical description.[80] Still another type of personal document was issued by the civil committee to an individual desiring to work in gathering the harvest. The citizen was fully described and his destination given. The president and secretary of the section signed the document, stating that it was being issued in conformity with article 5 of the decree of 19 thermidor, Year II (6 August 1794) of the Committee of Public Safety.[81] A forced loan was also recorded on a form under the heading of "Commission of Direct Contributions of the Commune of Paris" that was addressed to the president of the civil committee.[82] Among the more popular vouchers were those authorizing an individual to purchase a certain amount of soap or cords of wood. The certificate read as follows: date, section, number of certificate, applicant, occupation, street, quantity to be delivered for purchase, date issued by civil committee, and signatures.[83]

[78] B.N., Lb[40] 1794, contains a permit to vote in assemblies of section Droits-de-l'Homme for Marie-François-Maris l'Hommandie, residing at 70 rue Saint Antoine.

[79] B.N., Lb[40] 2104 (reservé), unmarked and in a perfect state of preservation for section Roi-de-Sicile. It reads "Inscription of Active Citizen, for Service in the National Guard . . . street . . . 179—" A number is provided on the left side, above the name of the section.

[80] B.H.V.P., MS 748, fol. 49, a passport issued to Denis-Joseph Grodard, a wine merchant.

[81] B.N., Lb[40] 1799, a certificate entitled "Comité civil de la section des Droits-de-l'Homme. Travaux pour les récoltes."

[82] B.H.V.P., MS 748, fol. 35, 11 pluviôse, Year III (30 January 1795).

[83] B.H.V.P., MS 754, fol. 49, 5 prairial, Year II (24 May 1794); MS 748, fol. 38.

In addition to administrative matters, the civil committee was charged with the important task of providing employment for the poor and the unemployed of the section. To this end it registered citizens to work on army uniforms, from shoes to overcoats, in shops scattered throughout the section.[84] The committee also examined reports of those charged with supervising the manufacture of army uniforms. Where merchandise appeared defective, it ordered the manufacturer to discontinue such work, and if it felt that he had monopolized the order, or was inefficient, it directed him to retail the employment among other shops. To make certain that all would be in order it did not hesitate to appoint its own members to supervise the work and the drafting of a report by the manufacturer for the section's general assembly.[85]

The quality of army shoes was also of interest to the civil committee. Cobblers had confessed that the condition of the leather used was simply not good enough for military purposes. Of the sixty-seven cobblers in the section inscribed with the committee, twenty-eight signed a letter requesting a better grade of leather for army use.[86] Six months later the committee examined the state of production among the sixty-seven cobblers upon request of the department, and was reminded shortly thereafter that the right of preemption was forbidden by decree of the Committee of Public Safety of 16 May 1793, the implication being that the purchase of shoes was to be left free. The committee was also asked to report the number of shoes in possession of the section's cobblers and to have them deposited in the warehouse of Trenel.[87]

Among other functions of the civil committee was the supervision of the curriculum in the primary schools, to which it sent commis-

[84] A.N., F7* 2497, unpaginated, 14 January 1793. The general assembly was addressed in a letter by the police administration that work on army overcoats was available. The assembly provided that a proclamation to this effect be issued on the morrow and that persons desiring to participate should register with the civil committee.

[85] B.H.V.P., MS 748, fol. 32, 10 February 1793. This abstract from the minutes of the committee's proceedings deal with a manufacturer by name of Baulard whose work was under question.

[86] A. de P., 4 AZ 356, 14 germinal, Year II (3 April 1794).

[87] Ibid., 6 vendémiaire, Year III (27 September 1794). B.H.V.P., MS 748, fol. 54, 7 pluviôse, Year III (26 January 1795).

sioners, and the examination of "the patriotic poor" who received government asssistance.[88] The collection of cord and twine no longer of use to individuals was also organized by the committee,[89] and it heard and ruled on requests for financial assistance of various persons who often brought supporting testimony.[90] Occasionally the committee had to verify the occupational status of individuals who addressed it for help in acquiring scarce raw materials needed in their craft.[91] Various bureaus addressed it also to verify dates when a certain sectional institution had been organized—its cannoneers, for example.[92] Finally, positions left vacant temporarily and requiring appointment of tried and capable patriots also came under the purview of the committee.[93]

Those unable or unwilling to serve personally in the National Guard were required to pay a tax as a substitute. It was this extra burden to older citizens that became the subject of complaints and requests for exemption. Since the law held that such contribution would be exacted only from those whose income was at least 1,500 livres per year, a number of supplicants sought to prove that their modest earnings exempted them from this tax. In addition to these were individuals who suffered physical disabilities, which if proven, excused them.[94]

[88] A. de P., 4 AZ 356, 20 messidor, Year II (8 July 1794).

[89] B.H.V.P., MS 748, fol. 54, 13 fructidor, Year II (30 August 1794), containing the appeal of the national agent to the section's civil committee; A. de P., 4 AZ 698, 15 fructidor, Year II (1 September 1794) is the appeal of the section's committee for citizens to deposit rope and string no longer needed.

[90] B.H.V.P., MS 748, fol. 47, 17 pluviôse, Year II (5 February 1794).

[91] A. de P., 4 AZ 356, 2 brumaire, Year III (23 October 1794), a letter by a grocer who also claimed to be a chandler and needed tallow to manufacture candles; ibid., 3 nivôse, Year III (23 December 1794), a letter of a carpenter, Galland, who needed candles in order to continue working or be forced to close his shop. The committee took no action on these requests.

[92] B.H.V.P., MS 748, fol. 56, 3 brumaire, Year III (24 October 1794), requested by the Bureau de l'organisation de l'artillerie.

[93] A. de P., 4 AZ 356, 3e sans-culottide, Year II (19 September 1794), a request by the Civil, Police, and Tribunal Commission.

[94] A. de P., 4 AZ 356, 9 pluviôse, Year III (28 January 1795), a memoir written to the civil committee by Jean-Félix Belu, a septuagenarian, requesting exemption as his income was only 1,136 livres for the year. The committee failed to excuse him. On the other hand, the committee excused a number of petitioners: Hamel, on 16 nivôse (5 January); Peck, on 15 pluviôse (3 February); Durand, on 21 pluviôse (9 February), and so on. Bertrand was excused because of a bad knee, 16 pluviôse, Year III (4 February 1795).

A petition reflecting the pathetic state of some suppliants, one with warm human appeal even today, is worth quoting in full:

> I have neither houses nor income; I am, thus, obliged to work for a living.
>
> I teach mathematics, geography, and history.
>
> The Revolution had deprived me of my students. Some retired to the country, others left France.
>
> I am in my 75th year; I suffer from asthma which torments me very much and deprives me of sleep. I have a hernia. In addition to this, it is three years since I was frightened by a clap of thunder (*que le Tonnere est tombé près de moi*) and by its concussion which deprived me of some intellectual faculties, memory, so essential to my profession, my hearing, and almost the use of my legs, so that I cannot work. The woman to whom I have been married for almost 51 years who is 73 years of age, has been attacked by a nervous illness, and for this reason, is unable to work. We have been obliged, therefore, to sell our possessions in order to live.
>
> Permit me to pose a hypothetical question. If a man is dependent solely upon his arms for a living, and if he loses them, he cannot exist. I am in the same state as such a workingman.
>
> The workman, whoever he may be, possesses more resources than I; he has his daily wages, paid him according to the cost of living. He has his youth and his strength. I am deprived of all these advantages.
>
> The committee has asked me to furnish two witnesses. I present it with Citizen Norin, my landlord of 24 years, and Citizen Cosson, my surgeon, who can only repeat and confirm what I have put forth.
>
> I appeal, therefore, citizen commissioners, to your prudence and justice, to exempt me from paying my military contribution, taking note of my sad situation, physical, as well as moral.[95]

On the eve of the hunger insurrection of 12 germinal 1795, the civil committee was empowered by the general assembly to distribute bread among inhabitants of other sections who were awaiting the re-

---

[95] A. de P., 4 AZ 356, written by Charpentier, 22 rue des Juifs, sometime in Year III. Richebourg, for the civil committee, in a marginal note, endorsed deliverance of the certificate of exemption.

newal of civic cards, asking, in return, that its fellow citizens of the section be accorded the same consideration.[96] A month later the Agency of Weights and Measures requested the committee to inform the general assembly, as well as the merchants and manufacturers in the section, of the provisions of the law of 18 germinal, Year III (7 April 1795)[97] on establishing a uniform system of weights and measures. It then addressed a number of questions to the committee, the answers to which could have been answered only by taking an exact census and inventory.[98]

Among requests to the civil committee were occasional appeals to be freed from the onerous duty of guarding effects placed under seal by the revolutionary committee, effects whose owners had been imprisoned. Maintenance of these seals and the continued duty to guard them made for inconvenience for an individual about to move to another dwelling. This was a power beyond the committee, however, which was forced to transmit the original petition to the Committee of General Security.[99] Veterans in quest of pensions also appeared before it, testifying to their army service, and bringing the necessary proofs in addition to witnesses residing in the section.[100]

Occasionally a note of irritation crept into replies of the civil committee as it was bombarded by various agencies and departments of the revolutionary government. The national agent, for example, wrote to the committee that he was astonished at their response to his inquiry on the state of passports in the section; it had dismissed his request with the scornful remark "that the Committee cannot occupy

[96] B.H.V.P., MS 748, fol. 127, 10 germinal, Year III (30 March 1795). Thiébart and Millet were authorized to inform section Indivisibilité of this decision. This was in joint meeting of the civil and welfare committees.

[97] Duvergier, VIII, 71-74, 28 articles.

[98] A. de P., 4 AZ 356, 15 floréal, Year III (4 May 1795), "L'Agence temporaire des poids et mesures."

[99] A.N., F⁷ 4661, d. 3, 16 messidor, Year III (4 July 1795), Dariencourt's appeal to the revolutionary committee of the 7th arrondissement for permission either to move the cabinet containing the papers of his father still in prison, or "better yet," to have the seals removed. There is no indication how the Committee of General Security ruled on this request.

[100] B.H.V.P., MS 754, fol. 51, 4 vendémiaire, Year IV (?) (26 September 1795), petition of Raymond Bordiers asking for a retirement pension. The endorsement of such a request by the civil committee presumably gave added strength to such an appeal.

itself with such useless work." Replying indignantly that "obedience to the law" could not be "useless work," he insisted upon an answer to his inquiry.[101] At times the Civil, Police, and Tribunal Administration berated the civil committee for negligence in carrying out its duties. People were forced to wait in line for hours before doors of merchants, it accused, because members of the committee who should have been present to supervise the distribution of merchandise failed to arrive in time.[102] Another complaint voiced by various agencies was the tardiness of the committee's replies to their many requests, letters, and bulletins. One explanation for this tardiness was surely the great pressure of work imposed on the committee. Michon, president of the committee, for example, asked the indulgence of the Civil Administration for not having submitted, as yet, the signatures of members of the committee requested by the agency. Explaining that he had to respond to all committees of the Convention as well as to all the different commissions, he simply lacked time to answer promptly as he alone was charged with this correspondence by the civil committee.[103]

Without the daily work of the civil committee, it is inconceivable that the municipal government could have managed its task alone. Had this institution not existed a similar one would have had to be created. Moreover, so long as the principle of decentralization and local autonomy prevailed, the committee continued to express it. It was only with its suppression by decree of the Convention on 19 vendémiaire, Year IV (11 October 1795) that whatever remnant of sectional independence still remained was finally ended.

Equally important, its membership represented stability and continuity in the section, whatever the changes in personnel. It is of some significance, surely, that of the sixteen original members who served on the committee, four had signed the militia list of 13-14 July of district Petit-Saint-Antoine. These signatories, Louis-Pierre Thiébart fils, Philippe (Jean) Hardy, Charles-Denis Saulnier (Saunier), and Ga-

[101] B.H.V.P., MS 748, fol. 67, 5 ventôse, Year III (23 February 1795).

[102] A.N., D III, 255-6¹, 4 pluviôse, Year III (22 February 1795). This is a printed document addressed to the civil committees of all the sections. The negligence noted above must have been common. This dossier contains numerous complaints of similar neglect.

[103] A.N., F¹ᵇ II, Seine 18, 13 vendémiaire, Year III (4 October 1794). This dossier contains many responses of other sections.

briel-Christophe-Agnet Rossignol could hardly be described as *sans-culottes*. Thiébart and Rossignol were *rentiers*, Hardy had been a master cobbler and an officer in the armed force before becoming a registrar in the police court, and Saulnier was a bailiff in the court of appeals. The others, as seen above, with the exception of Roger and Ponsard, were either members of a liberal profession or were property holders of one type or another. Thus, only Roger and Ponsard could be called *sans-culottes* in the traditional sense given this term by revolutionaries of the day.

The majority of the committee were relatively new men, since they do not appear until after the republic had been established. The fact that they failed to volunteer for the militia in July 1789 could be due to a variety of reasons, from the personal and social to the accidental and geographic. In any case, all these men had fixed dwellings, possessed skills, property, or a profession, and must have been known to their neighbors. They could well have expressed a certain class bias while, at the same time, have continued to defend the local interests of the section—there is no contradiction in this. Yet, as agents of a central political authority, the tendency of such an organ of administrative power, as we know, is to do its bidding. How better to impose a law or ordinance in a precinct than to have it applied by trusted men of the section? Here, too, the civil committee, oriented though it was toward administrative matters, played an important political role.

IX

The Revolutionary Committee

The destruction of the Old Regime ended the old police system in 1789 and gave way to the *comité permanent* of the Paris Commune. Police commissioners were suppressed on 4 August and on the 6th the newly established district committees were sanctioned by the Provisional Commune. On 21 October a *comité des recherches* (an investigating committee), was established with the right to interrogate and arrest suspects, a function that it continued to perform until 1 October 1791. The municipal law of May-June 1790, Title IV, granted police powers to commissioners acting jointly with their civil committees. In February 1791 these powers were placed under the departments,[1] and after the overthrow of the king municipalities were given police authority of a general nature.[2] By the fall of 1792 section Droits-de-l'Homme, for example, was ordered by the Department of Police to arrest certain individuals designated as suspects by the minister of war.[3]

The Convention formally decreed the establishment of revolutionary committees on 21 March 1793, though they had been launched by a number of sections months earlier.[4] The law provided for the surveillance of foreign residents or enemy aliens, and demanded proof of their good conduct. Composed of twelve members and six assistants elected by simple plurality of the voters in each section, the committees excluded certain categories in advance—ecclesiastics, former no-

[1] Mellié, pp. 178-179.

[2] Duvergier, IV, 295-296, 11 August-30 September 1792. Even before 10 August there were demands for sectional surveillance committees. A.N., D III, 251-252, d. 5, pc. 15, 28 May 1792 contains numerous signatures to a petition urging the above.

[3] B.N., MSS, Nouv. acq. fr. 2691, fol. 222, 15 November 1792.

[4] Mellié, pp. 178-180. The first one seems to have been that of section Amis-de-la-Patrie, 14 August 1792, followed by that of Postes, 21 August 1792.

blemen, seigneurs, or their agents.[5] These committees assumed their functions a week later, 28 March 1793.

The decree against foreigners was followed by one against suspects on 17 September 1793, which extended immeasurably the committees' jurisdiction.[6] They were now authorized to issue warrants of arrest and to seal the papers of a broad category of men and women loosely defined as "suspected persons." The new authority and the provision that they correspond directly with the Committee of General Security tended to make them independent of the Commune, and even of their sectional assemblies. At the same time, it converted them gradually into organs of centralization of the revolutionary government so that eventually they became powerful enough to control the political life of the section. This tendency was strengthened by the law of 14 frimaire, Year II (4 December 1793).[7] Whatever independence they still possessed while they remained unsalaried ceased when they became paid functionaries of the government. On 12 July 1793, the Committee of Public Safety of the Paris department accorded each member 3 livres per day, and paid their office expenses.[8] Shortly thereafter the Convention's Committee of Public Safety deposited 50,000 livres with the mayor for "the less fortunate members of the committees of surveillance."[9] On 5 September 1793, the Convention decreed the 3 livres per day for all, raised to 5 livres on 18 brumaire, Year II (8 November 1793).[10]

Local authorities were not pleased to see the growing alienation between the revolutionary committees and themselves. Pache, for ex-

[5] Duvergier, V, 206-207 in thirteen articles. A.P., LX, 389-390, reported on by Jean Debry (of Aisne) for the diplomatic committee.

[6] Duvergier, VI, 172-173 in ten articles; A.P., LXXIV, 303-304.

[7] Duvergier, VI, 317-322; A.P., LXXX, 629-635; B. & R., XXX, 254-266. See especially Section II, Articles 8, 9, 14, 16, 17, and Section III, Article 7. For an analysis of revolutionary institutions written with clarity and perception see Jacques Godechot, Les Institutions de la France sous la Révolution et l'Empire (Paris, 1951), where the role of revolutionary committees is discussed, pp. 291-297, passim. See also Sirich, The Revolutionary Committees.

[8] Mellié, p. 209.

[9] François V. A. Aulard, ed., Recueil des Actes du Comité de salut public . . . (Paris, 1889-1918), V, 497. This was on 7 August.

[10] Duvergier, VI, 147, 280. These decrees are only mentioned, not given. A.P., LXXVIII, 593-594, for the latter after a report of the Finance Committee of the Convention.

ample, requested that they continue their correspondence with the Commune on all matters except the arrest of suspects.[11] A more dramatic, if equally futile attempt, was made by Chaumette on the very eve of enacting the decree of 14 frimaire, which subordinated local authorities to national agents.[12] The destruction of the Hébertists hastened the process of depriving local officials of whatever influence they still retained over their committees. The Committee of Public Safety now began to appoint their members, an act that undermined still further the remnants of those democratic procedures which yet remained. Protests of the general assemblies were simply ignored by the government. After being made independent of sectional authority, the new revolutionary committees began persecuting militant *sans-culottes* for refusing to accept their tutelage over the assemblies, denouncing them as Hébertists and clubbists.[13] Prior to the adoption of the law of 7 fructidor, Year II (31 August 1794), which reorganized the revolutionary committees of Paris, the debate in the Convention illustrates the need of the Thermidorians to maintain the essential features of a centralized government and, at the same time, to domesticate local administrations under their control. This was done by reducing the committees to one for every four sections under twelve arrondissements, limiting their powers, and changing their social composition.[14]

The Thermidorians roundly condemned proposals like those of section Muséum for "the people" to elect members of the committees, and applauded vigorously addresses of those sections like Mutius Scae-

[11] 27 brumaire, Year II (17 November 1793), cited by Mellié, pp. 216-217.

[12] Duvergier, VI, 318-319, Section II, Articles 14-17. Chaumette reminded the committees that it was the Commune that had obtained them their salaries from the Convention. "The revolutionary committees are an emanation of the Commune; they must not separate themselves from it," he pleaded. On the morning of 4 December, before the convoked members of revolutionary committees could open their meeting in the Hôtel de Ville, the Convention decreed a penalty of ten years' imprisonment for any member of a constituted authority who dared to meet in an unauthorized convocation. The proposed defiance of the Commune collapsed without a blow. B. & R., XXX, 306, 309.

[13] Tønnesson, p. 32.

[14] *Moniteur*, XXI, no. 332, pp. 525-527, 2 fructidor, Year II (19 August 1794); pp. 548-550, 5 fructidor (22 August); no. 339, pp. 581-583, 9 fructidor (26 August).

vola, who dissociated themselves from Muséum's design.[15] On 27 prairial, Year III (15 June 1795), the Convention suppressed the word "revolutionary" from application to public establishments and institutions.[16] Once again, as at their beginning, the revolutionary committees became known as surveillance committees.

Even before they were established by law, a number of them had begun to adopt a regular procedure as to time of meeting, place, division of functions among members, and the keeping of minutes. While some members, for example, took charge of delivering civic cards, others interested themselves in the arrest and interrogation of suspects.[17] The revolutionary committee of section Droits-de-l'Homme began meeting on 28 March 1793 and keeping a register of its proceedings, its last entry being that of 15 brumaire, Year IV (5 November 1795), thus maintaining an unbroken record of two years and seven months.[18]

Members of the revolutionary committees tended to be from the lower ranks of the *sans-culottes*, unlike their confreres of the civil committees. Of the 454 commissioners whose vocations are known, only 4.6 percent lived off their capital or property, in contrast to the 26.2 percent of the civil committee. Wage-workers or former domestics numbered 23 or 9.9 percent, whereas, members of the liberal professions made up 10.5 percent. The great majority were craftsmen and shopkeepers, who together numbered 290 or 63.8 percent; of this total 45.3 percent were artisans. Many accepted positions on the committee because the Revolution had destroyed their former occupations—as wigmakers, shoemakers, or domestics.[19]

Although it is difficult to give a precise analysis of the social composition of the revolutionary committee in section Droits-de-l'Homme

[15] *Ibid.*, XXI, no. 343, pp. 610-612, 13 fructidor, Year II (30 August 1794). This is discussed at greater length in the chapter on the popular societies below.

[16] *Ibid.*, XXIV, no. 267, p. 682.

[17] Soboul, pp. 610-612.

[18] A.N., F7* 2497 is a journal of 146 pages that begins with 28 March 1793 and is concluded on the 2d *sans-culottide*, Year II (18 September 1794). This register is formally closed the next day. The second journal begins on the 4th complementary day, Year II (20 September 1794), and runs for 409 pages. The last entry is for 15 brumaire, Year IV (5 November 1795). This second register is designated under A.N., F7* 2498.

[19] Soboul, pp. 444-446, 447.

(especially in its early stages) because not all members listed their occupation, sufficient information exists to make possible a tentative analysis. The largest group, as that of the capital as a whole, is that of the artisans and shopkeepers. It is not always possible to separate the two because the craftsman was so often a small retailer as well. The first committee numbered nine artisans and retailers: Duclos, a wigmaker; Dupaumier and Guéneau, jewelers; Houdaille, a merchant-jeweler; Cordier, a caterer; Temponnet (or Tamponnet), a mason-en-trepreneur; Charbonnier, a shoemaker; Mazin, an upholsterer; and Eude, a clockmaker. Six of the above were artisans, whereas three were craftsmen-merchants (Houdaille, Cordier, and Temponnet).[20] Five members were of the liberal professions: Descombes, a schoolmaster (master of languages); Pommer (or Pommez), a surgeon-dentist; two painters, Bernard and Dassin;[21] and Gervais, a surveyor. Two were government employees: Bergeret, in the police administration, and Pinet, a post office employee. The occupations of Donzel and Pétaud are unknown. Collet, a lawyer, was nominated but did not serve.[22] Not one was a collector of *rentes* or lived off his property or investments.

When the committee was reorganized against the moderates on 19 May 1793, as discussed above, eight members of the first committee were reelected.[23] After the minutes of the first register were completed

[20] It can be assumed that a wig or clockmaker, for example, did not merely manufacture wigs and clocks but sold them, probably in a shop attached to his dwelling. Richard Cobb in "Note sur la répression contre le personnel sans-culotte de 1795 à 1801," *Annales historiques*, 26 (1954), 23-49, found Eude (spelled Eudes) to be a clockmaker (*ibid.*, p. 45), and gives his first names as Jean-Louis. There is a placard, however, that lists him as a stonecutter and gives his Christian names as Jean-Pierre, B.H.V.P., 19 February (or March) 1793, listing 144 representatives to the Commune. The men listed above and those that follow are discussed below.

[21] Both are listed simply as painters rather than as house painters. The first appears in scattered references in A.N., F⁷* 2497; the latter in A.N., F³⁰ 145 and on Babeuf's list, B.N., Lb⁴² 232.

[22] Others who appeared but seem to have been replaced or who resigned were Varies (?), Rattier, Barthelémy, and Viard. Viard and Collet reappeared, however, and were elected to various posts, including that of the presidency of the section.

[23] See the discussion of this incident in Chapter V. These were Duclos, Eude, Gervais, Dupaumier, Guéneau, Descombes, Pétaud, and Mazin. Duclos was a wig-maker and owner of his own shop. Several whose occupations are unknown elected on the 19th were: Joiris, Dubois, Deschamps, and Ravel.

(18 September 1794), nine members of the committee signed them, demonstrating a continuity of service of eighteen months.[24] After thermidor, when Droits-de-l'Homme became one of four sections composing the 7th arrondissement, according to the law of 7 fructidor, Year II (24 August 1794), it contributed three men to the reconstructed revolutionary committee. These were Desgrouard, a chandler; Godard, a wine merchant; and Vivien, a hatter. The others were, from section Réunion, Mill(i)et, a wholesale merchant; Buffault, a former wine merchant; and Poupard, a carpenter. From section Homme-Armé: Le Duc, a surgeon; Grénon, a merchant of small wares; and Couturier, a clockmaker. From section Arcis: Le Belle, an upholsterer; Houet, *père*, a former upholsterer; and Maillet, a tailor.[25]

An examination of the social composition of this committee in the seventh arrondissement demonstrates little change from the membership of preceding committees. It is true that with the possible exception of Buffault and Houet, listed as "former" wine merchant and "former" upholsterer, respectively, which could signify that the two lived off their investments and/or savings, no other member except Le Duc, the surgeon, was a *rentier* or a member of the liberal professions. Were the rest *sans-culottes*? Here, again, much depends on the definition given this vague term. The tailor, Maillet, for example, asked to be relieved of the dubious honor of serving on the committee, because, in addition to his poor health, his precarious financial state, and his lack of property, he was needed by his workers,[26] thus demonstrating that he was a master worker. This, obviously, did not

[24] A.N., F7* 2497, p. 146, 2e jour *sans-culottide*, Year II (18 September 1794). These were: Bertram, Costain, Temponnet, Mazin, Gervais, Cordier, Deschamps, Pommer, and Guéneau. The occupations of Bertram and Costain are unknown.

[25] A.N., BB³ 83, "Tableau de la formation des douze comités révolutionnaires de Paris contenant les noms des sections qui doivent composer chacun des comités, et la liste des citoyens proposés pour en être membres," 2e jour *sans-culottide*, Year II (18 September 1794). The published list is in B.N., Lb⁴¹ 1191, *Tableau de la formation des douze comités révolutionnaires de Paris*. Section Droits-de-l'Homme appears under "Septième comité." Two Godards signed the list of 13-14 July, one a wine merchant residing on Cimetière-Saint-Jean; the other, a bourgeois on rue de la Verrerie. Neither carries a first name. Vivien, a hatter established at no. 76 rue Saint-Antoine, signed the militia list. B.H.V.P., MS 742.

[26] A.N., BB³ 83, 2 vendémiaire, Year II (23 September 1794). Yet he "burned with republican spirit," he wrote, and did not want public affairs to suffer if he were placed on the committee.

exclude him from the ranks of the *sans-culottes*, unless we accept a number of definitions given by the poorer workingmen and their defenders during 1793–Year II.[27] Like many *sans-culottes*, the rest of the members combined their craft with petty commerce, or as in the case of the three merchants (Godard, Mill[i]et, and Grenon) engaged solely in trade. It is possible that Poupard and Couturier were artisans exclusively, but the likelihood was that they, too, joined their craft with business.

The first meeting of the revolutionary committee of the arrondissement took place on the 4th day *sans-culottide*, Year II (20 September 1794). Nine members were installed, with two absent without explanation and one ill.[28] As resignations and replacements occurred throughout the winter and spring of 1795, the social composition of the committee remained unchanged. Individuals replaced their confreres, but neither their occupations nor their social role indicated any change in the class structure of the committee.[29] On 21 nivôse, Year III (10 January 1795), for example, five members of the former committee were replaced by two merchants, a mirror maker, a haberdasher, a dyer, and one without a listed occupation.[30] No significant change is evident; on the contrary, the emphasis on commerce or artisanship combined with business continued.

[27] See the well-known definition of a *sans-culotte* in "Réponse à l'impertinente question: Mais qu'est-ce qu'un sans-culotte?" from A.N., F⁷ 4775⁴⁸, dossier Vingternier, cited by Walter Markov and Albert Soboul, *Die Sansculotten von Paris Dokumente zur Geschichte der Volksbewegung* (Berlin, 1957), p. 2.

[28] The nine members installed were: Poupard (president), Milliet (secretary), Le Duc, Grénon, Couturier, Maillet, Le Belle, Houet père, and Vivien. Desgrouard was ill, and Buffault and Godard were absent. *Ibid.* Buffault asked to be relieved because of his "lack of intellectual capacity" to serve on the committee. He was replaced by Serre, a wholesale merchant, on 21 germinal, Year III (10 April 1795). A.N., F⁷* 2498, p. 257.

[29] For example: Desgrouard was replaced by Deronsoi, a painter; Houet was replaced by Tournay, a seller of soft drinks (*limonadier*); and Giroux (Giroust?), a distiller, replaced Maillet. A.N., F⁷* 2498, p. 257, 21 germinal, Year III (10 April 1795).

[30] A.N., F⁷* 2498, p. 152. On 21 nivôse, Year III (10 January 1795), for example, Le Duc, Milliet, Le Belle, Couturier, and Poupard were replaced by Jacques-Claude Delarone, a former mirror maker; Jacques Regnoust, a merchant; Pierre-Modeste Martin, a former merchant; Jean-Baptiste Tartreau (no occupation given); Jean-Baptiste Delaporte, a haberdasher; and François Pinelle, a dyer.

Without minimizing the importance of social classes in determining the general policy of revolutionary committees, it would be equally unsound to ignore the role of individuals in these institutions. After all, man does make his own history, even if "he does not make it out of whole cloth." This truism assumes a meaning especially in extreme situations, in times when terror is made the order of the day. Whether revolutionary committees applied a policy of terror harshly and indiscriminately or with a touch of humanity and selectively often depended on the character, the education, and the ideals of individuals serving on these committees.[31]

Who were the men elected to the sectional revolutionary committee in March 1793? Few in section Droits-de-l'Homme had a more distinguished revolutionary career than Antoine-Ignace-François Descombes. Born in Besançon, he earned a degree as master of languages at age nineteen. From the beginning of the Revolution he was a partisan of the Jacobins, became an elector in 1792, served as a representative to the General Council, and was elected secretary and president of his section, and to its revolutionary and civil committees. There was nothing particularly distinguished in his appearance. He was described as being five feet six inches in height, with hair and eyebrows of light blond color, a nose of middle size, an average mouth, and a round chin and face.[32]

When the Revolution broke out, he was in Marseilles, then returned to his native town of Besançon and must have shocked his neighbors, as he alone signed a petition in favor of the Jacobins. In April 1791 he arrived in Paris and found a position as an inspector of schools. Like Varlet, he attacked Lafayette, and was arrested for demonstrating against the king on 20 June 1792. Descombes revealed that he was a republican before 10 August, and that his championship of the principle of equality led to his expulsion from the general assembly of his section.[33] A modest donation reinstated him and gained

[31] See my article, "The Terror in Miniature: Section Droits-de-l'Homme of Paris, 1793-1795," in *The Historian*, 39 (February 1977), 292-306.

[32] This is from a passport given to him by Pache on 8 August 1793. A.N., F⁷ 4672; d. 1; Tuetey, *Répertoire*, X, no. 2557. He resided on rue Sainte-Croix-de-la-Bretonnerie at the time of this description. At his interrogation of 30 ventôse, Year II (20 March 1794), his age was given as 29.

[33] *Descombes, électeur, membre du Conseil général*, pp. 1-5, *passim*. It is not clear whether he was still a member of section Lombards or of Roi-de-Sicile at the time of his expulsion.

him the rights of active citizenship, he wrote ironically. After the overthrow of the king, he played a key role in reconciling sections Quinze-Vingts and Roi-de-Sicile after a dispute that had resulted from a misunderstanding.[34]

In December 1792 he was elected secretary and then president of his section, which was commended by the Commune for its energy and zeal during his term of office. In January he was elected to the General Council, where his conduct was always judged politically and morally correct. It was he more than any other individual who organized the fraternization movement with other sections to defeat the "aristocrats" in these sections, including his own. The Girondin Commission of Twelve denounced him by name, and shortly thereafter he was elected as one of the commissioners to the Evêché assembly to launch the insurrection of 31 May.[35]

After the assassination of Marat, he heard some wild proposals for vengeance in the section, but was able to combat them successfully. On 19 July he was appointed by the General Council to accompany deputies of the Convention into the departments of Seine-et-Marne and of Loiret, to help organize supplies of grain and flour for Paris. The following month he was asked by the Committee of Public Safety to return to the department of Seine-et-Marne to purchase grain, which duty he faithfully fulfilled. While most agents were paying 325 livres per sack of grain of 200 pounds, he proudly reported paying only 80 livres per sack of flour weighing 325 pounds, and denounced "the criminal speculation" of the bakers. His conduct during the five months in the town of Provins, where he acted as commissioner of provisions for Paris, earned him the commendation of his colleagues of the revolutionary committee of section Droits-de-l'Homme.[36]

Thus his political conduct and activity on behalf of the Revolution should have made him above suspicion—purer than the most incorruptible of men. Yet Descombes was arrested in December 1793 on a trumped-up charge of peculation and for manifesting what was called a "false and dangerous patriotism." There is little that can be added to his defense against the first charge. All authorities involved in the difficult task of supplying Paris testified to his honesty, energy, and

[34] *Ibid.*, pp. 5-6.
[35] *Ibid.*, pp. 7-9.
[36] *Ibid.*, pp. 10-13.

patriotism.[37] The accusation had been made by a grocer named Chollet,[38] who might have resented Descombes' denunciation of profiteers, or was simply repeating rumors spread by the latter's personal enemies.

More serious was the second indictment, leveled at him by Gervais of the revolutionary committee and by Pierre Carron, commissioner on profiteering in the section.[39] What did this "false and dangerous patriotism" consist of? Descombes had been moved by the pitiful plight of the former justice of the peace, Louis Fayel, and had given him a favorable letter of introduction to the authorities of Arcueil, a town in the Seine department south of Paris, to which Fayel had moved his family after being released from prison.

Who was Louis Fayel? He was born in Drieux, department of Eure-et-Loire, sometime in 1748, and had been an *avocat* and *procureur au parlement* before the Revolution. After the formation of the National Guard, he became captain of the 4th company of the battalion of district Petit-Saint-Antoine. In 1790 he was elected justice of the peace and had served as one of seventeen electors the following year.[40] His correct legal behavior in presiding over a court that tried the demonstrators of 20 June 1792, as was seen, could not erase the stigma of having placed patriots on trial. This antagonism was compounded when he carried off the register book of the sectional assembly on the eve of the insurrection against the king. Furthermore, he was accused of making contemptuous remarks against patriots, calling them *canaille*.[41] All this led to his arrest and imprisonment.

Upon his release, he decided to leave Paris for Arcueil because he

[37] A.N., W 94. This carton contains four bulky dossiers of Descombes' records when he was administrator of subsistences in Provins for supplying Paris. Many of these documents are reproduced by Tuetey in his volume X, the numbers of which with their dates are noted herein. Tuetey referred to five dossiers at the time of publication of his *Répertoire général*, not the four that may be found there today.

[38] Tuetey, *Répertoire*, X, no. 2566, 31 August 1793.

[39] A.N., F⁷ 4672, d. 1, 9 nivôse, Year II (29 December 1793). Carron is discussed below.

[40] A.N., F⁷ 4704, d. 1, 14 and 15 frimaire, Year II (4 and 5 December 1793); Charavay, *Assemblée électorale*, I, 49.

[41] These charges were repeated by Dumas during the interrogation of Fayel on 26 frimaire (16 December). "Voila la Sainte Nation! Canaille, crie donc Vive la Sainte Nation!" he was quoted as having shouted. Wallon, *Histoire*, II, 264-265, citing A.N., W 302, d. 341, pc. 2.

lacked a means of livelihood. He was rearrested in December 1793 by the revolutionary committee of section Droits-de-l'Homme, before which he admitted removing the register book, but denied acting against the insurrectionists of 10 August.[42] The committee having concluded, nevertheless, that he was a counterrevolutionary, sent him to the Conciergerie prison and transmitted the *procès-verbal* to the public prosecutor. The accusations of the revolutionary committee were repeated at his interrogation by René-François Dumas of the Revolutionary Criminal Court (*tribunal criminel-révolutionnaire*) on 26 frimaire, Year II (16 December 1793). The questions put to him were so obviously prejudiced that it was evident the prosecutor was merely performing a ritual, the outcome of which was already known. "Were you one of the justices of the peace paid by the court to support the tyranny and persecute patriots?" was the question put to him by Dumas. Fayel's reply was a curt "no." The next question was: "Why did you always appear as such in the section?" Fayel could only answer "that he did not appear as such." To the accusation that he did all in his power to bring on the civil war so that "tyranny might triumph," Fayel replied that he knew nothing of this.[43] On 29 frimaire, Year II (19 December 1793), Fayel was condemned to death and his property was confiscated.[44]

Descombes testified that although he had given the ex-judge the letter in question, he had also written to the municipal authorities of Arcueil informing them of Fayel's past conduct and reputation and warning them to keep him under surveillance.[45] He admitted that he had congratulated Fayel for having escaped the September massacres when the latter was sitting in prison, but defended this act by arguing that this only showed he harbored no personal hatred for the man

[42] A.N., F7 4704, 15 frimaire, Year II.

[43] A.N., W 302, 341, pc. 4, pp. 1 and 2. This interrogation was signed by the members of the panel of public prosecutors: Gaffier, Fouquier (Tinville), Goujon, and Dumas, and by Fayel.

[44] *Journal de la montagne*, no. 38, p. 297, 1 nivôse, Year II (21 December 1793); Wallon, *Histoire du Tribunal Révolutionnaire*, II, 260.

[45] A.N., F7 4704, d. 1, 12 frimaire, Year II. Fayel held a certificate of civic conduct issued him by Décourchant in his capacity as president of the section's civil committee. When Décourchant was arrested in the Year III, one of the charges against him was that he had been a friend of Fayel, as was discussed in Chapter VIII. A.N., F7 4665, d. 3.

despite his opinions. As for the massacres, he thought they had been unfortunate, "because humanity . . . was trodden under foot," as he phrased it, and had given an extra weapon to enemies of the Revolution.[46]

Nor was Descombes alone in feeling pity for Fayel and his family. Shortly after her husband's first arrest, Mme Fayel petitioned the general assembly to allow her and the children to visit him in prison. According to the *procès-verbal*, those present were "touched by her state and that of her children." The assembly elected commissioners to request the authorities to allow Mme Fayel this visit.[47]

Although Descombes' premises in Paris and in Provins had been searched by agents of the revolutionary committee, nothing even remotely suspicious had been uncovered.[48] As news of his detention reached Descombes' friends and colleagues, it aroused indignation and immediate efforts to free him. He was heatedly defended in the general assembly[49] and in petitions from his native town of Besançon.[50] Geoffroy, his coworker in Provins, also came to his support.[51] Meanwhile, the Administration of Provisions recalled "the important services rendered to public affairs by Descombes,"[52] while the sectional assembly paid homage to his patriotism, holding that his arrest had expiated "a weakness from which men are not exempt."[53] The popular society of the section, although some of its members had expressed their antagonism to Descombes,[54] decided to intervene on his behalf.

[46] A.N., F⁷ 4672, 29 frimaire, Year II (19 December 1793).

[47] B.H.V.P., MS 748, fol. 9, 13 August 1792.

[48] Tuetey, *Répertoire*, X, no. 2621, 8-27 nivôse, Year II (28 December 1793-17 January 1794). Descombes' wife, Jeanne-Antoine Bernard, was made guardian over his papers. Houdaille and Bernard reported from the communes of Coulommiers and Provins, 23 and 27 nivôse (12 and 16 January 1794). A.N., F⁷ 4704.

[49] A.N., F⁷ 4672, 28 nivôse, Year II (17 January 1794).

[50] Tuetey, *Répertoire*, X, nos. 2633, 2634, 2635. A letter from a woman by name of Maugras in Besançon contained this revealing remark: if her society of women had not been suppressed, its members would have rendered justice to him, she wrote.

[51] Tuetey, *Répertoire*, X, no. 2632, 26 pluviôse, Year II (14 February 1794).

[52] A.N., F⁷ 4672, 30 pluviôse, Year II (18 February 1794); Tuetey, *Répertoire*, X, no. 2639.

[53] *Ibid.*, 20 pluviôse, Year II (8 February 1794); this was signed by Eude as president, and Collet, secretary. Reproduced in Tuetey, *Répertoire*, X, no. 2636, without signatures.

[54] *Ibid.*, 8 nivôse, Year II (28 December 1793); Tuetey, *Répertoire*, X, no. 2060.

At its meeting of 25 ventôse (18 March), widely attended according to the police spy, Bacon, discussion was focused on the fate of Descombes. The revolutionary committee reported that four of its members had gone to the Committee of General Security and had remained in its antechamber for five hours without getting a hearing. This brought forth a commotion in the hall. A member then spoke up praising Descombes as one of the best patriots, urging the committee to return and to remain until the Committee of General Security should receive them. This was applauded vigorously, and his suggestion referred to the general assembly.[55]

While his friends were mobilizing, Descombes was being interrogated by Claude-Emmanuel Dobsen, now president of the revolutionary tribunal. The questions put by Dobsen were ominous, as they implied that the prisoner had plotted against the security of the Republic.[56] This took a more serious turn when Etienne Lasne, commander of the section's battalion, reported to the revolutionary committee Descombes' observation that he did not expect to be released by that same committee which had incarcerated him in the first place; that if there were five or six good patriots like himself in prison he would be out in a few days.[57] This alleged remark was turned over to the public accuser, Fouquier-Tinville. On 3 germinal (23 March), Dupaumier added his denunciation of Descombes, confirming his alleged determination to escape from prison.[58] That was all the prosecutor needed to link Descombes in the supposed plot of the Hébertists to create shortages.[59]

The final blow came when the revolutionary committee sent four commissioners to the Committee of General Security to express its regrets for having requested the release of Descombes. Now that he was accused of plotting against the very security of the state, it seemed to them that he was "greatly guilty."[60] Two days prior to his convic-

[55] Caron, *Paris*, IV, 376-377, 28 ventôse (18 March 1794).

[56] A.N., F⁷ 4672, 26 pluviôse, Year II (14 February 1794), wherein the revolutionary committee refers to Descombes' concern over Fayel as having been a "passing weakness" (not in Tuetey).

[57] Tuetey, *Répertoire*, X, nos. 2643 and 2644, 1 germinal, Year II (21 March 1794).

[58] A.N., T 724, liasse 4. Dupaumier's name is spelled in this source as Dupaumié.

[59] Tuetey, *Répertoire*, X, no. 2647.

[60] A.N., F⁷ 4672, 3 germinal, Year II (23 March 1794); Tuetey, *Répertoire*, X,

tion, Descombes wrote a letter to his wife, convinced that he would be freed shortly. On 4 germinal (24 March) he was guillotined.[61]

A lesser victim of the terror was Pierre-François-Marie Duclos, president of the section during the events of 9th thermidor, member of its welfare committee, and a cannoneer in its company. He was born in 1769 and began working as a wigmaker's apprentice in Rouen at age eleven. Welcoming the Revolution, he went to Paris, then to Caen in April 1790, returning to the capital in July of that year. The following month he obtained employment in a hairdresser's shop, and by care and application so impressed its bourgeois owner that he gave him the shop as dowry in marriage to his sister, on 1 July 1791. He was then twenty-two years old.[62]

As an active citizen, he joined the National Guard, but was not permitted to participate in the sectional assembly as he was not yet twenty-five years of age. On 20 June and 10 August 1792, he demonstrated and fought against the king, joining the marching battalions of faubourg Saint-Antoine. With the end of the monarchy, he began to attend meetings of the general assembly, becoming popular enough to get elected to the revolutionary committee when it was first established, and, of equal significance, to be reappointed on 19-20 May, that is, when the section's radicals triumphed over the moderates. His work on the committee brought him a certificate of merit testifying to his revolutionary conduct; nevertheless, he resigned from the committee in September and was sent to the department of Aisne with his company. Although remaining in the battalion, he left his company when it indicated its desire to become part of the revolutionary army of the interior, an opportune act that possibly saved his life when the Hébertists came under attack of the revolutionary government. He was elected to the welfare committee on 15 ventôse, Year II (5 March 1794), and served there until his arrest on the 9th of thermidor.[63]

The third member of the committee was Jean-Louis Eude, captain

---

no. 2648. The apologetic nature of the committee's resolution requesting the Committee of General Security to examine "in its wisdom" the petition of the general assembly for the release of Descombes shows clearly its opposition to the assembly and fear of the Committee of General Security. A.N., F⁷* 2497, p. 96.

[61] Tuetey, *Répertoire*, XI, no. 219.

[62] A.N., F⁷ 4684, d. 3.

[63] *Ibid.*

of cannoneers of the section and a clockmaker by profession, residing on rue Saint-Antoine. He had been elected to the first revolutionary committee on 28 March 1793, and was reappointed at the time of its reorganization 19-20 May. Eude was arrested on 10 thermidor, as seen above, for supporting "the rebellious Commune" during the events of the preceding day.[64] Upon his release he tried to regain his post in the army, as his craft was insufficient to give him a living wage. He succeeded, finally, in regaining his rank of captain in the Year IV until the layoffs of brumaire, Year IX (October-November 1800), and returned to his former position only in 1807.[65]

François Dupaumier had been one of the members of the revolutionary committee who had denounced Descombes to Fouquier-Tinville. A jeweler by trade, residing on rue de la Verrerie, he was elected secretary of the sectional assembly on 17 November 1792. Dupaumier served as representative of the section to the Commune, was a member of the police administration, and was elected to the revolutionary committee from its beginning.[66] He was also charged by the general assembly in late August 1792 to turn over to the Society of Jacobins the list of those who had signed the Petition of Twenty Thousand, that is, of the conservatives and moderates in the section. The General Council appointed him and a colleague (19 November 1793) to examine the names on this same petition and the one called Petition of Eight Thousand, and to report on his research within two days.[67] He was eventually condemned by the revolutionary tribunal, according to a note in his dossier of sequestered papers.

Bergeret lived in the same house on rue de la Verrerie in which Dupaumier had his residence, and was attached to the police administration for three years. After the prairial insurrection he was arrested and charged with being "the most zealous agent of the system of terror" by two personal enemies in the section. Bergeret, they charged, had always denounced to the former general assembly and the section's

---

[64] A.N., F⁷ 4684, d. 3, 13 thermidor, Year III (31 July 1795).

[65] Cobb, "Note sur la répression," pp. 23-29.

[66] A.N., T 724, liasse 4; A.N., F⁷* 2497, *passim*. His name appears after those of Descombes and Eude on the first *procès-verbal* of the committee of 28 March 1793.

[67] *Ibid*. The Petition of Eight Thousand was circulated by national guardsmen of conservative belief on the eve of the demonstration against the king, 20 June 1792. The Petition of Twenty Thousand was circulated after the demonstration against the king.

popular society all those who had disagreed with him. His wife, moreover, never ceased exciting those women in the section who seemed the most dissatisfied.

Bergeret replied that the registers of the sectional assembly and the popular society would prove that he had merely expressed his opinions like everyone else, without ever denouncing anyone. His arrest, he emphasized, was motivated by a vengeful action of two individuals who had been refused membership in the popular society and who held him responsible for their rejection. The civil committee observed that Bergeret often spoke like a terrorist, but that this might have been due to the influence of wine. Basically, he was a man of little education and of no principles, the committee held, for upon obtaining the post of police inspector he seldom attended meetings and rarely spoke. After being imprisoned for two months he was released by the Committee of General Security, and shortly later recovered his rights of citizenship.[68]

Jean Charbonnier, a shoemaker residing on rue des Ecouffes, was accused of having excited the women against the authorities during periods of bread shortage, of having roused the people to march on the Convention, and, together with Fayölle, with having threatened the civil committee.[69] Charbonnier replied in the form of a question to the Committee of General Security: could a father of five children and a husband of a pregnant wife expose himself to such extreme behavior? On the contrary, he had urged citizens to protect the Convention, not to march against it. The civil committee maintained that he had been widely known as a troublemaker and suggested that his commanding officer be consulted on whether he had fulfilled his military duty during the late insurrection. The committee saw him as "an agitator and an anarchist" whose "good intentions . . . do not free him from the crime of anarchy whose principles he sowed." The

[68] A.N., F7 4592, d. 2. He was accused of terrorism by Giraud, a hairdresser residing on rue Saint-Antoine, and Garnot, of rue des Ecouffes. The observations of the civil committee are under date of 8 thermidor, Year III (26 July 1795). He was released on 14 thermidor, Year III (1 August 1795), and restored to citizenship on 11 fructidor, Year III (28 August 1795).

[69] A.N., F7 4639, d. 3, 5 prairial, Year III (24 May 1795). This is an abstract from the register of the sectional assembly signed by Bellarte, president. Charbonnier's reply is on 5 thermidor, Year III (22 July 1795). Also in A.N., F7 4774^45. Fayölle(s) is discussed in connection with the insurrection of prairial below.

surveillance committee of the 7th arrondissement, on the other hand, took note of "his numerous family" and urged his release, which was granted under the direction of the local authorities.[70]

Cordier was a caterer by profession, had been elected captain of the section's armed force, and had served on the revolutionary committee from its beginning. After an unspecified interval he was drafted again in messidor, Year II (June-July 1794). Meanwhile, he had opened a shop dispensing soft drinks in section Arsenal, and requested to remain there, but informed the Committees of Public Safety and of General Security that if another were not appointed in his place he would remain and do his duty. He was released with full rights several months after his arrest.[71]

Donzel resided on rue Bourg-Tibourg. He was charged with having been one of "the agents of tyranny that preceded the 9th of thermidor; of having vexed all citizens of the section; of having outraged all the unfortunates whom they threw into prison; of having been [one of the] tyrants of the section."[72] The civil committee heard five witnesses who testified that he had helped "extinguish the flames" of the insurrection.[73] In his own letter to the Committee of General Security, Donzel pointed out that not a single person had come forward to present charges against any of the arrested members of the former revolutionary committee—this despite the fact that a special commission had been appointed to receive denunciations against them. If citizens were harassed by the former committee, why were there no protests, he asked.

The civil committee admitted that it had no knowledge of any

---

[70] A.N., F7 4639, 9 thermidor, Year III (27 July 1795). This was signed for the committee by its secretary, Lambin. The letter of the surveillance committee is dated 13 thermidor; the Committee of General Security acted the following day.

[71] A.N., F7 4653, d. 4. Cordier's letter was written on 9 messidor, Year II (27 June 1794); a note of his request bears the date of 19 messidor, Year II (7 July 1794). He was released on 14 fructidor, Year III (31 August 1795) as stated in a note to the civil committee of section Arsenal. There is no information on the precise date of his arrest or of his removal from section Droits-de-l'Homme.

[72] A.N., F7 4679, d. 2, 13 thermidor, Year III (31 July 1795); A.N., F7 4774⁴⁵.

[73] A.N., F7 4679, 7 thermidor, Year III (25 July 1795). It is not clear from the witnesses whether there had been an actual fire, or whether the words used—"torch," "flames," "extinguish," etc.—were meant only in a figurative sense in reference to the insurrection.

particular act of Donzel's while serving on the revolutionary committee, nor did any witness interrogated by it have more than hearsay evidence on his role during the late uprising. Nevertheless, it refused to support his plea for release because he had "the character of an agitator and of an anarchist." This was too much for the Committee of General Security, which restored him to full rights of citizenship and employment with the Commission of Subsistence.[74]

Eugène-Honoré Gervais, a surveyor by profession, residing at Place des Droits-de-l'Homme, was accused of attacking the Thermidorian regime and of having "eulogized the former government." It was to him that the hotheads of the section turned, the assembly charged, when it arrested him. Moreover, he was reproached with slandering the Convention and of having joined faubourg Saint-Antoine when its insurgents marched on that body.[75] In the spring of 1794 Gervais had lost the respect of his colleagues because of his frequent absences and refusal to share the duties of the revolutionary committee.[76] It is difficult to say what his ultimate fate was, but it can be assumed that he was probably released on the eve of vendémiaire.

Guéneau was a jeweler by vocation, residing on rue de la Tisseranderie. He had been appointed to the revolutionary committee at the time of its reorganization by the radicals, and had been elected as its secretary during the same session. In his letter to the Committee of General Security he reminded its members that at the time of his appointment revolutionary committees received no pay, that his request to be relieved was refused by the general assembly, and that he had never joined the Jacobins or any other popular society.[77] During the affair of 9 thermidor he had been the first to pledge support to the Convention and to persuade the cannoneers not to join "the rebellious Commune," thus avoiding a threatening civil war. Although

[74] *Ibid.* Provisional freedom was granted on 26 thermidor, Year III (13 August 1795) with full freedom the following month.

[75] A.N., F⁷ 4774⁴⁵, d. 2, 5 prairial, Year III (24 May 1795). Tuetey confused Eugène-Honoré Gervais with Jean-Baptiste-Lazard Gervais (A.N., F⁷ 4723, d. 2), arrested for shady dealing as a broker (*brocanteur*), in his *Répertoire*, X, Index. See also the reference to Gervais in A.N., F⁷ 4672, 9 nivôse, Year II (29 December 1793).

[76] A.N., F⁷* 2497, p. 85, 19 pluviôse, Year II (7 February 1794); and p. 114, 26 floréal, Year II (15 May 1794).

[77] A.N., F⁷ 4734, d. 5. "Mémoire du citoyen Guéneau"; F⁷* 2497, p. 24, 20 May 1793, when the committee elected him secretary.

he did not explain why he was disarmed during the *journée* of prairial, he must have been a participant in the events like others.

Referring to the many citizens freed after 9 thermidor who had praised the humaneness of the committee, he claimed to have been among its moderates, and cited a specific example as proof. Upon learning that an old man had been imprisoned by the section, he returned him to his own home under house arrest—all this with the consent of the Committee of General Security. Adducing testimony of public health officials that his wife had suffered a nervous breakdown and could not be left alone,[78] he requested provisional freedom. The civil committee admitted that nothing in particular was known against him, and noted that several citizens had verified his humaneness. The Committee of General Security granted him provisional liberty and shortly thereafter (4 fructidor, Year III–21 August 1795) restored him to full citizenship.

Louis Houdaille, a merchant jeweler residing on rue de la Verrerie was elected to the revolutionary committee in September 1793 and remained until it was replaced in fructidor (August-September 1794). He was arrested in prairial for his participation in the "tyranny" that allegedly ruled the section and for his harassment of citizens—the same accusation leveled at others. A new charge was that he had been one of the men responsible for the disturbance that had broken out in the assembly over the removal of the bust of Marat from the hall.[79]

Houdaille wrote the Committee of General Security that his "crime in the eyes of some of his co-citizens was to have been a member of the revolutionary committee before the 9th of thermidor." Three successive commissions, he pointed out, were appointed by the general assembly to examine the conduct of former members of the revolutionary committee, yet nothing was found against them. Could he be held as a criminal, he asked, for being a member of a committee whose conduct had been found to be irreproachable? His denunciation was the result of personal hatred, nothing else, he concluded. The

---

[78] *Ibid.*, 1 and 4 thermidor, Year III (19 and 22 July 1795). Dufour, the health officer, testified that she suffered from "nerves," and should not be left alone. The civil committee also submitted the same evidence. A public health official characterized her illness as not unlike an attack of epilepsy.

[79] A.N., F⁷ 4745, d. 1, 6 nivôse, Year III. He was interrogated by the committee of surveillance of the 7th arrondissement. Unless otherwise noted the material below is based on this dossier of fourteen *pièces*.

committee restored him to full citizenship on 30 fructidor, Year III (16 September 1795).[80]

Philippe-Denis Pinet was a captain in the section's armed force, employed in the post office and residing on rue des Billettes. He had been invited to serve on the committee primarily because of his fine script. Arrested as "an agent of tyranny," he protested that he had never harmed anyone and asked indignantly if it were not true that the revolutionary committee on which he had served was a legally constituted body. Was it right, he asked, to be destroyed because he had helped its members to keep minutes and address correspondence?[81] Submitting a document that carried the signatures of his commander, noncommissioned officers, and privates that he had carried out his duties on 1 prairial with courage and exactitude, Pinet added that he was the father of four infants, the oldest being but three years of age. He was dependent completely on his salary of 2,400 livres, which he stood to lose unless he was restored to full citizenship within two days. Although there are no other documents in his dossier it seems reasonable to believe, on the basis of other rulings by the Committee of General Security, that he was restored to full rights of citizenship.[82]

Pommer (or Pommez), a dental surgeon who resided on rue Renaud-Lefevre, was charged with having incited his company to march on the Convention. Pommer appealed to the civil committee, which knew that his function had been limited to issuing cards of security and passports. His testimony revealed how he had been swept up by the mass of demonstrators on 1 prairial, an irresistible wave that carried everything before it. Pommer noticed that many men of his company had slogans written or chalked on their hats that read "Bread and 1793." One demonstrator asked him to sketch a large slice of bread on his hat and to add "93," confessing that he could not write. Then another dozen men presented themselves for the same purpose,

---

[80] *Ibid.*, Houdaille's first petition was on 2 messidor, Year III (2 June 1795). He was freed provisionally on 14 thermidor, Year III (1 August 1795), and appealed for restoration of full rights in a letter without date. His request was granted on 30 fructidor, Year III.

[81] A.N., F⁷ 4774⁷⁵, d. 5, 5 prairial, Year III and 19 prairial, Year III (7 June 1795).

[82] *Ibid.* The commander, Dupré, wrote "seen by me," and two commissioners of the civil committee verified the authenticity of the signatures on his appeal.

as he still had the chalk in his hand. He observed others performing the same task demanded of them. Several times he tried to erase his own inscription, but the pressing multitude would not let him. Meanwhile, he continued to march with his company to the aid of the Convention.[83]

Temponnet (or Tamponnet) was a mason-entrepreneur residing on rue Vieille-du-Temple with his wife and six children. He was charged with the usual "crimes"—being an agent of tyranny, of harassing citizens, and of agitating the demonstrators on 1 prairial. For good measure he was also accused of mistreating a septuagenarian paralytic, although the civil committee admitted that it was not certain that the accused was present when the alleged incident took place. Temponnet replied in a *tableau* tracing the history of his political conduct.[84] He denied having tyrannized over his fellow citizens or of being guilty of arbitrary acts. He had always interpreted the law humanely, he wrote, and had helped the oppressed and the unfortunate. Both the civil and surveillance committees admitted that the only charge against him was that he had been a member of the former revolutionary committee. The Committee of General Security granted him provisional freedom and then full rights of citizenship.

Jean-Baptiste Mazin, an upholsterer by trade, resided on rue de la Verrerie. He had been elected to the committee on 19-20 May 1793, at the time of its takeover by the militants, as discussed above. Like the others, he was charged with being responsible for "arbitrary actions with his former colleagues," and being "a partisan and agent of the former tyranny."[85] Although little else is known about him or his ultimate fate, it is quite probable that it differed little from that of his fellow members.

[83] A.N., F⁷ 4774⁷⁸, d. 6, 18 messidor, Year III (6 July 1795); A.N., F⁷ 4774⁴⁵.

[84] A.N., F⁷ 4775²⁶, d. 4, a dossier of thirteen *pièces*. A.N., F⁷ 4775²⁴ is a dossier of two *pièces*, which for some unaccountable reason is filed separately from the first reference above. The charge is the same in both dossiers under date of 5 prairial, Year III. One difference is that the latter is spelled Tamponnet, rather than Temponnet. A.N., F⁷* 699 also spells his name with an "a," Tamponnet. Temponnet, however, spelled his name with an "e." See his "Tableau de la conduite du Citoyen Temponnet détenue en la maison 3 à Plesis," 5 prairial, Year III.

[85] A.N., F⁷* 2497, p. 24. His first name appears in A.P.P., A A/136, fol. 44, 2 frimaire, Year II (22 November 1793). His occupation is given on Babeuf's list, B.N., Lb⁴² 232, and, as seen above, on the militia list of 13-14 July.

It is clear from the brief sketch of the revolutionary committee that its members did not differ in any significant degree from many others who were active politically in the section. Of course, they enjoyed power that had converted them from private individuals into functionaries of state. Six of the committee's members, and, possibly, eight (Charbonnier, Mazin, Pommer, Bernard, Vivien, Angar, Godard, and Dubois) had volunteered for the Paris militia in the early days of 13-14 July, thus demonstrating an involvement in the Revolution for most or all of its seven years. Several individuals made no effort to seek a post with the committee, but could hardly have refused to serve without incurring the serious charge of "uncivic conduct." After thermidor, as seen above, all members of this body became suspect; after prairial, the institution per se was rejected by the section. Those who had been associated with it were therefore held in suspicion, regardless of their individual role.

The police, for example, kept the following well-known members under surveillance: Gervais, Houdaille, Temponnet, Donzel, Dassin, and Pommer. In addition to these were several others who were included with the above, but whose revolutionary activities were less well known for the time being. Among the latter were Guéneau, Millet, and Serre.[86] Gervais, Houdaille, Guéneau, Temponnet, Donzel, and Dassin were "to be watched as dangerous," and Houdaille and Guéneau were to be removed from the welfare committee.[87] This repression led former members of revolutionary committees to suppress compromising records of registers.[88] Their colleagues, whatever

[86] A.N., F⁷* 699, no date. This is a loose sheet in the above register with a notation in the margin: "All citizens to be kept equally under surveillance." Guéneau is invariably spelled Guenault. There is a Serre on the militia list of 13-14 July, listed as a merchant, residing at no. 22 rue des Rosiers, but his first name is not given, nor is he identified in the police document.

[87] A.N., F⁷ 4748 (dossier 2, on Pierre Jacob), 5 pluviôse, Year III (24 January 1795). This is an eight-page manuscript containing descriptions of former revolutionaries and observations in the margin like "to be kept under surveillance; to be replaced; to be discharged; unworthy of occupying any position," and so on. One heading is "members of former bloody revolutionary committee."

[88] Marc Bouloiseau, "Les Comités de surveillance des arrondissements de Paris sous la réaction thermidorienne," in Annales historiques, 10 (1933), 317-337. The author has examined the minutes of the surveillance committees in the sections and has revealed the changed nature of their operations and composition in relation to former revolutionary committees. In addition to the above are his articles in the Annales entitled "Les Comités de surveillance des arrondissements parisiens," 10 (1933), 441-

their individual convictions as to the role of their former coworkers, were themselves regarded with some suspicion since they belonged to an institution held by many as abnormal, and which was destined to disappear when no longer needed.[89]

On 10 vendémiaire, Year III (1 October 1795), that is, on the very eve of the attempted royalist coup, it was moved in the general assembly of section Droits-de-l'Homme that former members of the revolutionary committee had lost its confidence. Another motion held that they had never enjoyed such confidence, and that the assembly had been violated in its rights by the committee. This proposition was adopted, and certificates of civic conduct were withdrawn from former members. Bent on vengeance, the reactionary assembly resolved to demand that the Convention disarm and expel these former officials from all civil and military functions.[90] Only the failure of the royalist coup put an end to further attempts at vengeance.

The duties of the revolutionary committee, although varied, tended to be repetitive; neither changes in personnel nor in political climate seemed to affect these pursuits.[91] They were limited, largely, to investigation of those individuals in the section who had come under suspicion by their political activities, their lack of zeal for the Revolution, their attitude toward the authorities, their signatures to former petitions, or, simply, by accident of class or profession. In addition to this effort of investigating and interrogating, the committee spent much time in enforcing decrees that required identification, proof of residency, or cards of civic conduct. The minutes of the committee give the impression that many citizens who were picked up by armed patrols were negligent, forgetful, or careless about their

---

453; 11 (1934), 233-249; "Les Comités de surveillance des arrondissements de Paris pendant les mois de germinal, floréal, prairial, an III," 13 (1936), pp. 42-60; "Les Comités de surveillance des arrondissements de Paris à la fin de l'an III," 14 (1936), 204-217. The developments in the 7th arrondissement correspond, with hardly an exception, to those analyzed by Professor Bouloiseau for the other arrondissements.

[89] *Ibid.*, X, 335.

[90] B.V.C., MS 120, fols. 160-161, 10 vendémiaire, Year III (1795).

[91] Colin Lucas demonstrates the varied concerns of revolutionary committees in the department of the Loire. The type of activity and the zeal shown by local organs differed widely because individual members were influenced by religious differences, different rates of illiteracy, local concerns, and personal caution. *The Structure of the Terror* (London, 1973), "The Comités de surveillance," pp. 125-155, *passim*.

numerous personal documents. Time and again the committee issued warnings to ordinary citizens (when it did not place them under arrest) who failed to carry proof of their identity.

The supply and orderly distribution of provisions, as might be expected, was also a pressing concern of the committee. Since riots and violence often resulted from long queues, the committee attempted to regulate and control crowds. Occasionally an individual appeared before it, and having been admonished, was not heard of again. At other times he reappeared on several occasions until discharged from further investigation. After the adoption of the *maximum*, incidents arising from its enforcement or circumvention appear regularly in the minutes. Confiscation and sale of contraband goods, mostly food, were also recorded, as was the deposit of guns, pistols, and sabers. Reports of displays of symbols of royalty, or more correctly, neglect to remove them, appeared occasionally. At times the committee seized horses and wagons belonging to civilians for use by the army.

Every two weeks the reelection of its officers was duly recorded in the *procès-verbal*, as well as the funds collected to pay its members' salaries and the expenses of its office. Quite often commissioners were sent to various neighborhoods of the section, or, sometimes, outside it on various missions. The commissioners on duty usually were sent in pairs, duly recording their misssion in a *procès-verbal* of their own, which became incorporated into that of the committee. At times the script of its secretary became less than elegant, if not quite illegible. Nor are the orthography, spelling, punctuation, or diacritical marks always reliable. As men of business or from the liberal professions began to keep the committee's minutes, especially after 9 thermidor, the more legible script of its secretary contrasts with the, at times, untrained hand of his former counterpart. It is tempting to see in this phenomenon a reflection of the shift from a *sans-culottist* composition toward the new, bourgeois makeup of the committee.

Its first meeting of 28 March 1793 contained all the elements and concerns of its police work of future years. An examination of the *procès-verbal* includes reports of house searches, requisitions, the return of lost civic cards, and the interrogation of suspects. The sergeant-major of the section's battalion, for example, was requested to furnish the names of nobles, refractory priests, and domestics who were still members of the armed companies, evidently in preparation for a purge.

Upon complaint of the adjutant that a number of citizens had failed to perform guard duty, the committee authorized him to recall these men to the colors.

The state of arms in various armorer shops also came under the committee's gaze as it sent commissioners to investigate. A number of men lacking civic cards were ordered to bring them on the morrow, while several who had been wounded in a personal dispute were remanded to the police commissioner for further investigation. A soldier without proof of leave was turned over to the police, and a number of hunting weapons confiscated from a nobleman's home were deposited with the committee. After several residents of the section were told to bring their cards of identity, the first session of the committee came to an end.[92]

The following day witnessed more developments of a similar nature, especially dealing with cards of security, a search of a marquis' house that yielded nothing suspicious, and the arrival of an agent to pick up rifles purchased for the Commune of Melun. On 30 March the committee cautioned an overzealous officer not to stop everyone in sight for cards of identity, but to limit the search to those who seemed suspicious to him—hardly a precise order. A letter from the mayor made inquiries on those arrested, the state of arms, and the number of saddle horses in the section. The following day the committee examined the register of the former armed company of the section and records of the current armed force. After turning over the sum of 11 livres following an examination of its receipts and expenditures, the sergeant-major, Pot(t)in, was discharged. On 2 April the committee examined papers of two non-juring priests, recording that "fanaticism was painted there on each line," and sent the priests to the police.[93]

On 25 April the committee was reconstituted, with new members replacing a number of original appointments. An interchange of membership with that of other committees (civil and welfare) may be recognized, in addition to the election of known activists of the section. In order to expedite business it was decided to appoint two commissioners to deliver cards of security and to set the time of de-

---

[92] A.N., F7* 2497, pp. 1-4, 28 March 1793. The *procès-verbal* was signed by Eude, president, and Bertrand, secretary.

[93] *Ibid.*, pp. 4, 5, 7, 9.

livery. Tuesday and Friday evenings were reserved for meetings of the full committee.[94]

After its reconstruction as a result of the internal revolution in the assembly by militants on 19-20 May 1793, the new committee met on 22 May. Modifying the previous order on the distribution of security cards, it limited them to thirty per day and requested the department to give it a mailbox for receiving communications from other constituted bodies, writing tablets, and a lock on the door. Then the committee appointed Isnard, a porter, as *garçon* and decided to keep a register with a blue cover for entries of denunciations received. Daily meetings were to commence at 6 p.m., with two members to be on duty every day during six days of the week.[95]

In the week preceding the revolution of 31 May, no noticeable changes can be discerned, in either its activity or its procedure. The committee continued to interrogate suspects, deliver civic cards, and receive reports. On the very eve of the insurrection it received an invitation from the civil and revolutionary committees of the neighboring section, Maison Commune, to help draft a plan for a primary school in the parish of Saint-Gervais.[96]

During the days following the overthrow of the Gironde, the committee carried on its normal activities. It prepared a list of those who had served under arms during the insurrection and sent them to the Comité central révolutionnaire. Being authorized by the Commune to search lodging houses for suspects, it appointed trustworthy citizens to help in this task. To enforce its actions the committee decreed that the commander of the armed force furnish each commissioner sent to make a search an escort of five armed men. A number of suspects found in lodging houses were questioned, and the usual number of citizens without their cards of security were brought before it. By the end of the week the committee was besieged by residents seeking these cards.[97]

[94] *Ibid.*, p. 17. The membership now was as follows: Saint Hubert (president), Angar, Bernard, Michon, Richebourg, Mazin, Pollet, Ravel, Sauvegrain, Dubois, Dupaumier, and Thiébart fils as secretary. By the end of the month Richebourg was president; Thiébart remained as secretary (p. 21). François-Charles Angar(d), *avocat*, no. 60 rue Saint-Antoine, signed the militia list of 13-14 July. He served twice as president of the section.

[95] *Ibid.*, p. 25.

[96] *Ibid.*, pp. 26-27.

[97] *Ibid.*, see the sessions for June 4, 5, 6, 7, and 9, pp. 29-31.

After the insurrection against the Gironde, the committee remained active in making house searches and depositing in an arsenal the weapons found. Its members were especially zealous in ferreting out those without civic cards and in turning over accused deserters from the armed forces to proper authorities, this after carefully examining the personal papers and effects of many whose homes were being searched. In one case they overreached themselves in entering the house of the Portuguese consul, but stopped in time to avoid an embarrassing diplomatic incident. On 25 June the committee took the initiative in inviting other sections to draw up lists of suspects of men "who [had] demonstrated their evil intentions during the revolution" and to send two commissioners each to the Evêché on Sunday, 30 June, to deliberate on what further steps ought to be taken under the circumstances.[98]

Throughout the month of July the committee was busy with interrogations of individuals who desired certificates of civic conduct, and upon orders of the Commune and department, collected guns and pistols, and requisitioned horses in the section. All these were tasks performed repeatedly by the committee throughout the Revolution. In a number of cases its overzealous role, judged by some questionable incidents, must have left behind a good deal of rancor. It arrested a "conforming priest," for example, because he had continued to ask a baker to sell him bread despite her insistence that she had none. He had never asked for alms, he protested, and was ready to pay for his morsel of bread, yet the committee picked him up on the baker's complaint.[99] Another case of overeagerness, if not petty tyranny, was the committee's warning given to a woman shoemaker, a widow who had been taught the craft by her deceased husband, who had gone marketing wearing man's clothes. The inconvenience of women's garb in practicing this trade evidently made no impression on the revolutionary committee, which warned her to assume the clothes of her sex or face the penalty of the law.[100] Male chauvinism and sexism were

[98] *Ibid.*, p. 35.

[99] A.P.P., A A/265, pc. 86, 7 August [1793]. Jean-Honoré Gundinard was arrested on rue Bourg-Tibourg at Letan's bakery. He refused to sign the *procès-verbal* and was turned over to the police. On the 19th, the police commissioner signed a note that he should be released as he was ill and had come to Paris to treat his illness.

[100] A.N., F⁷* 2497, pp. 49-50, 8 August 1793. That this was no idle threat may be seen by the actual arrest of a seamstress who had worn man's clothing. B.H.V.P., MS 748, fol. 109, 14 messidor, Year II (2 July 1794).

hardly modified by the change experienced by French society in so many other fields after 1789.

Although some of the foregoing undoubtedly contributed little to the Revolution, other activities were on a higher level. After the workers' demonstration of 4-5 September, the committee was asked to draft a list of citizens who were to compose the revolutionary army then being formed.[101] On 5 nivôse (25 December) it was asked by the Commission of Subsistences and Provisions to appoint two of its members and an expert shoemaker to requisition shoes of good quality in the section,[102] which was done on the following day. The next month it appointed commissioners to go jointly with delegates of the popular society of the section to present gifts donated by various citizens to the Convention. At the same time, it decided to turn over shoes and other articles collected to the *conseil exécutif de l'administration d'habillement*.[103]

During much of ventôse the committee distributed certificates of *civisme*, having decreed, however, on the 8th not to grant them to anyone who could not demonstrate his patriotic conduct prior to 10 August, a measure obviously aimed at former royalists or their sympathizers. At the same time it continued to oversee the distribution of food in public markets, to receive denunciations, and to hear reports and suggestions from the popular society of the section.[104] Its increased activity did not allow it to drop its defense against reported suspects in the section, as the following incident illustrates. When a citizen reported that a tailor had made some derogatory remarks against the popular society, it promptly decided to call him before it to explain his charges.[105] Occasionally it intervened on the request of a commune in behalf of a citizen residing in its section who had been arrested for some reason by authorities of another section.[106] In an-

[101] A.N., F7* 2497, p. 53, 7 September 1793.

[102] *Ibid.*, p. 67.

[103] *Ibid.*, pp. 77-78, 1 pluviôse, Year II (20 January 1794).

[104] *Ibid.*, p. 82. Revolutionary committees shared with civil committees the supervision of distributing articles of necessity. See, for example, B.H.V.P., MS 748, fols. 72-107, many of which deal with certificates authorizing the purchase of wood for fuel during 1793 (Year II); see also MS 769, fol. 304, 8 October 1793; and MS 770, fol. 66, 11 brumaire, Year II (1 November 1793).

[105] A.N., F7* 2497, p. 97, 5 germinal, Year II (25 March 1794).

[106] *Ibid.*, p. 97. This was a protest from the Commune of Chatenay on the arrest of a person by the committee of section Mutius Scaevola.

other case, it sent its own commissioners to Versailles on orders of the Committee of General Security to investigate suspects,[107] and received lists of products on the *maximum* to be enforced. Shortly thereafter it launched a campaign to gather saltpeter and gun powder,[108] and on orders of the Committee of Public Safety it requisitioned horses, wagons, and harness for military transport.[109]

Occasionally it found symbols of royalty slowly decaying on private buildings or grounds, symbols that had long served as decorations but neglected after 10 August. One such image was discovered on a building housing an ex-nobleman on rue Vieille-du-Temple. This ex-noble, now citizen Le Peletier de Morfontaine, a short time after the visit of four members of the committee, found it prudent to donate 300 livres for widows and children of volunteers of the section.[110] On 27 June Bertrand and Guéneau searched the premises of a Chierry reported to be in possession of a cross of Saint Louis, but found nothing.[111] In one case, a summer house on rue Tiron was found with a *fleur de lys* clearly visible. Carron, Houdaille, and Gervais, accompanied by police commissioner Auzolles, reported this contravention of the law, surely an example of overzealousness.[112]

In one case the committee was forced to apologize to the Committee of General Security for having proposed Duhamel, who had been duly appointed. His continual state of drunkenness and frequent absence as well as his unauthorized actions had embarrassed his colleagues. Some months later the committee was forced to send two of its members, Houet and Milliet, to make a formal complaint on the conduct of Duhamel, who, drunk again, complained loudly that all were against him.[113] Two days later it was Duhamel who reported that he had attended a dance where there were many volunteers and gendarmes present, whom he had forced to retire before midnight,

[107] *Ibid.*, p. 101, 12-13 germinal, Year II (1-2 April 1794).

[108] *Ibid.*, p. 114, 12-13 germinal and 9 floréal, Year II (1-2 and 28 April 1794).

[109] *Ibid.*, p. 132, 18 messidor, Year II (6 July 1794).

[110] *Ibid.*, Gervais, Guéneau, Bertrand, and Mazin paid him a visit on 12 pluviôse, Year II (31 January 1794). The donation was made on 17 pluviôse (5 February), p. 84.

[111] *Ibid.*, p. 128.

[112] A.P.P., A A/136, fol. 43, 11 brumaire, Year II (1 November 1793).

[113] A.N., F7* 2498, pp. 118, 151, 22 frimaire, Year III (12 December 1794) and 19 nivôse, Year III (8 January 1795).

ignoring their complaints.[114] For the time being, then, Duhamel continued in his post. Another instance of dereliction of duty was the
inattendance of Godard throughout the month of vendémiaire (September-October), duly noted by the secretary.[115] These two examples
seem to be the only record of neglect of duty by committee members.

Committeemen were careful to follow regular and accepted procedure in the examination of suspects, the confiscation of weapons, or
the sealing of personal papers and effects. It is surprising, given the
improvised nature of its early activity and the commotion and tension
surrounding it, that so few complaints of irregularity were leveled
against the committee. When they did appear they were politically
motivated after the fall of Robespierre, and, even more so, after the
abortive insurrection of prairial in 1795.

The committee seemed genuinely concerned with procedure to be
followed when it freed prisoners. Should witnesses be provided by
itself upon removing seals on papers, or, should they be selected from
outsiders? In a number of cases it freed those arrested on grounds of
irregularity with respect to their lack of civic cards, on the responsibility of two citizens who were willing to rescue the delinquents.[116]
An examination of its *procès-verbal* reveals no act of brutality, although
questionable interrogations and instances of petty tyranny can be leveled against it. Considering the untutored and inexperienced nature
of many of its members, it is not surprising that occasional acts of
injustice took place.

After thermidor, the new committee was kept busy in removing
seals placed on papers and effects of former suspects. Individuals who
felt that they had been wronged or who were seeking personal vengeance now began to bombard it with protests of pretended infractions
in the conduct of former members. The new members spent much
time throughout the month of September examining the *procès-verbal*
for these irregularities.[117] The following month four members of the

---

[114] *Ibid.*, p. 152, 21 nivôse (10 January).

[115] *Ibid.*, p. 116, 20 frimaire, Year III (10 December 1794). The treasurer of the
committee, Desgrouard, had paid each member 160 livres for the month of vendémiaire except to Godard, who had been present only once throughout the month.
The committee reported this breach to the Committee of General Security. *Ibid.*, p.
87.

[116] *Ibid.*, pp. 120-121, 122, and *passim*.

[117] A.N., F7* 2498, *passim*. After the decree of 18 thermidor, Year II (5 August

former committee (Guéneau, Pommer, Mazin, and Deschamps) were forced to make a formal denial of having misappropriated funds of the national treasury allotted for army equipment, giving a complete account of the money in question and protesting indignantly that they had not touched a sou of this sum.[118]

By April 1795 members of this reconstituted body received a communication from the Committee of General Security authorizing all citizens who had complaints against the former institution to examine registers in order to regain their confiscated effects or be compensated for losses resulting from these confiscations. If their grievances were well founded, they were to specify who were the men responsible for illegal actions.[119] It should be noted that this decree was adopted after the failure of the *journée* of 12 germinal. The directive undoubtedly encouraged further attacks on the old committeemen.

When the committee began to deal with these complaints, it was observed that many who had asked for the return of their weapons ostensibly seized from them before thermidor were not even mentioned in the minutes. Was this sheer negligence on the part of former commissioners, or were these complaints based on nothing but vindictiveness? It is difficult to believe that at a time when officials took note of every civic card granted they would be careless in recording the names of individuals whose weapons were being confiscated. Moreover, it was customary to have a number for each weapon or article placed in a warehouse. Whether their owners had copies of these receipts is not clear. In any case, it was decided now to maintain a separate journal where these demands would be recorded daily and appropriate comments placed beside each such request.[120]

In addition to the removal of seals on the effects of former suspects, the habitual concerns of former authorities continued. There were always new suspects to investigate and prison plots to foil. A released

---

1794), revolutionary committees were authorized to release suspects imprisoned prior to 9 thermidor. This was done despite the danger to their position by such releases. The Committee of General Security tempered this act, however, by declaring that it would pay no heed to complaints of the general assemblies, unless supported by the constituted authorities, that is, the civil committees. A.N., F7* 2411; 26, 28 thermidor (13, 15 August).

[118] B.H.V.P., MS 748, fol. 113, 8 brumaire, Year III (29 October 1794).

[119] A.N., F7* 2498, p. 258, 21 germinal, Year III (10 April 1795).

[120] *Ibid.*, p. 80, 26 brumaire, Year III (16 November 1794).

prisoner by name of Rozier, for example, informed the committee of a planned break in the Luxembourg prison.[121] Royalist slogans chalked on walls also brought flurries of activity.[122] Occasionally the committee was guilty of acts of petty tyranny, as when it ordered an armed force to surround a dance hall in order to check cards of security. One irate citizen, Caron, insulted its commissioners for interfering with his amusement, and spent the night in jail for his pains.[123]

Sometimes a false alarm disturbed the committee, as when a patriot reported that seals placed on doors and windows of a house had been broken. When its commissioners investigated the matter they found nothing more serious than that the wind had forced a casement window, leaving the original seal intact.[124] This false alarm was balanced, however, by genuine concern when the authorities received a warning from the police administration to gauge the effect produced by a poster entitled "People, Awake, it is Time."[125] Occasionally a case involving an individual reappears in the minutes of the committee until the matter under investigation or in dispute is resolved, or, at times, simply drops from view.[126] At other times a personal quarrel, as between husband and wife, involved the committee, judicial authorities, and even the regular army.[127]

Salaries of members remained unchanged at 5 livres per day,[128] but

[121] *Ibid.*, pp. 26-27, 16 vendémiaire, Year III (7 October 1794). This supposedly involved the son of a former minister, a Prussian colonel, and an English national.

[122] *Ibid.*, pp. 64, 68, 77; 16, 18, 24 brumaire, Year III (6, 8, 14 November 1794), dealing with an investigation of a slogan, "long live Louis XVII" chalked on the wall of a workshop.

[123] *Ibid.*, p. 143, 12 nivôse, Year III (1 January 1795).

[124] *Ibid.*, p. 220, 16 ventôse, Year III (6 March 1795).

[125] *Ibid.*, p. 229, 24 ventôse, Year III (14 March 1795).

[126] One of these involved a dispute with a shoe and leather merchant, Augustin Robillard, and upon his death, with his widow. The committee even allowed its colleagues of the civil committee to rule between it and Mme Robillard. *Ibid.*, pp. 118-119, 121, 150-151, 162, 214, 216, 217, 219, continuing on and off from 22 frimaire, Year III (12 December 1794) to 15 ventôse, Year III (5 March 1795).

[127] *Ibid.*, pp. 63-64, 66, 71, 74, 79, 96, 145, dealing with a Mathurin Pilleul, a shady character.

[128] On 1 frimaire, Year III (21 November 1794), treasurer Desgrouard reported paying individual members for the quarter beginning with 1 vendémiaire 160 livres per person for a total of 1,760 livres. (The difference from 1,920 livres, that is, 160 x 12 is accounted for by the absence of Godard, and, probably, occasional nonattendance of others.) *Ibid.*, p. 87.

daily expenses varied. The secretary, commissioners, the *garçon de bureau*, and the concierge all had to be paid. In addition, the committee had to purchase wood, candles, oil, paper, and pay for the printing of circulars. Thus, for the last quarter of 1794 the committee's total expenses amounted to 7,262 livres 13 sous.[129]

The surveillance committee of section Droits-de-l'Homme continued in office until 15 brumaire, Year IV (6 November 1795). A letter from the minister of the interior advised it that since the installation of the Executive Directory and the dissolution of the Committee of General Security, the functions and salaries of the committee would cease. Its members were requested, therefore, to surrender their official papers and effects.[130] The journal of the committee closed on that day after an unbroken record of more than two years and seven months.

How harsh was the terror in section Droits-de-l'Homme? The revolutionary committee was responsible for the arrest and incarceration of thirty prisoners brought to La Force between 9 September 1793 and 21 April 1794.[131] This is approximately one person arrested for each of the thirty-two weeks of the period. These thirty may be broken down further into the following: nineteen were held as suspects, two were accused of anticivic behavior, one had insulted a patriotic procession, one was guilty of violating the *maximum*, one of profiteering, and another had insulted the armed forces. These twenty-five individuals could be charged with "counterrevolutionary" activity against the government. The last five were indicted for the following reasons: one had allegedly manufactured badly made shoes; another either made

[129] Expenditures were as follows: for the office, 1,452 livres, 13 sous; for a secretary, 600 livres of annual salary of 2,400 livres; for two commissioners, 1,800 livres; for the *garçon de bureau*, 1,000 livres; and for the concierge, 2,400 livres. *Ibid.*, p. 161, 24 nivôse, Year III (13 January 1795), report of Desgrouard; see Bouloiseau, "Les Comités de surveillance," *Annales Historiques*, 10, wherein the author describes the functions of each employee. Receipts and expenditures varied each quarter. See Desgrouard's report in A.N., F⁷* 2498, pp. 87, 144, 255, 332, and 342 for the period from 18 germinal, Year III (7 April 1795) to 20 messidor, Year III (8 July 1795).

[130] *Ibid.*, p. 409. This letter was addressed to the committee at its address, 160 rue Avoye.

[131] A.P.P., A B/327 and A B/326, the *ecrous* of La Force prison. The names of committee members that appear on the prison register are those of Deschamps, Guéneau, Mazin, Pommez(r), Bertrand, Gervais, Bernard, Cordier, Houdaille, Gibois(y), Roger, and Desouches.

or had on his person false *assignats*; a third had committed an act of violence; one had stolen public property; and the last was held without an explanation.[132]

Were these the only imprisonments, it could be argued that the terror in the section was not particularly frightful. Not all who were arrested by the revolutionary committee were incarcerated in La Force prison, however; other places of confinement in Paris were also used. Moreover, the so-called Great Terror did not begin until after the decree of the 22d prairial, Year II (10 June 1794), subsequent to the period discussed above. Although it is true that no one was executed in the section for violating the *maximum* and few were arrested, most being fined and their goods confiscated, the guillotining of such former officials as Fayel, on the one hand, and of Descombes, on the other, must have frightened both the Right and Left in the section.[133]

[132] A.P.P., A B/327, pp. 378, 379, 396, 405, 406, 412, 420, 421, 435, 441, 452, and 459, for September-October 1793. Among those arrested was Philippe Hardy, age 33, listed as a registrar at the police tribunal and former commissioner of section Droits-de-l'Homme to the Commune of 10 August. He was accused of giving asylum to ex-nobles, including a princess Talmont. *Ibid.*, p. 420, 22 September 1793. A.P.P. A B/326 (unpaginated), from November 1793 to June 1794.

[133] There is a document, A.N., F⁷* 53, "Région de Paris deuxième division," which lists the names of those arrested in section Droits-de-l'Homme. It is impossible to know with certainty their fate, however. Descombes' name appears on this list, but not that of Fayel. The first name is that of Gaudin, an ex-*chanoine* of St. Croix imprisoned in Bicêtre. Thirty-five individual names appear, with Le Pel(l)etier Morfontain's name recorded twice. Among these is a woman, Marie-Alexandre Martinville, veuve Duvaugarnier, born in Paris and executed on 4 thermidor, Year II (22 July 1794). Charles Blanquet, called Cocu de Rouville, born in Marvejols, was executed at age thirty-seven on 18 messidor, Year II (6 July 1794). A Barton de Montbas (Gaspard-Siméon), born in Belac, was executed at age fifty on the 9th of thermidor, Year II (27 July 1794). See *Liste des victimes du tribunal révolutionnaire à Paris* (Paris, 1911), nos. 2420, 1946, 2624.

X

The Committee of Welfare,
the Justice of the Peace,
and the Police Commissioner

Poverty in the eighteenth century was as much a product of nature as of social institutions. Disease and the plague, loss of work due to declining demand caused by the changing seasons, illiteracy, unsanitary living conditions, the birth of an unwanted child—all made for chronic misery. In 1788 Condorcet observed: "any family which possesses neither real estate, personal property, nor capital, is subject to fall into poverty at the least accident."[1] This lack of the slightest reserve to fall back on was itself a product of myriad causes rooted in nature and history.[2]

In 1778, the curé Saint-Etienne-du-Mont estimated that there were 120,000 paupers in Paris, not counting the "privileged elite amongst the poor" (*pauvres honteux*),[3] receiving aid in kind at home. Nine years later a brochure entitled *Voeu de la dernière classe du peuple* calculated that there were 200,000 paupers employed in public workshops (*ateliers publics*) or in public spinning workrooms (*ateliers de filature*). Of the 600,000 inhabitants estimated to be in Paris, 10 percent or 60,000 were thought to be indigent, of whom half, or 30,000, were consid-

---

[1] Cited by Camille Bloch, *L'Assistance & l'état en France à la veille de la Révolution (1764-1790)* (Paris, 1908), p. 14. "It needed only some everyday occurrence, a sickness of the main earner, his death, the drying up of domestic industry, the birth of a third or fourth child, to plunge the family into difficulties from which recovery was almost impossible." "Life and Death among the Very Poor," by Olwen Hufton, in *The Eighteenth Century; Europe in the Age of Enlightenment*, edited by Alfred Cobban (New York, 1969), p. 300. This illustrated volume is as scholarly as it is attractive.

[2] Bloch, *L'Assistance*, pp. 380-381.

[3] As defined by Olwen Hufton in her study, *The Poor of Eighteenth-Century France 1750-1789* (Oxford, 1974), p. 215.

ered to be invalids incapable of work; the rest were children, the old, and vagabonds.[4] Mathiez was convinced that the figure of 10 percent poor, which was also the estimate of the Assembly's *comité de mendicité*, was substantially below the real number.[5]

The total of registered poor employed in public works rose from 12,000 in May 1789 to 22,000 in August.[6] In the charitable workshops of Montmartre alone during the latter month there were 17,000. By October 1790 the number employed in these *ateliers* had risen to 19,000 and by June 1791 they reached a new high with 31,000, costing the public treasury 950,000 livres monthly.[7] Bailly reported that merchants, grocers, and jewelers, unemployed or bankrupt in the spring of 1789, begged for the favor to work for 20 sous a day, and women engaged in retailing second-hand goods disguised themselves as men in a desperate effort to earn a man's wages.[8] It was this desperation and the fear of bread riots that finally moved both the National Assembly and the Paris Commune to provide temporary relief.[9]

The type of work that was provided required neither experience nor skill, and paid from 10 to 15 sous per day for women and children and 18 sous for men.[10] That these wages were low even by the standards of their day may be seen if we accept the estimate of the *comité de mendicité*, which held that a family of five needed "a strict minimum of 435 livres a year to survive."[11] Assuming that a man collected his 18 sous a day and worked steadily for six days a week, his earnings would have fallen far short of the modest requirements set by the

[4] *Ibid.*, p. 6. The totals would rise by 10,000 if we accept an additional 100,000 inhabitants for the capital.

[5] "Notes sur l'importance du prolétariat en France à la veille de la Révolution," in *Annales historiques*, 7 (1930), 512-513. Mathiez based this assertion on the results of the bad harvest of 1788 and the unemployment caused by the commercial treaty of 1786 with Britain.

[6] Bloch, *L'Assistance*, p. 418.

[7] Lacroix, I, 192-193, citing the report of the duke la Rochefoucauld-Liancourt, for the Comité de mendicité to the National Assembly, 16 June 1791.

[8] *Mémoires*, II, 316-317, cited by Lacroix, I, 411.

[9] Bailly, *Mémoires*, II, 254, in which he revealed fear of a mutiny, cited by Lacroix, I, 192.

[10] Tuetey, *L'Assistance*, I, Introduction, p. CXLII.

[11] Kaplow, p. 165, citing François Furet, "Definition," in *Annales: economies, sociétés, civilisations*, 18 (1963), 459-474.

committee.[12] The alternative to working in these *ateliers*, however, was to face starvation and the elements.

The social makeup of those employed in the charitable workshops did not differ substantially from those arrested in the riots and demonstrations between January and June 1789. Most of the latter were hungry and unemployed, certainly not criminals in the modern sense of the term. After 14 July they would be known as "conquerors of the Bastille."[13] Conquerors or vagabonds, the concentration of thousands of ill-disciplined and disaffected men aroused uneasiness and even fear in the authorities. They met with the director of the *atelier* of Montmartre, and even sent a delegation to visit Necker in Versailles to confer on the problem. Among the latter was a representative of district Petit-Saint-Antoine.[14]

This fear was real enough, since the Assembly of Representatives of the Commune had to revoke its own measure, which had lowered the wages of workers employed in the *ateliers*, an act termed by Bailly a "provocation."[15] The reaction of the unemployed was so threatening that on 15 August Lafayette had to reassure them in person that the obnoxious decree had been revoked. The same day, the Assembly was forced to agree to open the *ateliers* on a Sunday so that the workers of Montmartre might earn wages that they had lost during a two-day holiday some time before.[16] Fearing another riot, the authorities had even mounted cannon at the barriers of Montmartre,[17] and a week

[12] If he worked 313 days, he would have earned 5,634 sous or 281.7 livres.

[13] Marcel Rouff, "Le Personnel des premières émeutes de 1789" in *La Révolution française, revue d'histoire moderne et contemporaine*, 57 (Paris, 1909), 213-238. The author limited his study to three districts: St.-Jacques-de-la-Boucherie, St.-André-des-Arts, and St.-Germain-l'Auxerrois. The occupations of those arrested as compiled by the authorities of the Châtelet are listed on pp. 219-224. The embryo of Rudé's crowd is contained in these reports. Georges Rudé, "La Composition sociale des insurrections parisiennes de 1789 à 1791," in *Annales historiques*, 24 (1952), 256-288, points out that 58 of the 71 arrested at Reveillon were workers, and then traces their role in the Revolution from the fall of the Bastille to the massacre of the Champs de Mars, 17 July 1791. Although they played no special role, they formed a large portion of the demonstrators in these events.

[14] Menessier was from district Petit-Saint-Antoine. Lacroix, *Actes*, I, 168, 177-178, 11 and 12 August 1789.

[15] Bailly, II, 265, cited by Lacroix, I, 212, and 204-205, 13 August 1789; Tuetey, *L'Assistance*, I, #34, 23 August 1789.

[16] Lacroix, I, 225.

[17] Tuetey, *L'Assistance*, I, Introduction, p. CXLVI, 24 August 1789.

later commissioners of the *ateliers* asked Lafayette to take measures against possible disturbances.[18] When one hundred poor workers from Chaillot were refused admission to the *ateliers de charité* on the pretext that they had failed to register in time, their curé warned the authorities: "You must understand, gentlemen, the danger that would result from leaving such a number of poor workers without occupation or resources."[19] That the latter could, indeed, be driven to desperation may be believed even if their portrait as sketched by the *Révolutions de Paris* smacks of literary exaggeration. The journal saw them as "in rags, [with] haggard faces, sunken eyes and hollow cheeks, the brow beset with fear and anxiety, and at times with remorse."[20]

The atmosphere of uncertainty and fear gave rise to strange rumors that the men employed in these *ateliers* were building fortifications and redoubts for royalist artillery to be directed against the people of Paris. It was district Petit-Saint-Antoine that responded to these vague threats by sending observers to investigate and report their results to the general assembly. Its commissioners made a thorough study of the workshops of Montmartre and expressly denied that the work had anything to do with military entrenchments. On the contrary, they stressed, it was designed to improve roads to facilitate the transport of grain and flour to the capital. The benefit to the people, rich and poor alike, would be obvious. Furthermore, they found that the great mass of workingmen was orderly and peaceable.[21]

While the municipality and the National Assembly were taking practical steps to suppress want, the districts also adopted specific proposals. On 16 November 1789, Jacobins-Saint Dominique established the first lay committee on poverty, dividing its *comité de bienfaisance* into eight departments, with several streets under one com-

[18] Lacroix, 399, 30 August 1789.

[19] B.H.V.P., MS 741, fol. 26, "Du Comité des ateliers du charité de Paris," Versailles, 17 September 1789.

[20] Cited by Lacroix, I, 233, n.d.

[21] B.N., MSS, Nouv. acq. fr. 2654, fol. 156, *Procès-verbal de visite à Montmartre, 12 août 1789*. The members of the commission were Saint-Far, an engineer and member of the district's military committee; Plou and Desjardins, architects; and Beaulieu and Usquin, also of the military committee. Their specific instructions had been "to verify the condition of the place, and notably the possibility of a mine." A chevalier Quesnoy de Beaurepaire had published a pamphlet of 32 pages spreading the above rumor.

missioner of the committee. The latter submitted a plan of organization to the general assembly for endorsement, which included a survey of the poor in its district without publishing their names or listing the amount given. Aid was to be extended to those who did not earn enough from their labors, and to the partly and fully unemployed. To facilitate this help, its offices were to be kept open during prescribed hours and a special treasurer of the poor was appointed. Free medical service and drugs were also provided, and one butcher and one baker were selected in the district to distribute meat and bread to the needy, paid for by its treasury.[22] District Petit-Saint-Antoine appropriated 600 livres for this purpose, which were distributed by the curés of Saint Paul, Saint Jean, and Saint Gervais.[23] District Blancs-Manteaux opened a voluntary subscription on 29 August and extended it into October 1789.[24] On 20 February 1790, commissioners of the Commune reported that 66,000 livres had been disbursed among the districts, of which sum Petit-Saint-Antoine had received 650 livres and Blancs-Manteaux 200 livres.[25]

Among the many schemes on how to deal with poverty, some were surprisingly civilized in their recognition of the social elements of the problem. Almost all writers emphasized the need to encourage work and to discourage indolence.[26] Bailly wrote to the Assembly, for example, proposing the establishment of *ateliers de filature* for women, and suggesting a subscription of funds for the poor to be contributed by the more affluent citizens of the capital. This was followed by the adoption of Barnave's motion to gather contributions from members of the Assembly to relieve distress in the capital, but it was recognized as inadequate, shortly thereafter. To deal with the problem, the As-

[22] B.N., Lb[40] 1413, *District des Jacobins Saint-Dominique, Comité de Bienfaisance* (Paris, 1789), 33 pp. By 1 May 1790 the welfare committee had helped 1,091 poor, having received 32,233 livres and spent 16,330 livres. Garrigues, p. 234. This made for less than 15 livres per person for approximately six months, not exactly a generous welfare program.

[23] B.H.V.P., MS 800, fols. 486, 496-497, 18 August 1789.

[24] B.N., Lb[40] 233, *Arrêté de district des Blancs-Manteaux* ([Paris], 29 August 1789), 6 pp.; B.N., MSS, Nouv. acq. fr. 2681, fols. 311-313 ([Paris], 29 August 1789), 6 pp.

[25] Lacroix, *Actes*, IV, 161-162. The exact total was 66,764 l., 12 s., 8 d.

[26] Bloch, *L'Assistance*, pp. 420-422, mentions various proposals; Chassin, *Elections* II, 578-579.

sembly created the *comité de mendicité* on 21 January 1790, reflecting a new spirit in approach to the problem of poverty.[27] Relief was now seen as a social duty, not haphazard charity. Poverty had to be studied seriously and relief was to be dispensed by official governmental bodies. It had to be defined, and work was to be provided for the able and distributed at home in as economic a fashion as possible.[28]

Forming its own relief commission on 2 April 1791, the Paris Commune established parish committees on 12 October, and two weeks later gained the right to administer revenues of the poor, continuing its functions until the last day of August 1793. In October 1791 the municipality gave a new organization to the parish committees, directing them to correspond with the Hôtel de Ville and authorizing them to receive all gifts for the poor. At the same time it forbade them to discriminate on the basis of religion in assigning aid to applicants, an important step in secularizing relief. The existence of parish commissions side-by-side with sectional committees could not continue, however. By December 1791 the latter began demanding the suppression of parish committees and the concentration of relief in their own hands. After 10 August the sections, gaining in strength, redoubled the campaign to destroy their rivals. The Commune finally decided to comply on 8 December 1792, fixing the date of 1 January 1793 for their demise. Delays due to administrative difficulties post-

[27] Lacroix, III, 488-489. The committee consisted of four members at first, and held its first meeting on 2 February 1790. On 17 March, six more members were added. (The motion of Barnave is in A.P., XI, 264-265.) The president of the committee was the duke of Rochefoucauld-Liancourt. Dr. Guillotin was made a member in March, and Barère became a substitute at the same time. The committee sought to define the basis for relief and agreed that it was important to demand work of the unemployed rather than encourage idleness. It was better to provide below the need rather than above it, so as not to encourage the indolent, the committee felt. Camille Bloch and Alexandre Tuetey, *Procès-verbaux et rapports du Comité de mendicité de la constituante 1790-1791* (Paris, 1911), "Annexes à la séance du 26 février 1790," pp. 2-5.

[28] Bloch, *L'Assistance*, pp. 430-434. See especially the "Second rapport du Comité de mendicité, état actuel de la législation du royaume, relativement aux hôpitaux et à la mendicité," which deals with a history of the *hôpitaux*: Bloch and Tuetey, *Procès-verbaux*, pp. 334-350, and the section entitled "Historique de la législation contre les mendiants," pp. 350-355. See also Bloch's discussion on the approach and program of the committee, *L'Assistance*, p. 435-448, *passim*. In a number of respects the ideas of the committee were in advance of the practices in Britain.

poned action on this decree until March, by which time the Convention launched its own plan of relief.[29]

It did so by adopting a decree with a preamble (19 March 1793), which declared that "every man has a right to his subsistence through work, if he is physically fit, and through free aid if he is incapable of working; . . . the care of providing for the maintenance of the poor is a national obligation." Article 8 provided relief for able-bodied unemployed; relief at home for invalids, children, and the ill; private hospitals for sick persons, asylums for abandoned children, the non-resident old and the infirm; and help for victims of unforeseen accidents.[30] Recognition that society owed an obligation to the indigent, the helpless, and the infirm was a step forward from traditional acceptance of destitution as a merited curse on the descendants of Adam. Critics of this theological conception noted that the curse was unevenly distributed, and seemed to have escaped some of his descendants altogether. The Declaration of Rights of the Constitution of 1793 had proclaimed that "public relief is a sacred obligation."[31] On 28 March 1793, the Convention created a central commission of relief (*commission centrale de bienfaisance*) for all Paris, thus formally secularizing aid to the poor.[32] The delegate elected to this commission from section Droits-de-l'Homme was Pierre Michon, residing on rue des Droits-de-l'Homme.[33]

The General Council supplemented the plan of the Convention on 25 July 1793 by providing for the election by majority vote of the general assemblies of members of relief committees. The latter were to serve for two-year terms, take a careful census of the poor in their

[29] Mellié, pp. 235-238.

[30] See the report of Bô for the *comité de secours publics* to the Convention and the discussion that followed. A.P., LX, 322-328, 19 March 1793. Duvergier, V, 204-205, lacks a preamble. "Décret concernant la nouvelle organisation de secours publics," 19-24 March 1793, in 16 articles.

[31] Article 21: "Public relief is a sacred obligation. Society owes subsistence to unfortunate citizens, either by procuring work for them or by providing the means of existence for those unable to work."

[32] Tuetey, *L'Assistance* IV, #293, "Décret de la Convention nationale instituant une commission centrale de bienfaisance pour administrer les revenus de dotation appartenant aux pauvres des paroisses de Paris." Art. 15 suppressed parish commissions.

[33] *Ibid.*, IV, #293, 28 March 1793. For Michon, see the chapter on the civil committee.

respective sections, and distribute relief in kind every week.[34] These sectional committees were installed on 20-22 September 1793, and often deliberated in common with civil committees, discussing jointly the grave problem of provisions for the capital. Members of these welfare committees also helped to distribute bread and meat in their sections.[35] With the consolidation of the revolutionary government, their members became subject to appointment by the Committees of Public Safety and of General Security. On 12 December 1794 they were placed under the jurisdiction of the Convention's Committee of Public Assistance (*comité de secours publics*).[36] The *commission centrale* was replaced by the Directory on 16 floréal, Year V (5 May 1796) by a *bureau général de bienfaisance*, while the relief committees disappeared with the liquidation of the sections themselves.[37]

There is little doubt that without the constant pressure of the sections, the nature and amount of relief would have been far more modest than it was.[38] The right of the poor, the old, and the orphans to treatment equal to that received "by the rich in their mansions," in the words of section Homme Armé, was echoed by many others.[39] Petitions like those of faubourg Saint-Antoine to levy a tax on the rich and to deposit the proceeds in a common treasury that would divide the sums among needy citizens was an impulse and an echo of popular agitation for relief.[40] The very language of the provisions adopted by the Commune in establishing relief committees may be found in petitions and resolutions of the sections.[41]

[34] Tuetey, *L'Assistance*, IV, #317, in 6 chapters. "Plan d'organisation des quarante-huit comités de bienfaisance dans les quarante-huit sections de la ville de Paris." The three classes of poor differ slightly from those recognized in the winter of 1794. A.N., H 2121, pcs. 14 and 15, "Municipalité de Paris, départements des établissemens publics," 26 pluviôse, Year II (14 February 1794).

[35] Mellié, pp. 243, 244. Members of the committee held their posts for one month, and the committee was renewed by one-third every *décade*. *Ibid.*, pp. 244-245.

[36] Tuetey, *L'Assistance*, IV, #339, "Décret de la Convention nationale, donnant au comité de secours publics la surveillance sur les comités de bienfaisance de la commune de Paris."

[37] Mellié, p. 246.

[38] See the discussion of Soboul on the right to work and to relief, pp. 491-493. These demands appeared "as corollaries to the right of existence."

[39] B.N., MSS, Nouv. acq. fr. 2647, fols. 144-145, n.d. [1792].

[40] B. & R., XXVI, 317-318, 1 May 1793.

[41] A good example is B.N., MSS, Nouv. acq. fr. 2647, fols 156-165, *Adresse à la*

As to the effectiveness of the relief provided and the plight of the poor during 1793-Year II, this is more difficult to assess. The recognition of the right to relief and the new dignity given to penury must have had a profound effect on the militant *sans-culottes*. On the other hand, the harsher laws of the Terror and the less tolerant attitude of revolutionaries to their infraction might have made the position of the indigent less secure than before the Revolution.[42] Daujon, administrator of poorhouses, reported to the General Council that one Parisian out of every nine was receiving relief in the spring of 1794.[43]

What proportion this registered number of poor held to the total mass of indigents is impossible to say, however. Observers cited at the beginning of the chapter thought the number was far higher. Officially, section Quinze-Vingts had the most poor with 6,601. In the center of the capital, section Maison-Commune, a neighbor of Droits-de-l'Homme, reported 4,258, or 1 for every 2.9 inhabitants, a high percentage indeed.[44] Yet the funds appropriated by the Convention for use by its Committee of Public Assistance were, as a total figure, impressive.[45] It is only in relation to the immensity of the task facing the Convention that the adequacy of the sums can be questioned, even if the amounts contributed by departments, communes, and individual sections are added. This is hardly astounding, if the effectiveness of relief in contemporary life is compared with that of the eighteenth century.

It is unfortunate that so few records exist on the work of the welfare committee in section Droits-de-l'Homme. Many references are to the joint sessions of the civil and welfare committees, but what precisely

Convention nationale contenant projet de décret pour l'établissement d'une commission municipale de bienfaisance pour la Ville de Paris, 19 pp.

[42] Richard Cobb in his *Reactions to the French Revolution* (London, 1972), holds that the plight of the poor during the Revolution became worse than it had been before 1789, pp. 140-142, and *passim*.

[43] Daujon cited 72,801 registered indigents, 14 germinal, Year II (3 April 1794), in *Journal de la montagne*, no. 144, p. 1,162, 17 germinal, Year II (6 April 1794). If one accepts the number of inhabitants in the capital in 1795 as being 636,772 (according to A.N., F⁷ 3688⁴, "Etat général de la population de Paris"), the proportion of indigent was roughly 11 percent. Raising the population to 700,000 would make the proportion 10 percent.

[44] Soboul, p. 438.

[45] A.N., F⁴* 33, "Fonds mis à la disposition de la commission de secours publics" (for years II and III).

was discussed, how indigence was determined, what questions were asked of applicants for assistance, or the subsidy determined upon— these pursuits are lost to history. The number of poor in the section, that is, those officially registered as such by the census conducted, was 1,265, or 10.3 percent if the population figure of 13 pluviôse, Year III is accepted.[46] Viar, as president of the section's *comité de bienfaisance*, wrote to the civil commission that the section had an "immensity of indigents."[47] If this vague phrase meant that of the 1,265 of the section's poor the same proportion received a subsidy as in its neighbor section of Arcis (40 percent), this would have allowed 506 to collect help for attending sessions of the general assembly, probably too high a figure. But even if the latter were cut in half, about 258 *sectionnaires* could have pocketed the 40-sous subsidy.

Nine sections had substantially higher numbers of poor (double and triple the number of Droits-de-l'Homme); seven had somewhat higher numbers; three were approximately the same; and twenty-eight sections were below.[48] If the number of working men and women in the section who were unemployed regularly because of seasonal changes or periodic fluctuations of the market are included, the number of poor must have been substantially higher. Moreover, the drastic decline in property values between 1790 and 1795 (as shown in Chapter I) undoubtedly both aggravated and was the consequence of the economic crisis in the section. In either case, it must have raised the number on relief or forced others to abandon the capital.

Upon receiving notification of the creation of the *commission central de bienfaisance*, the general assembly of section Droits-de-l'Homme resolved to proclaim the news to all inhabitants of the section.[49] It

[46] *Journal de la montagne*, 17 germinal, Year II, and A.N., F⁷ 3688⁴, "Etat général."

[47] A.N., F¹⁵ 133, 12 vendémiaire, Year III (3 October 1795).

[48] These were Poissonnière (21.9%), Popincourt (36%), Montreuil (31.2%), Quinze-Vingts (36.1%), Maison-Commune (34.8%), Fraternité (24.3%), Observatoire (21.2%), Sans-Culottes (26.1%), and Finistère (42%). The slightly higher were: République (12%), Bonne-Nouvelle (12.2%), Faubourg-Montmartre (15.5%), Bondy (15%), Temple (11.2%), Faubourg-du-Nord (16.7%), Invalides (16%), Bonnet-Rouge (12.2%). About the same were: Champs-Elysées (10.9%), Chalier (10.1%), and Panthéon-Français (10.5%). These percentages are taken from the table of Soboul, pp. 1,091-1,092.

[49] B.N., MSS, Nouv. acq. fr. 2691, fol. 269, 29 April 1793 in a letter from Pache. The resolution of the assembly followed, signed by Picard, fils.

must have proceeded to take a census of the poor, and after the establishment of sectional welfare committees (25 July 1793), it elected its
own committee.[50] What evidence does exist is indirect, some based
on records of the section's revolutionary committee, some other on
those of the police commissioner. A baker sought assistance from the
welfare committee, for example. Since he was employed, however,
and in a state of requisition because of his occupation, he was sent to
the revolutionary committee. Although the latter admitted that his
earnings were insufficient, he was prohibited by law from seeking
more remunerative employment. It justified his efforts, therefore, at
seeking help and returned him to the welfare committee.[51]

Another case came to the attention of the police commissioner. A
Jean-Marie Delisle, femme Gentil, age 64, a lodger in the house of
Joseph Levasseur, a painter-gilder, lived in dire poverty, abandoned
and alone, shivering with cold. Although given assistance by the welfare committee, she was too ill to care for herself, but refused all
efforts on the part of Levasseur and his wife to send her to the hospital
(*hospice de l'humanité*). She had called for a little heat, but Levasseur
was afraid that it might lead to a fire in his lodging house, and
sought, instead, to put her to bed. She refused, and shortly after, was
found dead in her room. After burying her corpse and paying the
expenses of the funeral, a sum of 13 livres was deposited with the
justice of the peace and, in the absence of heirs, the room was sealed
with her effects.[52]

Appeals to the welfare committee by individuals who had no means
to pay a tax due led to investigations of the economic status of the
appellant. If the committee was satisfied that the applicant did, indeed, lack the means to pay his obligation, he was issued a certificate
to that effect duly signed by members of the committee.[53] The com-

---

[50] There is no reference either to the welfare commission or to an election of a
welfare committee in the *procès-verbal* of the assembly as it appears in B.V.C., MS
120. Members of the committee are discussed below.

[51] A.N., F⁷* 2497, p. 74, 22 nivôse, Year II (11 January 1794).

[52] A.P.P., A A/136, fols. 220-221. Among her papers was a petition for help to
the Convention dated 1 brumaire, Year III (22 October 1794), in which she claimed
to have lost 2,000 *écus* seized by authorities of the Old Regime (how, she failed to
explain), and mentioned that her husband had disappeared twelve years previously.

[53] B.H.V.P., MS 754, fol. 53, 26 fructidor, Year III (12 September 1794). This
is a certificate issued to *citoyenne* Fagotte testifying to her inability to pay any kind of

mittee also sought to place blind beggars in houses of asylum created for that purpose, and asked the *commissaires de secours publics* to determine the quota of funds due the section for its work among the poor.[54] At times the revolutionary committee initiated action without consulting the relief committee, as when Philippe Garnier, age seventy, with one son in the army and another employed as an apprentice baker, was referred to the Commission of Subsistence for help.[55] The committee also gave certificates of indigence upon the request of poor citizens appearing before it.[56]

Among the various certificates delivered were those entitling individuals to purchase a modest amount of sugar, usually one pound, occasionally two. Sugar was thought to possess medicinal qualities, and the 200-odd customers of the section who were given the right to purchase it did so only with the authorization of a doctor, a surgeon, a health officer, or a midwife.[57] A register of those receiving the sugar with their addresses and certificates of authorization was kept by the sectional authorities, probably the civil and welfare committees. Although it was the general assembly that legalized its purchase, the processing of certificates must have been done by the *comité de bienfaisance* together with the civil committee.

Although it could be argued that the subsidy paid by the Convention to the workingmen for overthrowing the Gironde was a political act, it was, undoubtedly, a form of relief as well, and was conceived as such by the Mountain and its supporters.[58] The amount varied for each of the thirty-three sections whose records are extant, from the high of 17,562 livres paid to citizens of section Montreuil to the low of 276 livres for the forty-six men of section Gardes-Françaises.[59] The

---

tax. It was then submitted to the civil committee and, finally, to departmental authorities.

[54] Tuetey, *L'Assistance*, IV, #195, 28 prairial, Year II (16 June 1794), "Lettre du comité de bienfaisance de la section des Droits-de-l'Homme." This was in reference to the *maison d'humanité*, Quinze-Vingts.

[55] A.N., F7* 2497, p. 123, 27 prairial, Year II (15 June 1794).

[56] A.N., F7* 2498, p. 165, 27 nivôse, Year III (16 January 1794). The request was made by Montauzun de Saint Eÿs, possibly an impoverished noble.

[57] A. de P., D 3 AZ 287, pc. 51, "Registre pour les bons de sucre délivrés par l'assemblée populaire des Droits-de-l'Homme, chez le citoyen Guiot, épicier, Vieille rue du Temple, no. 84." This is a folio of 26 pp.

[58] A.N., BB3 80, d. 16, pcs. 2, 8 on 3 June and 21 (?) July 1793, as examples.

[59] *Ibid.* and Calvet, "Remarques sur la participation des sections."

40 sous earned per day assured workingmen who remained under arms they would not suffer an economic loss.[60] It is unfortunate that the records for section Droits-de-l'Homme are missing, as it would be interesting to compare the sums expended in the section per individual to see if Varlet's agitation against the subsidy had any effect.

Another form of relief (discussed in Chapter VII) was the 40-sous subsidy given to poorer citizens for attending sessions of the general assemblies. As was noted above, not everyone supported this kind of relief, and its opponents numbered conservatives as well as radicals such as Jean Varlet. Being a champion of equality, the young *enragé* did not think it possible for indigent citizens to maintain this principle unless they enjoyed a position of human dignity that would be lost if they were paid for services to the state. He had converted the sectional assembly of Droits-de-l'Homme to his views as early as 4 June, when its delegation declared publicly, in the General Council, that it refused the proffered aid voted for the poorer citizens who had been under arms during the late insurrection. The council praised the delegation for its spirit of self-sacrifice, as was seen, but held that good patriots could accept the pay with honor.[61] That Varlet's section was not alone in this conviction was evident, as the armed force of section Panthéon Français refused the gift the same day.[62] By September, sections Sans-Culottes and Marchés had endorsed the same principle,[63] and on 16 September the general assembly of Droits-de-l'Homme again renounced the bounty.[64] Shortly thereafter sections Marchés and Contrat-Social petitioned against the decree as "an attack against the sovereignty of the people," and swore not to accept the offering voted by the Convention.[65]

[60] The amount earned per individual varied slightly from the 6 livres for section Gravilliers to 5.96 for Montreuil and 5.92 of Quinze-Vingts. This varied further if the sums paid are divided by the total number of *journées* listed. For example: the number of days under arms for section Gravilliers was 4,372, which made it exactly 3 days per individual. For Montreuil it was 8,781, thus being 2.98 per person, and so on.

[61] B.N., MSS, Nouv. acq. fr., 2647, fol. 179, 4 June 1793.

[62] Fillon, *Inventaire des autographes*, no. 547, p. 67; Charavay, *Catalogue* (1862), no. 98, items 22 and 23.

[63] B.V.C., MS 120, fols. 144, 146, 15 September 1793.

[64] *Moniteur*, XVII, no. 259, p. 654.

[65] A.N., C 275, d. 710, pc. 15, 15 vendémiaire, Year II (6 October 1793).

On 17 September 1793, Varlet made a provocative and ill-timed speech in the Convention attacking its decree to limit sectional assemblies to two a week (later twice a *décade*), and rejecting with indignation the proposed subsidy of 40 sous.[66] "In a free state the people cannot pay themselves to exercise their rights," he declared, and refused the help voted "in the name of the *sans-culottes* of Paris."[67] In criticizing the decree, Varlet attacked heatedly "the mandatories of the people" who, having just promulgated the Constitution had promptly forgotten it. "You decree the rights of man and you dishonor it," he charged. These immoderate words brought forth an angry counterattack. The enraged deputies, including Robespierre, called his petition "counterrevolutionary . . . a piece of metaphysical nonsense," and accused its author of being in the pay of Pitt and Coburg.[68] The following day the Committee of General Security ordered Varlet's arrest and detention in the Madelonnettes prison.[69]

A few weeks before Varlet's appearance in the Convention, and even prior to the formal establishment of the *comités de bienfaisance*, section Droits-de-l'Homme held an election for the office of president of this committee on 25 August 1793. As was mentioned above, Etienne Décourchant and Joseph Giboy received an equal number of votes, with the former becoming president because of his greater age.[70] Most

[66] On 9 September 1793, the Convention decreed that meetings of general assemblies be limited to Sundays and Thursdays and that wage-workers be paid 40 sous per session for attendance. A.P., LXXIII, 601.

[67] *Ibid.*, LXXIV, 311-313; *Moniteur*, XVII, no. 262, p. 682, 19 September 1793; B. & R., XXIX, 112; B.N., Lc² 563, *Mercure universel*, XXXI, no. 927, p. 293, 19 September 1793.

[68] A.P., LXXIV, 311-313; B. & R., XXIX, 113-115; *Moniteur*, XVII, no. 262, p. 682; *Mercure universel*, XXXI, no. 927, pp. 293-294.

[69] A.N., AF* II, 286, signed by Geoffroy, Lavicomterie, and Vadier. Tuetey, *Répertoire*, IX, no. 1336, 18 September 1793. Antoine Arnault Chemitte testified before the Committee of General Security on various "anti-civic proposals" made by Varlet. A copy of the warrant for the arrest of Varlet "for having made counterrevolutionary proposals" is in this dossier. A.N., F⁷ 4645, d. 2. The subsequent career and ideas of Varlet may be found in Morris Slavin, "L'Autre enragé: Jean-François Varlet," pp. 34-67, in *Eine Jury für Jacques Roux* (Berlin, 1981); and "Jean Varlet as Defender of Direct Democracy," *Journal of Modern History*, 39 (December 1967), 387-404.

[70] A.N., F⁷ 4665, d. 2. Neither Décourchant's nor Targé's name appears, however, on the obverse side of the document. According to the record of this session, the following fourteen names appear as members of the committee of welfare: Porcher (outgoing president), Dufour, Boussière (*président adjoint*), Rossignol, Doublet, Au-

members of the welfare committee had served on the civil committee by the fall of 1794, and a number had been on its revolutionary committee; few were relatively new men.[71]

Two days before the list mentioned above was drafted, the president of the section's welfare committee, Viar, wrote to the Commission des administrations civiles, police et tribunaux, informing it of the section's action in electing the eighteen members to the welfare committee, divided into nine departments. His reasons for electing this number were two: the extent of the territory included in the section and "the immensity of indigents" within its borders. Viar mentioned that the committee lacked one member because of the detention of Duclos (arrested on 9-10 thermidor). Several might have to be replaced if the Committee of Legislation should rule that members of the civil committee could not serve on the welfare committee at the same time. Among these were Doublet, Giboy, Hardy, and Rossignol (whose name does not appear on the list of 14 vendémiaire).[72] On the

---

zolles, Hardy, Pommer, Collet, Viar, Giboy, David, Gamain, and Thiébart fils (?). These fourteen plus Décourchant make a total of fifteen commissioners. The last name is Targé, *secrétaire adjoint* of the committee.

[71] A.N., F[1b] 11, Seine 18. The sketch below is based on this list, in addition to references already made to most of them in the chapters on the civil and revolutionary committees. As of 14 vendémiaire, Year III (5 October 1794), members of the civil committee were Boussière, Doublet, Rossignol, Giboy, and Hardy. Houdaille and Bernard had been on the revolutionary committee. Viar had been an elector in 1790. Grandjean, a leading Thermidorian in the section, was to be secretary of the general assembly during the arrest of the militants in prairial. Porcher was a judge, and prior to that, had been on the civil committee. Gamain, the pastry shop owner (*patissier*), had been nominated to the civil committee but had refused the post. Collet, the lawyer, had been appointed to the revolutionary committee at its formation but did not accept service. Duclos, the wigmaker, had served on the revolutionary committee. Jambon, also a wigmaker, was to serve on the civil committee for a time. Dupré was to be nominated to the civil committee. The three members who had not been on either the civil or revolutionary committee were: Targé, a professor of mathematics, residing on rue des Rosiers; Parisot, a *receveur des rentes*, located on rue Saint-Antoine; and David, a haberdasher installed on rue de la Tisseranderie. Pierre Michon remained the section's representative to the Commission centrale de bienfaisance. A.N., D III, 255-256[1], d. 2, 14 vendémiaire, Year III. Viar, president of the welfare committee, gave names, occupations, and addresses of the eighteen members in A.N., F[15] 133, 12 vendémiaire, Year III (3 October 1794).

[72] Tuetey, *L'Assistance*, IV, #327, 12 vendémiaire, Year III (3 October 1794), "Lettre du comité de bienfaisance de la section des Droits-de-l'Homme."

other hand, Gamain refused an appointment to the civil committee because he preferred to remain on the committee of welfare, and viewed his service on both as incompatible,[73] whereas François Gorguereau asked to be replaced because of his public duties on other boards.[74] Pollet, who had served on various committees since 10 August 1792, was charged anonymously with peculation and dishonesty in the distribution of supplies, a grave accusation that the Committee of Legislation felt should be investigated. Viar explained that Pollet was responsible for the supervision of the thirty-five butchers in the section, and that after examining his conduct closely the committee could attest to his absolute honesty. The denunciation, he thought, resulted from "the zeal and firmness of C{itizen} Pollet in the exercise of his duties."[75]

Whatever failures may be charged against members of welfare committees, there is no question that they raised the poor to a new dignity and convinced society to recognize the social roots of poverty. The liquidation of these committees at a time when inflation struck so cruelly at the working classes aggravated, especially, the condition of the poor.[76] The failure of the popular insurrections of germinal and prairial stripped the workers of means of defense and pushed thousands of them across the line of poverty into famine.[77] They were not to emerge from this sad plight until long after the *comités de bienfaisance* had passed into history.

If relief committees were limited in their jurisdiction to concern with the poor, justices of the peace had a far broader commission.

---

[73] A.N., D III, 256³, pcs. 28, 29, 12 nivôse, Year III (1 January 1795).

[74] A.N., D III, 255-256¹, d. 3, 8 floréal, Year III (27 April 1795). He was an elector in 1791 and a deputy to the Legislative Assembly. Charavay, *Assemblée electorale*, I, 49.

[75] A.N., D III, 256³, d. 10, pcs. 59 and 12; 19 and 24 prairial, Year III (7 and 12 June 1795).

[76] Richard Cobb, "Disette et Mortalité," in *Terreur et Subsistances 1793-1795* (Paris, 1965), pp. 307-342, paints a graphic picture of the plight of the poor in Rouen. In Paris, police reported a rising tide of suicides, many young women casting themselves with their infants into the Seine, especially after the prairial insurrection. *Ibid.*, p. 315.

[77] B.H.V.P., MS 770, for the Year IV is a collection of certificates and letters dealing with relief, pensions, public works, and petitions for economic assistance. See, especially, fols. 70, 71, 72, 74, 78-79, 80, and 111 for the months of germinal, prairial, floréal, and messidor 1796 for developments in the 7th arrondissement.

The reorganization of the judiciary had provided for great powers conferred on these judges. Endowed with authority to deal without appeal with all cases of persons or property whose value did not exceed 50 livres, and subject to appeal in cases of up to 100 livres, the justices ruled in disputes that included damage done by animals, litigations involving salaries of workmen, wages of domestics, and actions for verbal injuries and brawls. The affixing and removal of seals was also placed under their jurisdiction. Elected by primary assemblies for two years and made eligible for reelection without limit,[78] the two highest candidates became justice of the peace and clerk, respectively. Of the remaining sixteen commissioners on the civil committee, the first six candidates receiving the highest number of votes became *assesseurs*. The yearly salary of the justice of the peace was fixed at 2,400 livres; in addition he received fees from the affixing and removal of seals. At first justices were elected, but by decrees of 8 nivôse and 23 floréal, Year II (28 December 1793 and 12 May 1794), their nomination was assigned to the General Council of the Commune, not to be elected again until 5 fructidor, Year III (22 August 1795).[79]

At the time of the establishment of this office in the section, Fayel, as was seen, became its first justice of the peace, with Thiébart fils as clerk. A number of bailiffs and assessors occupied posts until 10 August 1792, when several changes occurred, and vacancies were filled from time to time by the civil committee.[80] François-Charles Angar,

---

[78] Duvergier, I, Title III, in twelve articles, pp. 313-318; A.P., XVIII, pp. 105-106, in thirteen articles. The law of 25 August-29 September 1790 provided for the Paris courts.

[79] Duvergier, VI, 359, art. 2; VII, 174 on *assesseurs*; VIII, 234. Mellié, pp. 274-275. The secretary-registrars earned 800 livres.

[80] The assessors were Saint Aubin and Louis Billaudel, the latter an elector in 1790 and in 1791. When they resigned, Jean Guyet; Charles Pointard; Regnault fils; Mouchon, a *rentier*; Le Boursier, an architect; and Charpentier, a bailiff became assessors. After 10 August, when Pointard became judge, Thiébart fils remained as clerk until ventôse (1794), when Rives took his place. The assessors were Auzolles (until appointed police commissioner); Ravel, a surgeon, who died after his appointment (date unknown); Pollet, the teacher; Hubert, a *rentier* who died; Vaubertrand, who moved and was replaced by Thiébart fils; Roger, of the civil committee; and Le Boursier, the architect. When two vacancies appeared, the civil committee nominated François Richebourg, Antoine Collet, Paul Porcher, and Lefebvre de Corbinière. A.N., D III, 254, d. 4, pc. 10, 3 frimaire, Year III (23 November 1794). This was signed for the civil committee by Rossignol as president.

the *avocat*, who had signed the militia list of 13-14 July, was among the latter. Elected twice as president of his section and described as "a true republican," he became clerk of the tribunal in the second arrondissement at age forty-eight. He was a native of Paris, residing on rue des Rosiers with his four children (there is no mention of his wife), two of whom had been serving at the front since July 1791. Having completed his studies at age sixteen, he obtained employment with a *procureur* at the Châtelet. When the Revolution broke out, he volunteered to comb the countryside for provisions to send to Paris.[81]

The office of the judge was always crowded by citizens desiring to consult him on their affairs and problems—this, according to a report of an *assesseur* of section Droits-de-l'Homme. For among his many duties were those of conciliation between parties to a dispute.[82] As for the social levels from which these justices were drawn, they were mostly from the upper ranks of the petty bourgeoisie; some had been lawyers in one capacity or another under the Old Regime who had embraced the people's cause in the Revolution.[83]

The removal of Fayel as justice of the peace after the 10th of August brought Claude-Charles Pointard, a former *avocat au parlement*, to the post. Chosen as an elector in 1790 by the primary assembly and re-elected the following year, he was forty-seven years old when he assumed his duties as justice. Having served as a volunteer in the section's armed force, he became an assessor to the justice of the peace before filling the post upon the resignation of Fayel. He held regular office hours during two days of each *décade*, and granted audiences to

[81] A.N., D III, 231, d. 4, 21 thermidor, Year II (8 August 1794).

[82] B.N., Lb⁴⁰ 1789, *Réflexions sur la justice de paix presentées à la section Droits-de-l'Homme par un de ses membres, assesseur* (Versailles, 1792), 4 pp. The author was Barbier, *assesseur* to the justice of the peace of Versailles, arrondissement du Nord, who praised the institution he described.

[83] Soboul, p. 604. Richard Andrews, "The Justices of the Peace of Revolutionary Paris, September 1792-November 1794 (Frimaire Year III)," *Past and Present*, no. 52 (August 1971), pp. 56-105, argues that the personnel which made up the justices of the peace during the period of 1792-Year II was composed of men of local *quartiers* with long family roots and social ties in the sections. The great majority came to the fore after 10 August. Moreover, they were not *sans-culottes* but rather bourgeois from the upper and middle ranks. They were dismissed during the period of reaction in the Year III, not, however, because of class differences, but rather because of factional disputes within the sections. See the critique of this article by Michel Pertué in *Annales historiques*, no. 208 (April-June 1972), pp. 313-317.

all who wished to consult him.[84] Pointard remained as justice until his death on 15 September 1795,[85] that is, for more than three years, reflecting a stability of office rare during times of rapid change. His six assessors were well-known political activists and members of the civil committee, as was his clerk and bailiff.[86]

The cases that came before the justice of the peace dealt with minor complaints, verbal abuse, the affixing and removal of seals, entertainment of testimonials regarding minors, the fixing of paternity of illegitimate children, and the sealing of effects of deceased.[87] Occasionally an appeal reached the National (Legislative) Assembly, as when Fayel requested that his decision be heard in a case where an official had entered a private home without warrant and had struck its dweller.[88] Throughout 1793-Year II the cases heard by Pointard were the same as those that had appeared in less revolutionary days: guardianship of minors, the declaration of a state of minority of imbeciles, affirmation of conditions of pregnancy, and the affixing of seals.[89]

When François-Jacques Richebourg became justice of the peace upon the death of Pointard, the cases before him, as revealed by the register of La Force prison, dealt mainly with accused burglars. An occasional act of violence punctuates the monotony of these entries, and, a few

[84] A.N., D III, 254, d. 4, pc. 5, n.d., a large placard.

[85] A.N., F[1b] 11, Seine 18, 14 vendémiaire, Year III (5 October 1795); Charavay, *Assemblée électorale*, I, 48, II, 41; A.N., D III, 256[3], pcs. 38-39, 30 fructidor and 2e jour complementaire, Year III (16 and 18 September 1795).

[86] *Ibid.* The assessors were Pollet, Roger, Thiébart fils, Le Boursier, Richebourg, and Collet. Joseph-François Rives, residing on rue de la Tisseranderie, a former scribe, was clerk, and Saulnier was the bailiff. In the fall of 1795 Pavace Le Roy and Lefebvre replaced Le Boursier and Collet. In the summer of the same year the general assembly recommended Bellard and Dommanger for position of assessors. Their addresses are given on this placard, but since they were noted above in the chapter on the civil committee I have given only the address of the court clerk, Rives. A.N., F[1b] 11, Seine 18; A.N., D III, 254, d. 4, pc. 10, 3 frimaire, Year III (23 November 1795), and d. 23, fol. 1. A.N., D III, 254, d. 4, pc. 19, 20 messidor, Year III (8 July 1795) and pc. 20, 21 thermidor (8 August).

[87] A. de P., D⁷U¹ 33, 1791. The first entry is for 26 January 1791.

[88] A.P., XLI, 37, 31 March 1792. Antoine-Nicolas Legros had struck Claude-Nicolas Lebas, whose house he had entered without a proper warrant. Fayel asked the Assembly to hear the court of the *police correctionnelle* on his decision of a few days back.

[89] A. de P., D⁷U¹ 33.

rare arrests for suspicious behavior appear.[90] Neither the class of the accused nor the type of crime underwent a change in section Droits-de-l'Homme from the time of the institution of justice of the peace until the end of the period considered. The Revolution might have aggravated some personal problems and ameliorated others, but individual difficulties requiring the intervention of the justice of the peace remained unchanged by political transformations.

To find jurors for criminal cases, the *procureur-général-syndic* of the department had to appeal to the section's civil committee. The law of 14 March 1793, which had divided the criminal court of Paris into two sections, made it difficult to fill these juries with good patriots, he explained. Those whose daily work supported families had to be excluded, which further diminished possible candidates. The civil committee, after some deliberation, submitted a list of twenty-nine names for consideration. Among the listed occupations of these prospective jurors were seven lawyers and two notaries, five architects, a *receveur des rentes*, a pharmacist, one former merchant, a perfumer, and one bailiff-assessor (*huissier-priseur*).[91]

If the social composition of jurors for 1793-Year II is compared with that of the Years VI, VII, and VIII (well beyond our period), it can be seen that it remained fairly constant.[92] Administrators of the Seine department continued to stress the importance of jury duty as they requested lists of prospective candidates from the municipal authorities of the 7th arrondissement. That the section accepted the importance of this duty may be seen in the relatively heavy vote cast for jurors, a total of 224 voting in the summer of 1794.[93]

The municipal law of 21 May 1790 also provided for the creation of police commissioners in each section, elected by simple plurality for a term of two years with the right to succeed themselves. Given deliberative voice on civil committees, they were endowed with the

[90] A.P.P., A B/328. See the entries for the Year IV (1795-1796). See also A.P.P., AB/329 for the same year. These entries continue through 27 messidor, Year VI (15 July 1798), well beyond our period.

[91] B.N., MSS, Nouv. acq. fr. 2691, fol. 243, 1 April 1793. Two names out of thirty-one had been crossed out.

[92] B.H.V.P., MS 763, fols. 171-172, for the Year V. Master craftsmen appear in large numbers. In addition to the lawyers there were grocers, assessors, merchants, cabinetmakers, bondholders, soft drink dispensers, and so on.

[93] B.V.C., MS 120, fol. 160, 10 fructidor, Year II (27 August 1794).

right to arrest lawbreakers *in flagrante delicto* and to send them to prison upon obtaining the signature of one civil commissioner. Daily reports were to be submitted to the officer on duty, and each police commissioner was provided with a secretary-registrar for this purpose. Among other duties, the latter also took minutes of meetings of the civil committee, prepared copies and extracts of the *procès-verbaux*, transmitted them to proper authorities, and kept registers.[94]

Police commissioners were directed by numerous decrees of the General Council to perform a variety of duties. Among these were to watch bill-posters, pedlars, and street-orators; the comings and goings of strangers, and lessors of furnished rooms; the cleaning of streets, the verification of weights and measures, and the price of bread. They also interrogated the accused, affixed or removed seals, drafted the *procès-verbaux* on violation of the law or on accidents, and delivered passports. Their salaries were determined by the Commune, ultimately set at 3,000 livres for themselves and at 1,800 for their secretary-registrars. Suspended on 10 August 1792, they were reelected on 19 September, but lost their importance in the fall of 1793, becoming auxiliaries of revolutionary committees.[95]

Before Pierre Auzolles assumed his duties, there were two police commissioners in the section who had preceded him. Jean-François-Rodolphe Tessier, elected in 1790, was thirty years old, residing on rue des Rosiers, and had served as an elector in the section's primary assembly.[96] He was succeeded by Duillier, who remained in this post until the overthrow of the king when he was suspended by the Commune on 16 August. Duillier complained to the Legislative Assembly that his expulsion was illegal and demanded to be reinstated, a demand that the Commune categorically refused.[97]

Auzolles served as police commissioner of the section from 8 October 1792 until 26 vendémiaire, Year IV (17 October 1795), and was one of eighteen electors sent by the primary assembly after 10 August 1792. At this time he was thirty-six years old, resided on rue Bourg-Tibourg, and was listed as a former teacher and collector of lotteries.[98] After the attempted royalist insurrection of 13 vendé-

[94] Title IV, articles, 3, 6, 12-15, 19-20, 22-23.
[95] Mellié, p. 272.
[96] Charavay, *Assemblée électorale*, I, 50.
[97] A.N., C 161, 357, p. 6, 21 August 1792.
[98] Charavay, *Assemblée électorale*, III, 52; A.N., F⁷ 4583, plaque 5.

miaire, he was arrested on a writ issued by the Committee of General Security. The police commissioner of section Arcis searched his home but found nothing suspicious, and sealed his papers.[99]

The day of his arrest, Auzolles dispatched a letter to the Committee of General Security protesting that he had always executed the law faithfully and citing his experience on 9 thermidor, 12 germinal, and the first days of prairial—all expressing his respect for the law. How could he have had anything to do with provoking the *journée* of 13 vendémiaire, he asked. Throughout most of the day in question he had been busy quelling a serious riot that had broken out in La Force prison. Once he had realized the gravity of this threat, he had gone immediately to the general assembly of the section asking the members to join their armed companies at once, not to waste time in deliberation, but to march immediately on the prison.[100]

That he did not exaggerate the gravity of the situation may be seen in the report of the section's civil committee. Rumors of a prison massacre had made the inmates frantic and rebellious—so rebellious, indeed, that six hundred armed men could not force them back into their cells. Auzolles was forced to fire over the heads of the prisoners and to threaten to shoot four of their leaders who were especially defiant before, finally, breaking the riot.[101]

Over forty members of the section had signed Auzolles's letter to the Committee of General Security, testifying to the truth of his report. In addition to this was the certification of Antoine Bault, the concierge of La Force, that Auzolles had been at the prison from 3 p.m. until the reestablishment of order, that he had left and reentered several times, and that without his help it would have been impossible to put an end to the riot. The civil committee, moreover, testified that Auzolles had always carried out his duties faithfully and zealously, and that such was his standing in the section that he had received support for the office of justice of the peace presented by the section to the Convention's Committee of Legislation. Convinced by this testimony, the Committee of General Security rescinded its writ of arrest against Auzolles on 3 brumaire, Year IV (25 October 1795),

---

[99] A.N., F⁷ 4583, d. 5, 26 vendémiaire, Year IV (18 October 1795).

[100] *Ibid.*, 26 vendémiaire, Year IV.

[101] *Ibid.*, 12 vendémiaire (4 October). The riot broke out because of rumors that another September massacre was being planned.

and Fremy, police commissioner of section Arcis, removed the seals from his papers.[102]

In addition to the police commissioner there were police inspectors, one of whom was Pavas Le Roy, residing on rue Bourg-Tibourg. His colleague, Jean Chevalier, and he were charged by the section's revolutionary committee with having acted arbitrarily and with having abused their authority. At the time of his arrest on 22 nivôse, Year II (11 January 1794), Le Roy was fifty-two years old. The two men had been pressed into service by Simon Robert (probably a member of the Commune's military force), to arrest a runner (*garçon courreur*) for failure to perform his military duty and for fraudulently collecting money for service he had not performed (31 May-2 June). This jurisdictional dispute between the revolutionary committee and the police department of which Le Roy and Chevalier were victims was resolved, finally, when the administration of police of the Paris Commune stepped in and released them from Conciergerie prison.[103] It is possible that the dispute between the two agencies had arisen in the course of the hectic days of 31 May-2 June, when a clear demarcation between the authority of the police commissioners and the revolutionary committee could not be definitely established.

Le Roy was arrested again on 5 prairial, Year III (24 May 1795) by the general assembly on a charge of Petit fils for ostensibly holding "anti-civic sentiments and of preaching a system of pillage." Added to this was the usual accusation that he had been "a partisan of the old tyranny," and that he had disapproved of "the measures of 11 and 12 germinal taken by the Convention."[104] Le Roy replied to the charge of terrorism leveled against him by inviting the Committee of General Security to inspect his morals, pointing to his service as police in-

---

[102] *Ibid.* A copy of Auzolles's letter of 26 vendémiaire contains 46 signatures. The testimonial of the civil committee is signed by Lambin and bears the date of 28 vendémiaire. The certificate of Bault is for 29 vendémiaire. Fremy quoted from the *procès-verbal* of the civil committee that Auzolles had been constantly at his post during the rebellion of the prisoners at La Force and had prevented their escape.

[103] A.N., F[7] 4774[19], d. 4. The revolutionary committee condemned the two police inspectors for drafting a *procès-verbal*, a power they did not possess. Jean Chevalier was the commissioner elected by the general assembly to replace Pollet on the night of 9-10 August 1792.

[104] A.N., F[7] 4774[45]; A.N., F[7] 4774[19]. His name is spelled Pavasse in A.N., F[1b] 11, Seine 18.

spector for three years. His proposal to the sectional assembly to invite the civil and welfare committees to distribute bread and wine among the poor of the section had been adopted—hardly a proposal to "pillage." Furthermore, he denied vexing or oppressing citizens and knew nothing of Petit's accusation that he had repudiated the measures adopted by the Convention on 12 germinal.[105]

In his appeal to the Committee of General Security, Le Roy revealed that his wife had died several months after his release, that his oldest son was in prison, and that his youngest was in the army. His funds were exhausted and he needed his former job.[106] The civil committee of the section, in examining Le Roy's petition for release, observed that he often spoke with assurance—hardly a valid reason to imprison him—and that he had been linked to Dassin, a man who was "generally regarded as being ill-disposed toward his fellow citizens." A Mouvoison had accused Le Roy, when he had been president of the popular society, of showing contempt and arrogance toward others. Once, when Dassin was about to leave for the Jacobins, Le Roy had supposedly cried out to him to wait, as there was need of him for the "purge," and addressed him as "the little Robespierre."[107] The committee failed to reveal, however, that ten months previous to these events it had assured the *comité de législation* that when presiding over the popular assembly Le Roy had shown himself to be a man of moderation.[108]

The surveillance committee of the 7th arrondissement was more forthright than its colleagues of the civil committee. It frankly stated that the charges against him were vague and without proof, and recommended his release. The Committee of General Security granted him provisional freedom on 1 fructidor, Year III (18 August 1795). A week later, after Le Roy's appeal, it restored him to full citizenship and allowed him to resume his former position in the police administration.[109]

---

[105] A.N., F⁷ 4774¹⁹, 2 thermidor, Year III (20 July 1795).

[106] *Ibid.*, 7 thermidor, Year III (25 July 1795). For the imprisonment of his son, see Chapter XII.

[107] *Ibid.*, 24 thermidor, Year III (11 August 1795), signed by Lambin.

[108] A.N., D III, 254, d. 4, pc. 11, 3 brumaire, Year III (24 October 1794).

[109] A.N., F⁷ 4774¹⁹. The surveillance committee recommended his release on 29 thermidor (16 August). The police administration of Paris testified that Le Roy was "a man of wisdom, and honesty," as well as being a good worker.

In examining the functions of the police commissioners, one is confronted by an aspect of life far removed from political concerns and ideological struggles. Narrowly considered, it deals only with those human activities that somehow run afoul of the prevailing law. Suspects are arrested and interrogated, prisoners are prevented from breaking out of La Force, personal belongings of the deceased are meticulously enumerated, and women pregnant and betrayed file their complaints. Yet beneath these prosaic events, from time to time a richer and more complex life makes its appearance. The record of this life is embodied in a register that begins in the fall of 1792 and ends only with the Consulate, in 1800.[110]

The police commissioner, like his colleagues of the revolutionary committee, was much concerned with the threat posed by those deemed to be suspect. His role in ferreting out counterrevolutionaries or political opponents did not alter despite changes in regime from 1792 to 1800. Only the nature of the opposition changed and, hence, the direction of police action. Whatever commitments the commissioner had to the Revolution, loyalty to his superiors and to his profession rather than to principles or to parties of the day seemed to motivate his behavior. He continued to perform his task regardless of whether the regime was revolutionary, Thermidorian, Directorial, or consular.

When a pharmacist, for example, received an anonymous letter containing an uncompromising royalist program it was to the police commissioner that he brought its contents, for his own peace of mind, as he explained.[111] It would be interesting to know how many such anonymous letters came before the police, because, for obvious reasons, not all recipients turned them over to the commissioner or to the revolutionary committee. Sometimes Auzolles was called in by the authorities to hear charges against suspects. In one case it was against an accused stemming from the events of 10 August; in another, it

[110] The register in question is in the A.P.P., A A/136. The first entry is fol. 1, 30 October 1792, ending with fol. 394, 5 germinal, Year VIII (26 March 1800). This is subdivided into three parts: from fol. 1 to fol. 149 (to 28 fructidor, Year II–14 September 1794); from fol. 150, 16 brumaire, Year III (6 November 1794) to fol. 252, 19 thermidor, Year IV and from fol. 253, 3 vendémiaire, Year V (24 September 1796) to fol. 394, for the years V to VIII. Unless otherwise noted, references to the police commissioner's activities are to this collection.

[111] *Ibid.*, fols. 15 and 16, 31 January 1793.

was for allegedly impersonating a police commissioner.[112] Occasionally the suspect was a nationally prominent deputy, as François Gorguereau, who had sat in the Legislative Assembly. The writ of arrest having been issued against him by the Committee of General Security, he was questioned by Auzolles. Gorguereau testified that he lived by his own labors, supporting an old father and mother together with three sisters, and that he had contributed a sum of 280 livres for patriotic causes since 1790. Despite his testimony he was imprisoned and his papers were sealed; not until six months later was he finally released.[113]

When the premises of a public gathering place, such as a restaurant or a café, had to be searched, the number of men helping Auzolles took on the aspects of a police raid. Ordered to seize the account book of an owner of a Café Franquelin, the commissioner, accompanied by fifteen men, questioned both the owner and his customers, but all to no avail. The mysterious account book was nowhere to be found.[114] Printers were also searched for "incendiary materials," but here, again, nothing of an incriminatory nature was discovered.[115]

An amusing incident occasionally relieves the rather grim proceedings. Auzolles was called to the Theater of the Marais, in one such instance, to reestablish order. The altercation involved two young men who had paid their money for seats up front, not to see the play, as they confessed, but to view an actress in the performance. Having bought their tickets they were conducted to their seats, which turned out to be toward the rear of the theater. In rage and disgust they threw their tickets to the floor and demanded the return of their money. They were conducted to the revolutionary committee, and Auzolles tried to reason with them, after the director of the theater had given his own version of the fracas. Although neither possessed his card of citizenship, they were returned to their homes in custody of their parents, chastened if not purified.[116]

[112] *Ibid.*, fol. 6, 26 nivôse, Year II (15 January 1794); fol. 22, 11 March 1793.

[113] *Ibid.*, fol. 55, 15 ventôse, Year II (5 March 1794). He was freed on 6 fructidor (23 August).

[114] *Ibid.*, fols. 184-186, 21 ventôse, Year III (11 March 1795).

[115] *Ibid.*, fol. 187, 25 ventôse, Year III (15 March 1795). There seem to have been two printers in the section: Darregladet and Cholet de Jetphort.

[116] *Ibid.*, fol. 9, 26 December 1792. Charles Cuel a volunteer, and Alexandre Decorbie, both age 20, were the young men in question.

The manager of the theater, Paul-Marie Langlois, faced other problems in addition to those caused by disappointed viewers. Several of his actors failed to appear at regularly scheduled performances, causing inconvenience and delay. Auzolles permitted him and his stage manager to swear out a complaint against them, ostensibly for breach of contract. Several months later Langlois complained again that he was the victim of an illegal act of a neighboring section, Place-des-Fédérés, which had appointed a receiver at his theater. Auzolles investigated the matter and found that three employees of Langlois had launched a complaint against him, which led to the action of section Place-des-Fédérés. It is not possible to say whether the conflict was personal or, as happened in other theaters, political in nature.[117]

Of a more serious character were several attempted prison breaks, long before the violent effort of 14 vendémiaire mentioned above. There is no evidence that they were politically motivated, excluding the possible attempt to act in conjunction with the royalist coup. Rather, they were the usual desperate attempts of men deprived of their liberty for too long. Crude ladders, often made from bed sheets torn into narrow strips and knotted together, then hidden in bed, would be found by Auzolles after a call from Bault, the concierge of La Force. Interrogated by him, the prisoners usually denied knowledge of these attempted breaks. Sometimes a suspicious noise gave the plotters away, such as the rasping of a saw on iron bars, or the fall of pieces of slate that brought the concierge into the prison chamber to find evidence of their work. Ropes found tied to bars and dangling from windows gave their owners away, and missing sheets often became a means of discovering an attempted flight. Unable to carry out an escape, prisoners jettisoned ladders into the latrine.[118] In

[117] *Ibid.*, fols. 21 and 35, 1 March and 18 June 1793.

[118] *Ibid.*, fol. 23, 13 March 1793. Rope ladders, iron hooks, and crowbars were found by Auzolles and Bault, but the nine prisoners involved denied any knowledge of the attempted escape. Fol. 33, 7 May 1793: a package made up of strips of bed linen was discovered. Fol. 52, 17 pluviôse, Year II (5 February 1794): Bault discovered a large opening in the wall of a chamber holding sixty prisoners. Auzolles interrogated eight prisoners who had marks of masonry on their persons or clothing, and had them transferred to a more secure cell. Fols. 60-61, 28 ventôse, Year II (18 March 1794): a "counterrevolutionary plot" (no less) was uncovered and all tools and objects that might have been used for purposes of escape were confiscated by Bault. All interrogated denied knowledge of the plot. Fol. 162, 19 pluviôse, Year III (7

one case a police inspector was implicated; he was allegedly responsible for smuggling three saws into the prison for a bribe of 200 livres, and even promised the wife of a prisoner to find a job for her husband in the police administration once he had escaped.[119]

The most dramatic effort to flee, one which seems to have come close to success, was the attempted break that came on the eve of the royalist coup of 14 vendémiaire. This was the *putsch* that Auzolles foiled, as he described in his justification after his own arrest. It seems that rumors were widespread that another September massacre was about to occur as prisoners milled desperately in front of the gates. Bault tried to calm them, and had extracted a promise from their spokesmen that if he took certain measures for their safety they would make no effort to escape. Instead, he found them tunneling under the walls. When he tried to recall them to their agreement they seized him, his wife, and his son and held them all as hostages. By this time Auzolles had arrived with an imposing armed force, but found the prisoners armed with various weapons and the Bault family captive in their midst. Ordering the guard to use caution and humanity, the latter began to discharge their weapons, but fired only blanks. The crowd still continued to press against the gate, however, seeking to escape. Meanwhile, Auzolles notified the Administration of Police as to what was going on. Upon returning he found that the crowd had dispersed—discouraged, evidently, by his firmness, and frightened, perhaps, by the continuous discharge of rifles of the National Guard.

Later, when calm was restored, and the Bault hostages were freed, an assessment of the damage done to the prison was made. Tunnels were found under walls; there were cracks in the wall made by a heavy log, wielded, evidently, by several prisoners, and wreckage was strewn in the prison yard.[120] Whether this prison riot was directly inspired

---

February 1795): a rope attached to the window was found. Fols. 167-170, 10 ventôse, Year III (28 February 1795): Bault found that fifteen pairs of bed sheets were missing. An ordnance surveyor (*ingénieur-géographe*), Jean-Louis Queblemont, revealed the plot and his refusal to participate in it. He was roundly abused by the others and was transferred to another part of the prison for his own safety. It was after this that he revealed the details of the plot.

[119] *Ibid.*, fols. 216-217, 18 messidor, Year III (6 July 1795); Guillaume Lenoble testified that a police commissioner by name of Prudhomme had given his wife three saws for the above sum.

[120] *Ibid.*, fol. 224, 13 vendémiaire, Year IV (4 October 1795).

by royalist plotters, or whether it was an outgrowth of fear, as is more likely, it is difficult to say. In any case, the climate of insecurity and near-panic that resulted, stimulated perhaps by well-planted rumors of an approaching massacre, must have contributed greatly to this outbreak. The prudence of the prisoners and National Guard, directed by Auzolles, says much for the humanity of both, and stands in marked contrast with the way prison riots are suppressed in our more enlightened age. Even after this all-out effort, some hardy women in La Petite Force tried to make their escape, but were foiled by an alert guardsman who discovered their plot in time.[121]

Mistreatment of prisoners by the hardened elements and complaints of victims occasionally came to the attention of the commissioner. The enforcement of a custom which required that a new arrival pay a sum called "the welcome" (la bonne venue) stripped the poor victim of his meager livres. The accused, naturally, swore that it was given voluntarily.[122] Outright thievery of personal funds was also a source of complaint. Prisoners working in collaboration with guards and doorkeepers must have had means of stripping their victims if any of the latter had been foolish enough to arrive with large sums of assignats on their person. The usual interrogations and searches were followed with occasional discovery of the missing sum and their return to their rightful owner.[123]

Sometimes prisoners in a state of depression and hopelessness attempted to commit suicide, and, at times, succeeded. The long delay of revolutionary justice coupled with a long confinement led them to desperate measures.[124] "The pangs of despised love" led still others to seek oblivion.[125] Many of these wounded themselves only superficially

---

[121] Ibid., fol. 235, 7 nivôse, Year IV (27 December 1795). Twenty-three women locked in a portion of the prison that adjoined the garden of a house at no. 1 rue Pavée were discovered in a prison break.

[122] Ibid., fol. 29, 13 April 1793. André Bourgeois complained that he had been deprived of his 6 livres by two prisoners who had spent it on drink. They maintained that he had offered to treat them.

[123] Ibid., fol. 42, 28 vendémiaire, Year II (19 October 1793).

[124] Ibid., fol. 125, 11 thermidor, Year II (29 July 1794); fol. 134, 26 thermidor, Year II (13 August 1794); fol. 200, 4 floréal, Year III (23 April 1795).

[125] Ibid., fol. 214, 10 messidor, Year III (28 June 1795). Paul Duguet struck himself with a knife. His mistress had abandoned him: "c'est une coquine qui m'a abandonné."

and were discovered, usually in the latrine, in time for medical assistance. Prisoners who died in the infirmary or in their cells were duly recorded in the *procès-verbal* and their decease verified by authorities.[126]

An incident involving a young woman prisoner and two police inspectors reads like a modern version of "Rashomon"; it is impossible to determine who told the truth. Marie Paul lodged a complaint against Dunant and Le Bague, the two inspectors in question, testifying that she had been confined in Sainte Pélagie for reasons unknown to her, and that Dunant had conducted her from prison to a furnished room in a house where Le Bague, his colleague, lodged. After lifting the seals from her home in section Poissonnière, they made "improper advances" to her, threatening her if she refused to give in. She was forced to remain with Dunant for five or six days, during which time she had been compelled to perform fellatio and to satisfy his passion in every way. After this Dunant had robbed her of her possessions, then sold and pocketed the proceeds, amounting to 227 livres.

Pierre Benoist Dunant was thirty-four years old when confined in La Force. He refuted her story as a calumny, and gave quite a different version of the events. She had been under his guard for three months, he testified, during which time it had never occurred to him to seek her favors. In fact, he knew five or six men to whom she had given herself. He had always carried out his duties to the letter, which is why she was seeking vengeance, nor had he taken anything from her, as could be verified by both the police commissioner and the concierge of the prison. On the contrary, his role had been to get the confidence of a woman, Ozanne, with whom Marie Paul was imprisoned, because the former was suspected of dealing in false *assignats*.

Le Bague was interrogated at the Conciergerie on the following day. He, too, called the charge a calumny. He could prove that he had made no dubious proposals and doubted if anything happened between her and his colleague Dunant because she was widely known as "a most unbridled libertine since her most delicate years." Moreover, not only had he taken nothing from her but had actually advanced her 35 livres to pay for necessities, and had turned over to her a sum of 100 livres gained from the sale of her possessions, this in the pres-

[126] *Ibid.*, fol. 210, 3 messidor, Year III (21 June 1795); fol. 213, 9 messidor, Year III (27 June 1795).

ence of Dunant. The gold from her trinkets had been weighed by a goldsmith in her presence, and all money realized from the sale of her effects had been turned over to her. This included the disposal of her silk stockings, which he had sold for her.[127] Upon conclusion of his testimony the *procès-verbal* was turned over to the prosecutor.

In contrast to the worldly Marie Paul were the young women who had loved too well, if not wisely. They came with their predictable tale of woe, innocent and trusting of the young men who had declared their love and promised them marriage, but having once surrendered their virtue they learned, to their regret, how false were the vows of young men made in the heat of passion. Only rarely did a man admit his paternity and willingness to do the right thing. Sometimes a young woman was granted the right to bring charges in court against her seducer, but it is difficult to see just what the police commissioner could have done to change the way of a man with a maid, especially if she were no longer such.[128] Sometimes infants born of these affairs were turned over to orphanages. Even if their mothers would have liked to keep them, their lack of resources probably prohibited it.[129]

Illness and disappearance of persons feared mentally disturbed also became the concern of the commissioner. A son suspecting that his old father lay helpless behind locked doors sought help from the commissioner, who found the father lying at the foot of his bed.[130] A mother of a two-year-old infant was forced to seek the commissioner's assistance because her husband had been suffering "fits" and had threatened her and the child. In the end, the man committed suicide.[131] A laundress who had sold the linen of a customer whom she accused of owing her money threw herself out of a window.[132] Another

---

[127] *Ibid.*, fols. 82-83, 86, 13 floréal, Year II (2 May 1794).

[128] *Ibid.*, fols. 17, 25, 141, 145, 146, 157, 166, 199.

[129] *Ibid.*, fols. 211, 212, 218, 223, 7 messidor, 23 messidor, 23 fructidor, Year III (25 June, 11 July, 9 September 1795).

[130] *Ibid.*, fol. 165, 27 pluviôse, Year III (15 February 1795). Morillon, a man in his seventies, was found lying at the foot of his bed. The public health officer diagnosed his illness as a stroke (*apoplexie*).

[131] *Ibid.*, fols. 177-179, 15 ventôse, Year III (5 March 1795). Suzanne Forest was married to Louis Magnion, a maker of buttons, who became obsessed with fear of the guillotine. When guards were about to take him away to the hospital (*hospice de l'humanité*), they found him lying in a pool of blood. He had slit his own throat, as the public health officer reported.

[132] *Ibid.*, fols. 180-181, 15 ventôse, Year III (5 March 1795). Marie Catherine

revealed that she had given her husband 200 livres to go out and buy a hat, but that he had never returned.[133]

Inhabitants of the section who died in unexplained circumstances, not always mysteriously, had to be accounted for. Some simply failed to appear until the odor of death roused fellow dwellers, wheareas others dropped in the street on their way to or from their homes. Still others became violently ill and died before aid could arrive. In some cases there was more than suspicion of suicide. All these had to be verified, their effects enumerated, their creditors or heirs satisfied, and their records finally closed. In a few instances bodies of prisoners in La Force were examined and prisoners suspected of possessing knowledge of the victims or circumstances of their death were questioned. Those who died of natural causes or as the result of accidents had their names duly recorded, the circumstances investigated, and their effects sold, sometimes to pay the cost of the funeral.[134]

Among crimes investigated by the commissioner was the manufacture of false *assignats* that appeared periodically. Seldom was Auzolles able to discover these *assignat* notes, however. When caught, the counterfeiters were conducted to La Force, interrogated, and their documents, at times carrying forged signatures, were closely examined.[135] The reporting of a false address by a madam in charge of a house of prostitution also led to lengthy investigations. The net result

---

Albout, thirty-six years old, with a reputation for infidelity, threw herself out of a fifth-story window.

[133] *Ibid.*, fol. 226, 8 brumaire, Year IV (29 October 1795). Thérèse Astruc described her husband as "feeble-minded" ("homme dont la tête est très faible") and said that he might have had another 400 livres in *assignats* on his person when he went off to buy his hat.

[134] *Ibid.*, fol. 4, 26 November 1792; fol. 10, 19 January 1793; fols. 11-13; fol. 27, 2 April 1793; fols. 28, 38, 152-155, 183, 190, 197, 198, 207, 208, 227-230, 250-251.

[135] *Ibid.*, fol. 18, 16 February 1793; fol. 34, 8 June 1793 describes a long interrogation of a Jacques Meuton reflecting a rivalry between him and his denunciator with jealousy as a motive involved; fol. 64, 17 germinal, Year II (6 April 1794), a search for false *assignats* that yielded nothing; fol. 67, 22 germinal, Year II (11 April 1794), deals with a sum of 13,000 livres in *assignats* involving Jacques-Germain Horaist who was imprisoned in La Force; fol. 73, 25 floréal, Year II (14 May 1794), Horaist refused to sign the *procès-verbal*; fol. 158, 26 nivôse, Year III (15 January 1795), concerns the interrogation of suspects in La Force; fol. 203, 26 floréal, Year III (15 May 1795) deals with plates for manufacturing false *assignats*.

simply showed that she had moved about quite a bit with her ladies of joy in tow. Swindling of volunteers also came to the attention of Auzolles. Rarely was there a report of violent death suffered by a resident of the section; if it occurred it must have escaped the attention of the police. When a prisoner long held on slim evidence in La Force convinced the commissioner that he had been falsely incarcerated, Auzolles reported the facts promptly and had him released. In contrast to so many other cases, this must have given Auzolles some satisfaction.[136]

The police commissioner arrested common thieves and burglars and sent them to La Force prison, until sentence was passed by proper judicial authorities or after such sentence. The register of La Force contains numerous references to his activities, as prisoners were recorded upon arrival.[137] The picture that emerges is that of relatively young men, many from the provinces, who for one reason or another resorted to burglary or robbery, seldom to anything worse. Naturally, there were occasional incidents of violence and armed robbery. Frequently those arrested were transferred to other prisons after staying in La Force. Among these were artisans, professionals, military men, and the unemployed.[138]

Of the sixteen prisoners in La Force arrested by Auzolles, exactly half were imprisoned on the charge of theft. Only two were held for suspicious behavior, one was charged with murder but immediately released, whereas two were arrested for violent conduct—one against the duly constituted authorities, and one against a private individual. The only prisoner who was a member of a liberal profession was charged with fraud, one had been picked up for lack of a card of security, and another had been arrested without a specific charge entered on the register. Crime against property, as has been shown by students of the eighteenth century, was by far the most common type of lawbreaking.[139]

The many activities of the police commissioner illustrate not only

[136] *Ibid.*, fols. 239, 240, 107, 135-140, 188-189.

[137] A.P.P., A B/327 and A B/326. References to the material below are based on these jail entries.

[138] A.P.P., A B/327, pp. 53, 194, 195, 214, 271, 308, and 422, from March to October 1793. A.P.P., A B/326, from January 1793 to February 1794.

[139] No effort is made here to reach any quantitative conclusion from the meager figures cited.

infractions of the law he was enjoined to uphold but the element of stability in the section which he represented. He was the direct and immediate representative of authority between inhabitants who were victims of private violence, and, at times, even personal misfortune. Pierre Auzolles as an individual and as an official enjoyed the esteem and support of his fellow citizens in the section, whatever the political changes. This, too, was an element of stability in a rapidly changing society.

XI

The Armed Force and the Popular Society

The organization of the National Guard and the contribution of the districts and Commune to its early consolidation in the summer of 1789 could not advance it beyond the limits of its bourgeois form. The division between active and passive citizens perpetuated by the law of 12-23 September 1791[1] was abolished only by a decree of the General Council on 13 August 1792 that authorized each section to form military companies without distinction, enrolling all citizens for personal service, and reducing the sixty battalions to forty-eight to correspond to the new structure of the capital. At the same time an energetic effort was made to arm the new recruits. The legislature confirmed this new division on August 19,[2] which authorized each company to enroll 126 men and one or several batteries of artillery. Officers and non-commissioned officers were elected by the men; assembled in companies they also elected their commanding general for three months, subject to reelection for one year.[3]

The sections had created military committees (*comités militaires* or *comités de guerre*) that became councils of discipline in 1793. They distributed aid to parents and families of volunteers, corresponded

[1] A.P., 573-574, 12 September 1791, art. 4; *Moniteur*, IX, no. 258, p. 660, 15 September 1791; A.P., XXXI, 625-632, report of Rabaut Saint-Etienne for the Comité de constitution, 29 September 1791. Art. 3 stipulated that those passive citizens who were in actual service were to remain in the guard.

[2] Tuetey, *Répertoire*, V, no. 942, 19 August 1792; Braesch, *La Commune*, pp. 327-331; Braesch cites the *Procès-verbaux de Chaumette*, pp. 18 and 27, among other sources. See his Appendix, pp. 165-168.

[3] A.P., XLVIII, 393, "Organisation de la gendarmerie parisienne" in twelve articles. Of the 126 men, 107 were privates (citizen-soldiers), and the rest were officers, non-coms, and specialists: 1 captain, 1 lieutenant, 2 second lieutenants, 1 sergeant-major, 4 sergeants, 8 corporals, and 2 drummers. The battalion was commanded by a commander-in-chief, a second-in-command, an adjutant, and a colors-bearer (*porte-drapeau*).

with battalions serving at the front, armed and equipped them, and maintained their morale—thus perpetuating the rapport between the nation and its army. The councils of discipline, moreover, were open to all grades. This democratic structure was undermined on the 19th of thermidor (6 August 1794), when the commander and his staff were placed directly under the Convention and its committees of Public Safety and of General Security. By the Year III this trend continued, as the government assumed greater control at the expense of popular forms. By decree of 13 frimaire, Year III (3 December 1794), members of the council of discipline had to be literate. After the germinal insurrection, on the 28th of the month (16 April 1795), correspondence between the battalion and its section was forbidden, and the National Guard was placed under the Convention and its *comité de guerre*. Following the prairial uprising, the sections were forced to surrender their cannon. On 16 vendémiaire, Year IV (7 October 1795) the National Guard was placed under the general-in-chief of the Army of the Interior and all semblance of popular control came to an end.[4]

The transition from a bourgeois to a popular structure can be seen in the evolution of the armed forces of districts Blancs-Manteaux and Petit-Saint-Antoine into those of section Droits-de-l'Homme. In April 1790 both districts pledged loyalty to the Assembly in support of its decree establishing their permanence.[5] The following year, the 3d battalion of Petit-Saint-Antoine adopted a strong resolution in favor of Lafayette, threatening to expel any guardsman who refused to obey the national commander "under all circumstances" whatsoever.[6] The following day an individual was arrested for uttering "seditious" re-

---

[4] Mellié, pp. 258-261; *Moniteur*, XXIV, no. 207, pp. 211-212, 28 germinal, Year III (20 April 1795); XXVI, no. 17, p. 136 note, 17 vendémiaire, Year IV (9 October 1795); no. 21, pp. 163-164, 21 vendémiaire, Year IV (13 October 1795). Duvergier mentions the following decrees on the reorganization of the National Guard without listing their provisions, however: 19 thermidor, Year II (6 August 1794), VII, 243, 28 germinal, Year III (17 April 1795), VIII, 79; 16 vendémiaire, Year IV (8 October 1795), VIII, 310.

[5] Tuetey, *Répertoire*, IV, no. 4213, 15 April (Petit-Saint-Antoine); II, no. 4421, 20 April (Blancs-Manteaux).

[6] B.V.C., MS 119, fol. 109, 22 April 1791, *Arrêté du bataillon du Petit-Saint-Antoine Ve division, IIIe bataillon* (Paris, 22 April 1791), 1 p., signed by Chapuis, *commandant*, and Coulombeau, *secrétaire du bataillon*.

marks at the moment of taking the oath of loyalty to Lafayette by the battalion of district Blancs-Manteaux,[7] although it is not clear whether this opposition came from the Right or from the Left. This loyalty remained firm throughout the events of the demonstration on the Champs de Mars, when a sergeant-major of the battalion was arrested for criticizing its behavior in firing upon the people.[8]

On the eve of the June 1792 demonstration, a marked change had taken place in the armed forces of section Roi-de-Sicile, reflecting the drift to the Left of the section itself. A number of guardsmen, individually and jointly, repudiated pro-Lafayette petitions that they had signed, evidently without realizing the implication of their contents or the principles expressed.[9] The battalion itself, however, remained under control of its officers still loyal to established authorities. Immediately after the demonstration of 20 June 1792, it issued an appeal to the Legislative Assembly complaining that the law and the Constitution had been violated and that the National Guard had been placed in an impossible position.[10] After 10 August the change was dramatic—as reflected in the censure and dismissal of the battalion's commanding officer, Herbault.

The new democratic structure evinced a spirit of egalitarianism and a suspicion of elitism in military affairs. When a question arose of creating a special armed force to guard the Convention, delegates of the sections vehemently opposed this step, condemning it as making for tyranny, and insisting that the legislative body rely on their own military organization. Chaumette, in endorsing their view, reminded them that if the ears of their mandatories were closed to them, "the ear of the sovereign body [that is, the people] is open to us."[11] The same commissioners demanded that the daily pay of young conscripts be set at 40 sous until their actual departure for the front.[12] On 30

[7] Tuetey, *Répertoire*, II, no. 1256, 23 April 1791.

[8] *Ibid.*, II, no. 1379, 18 July 1791. He was a member of section Enfants-Rouges, and said "that the National Guard dishonored itself yesterday in firing upon the people."

[9] *Ibid.*, IV, no. 586, 12 June 1792; IV, no. 592, 12 June 1792; V, no. 4186, 14 June 1792; IV, no. 622, 18 June 1792.

[10] B.V.C., MS 119, fol. 113, n.d., 2 pp. unsigned.

[11] A.N., F¹ᶜ III, Seine 27, d. 4, 19 October 1792. This is a printed brochure the second portion of which contains the "Réponse du citoyen Chaumet" to the resolution of the delegates of the forty-eight sections ([Paris], 19 October 1792), 7 pp.

[12] A.P., LXXVI, 367, 11 October 1793.

October 1792 the armed force of the section adopted a resolution which underscored the political change that had occurred since 10 August. In its address to the Convention it demanded a severe law against anyone who refused to mount guard." In a Republic, every citizen is a soldier," it declared. Those who declined to do their share of military duty were unworthy of enjoying liberty. Moreover, mounting guard in person would abolish distinctions among classes that had existed in previous times, as the poorer citizens could now approach the richer in a spirit of equality. This, in turn, would teach the latter to realize the value of the common people, and by mutual association and exchange of opinions would help instruct the less educated by the better educated. The battalion concluded by urging support for a law punishing refusal to do military service.[13]

Having adopted the above proposal, the companies added regulations for the armed forces, beginning with: "the adjutant of the section should have control over officers of all grades." The rules provided punishment for failing to fulfill regular military duties, which included provisions for stripping officers of their rank. All citizens were to perform service except sexagenarians, the infirm, and public functionaries, who could replace themselves with other citizens of the company or pay a tax for this purpose. Parents could not be replaced by minors, but physicians, surgeons, and *accoucheurs* (attendants at childbirth) were excused, together with workers in bakeries. Finally, the council of discipline was given power to act in military matters when the general assembly was not in permanent session.[14]

The abolition of distinctions in types of military companies led to the abandonment of different uniforms, such as those of grenadiers. Citizens of section Droits-de-l'Homme were reminded by the general assembly that caps worn by the latter were expressly forbidden by law when they presented themselves for military service.[15] Matters of a more technical nature, such as the manufacture of pikes, were turned over by the assembly to its military committee,[16] and a list of the

[13] A. de P., D 1 AZ 159², *Force armée de la section des Droits-de-l'Homme. Projet de service militaire arrêté par ladite section.* (Paris, [30 October 1792]), 16 pp. The same brochure in B.H.V.P., 104.095.

[14] *Ibid.*, punishments are treated in Title Two in twenty-one articles; replacements in Title Three, and the council of discipline is discussed in Title Four.

[15] A. de P., Seine, 3 AZ 287, 28 February 1793.

[16] B.H.V.P., MS 748, fol. 1, 21 May 1793, in a letter from the commander of artillery of the arsenal of Paris to the president of the section.

health officers, physicians, surgeons, and pharmacists, prepared by the section's revolutionary committee, was shared by the military committee for obvious reasons.[17] Minor irritations occasionally plagued the battalion, such as destruction of property in a guardhouse, which led to investigations by commissioners of the assembly, but with what results it is impossible to say.[18] A much more serious matter was the prevention of counterrevolutionaries from undermining the loyalty of recruits, a concern of all departments of municipal government.[19]

On 11 March 1793, the cannoneers of the section adopted an oath that stated: "We swear to smash the brains of anyone who gives way an inch before the enemy or dares cry every man for himself."[20] That this militancy was not all verbal may be seen in their role during the events of 9 thermidor and the insurrection of prairial. After the overthrow of the Gironde, the section was one of three to donate a cannon to the Ministry of War for the Vendée, a tribute, in part, to its own cannoneers.[21] Yet it rejected a proposal for the creation of a revolutionary army when it was first broached.[22]

Certificates of merit issued by the military committee or the commanding officers, or testimonials of honorable service, were eagerly sought by those who had served. Such phrases as that a soldier "showed the civic conduct of a true *sans-culotte*," that he was "a true republican," records of battles a veteran engaged in and where he was wounded, that one had volunteered for the Vendée, or testimonials to a man's honesty and patriotism abound in these certificates.[23] Often the service performed was perfunctory—of patrolling streets or squares, main-

---

[17] A. de P., 4 AZ 698, 3 vendémiaire, Year III (24 September 1794), from the military bureau of the department of Paris.

[18] B.H.V.P., MS 748, fol. 8, 2 September 1792.

[19] The reference to the above is beyond the limits of the period studied, but illustrates what must have been a concern from the very beginning of the Revolution. B.H.V.P., MS 750, fols. 200-201, 13 floréal, Year IV and 6 Frimaire, Year V (2 May 1796 and 26 November 1796).

[20] B.V.C., MS 120, fol. 135. This was signed by eleven cannoneers.

[21] *Affiches de la Commune*, no. 3, 16 June 1793. Sections Temple and Contrat-Social also contributed a cannon on 15 June.

[22] *Moniteur*, XVI, no. 167, p. 638, 16 June 1793.

[23] B.H.V.P., MS 798, fols. 222, 223-225, 226, 227, 228, 235-238, May-June 1792, August 1793-7 brumaire, Year II (28 October 1793); MS 781, fol. 56, 20 ventôse, Year II (10 March 1794); MS 780, fol. 210, 22 germinal, Year II (11 April 1794), fol. 211, 26 germinal, Year IV (15 April 1796).

taining order in crowds, accompanying members of a revolutionary committee on its rounds, or simply waiting patiently in the guardhouse for orders. Occasionally returning a stray child to his parents via the police is also recorded.[24] Those who served in the regular forces at the front had experiences of quite a different nature, of course. Their records reflect the universal impressions and concerns of soldiers in war. Leaves of absence to settle pressing family business, permits to join parents for a limited time while recovering from a wound, testimonials of accidents leading to dismemberment, and even denunciations of the conduct of commanders testify to these experiences of soldiers and officers.[25]

Whether one was a veteran or had remained a civilian, he had to find work, especially at a time when so many occupations had declined or had disappeared as the Revolution continued. The proliferation of official positions, coupled with the difficulty of finding suitable work, made government employment attractive, as the numerous petitions and requests for jobs testify. In some cases the pressure of work or additional functions placed extra demands on departments or individual functionaries, which also called for expansion of employment.[26] Testimonials of good conduct, or more correctly, of patriotic behavior, also were sought by individuals from officials, especially from the section's civil committee. A document bearing the endorsement of one's captain or another officer of the armed force in which the petitioner served, or was still in the process of serving, was also eagerly solicited. Others simply appealed on the basis of their past experience. Proof of "irreproachable behavior" during the night of 9 thermidor, as one petition reads, was a demonstration of reliability and worth. In a few instances those who had positions in various departments were forced to mobilize support to maintain themselves against the insistent demands of those who wanted to oust them.[27]

[24] A. de P., 4 AZ 698, "Force armée de Paris 5me légion, 4me section armée des Droits-de-l'Homme." This collection contains many examples of certificates of military service. An official notification to perform guard duty is in A. de P., 4 AZ 498.

[25] B.H.V.P., MS 798, fols. 229-233.

[26] See, for example, A.N., D III, 239, d. 2, pc. 45, a request for a concierge for the section's archives made by Gunnion of the Garde des Archives of the 7th arrondissement, on 25 prairial, Year III (13 June 1795). Dossier 2 of the above deals with employment.

[27] A.N., D III, 231, 25 prairial, Year III (13 June 1795).

A blunt request for an appointment to a higher post was made on occasion simply because the petitioner was unable to make ends meet on his salary.[28] A more ingenious way was to propose some scheme or a solution to a problem and then offer one's services to administer the agency to be created. A resident of section Droits-de-l'Homme wrote to the Convention suggesting that "a republican lottery" be established to raise money and at the same time to reduce the number of *assignats* in circulation. Were such a plan adopted, he offered his services as a director of the enterprise.[29]

When it was decided to establish a bureau of vital statistics, the Legislative Committee requested the section's civil committee to nominate reliable citizens who would verify births, marriages, divorces, and deaths in the section. The latter proposed eleven men, describing each one as "a good patriot," "an honest man," or "a good citizen."[30]

More important than the keeping of records, at least for the time being, was the need to organize the country's defenses. In order to manufacture gunpowder it was necessary to extract saltpeter from the soil or from heaps of decaying organic matter mixed with lime and other such alkaline substance that creates nitrates. To facilitate this activity, commissions of saltpeter were established by law (14 frimaire, Year II–4 December 1793), elected by sectional assemblies and placed under the supervision of revolutionary committees. If necessary, these commissions were authorized to employ workers in their search for and extraction of nitrates. Shortly thereafter the Commune established a central committee for this purpose by convoking delegates (one from each section) to serve on the committee, and arranged for lessons given at the Arsenal on how to extract the saltpeter. After

---

[28] Pavas Le Roy, inspector of police of section Droits-de-l'Homme, earned a salary of 1,500 livres a year. In his appeal he asked for the position of justice of the peace as he could not live on his salary. D III, 254, d. 4, 7 frimaire, Year III (7 November 1795). He added a document, however, listing his merits. *Ibid.*, 26 brumaire, Year III (16 November 1795).

[29] A.N., C 271, 670, p. 25, 16 September 1793. The author was Lefebvre, who signed himself "ami de la République" of no. 8 rue de la Verrerie.

[30] A.N., D III, 239, pcs. 39-40, 22 fructidor, Year II (8 September 1794). These were: Auzolles, Collet, Porisses (an ex-lawyer), Gérard, Lambin, Chappe, Ferret (a merchant haberdasher), Pellerin (an ex-business man), Gamain (the pastry cook), Le Roy (an ex-soft-drink dispenser), and Gervais (an inspector of buildings, *toiseur verificateur de hâtiments*).

the twelve arrondissements were formed, some sections paid their commissioners, who were placed under the control of civil committees.[31]

In addition to the lessons at the Arsenal, the Committee of Public Safety ordered that they be offered in the amphitheater of the Museum of Natural History and in the Hall of the Electors (formerly the Evêché). Upon conclusion of the session, a "frugal repast" followed, with dancing, singing, and the planting of a tree of liberty.[32]

Section Droits-de-l'Homme had an *atelier* devoted to the production of saltpeter in full activity,[33] and reported that it had furnished 3,117 lbs. of this ingredient for the war effort.[34] The popular society of the section, like others, also promoted the extraction and collection of saltpeter. At its meeting of 1 ventôse, Year II (19 February 1794), for example, the society resolved to present a quantity of saltpeter, "unrefined, fine, and very pure," to the Convention.[35] The commission was dissolved on 23 frimaire, Year IV (13 January 1796), and its effects and tools appraised and sold by Joly, Dommanget, and Dervin, civil commissioners of the section.[36]

In addition to these various activities, inhabitants of section Droits-de-l'Homme were aware of the contributions and, at times, disturbances, caused by political clubs. These clubs began as *sociétés de pensée* about 1770 under the influence of freemasonry,[37] becoming established in all large towns, where they served as nuclei of the future revolutionary clubs.[38] When deputies arrived in the capital in the

[31] Mellié, pp. 262-266. The number of commissioners varied. Section Brutus began with eight, then added another four, then eight more. *Ibid.*, p. 263.

[32] *Moniteur*, XIX, no. 161, p. 588, II ventôse, Year II (1 March 1794).

[33] *Journal de la montagne*, no. 72, p. 571, 5 pluviôse, Year II (24 January 1794). This was reported to the General Council by Eude (spelled Heude) on 3 pluviôse (22 January).

[34] *Ibid.*, no. 152, p. 1,224, 25 germinal, Year II (14 April 1794). This compared with the other three sections of the arrondissement as follows: Arcis, 3,410 lbs.; Réunion, 5,241 lbs.; and Homme-Armé, 1,208 lbs.

[35] Caron, *Paris*, IV, 198.

[36] A. de P., 4 AZ 53, "Du Registre des délibérations et arrêtés du comité de la section des Droits-de-l'Homme et la Commune de Paris," signed by Lambin.

[37] This masonic influence is clearly reflected in the publications of the Cercle social, which played an important role in the events of the spring and summer of 1791.

[38] Godechot, *Institutions*, pp. 63-68. But see Michael L. Kennedy, "The Foundation of the Jacobin Clubs and the Development of the Jacobins Club Network, 1789-

spring of 1789, what was more natural than to discuss the business of the National Assembly over a cup of coffee and then to formalize this discussion? Among the earliest of these gatherings was the Club national, conveniently located across from the gardens of the Palais Royal. For a nominal fee members could relax within its premises, which were open from 8 a.m. to 2 a.m.[39] The Friends of the Constitution (Jacobin Society), as is well known, originated in the Club Breton, founded by deputies from Brittany, who met probably in a café Amaury, and after the events of 5-6 October moved to the convent of the Jacobins Saint-Honoré.[40] The Club Cordeliers was founded on 27 April 1790, but unlike its predecessors became less a discussion society and more an organization for political action. The Cordeliers denounced officials deemed arrogant and unjust, undertook inquests into public scandals, visited oppressed patriots in prison, and offered financial assistance to their families. It became more powerful after rallying behind it the numerous fraternal societies that had sprung up in the capital.[41]

Unlike the bourgeois clubs with their relatively high dues, the more democratic societies recruited both active and passive citizens without discrimination. The latter were composed of "merchants of fruit and vegetables," and "carriers of water and other good people."[42] Most members were illiterate, and often employed a bombastic and exaggerated style of speech. Contributions were both infrequent and irregular, the treasury was usually empty, and, at times, the modest quorum of twenty members could not be met. Only on rare occasions was there a sizeable crowd.[43]

From the very beginning, moderates and patriots differed on the role of these clubs. The former wanted to limit their activities to educational endeavors, while the latter sought to point them toward

---

1791," *Journal of Modern History*, 51 (December 1979), p. 702: "it is now possible to discard a number of once-popular theories about their [the clubs'] masonic origins."

[39] B.N., Lb[40] 2371, which is an invitation from Marquis de Villette to the deputies to relax after their "patriotic work." ([Paris], n.d.), 1 p.

[40] Crane Brinton, *The Jacobins, an Essay in the New History* (New York, 1930); Aulard, *Jacobins*, I, Introduction, pp. I-xxx.

[41] Mathiez, *Club des Cordeliers*, pp. 8-9, 14-15, 19, 21-22.

[42] Isabelle Bourdin, *Les Sociétés populaires à Paris pendant la Révolution* (Paris, 1937), p. 132 nn. 1, 2, 3.

[43] *Ibid.*, pp. 132-138.

political goals. The decree of 29 September 1791 aimed at restricting their political life by prohibiting pressure on government authorities, the bearing of collective petitions, or the sending of delegations.[44] The law and its defenders were sharply attacked by leaders of the democratic party. Robespierre replied to Le Chapelier, who had argued that now that the Revolution had been completed it was high time to curb the clubs with their collective petitions, their denunciations, and their political meddling. Robespierre reasoned that the Constitution guaranteed citizens the right to assemble unarmed and to communicate with one another. How, therefore, could one proscribe this right in the name of the Constitution? Besides, the Revolution was far from finished; clubs were more necessary than ever to help defend freedom.[45] Marat, too, favored a more active role for patriots, and even urged them to open letters of suspects, correspond among themselves, and continue to expose aristocrats and their agents.[46] Brissot also defended the role of popular societies in a well-prepared address to the Jacobins, later issued as a tract. The clubs, he argued, made no pretense of competing with legislators, but their members had every right to discuss laws proposed or passed. If the law was good, its discussion would make it popular, if bad, discussion would reform it.[47] Robespierre, Marat, and Brissot were not the only ones to argue in favor of these clubs, of course. Moderates and even conservatives favored them, as well, although their approach and goals differed.[48]

The decree of 9 September 1793 limiting sectional assemblies to two a *décade* had called out energetic protests by Varlet and other militants, as we have seen. The police observer, Béraud, reported a week later that faubourg Saint-Antoine complained bitterly against this restriction. To circumvent this limitation, militants and their followers began to meet in popular societies formed largely in response

---

[44] *Moniteur*, IX, no. 273, p. 808, 30 September 1791.

[45] *Moniteur*, X, no. 275, pp. 9-10, 2 October 1791.

[46] *L'Ami du peuple*, no. 364, p. 4, 7 February 1791.

[47] B.N., Lb⁴⁰ 638, *Discours sur l'utilité des sociétés populaires, sur la necessité de les maintenir et de les multiplier par tout* . . . (Paris), 23 pp., 28 September 1791.

[48] Lack of space prevents the listing of the numerous individual items. Instead, numbers of the references are cited as presented by Maurice Tourneux in his *Bibliographie*, II, 375-474, of his Chapter VII entitled "Actes et deliberations des clubs et sociétés populaires." See items #10055, 9883, 9907, 9899, 9907.

to this law.[49] Acting like a modern political caucus, or a committee of the whole, these sectional societies could discuss any business they pleased, decide on a course of action, and then record their decisions in formal session of the general assembly. Permanence of sessions was thus transferred from the section's assembly to its popular club. The shoemaker, Mallais, of the revolutionary committee of section Temple, must have spoken for many militants in rejecting a decision of his sectional assembly when he said: "We'll quash all that. That won't hold. We'll reject it in our club."[50] Often it was impossible to draw a clear line of demarcation between the section's assembly and its popular society.[51] Such matters as formal appointments, examination of officials, scrutiny of justices of the peace and police commissioners, intervention in sectional elections, and delivery of civic cards became regular concerns of popular clubs.[52] Moreover, their role in rousing patriotic feeling was significant.[53] The assassination of Marat, for example, brought forth a rash of demonstrations, processions, memorials, and pamphlets directed at kindling these patriotic sentiments.[54] Petitions in support of revolutionary measures or in urging the Convention to take such measures were also characteristic activities.[55]

Criticism of popular societies became cause for suspicion and the Convention punished officials who interfered with them[56] by decreeing

[49] Pierre Caron, *Paris*, I, 112, 16 September 1793; Mellié, pp. 276-277.

[50] A.N., F⁷ 4774³⁷, cited by Soboul, pp. 636-637 n. 230.

[51] Mellié, pp. 278-283; Soboul cites numerous examples, p. 637. Often the general assembly would refer a matter to its society or even act as a referee in a sectional dispute. See his discussion, pp. 360-371, 614-653, *passim*.

[52] *Ibid.*, pp. 637-639; Mellié, pp. 279-281.

[53] See the following pertinent items in Tourneux's *Bibliographie*, II: #10023, 9910, 10017, 9914, 10069, 10062, 10075, 10089.

[54] *Ibid.*, #9891, 10019, 10010; B.V.C., MS 119, fol. 125, 26 July 1793, in which the Club Cordeliers proposed a special fête to honor Marat. See also *Affiches de la Commune* for 15 August 1793, which carried the memorial service for Marat in a popular society.

[55] Tourneux, *Bibliographie*, #9837, 9899, 9895, 10012; B.N., Lb⁴⁰ 2372, *Pétition à la Convention nationale, arrêté au comité centrale des sociétés patriotiques* . . . ([Paris], 13 September 1793), 4 pp. in which petitioners demanded trial of the Girondists; B.V.C., MS 119, fols. 35-140, the numerous resolutions and addresses of the Cordeliers under the presidency of Hébert, Momoro, etc.; *ibid.*, fols. 142-169, the addresses of section Louvre (Muséum) to the Legislature and Convention.

[56] *Moniteur*, XVII, no. 187, p. 47, 6 July 1793, on a motion of Delacroix de la Marne on 4 July 1793.

penalties (25 July 1793) against those who attacked them.[57] From the summer of 1793, government committees began to call on societies to help in the war effort, to recommend personnel for various administrative duties, to give aid to representatives on mission, and to carry out the many tasks of mobilizing the population in support of specific measures of the government.[58] Societies had interests of their own, of course, in addition to governmental duties. By September 1793, twenty-six clubs had been founded to nullify the restriction on meetings of the sectional assemblies.[59]

The regulations adopted by them were similar in all essentials, there being little difference in goals between these sectional clubs and the older organizations. The orator who said the following could have spoken for all: "We make up a part of the mass of people in whom all sovereignty is embodied. Here we maintain an active vigilance over our administration. Within the popular societies we are but brothers, friends who come together for the purpose of instruction."[60] All emphasized the need to study the laws, watch "traitors," as well as the legal authorities, protect the oppressed, and correspond with their brothers. Le Club centrale du département de Paris announced that its principles were based on the good of all, ardent love of country, the establishment of liberty and equality, help for the unfortunate, and respect for virtue.[61] The society of Sans-culottes des deux sexes met in order to enlighten themselves, to guarantee the triumph of liberty and equality, and to assure the maintenance of the republic. Women were to be admitted equally with men "to share the patriotic

---

[57] Ibid., XVII, no. 207, 26 July 1793. Functionaries who dissolved them or removed their registers or other documents were subject to ten years' imprisonment.

[58] As late as 4 February 1794, that is, after popular societies had come under attack of the government, the Committee of Public Safety called on them to help it "to expose treachery and to rip off the mask of hypocritical patriotism and superstition." It praised their work and called on them to continue the battle. B.V.C., MS 119, fols. 127-129.

[59] Soboul, pp. 617-619.

[60] B.N., MSS, Nouv. acq. fr. 2705, fol. 273, n.d. The remarks of the unknown orator are in fols. 272-278.

[61] B.N., Lb⁴⁰ 2370, Le Club central du département de Paris séant à l'Evêché à ses frères les républicains ([Paris], 21 September 1793), 4 pp. It invited the sections and all popular societies to send two commissioners each to participate in its sessions. The same brochure in A.N., AD XVI, 70.

work of the society."[62] The important Comité central des sociétés populaires, in addition to corresponding with other societies and acting as a center for affiliated organizations, meant "to denounce unfaithful agents of the Republic," help the unfortunate, clarify public opinion, and affirm "the liberty, equality, and unity of the Republic."[63] The society of section Homme-Armé declared that its aim was "to propagate the principles of liberty, of equality, of love of country; to unmask the plots of enemies of the public good, to thwart their intrigues, to revive weak or wavering patriots, to keep a sharp eye on authorities and functionaries who govern the section, to maintain the laws."[64]

To be admitted, an applicant had to prove that he had never signed any "anti-civic petition" and had accounted himself well during the great *journées* of the Revolution. Questions such as the following were put to him:

> Were you a noble, priest (an agent of one or the other), an agent of the exchange, profiteer, money merchant, banker, notary, monarchist, royalist, chaplain, Brissotin, Feuillant, federalist, moderate?

> Have you ever signed any anti-civic petitions? Have you ever attended any clubs of such nature? Have you ever spoken out against the revolutions of 20 June, 10 August 1792, 31 May, 1st and 2d June 1793? Have you accepted the Republican Constitution?

> What have you done for the Revolution?
> What are your means of support?
> What was your worth before 1789?
> What is your actual worth today?
> Do you have a certificate of *civisme*?[65]

Candidates were as a rule presented by members of a society and examined publicly. The minimum age was usually sixteen when spec-

[62] B.N., Lb⁴⁰ 2393, *Règlemens de la Société de l'harmonie sociale des sans-culottes des deux sexes défenseurs de la Constitution* ([Paris], n.d.), 8 pp.

[63] B.N., Lb⁴⁰ 2373, *Règlement du comité central des sociétés populaires séant à l'Evêché* ([Paris], 29 vendémiaire, Year II), 8 pp.

[64] Other examples may be found in the following: B.N., Lb⁴⁰ 2444, *Règlement de la société fraternelle, dite le club républicain de la section de l'Homme Armé* ([Paris], Year II), 15 pp. See also the following in Tourneux's *Bibliographie*, II: #9877, 9882, 10066, 9906, 10016, 9911, 9886, 9878, 10088, 10097.

[65] A.P.P., A A/266, fol. 194, Section Faubourg du Nord, n.d.

ified, and dues were deliberately kept low so as not to exclude anyone. Section Homme-Armé rejected all pecuniary considerations for admission,[66] as did the society of sections Poissonnière and Lepeletier.[67] All clubs had officers, of course, elected for brief intervals and subject to both reelection and to recall. These included a president, a vice president, one or several secretaries, a treasurer, and an archivist,[68] some adding inspectors and censors, and a committee of correspondence.[69] Meetings were held during days when general assemblies did not meet, or, in some cases, when the Jacobins were not in session.[70] After reading the minutes and correspondence, candidates were presented for consideration; there followed various committee or individual reports and then the reading of journals and bulletins. About 8 p.m. the society began to consider the important questions of the day. Orators wore the red cap of liberty and were heard, in theory, without interruption. The second person singular, *tu*, was invariably used, and all balloting was done in the open. Often the entire society would be seized by enthusiasm, all would rise and sing, take the oath to live free or die, and give other evidence of these "republican transports" (*transports républicains*).[71]

Feminism also appeared in a number of clubs, but received little encouragement from their male members.[72] Santerre must have spoken for many of his sex, militant and moderate alike, when he admonished Théroigne de Mericourt, who had attempted to organize the women of faubourg Saint-Antoine: "the men of this faubourg . . .

---

[66] B.N., Lb[40] 2444, *Règlement*, article 2.

[67] Mellié, p. 279; Soboul, p. 625, in both cases for those *sans-culottes* who could not afford to pay.

[68] B.V.C., MS 118, fol. 22, "Règlement de la Société adopté dans la séance du 30 7bre 1793" is typical except for the absence of an archivist. It was called La Société républicaine & révolutionnaire de la section des marchés.

[69] In addition to the references above see B.N., Lb[40] 2343, *Règlement de la société des amis de la liberté, de l'egalité, et de l'humanité séant à Paris, rue Vert-Bois* ([Paris], n.d.), 15 pp. This was the society in section Gravilliers, established in 1791. The above copy in the Bibliothèque nationale is defective, as pp. 4-13 are blank. No mention of imperfection in Tourneux, #10095, given as containing 4 pp.

[70] Art. XIII of the Règlemens de la Société des deux-sexes.

[71] Mellié, pp. 279-281; Soboul, pp. 626-629. These emotional displays were similar to those experienced by members of sectional assemblies.

[72] See the eloquent plea of Etta Palm d'Aelders of Holland to the Cercle social, where her letter was read, in which she asked for equal education to make women worthy companions of men. B.N., Lc[2] 317, *La Bouche de fer*, no. 1, 3 January 1791.

arriving from work prefer to find their household in order rather than to see their women returning from assemblies where they do not always acquire a spirit of gentleness."[73] To the charge that the fraternal society of section Panthéon Français was "hermaphrodite," its spokesman replied that intriguers feared the observing eyes of the women.[74] A man like Prudhomme, publisher of *Les Révolutions de Paris*, was rare. Not only did he support women in their efforts to go beyond the kitchen and the nursery, but even encouraged his wife to preside over the Société des indigents.[75] Jacobins, too, praised a few militants like Claire Lacombe and Pauline Léon, who led the Revolutionary Women's Republican Club, but only for a moment.[76] In May 1793 a delegation of the Société des républicaines révolutionnaires (which sat in the Cordeliers) was received with applause by the Convention and given the honors of the session by the General Council.[77] After the overthrow of the Gironde, when Lacombe announced that her revolutionary women would devote themselves to matters of public concern, she was applauded by the Jacobins.[78] A month later, because of her defense of Roux and Leclerc, she was violently attacked in the Jacobin Society. Lacombe had the temerity to address Robespierre as "monsieur," or so it was charged by Chabot.[79] When the Republican women clashed physically with those of les Halles over the latter's refusal to wear the national colors, the Convention stepped in with a decree supporting the right to dress as one pleased.[80] On the following

---

[73] Cited by Bourdin, p. 153. When a delegation of men and women arrived during a meeting of a fraternal club of the Jacobins, its presiding officer, Chabrou, announced regretfully that he would receive only the men delegates. B.N., Lb[40] 2416, *Discours, imprimé par ordre de la Société fraternelle de patriotes, de l'un et de l'autre sexe . . . séant aux Jacobins* (Paris, November 1790), 14 pp.

[74] B.N., Lb[40] 2456, *Guerre aux intrigans. Réponse de la société fraternelle du Panthéon . . .* ([Paris], primidi ventôse [2e]), 8 pp.

[75] Bourdin, p. 149.

[76] For Claire Lacombe, see A.N., F[7] 4756 and T 1001[1-3]; for Pauline Léon, A.N., F[7] 4774[9], which includes documents on Théophile Leclerc, her *enragé* husband.

[77] A.N., F[1c] III, Seine, 13, liasse 1, 20 May 1793; A.N., C 355, 1865, same date.

[78] Aulard, *Jacobins*, V, 360, 18 August 1793.

[79] A.N., T 1001[2], 16 September 1793. The riot in the Jacobins when Lacombe tried to defend herself is treated in the following sources: Aulard, *Jacobins*, V, 406-408; B. & R., XXIX, 115-120; *Moniteur*, XVII, no. 264, 21 September 1793; Tuetey, *Répertoire*, IX, no. 1234.

[80] *Moniteur*, XVIII, no. 39, p. 290, 30 October 1793, session of 8 brumaire. See

day, 31 October, after the report of Amar, the Convention dissolved all women's popular societies and prohibited their reconstitution.[81]

The Société populaire républicaine des Droits-de-l'Homme was founded by a nucleus of thirty members on 20 September 1793, and met in the same hall used by the sectional assembly on rue de la Verrerie. Although it limited its membership to males, it provided a separate tribunal from which women could address the club. Candidates for membership were introduced by a special committee, and sessions were scheduled for the fifth and last days of the *décade*. Although a number of sections counted more than one popular society within their precincts, section Droits-de-l'Homme had only this one club.[82]

Four days later the society adopted a detailed set of regulations that provided for the usual officers and duties, stipulated that all sessions were to be public, and guaranteed freedom of expression. The club met every day except when the general assembly was in session, and a committee of seven (not twelve, as stated in the reply to the national agent) presented candidates for membership. Those denounced for any reason were given a hearing before members acted on the accusation; dues, in the form of a contribution, were levied monthly, with indigent members being given relief by a voluntary collection. Since the goal of the society was to instruct one another, patriotic journals were subscribed to and delegates were appointed to seek affiliation with other societies. Certain categories of people were excluded in advance as being unworthy of membership.[83]

A.N., C 271, 666, 20 September 1793, for a report in the Commune to petition the Convention for the above.

[81] *Moniteur*, XVIII, no. 40, pp. 299-300, 31 October 1793.

[82] B.H.V.P., MS 807, fol. 208, ventôse, Year II. This is from a communication of the civil committee to Lullier, the national agent, in reply to his questionnaire of 11 ventôse, Year II (1 March 1794), *ibid.*, fol. 207. The committee's reply was signed by Doublet. In addition to this source there is the following: A. de P., D 4 AZ 79, 20 September 1793, Commune de Paris: "section Droits-de-l'Homme just announces that it has established a popular society in its usual meeting place. The General Council acknowledges this declaration and invites it to [the honors of] the session." Signed by Lubin, secretary-president.

[83] The John Reynolds Library (French Historical Tracts), *Règlement adopté par la Société populaire de la section des Droits-de-l'Homme* (Paris, 24 September 1793), 9 pp. There is no copy of this brochure in either the Bibliothèque nationale or the British Museum. No mention in Tourneux.

Among its first public acts was the presentation of a pennant (*guidon*) to the Society of Revolutionary Republican Women. "Your society," the spokesman began, "is one of the elements of the social body, and not the least important. Liberty finds a new school here." Praising the women for having broken a link in the chain of prejudice that had kept them isolated at home, and lauding their contribution "to the common good," he welcomed their participation in public affairs, in fraternal societies, in maintaining surveillance, and in teaching. Why should not women participate in public affairs? he asked. The Declaration of Rights was common to both sexes. Despite the demands of nature it was possible to reconcile needs of family with love of the public good. Then, presenting the pennant upon which was inscribed the Declaration of the Rights of Man, he urged them to carry it as a sign of equality side-by-side with the tricolor.[84] One can imagine the mutual satisfaction that must have permeated the hearts and minds of his hearers of both sexes as this symbolic gesture of love and respect was acknowledged.

Fragments of documents and partial reports give an imperfect insight into the society's operations and concerns. The session of 18 nivôse, Year II (7 January 1794) has come down to us almost intact. What can it tell the reader of the debates and motions in its hall? The president, Pavas Leroy, opened the session by calling on the secretary to read a letter from the society's ex-president, Hubert, expressing his regrets at being unavoidably absent because of the death of his father-in-law, and assuring his colleagues that he was waiting impatiently to rejoin them. Following this was a communication from its sister society of Lepeletier acknowledging receipt of an unspecified resolution transmitted to it by society Droits-de-l'Homme and assuring it that it would be presented to the general assembly of the section. The discussion then turned on the effort to obtain and examine a list of those residents in the section who had signed the Petition of Twenty Thousand. David was authorized to obtain these names from the original petition deposited with the police of section Fontaine-de-Grenelle. A discussion then arose on an observation made by a member that since the renewal of the society almost all new members had

[84] B.N., Lb⁴⁰ 2411, *Discours prononcé à la Société républicaines révolutionnaires par les citoyens de la section des Droits-de-l'Homme en lui donnant un guidon sur lequelle est la déclaration des Droits-de-l'Homme* ([Paris], [1793]), 6 pp.

been presented by the same persons and witnesses. This could result in abuses, he warned, the implication being that it could lead to factionalism or personal jealousies. Another member countered that regardless of who presented a candidate, the *comité de presentation* reported to the whole society, which ruled ultimately on his acceptance or rejection. No motion of any sort was recorded to bring the question to a vote, so that it can be assumed that the traditional practice continued.[85]

Once this matter was disposed, a young student, prepared evidently by his teacher, who was a member of the society, declaimed on the virtues of republicanism. When the enthusiastic applause had died down, the screening committee presented a candidate by name of Nicolas. His replies to questions put to him failed to impress the membership, and his application was postponed for three months. Nicolas then pointed out that he had been one of the guards or, more likely, that he had been appointed to fulfill this function in the society (the minutes are not clear on this point). The society then appointed another guard for the time being.

Among the three men accepted by the society was the future Thermidorian, Grandjean. Interestingly, not a single vote was cast against him.[86] The corporal of the 2nd company, Doubledaut, then presented himself and complained that he had been demoted because of accusations that he had rejected the republican Constitution. No action on this complaint was recorded, nor is it clear from the minutes whether the charge had originated in the society itself.

This was followed by specific complaints against three citizens of the section accused of shoddy work. The first was the shoemaker Hardy, member of the revolutionary and civil committees, charged with having manufactured two hundred pairs of worthless army boots. Citizen Robert was accused of turning out poor uniforms, and Chartrain of profiteering in books.[87] The society then resolved to invite the accused to come on the morrow and make their defense. What these men said and how they refuted the charges against them is unknown, since, unfortunately, the records of the next day's session are missing.

Before adjourning, the gathering was informed that its sister soci-

[85] *Ibid.*, B.H.V.P., MS 748, fol. 120.
[86] *Ibid.* The others were Guyon and Cuvilier.
[87] *Ibid.*, the latter charge is not clear, as the document is partially destroyed.

ety of section Amis-de-la-Patrie wished to inform it of a patriotic work entitled *Le Chêne de la liberté ou le pied civique idylle*, which aroused no comment or discussion. Finally, a member proposed that the society devote a portion of its session on the morrow to the problem of gathering saltpeter. There is no record of discussion on the important political questions of the day.[88]

The close relationship of the society with its general assembly may be seen in the *procès-verbal* of 21 nivôse (10 January), since the day preceding it was devoted to the sectional meeting. The assembly had adopted a resolution asking the society to present a list of eight candidates to fill vacancies on the civil committee, which it did.[89] On the following day, when commissioners for saltpeter reported that they lacked sufficient powers to fulfill their mission, the society simply referred this matter to the general assembly for official authorization. Two days later it heard a report that there were abuses in the administration charged with the care and provision of horses. This matter, too, was referred to the general assembly.[90] As might be expected, the society kept a close watch on prices in the section even though specific legal remedies were referred to the general assembly. The commissioner on profiteering was alerted by a member who complained that wine merchants had combined to raise the price of their product, making it prohibitive for many residents of the section. Here, again, the society requested the assembly to deal with the problem, suggesting it as the first item of business.[91]

There is some evidence also that the section's young men serving at the front corresponded with the society. Mention of a letter from a Marion fils, was duly noted and transmitted to the general assembly.[92] The promotion of patriotic feeling was certainly one of the pervading activities of the society. When, for example, Varlet was freed from prison in brumaire, he was invited to compose a hymn for the installation of the busts of Lepeletier and of Marat, presented by the soci-

---

[88] *Ibid.* This *procès-verbal* was recorded and signed by secretary Vacheloz.

[89] *Ibid.*, fol. 121. Those named were Jambon, Boison, Jean Chevalier, Collet, Bouquet (of rue de la Verrerie), its president Leroy, David, and someone by name of Quinier (?).

[90] *Ibid.*, 24 nivôse, Year II (13 January 1794). Bonnefont was secretary.

[91] *Ibid.*, fol. 122, 14 nivôse, Year II (3 January 1794).

[92] *Ibid.*, fol. 122, 14 nivôse, Year II (3 January 1794).

ety.[93] The renaming of the section's square of the Market of Saint Jean to Droits-de-l'Homme was also an outgrowth of its suggestion.[94]

Recommendations of the society to fill administrative posts were eagerly sought by those seeking employment. Sevice in the army, as discussed above, was proof of patriotism, and an introduction to the society by a member assured a candidate that his application would be received with sympathy.[95] That the society was interested in purifying the civil service may be seen from an acknowledgment by the popular club of section Brutus of receipt of a resolution from Droits-de-l'Homme's society urging revolutionary committees to investigate and purge public officials occupying various administrative posts. It demanded, for example, the expulsion of all subject to the draft (*la première requisition*) and an examination of their incomes and property. Those who were too wealthy were to be expelled to make room for "the good *sans-culottes* who had the ability" to carry out the necessary functions.[96]

That the society abused its position in removing moderates and other oppositionists can hardly be challenged. The pressure of militants to exclude signers of the so-called anticivic petitions from all government posts and even from general assemblies, if acquiesced in by the Commune and Convention, would have divided the country even more sharply. Moreover, when those who retracted their signatures a few days after signing, as happened in section Droits-de-l'Homme, were refused recognition of this retraction by the popular society, their "error" now became an excuse for intolerance and tyranny. Seven citizens of the section menaced with being excluded from

[93] B.V.C., MS 120, fols. 153, 156, 15 vendémiaire and 10 frimaire, Year II (6 October and 5 November 1793). These busts, it was ruled by the general assembly, could be placed only in the hall of the assembly or committee rooms. *Ibid.*, fol. 156, 10 frimaire, Year II (30 November 1793).

[94] *Ibid.*, fol. 155, 15 brumaire, Year II (5 November 1793); *Affiches de la Commune*, no. 140, 23 brumaire, Year II (13 November 1793); *Affiches de la Commune*, no. 140, 23 brumaire, Year II (13 November 1793), in session of the Commune, 21 brumaire. The society also recommended that market stalls (*baraques*) be replaced by open booths with overhangs shaded from the sun (*parasols*). This proposal was referred to the Administration of Public Works.

[95] A. de P., 4 AZ 53, 19 brumaire 1793 (9 November).

[96] B.V.C., MS 118, fol. 49, 9 nivôse, Year III, (29 December 1794). This is a prejudiced report by a commissioner, Poulletier, directed against former militants in the popular society of section Brutus.

the general assembly for having signed the Petition of Eight-Thousand appealed to the Convention for assistance.[97]

The seven protesters maintained that they had been deceived by their officers in signing the Petition of Eight Thousand, which they retracted three days later (18 June 1792) in a petition to the Legislative Assembly. They thought that the matter was finished until the general assembly reopened discussion on this old affair and had refused to recognize their retraction. Now they requested documentary evidence of their abrogation from the Convention in order to present it to the general assembly. This petition was referred to the Committee of General Security, which let the matter rest for the time being.[98]

In addition to watching prices of necessities, the society also examined the quality of products produced and sold in the markets of the section. When a member reported that the poor quality of bread baked was endangering the ill in the section, the society was quick to persuade the sectional assembly to demand that the General Council appoint one baker in each section who would specialize in preparing bread for the sick. It was to be made of the purest flour available, containing no cheap ingredients (such as rye or barley), and was to be delivered to the ill upon certification of health officials.[99] Meat was also to be made available, and a report on how to cultivate the potato was discussed.[100] On the other hand, when it was reported that rich prisoners were supposedly receiving beef and mutton in their prison fare, there was an outcry of general indignation and it was resolved to denounce this violation to the police.[101]

The society was equally interested in the political tone of plays produced on the stages of the capital. One such drama, entitled *L'Ecole*

[97] A.N., C 286, pl. 840, p. 19, 22 frimaire, Year II (12 December 1793). These were Magnenoz, an inspector (*toiseur de bâtiment*); Cailloué, a merchant butcher; Fournier and Gallant, mason-entrepreneurs; Régnier, a basketmaker; d'Aubigni, a glazier; and Georget, a "citizen." Only Régnier was an artisan, although d'Aubigni could have been one, too. This could have reflected a class antagonism, as Soboul points out, p. 247 n. 17.

[98] A.P., LXXXI, 383, 22 frimaire, Year II (12 December 1793). The petitioners admitted that they had been deceived in asking that the cannon held by the section's armed force be surrendered to the authorities.

[99] A. de P., 4 AZ 698, 3 pluviôse, Year II (22 January 1794).

[100] Caron, *Paris*, IV, 277, 4 ventôse, Year II (22 February 1794).

[101] *Ibid.*, IV, 340, 8 ventôse (26 February).

de Cartouche, performed in a theater on Boulevard du Temple, was denounced to the General Council as "a very dangerous play." The Council referred this complaint to the administration of police.[102] A harsher note was its proposal to the Committee of Public Safety, observing that those entrepreneurs who had undertaken to manufacture arms for the nation but who had not fulfilled their task should be regarded as being guilty of *lèse-nation*. The society even demanded the death penalty for dishonest businessmen, for suppliers who had been advanced funds that they used for speculation.[103] When expulsion of politically unreliable elements seemed necessary, the society did not hesitate to help purge the section's armed forces and its own membership, as well.[104] More tangible, perhaps, was its contribution of financial and other gifts to the Convention,[105] and the arming and equipping of "cavaliers" at its own expense.[106] Nor was it slow in coming to the defense of the section's civil commissioners when they were accused of malfeasance in the distribution of eggs and butter,[107] yet its members did not hesitate to accuse leaders of the section of lining their own pockets.[108]

It would be interesting to have a list of members, starting with the original thirty and ending with those who remained on the eve of its dissolution. The changes in the political climate and, especially, the attacks on popular societies launched by the government after the execution of the Hébertists led to the destruction of these lists and even records of the clubs. From the few names that make their ap-

[102] *Journal de la montagne*, no. 77, p. 610, 10 pluviôse, Year II (29 January 1794) in the Commune of 8 pluviôse. The play was being presented at the theater of a citizen Lazzari.

[103] B.N., Nouv. acq. fr. MSS, 2691, fol. 129, 17 nivôse, Year II (6 January 1794).

[104] *Journal de la montagne*, no. 110, p. 876, 13 ventôse, Year II (3 March 1794), reported in the Commune, 11 ventôse. Bacon reported a purge on 23 ventôse (13 March). Caron, *Paris*, IV, 268.

[105] A.N., F7* 2497, p. 81, 1 pluviôse, Year II (21 January 1794). Delegates of the society joined commissioners appointed by the section's revolutionary committee to deposit gifts in the Convention.

[106] A. de P., 4 AZ 698, 3 pluviôse, Year II (22 January 1794).

[107] *Moniteur*, XX, no. 197, p. 138, 17 germinal, Year II (6 April 1794), in Commune, 14 germinal. The charge was brought by an elector by name of Jobert. The Council referred it to the police.

[108] Caron, *Paris*, IV, 340, 8 ventôse, Year II (26 February 1794).

pearance, however, it is evident that the same activists who staffed the local committees, regularly attended the general assemblies, and contributed to patriotic activities in the section were among the militants who composed the society. Such names as Auzolles and Le Roy, police commissioners with a long background in the politics of the section, are among the first to appear. Members of the revolutionary committee such as Pommer, Collet, Duclos, Dommanget, Bergeret, Dassin, Gattrez, Ravel, Houdaille, and Temponnet were members. Civil committee members such as Hubert, Jambon, and Pollet; the battalion commander, Lasne; and the commissioners on profiteering, Carron and Perrin were also members. Names of occasional signatories to the *procès-verbaux* such as Vacheloz and Quinier (?) also appear. Varlet was a member of the society, as may be seen in his own testimony on Descombes and in that of Oudart.

In the absence of more specific information, it is difficult to establish the social composition of the society or the number who attended its sessions, either as members or as visitors. If the latter figures correspond to those of other sections, the number of members must have represented a small proportion of the total body of citizens in the section. The figures of neighboring sections may give some indication of what might have been true of Droits-de-l'Homme, as well. The society of Homme-Armé had 200 out of 2,000 men who bore arms in the section. Réunion had 148, while 4,378 voted in the section. The total number who belonged in all sections did not exceed 10 percent of those eligible.[109]

This observation must be modified during the crisis of ventôse, when the Hébertists faced suppression. In his reports to the minister of interior, the police observer, Bacon, reported on five different occasions that the popular society of section Droits-de-l'Homme "was extremely numerous."[110] Political activists were aware of the fierce struggle among the factions in the government and outside of it, and were personally involved in many cases. The fate of their own militant, Descombes, brought the attack home to them.[111]

[109] Soboul, pp. 639-640.

[110] Caron, *Paris*, IV, 197, 1 ventôse, Year II (19 February 1794); pp. 266-267, 4 ventôse, (22 February); p. 340, 8 ventôse (26 February); p. 268, 23 ventôse (13 March); p. 376, 28 ventôse (18 March).

[111] *Ibid.*, IV, 376-377, 28 ventôse, Year II (18 March 1794).

Writing on 9 pluviôse, Year II (28 January 1794), the police spy, Le Harivel, reported that there was much talk of the approaching dissolution of popular societies. Then he made this shrewd observation in explaining why the government committees favored such a move: "it is the only way to concentrate authority within a sole and single point."[112] The trend toward centralization embodied in the decree of 14 frimaire, Year II (4 December 1793), the subordination of the Convention to its committees, the sacrifice of dissent to the concept of unity demanded by the war, the growing impatience with nonconformist ideas and personalities, the fear that local autonomy undermined national unity, all placed sectional independence in jeopardy. The attack of government committees, so closely intertwined now with the Jacobin Society, against these independent popular societies was an inevitable consequence of this trend toward centralization and the concentration of political power in the executive organs of government. An autonomous organism like a section controlling its own armed force, and influenced so deeply by its more conscious political elements gathered in a popular society could not be tolerated for long. There was undoubtedly some truth in the observation of the police agent, Bacon, who wrote that he had witnessed men under the guise of patriotism deliberately set at odds popular societies against committees of surveillance.[113] Even if this was a rare occurrence, the antagonism between a voluntary body such as a popular club and an official institution such as a surveillance committee undoubtedly existed.

Robespierre had criticized popular societies as early as 9 November 1793 for not being sufficiently patriotic. He had demanded the suspension of the request to affiliate by the popular club of section Invalides because there were few men of 10 August within it, and even fewer of the men of 31 May. "Today," he declared, "all royalists are republicans, all Brissotins are Montagnards," and demanded that the society purge its ranks.[114] Even Varlet had joined the attack on the Club central des sociétés populaires when the Club central des élec-

---

[112] Caron, *Paris*, III, 194.

[113] *Ibid.*, IV, 223, 2 ventôse, Year II (20 February 1794).

[114] Aulard, *Jacobins*, V, 503-504, 19 brumaire, Year II (9 November 1793). Before Robespierre took the floor, the Jacobins had applauded the address presented by the delegates of Invalides.

teurs complained to the Jacobins that a society calling itself Club central was holding secret sessions near its own premises. Varlet had chimed in: "This so-called Club central has regulations; it is thus not a *comité*, it is a society," explaining that people confused it with the Club central des électeurs. Dufourny and Hébert added that its members should be prosecuted.[115]

On November 28, Robespierre urged a purge of the Jacobins,[116] and on December 26 reminded them that he had opposed the affiliation of the popular society of section Invalides, Bonnet Rouge. He was convinced, Robespierre added, that these sectional societies were "the ultimate resource of the malevolent opposed to liberty." Then, resorting to demagogy, he linked these societies to agents of foreign powers. "The great popular society is the French people," he continued, praising the Jacobins and those clubs that had been affiliated to them for a long time. "The so-called popular societies multiplying ad infinitum since 31 May are bastard societies and do not merit this sacred name."[117]

By the end of January 1794, the police spy, Rolin, reported that many expected the dissolution of sectional, fraternal societies. Only the Jacobins and the Cordeliers, and, possibly, the Club central du département de Paris (Club électoral), would remain.[118] His report was based largely on what had transpired in the Jacobins at its session of 8 nivôse (28 January 1794). Most speakers vehemently attacked all new societies formed since 31 May, saw the hand of Pitt behind their machinations, scoffed at their pretensions of being more patriotic than the true and tested Jacobins, and accused them, like Hébert, of counterrevolutionary activity in the sections. A lone dissenter, Saintexte, reminded the Jacobins how essential it was to have clubs in localities

[115] *Ibid.*, V, 538, 8 frimaire, Year II (28 November 1793); *Journal de la montagne*, II, no. 17, p. 134, 10 frimaire, Year II (30 November 1793).

[116] *Moniteur*, XVIII, no. 71, p. 549, 11 frimaire, Year II (1 December 1793).

[117] *Journal de la montagne*, nos. 45 and 46, pp. 356-358 and 363-364, 8 nivôse and 9 nivôse, Year II (28 and 29 December 1793), the most complete version of the session in the Jacobin Society of 6 nivôse. See also Aulard, *Jacobins*, V, 578-581; and *Moniteur*, XXI, no. 101, pp. 86-87, 6 nivôse, Year II, both describing the session of December 26 (6 nivôse).

[118] Caron, *Paris*, III, 12 pluviôse, Year II (31 January 1794). Rolin paraphrased those he overheard as saying that if these societies were closed down, things would go better and fear of civil war would abate.

far removed from the center of the Revolution to help rouse a "love of country." He was ignored, however, as the Jacobins withdrew affiliation of clubs formed since 13 May, demanding a thorough purge of those remaining, and resolving no longer to recognize sectional societies.[119]

After the execution of the Hébertists, it was only a question of time until the final blow fell. On 15 May 1794 the Jacobins ruled that their members could no longer belong to sectional societies, and were given ten days to withdraw or lose their membership. A demagogic oration by Collot d'Herbois in connection with efforts by the popular society of section Lepeletier both to dissolve itself and to maintain its affiliation with the Jacobins ended with a motion no longer to admit delegations of sectional societies to the tribune.[120] Under this kind of pressure the sectional societies began to dissolve themselves.[121]

Throughout the months of floréal and prairial these societies closed their doors, some not without an effort to maintain themselves. Several considered changing their name in order to appear less sectional.[122] Others faced the practical problem of where to deposit their records and to what body to entrust the investigation of applicants for civic cards, a function formerly performed by the club.[123] Still others asked if theirs was a true, popular society or merely a sectional club,

[119] *Moniteur*, XXI, no. 132, pp. 337-339, 12 pluviôse, Year II (31 January 1794); Aulard, *Jacobins*, V, 689-691, 24 ventôse, Year II (14 March 1794). A.N., AF 11, 66, pl. 488, n.d. The Committee of Public Safety, "in order to maintain the unity of the Republic," proposed prohibiting new societies except those which were affiliated with the Jacobins. Clubs like the Société fraternelle des deux sexes, which were general rather than sectional, remained affiliated to the Jacobins even after the fall of Robespierre. A.N., D III, 240-242, d. 1, pc. 11, 17 thermidor, Year II (4 August 1794).

[120] *Moniteur*, XX, nos. 236, 238, pp. 467-468, 482-483, 26 and 28 floréal, Year II (15 and 17 May 1794) reporting the sessions of the Jacobins for 23 and 25 floréal. Collot accused the Lepeletier society of lack of patriotism, of staging religious masquerades, and of "a new federalism."

[121] See the following items in Tourneux's *Bibliographie*, II: #10053, 10070, 10080, 9764.

[122] Caron, *Paris*, IV, 222, 2 ventôse, Year II (20 February 1794) for Guillaume-Tell.

[123] A.P.P., A A/266, fol. 6, 10 floréal, Year II (29 April 1794). The society of section Arcis had dissolved itself the day before.

and scanned the remarks of Jacobin orators in seeking answers.[124] What to do about pledges to maintain a volunteer's wife and family, to whom turn over the treasury and the effects of the club, and even whether to surrender their membership cards were questions discussed.[125] The same uncertainty is reflected in the popular society of Sans-culottes révolutionnaires at its session of 21 May.[126] On May 4, the society of section Brutus dissolved itself.[127]

The popular society of Droits-de-l'Homme terminated its session on 21 May 1794. Three days later, five commissioners of the club informed the National Convention that the former "Société populaire républicaine" of Droits-de-l'Homme had ceased to meet. In acknowledging its dissolution, they referred to the alleged "horrible project of perverse men [Hébertists] to struggle against the supreme power and to overthrow the National Colossus [that is, the Convention], before whom they should have prostrated themselves"—not the most republican sentiment or form of expression, it might be noted.[128]

After closing down the Jacobin Club on 12 November 1794, the Convention allowed the few scattered societies to continue their precarious existence. Since they were no longer deemed dangerous, a routine surveillance was thought to be sufficient. The law of 25 vendémiaire, Year III (16 October 1794) prohibited them from acting in a collective manner—to affiliate with one another, correspond, or present petitions. Furthermore, it required that a list of members be furnished the government quarterly.[129] The debate that followed the law's introduction revealed that although there were still men of principle and integrity sitting in the Convention, the majority supported the

---

[124] B.V.C., MS 119, fols. 105-106, 29 floréal, Year II (18 May 1794), société populaire, séante rue de Vendôme. After a long discussion, the society wrote to the Convention that although it had never abandoned its republican principles, it dissolved itself out of "regard for public opinion."

[125] Ibid.

[126] A.N., C 306, pl. 1155, p. 15, 2 prairial, Year II, séante place Chalier.

[127] B.V.C., MS 118, fol. 48, 15 floréal, Year II. The commissioner of the club in his report to the general assembly listed the following inventory of records: a register of denunciations, reports of the committee on presentation of candidates for admission, candidates on whom action was postponed, and the procès-verbaux of the sessions.

[128] A.N., C 306, pl. 1154, p. 74, 5 prairial, Year II (24 May 1794). This letter was signed by Duclos, Houdaille, Carron, Temponnet, and Donzel.

[129] Aulard, Jacobins, VI, 570-571.

demagogues.[130] The Conventionnels who argued that they were not attacking the clubs as such, but only their abuses, must surely have realized that prohibiting them to act collectively destroyed them as a political force. This was precisely what the Thermidorians intended. It was to be a long time before any meaningful revival of political societies was to take place.[131]

A feeble attempt was made to revive a popular society in the 7th arrondissement when two delegates, Gaudichot and David, requested a charter for "Les Hommes du Quatorze Juillet, du Dix Août et du Trente un May" (sic). After they declared that they intended to hold their sessions in the hall of the (former) popular society on the second, fourth and eighth day of each *décade*, the revolutionary committee immediately granted this request.[132] On 9 frimaire (29 November), the surveillance committee received a request for information from the national agent of the department of Paris on the existence, if any, of popular societies under its care. Le Duc replied for the committee four days later that he had information on "Les Hommes du Quatorze Juillet" society, which counted a mere six members who met in a café nearby. On 22 pluviôse and 5 ventôse (10 and 23 February 1795), the national agent requested a report every *décade* on meetings that might be contrary to the law of 25 vendémiaire. The committee delegated two of its members to give such a report in person, but it is doubtful whether there was anything to communicate.[133]

[130] *Ibid.*, VI, 572-588; *Moniteur*, XXII, no. 28, pp. 255-260, 28 vendémiaire, Year III (19 October 1794). See, especially, the defense of popular societies by Thibadeau, Lejeune, Chassous, Dubarran, and Romme. Defenders of the law were Merlin (de Thionville), Reubell, Bentabole, and Bourdon de l'Oise. An effort made to postpone the vote on this decree was defeated. Lejeune reminded his audience: "We must not forget the immortal services rendered by these societies so much calumnied."

[131] An interesting and long struggle over its popular society, Jean Jacques Rousseau, took place in section Beaurepaire (Thermes de Julien). B.V.C., MS 119, fols. 35-66.

[132] A.N., F7* 2498, p. 37, 22 vendémiaire, Year III (13 October 1794). Note that this is before the termination of the Jacobin Club.

[133] *Ibid.*, p. 107, 13 frimaire; p. 197, 22 pluviôse; p. 209, 5 ventôse. For developments in the 7th arrondissement under the Directory see: A.N., AF III, 260 Seine; A.N., F7 7353, fol. 9846. Isser Woloch, *Jacobin Legacy; the Democratic Movement under the Directory* (Princeton, 1970), Appendix I, p. 405. There was a total of 75 names that appeared on various petitions of the arrondissement, Figure I, p. 210. This is an excellent study of the resurgence and ultimate suppression of the republican movement under the Directory.

There is an atmosphere of depression and disillusionment permeating the final sessions of these societies. They had contributed so much to the Revolution and were now the objects of so much calumny. Yet it cannot be denied that many of them tended to form elitist groups in their sections, which must have irritated ordinary citizens and alarmed supporters of the principle of equality. The display of medals and ribbons and the sporting of liberty caps, coupled with an air of arrogance and exclusiveness, contained seeds of trouble.[134] It would be interesting to know how many applicants were rejected solely on the basis of class, and how many because of personal jealousies, petty conflicts, and personality clashes. How much resentment must have been stored up in the hearts of those thus turned down? There is evidence also of the tempestuous nature of their sessions. The cries, the brawls, the denunciations of intemperate men made warm by political fanaticism, and, sometimes, by wine, must have disconcerted the more moderate and self-sacrificing members.[135]

Modeling themselves on their elders, the young formed their own organizations. If not quite a cultural revolution, their attitude of superiority must have irritated their parents. When the Elèves de la patrie of section Arcis complained to the General Council that they had been maligned by journalists who accused them of hoping to become rivals of the popular society, the secretary noted the "prolixity and twisted style" in which their procès-verbal was couched; he was convinced that it could not have been edited by anyone above the age

[134] Caron, Paris, III, 393, 20 pluviôse, Year II (8 February 1794), report of Charmont: "There are actually two clearly pronounced parties in Paris: members of societies and those who are not members." Ibid., IV, 13, 12 pluviôse, Year II (9 February 1794), report of Rolin.

[135] Ibid., IV, 56, 24 pluviôse, Year II (12 February 1794), report of Bacon on a session of the society in section Arcis. When extracts of various journals were read, there was much hooting and shouting. Two days later (February 14), Bacon reported on the session of the popular society of faubourg Montmartre at which Bouchotte, minister of war, was accused of feeding horses for his own pleasure. On February 17 he observed an agitated meeting of the club in section Bonne-Nouvelle, whose secretary was accused of favoring small property holders. Ibid., IV, 94, 162; 26 and 29 pluviôse, Year II (14 and 17 February 1794). When, for example, a member of the society of section Droits-de-l'Homme denounced section Indivisibilité "as wavering in revolutionary principles," a great commotion broke out. Ibid., IV, 267, 4 ventôse, Year II (22 February 1794).

of twelve. The Council could easily have believed, therefore, that they were ripe for the machinations of intriguers and the ambitious.[136] Moreover, it must have been upsetting to waste time on such trivia. When delegates of the society of young men of section République denied to the Council that their club was composed of a majority of those rejected from the established society, a member of the Council, Bernard, warned "these societies of children can be dangerous" and could be misguided as easily as women's clubs already banned by the Convention. The Commune ruled, finally, that no primary school children could establish popular societies, and those so formed must be dissolved forthwith.[137]

The Council could hardly have forgotten an incident involving the youth of section Droits-de-l'Homme who in their overzealousness had incurred the wrath of the deputies and their elders in the section, as well. The affair began with their endorsement of the position taken by the young men of section Arcis who demanded that the Convention make no distinction among the three classes called to the colors. Their argument, simply expressed, was that since the Republic had need of men, all should serve without distinction. In repeating this stand, the youth of section Droits-de-l'Homme affirmed their burning desire to win glory against the enemies of France, but stressed that to divide conscripts into three different classes destroyed the essential state of equality that had been established by the Revolution.[138]

Other petitioners, some of popular societies, were not permitted to enter the hall and were hooted down by the deputies.[139] That this aroused an unusually sharp reaction may be seen in the forthright condemnation of their address by the general assembly of the section.[140] This repudiation, coupled with the hostile reception of its

---

[136] *Moniteur*, XIX, no. 118, p. 221, 28 nivôse, Year II (17 January 1794), session of Commune of 24 nivôse. The Council told the young delegates to complain to the journalists in question.

[137] *Ibid.*, no. 128, p. 305, 8 pluviôse, Year II (27 January 1794).

[138] A.N., C 271, d. 665, pc. 34, 5 September 1793. Among the sixty-seven signatures that of Pétaud is prominent. An unspecified number expressed support of the petition but were unable to sign their names.

[139] A.P., LXXIII, 420-421, 5 September 1793. The decree in question was that of 23 August.

[140] B.V.C., MS 120, fol. 145, 4 September 1793.

petition by the Convention, brought an immediate retraction and regret. Pétaud apologized to the Convention, and explained to the General Council that together with his comrades he had been misled by the resolution of the young men of section Arcis.[141] The general assembly had meanwhile communicated its own resolution to the Convention attesting to the repentance of the brash young protesters, testifying to the patriotism of Pétaud, and repudiating "the slander" that the youth of sections Droits-de-l'Homme or Arcis were *muscadins*.[142] A few days later, to demonstrate their patriotism, the petitioners declared publicly that they were ready to depart for the front, asking only for weapons and instruction in their use.[143] A week later citizens of section Droits-de-l'Homme, together with six other sections, marched through the hall of the Convention in support of its decree of the *levée en masse*.[144]

More threatening to the government committees were proposals to limit the authority of constituted bodies such as revolutionary committees in favor of popular societies.[145] This struck at the very base of the revolutionary government. The observation of Grivel that the Jacobins and the Cordeliers differed absolutely "in their opinions, views, and resolutions"[146] underscored even more clearly the differences between the Jacobins and the mass of adherents in the popular societies. A government that used the network of Jacobin societies to reenforce its decrees could hardly have tolerated, let alone encouraged, the independence and free development of rival organizations. Whatever the

[141] A.P., LXXIII, 531, 8 September 1793. The Convention applauded this action. *Moniteur*, XVII, no. 251, p. 550, 8 September 1793.

[142] *Affiches de la Commune*, no. 79, 6 September 1793; B.V.C., MS 120, fol. 145, 6 September 1793; *Moniteur*, XIX, no. 128, p. 305, 8 pluviôse, Year II (27 January 1794), session of 4 pluviôse.

[143] A.N., C 271, d. 667, pc. 37, 11 September 1793; the same in A.P., LXXIII, 675, same date. B.H.V.P., 952.361, *Petition des jeunes gens en requisition de la section des Droits-de-l'Homme; imprimé par ordre de la Convention nationale* (Paris, n.d.), 2 pp.; *Moniteur*, XVII, no. 252, p. 603, 9 September 1793.

[144] A.P., LXXIV, 403, 19 September 1793. Sections Cité, Bonne-Nouvelle, Réunion, Contrat-Social, Montreuil, and Quinze-Vingts joined Droits-de-l'Homme.

[145] Caron, *Paris*, III, 369-370, 19 pluviôse, Year II (7 February 1794), report of Grivel on Vincent's proposal in the Cordeliers.

[146] Grivel expressed the sensible view that in his opinion the injustice, intolerance, and cruelty of which revolutionary committees were accused did not necessarily make the popular societies superior.

merits of these societies, there was no question that they criticized too often and not always wisely, that their spokesmen were, at times, unrestrained in their attacks on the government and its decrees, and that they indulged in the same immoderation, intolerance, and suspicion that characterized the duly constituted authorities.

XII

Patriotism and Religion

If there was one common sentiment among Frenchmen of the middle and lower classes, it was their devotion to the *patrie*. Enragés and Girondists, laborers and shopkeepers, men and women, became zealous partisans of the fatherland. The sacrifices at the front or the Vendée, the financial contributions, the reverence for the colors, all bespoke a new creed—patriotism. Beginning with a veneration of king and country, it changed to a republican cult with its own symbols, heroes, and martyrs, gradually supplanting the worship of the cross with a salute to the flag.[1]

Residents of section Droits-de-l'Homme published numerous manifestos expressing their hatred of "tyrants" and praising the Parisians for their heroic defense of liberty. Focusing on the trial of Louis, they exploited this theme as they turned to an ardent defense of patriots against opposing factions.[2] An equally eloquent appeal to defend the country was written in February 1793, concluding: "The war that we have undertaken is a combat to the death against the despots. . . . Wherever you see a king be implacable. . . . Strike. . . . Everywhere you see brothers, embrace them, protect them, be indissoluble."[3] Two months later the armed force of the section issued a fiery vindication

[1] B.N., Lb⁴⁰ 2105, *Adresse de la section du Roi de Sicile à l'Assemblée nationale* (Paris, n.d.), 3 pp. This expressed a determination to defend France, liberty under law, and equality of duties. It was signed by Billaudel, president, and Pointard, secretary.

[2] B.N., MSS, Nouv. acq. fr. 2684, fol. 165, 8 January 1793, *Adresse des citoyens de la section des Droits-de-l'Homme à leurs frères* . . . (Paris, 1793). A thousand copies were published, signed by Dubois, president, and Dupaumié(r), secretary.

[3] B.N., Lb⁴⁰ 1795, *Adresse de la section des Droits-de-l'Homme aux quarante-sept autres sections* ([Paris], n.d.), 4 pp. The quotation is from p. 4, with elisions as in the original. The same in B.H.V.P., 104.095, and among placards of the Commune that bear the date of February 1793, in reference to the section's general assembly session of 22 February. Six hundred copies of this appeal were published.

Figure 8. The Arrest of Charlotte Corday

of Parisians and their role in the Revolution. Pledging to serve under the banner of liberty and equality, they appealed to the deputies on the eve of the overthrow of the Gironde to remain firm and united. The Convention was pleased with the address and published it at its own expense.[4]

In addition to calls to defend the fatherland, the death of prominent popular leaders like Claude-François Lazowski[5] and Marat called out expressions of both mourning and rededication to the ideals of the Revolution. On 13 July Hébert delivered a eulogy on Marat and proposed that he be apotheosized by the Convention.[6] Section Droits-de-

[4] B.N., Lc[38] 2444, 27 April 1793, *Adresse de la section armée des Droits-de-l'Homme à la Convention nat'le imprimée par ordre de la Convention nat'le* (Paris, 1793), 4 pp. This was signed by Polle[t] as president and Picard fils, secretary.

[5] B.N., MSS, Nouv. acq. fr. 2691, fol. 267, 27 April 1793, which is an invitation to section Droits-de-l'Homme by the Commune to attend the funeral ceremonies for Lazowski.

[6] *Moniteur*, XVII, no. 197, p. 125, 16 July 1793.

l'Homme lent support to this proposal, and was among the first to express its sorrow over his death, swearing to avenge him.[7] Other sections joined the demand to grant him special honors. Battalions of the National Guard, provincial communes, popular societies swelled the universal chorus.[8] In November, section Droits-de-l'Homme joined Indivisibilité to plan a commemoration for Marat and Lepeletier.[9] The installation of the bust of Marat in the halls of assemblies and clubs pushed this movement still further.[10] In December, the section was to note that the Panthéon was reserved only for patriots, excluding all who had been guilty of uncivic or even moderate conduct.[11] A swelling chorus of patriotic feeling was unloosed immediately after an attempted assassination of Robespierre and Collot d'Herbois on 3 prairial, Year II (22 May 1794). Pledges of support for the deputies, congratulations, fiery resolutions, all came pouring in from sections, communes, and popular societies.[12]

This feeling also found expression in collective and personal acts of kindness, voluntary contributions and gifts, and offers of professional service to the poor, all reflecting a spirit of solidarity developed by common sacrifice and effort. Humble working people gave their share, and, perhaps, more than their share. Women cooks of section Droits-de-l'Homme, for example, contributed money to the widows and orphans of 10 August.[13] When a cannoneer returning from a session of the National Assembly lost his purse, the general assembly of the section immediately took up a collection to indemnify him.[14] An unusual act of kindness and generosity was the collection of 75 livres to purchase food for six Swiss soldiers, not the most popular foreigners

[7] A.N., C 262, d. 578, pc. 27, 13-14 July 1793; *Affiches de la Commune*, no. 29, 15 July 1793, together with sections Sans-Culottes and Fraternité, A.P., LXVIII, 711, 14 July 1793. The address was signed by Pétaud, president.

[8] A.N., C 262, d. 578-586. Among the more emotional testimonials was that of section Contrat-Social: "People! You have lost your friend, Marat. He is no more."

[9] A.P., LXXX, 102, 5 frimaire, Year II (25 November 1793). This was on a petition presented by section Quinze-Vingts for a festival to honor the martyrs.

[10] A.N., C 275, d. 710, pc. 18, 14 September 1793.

[11] B.V.C., MS 120, fol. 157, 30 frimaire, Year II (20 December 1793).

[12] A.N., C 306, C II, 1155, pcs. 9-35, 6 prairial, Year II (23 May 1794). See also A.N., 306, 1157, *passim*.

[13] A.P., LXIX, 146, 31 August 1792. They contributed a total of 70 livres 10 sous, and were extended the honors of the session by the Assembly.

[14] B.V.C., MS 120, fol. 132, 12 September 1792.

in Paris at the time.[15] A teacher of mathematics, astronomy, marine science, and artillery offered to instruct the young without fee.[16] An orphan whose father had died in the Vendée and whose mother had passed away some time later was adopted by the section immediately upon learning of the decease of the mother.[17] Gifts in kind were also deposited regularly. Shirts, stockings, shoes, gaiters, bandages—all were donated for the armed forces,[18] with appropriate patriotic remarks accompanying these donations. Three months after the first large contribution, the revolutionary committee made another to the Convention.

The section also presented a whole company equipped and ready to join the army. Its orator had come, he said, to offer *bonsoir* to the Convention before giving a *bonjour* to the enemy. The Convention applauded as the young men defiled before it.[19] A week later a second company, calling itself *compagnie de la liberté*, which included a number of Swiss soldiers who had enrolled in it, announced that it was ready to join the first company of the section, and its sergeant made a contribution to the wives and children of the poor whose husbands and fathers were fighting at the front.[20]

A delegation of section Droits-de-l'Homme reported with pride to the Convention that its number of volunteers exceeded the quota that had been set for it, and asked for a loan to equip its men for the Vendée.[21] Three days later its president, Taller, used the occasion to call for "death to tyrants and to anarchists." Isnard, presiding, replied, "never forget that liberty is far from license," amidst applause from the Right and mutterings of disapproval from the Left. Despite this jarring note, the section received its loan from the Finance Committee,[22] which, in order to repay, forced the assembly to appeal to

[15] *Ibid.*, fol. 132, 16 September 1792.

[16] B.N., MSS, Nouv. acq. fr. 2691, fol. 264, 23 April 1793. The teacher, Targé, asked the general assembly to select five young men for the purpose of instruction.

[17] B.V.C., MS 120, fol. 157, 30 frimaire, Year II (20 December 1793).

[18] A.N., F⁷ * 2497, p. 81, 6 pluviôse, Year II (25 January 1794); A.P., LXXXIII, 645-646, same date. A.N., F⁷* 2497, p. 112, 3 floréal, Year II (22 April 1794).

[19] A.P., XLIX, 417, 6 September 1792.

[20] *Ibid.*, XLIX, 618, 13 September 1792. Jean Julien Liard, 1st sergeant, contributed a silver sword and money.

[21] *Ibid.*, LXIV, 719, 16 May 1793. The request was for a loan of 70,000 francs, which was referred to the Finance Committee.

[22] *Ibid.*, LXV, 61, 19 May 1793; p. 667, 1 July 1793. This was on the eve of the section's reorganization by the militants.

the inhabitants, designating the home of Pointard, treasurer of the section, as a depository for contributions. The section had promised to pay 20 sous a day for each woman dependent of a volunteer and 10 sous per child, an obligation that had to be met eventually. Commissioners of the civil committee had to remind their fellow citizens that because of the economic crisis the debt incurred by the section had risen to 25,000 livres,[23] and urged them to meet their obligations. A warning to publish names of those who had failed to pay their pledges, or charging delinquents with being "false patriots," was always an available weapon, of course.[24]

In October 1793 the revolutionary committee of section Droits-de-l'Homme prepared a list of twelve volunteers, one of whom was to be accepted for special military duty to help crush the federalist revolt in Lyons and Bordeaux.[25] The same day a resident, fifty-four years of age, scheduled to depart with his company and unable to do so because of a hernia, insisted that his son of sixteen years replace him. The assembly applauded father and son and gave them honorable mention.[26] On 13 February the section, together with a delegation of Jacobins, presented to the Convention a volunteer from the district of Vendôme, hailed as a hero who had saved eleven children from drowing and who had volunteered to fight the enemies of his country to the death. Then, addressing the Convention, "the hero" declared, amidst loud applause, that should an offspring of his refuse to serve in the Vendée he would personally break his neck.[27]

Wounded veterans were given preference in jobs, of course. When a young man of twenty-six who had been seriously injured in battle and who, according to his sponsors, had given proof of his devotion to the Revolution, sought work, he was presented by Gattrez, a former member of the General Council, and by citizen Ravet, in the name of section Droits-de-l'Homme. After lively applause by the General Council, he was given the position of a former commissioner who had been refused a certificate of civic conduct.[28]

[23] B.N., Lb⁴⁰ 1793, n.d., 1 page.

[24] B.N., MSS, Nouv. acq. fr. 2691, fol. 276, 1 May 1793, contains a warning by the Commune to meet the pledges made.

[25] B.V.C., MS 120, fol. 154 (25?) vendémiaire. This was after a resolution by the Jacobin Society to send twelve members plus one volunteer from each section.

[26] Ibid., Jean and Jean-Pierre Génitier.

[27] A.P., LXXXIV, 677, 25 pluviôse, Year II. His name was Durand.

[28] Journal de la montagne, no. 97, p. 772, 30 pluviôse, Year II (18 February 1794).

This patriotic zeal, however, brought its share of intolerance and injustice in the section. A man arrested for having said that women who wore gold earrings insulted public poverty was sent before the commissioners of the section, probably the revolutionary committee or its police.[29] That this intolerance could reach ludicrous proportions may be illustrated by an incident in the General Council as its commission on certificates of civic conduct made its report. A name in dispute was "Marat," which was challenged by a member of the commission who demanded that the citizen abusing this name give his true one. Lubin, who presided, observed that it was not the name that reflected a man, but vice-versa. A man who carried the name of Cicero could be a bad orator; another who took the name of Marat could be a bad patriot. Finally, the candidate in question was allowed to explain himself. He revealed that his name was Marras, not Marat, after which his certificate was duly granted.[30]

A more serious case started with an innocent prank. A young worker, Harpin, age sixteen, was caught from behind by a fellow worker who tried to force him to say "uncle" by twisting his arms. The first slogan shouted by the young man was "long live the republic!" When the pressure continued he changed to "long live the king!" His fellow workers were properly shocked, and levied a fine on him for the benefit of the Republic in what probably was a kangaroo court. Although he was in tears and promised not to utter such vile words again, he was denounced by a fellow worker, Joseph-Bartin Lefevre. The revolutionary committee of the section issued a summons for him to learn "his motive in expressing himself in such manner." If he did report and was interrogated, there is no further information on this matter.[31] It is possible, of course, that the committee, upon learning the circumstances of this prank, allowed the matter to drop.

The police commissioner investigated a different incident about a year later. The entrepreneur of the Théâtre du Marais, Jean-Baptiste Dugas, had produced an opera entitled Le Milicien. In one scene the principal actor was about to be given a uniform of the National Guard by a corporal. Hesitating to put it on, he heard the corporal urge him

[29] B.V.C., MS 120, fol. 132, 12 September 1792. This is an unusual action, since public opinion tended to agree with him more and more, especially as shortages made themselves felt.

[30] Journal de la montagne, no. 83, p. 659, 16 pluviôse, Year II (4 February 1794).

[31] A.N., F⁷* 2498, p. 141, 9 nivôse, Year III (29 December 1794).

to do so with the reminder that "it is the uniform of the nation." The protagonist then replied: "It is because of that . . ." when the audience broke out into warm applause. It did not wait for him to finish, "I am unworthy of wearing it." This applause was malicious, reported Auzolles, and was difficult to understand since the same audience approved patriotic plays of the past.[32]

Another incident involving reaction to a historic drama dealt with the arrest of François Maillet, a native of Paris, age twenty-nine, who resided on rue des Droits-de-l'Homme. While attending a play entitled *Charles et Carroline* given at the Théâtre de la République, during a scene when Charles is about to be arrested, he allegedly exclaimed: "This is just like the revolutionary committees do." His accuser, a Vauthier, testified that his own remark had been that this was just the way the revolutionary committees had behaved under Robespierre, to which Maillet replied that the Committee of General Security did the same today. Vauthier objected that he was attacking a constituted authority whose justice was common knowledge. Maillet then menaced him with violence.[33] Whatever the truth of the above, Maillet was imprisoned for a time, but was released upon presenting a document signed by his lieutenant and other citizens testifying to his good conduct. Among those urging his release was Pierre Auzolles, who wrote that Maillet was a good citizen and known for his *bon ordre*. There is no indication, however, whether the Committee of General Security allowed his full restoration to citizenship.[34]

Several months later Auzolles and Grandhomme summoned the company of the theater, warning them that if they continued to refuse to sing patriotic songs the authorities would close down their play. In rebuttal, signed by eleven members of the company, they vigorously denied plotting to withhold expressions of patriotism and protested their love of republican compositions.[35]

The company must have had its share of harassment in trying to satisfy the confusing rulings on when to employ the word *citoyen* and when to resort to the traditional *monsieur* on the stage. In a letter to

[32] A.P.P., A A/136, fol. 233, 5 nivôse, Year IV (25 December 1795).

[33] A.N., F⁷ 4774³⁰, d. 3, 8 germinal, Year III (25 March 1795).

[34] *Ibid.*, the document testifying to Maillet's good conduct is of 26 floréal, Year III (15 May 1795).

[35] A.P.P., A A/136, fols. 243, 244, 10 pluviôse, Year IV (29 January 1796).

the Committee of Public Safety, Payan, the national agent, concluded that it was proper to use the latter form of address only in older plays or as a term of opprobrium.[36] There is little question that actors must have experienced difficulties in portraying roles that caused contradictory reactions in the audience.[37]

In addition to the censorship of stage terms, such marks of "feudality" as king, queen, and jack on playing cards had also to be replaced by appropriate republican symbols. The General Council empowered the section's police commissioner to search the premises of a merchant in order to confiscate the hateful signs. Auzolles examined the merchandise in question after its owner had assured him that he had none of such nature in his possession. Upon examining the many cartons of playing cards, he found nothing but republican figures, and so reported.[38]

That this was no isolated incident may be seen in the section's solicitation of the General Council to change the postmark, which still carried the word "king."[39] Some months later it was reported that among the engravings found on the premises of a private citizen were several representing Charlotte Corday and the duke of York shown in a "proud attitude" which seemed to say "you need a king." The police were directed to check into this matter.[40] Among those who had their effects sealed were two residents who had a *fleur de lys* above the service door, a symbol whose existence no one in the house had ever been aware of.[41]

In another incident, Catherine Gillot, a *femme de confiance*, testified that she had asked one of her lodgers, Etienne-Pierre Duchosal, to remove engravings of the royal family still hanging in his room. Finally, after a quarrel with him, she asked him to leave her house. Duchosal was duly interrogated by Bertrand and Donzel of the revo-

[36] A.N., F¹ᶜ III, Seine 27, 14 floréal, Year II (3 May 1794).

[37] A.N., F⁷ 4679, d. 2, 22 June 1793, deals with the arrest and interrogation of Christophe Amroise Donnon, who had played with an unspecified *comédie*, probably the Comédie française. For the controversy between supporters and opponents of the Revolution in the Comédie française, see Marvin Carlson, *The Theater of the French Revolution* (Ithaca, 1966).

[38] A.P.P., A A/136, fols. 80, 81, 13 floréal, Year II (2 May 1794).

[39] *Moniteur*, XVII, no. 179, p. 746, 28 June 1793.

[40] *Ibid.*, XVII, no. 251, p. 590, 8 September 1793.

[41] A.N., F⁷* 2498, p. 93, 4 frimaire, Year III (24 November 1794).

lutionary committee, revealing that he was a native of Paris, sixty-four years of age, and had been a tapestry merchant. After searching his room and not finding anything suspicious, they asked him why he had not removed the offensive impressions. Duchosal replied that he had intended to do so but had neglected to dispose of them. The officials released him after ordering its commissioners to deposit the engravings with the committee but allowing him to keep his other etchings that did not represent "the tyrants."[42]

When delegates from the departments arrived in Paris to celebrate the anniversary of 10 August and the acceptance of the newly proclaimed Constitution, sixty-one patriots of section Droits-de-l'Homme offered their homes to lodge them during their stay. This produced an interesting register listing the activists of the section, members of its popular society, commissioners of its various committees, and militants of the general assembly. The first name is that of Ladoubé(t) who asked to share his home with a delegate from Orléans or Rouen. Giboy and Dufour, also of the civil committee, joined him, as did Pointard, the justice of the peace, Antoine Bault, the concierge of La Force prison, and Jean-François Millet, clerk of the civil court. Among other familiar names were Mazin, Gervais, Boussière, Oudart, Pétaud, Saulnier, Targé (the professor of mathematics), and Godard. The rest were citizens of the section who held no special position in its administration, most undefined by profession; several volunteered to put up more than one visitor.[43] Perhaps this is not an impressive list in terms of numbers if the modest figure of volunteers is compared to the total number of residents in the section. On the other hand, multiplied by

[42] A.N., F⁷ 4684, d. 3, 7 and 23 pluviôse, Year II (26 January and 11 February 1794). Mme Gillot had also accused Duchosal of neglecting to contribute to his natural son, living with another. The law of 18 vendémiaire and 3 brumaire, Year II prohibited exhibition of symbols of feudality. Duvergier, VI, 218, 18-20 vendémiaire (9-11 October), 1793. The decree is mentioned but is not given. No mention of the decree of 3 brumaire (24 October).

[43] A. de P., D⁴ AZ 101, 10 August 1793, "Liste des citoyens de la section des Droits-de-l'Homme qui ont déclarés vouloir au désir du décret du 11 du courante offrir l'hospitalité à servir concitoyens des départements qui se rendent à Paris pour l'acceptation de la Constitution et la feste du 10 août 1793. 2e de la République." Among those whose occupation was given were nine merchants, seven artisans, two architects, a painter, a lawyer, a *huissier*, a dispenser of soft drinks, a professor, and a notary.

the forty-eight sections, it probably represented a proportionate share of those who volunteered to lodge the celebrants.

That love of country can turn into hatred of dissenters is a phenomenon not unknown to our own epoch. A classic example of revolutionary intolerance involved the son of the section's police administrator, Jean-Charles-Hubert Leroy (or Le Roy) fils. He was employed in the Mont de Piété when he was arrested at age twenty-six. The revolutionary committee was informed by several of his fellow employees of remarks made by him prejudicial to the government. Accusing the authorities of shedding blood, he declared boldly that he would give 500 francs a month "to see the end of the revolutionary government." One of his coworkers reported that he had remarked "that we were not free, that we were more enslaved than ever." When his colleagues objected, he had called them *des Jean foutres*, boasting that "he feared nothing, that he had the whole section behind him."[44] The head of his office testified on the "irregular conduct" of the young man, charging him with carelessness in his work and harsh manners toward the public. The paymaster, Richard, wanted him dismissed after he had been transferred from one office to another, fearing that all employees would be compromised if he continued in his position. Le Roy, he declared, suffered from a "restlessness of spirits" (*de l'effervescence de la tête*), had shown signs of derangement, and when angry had made counterrevolutionary proposals. Another employee added that his parents thought he was a "hothead" (*comme une tête exaltée*). His younger brother admitted that Le Roy had "moments of restlessness." Another fellow worker simply thought him to be "cracked" (*timbré*).[45]

When Le Roy appeared before the revolutionary committee, he gave quite a contrary version to the reports against him. Admitting that he had been suspended by his department, he claimed that the circumstances were quite different. According to him, two citizens had complained of bad treatment received at the hands of a fellow employee, to whom he had gone in a friendly spirit to try and resolve

[44] A.N., F⁷ 4774¹⁹, d. 4; 6 and 7 thermidor, Year II (24, 25 July 1794). A number of employees testified before the committee to the above. Not all of this testimony was given through fear. Leroy fils, evidently, had succeeded in alienating all his coworkers.

[45] *Ibid.*, 7 thermidor. This is from the *procès-verbal* of the administration of the department that employed Leroy fils.

the complaints. When his coworker had grabbed him by the wrists to bring him to his knees, he had protested that "a republican does not kneel down." This shrewd remark, although it did not change Le Roy's ultimate fate, does not reflect a troubled spirit, at least not at the moment when it was made. Furthermore, he denied having made counterrevolutionary proposals, although he admitted that after the execution of an employee by name of Rogé, he had discussed the meaning of the word "liberty" with two colleagues. Le Roy asserted that liberty had been more effective before the establishment of the revolutionary government. When he realized that neither of the two men understood him, he had simply walked away. This testimony, too, does not reflect a deranged mind. Nevertheless, the committee found him strongly suspect of counterrevolutionary suggestions and sent him to Luxembourg prison. The Committee of General Security freed him two months later.[46]

Upon his liberation, he appealed to the latter committee to help him recover his former job with the Mont de Piété, since he did not want to be a burden on his poor parents.[47] This request remained unanswered. On 27 messidor, Year III (15 July 1795) he was picked up by a patrol of section Montreuil for not having his card of security. The police commissioner, Pierre Auzolles, sketched his biography. His father had been arrested; his mother had died. Le Roy fils was destitute and was forced to live on credit, often eating in restaurants and then confessing that he had no money to pay for his meal. He had been brought before the police commissioner in the past, Auzolles reported. Although Le Roy was hot-headed he could be useful to society, having had a good education. It was true, moreover, that he had been arrested for opposition to the regime of Robespierre. Now he needed a card of security to begin his rehabilitation. There are no documents to trace his ultimate fate. One thing seems certain: if Le Roy fils was "cracked," he was *timbré* like King Lear's fool.[48]

That patriotism was a strong emotion is evidenced by the incidents discussed above. It could elevate men and women beyond egoism and personal concerns, or it could degenerate into simple chauvinism and irrationality. As such it made for intolerance and struck at victims

---

[46] *Ibid.*

[47] *Ibid.*, 29 brumaire, Year III (19 November 1794).

[48] *Ibid.* This was written to the revolutionary committee of the 8th arrondissement.

indiscriminately. Not the least of these were ardent patriots and revolutionists themselves.

If patriotism had become an important moral force in the section,
traditional religion had not disappeared but continued to exercise its
influence, weakened though it was by the Revolution. It was inevitable that cult of country should clash with the cult of Catholicism.
It is difficult to imagine a *dévote* such as Mercier painted in his "Portrait d'une dévote du Marais" maintaining the same kind of arrogance
and insolence toward her flock after the Revolution had unleashed its
attacks on the church. Mercier saw her as one who, instead of modestly casting her eyes downward, measures one from head to toe,
examines one for too much rouge, looks critically at the coiffure if it
will fit into a confessional, and responds in harsh monosyllables to the
worldly. Soon she speaks warmly of the horrors of depravity in other
quarters and of eternal damnation for those who do not attend mass
at the Capucins of the Marais.[49] This amusing sketch reflects to some
degree the self-confidence and status of the church on the eve of the
Revolution. There is no need to repeat what was recognized by contemporaries regarding the power, prestige, and property of the church.
More dramatic, perhaps, was the precipitous decline of the clergy
from its former social heights. The urgent admonitions of Bailly and
the municipal authorities shortly after the fall of the Bastille to "respect the ministers of your holy religion" as they "saw the excesses to
which ecclesiastics were being subjected" is sufficient proof of this
decline.[50]

The effort to establish a constitutional church, the break with the
pope, the growing division between the juring and refractory clergy,
the decree on the liberty of worship—nothing that the National Assembly did could prevent the growing rift between the church and its
antagonists. In the end, a civic cult challenged the allegiance of the
French formerly monopolized by religion.[51] By the spring and summer of 1792, Catholic worship, not only its priests, came under at-

[49] *Tableau*, I, pp. 276-277.

[50] A. de P., 1 AZ 138, 15 October 1789.

[51] See the discussion of A. Aulard, *Le Christianisme et la Révolution française* (Paris,
1925), especially the chapters in Part III entitled "La Tentative de déchristianisation," pp. 85-123; and "Le Culte de l'Etre suprême," pp. 116-123.

tack.[52] After 10 August, repressive legislation against Catholics and arrests of nonjuring priests multiplied, and instances of harshness against them became more frequent. A denunciation by an individual of section Roi-de-Sicile against an abbé who allegedly had "turned his head by confession" reflects this anticlerical climate.[53] The massacre of imprisoned priests, the outburst in the Vendée, the draconian measures against churchmen (now, in their turn, among the persecuted) led to an attempt to break with traditional religion itself—a break dubbed by historians dechristianization.[54]

[52] A.N., F[1c] III, Seine 27, 12 June 1792. The directory of the department of Paris admitted that it was opposed to the "absolute freedom of religion" because it was a source of trouble. It was supported in this position by the Commune.

[53] Tuetey, Répertoire, V, no. 2954, 18 August 1792.

[54] In this connection, see the following sources: Mathiez, Autour de Robespierre (Paris, 1925); and his articles "Robespierre et la déchristianisation," and "Robespierre et le culte d'Etre suprême" in the Annales révolutionnaires, II, 321-355 and III, 209-238.

Maurice Dommanget agrees with the basic arguments of Mathiez that only scoundrels used dechristianization for their own purpose, and praises Robespierre for his statesmanship in using religion for its social value. "Robespierre et les cultes," Annales historiques, 1 (1924), 192-216. See especially the interesting discussion of Guérin, I, 250-305 and 405-470, in which he holds that dechristianization was a maneuver of the plebeians (that is, the Hébertists) to divert the popular movement from pressing economic demands so as not to alienate the bourgeoisie.

Soboul sees hostility to religion and the clergy as a trait of popular mentality, but rejects Guérin's thesis of a pression populaire, a spontaneous popular movement. It "was imposed from the outside . . . the people are absent from decisive journées" (Sansculottes, p. 291). See his discussion of this phenomenon and the cult of Reason, ibid., pp. 283-317.

Richard Cobb in Les Armées révolutionnaires, instrument de la Terreur dans les départements, avril 1793-floréal an II, II (The Hague, 1963), 641, agrees that "Dechristianization, in its form of primitive violence, is a manifestation of popular mentality." In analyzing the diverse elements that composed it, he reached the conclusion that anti-clerical and popular iconoclasm were fed by the political alliance between clergy and monarchy; anti-feminism due to the influence of ecclesiastics on women, fear of counterrevolutionary assemblies in the countryside, hatred of peasant greed and meanness, a general indulgence in violence, and individual drunkenness—all played a part. This work is a model of research, organization, and exposition. See his discussion, II, 636-690, much of it filled with subtle psychological analysis.

John McManners in French Ecclesiastical Society under the Ancien Régime; a Study of Angers in the Eighteenth Century (Manchester, 1960), p. 287 writes that it was not "a popular movement, but rather an introduction from outside by représentants en mission and revolutionary committeemen [yet] it was . . . powerful and menacing enough to drive bishop Pelletier to abjure his orders." For the genesis of the movement, see

The contributions of Fouché and Chaumette to this movement have been noted by various scholars and need not be repeated here.[55] The proposal to substitute the new civic cult for Catholicism reached a high point on 17 brumaire (7 November 1793) with the renunciation of his ministry by Jean-Baptiste-Joseph Gobel, bishop of Paris.[56] Three days later, on 20 brumaire (10 November), the famous festival of liberty was held in Notre Dame, converted for that purpose into a Temple of Reason. Included in the new cult was the substitution of the martyrs of the Revolution for the saints of the church. As early as 9 February 1793, section Droits-de-l'Homme had inaugurated the cult of Michel Lepeletier. As it planned a funeral oration in his honor and the installation of his bust, the section invited the Convention to send a delegation to the ceremony, to which the representatives sent twelve of their members.[57]

While still in prison, Varlet had been requested by the general assembly, on the initiative of the section's popular society, to compose a hymn for the Festival of Reason planned by the Commune for 10 November. In reply Varlet revealed that he had not been indifferent to the movement against priests (that is, dechristianization), and enclosed one of his publications of 1792 on the subject, which was read approvingly in the assembly.[58] The following day, section Droits-de-l'Homme, together with six others, proclaimed in the General Council that they had closed their churches and would recognize, henceforth, only the cult of Reason and Philosophy. Depositing precious objects confiscated from their churches for the good of the nation, their spokesman announced: "We shall carry to the Convention the keys of Saint Peter. Paradise is open for all to enter."[59]

Maurice Dommanget, *Sylvain Maréchal l'egalitaire "l'homme sans Dieu"; sa vie—son oeuvre (1750-1803)* (Paris, n.d.), pp. 223-224, 227, 229-230; and Robinet (le docteur), *Le Mouvement religieux à Paris pendant la Révolution (1789-1801)*, II (Paris, 1898), 538-560, *passim*.

[55] The work of Fouché in Nevers and Chaumette's report of his trip to Nièvre may be followed in the *Moniteur*, XVII, nos. 259, 267, 272, and XVIII, nos. 25, 27, 30, 34, 43, 48, 49, 50, and 53, from 16 September 1793 to 13 November 1793.

[56] *Moniteur*, XVIII, no. 49, p. 369, 19 brumaire, Year II (9 November 1793).

[57] A.P., LVIII, 400.

[58] B.V.C., MS 120, fol. 155, 20 brumaire, Year II (10 November 1793). The brochure of 1792 was probably his *Plan d'une nouvelle organisation*.

[59] *Moniteur*, XVIII, no. 53, p. 397, 23 brumaire, Year II (13 November 1793). The other sections were Quinze-Vingts, Lombards, Gravilliers, Arsenal, Indivisibi-

That the celebration enthroning Reason in the former Notre Dame cathedral made a great impression on the section may be seen from the minutes of the assembly, read in the Commune. A number of participants spoke with feeling of the festival, which they had found touching and sublime. The orator reminded his hearers that in order to break the bonds of superstition and fanaticism they must substitute the cult of reason and liberty, while the huge crowd swore to the golden rule.[60] The new cult was established formally when the revolutionary committee of the section so informed the General Council on 25 brumaire (15 November).[61]

Acts of violence against ecclesiastics in the section were few. Before the official closing of churches a case arose of a corporal Proux, who took it upon himself to halt the celebration of a midnight mass in Saint Gervais church. A delegation from the General Council escorted him to the general assembly of the section (probably after a complaint of the vicar, to whom he had admitted being from section Droits-de-l'Homme). The assembly, after a long discussion (for it was obvious that Proux had sympathizers), turned him over to the police commissioner and reported the affair to the military committee of the section.[62]

The few priests arrested in the section, although victims of the stern laws directed against them, did not undergo any particular severity different from that of the general class of suspects. An interrogation conducted by members of the revolutionary committee in the early hours of the morning and several months of imprisonment are not to be dismissed lightly, of course, especially when the sufferers were old and not in robust health. Moreover, to feel isolated and abandoned, despised and sometimes slandered, might make the anguish worse, except for those few who felt a spiritual exaltation in their ordeal.

---

lité, and Muséum. The *Affiches de la Commune*, no. 139, 22 brumaire, mentions only Arsenal, Droits-de-l'Hommme, and Indivisibilité. B.V.C., MS 120, fol. 155, 20 brumaire.

[60] *Affiches de la Commune*, no. 141, 24 brumaire, Year II (14 November 1793). The last portion of the *procès-verbal* repeated the resolution of the assembly prior to the celebration and was signed by Thiébart, secretary.

[61] *Journal de la montagne*, II, no. 4, p. 27, 27 brumaire, Year II (17 November 1793).

[62] A.P.P., A A/136, p. 8, n.d. This is from the minutes of the general assembly, when Descombes was president and Dupaumier secretary.

The experience of Jean-Louis Mercier, a *religieux* formerly of the order of Grands Carmes, arrested on 19 September 1793, was not unusual. The charges against him were that he had associated with "fanatics," had celebrated communion, had hidden his profession in order to obtain a *carte de sureté*, and that he possessed a *caractère tartuf{e}*. After his arrest, Mercier, who was sixty-seven years old, replied to these charges from the infirmary of La Force prison. He had always recommended submission to the law, he wrote. The two priests who had been arrested with him simply lived in the same house and were mutual acquaintances with whom he had dined occasionally. As for the ornaments found in his home by commissioners of the revolutionary committee (Mazin, Le Roy, and Bertrand), they consisted of some ecclesiastical robes and a mass book, which he hardly could have hidden since he was a pensioner. Moreover, had he been such a bad citizen he would not have received his certificate of citizenship from the section's revolutionary committee. As for the charge that an almanac was found on his premises entitled *Almanach des honnêtes gens*, he denied that it had been present among his papers when they were placed under seal, insisting that it had been added as additional evidence after the *procès-verbal* had already been drawn up. On the accusation of his making uncivic proposals, he asked for their specific nature and witnesses to these alleged suggestions. The charge that he had seldom attended meetings of the general section he did not bother to refute. After a juror of the revolutionary tribunal, Bazaine, wrote on his behalf to the Committee of General Security, he was released on 22 frimaire, Year II (12 December 1793).[63]

An occasional report indicates that officials and committees of the section took the usual precautions, but there seems to have been no concerted drive against priests and vicars of section Droits-de-l'Homme. In the spring of 1793, Auzolles and Descombes examined the premises of a deceased "relative to matters of religion." A number of religious objects were found and listed, and a guard was placed over the papers—this after a search conducted twice, the second at 4 a.m.[64]

Former nuns who wished to return home upon the dissolution of their religious houses were encouraged to do so after carefully and

[63] A.N., F⁷ 4774⁴², d. 4.
[64] A.P.P., A A/136, fol. 32, 22 April 1793. Among the papers of the deceased, Michel André Le Maire, were such journals as *Le Père Duchesne*, *l'Ami du peuple*, and *Les Révolutions de Paris*, as noted by the commissioners.

patiently being informed of their rights as their personal effects were minutely inventoried and listed.[65] The administration of *hôpitaux* informed the civil committee of the section that it had given permission to eight *ex-religieuses* of the *maison hospitalière dite de Gervais* situated on rue Vieille-du-Temple, to leave the house and to dispose of their effects as they saw fit. Michon, as president of the committee, and Jean-Louis Alexandre then went to the above establishment and interrogated its administrator, Marie-Gilbert Graudin, age forty-seven. Upon verifying that the eight in question did indeed desire to leave, they listed their furniture and effects, each woman receiving a sum of 100 livres and being told that she had the right to settle where she pleased.[66]

Of a different nature was an incident involving an ex-priest who was brought before the surveillance committee still wearing the habit of his profession (black garb, short coat, and clerical band). After taking note of his replies and listening to the testimony of several witnesses, the committee became convinced that there was no treacherous intention on his part, and conveniently blamed his action on "the long and sad arrest which he had suffered at the time of Robespierre."[67] Sectional authorities continued to keep under surveillance, however, all priests and *curés* who had been freed by revolutionary tribunals.[68] The police commissioner also inspected and reported on the state of premises set aside for religious worship and whatever incidents developed there.[69] This report seems to have resulted, however, from a protest by unnamed citizens that their right to worship in the church of Carmes Billettes (Eglise des Carmes Billettes) had been interfered with.[70]

[65] *Ibid.*, fols. 30-31, 19 April 1793. The effects of a former *religieuse*, Louise-Marie-Aimé-Elizabeth Lescouvé of Saint Anastasse dite Saint Gervais, were carefully enumerated by Auzolles.

[66] A. de P., 3 AZ 287, pc. 42, 2, 15, 29 fructidor and 3e jour *sans-culottide* (19 August, 1, 15, and 19 September 1794).

[67] A.N., F7* 2498, p. 366, 22 thermidor, Year III (9 August 1795). The victim was Jean-François Caffin, whose long confinement had evidently undermined his mental health.

[68] *Ibid.*, p. 48, 29 vendémiaire, Year III (20 October 1794). The person in question was Jean-Antoine Chevalier.

[69] *Ibid.*, pp. 219, 222, 16 and 18 ventôse, Year III (6 and 8 March 1795). The latter was a report on the Eglise des Billettes, where all was "calm and decent."

[70] A.P.P., A A/136, fol. 171, 10 ventôse, Year III (28 February 1795). The protest carried some ten signatures.

Occasionally too much zeal by individuals had to be curbed by the police. On 12 ventôse, Year III (2 March 1795), the Paris police administration informed Auzolles that it had received reports of a man going through the section with a bell calling on the believers to attend mass at the church of Billettes. The accused, Charles-François Prou, age forty-three and employed in the fabrication of saltpeter, was brought before the police commissioner, and readily admitted that he had indeed been calling "the bakers and dyers" to worship the following Sunday. Although he was guilty of violating the law, no punitive measure was taken against him by Auzolles.[71]

Political shifts in the section were reflected in changing policies on religion. When it was popular to join dechristianizers, people did so. When the worship of the Supreme Being replaced that of Reason, the section enthusiastically congratulated the Convention on its decree regarding the immortality of the soul.[72] When the churches were reopened and Catholicism was again permitted to revive, the section, again, accepted the new state of things.[73]

It is difficult to ascertain the effect of the cult of Reason on residents of the section, as there is no conclusive evidence on this matter. Aside from the militants in the general assembly and in the popular club, how much of an impression did the new worship make? Section Droits-de-l'Homme's citizens must have experienced the same reaction that seemed to characterize others. Could any workingman have been happy over losing his day of rest every seventh day, to celebrate it every tenth day? The *décade* might have pleased calendar makers, mathematicians, and employers, but it could hardly have appealed to those who had to work hard twelve to sixteen hours a day.

[71] *Ibid.*, fols. 172-174, 12 and 14 ventôse, Year III (2 and 4 March 1795); A. Aulard, *Paris pendant la réaction thermidorienne et sous le Directoire*, I (Paris, 1898), 521, 527.

[72] B.V.C., MS 120, fol. 159, 3 prairial, Year II (22 May 1794).

[73] At his trial after thermidor, Lebon claimed that there was continuity between his life as an Oratorian and his work as a terrorist. "I derived most of my revolutionary maxims from the Gospels which, from beginning to end, preach against the rich and against priests," he stated. Cited by John McManners in *The French Revolution and the Church* (London, 1969), p. 91. On 4 floréal, Year V (23 April 1797), the commissioner of police of the seventh arrondissement, Lafond, reported the celebration of a mass by the minister of Saint Méry church, Rollin. The constituted authorities were well represented. B.H.V.P., MS 750, fol. 187.

Although there is some evidence that Parisians were not the most pious of Frenchmen, the idea of worshiping Reason, and, later, the Supreme Being, could hardly have taken the place of praying to a living, bleeding God. The new worship was simply too abstract. A civic cult, on the other hand, was of a different nature, as beleagured Frenchmen could easily understand the importance of unity and indivisibility in the face of foreign and domestic threats. Republican virtues, egalitarianism, political democracy, martyrs of the Revolution, the new symbols—tricolor, *bonnet rouge*, the Declaration of the Rights of Man, the watchful eye of the Jacobins—these could indeed be comprehended.[74] Mass processions, festivals, public outdoor suppers—in time, perhaps, they could and did replace traditional worship. In doing so the dechristianizers unleashed a profound and an "irresistable torrent."[75]

Lack of education was also an inhibiting factor in replacing traditional worship by a secular cult. The illiteracy rate, especially in the countryside, was appalling. Prolonged debates in the Convention on projects to introduce compulsory, free, and universal education, culminating, finally, in the plan proposed by Gabriel Bousquier, might have transformed France, given time.[76] There is evidence, however, that one reason for the acceptance of the Bousquier proposal by the government was the possibility the governing committees saw in using the law against the Hébertists. The provision for private initiative in education gave them an opportunity to use the services of loyal priests against the preachers of atheism.[77] In any case, education, too, became subject to a struggle between the factions, and its benefits became subordinated to politics. Thermidor reversed still further the original intent of elevating the intellectual sights of the *sans-culottes*, and the Napoleonic reforms established a different goal for them al-

[74] E. F. Henderson, *Symbol and Satire in the French Revolution* (New York, 1912).

[75] Guérin, I, 273-278. The author entitles this section "Un Torrent irresistible," and quotes Edgar Quinet as saying of this popular movement, "it was the Revolution itself." *Ibid.*, p. 276.

[76] A.P., LXXXI, 136-138, 18 frimaire, Year II (8 December 1793). See the *Moniteur*, XVIII, no. 83, pp. 646-647, 23 frimaire, Year II (13 December 1793) for conclusion of the debate on Bousquier's proposal.

[77] Albert Duruy, *L'Instruction publique et la Révolution* (Paris, 1882), p. 105; James Guillaume, ed., *Procès-verbaux du Comité d'instruction publique de la Convention nationale*, III (Paris, 1897), 39.

together. Above all, the poverty, the isolation—mental as well as physical—the hazards and uncertainties of life, the low productivity, the dependence on nature—all called for a belief in God, for consolation, for compensation. As Guérin puts it so convincingly: when the Jacobins preached the right to happiness and then asked for sacrifice and more work, they repeated the language of the priests.[78]

As is well known, the government could not afford yet another division between believer and nonbeliever added to that of loyal priests against papists. On 16 frimaire (6 December), the Convention decreed that "all violence and measures against liberty of worship are forbidden."[79] The Commune had already recoiled from its bold position when Robespierre and others had begun their attacks in the Jacobin Club and in Convention against the dechristianizers. On 8 frimaire (28 November) Chaumette made an apologetic speech in the General Council protesting that the Commune had never meant to proscribe constitutionally guaranteed freedom of worship. The Council then decreed "that it declares that the exercise of religion was free. It had never intended to prevent citizens from renting houses, of paying their ministers, for whatever cult it may be, provided that the exercise of this cult does not injure society by its practice."[80] Dechristianization was over; it was followed by the worship of the Supreme Being, which in turn gave way to the restoration of Catholicism.[81]

[78] *La Lutte*, I, 304. See his discussion in the section entitled "Mais la Révolution ne s'attaque pas aux racines materielles de la religion," pp. 299-305.

[79] A.P., LXXXI, 120-121; the debate between Robespierre and Cambon is in B. & R., XXX, 321-324 with the decree following.

[80] *Moniteur*, XVIII, no. 71, p. 547, 11 frimaire, Year II (1 December 1793), Article 2. Chaumette's remarks are on pp. 546-547.

[81] Aulard, *Le Christianisme*, pp. 85-123, *passim. Moniteur*, XX, no. 229, p. 411, 19 floréal, Year II (8 May 1794). After Robespierre's speech (pp. 403-411), the Convention decreed the worship of the Supreme Being.

XIII

Germinal, Prairial, Vendémiaire

The insurrections of germinal and prairial, although motivated to some extent by political developments, were fundamentally caused by hunger. Inflation, shortages, and high prices continued to ravage the troubled capital, as the *assignat* fell to new depths. Its precipitous decline tells a dramatic story—from 36 percent in July 1794, to 20 percent in December and to the low of 7½ percent in May 1795.[1] The abolition of the *maximum* on 4 nivôse, Year III (24 December 1794) raised prices to new levels, making it impossible for the government to supply food at controlled costs as in the past, and forcing consumers to spend their last sou in the open market if they wanted to eat at all.[2] The rise in the price of bread was especially disastrous, as it climbed from 25 sous per pound on 7 germinal (March 28) to the dreadful level of 16 livres a pound on 29 floréal (May 18), just two days before the last insurrection.[3] The index of retail prices, using June 1790 as the base, shows an increase from 500 in January 1795 to 900 in April,[4] while real wages sank lower than they had been throughout the whole period

[1] Harris, *Assignats*, p. 186. Caron's *Tableau* gives 34 percent for July 1794, p. LII. The fall of the *assignat* was uninterrupted from August 1794 to March 1796, when the *mandat* was substituted.

[2] Aulard, *Paris*, I. The daily reports of police observers on the economic situation in the capital are eloquent proof of hunger on a mass scale that pushed the women, especially, to seek remedy by an uprising against the government.

[3] *Ibid.*, I, 610, citing *Messager du soir* of 8 germinal. See also the reports on bakeries and pastry shops, pp. 675, 715, 729. Tallien reported in the Convention that provincials in the southern departments were reduced to one-half loaf of bread per head. *Moniteur*, XXIII, no. 178, p. 700, 28 ventôse, Year III (18 March 1795), session of 25 ventôse.

[4] Harris, *Assignats*, pp. 107-108. Meat that sold at 34 sous per lb. in December 1794 went to 7 livres 10 sous on 12 germinal (April 1), the day of the insurrection. Aulard, *Paris*, I, 341, 629, for beef and mutton.

of 1793-1794, or even, perhaps, fell "to the catastrophic level of the early months of 1789."[5]

Section Droits-de-l'Homme was among the hardest hit. As early as 6 pluviôse (25 January 1795), most of its bakers complained of failure to receive flour;[6] one of them, Calix, of rue Droits-de-l'Homme, warned publicly that unless he were supplied he would have nothing to bake. Instead of providing him with flour, the authorities turned him over to the police amidst angry muttering of the crowd.[7] A month later the committees of the section were instructed by the Department of Subsistences to reduce the quantity of bread distributed; as a result, an armed force had to maintain order in queues before the doors of bakeries.[8] Bakers Bizouard, Patriarche, and Garnier lacked sufficient flour to provide bread even for those who had ration cards, and a patrol had to reestablish order on rue Vieille-du-Temple.[9] Observers noted that in sections Droits-de-l'Homme, Indivisibilité, Marchés, and Lombards many families lacked even a morsel of bread, which, naturally, led to bitter complaints. Men and women spent whole nights before the doors of bakeries, while others had to wait because of late deliveries of flour, or accept spoiled, unleavened bread.[10]

Two days before the uprising, bread riots broke out in section Droits-de-l'Homme. As queues started to form at 11 p.m., the police administrator, Le Roy père, reported that the stronger men seized control of the doorways of bakeries, pushing aside everyone, including pregnant women and children. The following evening crowds began to gather at 7 p.m., and when commissioners of police asked all to disperse and to come back at 5 a.m., they replied that not having eaten bread for several days they intended to hold their places in line, come what may.[11]

While this was taking place, another large crowd formed shortly after 8 a.m. (11 germinal—31 March) because flour destined for the section had not yet arrived. Demands were then raised that the president of the section (Grandjean?) call an emergency meeting of the

[5] Rudé, The Crowd, p. 145.
[6] Aulard, Paris, I, 425.
[7] Ibid., I, 436, 11 pluviôse (30 January).
[8] Ibid., I, 514, 9 ventôse (27 February).
[9] Ibid., I, 585-586, 30 ventôse (20 March).
[10] Ibid., I, 599, 4 germinal (24 March).
[11] Ibid., I, 629.

general assembly, but he refused, citing the law against it. Upon rejection of this proposal, one of the bolder men seized a bell and began to ring it, crying up and down the streets: *"Citizens, you are invited to gather immediately on the main square of the section to deliberate on provisions,"* while the crowds in front of bakeries applauded him enthusiastically. Auzolles admitted that he was powerless to stop him, and reported that "the piercing and unanimous cry of *'bread, we want bread'* was the *sole response."* Advising the central police administration of what was transpiring, he met with the joint civil and revolutionary committees, all of whose measures to calm the situation proved ineffective. Upon entering the hall of the general assembly, he found a large crowd there which insisted that he take the chair. Refusing this demand, he asked instead that all disperse to their homes—a suggestion in turn rejected by the assembly, although no one tried to shout him down. "They only wanted a legal way to make the National Convention become aware of their demands," he wrote. Although the assembly was illegal, no one suggested that it elect officers or take official minutes, thus demonstrating its own irresolution. Auzolles then recommended that the gathering send a delegation to the joint meeting of the section's committees, and to transmit their demands to the representatives of the people, a suggestion adopted by the crowd.[12] That the meeting was an act of desperation may be understood when it is realized that on the very day of the insurrection of 12 germinal (April 1), police noted that there were people in the section who literally had not eaten any bread for three days—which means that they had not eaten at all.

Unlike the illegal assembly of section Droits-de-l'Homme, most gatherings in other sections were far stormier, with cries of "give us bread!" punctuating the sessions. Lack of food was the principal topic of conversation in the cafés as bread rations were reduced from the one pound provided by law to one-half of this inadequate amount. The 6 ounces of rice given to supplement the bread ration was practically useless as the cost of firewood to boil it was prohibitive. While muttering against authorities increased, inhabitants of section Droits-de-l'Homme and its neighbor, Homme-Armé, proposed to go to the Convention on 30 March to demand bread. On the following day, the

[12] A.P.P., A A/136, fol. 193, italics as in original.

assembly in the former section also met in illegal session and drafted a petition on shortages to the Convention.[13]

The following day crowds gathered in front of bakeries, shouting they would rather be shot than die of hunger. Everywhere shortages and hunger were the sole topic of conversation. Many, resenting the affluence of the rich in contrast to their own condition, claimed that caterers and pastry cooks were better supplied than ever.[14] More dangerous was a delegation of section Quinze-Vingts which reminded the Convention in a powerful petition that under certain circumstances an insurrection was a sacred duty.[15]

The storm long gathering finally broke the next day, 12 germinal (1 April). In section Droits-de-l'Homme great crowds milled about at doors of bakeries as women fought each other for loaves of bread, snatching them from one another's hands; several were wounded in the struggle.[16] In some sections there was no bread at all, while in others a mere four to eight ounces were distributed. Meanwhile, as processions and meetings were sweeping the capital,[17] the authorities seemed impervious to the crisis. The Committee of General Security, incredibly, sent a letter to the surveillance committee of the 7th arrondissement blaming the troubles on "malevolence" that was troubling public order, and ordered it to meet in permanent session so as to keep watch on these desperate men and women.[18]

Of course there was little need to report on these spontaneous and open manifestations of discontent, especially when crowds invaded the Convention itself and interrupted Boissy d'Anglas with cries of "bread!" The Montagnard deputies, however, playing an ambivalent role in

---

[13] Aulard, *Paris*, I, 620; Rudé, *The Crowd*, p. 148.

[14] Aulard, *Paris*, I, 622-623.

[15] *Ibid.*, I, 623 n. 1. The petitioners asked why Paris still lacked an independent municipality, why popular societies had been dissolved, and why the *assignats* were in a continual state of decline, thus combining political and economic demands. This petition is reproduced in the *Moniteur*, XXIV, no. 194, p. 106, 14 germinal, Year III (3 April 1795).

[16] Aulard, *Paris*, I, 629-630.

[17] For a dramatic description of this day see Mathiez, *La Réaction thermidorienne* (Paris, 1929), p. 186 ff., or chapter VIII, entitled "La Première Emeute de la faim," pp. 186-209; Tønnesson's *La Défaite*, "Les Journées du 12 et 13 germinal," pp. 187-222; and E. Tarlé, *Germinal et prairial* (Moscow, 1959), pp. 8-49, 162-164.

[18] A.N., F⁷* 2498, p. 251, 12 germinal, Year III.

their desire to curb reaction without relying on the people, persuaded the demonstrators to evacuate the hall. Nothing had been gained by the hungry thousands, and by the time they might have realized this, loyal detachments of the National Guard, arriving from the middle-class sections of the west end, dispersed those who had lingered. Paris was declared in a state of siege, and its armed forces were placed under the command of General Pichegru. Leaders of the *sans-culottes* were arrested in their sections together with former principal Thermidorians such as Léonard Bourdon, Amar, and Cambon, while Barère, Billaud-Varennes, and Collot d'Herbois were condemned to deportation.[19]

Conditions failed to improve following this demonstration, as long queues continued to wind around the doors of bakeries. Fathers of families were observed weeping upon obtaining a mere one-half pound of bread after waiting all night, while others received no bread at all. The more desperate were heard to express a desire for the return of the monarchy so as to assure bread, amidst the applause of others.[20] Robillard's shop on *marché* Sainte Catherine was pillaged, and a man was arrested for agitating crowds at baker Patriarche's, rue Culture-Sainte-Catherine, while police commissioners were roundly abused.[21] Reports of suicides were bruited about as people blamed the government.[22] Hungry women of the section halted a wagon of flour and forced the commissioner to deliver one sack that had been consigned to a different baker on rue des Rosiers. While police went looking for them, others emptied their chamber pots on the armed force.[23] The revolutionary committee of the section noted that the state of public feeling was "uncertain" in Droits-de-l'Homme,[24] a rather obvious understatement.

A pamphlet entitled *Insurrection du peuple, pour obtenir du pain et reconquérir ses droits*, published on the evening of 30 floréal (19 May)

[19] Mathiez, *La Réaction*, p. 186 ff. See also the *Moniteur*, XXIV, no. 194, pp. 109-112, 14 germinal (3 April 1795); no. 195, pp. 113-120, 15 germinal; and no. 196, pp. 121-124, 16 germinal.

[20] Aulard, *Paris*, I, 632, 648.

[21] *Ibid.*, I, 650, 21 germinal (10 April); 652, 22 germinal (11 April); 668, 29 germinal (18 April).

[22] *Ibid.*, I, 657, 24 germinal (13 April); 673, 1 floréal (20 April).

[23] *Ibid.*, I, 687-688, 7 floréal (26 April).

[24] A.N., F7* 2498, p. 295, 23 floréal (12 May).

gave the signal for the last popular insurrection of the Revolution. Beginning with a demand for bread, it launched into a fundamental attack on the Thermidorian system of repression and its organs of government. In its stead it called for the establishment of the principles of the Rights of Man and of the Constitution of 1793. Appealing to the troops to join the people, it also invited the forty-eight sections to convoke the primary assemblies to take control of the government. To force the Convention to do their bidding, the people were induced to march en masse upon their representatives and to do so without waiting to range themselves by section, but rather in a "fraternal disorder."[25] No better expression of mistrust of sectional authorities could have been revealed than in this call for the people to march pell-mell.

It is against this background that the concern of the civil committee of section Droits-de-l'Homme must be viewed. Immediately after the sounding of the general alarm, it met together with the revolutionary committee to distribute bread under guard of the section's armed force. Just as the committees began their session, several armed men forced their way into the room led by a citizen Lory, quartered on rue Cloche-Perce, and by Lointier, of rue Francs-Bourgeois. Wearing in their hats the prescribed band with the slogan "Bread and the Constitution of 1793," the two spokesmen demanded that the committees place themselves at their head and march on the Convention, admonishing their members not to fear anything, as their lives were no more precious to them than were their own.[26]

---

[25] *Moniteur*, XXIV, no. 244, pp. 497-498, 4 prairial, Year III (23 May 1795). The slogan was "Bread and the Democratic Constitution of 1793." Whoever failed to carry this slogan chalked on his hat was to be regarded as an enemy. An address to departments and to the army was also to be drafted. The manifesto was drawn up in the form of resolutions beginning with: "The people, considering that the government allows them to starve inhumanely . . . .," etc., and concluding in eleven separate articles. See the discussion of F. Dieudonné, "Préliminaires et causes des journées de prairial an III," in *La Révolution française*, 43 (November 1902), 442-465, and 44 (December 1902), 504-527. The author cites the food crisis and objections to the reorganization of the National Guard along with the presence of regular troops as important causes of the insurrection. Both Babeuf and Brutus Magnier, who preached insurrection, were in jail, he points out.

[26] A.N., F⁷ 4633, d. 4 (dossier Carnonkel), 1 prairial, Year III, "Procès-verbal du Comité civil de la section des Droits-de-l'Homme." This document was brought to my attention by M. François Gendron, Professeur au Collège Militaire Royal, Qué-

Meanwhile women bombarded the committees with complaints of shortages, and one remarked that it was strange indeed to see members of the committees sitting in the room while their own husbands were under arms at the Convention. All that the officials could reply was that they had no provisions. Yet they sent out patrols to see that whatever bread was available should be distributed, and that commissioners in charge of distribution be at their posts. The latter reported, however, that there was danger in distributing bread at the moment because of the great agitation of crowds. The committees then decided to wait until calm returned to the section, even though it was already 8 p.m.[27]

The popular outburst was so spontaneous and powerful that officers of the armed forces lost control over their men. Fayölle, the second in command, who had played an important role in suppressing the supporters of the Commune on the 9th of thermidor, now was swept along by the powerful popular current. Arriving at 10 p.m. with an armed force on the premises of the committee, he demanded that the *procès-verbal* be read out loud to the battalion because he had heard that a hostile decree directed against him had been adopted by the joint committees. Actually, the Committee of General Security had ordered his arrest. As the secretary was forced to accompany Fayölle, with pen in hand, to read the *procès-verbal* to the battalion, other members of the committee were compelled to remain in their seats. Upon returning, the secretary reported that he had declared to Fayölle that he would remain silent and would hold him personally responsible if he or his colleagues suffered abuse. Fayölle then ordered the drums to roll, and declared that no harm would come to members of the committees. After having read the *procès-verbal*, he observed, critically, that while the general alarm was sounding in the section members of the committees remained at their posts, that is, they had refused to join the people. A few members of the battalion spoke up in support, but most remained silent.[28]

The joint committees had realized that the decree of arrest against

---

bec. See also, François Gendron, *La Jeunesse dorée épisode de la Révolution française* (Québec, 1979). Because of the joint meeting with the civil committee, the *procès-verbal* of the revolutionary committee contains little of importance for its session of 1 prairial.

[27] *Ibid.*

[28] *Ibid.*

Fayölle could not be executed due to the great excitement in the section, and had returned the writ to the Committee of General Security. It was only after the uprising had been suppressed that several individuals came forward to testify against Fayölle. The burden of their charges was that he had declared openly to the general assembly that certain decrees of the Convention were unjust and hence should not be executed, that he had ordered a march on the Convention, and that he had taken the battalion in a direction where it might join those of sections Quinze-Vingts and of Observatoire in a hostile act directed against that body.[29] In his own justification, Fayölle later argued that his express order (no. 4 of the general staff), was to take the armed force of the section, including the cannon, to the Convention; this order had superseded the previous command to take his men to the Temple. Moreover, he had been given a precise order by the general staff on where to take up his post.[30] Whatever the technical merits of Fayölle's argument, his hostile action against the civil and revolutionary committees of section Droits-de-l'Homme placed him squarely on the side of the insurgents.

The decree of the Convention, enjoining citizens from marching armed to the various public squares of their respective sections, could not be proclaimed because commissioners charged with making this and other commands public at 10:30 p.m. were shouted down and threatened. The armed detachment accompanying them was attacked and dispersed on rue Sainte-Croix-de-la-Bretonnerie, thus preventing them from advertising the decrees of the Convention and even from returning to the hall where the committees were sitting.[31] It was clear that local authorities were repudiated no less than the Convention itself.

An hour later, two workingmen informed the committees that having just returned from the Convention they had witnessed a large armed force disarm the people in the hall and arrest those deputies who had defended their interests so well. Suddenly a cry was heard in the courtyard: "To arms, to arms! They are massacring the patriots

[29] A.N., F⁷ 4704, d. 1; 1, 3, 7 prairial (May 20, 23, 27) (dossier Fayölle).

[30] Ibid., 22 thermidor, Year III (9 August 1795), "Réponse de Fayölle . . . du Plessis." Fayölle underscored the order of the general staff signed by the commanding officer, Nonnoille, which read: *You will take section to the Convention armed with your cannon.*

[31] Ibid.; A.N., F⁷ 4633, d. 4.

and the honest representatives!" Several men came rushing into the room demanding the key to unlock the hall of the general assembly. Although the committees refused to comply, the door had already been opened and a crowd assembled there. Among those who took the floor were Fayölle, Carron, and the musician Perrin, whose voices were clearly heard—but in what cause it is impossible to say. In any case, the local authorities found it impossible to reestablish order, and so informed the Committee of General Security, which armed its commissioners with warrants of arrest against the three whose voices had been heard in the hall. Nothing concrete had been accomplished, and sensing defeat, perhaps, the general assembly had dissolved itself; shortly thereafter a large force of infantry, cavalry, and artillery arrived. The officer in command and his staff observed to the joint committees that order seemed to reign in the section, and withdrew. It was then about 3 a.m.[32]

At 5 a.m. members of the joint committees returned from a session with the Committee of General Security, which, after praising their action, had withdrawn the arrest warrants issued by it without explanation. Perhaps members of the Committee had been persuaded to let sleeping dogs lie. At 8 a.m., however, several members returned and reported that a more alarming movement was being organized, "that the agitators of the section are proclaiming loudly that blood will flow in great torrents today in Paris," and that committee members were being threatened again. Among the agitators of the moment appeared to be the musician Perrin, who had entered the room with his supporters while most committee members had gone out to eat. A cry arose that the latter were in contempt of the law; that they should have been sitting in permanent session, and that this "desertion" of their posts should be noted in the *procès-verbal*. Naturally, members of the committees who were present refused to act on this demand. At 10 a.m. the joint committees were again reunited, awaiting "with calm and tranquillity" the developments of the day,[33] a calm few of them felt despite the assurances of their secretary.

While the committees were meeting the general alarm sounded in

---

[32] A.N., F⁷ 4633; A.N., F⁷ 4704, 1 prairial, Year III.

[33] A.N., F⁷ 4633. This *procès-verbal* was signed by Grandhomme as "secretary-registrar of the police fulfilling the functions of secretary of the joint committees because of [extraordinary] circumstances."

the section at 10 a.m.,[34] five hours after it was first given in faubourgs Saint-Antoine and Saint-Marcel.[35] Never had such huge crowds been seen in Paris, not even in the dramatic *journées* of the past.[36] Police observers, although repeating the propaganda of the government that it was largely a conspiracy of former Jacobins and Montagnards, and that the movement had been organized long before, admitted that dearth "was the pretext" but, "unfortunately," a plausible one.[37] This was one reason why women took the lead, dragging the men after them. Many of them had been standing in queues as usual, sharing seditious utterances with the crowd.[38]

Once again, as in germinal, food riots broke out in sections Droits-de-l'Homme, Popincourt, and Gravilliers.[39] On the left bank women demanded that the civil committees lead them to the Convention, and in faubourg Saint-Antoine they closed all shops and started for the Tuileries about 1:30 p.m. Ejected from the hall, they returned with armed companies of the National Guard. Shortly thereafter the general call to arms was sounded in faubourgs Saint-Antoine and Saint-Marcel, as well as in the sections of the center. Although a number of sections from the more affluent neighborhoods of the west end arrived to defend the Assembly, they became mixed up with the contingents of armed men who were milling about at the Tuileries. Shortly

---

[34] A.N., AF II, 50, pl. 385, pc. 10, 3 prairial (22 May).

[35] *Moniteur*, XXIV, no. 244, p. 497, 4 prairial.

[36] The *Messager du soir* of 2 prairial wrote that such crowds had not been seen since 1789, and the *Courier républicain* of 3 prairial reported that Paris resembled an armed camp. Never had such an immense armed throng been witnessed in the capital, not on 14 July, 10 August, or 31 May. Cited by Aulard, *Paris*, I, 735, 1 prairial.

[37] *Ibid.*, I, 733, 1 prairial. The police spy listed the reestablishment of the Commune as among the political demands of the insurgents. Rudé calls this "a piece of deliberate embroidery by the police," as no such demand occurs among the slogans of the insurrectionists of either germinal or prairial. *The Crowd*, p. 156 n. 2. The petitioners of section Quinze-Vingts, however, raised the quesiton of why Paris still had no independent municipal government on the eve of the germinal insurrection, as was seen above.

[38] Aulard, *Paris*, I, 733, 1 prairial. A brief description of the events from the sounding of the tocsin to the arrest of the man who had carried Féraud's head on his pike is contained in the police reports for 1 prairial in the above reference, pp. 734-735, and for 2 prairial on pp. 736-737. On the latter day markets were well supplied but prices remained high.

[39] Rudé, *The Crowd*, p. 152.

after 3:30 p.m. armed companies of insurgents broke into the hall, while deputies of the Right shouted that they were victims of a foreign conspiracy, the universal cry against dissenters of the Left. While the more moderate members appealed for patience to the crowd now master of the hall, cries of "bread!" punctuated the session as time and again the president was forced to suspend the proceedings. It was then that deputy Féraud was shot, dragged away, and his head was mounted on a pike,[40] an act that silenced the Thermidorians. Open demonstrations for the Jacobins and Montagnards now broke out, and demands were raised to implement the Constitution of 1793 and to establish effective controls to assure food for the people.

The demonstrators carried all before them—but in the form of paper decrees and fatuous resolutions as they wasted time in idle addresses and meaningless chatter. The one ingredient lacking to make the insurrection a success was a Committee of Nine, as on 31 May. Remnants of the old Mountain made no effort to organize the people, arrest leading Thermidorians, and surround the hall with troops of the radical sections. Instead, they only compromised themselves and sealed their own doom. Given time so generously by the people and the Montagnards, the Thermidorians brought up troops from the loyal sections, and to the cries of "Down with the Jacobins!" drove the insurgents out of the hall.[41] Montagnards were immediately attacked and arrested as the Thermidorians authorized the sections to disarm the *buveurs de sang* and the "agents of tyranny that had preceded the 9th of thermidor."[42]

Yet all was not lost, for on the morrow the armed rebellion, more menacing than ever, renewed itself. The call to arms sounded in section Quinze-Vingts at 2 a.m., and at 10 a.m. the tocsin rang out in

---

[40] A member of the revolutionary committee of the 7th arrondissement described the carrying "in triumph" of the head of Féraud by the "terrorists and partisans of tyranny." A.N., F7* 2498, pp. 302-303, 3 prairial.

[41] *Moniteur*, XXIV, no. 244, pp. 498-499, 4 prairial; no. 245, pp. 501-507, 5 prairial; no. 246, pp. 510-515, 6 prairial. See, especially, the dramatic version of Mathiez, *Réaction*, pp. 245-253; Tønnesson, *La Défaite*, chapters XI-XIV, pp. 253-344, perhaps the clearest and fullest version of all. Tønnesson cites evidence that the Thermidorians plotted to provoke the insurrection so as to compromise former Montagnards and their supporters. See also the brief but intelligent summary of these events by Rudé, *The Crowd*, pp. 152-159.

[42] *Moniteur*, XXIV, no. 246, p. 515, 6 prairial.

section Droits-de-l'Homme, where an illegal assembly was being held.[43] Sections Fidelité, Arcis, Gravilliers, and Popincourt also convoked their general assemblies illegally. The three sections of faubourg Saint-Antoine and the sections of the center arrived at the Place du Carrousel at 3:30 p.m., armed and with their cannon. The decisive moment approached as the insurgents trained their guns on the Convention, whose troops under General Dubois numbered 40,000 to their own 20,000. Suddenly the cannoneers and gendarmes of the Convention deserted the Thermidorians and went over to the side of the revolutionaries. A Varlet might have quickly converted this tactical victory into a decisive triumph. Unfortunatley for the insurgents, there was no Varlet. Once again, the insurrectionists, lacking leaders, retired with false promises and paper resolutions. They would not have another such opportunity. Among the tactics to defeat them was a rumor that peace with Holland had been signed.

On the 3rd of prairial, faubourg Saint-Antoine was ringed with soldiers of the regular army and troops from the loyal sections. The following day the faubourg faced starvation and an all-out attack as several half-hearted efforts by those outside failed to bring relief. In the end, the revolutionary faubourg was forced to surrender and to give up its arms. Military commissions carried out their task of repression; six deputies were immediately condemned to death, while Thermidorians in the sections settled old scores and incarcerated some 10,000 former revolutionaries.[44] Militants and former commissioners of the old committees were now conveniently labeled "agents of tyranny," according to the happy formula hatched by the Thermidorians. If no proof of tyranny existed it was sufficient that they had been partisans or friends of partisans of those who had administered the section before 9 thermidor.[45] Grandjean presided at the assembly session of 5 prairial and set the stage for the arrests. It was time, he declared, to purge the section of "the men of blood" who had dem-

[43] A.N., F[7] 4633, at 10 a.m., when the joint committees awaited "with calm and tranquillity" the events of the day.

[44] *Moniteur*, XXIV, nos. 246, 247, 248, pp. 515-516, 517-524, 525-526, 6, 7, 8 prairial; and the appropriate references in Mathiez, Tønnesson, and Rudé, as above.

[45] A.N., F[7]* 2498, pp. 304-306, 4 prairial. After a long discussion it was observed by various members of the revolutionary committee that among the partisans of "anarchy" in the general assemblies of the sections and among the former local authorities almost all were old Robespierrists.

onstrated their perfidious intentions in the late revolt. The law itself demanded that they be unmasked. "Do not think that you can buy safety by keeping silent," he affirmed, addressing his remarks to the assembly members who tried to remain neutral and uninvolved. If these men ever regained power there would be no safety for anyone because "the men of Robespierre strike indiscriminately." The assembly probably needed no urging, and promptly voted the arrest of thirty-four members.[46]

For the next few days the general assembly occupied itself with the purge. The Committee of Public Safety ordered it to continue disarming suspects and expressly forbade it to consider any other matter.[47] The same day (6 prairial), Leclerc and Lenfant were arrested on trumped-up charges of being responsible for the September massacres.[48] Varlet was also attacked, charged with having opposed the attempt to halt the massacres in September, saying that patriotic justice should be above the law.[49] Since Varlet was in prison at the time, what his enemies hoped to gain was to have him kept there as long as possible by concocting fresh charges against him. Finally, the battery of cannoneers was disarmed and their guns offered to the Convention. Had they been among those who had deserted the troops of the Convention and joined the insurgents on 2 prairial? There is no such charge against them, yet the Thermidorians must have recognized that these were not their men.

By the evening of 10 prairial, forty-seven revolutionists, or men accused of being insurrectionists, had been arrested in the section and another eighteen had been disarmed. This elimination of sixty-five militants, former officials, members of the section's popular society, and general dissenters must have pushed the section still further to the Right.[50] A number of those imprisoned or disarmed were rela-

[46] B.V.C., MS 120, fols. 161-163, 5 prairial. See my article, "L'Epuration de prairial an III dans la section des Droits-de-l'Homme," *Annales historiques*, no. 232 (April-June 1978), pp. 283-304.

[47] *Ibid.*, fol. 163, from 12 m. to 7 p.m. by order of the Committee of Public Safety.

[48] *Ibid.*, fols. 163-165, 6 and 7 prairial, 1795. These charges and their refutations are discussed in the chapter on the insurrection of 10 August above.

[49] *Ibid.*, fol. 163, 7 prairial 1795. "Varlet s'y opposa disant que la justice nationale devait avoir le dessus."

[50] The purge was completed by 10 p.m. of 10 prairial, and on the following day

tively unknown, having neither held official posts nor been conspicuous by their political activity. It was enough, evidently, that they had supported or befriended those who had led the section in the past. The reasons for their denunciation, although varied, are essentially that they had been militant, conspicuous, or popular in the days before 9 thermidor. Some were charged with having excited the people against the Convention or bakeries; others for having supposedly been among the *Septembriseurs* at La Force prison in 1792. Several were accused of having seconded Fayölle in threatening the joint committees during the events of prairial. One, Beudelot, was indicted because he had allegedly shown "a forced joy" at the execution of Robespierre and the chiefs of the Commune, while another, Leclerc, rejoiced at the execution "of unfortunate victims of tyranny." A number had participated in the illegal assembly; Monneuse was charged with having been a judge at La Force prison during the massacres. Diversin had threatened "to eat the heart of Grandjean [the president of the section during the repression] with pleasure." Leleu was held responsible for having inculpated a young patriot, which led to the latter's execution. Prou had been a former member of the revolutionary army, which was sufficient to indict him, whereas Barré had supposedly advocated the calling of a new primary assembly to elect another representative. Two were women—Barbot, who had left her section of Indivisibilité in order to hide in Droits-de-l'Homme, and Le Blanc, who had been conspicuous in all "seditious demonstrations" of women and who allegedly had forced a citizen (Larue) to beat the general alarm on 11 germinal.[51] In short, whole categories of former revolutionists were disarmed or imprisoned, which made the section safe for the Thermidorians.[52]

Among the others arrested was Carnonkel, *garçon de bureau* of the civil and revolutionary committees, who had resided on their premises, accused of having insulted members of the committees, of pro-

---

a number of women denounced former members of the old revolutionary committee. *Ibid.*, fol. 166. A.N., F⁷ 4774⁴⁶, "Extraits des registres de l'assemblée générale de la section des Droits-de-l'Homme des cinq, six, sept, huit, neuf, dix et onze prairial l'an troisième de la République une et indivisible."

[51] *Ibid.* See also A.N., F⁷ 4597, pl. 8, 4e jour complementaire, Year III (20 September 1794) (dossier Beudelot).

[52] Cobb, "Note sur la répression," points out that the repression of prairial was against categories, not individuals.

posing seditious measures, and of having delivered the key to the hall of the general assembly to the insurgents.[53] Caval, Chartrain, and Monneuse were accused of having participated in the September massacres, and were transferred by order of the Committee of General Security from Plessis Prison to the Conciergerie, and their *procès* transmitted to the public accuser.[54] Diversin, a cannoneer, lodged on rue Bercy, was accused by a fellow cannoneer, Dupré, of threatening Grandjean, making seditious proposals, and exciting others to revolt. Diversin replied that not one of the accusations bore a date or mentioned a specific fact, that he did not even know Grandjean, and that the whole accusation was a slander. On 16 thermidor (3 August) the surveillance committee of the seventh arrondissement resolved to free him, as only one witness had testified against him. Three days later the Committee of General Security granted him provisional freedom.[55] It can be assumed that he gained full freedom like the others before the royalist attack.

Toussaint Fouque was a saddler by trade, established on rue des Ecouffes, and a signatory of the militia list of 13-14 July. He was arrested because he had served in the Revolutionary Army, although the charge was that he had excited citizens to march on the Convention. The civil committee knew nothing of this, but reported that he had indulged in wine, which made him suspect of upsetting public tranquillity! His officers, noncommissioned officers, and others testified in his behalf, including the surveillance committee, which recommended his release. The Committee of General Security freed him provisionally on 29 thermidor, Year III (16 August 1795).[56] Linked to Fouque was François Gamain, a pastry cook installed on rue de la Verrerie, who had been an active member of the relief committee. In August 1793 he had engaged in a fracas with a colleague and had been deprived of his functions for this act. After prairial he was accused of having testified in favor of Dupaumier, the former member

[53] A.N., F⁷ 4633, d. 4. He was restored to full citizenship by the Committee of General Security on 9 vendémiaire, Year III (30 September 1795).

[54] A.N., F⁷ 4774⁶⁰, d. 3, 13 fructidor, Year III (30 August 1795).

[55] A.N., F⁷ 4677, d. 5. The release of Diversin was on 19 thermidor, Year III (6 August 1795).

[56] A.N., F⁷ 4710, d. 4; B.H.V.P., MS 742.

of the revolutionary committee, and of having been involved in an unexplained affair dealing with a citizen Colivet. The united civil and relief committees testified, however, that he had always been exacting in his duties and had shown warm concern for the welfare of the section's poor. Released provisionally by the Committee of General Security at an unspecified date, he appealed for the restoration of full rights on 24 messidor, Year III (12 July 1795).[57]

Joly, member of the civil committee residing on rue des Rosiers, had been denounced by one member of the assembly and on this basis alone was disarmed. The civil committee took no position on his demand for rearmament, surely a trimming of sails unusual even for the most cautious member of the committee. Only on the eve of the attempted royalist coup did the surveillance committee request his rearmament, which was promptly granted by the Committee of General Security.[58] Another official was S. N. Larivièrre, probably employed by the police administration. He had been adjutant-major of the section's armed force during the events of 9 thermidor, and in that capacity was empowered to distribute the 40-sous subsidy voted by the grateful Convention to participants in the overthrow of Robespierre. While serving with his company, he complained that unknown persons had threatened his wife if they did not receive the money due them. Although disarmed by the assembly during its purge of prairial, he seems to have been restored to his former position shortly thereafter.[59]

Lelièvre resided on rue de la Verrerie and served in the section's 9th company. He was denounced by a Bernardeau on 5 prairial for having allegedly urged "measures" to punish the guilty on the eve of the September massacres. Since he had been disarmed by the assembly and was illiterate, his wife had to undertake his defense. The civil committee could only report that Lelièvre often took the floor in the general assembly and spoke "with great vivacity," a new reason for

[57] A.N., F⁷ 4715, d. 2. Among the signatures on his behalf was that of Grandjean.

[58] A.N., F⁷ 4750, d. 4. He was rearmed on 12 vendémiaire, Year IV (4 October 1795).

[59] A.N., F⁷ 4765, d. 4. Larivièrre's complaint was written on 20 thermidor, Year II (7 August 1794), but he was sent on a mission by the Commission de police administrative de Paris on 19 thermidor, Year III (6 August 1795).

suspicion. The surveillance committee noted, however, that he had been accused without any proof and recommended his release, which was done by the Committee of General Security on 20 thermidor, Year III (7 August 1795).[60] Louis-Nicolas Vallée was probably a cobbler by trade,[61] accused of exciting others to march on the Convention and of having been among the armed men who had accompanied Fayölle when the civil committee was forced to read publicly its *procès-verbal* of 1 prairial. Vallée replied that he had been with his battalion throughout the events of prairial. As for his presence during the reading of the committee's minutes, he had carried out an order of his superior officer together with nine other men ordered to do so by Fayölle. On the final charge that he had attended an illegal assembly, Vallée denied any knowledge of such a meeting, adding, however, that even if this were true, was he more guilty than others who were found there? After the surveillance committee requested the Committee of General Security to rule on Vallée's arrest, the latter granted him provisional freedom.[62]

According to the minutes of the civil committee, one of the voices clearly heard by its members was that of a musician, Jean-Michel Perrin, who was charged with being "one of the leaders of the revolt of 1st prairial." Although the Committee of General Security issued a warrant for his arrest with orders to seal his papers, the revolutionary committee of the 7th arrondissement could not find him at home but did examine and seal his effects.[63] A number of witnesses came forward to implicate him in the insurrection. He was quoted as having said: "Here are the *muscadins*, f——them. There is Féraud killed; his head is being carried about. What a triumph for the patriots!" Others had heard him say that the Convention was engulfed in blood, cry out against commissioners, insult members of the committee, and declare that all authority had been overthrown. Grandjean, who presided at the meeting of the assembly, added that Perrin demanded that he open the hall of the general assembly on 11 germinal and

[60] A.N., F⁷ 4774¹⁴, d. 5.

[61] A.N., F⁷ 4775³⁸, d. 2. Vallée wrote a letter on 22 nivôse, Year III (11 January 1795) to the Administrator of Provisions requesting a job because he was unemployed due to the scarcity of leather, adding that he was a father of two volunteers.

[62] *Ibid.* He was released on 19 thermidor, Year III (6 August 1795).

[63] A.N., F⁷ 4774⁶⁸, d. 2, 1 prairial; A.N., F⁷* 2498, pp. 301-302, 4 prairial.

preside over it. Furthermore, that it was a comrade of his who had gone up and down the streets of the section with a bell, summoning the people to assemble.[64]

Perrin had gone into the country, probably trying to escape his persecutors, and was arrested some time later, as his appeals for release testify.[65] These appeals give a brief biographical sketch of his life. Born in 1764, he joined an infantry regiment at age fourteen and was mustered out five years later because of an infirmity. Upon recovering, he rejoined the army and was demobilized as a sergeant in 1791. Then, turning to poetry and music, he became proficient enough to command a subsidy to compose patriotic songs.[66] Although he enjoyed the esteem of his fellow citizens, he wrote, he had never been employed in any official capacity, joined the Jacobins, or been guilty of an act of tyranny. His only elective posts had been as vice president of the section, as its secretary on an unspecified occasion, and as an officer of the peace. Nor had he ever advocated the dissolution of the Convention or the restoration of royalty. Perrin was able to submit testimony of good conduct and patriotic behavior verified by members of the armed forces with whom he served, including a letter signed by his commanding officer. As a result, the Committee of General Security decreed the return of his arms on 24 floréal, Year III (13 May 1795).[67]

Among those arrested on 5 prairial was Nicolas Oudart, president of the criminal tribunal of Paris. What was the charge against him? He had presided over the assembly in brumaire 1793, when Varlet was freed, and when the latter began to read his discourse the assembly interrupted him before he was able to finish, a slight for which Varlet held Oudart responsible. After Varlet had been freed from prison in November 1793, Oudart admitted that he was pleased to have contributed to his release despite Varlet's attacks on him. In fact, it was he who had proposed to intervene on his behalf to the assembly,

[64] A.N., F⁷ 4774⁶⁸, 7 prairial, Year III (26 May 1795). In the margin of this document are written remarks like "this is true" or "this is false," probably by Perrin.

[65] *Ibid.*, 2 messidor (20 June); A.P.P., A A/22, pc. 367, 14 messidor, Year III (2 July 1795).

[66] "Section Droits-de-l'Homme . . . also submitted a patriotic song on the same subject [the taking of Toulon] composed by citizen Perrin." *Journal de la montagne*, no. 49, p. 387, 12 nivôse, Year III (1 January 1794).

[67] A.N., F⁷ 4774⁶⁸, 14 floréal, Year III (3 May 1795); 23 floréal (12 May).

promising to watch over his conduct. After being released, Oudart wrote, Varlet continued to attack him in the popular society of the section, but he had no other relations with him. As for Descombes, he had never received him at his home.[68]

The original charges had been brought against him by a Dommanget,[69] but the criminal court testified that Oudart had been at his post during the insurrection of 12 and 13 germinal and on 2, 3, and 4 prairial. In summarizing the charges and refutations of Oudart for the Committee of General Security, the civil committee pointed out that he had spent the night of 9 thermidor in the Hôtel de Ville. Oudart admitted it, but gave an acceptable explanation for his presence at the Commune. As for being appointed to the criminal tribunal because he was supported by the terrorists, Oudart claimed that he was nominated despite his statement expressly disclaiming terrorism, and submitted proof thereof. Referring to his own evidence and to the observations of the civil committee, the Committee of General Security ruled, therefore, that Oudart would continue "to enjoy his freedom."[70]

Another of those arrested in what seems to have been a comedy of errors was André Michel, of rue des Ecouffes, accused of "gravely insulting" and wounding Rossignol, a member of the civil committee, and of having roused the section to revolt. There is no indication who he was, exactly, as he held no formal post in the section, but he must have been a militant active in the assembly and the popular society. According to Michel, he met Rossignol when both were in a slight state of intoxication, and thinking that he was still a member of the civil committee, had urged him to return to his post. Rossignol took a step or two backwards, but unaware of a slight step, stumbled over it and fell down. Michel staggered over to lift him up, but fell over him, instead, whereupon another passerby, Fouque, helped them both up. This explanation was rejected by the civil committee as the common excuse of agitators who always pleaded that "I have drunk (too much)."[71]

---

[68] A.N., F7 4774⁶⁰, d. 2, 6 and 18 prairial, Year III (25 May and 6 June 1795).

[69] It is not clear, however, which Dommanget this was. The reference is merely to "a citizen Dommanget," probably not the civil commissioner. *Ibid.*, 5 prairial.

[70] *Ibid.*, containing eight signatures; 9 thermidor, Year III (27 July 1795), signed by Lambin as interim secretary for the committee; and 8 fructidor, Year III (25 August 1795), signed by the eleven members of the Committee of General Security.

[71] A.N., F7 4774⁴⁵, 5 and 7 thermidor, Year III (23 and 25 July 1795).

As for the charge that he had excited citizens to insurrection on 1 prairial, Michel asked the Committee of General Security to investigate his conduct. It would find that he had been on the side of the Convention from the beginning. Then, warming to the subject, he went over to the attack against the local authorities. This was how the best people of the section were treated during the first days of prairial "by several so-called citizens, who only joined the band of thieves in the sections to spread alarm and terror." It would be easy to convince you of this, he concluded, if you only knew "the morals of all *these vile accusers*."[72] There is no indication of how long Michel remained in prison, but it can be assumed that he, too, was released after the royalist rising in vendémiaire.

As late as 30 pluviôse (18 February 1795), the general assembly had resolved that no one was to apply such terms as "terrorist" to his political opponent, and pledged to respect the freedom of opinion of all.[73] This pious resolution was never meant to be taken seriously, however, for ten days later a discourse of an orator from section Bon-Conseil against "terrorists and men of blood" was loudly applauded by the same section that had just pledged not to abuse the meaning of words.[74] Roused by the speaker, the section resolved to go to the Convention on the morrow (21 ventôse—11 March 1795) and demand a report on the decrees that had suspended the prosecution of the *Septembriseurs*. Meanwhile, denunciations against those accused of being such continued in the section, as the order of the day was to let justice take its course.[75] Needless to say, this justice had a Thermidorian face.

Although threats of reviving Jacobinism caused panic in the ranks of the Thermidorians,[76] the assembly burned the list of citizens who had signed the adoption of the Constitution of 1793 with so much enthusiasm.[77] It was obvious that had it been published, only the royalists would have reaped a political advantage. Too many Ther-

[72] *Ibid.*

[73] B.V.C., MS 120, fol. 160.

[74] Ibid., 10 ventôse, 1795 (28 February).

[75] *Ibid.*, fol. 161. The section also offered its congratulations to the Convention on the return of the Girondist deputies shortly thereafter.

[76] *Ibid.*, MS 120, fol. 167, 21 prairial 1795. An anonymous note preaching terror and raising demands to revive the Jacobins when brought to the attention of the assembly caused indignation, it was reported.

[77] *Ibid.*, fols. 168-169, ler jour complémentaire 1795 (17 September).

midorians and moderates, innocent citizens and apolitical residents of the section, had committed themselves to support a document now anathema to the Center and the Right. Before this happened, however, royalism had to make its bid for power and be crushed.

The insurrection of 13 vendémiaire differed from those that preceded it in that it was organized and directed by sections and social classes of conservative persuasion. Those same sections of the west end, like Lepeletier and Théâtre-Français, which had helped the Convention repress the uprisings in the spring of 1795 now threatened the Thermidorians with a royalist coup. Despite this political difference, the motives that impelled the supporters of "law and order" to undermine that same order hardly differed from those of the *menu peuple* in germinal and prairial. The rampant inflation, shortages of essentials, the fall of the *assignat*, and the widespread hunger struck indiscriminately at the bourgeois sections of the west no less than at the *sans-culottes* of the radical faubourgs and the sections of the Center.

On the eve of vendémiaire appeared a table of prices contrasting the year 1790 with that of 1795. According to this comparison, the price of all goods had risen astronomically. Flour had gone from 2 livres 10 sous a bushel (*boisseau*) to 225 livres; sugar from 1 livre 18 sous to 62 livres; soap and tallow-candles from 1 livre 18 sous each to 41 livres; firewood from 20 livres a *voie* (56 cu. ft.) to 500 livres; shoes from 5 livres 8 sous a pair to 200 livres. The total for all items increased from 164 livres 17 sous to 5,642 livres, a rise of 3,319 percent. By October the *assignat* had fallen to 5 percent of its face value.[78]

More alarming was the steep increase in prices on essentials between June-July and September. Bread sold from 15 to 20 livres a pound on the open market, and often arrived spoiled.[79] Many bakers demanded 4 sous per ration instead of the 2 sous 6 deniers provided by law, and few were willing to sell it at the prescribed legal price of 3

[78] The *Gazette française* of 3 vendémiaire, Year IV (25 September 1795), cited in Aulard, *Paris*, II, 271; II, 325, 25 vendémiaire (17 October). Unless otherwise noted all references are to the year 1795.

[79] Aulard, *Paris*, I, 756, 10 prairial (10 May); *ibid.*, II, 36, 7 messidor (25 June); *ibid.*, pp. 186-187, 5 fructidor (22 August); p. 199, 10 fructidor (27 August); p. 139, 18 thermidor (5 August), workers expressed fear of the approaching winter and complained that merchants were demanding twenty to thirty times what they had asked a year previously.

sous per pound. Rations reached the pitiful state of 4 to 6 ounces per person, and meat, when available, rose from 8 livres a pound in June to 30 livres in September. These prices and shortages, as might be expected, caused rioting and disorders at butcher shops, one being that of citoyenne David, on rue Droits-de-l'Homme. When individuals ignored the queue and began to push their way to the front, an armed patrol had to intervene to restore order.[80] Late deliveries of flour aggravated the situation, and often men and women waited in vain through the night. Section Droits-de-l'Homme frequently failed to receive its quota until late in the morning, sometimes getting no flour at all, which forced its bakers to exhaust whatever reserves they had on hand or bake nothing for the day.[81]

Even worse, perhaps, than the conditions of the working classes was the distress of the middle classes, those with fixed incomes, the petty proprietors and the *rentiers*. A police spy observed: "The unfortunate *rentier* cannot live without selling his last piece of furniture, which becomes loot of the greedy speculator. The petty proprietor, stripped of all resources, eats up his capital as well as his income. The civil servant who has nothing but his salary also suffers the pangs of need."[82] Others made similar declarations. Only yeomen farmers and profiteers, thieves and whores were well off, they charged, while those with fixed incomes or with none at all were reduced to desperate circumstances.[83] It is these austere conditions that explain, in large part, the hostility to the Convention of such bourgeois sections as Lepeletier, Théâtre-Français, Butte-des-Moulins, and Place-Vendôme. They had been among the staunchest supporters of the Assembly in thermidor, germinal, and prairial. Now, in vendémiaire, they attempted to dissolve it.

The reaction unleashed against former militants and old patriots after prairial had changed the composition and leadership of previously radical sections. Only property holders now sat in their assem-

[80] *Ibid.*, II, 113, 7 thermidor (26 July).

[81] *Ibid.*, II, 315, 18 vendémiaire (10 October).

[82] *Ibid.*, II, 142, 19 thermidor (6 August).

[83] *Ibid.*, II, pp. 48-49, 13 messidor (1 July); p. 50, 14 messidor (2 July); p. 208, 14 fructidor (31 August). An observer wrote that in addition to the *rentiers* and petty proprietors, public officials and other *employés* without resources who were not paid in kind were at the lowest point of misery. See also pp. 209-210, same date, and p. 213, 15 and 16 fructidor (2 and 3 September).

blies, and the *sans-culottes* were excluded from the National Guard. On September 6 all sections accepted the new Constitution, inaugurating the period of the Directory, but forty-seven had rejected the two-thirds decree, an act that was more decisive than the nominal acceptance of the Constitution. This decree, passed on 5 and 13 fructidor, Year III (22 and 30 August 1795), provided that 500 of the 750 members of the Convention were to be returned to the new assembly,[84] thus guaranteeing control of the government by the Thermidorians. The sections launched a vigorous movement against it. Its rejection would have undermined, if not completely destroyed, the delicate balance so carefully erected by the Thermidorians in order not to fall prey either to royalism or to Jacobinism. To neutralize this opposition, the Convention admitted former terrorists into the primary assemblies, knowing full well that they would hardly support the disaffected bourgeoisie of the Right or the royalists with whom certain elements of the bourgeoisie were coming into contact. The ultimate resort, and it was to prove decisive, was to rely on the regular army to defend the Convention. It was these two measures that the insurgents of vendémiaire opposed.[85]

The nucleus of royalist agitation was in section Lepeletier, a center of finance and stock-jobbing with a long history of moderate and royalist sympathies. Its grenadiers had defended the monarchy in August 1792; it had rallied to the Convention on 9 thermidor, and in germinal and prairial it took the lead against the insurrectionists.[86] It was also the first to have removed the busts of Marat and of Chalier from its hall.[87] In its sessions of 21 and 26 fructidor (7 and 12 September) it had taken the initiative in repudiating the two-thirds de-

[84] Duvergier, VIII, 242, 5 fructidor, Year III (22 August 1795), Art. 2, Title I decreed that electoral assemblies could not take fewer than two-thirds of the members of the future Legislative body from the ranks of the Convention; *ibid.*, p. 250, 13 fructidor, Year III (30 August 1795). Art. 1 provided that electoral assemblies elect two-thirds of the deputies from delegations of their departments or from the Convention itself. *Moniteur*, XXV, no. 347, p. 623, 17 fructidor, Year III (3 September 1795), the same.

[85] Aulard, *Paris*, II, 187, 199, 218; 5, 10, 18 fructidor (22, 27 August, 4 September).

[86] B.N., MSS, Nouv. acq. fr. 2687, fols. 141-144; Henry Zivy, *Le Treize vendémiaire an IV* (Paris, 1898), pp. 28-31. This is the definitive study on vendémiaire.

[87] Aulard, *Paris*, I, 467.

cree by an "act of guarantee" that sought to assure the freedom of opinion to all, placing each individual so exercising this right under the safeguard of the sections. To rally support among the latter, it published an address which it proposed to communicate to the departments and the armies, as well.[88] In short, it was a direct challenge to the Convention.

Among the thirty sections that had endorsed this address was Droits-de-l'Homme.[89] Having examined the proposed Constitution in its primary assembly, it had rejected the two-thirds decree of the Convention. To enforce the right to "freedom of opinion" it had placed its members under the safeguard of the nation itself, pledging to oppose all arbitrary acts, that is, efforts of the Convention to enforce the law. Furthermore, it rejected the enfranchisement of the so-called terrorists and all who had been granted only provisional liberty. Although willing to deal generously, it declared, with those who had confessed their errors under the revolutionary government, it refused to recognize "the scoundrel(s) who had no excuse" for behaving as they did. Furthermore, it argued that the votes of the latter could give a majority to unworthy candidates who were running for the electoral assembly that was to choose deputies to the new Council of Elders and Council of Five Hundred. Finally, it resolved to act jointly with the other sections, and published six hundred copies of this resolution.[90]

The action of the other sections in rejecting the two-thirds decree followed closely a common formula, as they guaranteed freedom of opinion to their members and excluded former terrorists from the vote while at the same time adopting the proposed Constitution.[91] The

[88] Zivy, pp. 28-29, 114-116. The address was entitled "Les Citoyens de Paris, réunis en assemblées primaires, à toutes les assemblées primaires de la République française, à la Convention nationale et aux armées," B.N., Lb[41] 4598, cited by Zivy, p. 32.

[89] B.N., Lb[40] 3452, N. Karéiev, Les Comités révolutionnaires. The proceedings in section Réunion for 21 and 22 fructidor are especially dramatic. Ibid., pp. XIV-XVI; Zivy, p. 32 n. 3, lists the thirty sections.

[90] B.V.C., MS 120 fols. 166, 167, 20-22 fructidor, 1795 (6-8 September); B.N., MSS, Nouv. acq. fr. 2687, fol. 112, 22 fructidor, Year III (8 September 1795), Section des Droits-de-l'Homme. Extrait du registre des délibérations . . . ; B.N., Le[40] 36, the same in the form of a poster. The procès-verbal was signed by Grandjean, president, and Gorguereau, secretary.

[91] B.N., MSS, Nouv. acq. fr. 2687, fol. 88, Bonne-Nouvelle; fols. 90, 140, Amis-de-la-Patrie; fol. 91, Place-Vendôme; fol. 92, Brutus; fol. 93, Mail, adding clemency

sections also accepted the traditional practice of sending and receiving delegations in order to reinforce their own resolutions, the sole difference being that those militants who had launched this policy of fraternization in the past were now absent from the assemblies. Section Droits-de-l'Homme joined with others in this action, and visited section Observatoire to announce its own rejection of the decrees of 5 and 13 fructidor.[92]

The results of the vote on the proposed Constitution were announced on 1 vendémiaire (23 September). Voting in support were a total of 914,853 to 41,892 in opposition; the two-thirds decree also passed, but by a much smaller margin—167,758 to 95,373.[93] The electoral assembly was scheduled to meet on 12 October and the new legislative body on 6 November.

Section Droits-de-l'Homme, together with ten other sections, declaring the returns fraudulent, decided to ignore the order to disband its primary assembly. Of the 1,721 who voted in the section, 1,652 favored the adoption of the Constitution, while 51 were opposed (the other 18 votes were scattered).[94] All rejected the two-thirds decree.

for its "misled citizens"; fol. 94, Fidelité; fols. 95, 107, Butte-des-Moulins; fol. 96, Lepeletier defended its call for a meeting of commissioners of the sections; fols. 97, 117, Roule, which endorsed the resolution of Jardin-des-Plantes never again to allow revolutionary acts to take place, including "the existence of assassins under the suborder called revolutionary committees"; in fol. 118 it addressed the soldiers explaining its rejection of the two-thirds decree; fols. 98, 99, Montreuil; fols. 102, 103, Jardin-des-Plantes; fol. 104, Halle-au-Blé; fol. 106, Panthéon endorsed the concept of unity among the sections but said nothing on the two-thirds decree; fols. 109, 110, Indivisibilité; fol. 113, Faubourg-Montmartre; fol. 114, Arsenal, which insisted that it regarded the permanence of its assembly as incontestable until the meeting of the new legislative body; fol. 119, Quinze-Vingts was noncommital on the two-thirds decree but in fol. 125 announced its own permanence; fols. 120, 121, Cité explained to the army that it was neither royalist nor made up of intriguers; and fol. 126, Tuileries.

[92] Aulard, *Paris*, II, 236, 26 fructidor (12 September).

[93] Zivy, p. 35.

[94] A.N., B 11, 61, pcs. 86 and 87, 26 fructidor, Year III (12 September 1795). Two voted for a king, two accepted the Constitution with reservations, one demanded the Constitution of 1789, four accepted the Constitution provisionally, one favored the maintenance of the executive power by the people, one supported a suspensive veto, one accepted the provision on émigrés, and six ballots were declared void. The cover of this dossier is wrongfully labeled as section l'Homme-Armé. According to the *procès-verbal*, voting started in the section at 7 a.m. B.V.C., MS 120, fol. 167.

The primary assembly then adopted an address aimed at the other forty-seven sections in which it complained "energetically" that it was forbidden to communicate directly with delegates of other sections and spoke of breaking this new tyranny. Finally, the assembly burned all ballots.[95]

The following day, 24 September, section Droits-de-l'Homme repudiated the vote on the Constitution and the decrees of the Convention, defending boldly the concept that each primary assembly constituted a sovereign power to whom all civil and military authorities were responsible, and demanding the right to examine all decrees of the Convention before they were to be promulgated and published. (Shades of Jean Varlet!) Insisting that the overwhelming mass of voters had repudiated the two-thirds decree, it accused the minority of foisting its views on the majority, and employed such sharp terms of opprobrium as "lying declarations," "imbecilic," and "idiotic" in attacking the Convention. Finally, it resolved to suspend the results of the vote until the primary assemblies had declared themselves on the question.[96] Ten days later it rejected the rearmament of former terrorists, whom it called "brigands and assassins of Féraud," as being injurious both to troops of the line and to the National Guard. Suggesting that a delegation of fifty citizens chosen at random go to the Convention to manifest their outrage at its decree on rearmament of the ex-terrorists, it demanded that the legislature repudiate the conduct of its committees, and communicated this resolve to the other sections, soldiers, and citizens in general.[97]

[95] B.V.C., MS 120, fol. 168, 26 fructidor. In Br. M., Tab. 580. a.2., *A Collection of 520 broadsides . . . 1787-1813*, 5 vols., under *Tableau du dépouillement et recensement du voeu des assemblées primaires . . . sur la Constitution presentée par la Convention nationale.* The count for section Droits-de-l'Homme (Department de la Seine) is slightly different from A.N., B 11, 61 in that of the 1,721 voting, 1,661 accepted, 54 opposed, and 6 were nullified.

[96] B.N., Le⁴⁰ 36, *Section des Droits-de-l'Homme. Extrait des registres de l'assemblée primaire des Droits-de-l'Homme portion intégrante du peuple souverain.* This poster was signed by Grandjean, president, and Gorguereau, secretary.

B.N., Lb⁴⁰ 437, *Adresse des parisiens à la Convention nationale* ([Paris], n.d.), 8 pp. This brochure signed by Bellart as president of section Droits-de-l'Homme, and Gorguereau, secretary, warned of the danger of division among the French. It was published, according to its authors, in order to expose "the lies" that had been spread about the debates that had taken place in the section's primary assembly.

[97] *Ibid.*, 12 vendémiaire (3 October). This was on the eve of the uprising. The manifesto was signed by Dommanget fils. as president, and Beauquesne, secretary.

These resolutions and manifestoes were an outgrowth of a fervent agitation of major proportions in the sections. Clashes between *muscadins* (young royalists dressed in the height of fashion) and the army punctuated the political scene as monarchists now took advantage of the troubled situation. Twenty-three sections endorsed the address of Lepeletier to the Convention rejecting its decrees (8 vendémiaire–29 September). Three days later sections Lepeletier and Théâtre-Français invited the electors of the primary assemblies to meet in the hall of the latter and to come escorted by military force.[98] The *procès-verbal* of Droits-de-l'Homme reflects the ferment in the section as well as in the surrounding areas. On 22 September (*6e jour complémentaire*) the assembly denounced the terrorists of 12 germinal and 1 prairial who had been rearmed, and followed this up by repudiating its civil committee, which had transmitted the decrees of the department relative to the acceptance and implementation of the new Constitution (2 and 3 vendémiaire). Then came reports (4 to 9 vendémiaire) on resolutions of several sections rejecting the decrees of the Convention.[99] The stage was now set for the insurrection itself.

The *garçon* of the bureau of the surveillance committee of the 7th arrondissement reported on 23 fructidor (9 September) that royalist placards and slogans chalked on the walls had made their appearance in the section. "It is better to have an honest king than a false Constitution" read one. "Long live the king," and "we need a king before 1796" read others. After interrogating several people, not one of whom could enlighten the committee on who the royalitsts responsible for these appeals might be, it decided to have them erased and to keep a closer watch on its own premises by placing a guard in its vestibule.[100] On 12 vendémiaire (3 October) its members were informed of a decree of the Committee of Public Safety that all constituted authorities were to go into permanent session and to recall everyone to his post. Meanwhile, news of disturbances began to reach the committee, including reports of gunfire.[101] Police communications spoke of armed battalions being at the ready, as sections continued to protest the arming of ex-terrorists and to reject the decrees of the Convention

[98] Zivy, pp. 31-33, 36-37, 41-45, 116-118.
[99] B.V.C., MS 120, fol. 169.
[100] A.N., F7* 2498, pp. 377-379, 23 fructidor.
[101] *Ibid.*, p. 387.

dispersing the primary assemblies. Although several sections were prepared to go on the offensive, others assumed a purely defensive stance. In most there was confusion and uncertainty.[102]

On 11 vendémiaire (2 October) sections Lepeletier, Butte-des-Moulins, Théâtre-Français, and four others of the Center (Brutus, Temple, Poissonière, and Contrat-Social) declared themselves in a state of rebellion against the Convention. The Committee of Public Safety informed the deputies that the primary assemblies had formed a central committee like that of 2 September 1792 and of 2 June 1793; that patriots were being excluded from the general assemblies; and that a number of these meetings had declared themselves in permanent session. After reading the call of Lepeletier that had summoned the sections to meet under arms in the hall of Théâtre-Français, the reporter stressed that royalism and "anarchy" had combined against the Convention, which alone stood for moderation—the social and political slogan employed by Thermidorians and Directorials to justify their regime. Finally, in an obvious effort to appeal to the mass of republicans and *sans-culottes*, profiteers in these rebellious sections were roundly attacked.[103] Then, ordering all primary assemblies to dissolve by the fifteenth of the month and forbidding electors to meet under any pretext, the Convention, on a motion of Barras, declared itself in permanent session.[104] The following day it condemned the charge that the government was rearming former terrorists, and called on all patriots to rally around it, so as to vanquish both royalty and "anarchy."[105] In fact, the Convention, now happy to have their aid, did rearm "anarchists" among the 1,500 volunteers who joined in its defense.

Of all the sections, Lepeletier alone came out boldly for a king—an unpopular act, if police reports of 13 vendémiaire may be believed. The general indignation that it aroused against itself and its supporters in sections Brutus, Butte-des-Moulins, and Théâtre-Français became evident as *sans-culottes* and workingmen hastened to the aid of the Convention. They hoped, it is true, to see profiteers punished,

---

[102] Aulard, *Paris*, II, 293-298.

[103] *Moniteur*, XXVI, no. 16, pp. 123-127, 16 vendémiaire, Year IV (8 October 1795). The reporter was Daunou.

[104] *Ibid.*, no. 15, pp. 114-115, 15 vendémiaire (7 October).

[105] *Ibid.*, no. 15, pp. 117-118, 15 vendémiaire.

especially those in Lepeletier and Butte-des-Moulins, because so many were thought to have come from these sections.[106] Faubourg Saint-Antoine, which had no cause to love the government, rallied to its support, thus reflecting a remarkable political sophistication.[107]

During the night and early morning of 12-13 vendémiaire, section Droits-de-l'Homme remained calm,[108] but by evening and throughout the following night it had been stirred up as its residents responded to the general alarm sounded in the neighborhood. Its surveillance committee showed confusion and ignorance reflected in its *procès-verbal* of what exactly was transpiring in the capital, as it dispatched two members "to investigate the state of public feeling in various parts of Paris."[109] It should be added that in this respect it hardly differed from other sections of the city. Moreover, the distribution of a mere half pound of bread at 15 livres on the morrow hardly made for tran-

Figure 9. The Attempted Royalist Insurrection of 13 Vendémiaire, Year III

[106] Aulard, *Paris*, II, 297, 299-300, 12 and 13 vendémiaire (4 and 5 October).

[107] *Ibid.*, p. 303, 13 vendémiaire. Fréron reported that the sections of Saint-Antoine had come to the aid of the Convention. *Moniteur*, XXVI, no. 15, p. 119, 15 vendémiaire (7 October).

[108] Aulard, *Paris*, II, 301 n. 2.

[109] A.N., F7* 2498, p. 387, 13 vendémiaire.

quillity.[110] By then, of course, the rebels of Lepeletier had been dispersed, and the prisoners of La Force, as seen above, had been returned to their cells. Although some one hundred shots had been fired to frighten the prisoners, only one man had been wounded slightly in the arm,[111] a commentary on the relatively humanitarian policy pursued by Pierre Auzolles, the police commissioner.

After an attempt at parleying, General Menou, commanding the military forces of Paris, allowed the rebels of Lepeletier to go home—an act that only encouraged several sections to come to their assistance. A general staff now emerged led by a royalist journalist, Richer-Sérisy, as chairman, and General Danican of section Théâtre-Français as commander of the rebel forces. Although some 25,000 troops were available to the insurgents, only 7,000-8,000 from sections Lepeletier and Butte-des-Moulins were bold enough to take the field and to attack the Tuileries. This factor alone probably doomed the uprising to defeat.[112] Meanwhile, the Convention acted promptly and removed General Menou, replacing him with Barras, to whom it gave all power as it had on 9 thermidor.[113]

While the Convention awaited news of the battle, a stiff engagement took place during the evening of 13 vendémiaire, when Napoleon's famous "whiff of grape-shot" dispersed the attackers.[114] The combat lasted from 7 to 10 p.m., according to some sources; less time, according to others.[115] The following morning, 14 vendémiaire (5 October), after a final effort of the rebels to gather their forces again during the night, Saint Roche fell, and shortly thereafter, the headquarters of section Lepeletier.[116] The proclamation of the Conven-

[110] Aulard, *Paris*, II, 306.

[111] *Ibid.*, p. 307, 14 vendémiaire.

[112] Zivy, pp. 66-69, 84-85.

[113] *Moniteur*, XXVI, no. 15, p. 119, 15 vendémiaire.

[114] Zivy is skepitcal of Bonaparte's role and of the legendary episode itself, pp. 90-91.

[115] According to the *Journal du Bonhomme Richard* of 17 vendémiaire, Aulard, *Paris*, II, 304. The *Gazette française* of 14 vendémiaire and *Censeur des journaux* of 15 vendémiaire also carried stories on the fighting; *ibid.*, pp. 303-305. The version of *Moniteur* differs from that of *Journal du Bonhomme Richard*, which reported victory by 6:15 p.m., according to Merlin de Douai, during its session of 13 vendémiaire; XXVI, no. 16, pp. 127-128, 16 vendémiaire. Zivy describes the combat in some detail, pp. 85-97.

[116] Cavaignac reported to the Convention on the action at Saint Roche. *Moniteur*,

tion on the events of 13 vendémiaire likened the effort of the rebels to those of 31 May and 2 June 1793, thus deliberately confusing the Jacobin-*sans-culottes* insurrection against the Gironde with the royalist attack of 13 vendémiaire. Blaming émigrés and foreigners, the Convention swore never to allow a regime of Robespierre to rise again. The amalgam was complete—those who opposed the Thermidorians were either monarchists or terrorists and, in either case, the two factions were united in their efforts.[117]

The military victory over the insurgents of vendémiaire was followed by a mild coercion against their remnants, in sharp contrast to the repressive measures taken against those of prairial. This was not lost on various observers who contrasted the reaction of the Convention to the two events, some declaring that the rebels of prairial were less guilty than those of vendémiaire because, whereas the former wanted only bread, the latter desired the dissolution of the Convention itself. Despite this fact, the Convention pitied the fate of the vendémiaire rebels more than those of prairial.[118] It arrested commissioners of the section who had been sent to the departments by their general or primary assemblies to rally support for their cause, and dissolved the general staff of the Parisian National Guard as well as the companies of grenadiers and riflemen who had proved unreliable.[119] Military councils began judging those who were unfortunate enough to have been caught in sections Lepeletier, Butte-des-Moulins, and Théâtre-Français. A mere thirty persons were tried in person or in absentia; two were executed, eight acquitted, and the rest fined or imprisoned. A year later the survivors were amnestied.[120] The formula of the surveillance committee of the 7th arrondissement that "agents"

XXVI, no. 16, p. 128, 16 vendémiaire. That the fighting around the Convention was sharp may be seen from the report of the *Journal du Bonhomme Richard* describing the broken glass and debris in the streets. Aulard, *Paris*, II, 304.

[117] *Moniteur*, XXVI, no. 17, pp. 132-133, 17 vendémiaire (9 October), Louvet's report.

[118] Aulard, *Paris*, II, 319, 21 vendémiaire, Year IV (13 October). Zivy, pp. 99-101. "But soon, all was forgotten," wrote Zivy, p. 101.

[119] *Moniteur*, XXVI, no. 17, pp. 134-135, 17 vendémiaire (9 October).

[120] *Ibid.*, no. 21, p. 165, 21 vendémiaire (13 October). A few were condemned to death and only two men were executed, the president of section Théâtre-Français and Lafond, who had commanded the troops of Lepeletier. Zivy, p. 100; Rudé, *The Crowd*, p. 174.

had misled the people in their primary assemblies and had excited them to take up arms was meant to quash deeper probings.[121] Section Droits-de-l'Homme "unanimously" applauded the address of the Convention on the events of the 13th, rapturously affirming that everyone had been "electrified" by it.[122]

On the 10th vendémiaire, when the voting for the electoral assembly had been completed, the *procès-verbal* of section Droits-de-l'Homme confessed that "the number of voters diminishes each day." No further reference appears until 10 brumaire (31 October). By then, of course, the political situation had changed decisively in favor of the Thermidorians. From 10 brumaire until the 15th (31 October to 5 November), the section voted for various officials, with the totals fluctuating from 98 for justice of the peace to 283 for the administrators of the department. By the 15th the electoral process was completed and the section could look forward to implementing the new constitution.[123]

The electors returned by the 7th arrondissement reflected the trend since thermidor of placing men of property and of the liberal professions in positions of power at the expense of the artisans and petty proprietors. Lawyers, men of letters, a health officer, attorneys of the criminal court, journalists, and such well-known figures as Talleyrand, general Pichegru, and a former Constituent, Target, were elected to determine the composition of the government of the Directory.[124] Jacobinism was to revive on rare occasions and for brief periods, but its former influence on the Revolution was over. The *sans-culottes* for whom Varlet spoke in the section had been defeated in prairial. Not until 1830 were their descendants to finish the task begun by the generation that had preceded them.

[121] A.N., F7* 2498, pp. 388-389, 14 vendémiaire.

[122] A.N., C 322, d. 1353, pc. 47, 22 vendémiaire. This was signed by Auzolles as president, reflecting the change that had taken place in the section with the resignation or removal of Grandjean.

[123] B.V.C., MS 120, fol. 169.

[124] B.H.V.P., MS 750, fol. 118, "Elections. Liste de candidats inscrits sur le registre du 7e arrondissement pour les fonctions dont la nomination appartient [*sic*] aux assemblées électorales de l'an 3e." Then follow eighteen names.

Conclusion

The Revolution found an identity within the boundaries of section Droits-de-l'Homme, where it became both tangible and personal. Although residents of the section had more than a formal relationship with the Commune, the development of a sense of intimacy and closeness resulting from long association with neighbors and friends could be nourished only within a narrow precinct. Because of this intimacy, the proclamations or decisions of a local committee impinged directly on the lives of the inhabitants. Proximity developed new loyalties that sometimes clashed with the wider concerns of the capital and the nation. Yet it was this factor that made possible the prompt execution of the laws and decrees issued by the national assemblies and the municipal government of Paris. Above all, it was this loyalty that guaranteed social peace and avoided social warfare.

Nothing illustrates more clearly the emergence of new-found loyalties to the neighborhood than the desperate effort of district Blancs-Manteaux to maintain its integrity. Whatever the logic of its spokesmen's arguments, it is the desire to persist as a unit that strikes the observer most sharply. Undoubtedly, some of this feeling was due to the obvious loss of individual influence that had emerged in 1790. Two years of intense political agitation and controversy had established many a reputation. More important, the psychological security that familiarity with one's neighbors had developed, the tested work of a committee, the bonds established in the general assembly—all would be jeopardized or thrown away with the disappearance of the district. Much of this fear was probably exaggerated, since portions of the district did not vanish, after all, but were integrated into new units. Nevertheless, the traditional loyalties were broken up and new ones had to be developed to sections Roi-de-Sicile and to Enfants-Rouges, a process that took some time to complete.

The signatures to the militia list of 13-14 July 1789 reflect the early commitment to the Revolution of a substantial portion of the male population in district Petit-Saint-Antoine. One-third of its electors and between a fourth and a third of all those who staffed the various committees of the section could be found on this list. Considering the profound political changes experienced by Droits-de-l'Homme, this shows a remarkable consistency in those activists who remained at their posts regardless of the transformations in the section during the period from 1789 to 1795. A partial explanation lies, undoubtedly, in the need to hold on to government employment regardless of the political coloration of this government. Nevertheless, a number of members of the civil and relief committees were not economically dependent on this employment. This core of administrators gave continuity and stability to sectional authorities.

The labor force, as revealed by this list, illustrates the wide distribution of the many occupational and professional groups. Its wide diffusion in the section made for an egalitarian, if not a democratic, expression. Apprentices, journeymen, master workers—all manifested an interest in those political ideas that affected their economic situation. If few bothered to vote, their mass demonstrations during decisive moments in the course of the Revolution were a clear expression of their political involvement, clearer, perhaps, than that expressed by the ballot.

Tax assessments of both real and personal property demonstrate the prevalence of an economic crisis in the section. This in no way denies the political role of tax commissioners as they made their evaluations. Although the appraisal of real estate rose from 1792 to 1793, the number of contributors tended to decline on some of the more important streets. The general tendency during the years 1793-1794 was to impose forced loans and to requisition wealth in support of the Revolution. The trend in section Droits-de-l'Homme was in line with this inclination. A marked decline in the number of inhabitants for the years 1792-1795, as reflected in the census returns, naturally affected the price of houses whether for sale or rent. Their neglect by the principal *locataires* only encouraged this downward slide. Individual properties escaped this trend on some streets, but the overall fall in prices of empty houses and commercial establishments is unmistakable—this, despite the continuing decline of the *assignat*.

Loss of revenue from houses and stalls, together with the growing unemployment caused by the disappearance of whole trades due to emigration of nobles, clergy, and their agents, must have aggravated the crisis. The rise in the price of necessities, together with growing shortages, the uncertainty caused by the war, the disruption of supplies, and the general insecurity must have affected profoundly both the outlook and the personal plight of the *sectionnaires* in Droits-de-l'Homme. If many of them became skeptical of the benefits of free trade and the "law" of supply and demand, it was their desperate economic plight that had changed their outlook. The demand that government intervene in the economic process to help the consumer had a long tradition behind it. The *maximum*, therefore, was an outgrowth of this tradition and a practical response to desperate circumstances.

Although there may be no direct relationship between an economic crisis and its political expression, it is hardly conceivable that in time of revolution it would remain suppressed for long. Directly or indirectly, the economic plight of the section's inhabitants revealed itself in the growing radicalization of its politically active population. The at times violent language of the *sectionnaires* in their motions and resolutions was partially a manifestation of this economic distress. The refusal of some, like Varlet, to believe that such phenomena as the decline of the *assignat*, speculation, and the growing shortages were due to deep economic trends rather than to human malevolence gives further proof of the nature of this crisis. Needless to say, this does not weaken the argument of those who pointed to political policies as a partial cause of economic distress for the great mass of consumers in the section.

Changes in politics brought new men to the fore, but seldom did these purges make a clean sweep of former administrators and committees. The vast majority of sectional leaders had enjoyed long association with the section. The interchangeability of a core of revolutionaries among the committees, commissions, assemblies, and delegations gave an aspect of permanency to the revolutionary institutions of the section. Even after thermidor, men could be found whose origins dated back to the monarchy, and who would remain in office until the advent of the Directory. With the exception of the revolutionary committee, all other organs of power were of an administrative nature. Whatever political role the former enjoyed was strictly limited—despite the exaggerated claims of its enemies. The nature of the central regime, therefore, did not immediately affect the personnel of these committees in section Droits-de-l'Homme. Moreover, the lack of documents revealing the political history of some of these "new" men might account for their sudden appearance in assembly or committee. In short, there was stability in the neighborhood.

For despite the tensions and uncertainties created by the Revolution, a fair degree of order and discipline reigned in the section. Few transitions were so violent and chaotic that they severed completely the roots with the past. The transformation of district Petit-Saint-Antoine and a portion of Blancs-Manteaux into section Roi-de-Sicile was both rapid and smooth. It entailed no violent wrenching, and left no resentments or undying enmities. The assemblies, committees, and officials continued to function without interruption. Those who staffed the local organs of government persisted as before, modified only by the flux and flow of the Revolution. Had the district remained as it had been, it is difficult to see what changes would have resulted on a local level. There was nothing in its structure or in its official instruments of power that would have prevented it from experiencing as a district what it was to undergo as a section. If the history of the latter differed from its predecessor after shedding its original political skin, this was due far more to the rhythm of events than to changes of geography or of internal structure.

The social composition of Droits-de-l'Homme's electoral assembly illustrates this gradualism further. The electors chosen were all men of the legal or liberal professions, with a few merchants to underscore the bourgeois nature of the electoral college. Only after the overthrow of the monarchy were two artisans added to the assembly. Despite this relatively conservative tendency, the section never elected an ecclesiastic. The only consistent trend from 1790 through the election of 1792 that can be noted was the growing youthfulness of the electors. Had elections been held under the Constitution of 1793, the section undoubtedly would have returned its share of artisans and *sans-culottes*. It is true, of course that only three of the eighteen electors chosen previously were returned after 10 August 1792. Nevertheless, the occupational background of those elected hardly varied from that of the men of 1790, despite the presence of Jean Varlet. The three representatives sent to the General Council in 1793—Descombes, Gattrez, and Eude—reflected the same trend: a schoolmaster, an *avocat*, and an artisan turned military. Not one was a *sans-culotte*.

This is equally true of the civil committee. Of the twenty-six names submitted to the General Council in December 1792, the occupation of twenty-one is known. Of these only three were artisans, and it cannot be certain that they did not combine a retail business with

their craft. Although in March 1795 the number of craftsmen increased to four, it is doubtful if any of these were true *sans-culottes*.
The six craftsmen who served on the revolutionary committee in 1793,
on the other hand, made up a much higher percentage of artisans than
those on the civil committee. The trades they represented (wigmak-
ing, jewelry manufacture, catering, shoemaking, upholstering) were
trades that had been hard-hit in the Marais neighborhood. It is not
surprising then that these men sought other means of making a living
and must have been grateful to the government that employed them.
This undoubtedly strengthened their loyalty to the Committee of
General Security at the expense of allegiance to their own section.
After thermidor, the artisan-merchants of the committee in the 7th
arrondissement were even more clearly in evidence.

It is clear that the number of employers and workers generally
believed to have lived in the section must be revised upward. The
addition of 112 men divided among three categories of labor—bakers,
butchers, and shoemakers—raises the total from the 1,031 as given
by Braesch (1,028 according to his figures) to 1,143. How many more
were employed by the master workers among these 112 it is impossible to say. It is obvious, however, that the addition of the above to
the labor force would raise the aggregate population of the section by
some 1,400 individuals, substantially above the 11,000 or even the
12,321 reported by authorities from time to time. Nor do these in-
crements take into consideration the "floaters," all of whom must have
contributed to the turbulence in the section as shortages, lack of work,
and inflated prices unsettled the population. Moreover, it should be
noted that fewer than one-fourth of the employers hired almost two-
thirds of the labor force. It was these men, therefore, coupled with
the merchants, professionals, and civil servants, who possessed the
influence and prestige that property traditionally gives to its owners.
The *sans-culottes* were subordinate to them. So long as the employers
continued to exercise this influence, the politics of the section remained moderate or conservative. It was only when the economic
crisis became linked to military defeats and to political struggles that
this authority was undermined and *sans-culottism* emerged as an independent force.

Spokesmen of Petit-Saint-Antoine and of Roi-de-Sicile, each in turn,
endorsed the principle of the *mandat impératif*. The general assembly

of section Droits-de-l'Homme extended its practice further, but only because the section's social and political composition had changed after 10 August 1792. Defiance of royal authority evinced by the district merely changed into mutiny against Girondin power by its more radical successor. The conviction that government, any government, must express the will of the people embodied in a general or primary assembly was widespread. Representatives to the national assemblies, as delegates to the General Council, were only mandatories or proxies. If they failed to carry out this will the primary assembly assumed the power to replace them. This could be done in the normal course of elections, or, in times of emergency, by special commissioners for a specific purpose in defiance of the duly chosen authorities. Section Droits-de-l'Homme resorted to the latter method more than once in order to express its collective will.

The creation of revolutionary institutions in the section did not guarantee their revolutionary role, however. There was nothing inherent in their structure that prevented them from being used in an opposite manner. A revolutionary committee could be employed to uphold the status quo, so long as the central source of power rested with conservatives. When members of these committees were revolutionary they persecuted not only counterrevolutionaries, but moderates as well. When they were Thermidorian, they struck at former revolutionists. It is conceivable that even a Bonapartist regime could have used nonprofessional surveillance committees for its own ends. The organ itself was neutral—within limits. Obviously, if a Napoleon wished to suppress popular participation in government he had to discourage all institutions not salaried, staffed, and controlled by professional government servants. There are also examples of the employment of democratic principles and slogans for nondemocratic goals. Primary assemblies could overthrow a royalist regime, but, given time and a happy conjunction of forces, they could also overthrow Conventionnels, Thermidorians, or Directorials. After prairial, the *mandat impératif* became a weapon of reaction in the section.

This weapon rested on a consensus of class, but the will of the *sectionnaires* could be expressed in other forms, of course. Even before the fall of the Bastille, the electors of districts Petit-Saint-Antoine and of Blancs-Manteaux showed a surprising unanimity in opposing the agents of the Old Regime. That this opposition had been gathering for some time can be seen in the concerted action of the district assemblies and the universal agreement on the steps that had to be taken to guarantee the success of the Revolution. The bourgeois spokesmen were no less harsh toward their former rulers than the *sans-culottes* were to be toward them in 1793. At the same time, their understanding of the immediate tasks faced by the newly established districts, namely, the creation of a new administration, provision of supplies, and organization of a people's militia illustrates a political sophistication that seems to have arisen out of thin air. This tends to prove that the class as a whole was aware of both the basic problems of its society and the concrete remedies needed to bring about a change.

If the split between moderates and radicals was to some extent a class division, it would be more difficult to demonstrate the class consciousness of each group. Occasionally there appear references to the "egoism" of the rich and their lack of public spirit in contrast to the virtuous *sans-culottes*. These moral terms, however, lack class content. Both groups unhesitatingly invoked patriotism, republicanism, *sans-culottism*, or any other image made sacred by the Revolution. The difference was not in terminology but in concept. Nor does this mean that factional and personal differences never transcended class divisions. The persecution of social or occupational categories undoubtedly embodied class overtones. What is one to say, however, to the abuse of a Descombes or a Varlet? The motivation, in both cases, was political and factional. More conclusive was the persecution by the Thermidorians of former militants. Class divisions might have played a role in this molestation, but party and factional differences seemed to be more important. On the other hand, the sweeping arrests after prairial were clearly of a class nature—in addition to the usual personal harassment. There is no question that former "terrorists" became victims of personal vengeance and ambition, just as in some instances moderates suffered for the same reason. It would be difficult to be precise, therefore, in analyzing the exact proportion of class prejudice, party splits, and personal spite that accounted for divisions between radicals and moderates, Robespierrists and Brissotins, or Jacobins and Thermidorians.

The role of the section in overthrowing the monarchy must be reassessed. It is true, of course, that like others, its assembly wavered and vacillated. Nevertheless, it took the decisive step of sending commissioners to the illegal Commune that organized the insurrection on 9-10 August. This indicates that the democratic faction was willing to commit itself before the battle was joined. The success of the insurrection assured its triumph in the section and its leadership thereafter. Once again, it was the wave of radicalism in the capital—to which this faction had contributed, it should be noted—that determined the ultimate outcome. In short, it is impossible to characterize precisely the political conduct of section Droits-de-l'Homme on the eve of 10 August, if for no other reason than because it was in constant flux.

This is not to say that radicalism was a weak force in section Droits-de-l'Homme. On the contrary, the initiative taken by its general assembly in launching the Evêché committee by late March 1793 and the support it gained from the General Council and other sections testify to the strong radical current expressed by Jean Varlet and other militants. The Girondin supporters in the section were destined to lose the battle for control of the assembly and its committees, but only because the economic and military situation had undermined their position. By May, military defeats and growing shortages convinced the wavering or the indifferent that the policies of the Girondins, especially their championship of free trade and laissez-faire economics, had to be reversed. Nevertheless, it took the militants of six neighboring sections to help engineer the defeat of the moderates in Droits-de-l'Homme on 19-20 May. Once the revolutionary committee was in their hands, however, it became easier for the radicals to maintain control of the section. Their principles now had the official stamp of the government, and only the fall of the Hébertists and the Robespierrists ended their leadership in the section.

Radicalism triumphed on the eve of the 31 May insurrection and was consolidated shortly thereafter. The selection of Jean Varlet to give the signal for the overthrow of the Gironde was its most eloquent expression. If the uprising had the support of the Jacobins and the Montagnards, that is, the future rulers of the nation, this reflected their recognition of the need to involve the *sectionnaires* in support of the Revolution. To gain this support they had to give economic concessions to their representatives in the Evêché and in the General Council. This link between the formal organs of state power and of the insurrectionary committee led by Varlet was exemplified by the adoption of the *maximum*. No one championed more consistently the economic demands of the masses than did the *enragés*, whose general program Varlet shared. His early role in the insurrection, therefore, was an extralegal recognition that a policy of laissez-faire had to give way to a managed economy and a consolidation of power in the Convention and its Great Committees against all manifestations of federalism, economic as well as political.

As to how efficient the *maximum* proved to be in its operations, it is difficult to say. The average individual consumption of bread per day in "normal" times was slightly more than a pound. During more critical moments it fell to as little as 6 ounces. If, as Rudé has demonstrated, the amount consumed by a Parisian worker was 4 pounds, this was as much as an entire family on baker Perreau's list absorbed (4.01 pounds). These figures underscore the desperate situation of the consumer in the section. A few might have benefited by its enactment—the very poor whose wages rose in proportion to the controlled prices. Most were subjected, however, to the inconvenience and frustration of sharing the scarcity around them. The long queues, the continued shortages, the rationing, the suspicion of commercial enterprise—none of these could have made life easier in the section, or, it might be added, could have enhanced the popularity of local authorities forced to execute the law. The *procès-verbal* of the section's police commissioner is sufficient proof of how the *maximum*, essential though it was to ward off famine, embittered traditional relations between retailer and consumer, much as it did between farmer and town dweller.

The revolutionary committee, like the police commissioner, was absorbed in enforcing the regulations of the *maximum*, in addition to investigating suspects. Although guilty of occasional acts of petty tyranny, it seldom went beyond traditional norms of police behavior of the century. After prairial, when former members were arrested and imprisoned, nothing was proven against them except that they had staffed an institution now repudiated by the Thermidorians. The charge that they had supported "the tyranny" that allegedly had prevailed under Robespierre was so vague that neither the civil committee, nor, ultimately, the Committee of General Security was willing to sustain it. The few individuals who brought specific charges against members of the committee could not prove them. One reason for this lay in the correct and legal procedure adopted by the committee; another might have been in the character of the individuals who served on it. The relative independence manifested by its members when they were elected by the general assembly, as may be seen in their agitation for the release of Varlet in the fall of 1793, changed into sycophancy in the case of Descombes' arrest in the spring of 1794. By then, of course, they had become appointees of the Committee of General Security and shared the general fear that the suppression of the Hébertists had brought about. The Terror in the section was now controlled from the outside.

With the exception of the September massacres, neither the Terror nor the reaction against it, was particularly bloody in the section. The fate of prisoners was an unhappy one, as they were condemned by accident of birth or class. On the other hand, there is no instance of deliberate torture beyond the psychological one of not always knowing one's fate—or knowing it all too well. Moreover, it cannot be certain how magnanimous the Thermidorians would have proved without the threat of vendémiaire. Yet, in numerous individual cases, they released their political opponents and allowed them to return to normal life. Even those who were under continued surveillance were permitted to resume their former occupations. The "terrorists" were less tolerant, but their problems were more profound and the threats to the existence of the republic were more immediate.

Nevertheless, this terror was irrational, as it struck down political enemies and friends with equal impartiality. What possible purpose was there in the condemnation and execution of the former justice of the peace, Louis Fayel? He had lost all power and influence long before terror had become the order of the day. More irrational still was the guillotining of Antoine Descombes, whose contribution to the section and, indeed, to the capital itself, was beyond question. Political expediency combined with petty personal antagonism to end his life. Equally irrational was the arrest and imprisonment of Jean Le Roy fils, a young man of intemperate speech. Finally, the persecution of the section's leading *enragé*, Jean Varlet, for opposing the 40-sous subsidy, was out of proportion to the imagined threat to the revolutionary government. It would be difficult to determine how effective this type of action was in driving opposition in the section underground. It seems possible that it made some men more determined to put an end to the government at the first opportunity. Not all had the courage to utter their curses loudly, but many must have sworn silent but deep resolves to avenge their unjust fate.

Jean Varlet had dedicated a brochure (*Plan d'une nouvelle organisation de la Société mère* . . .) to the "respectable indigents," an expression of the change in attitude toward poverty. The latter was now recognized as a social problem, and its relief a social obligation. But the number of poor and destitute in the section must have been far higher than the official figure of 10.3 percent would indicate. If the statement of Viar, the chairman of the section's relief committee, that there was an "immensity of poor," can be taken literally, then the problem faced by the *comité de bienfaisance*, after its establishment in the summer of 1793, must have been insoluble. This is another example of the contradiction between the goals of the Revolution and the pitiful reality of the day.

Although the police commissioner was loyal to his profession, a man like Pierre Auzolles was more than the traditional officer of the law. He was by training and education a member of a liberal profession (being a former teacher); had been elected to several posts by the general assembly, including that of the presidency of the section; was a founding member of the popular society; and had been an elector. Men of his stamp were less open to corruption because they were committed to the principles of the Revolution and valued the esteem of their neighbors. Despite contact with lawbreakers of all sorts, there is no evidence that this experience had hardened his heart. His successful role in ending the riot in La Force without bloodshed, his gentle treatment of Pavas Le Roy fils, and his occasional intervention in favor of the imprisoned—all testify to his basic humanity. There is little question that such a man helped give stability and a sense of security to his neighbors in the section.

The most politically conscious institution in the section was its popular society, the Société populaire républicaine des Droits-de-l'Homme. Although its membership was small and attendance at its meetings no less so, the crisis of ventôse swelled the latter immeasurably, thus testifying to the political awareness of many citizens at critical moments of the Revolution. Its primary function was to defend its neighbors in the section as consumers, either by supervising prices of necessities, or by examining the quality of goods sold. Second in importance was its propaganda role in staging festivals, processions, and parades, in chalking slogans and placarding the walls of public buildings, thus popularizing the decrees and ordinances of the revolutionary government and the Commune. Moreover, the discussions within its premises raised the political levels of both its members and its audiences. In addition, its recommendations of personnel for the civil committee and its initiative in purging the less zealous from the civil service gave it an importance far beyond its small membership.

This positive role was negated, however, by its prosecution of signers of the so-called anticivic petitions and its rigorous exclusion of certain categories of citizens from membership. Such action helped develop an atmosphere of intolerance and zeal in the section—an atmosphere that did not encourage social peace, it might be added. Moreover, its own example of exclusiveness encouraged the arrogance of the youth, which led to the condemnation of the latter by the exasperated assembly and the Convention itself. How much success the society would have enjoyed in politicizing the neighborhood if given another decade to work in an atmosphere of freedom it is difficult to say. The bureaucratic and centralizing tendencies of the revolutionary government ended its existence before it could play out its historic role.

Of the many influences that encouraged a feeling of neighborliness and closeness in the section, none was as powerful as the cult of the *patrie*. The sentiment of sharing a common fate, of suffering the same hardships, of sacrificing for a cause—these profound feelings moulded the *sectionnaires* into a unified body. Of course, neither social classes nor individual differences disappeared, but the impact of a foreign invasion, the internal threat of a federalist uprising, or of counterrevolution in the Vendée, tended to unify the great mass of the section's inhabitants. Religion, however, was a divisive element—whether the dwellers of the section remained Catholic, embraced the new deism of the cult of the Supreme Being, or transformed the churches into temples of Reason. Although there must have been atheists in the neighborhood, they played no visible role. The twin elements of the civic cult—patriotism and deism—might have established firmer roots with time, but like so many other revolutionary developments were ended after thermidor.

The results of thermidor might have been reversed had the insurrection of prairial been successful. The magnitude of this uprising swept away the established authorities and isolated the civil and revolutionary committees in the section. Writs of arrest issued by the Committee of General Security became so much paper, as the local government had no means to enforce them. A number of officers who had remained loyal to the Convention on 9 thermidor were pushed into the ranks of rebels. Higher-grade commanders lost control of the armed forces as the latter began their march on the Convention. For the second time, the cannoneers of section Droits-de-l'Homme broke with the central government: the first time in thermidor, and on a more massive scale in prairial. Had they acted decisively, in concert with their fellows of the artillery in other sections, it is possible that they might have overwhelmed the forces of the Convention.

In revolutionary situations the coefficient of living action is often more important than numbers. This depends, however, on a determined and conscious leadership. Absence of this element doomed the insurrection. Had Varlet, Descombes, and their followers been on the scene and enjoyed the support of substantial numbers of armed men, and were this factor multiplied to include all the radical sections, the uprising of prairial might have succeeded. Without them, the *journée*, powerful as it was, could not triumph.

It is possible that one reason for the more radical behavior of the artillery, in contrast to the infantry, is that the cannoneers were more *sans-culotte* and less petty bourgeois in composition. The nature of *sans-culottism* remains vague and imprecise, however. This is partly due to its amalgam and to the politico-psychological factors involved in the definition. The fact that an employer and his worker considered themselves both to be *sans-culottes*, together with the retailer from whom they bought their groceries, makes it difficult to interpret this social category. In addition to this social reality there is the well-known factor that in times of revolution all men are *sans-culottes*. Despite this, it would be foolhardy to ignore the overwhelming evidence of this phenomenon, embodied in thousands of documents that speak of and to the *sans-culottes*. Equally rash would be to deny the psychology that this term embodied, even if the social reality in terms of class structure remains unclear.

An examination of the leading cadres in the section shows that they were from the middle ranks of society. They were small businessmen, professionals of the lower rung, retailers or modest wholesalers, a few *rentiers*, government employees, and artisans and craftsmen. Without exception they were constitutionalists or moderates in the early days of the district's and section's existence, becoming republican after the overthrow of the king, supporting the Great Committees in their heroic period, then accepting the Convention after thermidor. If they exaggerated the forms and rituals of egalitarianism, this hardly denies the psychological reality of this ideal. Their devotion to patriotism, republicanism, secularism, and egalitarianism gave them a common psychology, if not always a common politics or a common fate. Even if one were to admit the exaggerations of some modern historians as to their nature and political outlook, the belief that they were a class apart during the brief epoch of the Revolution was itself a social reality. This faith inspired them to act in common for well-defined goals of the Revolution—from instituting relief for the less fortunate to demanding price controls. *Sans-culottism* was therefore more than a psychological phenomenon or temporary aberration; it was a powerful social and political reality.

A characteristic that stands out throughout the period under consideration is the relatively high level of political sophistication in both district and section. How often did the national assemblies follow a program originating on a local level? The history of section Droits-de-l'Homme is filled with instances of initiative seized by obscure men sitting in general assembly or popular society, of innovative proposals first broached within its walls. The response of national assemblies to this initiative can be traced in many instances. Nor were all measures adopted by them caused by threats and demonstrations. A number were accepted on their merits alone. In most cases, of course, popular pressure was decisive—until the organs and means of sectional expression were finally curbed.

How did these innovative ideas arise? One can only speculate in tracing their origin. Many, obviously, were born in response to immediate problems of the day. Some evolved from an informal discussion in a café; some grew out of a popular society. Others stemmed from practical administrative tasks of a committee or an official post. Decrees, reports, pronouncements of authorities stimulated unknown individuals. A few, like Varlet, might have thought out the implication or necessity of certain actions in the quiet of their rooms. So long as there was popular ferment and discussion, there was no end of possibilities for ideas to arise in a local club or assembly.

It is difficult to say how committed sectional leaders were to conflicting political principles. That there was a sharp reaction to royalism in section Roi-de-Sicile may be seen in the role of militants on the eve of 10 August. Less than a year later they struck against the moderates or those considered to be such. Yet in the sharp struggle between the government and the Hébertists, there appears little to indicate their position. Descombes was linked to them only by judicial action, but whether and to what extent he shared their views remains obscure. That these leaders were patriots and republicans seems clear. The progress or retrogresssion of the Revolution modified or altered their earlier ideology. Nevertheless, the men who staffed the administrative agencies of the section were not mere time servers. If they did not always reflect accurately the politics of the section, at least they refracted them. Their early histories prove their devotion to the ideals of the Revolution.

This devotion was tested especially in the great *journées*. Nothing illustrates the elemental power of an aroused section more clearly than a spontaneous or directed outpouring of its inhabitants. It was then that its officials proved helpless to impose traditional controls. This was doubly true during the dramatic conflicts of thermidor and prairial. Despite this, a majority of the *hommes en place* remained true to their oath, acting as agents of higher authorities. Even the revolutionary committee became less than its name implied and more legalistic. This legal formalism was partly due to the salaried post per se and partly to faith in the national assemblies and their committees. Recognition of this conservative and inhibitive factor forced militants to launch periodic campaigns to bypass the regularly constituted authorities by sending commissioners to the assemblies of the Evêché. The organization of such committees assured victory of a particular *journée*. Its absence doomed to defeat any uprising, even a powerful one like that of prairial.

Devotion to revolutionary ideals did not mean that the humble dwellers of the section ceased going about their business of earning a living, enjoying their simple pleasures with family and friends, or doing what they had always done, revolution or no revolution. It would be a mistake, however, to deny the impact of the Revolution on their daily lives. Civic or ration cards to be obtained or renewed, a son or father to be seen off to the front, guard duty to perform, a parade or procession to join or to cheer, a wall placard or journal to read—these and a dozen such manifestations of the profound upheaval all around them could not insulate them from politics, much as they might have liked to ignore public developments at the expense of their private lives. If they failed to attend meetings of their assembly or abstained from casting their votes, this does not mean that they were uninvolved in public affairs. The reality of the Revolution was everywhere whether they willed it or not.

Life continued, but it no longer was the old life. Even the more obtuse would have noted the profound changes made by the Revolution. Although its slogans clashed with reality, their daily repetition, their persistent presence, their repudiation of the old, were bound to transform the psychology of the *sectionnaires* of Droits-de-l'Homme. Just as the ordinary life of an individual is sanctified in theology, so the daily life of the section's inhabitants was touched by the Revolution. For a short time "the bottom rail was on top"—or was thought to have been. The expectation of something different, of a new society, must have been a powerful psychological presence.

It woud be instructive to learn the ultimate fate of the leading *sectionnaires* of Droits-de-l'Homme. How did they fare under Napoleon? and under the Restoration? Did any reappear in the overthrow of Charles X? Like the mass of the population, they were forced to surrender their political experience gained during the Revolution. Undoubtedly politics was closed to them after vendémiaire. Yet, one wonders, how many movements, institutions, societies, and ideas were fructified by them because of their never-to-be-forgotten political and administrative experience? If politics was closed to them, other means of collective expression were open. Some, surely, must have enriched their lives; others equally, were enriched by them. Seven years of revolutionary experience could hardly have disappeared from history. For them, at least, the Revolution was no myth.

Bibliography

The bibliography that follows is select rather than complete; only the most significant references are listed. Individual documents, brochures, and folios are included, of course, in the footnotes. The collections are organized under the various archives and libraries after which individual references to published works are given in the two broad divisions, namely, primary sources and secondary sources.

Research on the origin and development of the sections may be greatly facilitated by consulting Albert Soboul, *Les Papiers des sections de Paris (1790-An IV) répertoire sommaire* (Paris: Maurice Lavergne, 1950). Individual catalogues and inventories in the possession of the archives and libraries listed herein are indispensable for an examination of manuscript sources. The most important of these are listed with a description of specific series or collections. For published sources, mostly in the Bibliothèque nationale, Maurice Tourneux, *Bibliographie de l'histoire de Paris pendant la Révolution française*, 5 vols. (Paris: Ville de Paris, 1890-1913), is essential.

ARCHIVES NATIONALES (MANUSCRIPTS)

A brief but practical guide to the National Archives may be purchased for a nominal sum, prepared by André Chamson, director general, entitled *Guide du lecteur* ([Paris]: Imprimerie Nationale [Ministère d'état/Affaires culturelles], 1966), 39 pp. The most important inventories and guides may be found readily in this source. *L'Etat des inventaires des Archives nationales* . . . (1937), together with a *supplément* that lists the holdings to 1955, may be consulted. In addition to these are such well-known published sources as Pierre Caron's *Manuel pratique pour l'étude de la Révolution française* (Paris: A. et J. Picard, 1912, 1947), and Alexandre Tuetey, *Répertoire général des sources manuscrits de l'histoire de Paris pendant la Révolution française*, 11 vols. (Paris: Imprimerie Nouvelle, 1890-1914).

Collection by Series

Série B, elections. The following proved useful: B I, 1 and 2, which give the names of electors and the number of active citizens participating; B II, 23 deals with the vote on the Constitution of the Year II; B II, 61 gives the totals and their divisions for the Constitution of the Year III. See Henri Forgeot, *Répertoire numerique, 1894, registre manuscrit*, no. 537 of *L'Etat des inventaires des Archives nationales* . . .

Série C, procès-verbaux, reports, motions, discussions, letters of representatives-on-mission, etc., of the national assemblies. Many cartons contain petitions of sections and popular societies and present a clear picture of the political situation of a particular period. The following were especially valuable: C 156, 304; C 161, 350; C 161, 351; C 233, pl. 190; C 256, pl. 488-489, 46 pcs., of letters and petitions of popular societies; C 261, pl. 564-570, 37 pcs. of addresses and letters of various communes and districts supporting the Convention after the insurrection of 31 May-2 June, 1793; C 262, pl. 578, pc. 27, section Droits-de-l'Homme's letter of support for the Convention, 14 July, Year II; C 271, pl. 665, 36 pcs., letters of support for the Convention; C 275, pl. 703-712, same; C 280, pl. 769, pcs. 39-63, petition of section Observatoire for payment of salaries to civil committees; C 355, pl. 1859-1871, contain the papers of sections deposited with the Commission des douze. See Alexandre Tuetey, *Les Papiers des assemblées de la Révolution aux Archives nationales, inventaire de la série C (constituante, législative, convention)*, (Paris: Société de l'histoire de la Révolution française, 1908).

Série D, contain correspondence of the Committee of Legislation of the Convention with the civil committee of section Droits-de-l'Homme, resignations and promotions to various official posts, and petitions dealing with jobs. Correspondence of Commissions of the Administrations civiles, police, et tribunaux, and replies of civil committees are contained in this series. The following proved valuable: D III, 231, seeking positions; D III, 239 give descriptions by the civil committee of individuals proposed for various posts; D III, 251-252, individual petitions; D III, 254, various matters in connection with the justice of the peace of the section; D III, 255-256¹, correspondence between the Administration civiles, police, et tribunaux with the civil committee, D III, 256³, correspondence with the Comité de législation of the Convention on jobs, resignations, civic cards, etc.; D III, 324, various legal questions; D IVbis 13 contain plans for the conversion of districts Petit-Saint-Antoine and Blancs-Manteaux into section Roi-de-Sicile.

Série F⁷ are the police dossiers dealing with arrests, detentions, and interrogations of individuals. See Pierre Caron, *Les Fonds du Comité de sûreté générale* (AF II*, F⁷, DXLIII) (Paris, 1954). The *procès-verbal* of the revolutionary committee of section Droits-de-l'Homme is in cartons F⁷* 2497 and 2498. The alphabetical series runs from F⁷ 4577 to 4775[53]. The following individual dossiers were consulted:

Name	F⁷ Carton	Dossier
Auzolles, Pierre	4583	5
Barré	4587	5
Bergeret	4595	2
Bernard, Anne Catherine Henriette	4595	5
Beudelot	4597	8
Bonneville, François	4608	2
Carnonkel	4633	4
Carron, Jean Pierre	4634	3
Caval (with Chartrain and Monneuse)	4774[60]	4
Charbonnier, Jean	4639	3
Chemitte (Chemite) Antoine Arnault	4645	2
Cordier	4653	4
Courchant (also Courchamp)	4655	3
Dariancourt	4661	3
Dariencourt	4684	3
Decomble, Henry Edme	4665	2
Décourchant, Etienne	4665	2
Descombes, Antoine Ignace François	4672	1
Diversin	4677	5
Donnon (Donon), Christophe Ambroise	4679	2
Donzel	4679	2
Duchosal, Etienne Pierre	4684	3
Duclos, Pierre François Marie	4684	3
Eude, Jean Louis	4684	3
Fyel, Louis Gille Camille	4704	1
Fayölle (or Fayolles)	4704	1
Fouque, Toussaint	4710	4

Name	F^7 Carton	Dossier
Fournier (l'Américain)	(4711)	2
	6504	
Gamain, François	4715	2
Gervais, Eugène Honoré	4723	2
Giboy, Joseph	4725	1
Giroux	4726	5
Guéneau	4734	5
Hardy, Philippe	4739	1
Houdaille, Louis	4745	1
Jacob, Pierre	4748	2
Joly	4750	4
Lambin, Jean Jacques	4761	4
Lambin, Louis Marie	4761	4
Larivierre, S. N.	4765	4
Leclerc, Etienne Pierre	4774^9	1
Lelievre	4774^{14}	5
Lenfant, Jean Baptiste Pierre	4774^{17}	1
Leroy, Pavas, père et fils	4774^{19}	4
Maillet, François	4774^{30}	3
Martin, Jean Baptiste	4774^{37}	1
Mazin, Jean Baptiste	4774^{45}	2
Mercier, Jean Louis	4774^{42}	4
Michel, André	4774^{45}	2
Millet, Jean François	4774^{46}	4
Oudart, Nicolas	4774^{60}	2
Perrin, Jean Michel	4774^{68}	3
Picard, Amable Antoine	4774^{72}	4
Pinet, Philippe Denis	4774^{75}	5
Pommez (Pommer)	4774^{78}	6
Ponsard, Jean	4774^{79}	2
Poupart, François	4774^{81}	4
Roger, Antoine Simpsonien	4774^{97}	1
Sallier, Guy Marie	4775^{12}	4
Saulnier	4775^{14}	1
Sonnois	4684	3
	(D. Duclos)	
Soubiran	4408	2

Name	F^7 Carton	Dossier
Tamponnet	4775^{24}	4
Temponnet	4775^{26}	2
Thiébart, Adrien Désiré	4775^{28}	2
Vallée, Louis Nicolas	4775^{38}	2
Varlet, Jean François	4775^{40}	2
	6586	(no separate dossier)

F^7 *7353*, fol. 9486; and *7402*[b], fol. 3960, on *cercles constitutionnelles*

F^7 *3688*[2] and *3688*[3], police observers; *3688*[4], census

F^{1b} *11 Seine 18*, correspondence of civil committee with Administrations civiles, police, et tribunaux

F^{1c} *III, Seine 13* and *27*, observations of police, letters to minister of interior, various papers of Paris Commune, and personal observations on political state of Paris

F^{7*} *699*, characterizations of former so-called terrorists by the Committee of General Security for information of local authorities

F^{11} *202, 205, and 218*, on state of subsistences in Year II; F^{11} *1181* is especially rich on the subject of feeding the poor, their letters for help, and amounts spent on their aid

F^{15} *133, Comité de bienfaisance* of section Droits-de-l'Homme

F^{20} *123, 255, 381*, contain statistics and census of the section

F^{30} *145*, list of workers and employers in section for 1790-1792

Série T. séquestre, T 724, papers seized from François Dupaumier

Série W, Military Commission of the Revolutionary Tribunal. W 546, on events of prairial, Year III; 94, on Descombes's role in Provins, W 79, civil committee's report on conflict with cannoneers, thermidor 9-10; W 302, d. 341, interrogation of Fayel

Série BB, deposits in the Ministry of Justice. See *Etat des versements faits aux Archives nationales* . . . , vol. IV, with an Introduction by Georges Bourgin (Paris, 1947). BB[3] 73, various items from sections and department of Paris on supplies; BB[3] 80, is the carton which deals with the insurrection of 31 May-2 June 1793; BB[3] 83, on organization of revolutionary committee of sections; BB[30] 17, on the events of 20 June 1792; 18, also on the same event and on criminal activity before and after 10 August 1792

Série AF, Secretaries of State (secrétairerie d'état). AF II* 286, 289, 292, arrest and release of Varlet; AF II, 47, events of 9 thermidor as reported by revolutionary committees and commanding officers; AF III, 260, d. 1073 on *cercle constitutionnelle* of 7th arrondissement; AF IV, 1470, the abortive coup of 9-10 March 1793

Série Q², 207, contains register of the national estates in the section

Série H 2121, carton is marked Police de Paris, and contains documents on the poor of the city

N II Seine 235, map of Parisian sections

Published Sources in Archives Nationales

Série AD I—ADXVII (collection Rondonneau); especially valuable were the printed sources in AD XVI, 70.

Série T 604², Liasse Aᵉ B, Chaumette, "Mémoires de Chaumette sur la révolutions du 31 mai."

ARCHIVES DE PARIS

A description of the collection in the Archives de Paris (formerly Archives de la Seine) may be found in *Archives du Département de la Seine et de la Ville de Paris; Inventaire sommaire des documents de 1889 à 1928* (Séries 1 à 4 AZ), edited by Marius Barroux (Paris, 1935). In addition to individual documents dealing with districts and sections, there are important brochures, addresses, reports, and lists of committee members in these archives. Of special value were *série 1 AZ 138*, beginnings of district political life, regulations of the municipal government, and brochures on proposals to reorganize the capital into sections; *série 1 AZ 145*, provisions, ordinances, reports of the mayor and the General Council; *série 1 AZ 159²*, armed force and its regulations; the *procès-verbal* of the revolutionary committee when it was reorganized on 20 May 1793; *série 3 AZ 287*, the register of orders for sugar, documents permitting the dissolution of a religious house in the section, and list of the *jardins de luxe*; and *série 4 AZ 53*, inventory of flour; *101*, offers of hospitality to lodge visitors on the anniversary of the overthrow of the monarchy; *356*, list of cobblers, many documents of the civil committee and its personnel; *813*, the report on events of 14 July 1789; and *1233*, names of civil committee members in December 1792.

The work of justices of the peace of section Droits-de-l'Homme is in D 7U¹ 33. Registers of property held, its sale and acquisition, the amount of taxes paid on real and personal property, tables of heirs, the deceased, and of verification are in the following references: D 4L¹ 37 and 38; D Q⁷ 1.761; D Q⁸ 47, 48, 126, and 282.

Note that *série 1 to 4 AZ* contains published materials, especially decrees and ordinances of the Paris Commune, individual brochures, and summaries from the *procès-verbaux* of general assemblies of districts and sections.

Archives de la Préfecture de Police

The valuable holdings that survived the fire of 1871 are described by Henri Malo, in a catalogue entitled *Inventaire sommaire des archives de la préfecture de police; Archives historiques série A A/*, cartons 1-445. Carton A A/136 is the collection on section Droits-de-l'Homme. Folios (termed numbers in the collection), 1 to 149 embrace 1792 to the Year II; folios 150 to 252 include the Years III and IV; folios 253 to 394 are for the Years V-VIII. A A/265, pièce 86 contains two documents on the section. A A/34 for 1-22 thermidor, Year II (19 July to 9 August 1794), pièces 1-290 is a collection on those arrested and released that is part of the larger collection, A A/9-A A/47, *Mises en arrestation, mises en liberté*. Unfortunately, the name of the section seldom appears with the individual arrested or released. The jail book for La Force prison is under A B/326-329. The *table analytique*, which is alphabetized, contains an error in the inventory for Pierre Auzolles, p. 461. This *table* is, of course, timesaving for the researcher.

Bibliothèque Nationale

The following two catalogues are indispensable: Marius Sepet, *Catalogue sommaire des ouvrages et documents relatifs à la période contemporaine*, vol. II, *Manuscrit*, 1891, pp. 193-208; and Henri Ormont, *Catalogue des manuscrits français de la Bibliothèque nationale*, vol. I, Paris, 1899, nos. 1-3060. The collection under Nouvelle acquisition française, 2638-

2718, is especially rich. The following references were especially useful: *2647*, resolutions and addresses of the General Council for 1793; *2680*, on districts Petit-Saint-Antoine and Blancs-Manteaux; *2681*, district Blancs-Manteaux; *2687*, opposition of the sections to the two-thirds decree in 1795; *2691*, events and resolutions in section Roi-de-Sicile after the fall of Louis, organization of the Evêché assembly in April 1793 against the Girondins, list of jurors in the section, correspondence with General Council, and miscellaneous documents; scattered references in *2644, 2654, 2659, 2665, 2684, 2705, 2715,* and *2716.*

Published Sources

Lb³⁹ 4211. *Refutation des principes exposés par M. le Maire de Paris.* . . . [1790]. 19 pp.

7837. *Tres-sérieuses Observations sur la mauvaise organisation de la Garde nationale-parisienne . . . par Coque (soldat-citoyen du district St. Germain-l'Auxerrois).* 15 September 1789. 58 pp.

9715. *Discours prononcés a l'assemblée electorale.* 1791. 284 pp.

Lb⁴⁰ 15. *Motifs des commissaires, pour adopter le plan de municipalité . . . par J.-P. Brissot de Warville.* 20 August 1789. 71 pp.

28. *Adresse de l'Assemblée-gén'e des représentans de la Commune de Paris.* . . . 10 October 1789. 4 pp.

36. *Assemblée des représentans de la Commune de Paris.* 14 November 1789. 3 pp.

36. *Section des Droits-de-l'Homme . . .* [a poster]. 2 vendémiaire, an IV.

233. *Arrêté du district des Blancs-Manteaux.* 29 August 1788. 6 pp.

234. *Extrait des registres des délibérations du district des Blancs-Manteaux.* . . . 30 July 1789. 14 pp.

235. *Discours prononcé dans l'église des Blancs-Manteaux.* . . . 12 September 1789. 23 pp.

295. *Adresse à M. Bailly.* 21 July 1789.

296. *Adresse à M. de La Fayette.* 21 July 1789.

297. *Extrait des délibérations du district des Petits-Augustins.* 6 August 1789. 3 pp.

437. *Adresse des parisiens, à la Convention nationale.* [1795]. 8 pp.

638. *Discours sur l'utilité des sociétés populaires* . . . *J.-P. Brissot.* 28 September 1791. 23 pp.

1226. (No title; catalogued as Lettre circulaire aux présidents des sections . . .). 4 June 1790.

1344. (*Blancs-Manteaux,* oath to defend Constitution, etc.). 5 February 1790.

1413. *District des Jacobins Saint-Dominique.* . . . 16 November 1789. 34 pp.

1488. *Petit-Saint-Antoine; extrait des registres.* . . . 13 August 1789. 8 pp.

1489. *Extrait des délibérations.* . . . 20 August 1789.

1489*. *Extrait des délibérations.* . . . 7 October 1789.

1706. *Liberté, égalité. Section de l'Arsenal.* . . . 20 ventôse, an III. 7 pp.

1790. *Extrait du registre.* . . . 20 December, Year I [1792]. 3 pp.

1791. *Section des Droits-de-l'Homme.* 2 February 1793. 4 pp.

1792. *Section des Droits-de-l'Homme.* 4 April, Year II. 4 pp.

1793. *Section des Droits-de-l'Homme* [circular]. N.p., n.d. 1 p.

1794. *Section des Droits-de-l'Homme.* [Billet de citoyen admissible à voter aux assemblées].

1795. *Adresse de la section des Droits-de-l'Homme.* . . . N.d. 4 pp.
1796 and 1796 A.
Adresse presentée à la Convention nat'le. . . . 30 September 1792. 4 pp.

1797. *Adresse à la Convention nationale.* 27 November 1792. 4 pp.

1798. *Réflexions sur la justice de paix.* . . . 1792. 4 pp.

1799. *Liberté, égalité* [a certificate for work on the harvest]. An II.

1892*. *Extrait du registre* . . . *de la section des Invalides* [a placard]. 8 May 1793.

1945. *Section de la Maison commune.* . . . 27 July 1793. 4 pp.

1993. *Arrêté de la section du Muséum.* 30 thermidor, an II. 7 pp.

2104. (Réserve) [certificate for service in Garde nationale].

2105. *Adresse de la section du Roi-de-Sicile.* . . . N.d. 3 pp.

2273. *Société des Amis de la constitution* . . . *par Pétion.* 8 July 1792. 2 pp.

2343. *Règlement de la Société des amis de la liberté.* . . . N.d. 15 pp.

2345. *Société des amis de la liberté et d'égalité.* 2e sans-culottide, an. 7 pp.

2346. *Extrait du registre des délibérations.* . . . 17 February 1791. 15 pp.

** 2359. *Du Cercle constitutionnel et des clubs en général.* N.d. 7 pp.

2363. *Résumé des travaux du cercle constitutionnel.* 8 ventôse, an VI. 16 pp.

2364. *Règlement de police intérieur.* . . . N.d. 4 pp.

** 2365. *Discours prononcé par le régulateur du cercle constitutionnel.* . . . 2 pluviôse, an VI. 8 pp.

2371. *Monsieur.* . . . N.d. 1 p.

2372. *Pétition à la convention nationale.* . . . 13 September 1793. 4 pp.

2373. *Règlement du comité central.* . . . 29 vendémiaire, an II. 8 pp.

2393. *Règlemens de la Société des l'harmonie sociale.* . . . N.d. 8 pp.

2394. *La Société des hommes libres.* . . . 2 October, an II. 1 p.

2396. *Pétition* . . . *de la Société des hommes révolutionnaires du 10 août, séante rue Saint-Denis.* . . . 15 July 1793. 1 p.

2397. *Deuxième rapport à la Société des hommes révolutionnaires.* . . . 18 October 1793. 8 pp.

2398. *Adresse de la Société des indigens.* . . . N.d. 4 pp.

2410. *Aux Montagnards.* . . . 20 frimaire, an II. 4 pp.

2411. *Discours prononcé à la Société républicaines révolutionnaires.* . . . N.d. 6 pp.

2413. *Prospectus.* . . . N.d. 4 pp.

2414. *Exposition patriotique du premier article.* . . . N.d. 8 pp.

2416. *Discours, imprimé par ordre de la Société fraternelle.* . . . November 1790. 14 pp.

2418. *Extrait des délibérations.* . . . 4 December, an III. 15 pp.

2428. *Les Membres composant la Société populaire du club.* . . . 7 ventôse, an II. 16 pp.

2429. *Société populaire séante en la salle électorale.* N.d. 14 pp.

2432. *Discours sur l'aristocratie mercantile.* 27 pluviôse, an II. 7 pp.

2433. *Discours philosophique.* 11 pluviôse, an II. 14 pp.

2434. *Société populaire de Brutus.* 24 brumaire, an II. 4 pp.

2435. *Section de Brutus.* . . . 30 germinal, an II. 7 pp.

2436. *Liberté aux abois.* . . . [a placard]. 25 May 1793.

2437. *Aux Patriotes âmes sensibles* . . . [a placard]. N.d.

2438. *Discours prononcé par le C. Camus.* . . . 11 ventôse, an II. 6 pp.

2439. *Organisation règlementaire de la Société de la fraternité.* 10 July 1790. 8 pp.

2440. *Projet de règlement pour la Société des gardes-françaises.* 24 September 1793. 15 pp.

2441. *Règlement.* . . . 1790. 11 pp.

2442. *Discours prononcé à l'ouverture du Club patriotique.* . . . N.d. 4 pp.

2443. *Règlement.* . . . Illegible date. 20 pp.

2444. *Règlement de la Société fraternelle.* . . . An II. 15 pp.

2445. *Projets de statuts.* . . . 28 January 1792. 16 pp.

2446. *Discours prononcé à la Société.* . . . 6 March 1792. 10 pp.

2448. *Adresse au peuple.* . . . 18 December 1792. 8 pp.

2449. *Règlement de la Société.* . . . 19 February 1793. 16 pp.

2451. *La Société patriotique* . . . [a placard]. 8 May 1793.

2452. *Extrait des procès-verbaux.* . . . 8 August [1793]. 8 pp.

2453. *Discours prononcé par le citoyen Darman Maison-Neuve.* 14 April 1792. 7 pp.

2454. *Règlement de la Société patriotique.* 19 June 1792. 8 pp.

2455. *Fête civique en l'honneur de Lepeletier.* . . . 1 frimaire, an II. 12 pp.

2456. *Guerre aux intrigans.* . . . 1 ventôse [an II]. 8 pp.

2457. *Société fraternelle des deux-sexes* . . . [a placard]. N.d.

2458. *Société populaire de la section des Piques.* . . . 22 pluviôse, an II. 23 pp.

2459. *Le Culte des arbres.* . . . 4 ventôse [an II]. 14 pp.

2460. *Règlement de la Société patriotique de Sainte-Genéviève.* 16 December 1790. 7 pp.

2461. *Société fraternelle des sans-culottes.* 24 brumaire, an II. 8 pp.

2462. *Société fraternelle des sans-culottes.* 27 ventôse [an II]. 4 pp.

2463. *Règlement de la Société populaire et rep'ne de l'unité.* 26 September, an II. 15 pp.

2464. *Discours prononcé à la Société populaire.* . . . N.d. 7pp.

2465. *Règlement de la Société des vertus républicaines.* . . . 4 germinal, an II. 18 pp.

2466. *Règlement pour la Société des zélés défenseurs de la constitution.* N.d. 6 pp.

3246. *Adresse de la section du Roi-de-Sicile.* . . . [August 1792]. 1 p.

3334. *Rapports des commissaires des quarante-huit sections.* . . . 1 August 1793. 10 pp.

Lb^{41} 201. *Donnez-nous du pain, ou égorgez-nous!* N.d. 7 pp.

715. *Bergoeing; député du département de la Gironde.* . . . Caen, 1793. 44 pp.

1191. *Tableau de la formation des douze comités révolutionnaires de Paris.* 2e jour sans-culottide, an II. 18 September 1794. 7 pp.

1328. *Cambon plaidant la cause des 73 collègues détenus.* . . . 13 vendémiaire, an III. 8 pp.

1476. *Mémoire justicatif de la conduite de la compagnie des canonniers.* . . . brumaire, an III. 11 pp.

2886. *Le Dernier cri des sans-culottes.* . . . N.d. 8 pp.

Lb^{42} 232. *Copie des pièces saisis dans le local que Babeuf occupait lors de son arrestation.* Paris: Imprimerie nationale, frimaire-nivôse, an V (1796).

Lc^{38} 2444. *Adresse de la section armée des Droits-de-l'Homme.* . . . 27 April 1793. 4 pp.

$**Le^{23}$127. *Remontrance de Messieurs les Electeurs.* . . . N.d. 4 pp.

Le^{29} 257. *Adresse repésentans de la Commune.* . . . 10 October 1789. 6 pp.

Le 36. *Assemblée primaire* . . . [a poster]. 22 fructidor, an III.

Ln^{27} 5894. *Descombes, électeur, membre du Conseil général.* . . . N.d. 16 pp.

BIBLIOTHÈQUE HISTORIQUE DE LA VILLE DE PARIS

The manuscript collection in this library is rich in reference to section Droits-de-l'Homme. These are numbered from MS 741 through MS 814. The most useful were the following collections: MS 742 includes documents with the food crisis in district Petit-Saint-Antoine, individual letters, problems of administration, and a valuable list of voters with their occupations in the district. MS 748 is especially profitable as it contains the *procès-verbaux* of the sectional assembly, examples of civic, residency, and ration cards; there are many extracts from the minutes of the civil committee and its correspondence on various matters; several printed forms of the revolutionary committee; communications from the Commune; problems of engrossment and of relief; and scattered minutes of the section's popular society.

MS 750 deals with elections and relief, mostly for the Year III and beyond, in the 7th arrondissement. MS 754 contains certificates of relief by the *comité de bienfaisance* and requests by individuals for pensions; MS 763, juries; MS 768, documents on the problem of shortages and provisions from 1789 to the Year IV—most of these are records of the civil committee. MS 769 is valuable for the problem of shortages and subsistences. The names of bakers in the section are in this collection. MS 770 has certificates and letters dealing with relief, pensions, public works, petitions, etc. Most deal with relief or economic assistance. MS 798 has documents on efforts of veterans to obtain pensions or jobs. MS 799 (Collection Etienne Charavay—Commune and department) has documents on the early period of the Revolution dealing with shortages.

MS 800 (Collection Etienne Charavay—districts) is especially useful for administrative and military matters in the summer and early fall of 1789. MS 806 (Collection Etienne Charavay—assemblées primaires), contains *procès-verbaux* of primary assemblies and some valuable documents on the events of 20 June 1792. MS 807 contains the reply of the civil committee on the section's popular society. MS 808 (Collection Etienne Charavay) has the resolution of the General Council condemning Varlet's attempted coup in March 1793.

Published Materials

The collection under the *côte* 104.095 has diverse addresses, petitions, decrees, brochures, and resolutions on multiple subjects. The defense of Varlet by an anonymous orator of the section's popular society, for example, is in this compilation. 100.64 is a collection of fourteen pamphlets entitled "Faubourgs" reflecting the growing radicalization of faubourgs Saint-Antoine and Saint-Marceau, from 1790 to 1793. *Côte* 100.65 is a collection of twenty-three brochures ranging from plans for converting districts to sections to military regulations for their battalions. Varlet's brochure, *Projet d'un mandat spécial . . .* is in 900.380; the petition of the young men of section Droits-de-l'Homme on the draft is in 952.361; Carra's memoirs on the secret directory which supposedly staged the insurrection against the monarchy is in 959.751.

Bibliothèque Victor Cousin

See Paul Deschamps, *Catalogue général des manuscrits des bibliothèques publiques de France, Université de Paris et universités des départements* (Paris, 1918). Barthélemy Saint Hilaire collected important documents on the Revolution in MSS 117-119. MS 117 has fragments of registers of general assemblies of various sections from 1792 to 1795. MS 118 contains other fragments from the same registers. (There is nothing on section Droits-de-l'Homme in either MS.) MS 119 has forty-six *pièces* from registers of the sections, including extracts of discussions on the dissolution of sectional societies. The most valuable and indispensable manuscript compiled by Saint Hilaire is MS 120, which contains summaries of proceedings in the assemblies of the sections. Section Droits-de-l'Homme's record is especially rich, with Jean Varlet's activities recorded in some detail. Resolutions, disputes, number voting—in short, the almost daily concerns of the section—may be found in this collection.

The British Museum

In addition to copies of Varlet's brochures, the British Museum has a number of publications dealing with district Petit-Saint-Antoine and section Droits-de-l'Homme. Folio Tab. 580.a.2 is entitled *A Collection of 520 Broadsides . . . 1787-1813* (5 vols.), where a number of pamphlets dealing with a wide variety of topics may be found.

Archives de la Loire-Atlantique

These archives have a number of references to Varlet, as under 1-M-64-65, *Liste électorale de 1831*, 2e arrondissement électoral (4e, 5e, 6e cantons de la ville de Nantes).

The John Rylands Library (Manchester)

In the collection marked French Historical Tracts is a copy of the constitution of the popular society of section Droits-de-l'Homme, which does not seem to exist in either the Bibliothèque nationale or in the British Museum. It is entitled *Règlement adopté par la Société populaire de la section des Droits-de-l'Homme* (Paris: de l'Imprimerie de Mayer, 24 September 1793), 9 pp.

Primary Sources (published)

Almanach de Paris. Paris: Lesclapart, 1789.

Almanach national. Paris: Cuchet, 1790.

Almanach royal. Année commune M. DCC.XCI. Edited by Laurent d'Houry. Paris: Imprimerie de la Veuve d'Houry, 1791.

Aulard, F. A., ed. *Paris pendant la réaction thermidorienne et sous le directoire*. 5 vols. Paris: Librairie Léopold Cerf; Librairie Noblet, 1898-1902.

————. *Recueil des actes du Comité de salut public avec la correspondance officielle des représentans en mission et le registre du conseil executive provisoire*. 28 vols. Paris: Imprimerie Nationale, 1889-1951.

————. *La Société des Jacobins, recueil de documents pour l'histoire du Club des Jacobins de Paris*. 6 vols. Paris: Librairie Léopold Cerf; Librairie Noblet, 1889-1897.

Bailly. *Mémoires de Bailly*. Edited by Saint-Albin Berville and Jean-François Barrière, 3 vols. Paris: Baudouin Fils, 1821-1822. In *Collection des mémoires relatifs à la Révolution française*. 56 vols. Paris, 1820-1828.

Bloch, Camille, and Alexandre Tuetey, eds. *Procès-verbaux et rapports du Comité de mendicité de la constituante 1790-1791*. Paris: Imprimerie Nationale, 1911.

Braesch, F., ed. *Procès-verbaux de l'assemblée générale de la section des Postes, 4 décembre 1790—5 septembre 1792*. Paris: Librairie Hachette, 1911.

Buchez, P.J.B., and P. C. Roux, eds. *Histoire parlementaire de la Révolution française*. 40 vols. Paris: Paulin, Libraire, 1834-1838.

Calvet, Henri. *L'Accaparement à Paris sous la Terreur; essai sur l'application de la loi du 26 juillet 1793*. Paris: Imprimerie Nationale, 1933. Commission de recherche et de publication des documents relatifs à la vie économique de la Révolution, mémoires et documents.

Caron, Pierre. *Le Commerce des céréals*. Paris: Imprimerie Nationale, 1907. Commission de recherche et de publication des documents relatifs à la vie économique de la Révolution. Edited by Ernest Leroux. Paris: Imprimerie Nationale, 1912.

———. *Paris pendant le Terreur; rapports des agents secrets du ministre de l'intérieur*. 6 vols. Paris: Librairie Alphonse Picard et Fils, 1910-1964.

———. *Tableau de dépréciation du papier-monnaie*. Paris: Imprimerie Nationale, 1909. Commission de recherche et de publication des documents relatifs à la vie économique de la Révolution. Edited by Ernest Leroux.

Charavay, Etienne, ed. *Assemblée électorale de Paris 18 novembre 1790– 15 juin 1791 par Etienne Charavay*. 3 vols. Paris: Maison Quantin, 1890.

Charavay, Jacques, ed. *Catalogue d'une importante collection de documents autographes et historiques sur la Révolution française depuis le 13 juillet 1789 jusqu'au 18 brumaire an VIII*. Paris: Charavay Librairie, 1862.

Charavay, Noel, ed. *Catalogue des autographes et des documents historiques composant la collection de M. Etienne Charavay*. Paris: Charavay, 1900.

Chassin, Charles L. *Les Elections et les cahiers de Paris en 1789*. 4 vols. Paris: Jouaust et Sigaux, 1888-1889.

———. *Les volontaires nationaux pendant la Révolution*. 3 vols. Paris: Librairie Léopold Cerf; Librairie Noblet, 1899-1906.

Chaumette, Pierre-Gaspard. *Papiers de. . . .* Edited by F. Braesch. Paris: *Société de l'histoire de la Révolution française*, 1908.

Dauban, C. A. *La Démogogie en 1793 à Paris, ou histoire, jour par jour, de l'année 1793*. Paris: Henri Plon, 1868.

Dawson, Philip, ed. *The French Revolution*. Englewood Cliffs, N.J.: Prentice Hall, [1967].

Duvergier, Jean, ed. *Collection complète de lois, décrets, ordonnances, règlemens, avis du Conseil d'état . . . de 1788 à 1830. . . .* 106 vols. Paris: Imprimerie Nationale, par Baudouin, 1834-1906.

Fillon, Benjamin. *Inventaire des autographes et des documents historiques composant la collection de M. Benjamin Fillon*. Series I and II. Edited by Etienne Charavay and Frederic Naylor. Paris and London: Charavay Frères, 1877.

Gerbaux, Fernand, and Charles Schmidt, eds. *Procès-verbaux des comités d'agriculture et de commerce de la constituante de la législative et de la convention*. 4 vols. Paris: Imprimerie Nationale, 1906-1910. Collection de documents inédits sur l'historie économique de la Révolution française.

Guillaume, James, ed. *Procès-verbaux du Comité d'instruction publique de la Convention nationale*. 6 vols. Paris: Imprimerie Nationale, 1891-1907.

Karéiev, N. *Les Comités révolutionnaires de Paris 1793-1795*. St. Petersburg: Imprimerie de Schroeder, 1913.

―――. *Neizdannie Protokolie Parizhskikh Sektsii 9 Thermidora II (Documents inédits . . .)*. *Mémoires de l'Académie impériale des sciences de St. Petersbourg, VIIe série*. Vol. XII, no. 4. St. Petersbourg: Imprimerie de l'Académie impériale des sciences, 1914.

―――. *Les Sections de Paris pendant la Révolution française*. St. Petersburg: Telegraphia M. M. Stasuleveecha, 1911.

Lacroix, Sigismond, ed. *Actes de la Commune de Paris pendant la Révolution*. Series, I, 7 vols.; series II, 8 vols. Paris: Librairie Léopold Cerf; Librairie Noblet, 1894-1900. Collections de documents relatifs à l'histoire de Paris pendant le Révolution française.

Lefebvre, Georges, ed. *Documents relatifs à l'histoire des subsistances dans le district de Bergues pendant la Révolution (1788–an V)*. 2 vols. Lille: C. Robbe, 1914. Collection de documents inédits sur l'histoire économique de la Révolution française.

Mathiez, Albert, *Le Club des Cordeliers pendant la crise de Varennes et le massacre du Champ de Mars*. Paris: Librairie Ancienne, 1910.

Mavidal, M. J., M. E. Laurent et al., eds. *Archives parlementaires de 1787 à 1860; recueil complet des débats législatifs et politiques des chambres françaises. Imprimés par ordre du sénat et de la chambre des députés*. Series 1, 90 vols. Paris: Librairie Administrative de Paul du Pont, 1879―.

Monin, H., and L. Lazard, eds. *Sommier des biens nationaux de la Ville de Paris*. 2 vols. Paris: Imprimerie Léopold Cerf, 1920.

Schmidt, Adolphe, ed. *Tableau de la Révolution française*. 3 vols. Leipzig: Veit & Comp., 1867.

Schmidt, Charles, ed. *L'Industrie; instruction, recueil de textes et notes.* Paris, Imprimerie Nationale, 1910. Commission de recherche.

Stewart, John Hall. *A Documentary Survey of the French Revolution.* New York: Macmillan, [1951].

Tourneux, Maurice. *Bibliographie de l'histoire de Paris pendant la Révolution française.* 5 vols. Paris: Ville de Paris, 1890-1913.

———, ed. *Procès-verbaux de la Commune de Paris (10 août 1792–1er juin 1793)* (Paris: Société de l'histoire de la Révolution française, 1894.

Tuetey, Alexandre, ed. *L'Assistance publique à Paris pendant la révolution,* 4 vols. Paris: Imprimerie Nationale, 1895-1897. Publications relatifs à la Révolution française.

———. *Répertoire général des sources manuscrites de l'histoire de Paris pendant la Révolution française.* 11 vols. Paris: Imprimerie Nouvelle, 1890-1914.

Journals

B.N., Lb^{40}	2	*Affiches de la commune*
B.N., Lc^2	704	*L'Ami du peuple* (Leclerc)
B.N., Lc^2	218	*Chronique de Paris*
B.N., Lc^2	710	*Feuille de Paris*
		Journal des débats et des décrets
		Journal de la liberté de la presse (Babeuf)
B.N., Lc^2	786	*Journal de la Montagne*
B.N., Lc^2	260-261	*Journal de la municipalité et des districts de Paris*
		Journal de Paris
B.N., Lc^2	80	*Journal de Paris national*
		Journal de la république française (Marat)
B.N., Lc^2	563	*Mercure universel*
		Réimpression de l'ancien moniteur
		Le Patriote françois
		Le Père Duchesne (Hébert)
B.N., Lc^2	227	*Le Publiciste de la république française* (Marat)
		Les Révolutions de Paris (Prudhomme)
		Tableau de Paris (Louis Sebastien Mercier)
		Le Tribun du peuple, ou le défenseur des droits-de-l'homme (Babeuf)

Secondary Sources

Monographs

Afanassiev, Georges. *Le Commerce des céréals en France au dix-huitième siècle.* Translated under the direction of Paul Boyer. Paris: Alphonse Picard et Fils, 1894.

Aulard, F. A. *Le Christianisme et la Révolution française.* Paris: F. Rieder, 1925.

Behrens, C.B.A. *The Ancien Régime.* In *History of European Civilization,* Geoffrey Barraclough, general editor. London: Harcourt, Brace & World, [1967].

Bloch, Camille, *L'Assistance & l'état en France à la veille de la Révolution (1764-1790).* Paris: Librairie Alphonse Picard et Fils, 1908.

―――. *La Monnaie et le papier-monnaie.* Paris: Ernest Leroux, 1912.

Bluche, J. François. *L'Origine des magistrats du Parlement de Paris au XVIIIe siècle.* Paris: Librairie C. Klincksieck, 1956. *Paris et Ile-de-France, Mémoires.* . . . Vols. V-VI, 1953-1954.

Bourdin, Isabelle. *Les Sociétés populaires à Paris pendant la Révolution.* Paris: Recueil Sirey, 1937.

Braesch, Frédéric. *La Commune du dix août 1792, étude sur l'histoire de Paris du 20 juin au 2 décembre 1792.* Paris: Librairie Hachette, 1911.

Calvet, Henri. *Un instrument de la terreur à Paris: le Comité de salut public ou de surveillance du département de Paris (8 juin 1793–21 messidor an II).* Paris: Librairie Nizet et Bastard, 1941.

Carlson, Marvin. *The Theater of the French Revolution.* Ithaca: Cornell University Press, 1966.

Caron, Pierre. *Les Massacres de septembre.* Paris: La Maison du Livre Français, 1935.

Christ, Yvan et al. *Promenades dans le Marais.* Paris: Editions André Balland, [1964].

Cobb, Richard. *Les Armées révolutionnaires, instrument de la terreur dans les départements, avril 1793–floréal an II.* 2 vols. The Hague: Mouton, 1961-1963.

―――. *Reactions to the French Revolution.* London: Oxford University Press, 1972.

―――. *Terreur et subsistances 1793-1795.* Paris: Librairie Clavreuil, 1965.

Daumard, Adeline. *La Bourgeoisie parisienne de 1815 à 1848*. Paris: S.E.Y.P.E.N., 1963.

Dommanget, Maurice. *Sylvain Maréchal, l'égalitaire "l'homme sans dieu"; sa vie—son oeuvre (1750-1803)*. Paris: Spartacus, n.d.

Egret, Jean. *La Pré-Révolution française (1787-1788)*. Paris: Presses Universitaires de France, 1962.

Festy, Octave. *L'Agriculture pendant la Révolution française*. Paris: Gallimard, 1947.

Franklin, Alfred. *La Vie privée d'autrefois; arts et métiers; modes, moeurs, usages des parisiens du XIIe au XVIIe siècle; commment on devenant patron*. Paris: Librairie Plon, 1889.

Garrigues, Georges. *Les Districts parisiens pendant la Révolution française*. Paris: Editions SPES, n.d.

Gendron, François. *La Jeunesse dorée épisode de la Révolution française*. Préface de Albert Soboul (Québec, Les presses de l'université du Québec, 1979).

Godechot, Jacques. *Les Institutions de la France sous la Révolution et l'Empire*. Paris: Presses Universitaires de France, 1951.

————. *La Prise de la Bastille 14 juillet 1789*. Paris: Gallimard, 1965.

Gottschalk, Louis, and Margaret Maddox. *Lafayette in the French Revolution; Through the October Days*. Chicago: University of Chicago Press, [1969].

Guérin, Daniel. *La Lutte de classes sous la première république; bourgeois et "bras nus" (1793-1797)*. 2 vols. Paris: Gallimard, 1946.

Harris, Seymour, E. *The Assignats*. Cambridge: Harvard University Press, 1930.

Henderson, E. F. *Symbol and Satire in the French Revolution*. New York: Putnam, 1912.

Hertzberg, Arthur. *The French Enlightenment and the Jews*. New York: Columbia University Press, 1968.

Hillairet, Jacques. *Dictionnaire historique des rues de Paris*. 2 vols. 5th ed. Paris: Editions de Minuit, n.d.

————. *Evocation du vieux Paris*. Paris: Editions de Minuit, [1952].

————. *La Rue Saint-Antoine*. Paris: Editions de Minuit, 1970.

Hufton, Olwen. *The Poor of Eighteenth-Century France 1750-1789*. Oxford: Clarendon Press, 1974.

Jacques, Jean. *Vie et mort des corporations; grèves et luttes sociales sous l'ancien régime*. Paris: Spartacus, [1948].

Jaurès, Jean, ed. *Histoire socialiste (1789-1900) sous la direction de Jean Jaurès*. 12 vols. Paris: Publications Jules Rouff, 1901-1909.

Kaplow, Jeffrey. *The Names of Kings; the Parisian Laboring Poor in the Eighteenth Century*. New York: Basic Books, 1972.

Karéiev, N. *La Densité de la population des différentes sections de Paris pendant la Révolution*. Translated by J. Patouillet. Paris: Honoré Champion, 1912.

Koch, Camille. *Les Origines françaises de la prohibition du mandat impératif*. Nancy: A. Crepin-Leblond, 1905.

Labrousse, C. E. *Esquisse du mouvement des prix et des revenus en France au XVIIIe siècle*. Paris: Librairie Dalloz, 1932.

La Monneraye, Jean de. *La Crise du logement à Paris pendant la Révolution*. Paris: Librairie Ancienne Edouard Champion, 1928.

Lazare, Félix and Louis Lazare. *Dictionnaire administratif et historique des rues de Paris et ses monuments*. Paris: Félix Lazare, 1844.

Lecocq, Georges. *La Prise de la Bastille et ses anniversaires d'après des documents inédits*. Paris: Charavay Frères, 1881.

Levasseur, Pierre Emile. *Histoire des classes ouvrières et de l'industrie en France de 1789 à 1870*. 2 vols. Paris: Arthur Rousseau, 1903-1904.

Lucas, Colin. *The Structure of the Terror; the Example of Javogues and the Loire*. London: Oxford University Press, 1973.

Mathiez, Albert. *Autour de Robespierre*. Paris: Payot, 1925.

———. *La Réaction thermidorienne*. Paris: Armand Colin, 1929.

———. *La Vie chère et le mouvement social sous la Terreur*. Paris: Payot, 1927.

McManners, John. *French Ecclesiastical Society under the Ancien Régime; a Study of Angers in the Eighteenth Century*. Manchester: University of Manchester Press, [1960].

———. *The French Revolution and the Church*. In *Church History Outlines*, edited by V.H.H. Green. London: Talbot Press, 1969.

Mellié, Ernest. *Les Sections de Paris pendant la Révolution française (21 mai 1790–19 vendémiaire an IV); organisation–fonctionnement*. Paris: Société de l'Histoire de la Révolution Française, 1898.

Mortimer-Ternaux, Louis. *Histoire de la Terreur 1792-1794*. 7 vols. Paris: Michel Lévy Frères, 1868-1881.

Perrot, Michelle. *Les Ouvriers en grève, France 1871-1890*. 2 vols. Paris: Mouton, 1974.

Pfeiffer, Laura B. *The Uprising of June 30, 1792*. New York, 1970. Reprinted from *University of Nebraska Studies*, 12:3 (1913).

Pinkney, David H. *Napoleon III and the Rebuilding of Paris*. Princeton: Princeton University Press, 1958.

Pronteau, Jeanne. *Les Numérotages des maisons de Paris du XVe siècle à nos jours*. Paris: Ville de Paris, 1966.

Reinhard, Marcel, ed. *Contributions à l'histoire démographique de la Révolution française. Etudes sur la population parisienne. Commission d'histoire économique et sociale de la Révolution française*. 3rd series. Paris: Bibliothèque Nationale, 1970.

———. *Etude de la population pendant la Révolution et l'Empire. Commission d'histoire économique et sociale de la Révolution française*. Gap: Imprimerie Louis Jean, 1961.

———. *Nouvelle histoire de Paris. La Révolution 1789-1799*. Paris: Hachette, 1971.

Robinet, le Docteur, *Le Mouvement religieux à Paris pendant la Révolution (1789-1801)*. 2 vols. Paris: Librairie Léopold Cerf–Charles Noblet, 1896-1898.

Robiquet, Paul. *Le Personnel municipal de Paris pendant la Révolution, période constitutionnelle*. Paris: D. Jouast, Charles Noblet, 1890.

Rose, R. B. *The Enragés: Socialists of the French Revolution?* London and New York: Melbourne University Press, 1965.

Rudé, George. *The Crowd in the French Revolution*. Oxford: Clarendon Press, 1959.

Sainte-Claire Deville, Paul. *La Commune de l'an II*. Paris: Librairie Plon, 1946.

Saint-Fargeau, Girault de. *Les Quarante-huit quartiers de Paris*. Paris: Firmin Didot Frères, 1846.

Sirich, John Black. *The Revolutionary Committees in the Departments of France, 1793-1794*. Cambridge: Harvard University Press, 1943.

Soboul, Albert. *Les Sans-culottes parisiens en l'an II*. Paris: Librairie Clavreuil, 1958.

Tarlé, Eugène. *Germinal et prairial*. Moscow: Editions en Langues Etrangères, 1959.

Tønnesson, Kåre D. *La Défaite des sans-culottes; mouvement populaire et réaction bourgeoise en l'an III*. Paris: Presses Universitaires et Librairie R. Clavreuil, 1959.

Wallon, Henri A. *Histoire du tribunal révolutionnaire de Paris*. 6 vols. Paris: Librairie Hachette, 1880-1882.

Wilhelm, Jacques. *La Vie quotidienne au Marais au XVIIe siècle*. Paris: Hachette, 1966.

Woloch, Isser. *Jacobin Legacy; the Democratic Movement under the Directory*. Princeton: Princeton University Press, 1970.

Zivy, Henry. *Le Treize vendémiaire an IV*. Paris: Ancienne Librairie Germer Baillière, 1898.

Articles

Andrews, Richard M. "The Justices of the Peace of Revolutionary Paris, September 1792–November 1794 (Frimaire Year III)." *Past and Present*, No. 52 (August 1971), pp. 56-105.

Bouloiseau, Marc. "Les Comités de surveillance des arrondissements de Paris sous la réaction thermidorienne." *Annales historiques*, 10 (1933), 317-337.

————. "Les Comités de surveillance des arrondissements parisiens." *Annales historiques*, 10 (1933), 441-453.

————. "Les Comités de surveillance des arrondissements parisiens." *Annales historiques*, 11 (1934), 233-249.

————. "Les Comités de surveillance des arrondissements de Paris pendant les mois de germinal, floréal, prairial, an III." *Annales historiques*, 13 (1936), 42-60.

————. "Les Comités de surveillance des arrondissements de Paris à la fin de l'an III." *Annales historiques*, 14 (1936), 204-217.

Braesch, Fritz. "Essai de statistique de la population ouvrière de Paris vers 1791." *La Révolution française; Revue d'histoire moderne et contemporaine*, 63 (1912), 289-321.

Calvet, Henri. "Les Origines du comité de l'Evêché." *Annales historiques*, 7 (1930), 12-23.

————. "Remarques sur la participation des sections au movement du 31 mai–1er-2 juin 1793." *Annales historiques*, 5 (1928), 366-369.

Cobb, Richard. "Note sur la répression contre le personnel sans-culotte de 1795 à 1801." *Annales historiques*, 26 (1954), 23-49.

Dieudonné, F. "Préliminaires et causes des journées de prairial an III." *La Révolution française*, 43 (November 1902), 442-465; and 44 (December 1902), 504-527.

Dommanget, Maurice. "Robespierre et les cultes." *Annales historiques*, 1 (1924), 192-216.

Eisenstein, Elizabeth L. "Who Intervened in 1788? A Commentary on the Coming of the French Revolution." *American Historical Review*, 71 (October 1965), 77-103.

Eisenstein, Elizabeth L., Jeffrey Kaplow, and Gilbert Shapiro. "Class in the French Revolution: A Discussion." *American Historical Review*, 72 (January 1967), 497-522.

Hufton, Olwen. "Life and Death among the Very Poor." In *The Eighteenth Century; Europe in the Age of Enlightenment*, edited by Alfred Cobban, pp. 293-310. New York: McGraw-Hill Book Company, 1969.

Kennedy, Michael L. "The Foundation of the Jacobin Clubs and the Development of the Jacobin Club Network, 1780-1791." *Journal of Modern History*, 51 (December 1979), 701-733.

Markov, Walter. "Robespierristen und Jacqueroutins." In *Maximilien Robespierre 1758-1794. Beiträge zu seinem 200. Geburtstag*, edited by Walter Markov, pp. 159-217. Berlin: Rütten & Loening, 1958.

Mathiez, Albert. "Notes sur l'importance du prolétariat en France à la veille de la Révolution." *Annales historiques*, 7 (1930), 497-524.

Pertué, Michel. "Critique" of R. Andrews' article on the justices of the peace. *Annales historiques*, No. 208 (April-June 1972), pp. 313-317.

Roche, D. "La Noblesse du Marais." In *Recherches sur la noblesse parisienne au milieu du XVIIIe siècle, actes du quatre-vingt-sixième Congrès national des sociétés savantes*, pp. 541-578. Montpelier, 1961; Paris: Imprimerie Nationale, 1962.

Rose, R. B. "How To Make a Revolution: The Paris Districts in 1789." *Bulletin of the John Rylands University Library of Manchester*, 59 (Spring 1977), 426-457.

Rouff, Marcel. "Le Personnel des premières émeutes de 1789." *La Révolution française*, 57 (September 1909), 213-238.

Rudé, George. "La Composition sociale des insurrections parisiennes de 1789 à 1791." *Annales historiques*, 24 (1952), 256-288.

———. "Les Emeutes des 25, 26 février à Paris." *Annales historiques*, 25 (1953), 33-57.

———. "La Population ouvrière parisienne de 1789 à 1791." *Annales historiques*, No. 187 (January-March 1967), pp. 15-33.

———, and A. Soboul. "Le Maximum des salaires parisiens et le 9 thermidor." *Annales historiques*, 26 (1954), 1-22.

Slavin, Morris. "L'Autre enragé: Jean-François Varlet." In *Eine Jury für Jacques Roux*, pp. 34-67. Berlin: Akademie Verlag, 1981.

―――――. "L'Epuration de prairial an III dans la section des Droits-de-l'Homme." *Annales historiques*, No. 232 (April-June 1978), pp. 283-304.

―――――. "Jacques Roux: A Victim of Vilification." *French Historical Studies*, 3 (Fall 1964), 525-537.

―――――. "Jean Varlet as Defender of Direct Democracy." *Journal of Modern History*, 39 (December 1967), 387-404.

―――――. "Section Roi-de-Sicile and the Fall of the Monarchy." In *Bourgeois, Sans-Culottes, and Other Frenchmen; Essays on the French Revolution in Honor of John Hall Stewart*, edited by Morris Slavin and Agnes M. Smith, pp. 59-74. Waterloo, Ontario: Wilfrid Laurier University Press, 1981.

―――――. "The Terror in Miniature: Section Droits-de-l'Homme of Paris, 1793-1795." *The Historian: A Journal of History*, 39 (February 1977), 292-306.

―――――. "Théophile Leclerc: An Anti-Jacobin Terrorist." *The Historian: A Journal of History*, 33 (May 1971), 398-414.

Soreau, Edmond. "Les Ouvriers aux journées des 4 et 5 septembre 1793." *Annales historiques*, 14 (1937), 436-447.

Taylor, George V. "Noncapitalist Wealth and the Origins of the French Revolution." *American Historical Review*, 72 (January 1967), 469-496.

Viola, Paolo. "Sur le mouvement populaire parisien de février-mars 1793." *Annales historiques*, no. 214 (October-December 1973), pp. 503-518.

Vovelle, M., and D. Roche. "Bourgeois, rentiers, propriétaires, 'éléments pour la définition d'une catégorie sociale,' " *Actes du quatre-vingt-quartrième Congrès national des sociétés savantes*, pp. 419-452. Dijon, 1959; Paris: Imprimerie Nationale, 1960.

Wick, Daniel L. "The Court Nobility and the French Revolution: the Example of the Society of Thirty." *Eighteenth-Century Studies*, 13 (Spring 1980), 263-284.

Index

LIBRARY OF CONGRESS CATALOGING IN PUBLICATION DATA

Slavin, Morris, 1913-
The French Revolution in miniature.

Bibliography: p.
Includes index.
1. Droits-de-l'Homme (Paris, France)—History.   2. Paris (France)—
History—Revolution, 1789-1799.   I. Title.
DC194.S57   1984   944.04   83-16034
ISBN 0-691-05415-0 (alk. paper)